# Business-to-
# BUSINESS
# MARKETING

# Business-to-
# BUSINESS
# MARKETING
## A Strategic Approach

# THIRD EDITION

## Michael H. Morris • Leyland F. Pitt
## Earl D. Honeycutt, Jr.

Sage Publications
*International Educational and Professional Publisher*
Thousand Oaks ■ London ■ New Delhi

*For information:*

 Sage Publications, Inc.
2455 Teller Road
Thousand Oaks, California 91320
E-mail: order@sagepub.com

Sage Publications Ltd.
6 Bonhill Street
London EC2A 4PU
United Kingdom

Sage Publications India Pvt. Ltd.
M-32 Market
Greater Kailash I
New Delhi 110 048 India

Printed in the United States of America

*Library of Congress Cataloging-in-Publication Data*

Morris, Michael H.
    Business-to-business marketing: A strategic approach / by Michael H.
Morris, Leyland F. Pitt, and Earl D. Honeycutt, Jr.— 3rd ed.
    p. cm.
    ISBN 0-8039-5964-8
  1.  Industrial marketing.  I. Pitt, Leyland F. II. Honeycutt, Earl D.
III. Title.
    HF5415.1263 .M666 2001
    658.8'4—dc21

                              00-012755

This book is printed on acid-free paper.

01  02  03  04  05  06  7  6  5  4  3  2  1

| | |
|---|---|
| *Acquiring Editor:* | Marquita Flemming |
| *Editorial Assistant:* | MaryAnn Vail |
| *Production Editor:* | Sanford Robinson |
| *Editorial Assistant:* | Candice Crosetti |
| *Typesetter:* | Rebecca Evans |
| *Indexer:* | Teri Greenberg |
| *Cover Designer:* | Michelle Lee |

*MHM: To the General . . . with love,*
*and to Julia and Katie, my special angels*

*LFP: To Lize, Linda, and Christine*

*EDH: To Laura, Travis, Angela, and Cole*

# Contents in Brief

# Contents

# Preface

The book you are about to read is concerned with marketing when the customer is a business or organization. This type of marketing goes by various names, including industrial marketing, business-to-business marketing, and organizational marketing. For simplicity, we will use the term *industrial* to distinguish the discussion from consumer marketing. But industrial marketing covers a lot of territory: Everything from Intel chips sold to IBM, to accounting services sold by Ernst and Young to a small business, as classroom desks sold to the local school authority falls under its umbrella. These markets are diverse, sizable (bigger in a number of ways than consumer markets), and experiencing dynamic growth.

The field of industrial marketing is relatively young. For many years, it took a back seat to consumer marketing and the challenges of selling to households through mass media and retail channels. This has changed in the past 25 years, with most universities now offering courses, the appearance of a number of academic journals, and conferences held annually around the world, all devoted to the challenges of the business-to-business market. In addition, scholars have produced a body of quality research on industrial selling and buying, and our knowledge base continues to expand. New tools continue to appear both for understanding these markets and for better managing marketing programs directed at these customers.

Three revolutions are occurring around the world today, each of which is fueling tremendous growth and change in industrial marketing. The first of these is the technological revolution. Never before has technology changed at the current pace. These changes affect the industrial marketer much faster and more directly than the consumer marketer. They result in a much faster pace of new product and service development. Meanwhile, product life cycles get shorter. Technology also affects how industrial firms make products, their approach to customer logistics, and the levels of support and service they provide customers. It makes it possible for buyer and seller to operate in "real time," conducting much of their business through electronic networks.

The second development driving industrial marketing is the entrepreneurial revolution. Companies have downsized, reengineered, and reinvented themselves in attempts to remain competitive. The essence of sustainable competitive advantage today lies in adaptability, flexibility, speed, aggressiveness, and innovativeness.

Whether large or small, it is the entrepreneurial firm that is today's winner. The marketing function is learning to play a leading role in the entrepreneurial efforts of companies. It is marketing that discovers the new market segments, identifies the untapped needs, finds new applications for existing products, and introduces innovative new processes for selling, distribution, and customer service.

Finally, there is a revolution within marketing itself, as we question traditional assumptions and adopt new frameworks, theories, models, and concepts. There has been a move away from the mass market and preoccupation with the transaction. Today, marketing is about relationships, partnerships, and alliances. One-to-one approaches, where marketing programs are customized to individual accounts, have replaced the old "one size fits all" way of thinking. Industrial marketers are at the forefront of this revolution. They have long recognized that success in the marketplace hinges on the ability to build long-term relationships one account at a time.

The purposes of this book are threefold: (a) to provide an introduction to the distinctive nature of the job of the marketer when the customer is a business or organization, (b) to provide an appreciation for the growing and changing role of marketing within industrial companies, and (c) to provide insights into ways in which a number of emerging principles, concepts, and techniques can be used successfully by the industrial marketer. Building on the experience of successful practitioners as well as the latest research, this text provides the reader with a state-of-the art view on where industrial marketing is today and where it is going. The book is intended for M.B.A. students and advanced undergraduate students with some background in marketing. Managers both in marketing and in technical functions that interface with marketing should also find it useful.

## Organization of the Text

The book is structured to be consistent with the logic of strategic thinking and acting. The first six chapters focus on developing an understanding of the industrial marketplace, whereas the next six chapters look at how to translate that understanding into creative and impactful marketing programs. We close with a discussion of how to track and evaluate the success of these programs.

A logical beginning point is to lay a foundation in terms of exactly what we mean by industrial or business-to-business marketing. Thus, we start in Chapter 1 with an introduction to the definition, scope, size, and distinct challenges of the business-to-business marketplace. This is followed by three chapters that look at various aspects of industrial customers. First, we consider their formal purchasing operation (Chapter 2), then we look at the ways in which they actually make buying decisions (Chapter 3), and then we examine the emerging area of relationship building with customers (Chapter 4). Next come two chapters that examine ways in which industrial markets are analyzed, first for the purposes of market segmentation (Chapter 5) and then when conducting market research (Chapter 6).

With a keen sense of the customer and the market, one can begin to design great marketing programs. First, one formulates a plan with strategies, which is the concern of Chapter 7. This chapter also provides a number of tools and analytical frameworks that facilitate strategic planning in industrial firms. These strategies are then translated into marketing mix programs.

The core element of the industrial marketing mix is the product or service itself. Accordingly, separate chapters are devoted to innovation and new product or service development (Chapter 8) and creative management of existing products and services (Chapter 9). Next comes a discussion of pricing and how the marketer can move toward value-based pricing approaches (Chapter 10). This is followed by two chapters on communications with customers. The industrial promotional mix is covered in Chapter 11, with separate discussions of advertising, sales promotion, and publicity. Because it is the central element in the promotional mix, personal selling receives separate attention (Chapter 12). Finally, the design and management of distribution channels is addressed in Chapter 13. This chapter also includes a look at logistics and customer service.

Having analyzed the market, and having designed and implemented marketing mix programs, the challenge becomes one of monitoring performance, then making corrections and adjustments to these programs. We explore these tracking and control issues in Chapter 14. A central theme is the need for accountability in marketing.

# Highlights

Some of the distinct features of *Business-to-Business Marketing: A Strategic Approach* include the following:

* A detailed summary of how industrial markets differ from consumer markets, and the implications of these differences for successful marketing efforts

* A separate chapter devoted to industrial purchasing practices, including treatment of some of the latest technological developments in just-in-time systems, Internet-based electronic data interchange, Web-based procurement, enterprise resource planning, and flexible manufacturing systems

* A comprehensive chapter on how businesses actually make buying decisions, with a number of tools for deciphering key buying influences and matching the selling process to the buying process

* An assessment of the fundamental changes taking place in the marketing function, including the move toward one-to-one marketing and the concept of customer equity

* Coverage of the latest developments in how to build and manage relationships with business customers

* A cost-benefit look at the concept of nested market segmentation

❖ A discussion of marketing intelligence systems and decision support systems as they relate to the traditional marketing research function in organizations

❖ An examination of the new NAICS system for organizing secondary data on the industrial marketplace

❖ Insights regarding the use of contribution analysis when selecting market segments, managing products and services, setting prices, and evaluating intermediaries

❖ A look at the need for entrepreneurship in the marketing efforts of industrial firms and at how entrepreneurship relates to the development of new products, services, and processes

❖ A value-based approach to pricing built around the concept of a strategic pricing program, along with extended discussion of negotiation, bidding, use of discounts, and transfer pricing

❖ Extensive treatment of the implications of the Internet for the design and management of marketing research, pricing, promotion, and distribution efforts

❖ New developments in the management of the personal selling effort, especially from a relationship vantage point

Each chapter includes a list of key concepts and learning objectives for the reader. Each chapter is followed by a set of discussion questions, in which the reader is encouraged to apply major ideas and principles. Every chapter also includes a Business Marketing Capsule in which interesting real-world illustrations of marketing issues are provided and key findings from the latest research are summarized. In addition, an index of key names and subjects cited in the text is provided.

# Acknowledgments

The authors would like to thank all those who made this project a reality. Chief among these is Minet Schindehutte, of Miami University, whose keen insights and critical eye were a source of both inspiration and quality control as the project unfolded. We owe a significant debt to Al Burns, of Louisiana State University, for his efforts in formulating many of the early ideas for the chapters on market segmentation, market research, and marketing planning. A number of reviewers made invaluable suggestions for revisions, additions, and deletions. The true value of these reviewers in not always apparent to the reader, but without them there would be no book. A big thank you goes to Thomas L. Baker at the University of North Carolina at Wilmington, David Berkowitz at the University of Alabama at Huntsville, Parimal S. Bhagat at William Paterson University, Roger Calantone at Michigan State University, Andrew C. Gross at Cleveland State University, and C. David Shepherd at Kennesaw State University. We are also deeply appreciative of the team at Sage and especially Marquita Flemming and MaryAnn Vail. It was in large part because of their many suggestions, encouragement, and patience that all the pieces came together. Finally, much gratitude is owed to Donna Hensley, who was in effect the project manager. Her efforts at word processing, formatting, finding errors, and handling the difficult task of coordinating the work of three authors were nothing short of superlative.

*Michael Morris*
*Leyland Pitt*
*Earl D. Honeycutt, Jr.*

# CHAPTER 1

# The Unique Nature of Industrial Marketing

*Marketing is everything.*
—Regis McKenna

## Key Concepts

B2B
Business-to-business marketing
Characteristics of industrial demand
Customer orientation
Customer value
Environmental turbulence
Exchange process
Industrial marketing
Information revolution

Marketing mix
Marketing concept
Marketing myopia
Organizational environment
Product attribute bundle
Product life cycle
Reciprocity
Relationships in marketing

## Learning Objectives

1. Define industrial marketing and the industrial marketing mix.

2. Establish the critical need for industrial firms to adopt a market orientation.

3. Describe the size and importance of the industrial marketplace.

4. Discuss the dynamic environment facing industrial marketers.

5. Identify key differences between consumer and industrial marketing management.

Countries throughout the world are in the midst of a market revolution. Everywhere we are witnessing shifts from market segmentation to mass customization as well as the emergence of new media that kill distance, homogenize time, and render location irrelevant. Historically conservative institutions such as banks and telephone companies have transformed themselves into aggressive competitors that have used creative means to displace fast-moving consumer goods companies as the "world champion marketers." The 1990s emerged as the "decade of entrepreneurial marketing." Social observers such as Alvin Toffler and John Naisbitt coined terms such as "de-massification" and the "multiple-option society" to describe a move away from an economy built on mass production, centralization, mass marketing, uniform technologies, standardization, and homogeneity, and their predictions have proved to be remarkably prescient.

Many firms have successfully followed Theodore Levitt's (1980) admonition that they find ways to differentiate such traditionally homogeneous commodities as isopropyl alcohol, strip steel, pork bellies, and plastics. By facilitating customer search, however, new marketing media such as the Internet and the World Wide Web have simultaneously had the effect of pressuring a huge range of products and services toward becoming commodities. These trends suggest that companies must become more knowledgeable in their understanding of marketplace demands and more sophisticated in their attempt to reach and satisfy their target audiences. A superior product or production process is no guarantee—indeed, they are almost minimum requirements—of market success. The implications are perhaps greatest for companies that compete in industrial, or business-to-business, markets, where changing growth patterns and environmental turbulence are a way of life. These markets are the focus of this book. They represent a distinctly different challenge, one that presents major opportunities for the application of marketing principles and concepts.

## Defining Industrial Marketing

Marketing is concerned with exchanges between and among buyers and sellers, and as such it is an attempt to match supply with demand. The subject of this exchange might be goods, services, technologies, business systems, people, information, concepts, or ideas. While the buyer is traditionally viewed as some household member purchasing finished goods through a retailer, in many instances a company or institution is doing the buying. When this is the case—where both parties to the exchange are organizations—our focus becomes industrial marketing, also referred to as *business-to-business marketing* or *organizational marketing.*

In recent years, it has been observed that the concern of marketing is not discrete, one-time exchanges or transactions. Rather, buyer-seller interactions tend to be of longer duration, with a good probability that the customer today will also be the customer tomorrow. Today, the objective of marketing is the management of mutually beneficial relationships (see Morgan & Hunt, 1994).

*Industrial marketing* can thus be formally defined as the creation and management of mutually beneficial relationships between organizational suppliers and organizational customers. The focus is on the flow of goods and services that produce or become part of other goods and services or that facilitate the operation of an enterprise. This enterprise can be a private firm, a public agency, or a nonprofit institution. The management of these relationships means deciding whom the organization wishes to have a relationship with in the first place, and then, once having begun the relationship, how to maintain it. In the language of today's marketing, this means that organizations have to make decisions about the acquisition of customers and on the retention of these customers (Blattberg & Deighton, 1996). Acquisition of customers means that marketers must find ways of creating value for them; retention of customers implies that this value be sustained and enhanced. It should be noted that what we have called industrial marketing also goes under a variety of other names—it is frequently referred to as *marketing to organizations* or *organizational marketing.* This is to emphasize that firms can market to other kinds of organizations, such as government and nonprofit organizations. It is also called *business-to-business marketing,* and more recently in electronic commerce, it is referred to simply as *B2B.*

## The Philosophy of Marketing

The essence of industrial marketing is creating value for customers with goods and services that address organizational needs and objectives. This idea is known as the *marketing concept*—probably best expressed more than 40 years ago by management guru Peter Drucker (1954) in his classic text *The Practice of Management,* in which Drucker states that "the purpose of a firm is to *create* and *serve* customers" (p. 64). As a philosophy of doing business, it has three major components. First, all company activities should begin with, and be based on, the recognition of a fundamental customer need. Second, a customer orientation should be integrated throughout the functional areas of the firm, including production, engineering, finance, and research and development (R&D). Third, customer satisfaction should be viewed as the means toward long-run profitability goals. Drucker explains, "the aim of marketing is to know and understand customers so well that the product or service fits them and sells itself" (1954, p. 65).

This orientation is especially critical with industrial customers, because the goods and services they buy have an impact on the performance of day-to-day business operations, and thus the viability of the enterprise. The buyer-seller relationship tends to involve mutual interdependence, with each party attempting to satisfy organizational objectives through the other.

The marketing concept has frequently been misunderstood and misinterpreted, embodied in such platitudes as "the customer is always right" or oversimplifications that marketing is about "finding out what customers want and giving it to them." Many business-to-business marketers have discovered that organizational customers frequently don't know what they want, nor do they always conceive of what is possible. Products and services often shape markets rather than markets shaping products and services. It is worthwhile remembering that Drucker emphasized the *creation* of customers and not just the serving of them. The fact is that technology in the form of new products and new services creates and shapes markets by shaping and creating customers. In consumer markets, Sony's[1] Walkman is frequently cited as an example of this; in business-to-business situations Boeing's[2] 707 in a very real way created and shaped the market for intercontinental jet aircraft travel.

Figure 1.1 provides a simple but effective way of illustrating this point (Berthon, Hulbert, & Pitt, 1996). The figure suggests that it is possible for a firm to focus on customers and technology (developing new products, services, processes), and the focus on each can be either high or low. Firms that operate in an "isolate" mode focus neither on customers nor on technology, but probably on themselves and their own activities. For example, a gold producer may find it has little opportunity to develop new products, as gold is a commodity traded on open markets. Gold mines tend to focus on their own efficiencies. Alternatively, a "follower" attempts to find out what customers want and to give it to them. As a case in point, Toyota's Lexus[3] was developed by focusing on the needs of corporate executives who wanted something better than a Mercedes[4] or BMW[5] and more affordable. Next, a "shaper" focuses on technology in the form of new products and services, in an attempt to shape customers and hence markets. Observing how radical business-to-business products such as Otis[6] Elevator's "mobile rooms" for mile-high buildings (called Odyssey) and General Electric's[7] development of digital X rays will "shape" future markets, Bentley College President Joseph G. Morone observes, "If you worship at the throne of the voice of the customer, you'll get only incremental advances, not brand-new ideas" ("Getting to Eureka," 1997, p. 37). Finally, an "interact" strategy involves the management of a dialogue between customer and technology, such as that facilitated by Boeing in the development of the 777. The company worked intimately with its largest customers—

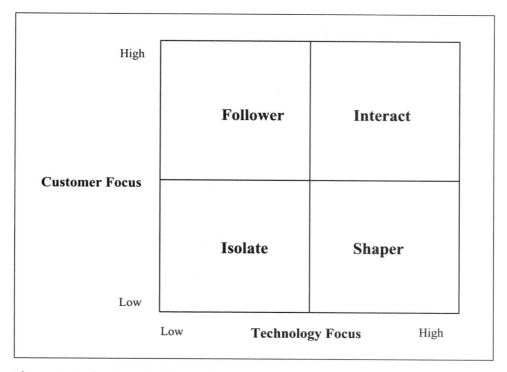

**Figure 1.1.** The Strategic Focus Grid

SOURCE: Adapted from Berthon, Hulbert, and Pitt, "To Serve or Create? Strategic Orientation Towards Technology and Customers." Copyright © 1999, by The Regents of the University of California. Reprinted from the *California Management Review, 42*, No. 1. By permission of The Regents.

such as British Airways,[8] United,[9] and Singapore Airlines[10]—to conceptualize and design the aircraft.

Although it is tempting to assume that there is a "best" focus (interact) and a "worst" (isolate), this is not necessarily the case. Rather, there is a most appropriate focus for a firm at any time, and the true application of the marketing concept requires fitting the firm's strategic focus to the business environment in which it operates. Indeed, successful organizations seem to be able to follow where appropriate and shape at other times, and then interact. There may even be occasions when an isolate strategy could be justified.

The marketing concept requires that the firm be effective at gathering information about the market, disseminating this information inside the organization, and being responsive to it (Kohli & Jaworski, 1990; Kohli, Jaworski, & Kumar, 1993). Frequently, business-to-business firms confuse the marketing concept with "having a marketing department," which has the responsibility of interfacing with customers. In truly market-oriented or market-driven firms, the focus of all within the organization is on their role in delivering on the firm's basic promise to the customer. Unfortunately, a "silo" mentality is often encountered along functional lines, with finance concentrating on profits and cost while operations concentrates on efficiency, human resources

## BUSINESS MARKETING CAPSULE

### *Replace Marketing Specialists With Company Marketing Orientation*

The key job of the marketer in any corporation is self-destruction.

The great cycle in marketing goes something like this: Manager discovers that customer satisfaction is important, manager hires experts to maximize customer satisfaction in exchange and use, manager delegates customer satisfaction to these new "high priests", the high priests then whisper largely among themselves about things that don't make a difference. The house falls down and is then rebuilt.

It's the job of the marketer to pursue intra- and extra-firm actions designed to maximize customer loyalty. But marketers don't and can't do the jobs that produce that loyalty: They don't make the hamburger, and they don't serve it. Marketers seldom control either the selling, buying, or using context in which the customer actually is pleased or displeased with the offering.

In addition, most corporate managers find the customer a difficult-to-understand, fickle, changeable, and profoundly complex beast who does not always behave according to clever engineering equations or even in accord with tradition and history. It's tempting for managers to stay where things are clearer, such as the computation of minimum inventory levels or of minimum distance paths in logistical science.

The rise of marketing as a profession and a science can actually signal disaster for the firm. When general managers mistake market organization for market orientation and allow a high-priest class of customer experts to be created and then delegate the management of customer satisfaction to them, disaster results. If marketers mumble to themselves about the arcane footnotes of their science, if they draw to their breasts "ownership" of the customer and the account, and if they allow others to relegate this function to their "professional judgment" by increasing their own ranks and specialization, marketing organizations balloon and market orientation shrinks.

If, instead, the woman working the lathe understands why it is useful that the spindles not be seriously out of spec, if the accountant believes that accurate and timely billing will increase company sales, and if the customer service person takes the time to tell the equipment owner about a lubricant that helps reduce repair calls, customer satisfaction will be maximized, as will market orientation.

Marketing is a general management function and cannot be delegated to "experts" without the serious risk of ruining the business by failing to inculcate care for the customer in all employees.

By this logic, the key jobs of the marketing person in the corporation and the key jobs of the researcher interested in discovering marketing "truths" read a little bit differently from what is encountered in the basic textbooks. They include:

> - Understanding the customer, company, and competition
> - Interpreting customer dynamics to key insiders, who may be motivated not to hear or to understand, as well as to potential customers
> - Leading others inside the corporation across every function, in the sense that customer requirements are key across all functions in the organization, not just something to be delegated to experts who "know that stuff"
> - Self-destructing, in the sense that the best marketing makes marketers of others and does away with much of the need for specialized marketing "expertise," because the culture of the corporation has been changed to total customer sensitivity
>
> So, if you see a lone marketer looking smug, with his or her feet up on the desk in a $1 billion corporation, don't assume incompetence. He or she may have succeeded in the true mission of marketing—to get every employee in the organization so committed to, and concerned about, what the customers want that arm-waving exhortations and the 49th awareness and usage study would be regarded as totally unnecessary.
>
> SOURCE: Adapted from "A Marketer's Job Is to Self-Destruct," *Marketing News* 24 (June 25, 1990), p. 10, Bonoma.

departments concentrate on developing employees, and administration is engrossed in moving paper. Correspondingly, the customer becomes the object of the marketing and/or sales department and is frequently seen as getting in the way of other functions as they attempt to get their work done. Ultimately, marketing is everybody's job in the truly market-oriented organization, as illustrated in the Business Marketing Capsule above.

## The Marketing Mission Statement

Because many industrial products and services are fairly complex, technical people such as engineers, designers, and manufacturing managers tend to play a dominant role in marketing-related activities. They usually bring a technical orientation to decision making. As a result, companies have to be wary of what Levitt (1960) many years ago called "marketing myopia," which is a tendency to see one's business in terms of products rather than customer needs. This indicates a narrow-minded view of business purpose. For example, is a maker of glue in the glue business or the industrial adhesives business? The marketer might insist that such a company is actually in the business of making things stick together. Although the distinction may seem insignificant, the way in which one defines the business boils down to a question of just how flexible and innovative the firm will be in satisfying the needs of a changing market.

As a rule, no product can sustain market growth indefinitely. This fundamental is the lesson of the product life cycle. The company that defines itself in terms of a specific product will fade as the product inevitably matures and declines. The firm must adapt to changes in technology, competition, and especially customers. It must develop, over time, new technological applications, new products, and new markets to meet these opportunities. By defining the firm in terms of customer needs, change and adaptation become normal parts of business operations.

The National Cash Register Corporation (NCR)[11] of Dayton, Ohio, is an example of a company that was almost destroyed by marketing myopia. By defining itself in terms of mechanical and electromechanical (key-driven) cash registers and accounting machines well after these products were mature, the company faced a disastrous situation during the 1970s. Not only had its management ignored the signs of inevitable technological change, but it also had lost touch with the operations of customers. The needs of major banks and of such retailing giants as Sears Roebuck[12] and J. C. Penney[13] had evolved beyond NCR's capability to fulfill them. Many investment analysts openly predicted imminent company failure. New management, in spite of a huge, outdated manufacturing complex and increasingly obsolete products, was able to turn the company around, but only at great cost. A $60 million loss was experienced in 1972. More than 13,000 manufacturing jobs were eliminated, creating havoc in the Dayton economy. A metamorphosis took place as NCR became a major player in computer-based systems. Changes included decentralized manufacturing, streamlined product lines, new technologies, greater reliance on vendors, and increased R&D (with an applied orientation). Most important, the sales and service organizations were restructured from a geographic and product focus to one based on customer groups. NCR grew to dominate the market for point-of-sale terminals used by banks and retail food establishments and developed its own lines of business and personal computers.

## The Industrial Marketing Mix

The industrial marketer is responsible for a wide range of activities. Some of the key ones include

- Identifying customer needs
- Researching buyer behavior
- Segmenting users into manageable groups
- Assisting in the development of new products and services
- Setting and negotiating prices
- Ensuring proper delivery, installation, and servicing of products
- Making products available at the right time and place, and in the right quantity
- Allocating marketing resources across product lines

❖ Communicating with target customers before, during, and after a sale

❖ Evaluating and controlling ongoing marketing programs

In reality, companies can create value for customers in an unlimited number of ways. To simplify the management of marketing activities, the major value-creating activities of the firm have been grouped conveniently into a general framework called the *marketing mix*. This mix consists of four components: product, price, promotion, and distribution. Each of these involves a category of decisions that are interdependent with one another.

Product decisions concern the specific attributes designed into a product: its packaging, warranties, adjunct services, customer training, and installation, among others. These decisions represent the core element of the mix in industrial markets, around which everything else revolves. Pricing involves establishing terms of sale, discounts, trade-ins, rebates, bidding strategies, and, possibly, financing. Promotional concerns include such areas as personal selling, sales management, trade advertising, free samples, trade shows, demonstrations, direct mail campaigns, and publicity. These are the communications component of the mix. Distribution decisions are those pertaining to the number and types of middlemen used, market coverage, delivery time, and inventory policies, as well as issues such as logistics and supply chain management.

Note that each of these components is a variable that can be manipulated—not a constant, which is indeed why we refer to a marketing "mix." Each requires a strategy. Although not all these activities are necessarily performed by someone called a marketer in any given firm, each can play a key role in the marketing function. Collectively, they combine to determine the value received by a customer from a given product or service. For this reason, decisions in any one of these areas must be closely coordinated with those in the other three areas. Specific questions that must be considered in formulating the industrial marketing mix are outlined in Table 1.1, but it should be borne in mind that the relative importance of the different components of the mix within a particular industry is likely to vary.

## The Size and Scope of the Industrial Marketplace

Although a market economy ultimately depends on the final consumer, the purchases of these consumers actually are substantially less than those of industrial customers. Much of this industrial activity concerns the raw materials and components that eventually become part of consumer goods. It also consists of a wide range of services sold to organizations.

To better understand the vast array of economic activity that constitutes the industrial market, consider the development of a consumer product such as a lawn mower. Before a lawn mower can be sold to a consumer, it has to be assembled, wholesaled,

**TABLE 1.1**  Questions Facing the Industrial Marketing Manager

1. How are my customers' markets changing? What changes can I expect in my customers' product lines and production processes?
2. Who are the key members of the decision-making unit in my customer's firms?
3. When should market research be performed, how much should I spend, and who should be the subject of this research?
4. What new forms of competition are impending, given anticipated technological, economic, and regulatory changes?
5. Are there more effective ways to segment my markets? Should I be focusing on industries, organizations, or specific people within organizations in my segmentation plan? What is the profit-maximizing service level for each target segment?
6. How long can I keep the customer organization sold after the sale? Should I organize our marketing effort around products, territories, customers, functions, or some combination?
7. What is the total amount my product will cost a customer over its useful life?
8. Are there gaps in my product line? Is it too broad? When do I decide to drop a product?
9. What products are in joint demand with mine? How will changes in their prices or availability affect my sales?
10. Are long-term contracts in our interest? Should I finance my customers' purchases?
11. Could discounts be used more effectively to achieve marketing objectives?
12. What effect will increased advertising have on the effectiveness of my sales force?
13. How do I evaluate the effectiveness of trade shows?
14. When should I use industrial distributors? Manufacturers' representatives? How should commission structures be designed for reps?
15. How should I use new media such as the Internet and the World Wide Web to interact more effectively with my new and existing customers?

and retailed. Before assembly, someone had to manufacture a frame, a motor, a blade, a starter system, wheels, a grass bag, and a variety of other components. Any number of firms were involved in making these parts—each of which, in turn, required machines, presses, tools, chemicals, lubricants, and paints for their manufacture. Again, these inputs had to be manufactured and marketed by someone. Finally, had not a variety of raw materials been developed, processed, and marketed in sufficient quantities, the entire process would never have begun. This set of developments is called the *production chain*. It concerns the process by which companies transform raw materials into components, parts, tools, and machines and by which these components are used to produce other products. The production chain ultimately facilitates the production of consumer goods from industrial products.

Figure 1.2 illustrates the production chain. For simplicity, six major stages in the process are presented, with examples of firms involved at each stage. There are, in

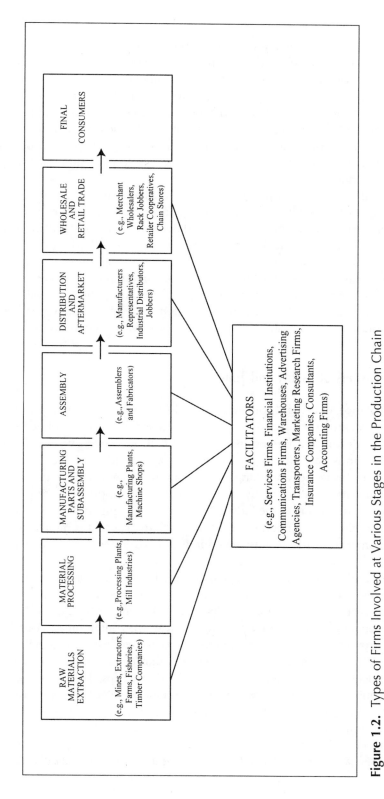

**Figure 1.2.** Types of Firms Involved at Various Stages in the Production Chain

SOURCES: Adapted from *Industrial Marketing Management*, Haas, © copyright 1982 by Kent Publishing and *Managerial Marketing for Industrial Firms*, Ames and Hlavacek. © Copyright 1984 by Random House.

addition, a number of facilitating firms that provide vital support services to companies throughout the process. In our lawn mower example, the manufacturer requires insurance, telecommunications, auditing, marketing research, and a host of other ancillary services. Although the consumer marketer focuses primarily on the link to the final consumer, industrial marketing includes a multiplicity of transactions leading up to this final link. This process involves an often complex network of interactions among many firms operating at different points in the production chain. Excluded from the domain of industrial marketing are the wholesaler and retailer of the final consumer product.

Despite the size and scope of business-to-business markets, engineers, technicians, or professionals who have little formal understanding of marketing principles and strategies make many marketing-related decisions. In fact, many industrial firms have no marketing department or marketing manager and fail to embrace the marketing concept in their operations. This situation must change, however, as firms find themselves unable to keep pace with the developments in their markets and the surrounding environment. In the meantime, programs and policies based on misconceptions regarding the marketing function often result in mediocre performance or outright failure. Table 1.2 highlights some of these misconceptions.

## Growth Markets of Today and Tomorrow

At first glance, one might conclude that industrial markets, regardless of their size, are on the decline. One has only to picture closed steel, automobile, and rubber plants and to recall the numerous obituaries that have been written for so-called smokestack industries. Although such dire predictions hold true for industries built on obsolete technologies and aging capital equipment, they hardly describe the overall industrial market. In fact, many of the major growth opportunities would appear to fall on the industrial side of the ledger. This is the case, in part, because many industries are retooling and adapting to the future—a process that stimulates demand for goods incorporating the newest technologies and goods that reduce production costs.

The postindustrial information age holds much promise for producers of products and services intended for organizational customers. As AT&T[14] closes plants that manufacture outdated telephone equipment, its Lucent Technologies[15] spin-off creates new technologies that are changing the way we communicate. Developed nations are growing primarily in such areas as computers, environmental and energy controls, optical instruments, electronic connectors, telecommunications equipment, robots, office machines, aerospace propulsion, plastics, biotechnology, electromedical equipment, and process control instruments. These are products sold, in large part, to organizational users—to factories, offices, hospitals, hotels, schools, and the government.

The laser field exemplifies the immense industrial potential represented by newer technologies. Worldwide sales of laser equipment now exceed $2 billion annually. It

---

**TABLE 1.2** Marketing Misconceptions Held by Managers
of Industrial Firms

---

The industrial manager is apt to make certain untrue assumptions about customers, products, and marketing. Some of these mistaken notions, or myths, are summarized below.

◆ **Myth:** Purchasing behavior is economically rational.

**Reality:** Subjective judgments and personal motives guide the behavior of organizational decision makers.

◆ **Myth:** New technology sells.

**Reality:** Many technologically superior products fail in the marketplace, while many technologically obsolete products continue to be purchased.

◆ **Myth:** The right product will sell itself.

**Reality:** One must have the right product at the right time, its benefits must be effectively communicated to the right people, and it must be made available through the right channels of distribution.

◆ **Myth:** "We can't waste time on marketing, we don't have the product designed yet."

**Reality:** Failure to perform market research throughout the product development process is likely to result in exaggerated estimates of market potential, in product features of little value to customers, and in prices that are too high or low.

◆ **Myth:** Sales and marketing are the same thing.

**Reality:** Selling is part of promotional strategy, which in turn is part of overall marketing strategy. Marketing includes product, price, promotion, and distribution activities that contribute to customer value.

◆ **Myth:** Purchasing can be ignored—focus on the engineers.

**Reality:** Those in purchasing can be instrumental in helping the marketer understand how buying decisions are made in a particular organization; they can also work to ensure that the firm does not buy from a particular vendor. Also, after a buying decision is made, the vendor must deal directly with the purchasing department.

◆ **Myth:** Low price is the customer's main concern.

**Reality:** Price is often a secondary concern to engineers and production managers, who will pay more for quality and reliability.

◆ **Myth:** Bookings and sales are the same thing.

**Reality:** Industrial customers rarely pay in advance; a booking or purchase order represents a potential sale, but orders are often canceled or changed, and revenue comes later.

---

seems that new applications for lasers are found daily, from their use in delicate ophthalmic surgery to the machining of extremely complex shapes within fine tolerances. The Fisher Body Division of General Motors[16] cut the labor time for making steel rule die boards (used to cut cloth and vinyl for automobile interiors) from 32

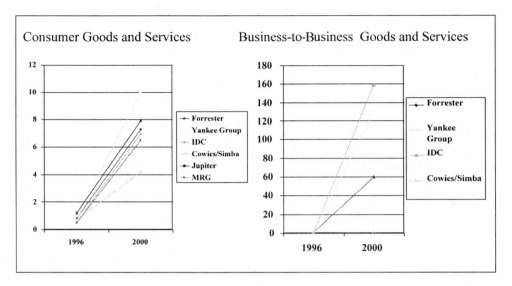

**Figure 1.3.** Forecasts of Sales on the Internet in US$ (billions), Consumer and Business-to-Business Markets

SOURCE: Cable News Network Web site (www.cnn.com), 1997.

hours to 4 hours through use of a laser. Firms are using laser-produced holograms (three-dimensional photographic images) for simulation purposes in new product testing. Supermarkets have increased customer checkout efficiency with bar code scanners, which use laser technology. Law enforcement agencies have found that marksmanship abilities can be enhanced by installing lasers into the gunsights of firearms. Homebuilders are now designing homes that employ optical disks to control energy consumption and related household functions. Laser technology can even assist in industrial espionage, enabling a company to eavesdrop in another room without having to enter and place a bugging device (although this behavior generally would be recognized to be unethical and, in most countries, illegal). The much heralded "information revolution" also presents growth opportunities for industrial marketers. As is shown in Figure 1.3, the potential for industrial marketing on the Internet far exceeds that of consumer goods and services.

At the same time, many consumer markets are maturing. Makers of soft drinks, blue jeans, and automobiles increasingly look to international markets for growth, and they segment the domestic market into smaller and smaller niches. Other consumer product categories, such as jewelry, lawn equipment, furs, leather goods, and food utensils, face zero growth or actual decline. This is not to say there are no dynamic opportunities on the consumer side—consider personal computers, bicycles, and specialty frozen foods. Rather, what is suggested is the need to broaden the focus in marketing to include organizational products and markets.

The attractiveness of opportunities on the industrial side can lead a firm with an established market position in consumer products to reposition itself completely. BF

Goodrich[17] is a household name as one of the top producers of automobile tires for consumer (and industrial) use. This traditional giant found itself in great difficulty as major competitive, economic, social, and demographic changes eroded its customer base. BF Goodrich's response was to redirect its resources and technologies toward aerospace and chemical markets, to become a major factor in aircraft modifying, repairing, and overhauling.

In a related vein, more than half of today's college graduates are finding employment in organizations that operate in industrial markets. A boom in entrepreneurial activity has been taking place in Western economies. Hundreds of thousands of new businesses are being created each year, many attributable to the technological opportunities just mentioned and many driven by information technologies such as the Internet.

College graduates work predominantly in white-collar jobs, most as professional and technical workers, managers, or salespeople. For the past two decades, growth in professional and technical workers increased at a faster rate than total employment. Most of these people work for manufacturing or service firms. Of the occupations projected to grow the fastest, a number involve industrial firms. Examples include electronic technicians, technical sales representatives, engineers (electrical, civil, mechanical), mold machine operators, computer programmers, systems analysts, service technicians, and operators.

Accompanying this growth in industrial markets are a number of profound changes in the environments surrounding these firms. Historically, industrial customers may have seemed virtually captive, while a firm's sales growth was fairly easy to extrapolate. Managers could afford to focus their efforts on product line extensions and production efficiencies, and a solely technical orientation could prevail. This situation is no longer the case; companies must plan for a future as different from today as today is from yesterday. These changes represent the most compelling reason for an enhanced understanding of industrial marketing management. Let us elaborate on some of these environmental issues.

## The External Environment of Industrial Firms

A failure to anticipate and act on changes in customer needs, technology, resource availability, regulation, market structure, competitor moves, or economic variables can doom even the most innovative of companies. These factors are part of a firm's external environment, defined as everything outside the organization itself. The environment also includes any social, political, geographic, and climatic developments that might affect the firm.

Organizational environments can be characterized by their degree of stability, complexity, diversity, and hostility. As a generalization, industrial firms must increasingly cope with instability, significant complexity, more diversification in their customer base, and a number of hostile forces in their surroundings. The experience of Digital Equipment Corporation (DEC),[18] one of the largest American computer manufacturers, provides an example. As this giant entered the mid-1980s, it found rapid technological change undermining environmental stability while the demands of new high-growth fields (such as office automation and computer-aided design and manufacturing) contributed to environmental complexity. It was forced to seek a broadened, more diverse customer base as growth opportunities shifted toward small business markets and desktop workstations. The presence of strong traditional competitors (e.g., IBM[19]), together with aggressive upstarts (e.g., Dell[20]), suggested a more hostile environment. DEC declined in market influence to the extent that it was taken over by Compaq[21] in 1998.

Industrial firms attempt to survive and prosper in what has been termed both the information age and the age of discontinuity. Environmental turbulence creates unplanned change divergent from past and present trends. Marketing strategy can play a major role in anticipating where the major changes will occur and in providing action plans for exploiting these changes or adapting to them. The next few pages elaborate on some of the specific changes taking place in the areas of technology, customers, competition, government regulation, and the economy—changes that represent both threats and opportunities for industrial marketing.

## Technological Environment

Technological change has been with us throughout history; it is not merely a fact of the human condition over the past 100 or so years. Every now and then, however, a technological change occurs that does not just change markets or circumstances; it changes society itself—the way we live. An early example of this is the adoption of the stirrup by the Franks in medieval times. The lowly stirrup changed the course of battle, particularly against the marauding Saracens, because it enabled cavalry soldiers to keep stable on a horse. It also changed the political, social, and economic structure of medieval Europe (White, 1962), for the military supremacy the stirrup gave Charles Martel, the Frankish leader, allowed him to break the power of the Catholic church and, in a very real way, to create a new world order. Similarly, the automobile did not just change the way we travel but also changed the way we live, work, shop, and enjoy leisure time.

Downes and Mui (1998) refer to technologies that do not just change markets or applications, but society itself, as "killer applications" or "killer apps." They also observe that the pace of development of "killer apps" has increased dramatically over the past 10 years. Whereas killer apps appeared roughly every 100 years or so in the Middle Ages, in the period of the Renaissance they appeared more frequently. This pace accelerated greatly during the Industrial Revolution, and throughout the 20th century they appeared at the rate of around one a year. In the past 5 or 6 years, killer apps have made their appearance at the rate of more than one a year (in the past 10 years, we think of cellular telephones, digital video disks, cloning, and of course the Internet). Dealing with this rate of change challenges the very nature of strategy itself.

Technical obsolescence poses a distinct threat, especially for more sophisticated industrial products. This threat has led some to conclude that the best way for industrial firms to remain competitive is by actively participating in the development of the latest technologies and by continually using these technologies in new products to satisfy ever-changing customer needs. For instance, Cincinnati Milacron,[22] a company that manufactured screws and taps 100 years ago, and milling and grinding machines 40 years ago, has prospered more recently as a maker of machines to form plastics, silicon exitaxial wafers used in integrated circuits, and computer-controlled robotic arms used in production lines. Marketing can play a key role in identifying likely changes in a customer's production process or in its delivery and service needs. Successful innovation requires the matching of a technological opportunity to a market need. Moreover, many industrial innovations originate in the customer firm, suggesting the need for a strong and continuous process of buyer-seller interaction.

Marketing can also identify potential technological developments through competitive analysis, interaction with suppliers and distributors, and trade show forums, among others. As new technologies are developed, countless opportunities for applying these technologies to products or processes become available. The firm must pick and choose among these opportunities. Too often, projects are pursued simply because they are technically interesting. One of the major reasons for new industrial product failure is the so-called better mousetrap that nobody wanted. This refers to a truly innovative product for which there is little real market potential. Marketing inputs can help ensure that technical projects properly reflect the demands of the marketplace.

Technology is also changing the way industrial customers do business. For example, Caterpillar[23] made its first attempt at serious on-line purchasing on June 24, 1997. The giant construction equipment manufacturer invited pre-approved suppliers to bid on a $2.4M order for hydraulic fittings—simple plastic parts which cost less than a dollar but that can bring a $2m dollar bulldozer to a standstill when they go wrong. Twenty-three suppliers elected to make bids in an on-line process on Caterpillar's Web site (Woolley, 1998). The first bids came in high, but by lunchtime only nine bidders were still left revising offers. By the time the session closed at the end of the day, the low bid was 22 cents. The previous low price paid on the component by Caterpillar had been 30 cents. Caterpillar now attains an average savings of 6% through its Web site supplier bidding system.

General Electric (GE) was one of the first major firms to exploit the Web's potential in purchasing: In 1996, the firm purchased $1Bn worth of goods from 1,400 suppliers over the Internet (Woolley, 1998). As a result, the company reports that the bidding process has been cut from 21 days to 10 and that the cost of goods has declined between 5% and 20%. Previously, GE had no foreign suppliers—now 15% of the company's suppliers are from outside North America. The company also now encourages suppliers to put their Web pages on the GE site, and this has been found to effectively attract other business.

## Customer Environment

The industrial marketer has faced, historically, a geographically concentrated customer base. This situation is changing as transportation, technological, and labor force developments enable companies to locate farther from their suppliers. Indeed, technology such as the World Wide Web allows even the smallest business-to-business marketer to have an international presence. DuPont Lubricants[24] markets a large range of lubricants for special applications to customers in many parts of the world. Its catalog has always been subject to change with regard to new products, new applications of existing products, changes to specifications, and price changes. Similarly, GE Plastics[25] a division of General Electric, offers a large range of plastics with applications in many fields, and the company has faced similar problems. Both firms now use virtual routinization by way of their Web sites to replace the physical routinization that updating of printed catalogs required previously. This can be done for customers regardless of distance, and the virtual catalog is in a real sense delivered instantaneously. Users are availed of the latest new product descriptions, specifications, and prices, and are also able to quiz the catalog on the best lubricant or plastic application for a particular job. In addition, many industrial firms find that their customer base is expanding as pressure for new products or product applications forces them to consider markets and segments with which they have had little previous experience.

Another significant challenge has to do with the buyer's training and qualifications. For a variety of reasons, the industrial buyer is increasingly more sophisticated and technically trained. More than half of the revenues earned by the average industrial firm were spent on purchases. In turbulent times, pressure is brought for more cost-effective practices for managing these expenditures. The buyer may well have earned the certified purchasing manager (CPM) designation or may even have a degree in purchasing and logistics management. He or she may have received training in materials planning, value analysis, contractual terms, negotiation strategy, financial analysis, bid appraisal, inventory management, and computer applications in purchasing and materials management. Organizations themselves are elevating purchasing management to a senior-level position. In many instances firms are reorganizing so that purchasing, materials handling, inventory, storage, and related activities are organized under one materials manager.

There is also some evidence that the future will bring more decentralized organizational structures and a greater demand for specialized goods and services. Markets themselves are becoming more fragmented. As these trends affect organizational buying, the industrial marketer must develop new strategies for need assessment, product management, and organizing the sales effort. Companies such as Hewlett-

Packard,[26] IBM, Rolls-Royce,[27] BMW, British Telecom,[28] General Electric, and Exxon[29] are experiencing shifts to smaller production runs and customized items in certain product areas.

Other trends in the customer environment include just-in-time purchasing, electronic commerce, and reverse reciprocity. Dell Computer is one of the real success stories of electronic commerce (Serwer, 1998), with estimates of daily sales from its Web site needing to be updated on a daily basis (in February of 1998, these were reckoned to be in excess of $4m each day). The company has been a sterling performer through the latter half of the 1990s, and much of this recent achievement has been attributed to its trading internationally over the Internet. Using Dell's Web site, a customer is able to customize his or her own computer by specifying (clicking on a range of options) such attributes as processor speed, RAM size, hard drive, CD-ROM, and modem type and speed. A handy calculator instantly updates customers on the cost of what they are specifying, so that they can then adjust their budgets accordingly. Once a customer is satisfied with a specified package, he or she can place an order and pay on-line. Only then does Dell commence work on the machine, which is delivered to the customer in a very short time. Even more important, Dell places orders only for items such as monitors from Sony or hard drives from Seagate[30] once a customer's order is confirmed. The PC industry leader Compaq's current rate of stock turn is 12 times per year; Dell's is 30. This may merely seem like attractive accounting performance until one realizes the tremendous strategic advantage it gives Dell: When Intel[31] launches a new, faster processor, Compaq effectively has to sell 6 weeks' old stock before it is able to launch machines with the new chip; Dell has to sell only 10 days' worth (Magretta, 1998). Dell's location is irrelevant to customers—the company is where customers want it to be. For its largest business-to-business customers, Dell even has dedicated Web sites so that these customers can order in complete privacy, and in ways most suitable to them.

Trends such as these are also leading to a general reduction in the supplier base relied on by industrial customers. This means that the firm that used to rely on three or four sources of supply for a particular item is now using only one or two.

## Competitive Environment

A company's competitive position is defined by the number, size, and intensity of rivalry among the firms that make up its industry. Other important factors include the availability of substitute products, the existence of barriers to market entry, and the bargaining power of the firm's suppliers and buyers (Porter, 1980). Basic changes in each of these areas indicate a much more threatening competitive environment for most industrial firms. Attractive growth opportunities and the sizable increase in new entrepreneurial activity suggest more competition in the industrial markets of the future. Some of these entrepreneurial ventures will come from established companies setting up semi-autonomous divisions in high-growth fields.

The market leaders of tomorrow may well be firms that are nonexistent or insignificant today. Rivalry among companies will intensify—especially where competitors are diverse, fixed costs are high, products are homogeneous, exit barriers are high, and production capacity tends to be increased in fairly large increments. Each of these conditions is frequently found in industrial markets. In response, marketers are continually being forced to find new ways to differentiate their products and services in an attempt to maintain some kind of competitive advantage in the minds of customers. Competition will be further affected by diseconomies of scale resulting from smaller production runs and less standardization in certain product areas, as well as by attempts at global standardization (and large cost reductions) in others. Similarly, new technologies are both eliminating and creating barriers to entry. They are also providing new types of product substitutes and alternative methods of production and distribution, undercutting a firm's competitive position. Vertical and horizontal integration of firms at different levels in the production chain is changing the bargaining power of the industrial firm in negotiations with its suppliers and buyers. Such integration may also be a tactic pursued by the firm's competitors, further undermining its competitive position.

## Legal Environment

The restrictions placed on a corporation by the government have multiplied dramatically during the past 50 years. One could argue that virtually no major marketing decision could be made without consulting a lawyer, or at least carefully considering legal ramifications. The marketing challenge is not only to satisfy customers' needs in a manner that provides the firm with a true competitive advantage but also to do so while meeting legal and regulatory constraints.

These constraints on business decision making include economic and social restrictions, both of which reduce the manager's flexibility. Economic regulation in most countries affects such customer-sensitive areas as pricing, discount policies, advertising practices, arrangements with distributors, and tax considerations. Social regulation defines corporate responsibilities in such areas as health and safety, product ingredients, pollution control, energy efficiency, and product liability. This type of regulation can drive costs up and make products or production processes obsolete.

Government regulation in industrial markets affects both buyer and seller. The marketer must increasingly play a key role in assessing the impact of regulation on a customer's operations, as well as on how and what that customer buys. With time, a customer's needs may be entirely reshaped.

## Economic Environment

Turbulence is pervasive in the economies of all the nations of the world. Business cycles bring alternating recessionary slowdowns and inflationary booms every few years, and interest rates and currency exchange rates vary daily. These trends impel companies to decrease or increase inventories, creating a magnified effect on industrial demand. In many economies there is a relative decline in the productivity of resources, especially labor. Productivity problems are due, in part, to aging machines and equipment in industrial plants. This fact represents a major opportunity for the marketer as industries retool and adapt the latest technologies, such as robotics and mass customization. This fact also means that many industries will simply cease to exist, given the costs of reindustrializaton. Labor force demands and government regulations also affect productivity. Unions bring pressures on management to limit the introduction of new technologies. Because of inflationary expectations, workers demand wage increases that outstrip increases in labor productivity. This, in turn, drives up the cost of finished goods, raising inventory costs of the buyer. In some countries, such as South Africa and Indonesia, the most efficient production methods cannot be used because of government regulation, making some industrial opportunities much less attractive. Another key economic development is resource shortages, which affect not only costs but also vendor relationships and contract terms. Shortages occur for a variety of reasons, including industrial cartels, international politics, and war.

Another major problem is that natural resources are being depleted, creating demand for equipment and processes that conserve resources. This problem also encourages the birth of entirely new industries and markets, such as those for synthetic materials. Up to this point, we have stressed that a greater understanding of marketing management is required to deal with the environmental opportunities and threats facing industrial organizations. One might question, however, whether industrial marketing is really any different from consumer marketing, and whether separate attention is warranted. As will be seen, these differences are actually quite profound when it comes to the practice of marketing.

## Distinctive Aspects of Industrial Marketing

The field of industrial marketing remains fairly underdeveloped. There are limited bodies of theory to help explain and predict the behavior of industrial buyers and sellers. Only moderate progress has been made in determining what works, and why, in terms of industrial marketing strategy. The quantity and quality of research performed on industrial customers are limited as well. Compared with consumer products and markets, industrial products and markets historically have received much less attention in textbooks, journals, and educational programs that deal with marketing. Industrial marketing, however, is clearly a distinct field with a number of unique characteristics and challenges.

What is different about marketing to an organization? Marketing might seem to be basically the same, regardless of the type of customer or what is being sold. This point is true to a certain extent because the basic tools and concepts—marketing concept, marketing mix, market segmentation, and the product life cycle—apply equally in both consumer and industrial markets. What differs is the design and implementation of marketing strategies and tactics to meet organizational versus consumer needs. In fact, industrial marketing represents quite a distinct challenge. The major distinguishing elements concern the importance of technical product characteristics, the fact that these products directly affect the operations and economic health (e.g., profitability) of the customer, and the fact that the customer is an organization rather than an individual consumer. Differences related to these three characteristics can be further broken down into several categories: the product itself, the nature of demand, buyer behavior, communication processes, and economic/financial factors (Table 1.3).

## Major Difference #1: The Products and Services Being Marketed

The extensive focus placed on consumer goods in marketing texts is due, in part, to the fact that most people can easily relate to the relevant properties of these products (e.g., brand name, style, color, performance, size). All of us have extensive daily experience with consumer goods. Industrial products tend to be more complex, and the relevant properties are typically more technical in nature. As Webster (1984) explains, "The same man who, as a consumer, settles for plain shaving cream if he cannot find lemon lime, will be unwilling as an industrial buyer to accept a bolt with 30 threads to the inch when his specifications call for 28" (p. 15). In fact, the industrial product represents a multiplicity of physical and performance-related specifications.

One of the most basic principles of marketing is the recognition that a product is a bundle of attributes. That is, customers buy a product based on its attributes (e.g., quality, price, durability, availability, speed) and the benefits that derive from these attributes. A distinction can be drawn between functional attributes (the product performs better, is less expensive, or is available sooner) and symbolic attributes (the product makes me feel important, young, feminine, smart, or sexy). For obvious reasons, functional attributes tend to be far more important in the industrial marketplace.

Many industrial goods carry a large unit dollar value, and most are sold in large quantities. Often they are custom made or tailored to the specific application needs of the customer organization. Furthermore, these products are marketed at different stages of completion, with much of what is sold taking the form of raw and semifinished goods. The buying firm may be purchasing for inventories as well as immediate usage. It may well purchase a given product for a number of differing uses. In some instances, the buyer has the option of making or leasing products rather than purchasing them.

The products and services sold in industrial markets can be categorized into three major groups:

**Foundation goods:** products that are used to make other products (e.g., a printing press) or to deliver services (an airplane). It is important that these do not become part of

**TABLE 1.3** How Industrial Marketing Is Different

| *Major Distinguishing Characteristics* | *What This Means to the Industrial Marketer* |
|---|---|
| Importance of technical product characteristics | Customer needs must be clearly understood and clearly monitored |
| | Marketers must consider all costs a customer will incur with a product over its useful life |
| | Product life cycle is shorter because of technological change, necessitating continual product innovation |
| | Product quality is critical |
| | Distribution channels are shorter and more direct |
| | There is a need for technically qualified sales personnel and knowledgeable, specialized middlemen |
| | Aftersale service, training, and technical assistance are stressed |
| | Packaging is more functional and less promotional |
| Products being marketed affect the operations and economic health of the user | Buyer/seller negotiation skills are crucial |
| | Formal contracts are drawn |
| | Strong vendor loyalty exists; marketers should strive to develop long-term relationships |
| | Conservative attitudes are encountered in purchase decision making; marketers need to lower the buyer's perceived risk |
| | Formal product and vendor evaluation occurs |
| | Purchases are for inventory as well as use; inventories may need to be financed |
| | Delivery reliability is critical |
| | Industry demand is fairly inelastic |
| | Size and cost of purchases are large |
| The customer is an organization rather than an individual consumer | Price bidding is used |
| | Discounts are prevalent |
| | There are fewer customers, often geographically concentrated |
| | Many people are involved in buying decisions |
| | Longer, more complex buying process |
| | Promotion is more focused, using personal selling over advertising |
| | Marketing research is more difficult |
| | A major customer can have a strong bargaining position, placing the marketer in a vulnerable position |
| | Make or buy option exists |
| | Reciprocity arrangements develop |
| | Tax and accounting implications of products and services being purchased affect what is bought as well as when and how it is bought |

those finished products. Many of these products represent major capital equipment, such as production machinery, that gets depreciated, but foundation goods also include smaller items that are expensed, such as hand tools.

**Entering goods:** products and services that actually become part of other products. Key examples include component parts (e.g., a windshield for an automobile), raw materials (e.g., lumber, iron ore, granite), and processed materials (e.g., specialty chemicals).

**Facilitating goods:** products and services that enable the day-to-day operation of an enterprise. Companies buy copiers, insurance, consulting services, cleaning supplies, and security systems that help them operate more efficiently and effectively.

Of course, the customer typically buys much more than just a product or service. The industrial product attribute bundle may also include technical assistance for installation and operation of equipment, service before and after the sale, and an emphasis on prompt, reliable delivery. In addition, the buyer organization may focus not just on a product's price but also on all the costs that will be incurred over its useful life, including installation, maintenance, and servicing. This viewpoint can be evident for even the simplest of products, such as a fluorescent light bulb that might be priced higher but saves the customer $20 in energy costs over its useful life. Another unique aspect concerns packaging requirements. For industrial products, packaging has more to do with protection than with providing promotional information. Finally, industrial products are distinctive because the daily operations and longer-term economic viability of the customer organization are directly affected by their satisfactory performance.

## Major Difference #2: The Nature of Demand

Industrial goods contribute directly or indirectly to the manufacture of consumer goods, either as part of a consumer product or as part of the production process. As a result, the demand for industrial goods is ultimately *derived* from the demand for consumer goods. For example, a maker of electrical components sells the components to a producer of small motors, who in turn sells the motors to a windshield-wiper assembler, who then sells these assemblies to a truck manufacturer. Each of these firms will find its demand dependent on the number of trucks being purchased. In fact, there is a multiplier effect, where changes in demand get magnified as one moves up or down the value-added chain. Thus, an increase in truck demand can lead to a much bigger increase in demand for the basic electrical components, principally due to inventory adjustments that occur in the various firms within the value-added chain. Derived demand also creates an interesting marketing opportunity. The marketer may be able to affect sales by appealing not just to direct customers but also to the ultimate consumer, or anyone in between. For example, the computer chip manufacturer Intel doesn't sell chips to computer users, but rather to computer manufacturers. Much of its advertising, however, has been directed to users with the "Intel Inside" campaign, which suggests to users that they should purchase a computer only if it has an Intel processor. Market activity must be analyzed at all levels of the marketing channel.

A related characteristic is termed *joint*, or *shared*, demand. Many industrial products can be used only in conjunction with other products, so the sale of one is dependent on the other. Particleboard used in construction requires wood chips, resins, and glue for its manufacture. The maker of gasoline products requires additives such as boron and lead. In each case, without any one of these components, the manufacturer does not need the others. Thus, such components have a joint demand. The industrial marketer must be knowledgeable about the products that involve joint demand. Supply shortages of joint demand products can erode sales.

A third characteristic of industrial demand is that it is frequently *concentrated*: a handful of companies may account for a disproportionate share of a firm's sales. Thus, the marketer who sells goods to companies making elevators, fire hydrants, X-ray machines, or floors for basketball courts may find that the entire market consists of fewer than 10 firms. Under such conditions, sellers find that they are much more dependent on a given customer and that the loss of a customer has a more serious impact on sales.

Finally, industrial demand is relatively *inelastic*. Where the product represents a key component, perhaps made to exact specifications, the buyer may be less sensitive to price changes. This occurs when an item is more of a necessity and fewer substitutes are available.

## Major Difference #3: How the Customer Buys

The most important point of departure between consumer and industrial marketing is *buying behavior*. The two types of buying behavior differ in terms of who buys, why, how, when, where, and what. When the customer is an organization, purchases typically involve a number of individuals. A given buying decision might include inputs from the people in engineering, production, finance, marketing, R&D, and purchasing departments. Although the goal for all is to make purchases that best fulfill organizational needs and objectives, various departments may find that their individual interests conflict when it comes to selecting a product or vendor. The manner in which these conflicts are addressed can create a very political buying process. The salesperson is placed in the difficult position of trying to figure out where to concentrate efforts in the buying firm to reach the key decision makers.

Industrial buying also involves a degree of formalization not found in consumer purchasing. Organizations can have formal policies regarding the determination of product and vendor specifications, the solicitation of bids or proposals, and the evaluation of available alternatives. Purchase requisitions, invoices, and contracts are used to specify the terms of sale. These terms frequently are negotiable.

The decision to purchase a product from a given industrial supplier may take a long time to make, often 6 months to 2 years. Once sold, a customer is likely to be source-loyal unless significant problems develop. At the same time, the customer's interest is better served if orders are spread between or among a few suppliers.

The economic performance (e.g., profitability) of the buying organization may hinge on the quality of its purchasing decisions. Keep in mind that customers are working people, responding to evaluation and reward systems within their organizations. As a result, products may represent significant risks and opportunities from the buyer's perspective.

## Major Difference #4: Communication Processes

Given the complexities of industrial products and organizational buying, the communication process between seller and buyer also differs from that typically found with consumer products—much less if any media advertising is used. Personal selling becomes the thrust of one's promotional efforts. In fact, frequently the seller goes to the buyer—not the other way around, as in consumer shopping. These contacts are supported with trade journal advertising, catalogs, industrial directories, trade shows, videos, direct mail appeals, Web sites, and other promotional tools.

The sometimes lengthy and involved buying decision produces a need for personal contact, with the sale taking on the appearance of a social negotiation process. Two-way interaction between buyer and seller over time will determine the outcome. Further, different media may be more or less effective depending on the stage of the buying process. For example, trade shows might be effective at creating awareness, while the Internet is used by the buyer to gather information, and closing the sale is best done by personal selling (Gopalakrishna, Lilien, Williams, & Sequeira, 1995).

The marketer's message must address the needs and orientations of technical people and specialists. Appeals are often more factual and descriptive (focusing on functional attributes, with less emotional or symbolic content); however, it is not unusual to also appeal to the buyer's sense of pride, security, intelligence, or innovativeness. Communication is also complicated by the fact that multiple people inside the buying organization can get involved in the buying decision. Ensuring that a given message reaches the intended member of the buying organization and that it does so at the intended time can be difficult.

## Major Difference #5: Economic/Financial Factors

Industrial marketing encompasses a number of interesting economic and financial aspects. For example, the marketer is likely to compete in an oligopolistic market, characterized by few competitors. In this situation, company strategies are much more interdependent, with whatever one firm does being strongly influenced by the anticipated reactions of its competitors. The result is often a strong competitive emphasis that can be price based on non–price based. Oligopolistic structures also give rise to price leadership.

In addition, the earlier-mentioned concentration among buyers suggests the possibility of considerable relative economic power on both sides of the market transaction. This economic concentration can be envisioned by considering the negotiation process between U.S. Steel[32] and General Motors, or between Intel and Compaq Computer. The outcomes are likely to follow from the nature of power/dependency relationships between buyer and seller. Does the seller need the buyer more than the buyer needs the seller?

Another aspect of industrial market structure is termed *reciprocity*. The customer can sometimes be a key supplier to the marketer's firm. The existence of such reciprocal relationships may indirectly affect either party's willingness to significantly change the terms of the sale. The dollar value of the product and the need for customers to maintain inventories make economic variables such as interest rates, inflation, and the business cycle critical concerns for industrial marketing. Inventories must be internally or externally financed, with inventories becoming more expensive when interest rates are higher. Inflation undermines the valuation of inventories and the replacement cost of capital, and it may encourage buyers to look for new, creative financing alternatives. They may seek inflation protection through longer-term contracts. Leasing is often a viable alternative to purchasing. So, too, might be the option of making the products instead of buying them.

# Where Are We Going From Here?

This text is concerned with the challenges and opportunities confronting the marketer in industrial/organizational markets. It is organized so that the reader can develop a logical approach to the planning, design, implementation, and control of marketing programs. Consistent with the marketing concept, we will first examine the industrial customer and how purchase decisions are made. Following this, we look at the types of analyses performed by the marketer to properly understand and evaluate industrial market opportunities. Specifically, we explore industrial market segmentation, marketing research, the assessment of competitors, and demand analysis. With this buyer and market assessment in mind, we then introduce a strategic approach to industrial marketing management. The nuts and bolts of developing specific strategies and tactics to meet customer needs profitably are examined. Individual chapters are devoted to innovation, product and service management, approaches to pricing, issues in marketing communication, managing the industrial sales force, and the design of distribution channels for industrial products. Lastly, we address the control or tracking aspects of individual marketing programs, attempting to answer the question, "What method do I use to make sure my plans are implemented correctly?" This last step should also alert industrial marketing managers to needed changes in objectives, strategies, or programs.

## Summary

Industrial marketing is concerned with exchange processes among organizations. The industrial marketer is trying to create value for organizational customers by satisfying their needs—at a profit. This goal is accomplished by manipulating a set of variables commonly referred to as the marketing mix: product, price, promotion, and distribution. In most of the economically developed nations, industrial markets make up the most significant sector of the economy. These markets represent not only a sizable number of transactions but also a major source of economic growth. As a case in point, many so-called high-tech industries are primarily involved in developing and marketing products and services sold to other organizations. Firms that compete in industrial markets have only begun to adopt a marketing orientation in their approach to producing and distributing goods and services. Technically oriented and production-oriented managers traditionally have dominated these organizations.

The change in orientation is due to a number of fundamental changes in the technological, customer, competitive, legal/regulatory, and economic environments facing industrial firms. As these companies place more emphasis on marketing skills, it becomes increasingly apparent that industrial marketing represents a challenge distinct from consumer marketing. Major differences exist in product characteristics, the nature of demand, buyer behavior, communication processes, and economic characteristics. These differences are investigated in more depth in the chapters to come. Each has important implications for the development of successful industrial marketing strategies and tactics.

## Notes

1. www.sony.com/
2. www.boeing.com/
3. www.lexus.com/
4. www.mercedes.com/
5. www.bmw.com/
6. www.otis.com/
7. www.ge.com/
8. www.britishairways.com/
9. www.ual.com/
10. www.singaporeair.com/
11. www.ncr.com/
12. www.sears.com/
13. www.jcpenny.com/
14. www.att.com/
15. www.lucent.com/
16. www.gm.com/

17. www.bfgoodrich.com/
18. www.dec.com/
19. www.ibm.com/
20. www.dell.com/
21. www.compaq.com/
22. www.milacron.com/
23. www.caterpillar.com/
24. www.lubricants.dupont.com/
25. www.ge.com/plastics/
26. www.hewlett-packard.com/
27. www.rolls-royce.com/
28. www.britishtelecom.com/
29. www.exxon.com/
30. www.seagate.com/
31. www.intel.com/
32. www.ussteel.com/

# Questions

1. Bob King is president of a medium-sized firm (300 employees) that manufactures and sells customized electronic components to companies that make sophisticated consumer electronic products (e.g., advanced home alarm systems, high-quality home stereo systems). Although Mr. King employs five salespeople, he has little use for marketing. Explain to Mr. King what the role of marketing should be in a firm such as his and how sales is different from marketing.

2. "Industrial marketing is the same as consumer marketing." Argue both sides of the issue.

3. "The information age holds much promise for producers of products and services intended for organizational customers." Do you agree or disagree? Support your position.

4. At a recent management seminar, a marketing vice president with 30 years of experience argued that "most industrial firms do not understand, and certainly do not practice, the marketing concept." What are some possible reasons for (a) their lack of understanding and (b) the failure to implement or follow the marketing concept?

5. What are some problems you would see in measuring customer satisfaction when the customer is an organization?

6. How can industrial organizations avoid marketing myopia? Identify specific problems in defining one's business too narrowly. Can a company define itself too broadly? What, if any, is the relationship between the marketing concept and marketing myopia?

7. Many of the activities we claim to be part of marketing are not actually performed by someone called a "marketer." For example, prices may be set by those in finance, distribution decisions made by those in production, and a product's design, features, and packaging determined by design engineers. What are some possible implications of this?

8. Using the five components of the environment described in the chapter, discuss some of the environmental opportunities and threats facing industrial firms in the next 5 years. How can marketing improve an organization's ability to face these challenges?

9. Singer Corporation, a traditional manufacturer of sewing machines, is now a major competitor in the flight simulator and navigation system industries. Identify and discuss major environmental trends that might have caused Singer to redirect its focus to the industrial product area.

10. Bestco Blade Co. manufactures blades used in snowplowing machines and vehicles. The company also produces blades for large industrial fans. How does the concept of derived demand apply to a firm such as this? Would the impact likely be different for its two major markets? How might they differ? Draw implications for the marketing efforts of Bestco.

11. Of the four elements in the marketing mix, marketers often place the most emphasis on promotion. Why do you think this area receives so much attention? Do you see potential dangers in a preoccupation with promotion when marketing industrial goods and services?

# Exploring the Customer's Purchasing Operation

*A dollar saved by the purchasing department*
*is a dollar of profit for the firm.*
—Gary J. Zenz

## Key Concepts

Electronic data interchange (EDI)
Enterprise resource planning (ERP)
Expediting
Forward buying
Hand-to-mouth buying
Job plan
Just-in-time inventory (JIT)
Life-cycle costing
Materials management concept
Materials requirement planning (MRP)

Purchasing process
Purchasing structure
Reverse engineering
Salvage value
Speculative buying
Time-based buying strategies
Value added networks (VANs)
Value analysis
World Wide Web (WWW)

## Learning Objectives

1. Introduce the customer's purchasing department as a major source of interface between the industrial marketer and the buying organization.

2. Summarize the formal procedures and paperwork a company relies on when making a purchase.

3. Characterize the ways in which companies organize their purchasing operations, with an emphasis on the materials management concept.

4. Assess the major tools used by purchasing professionals when evaluating vendors and selecting products/services.

5. Draw marketing implications from major new production operations technologies being used by industrial buyers, such as JIT, EDI, and MRP.

## Purchasing as a Point of Contact

To understand industrial marketing, one must first understand how the industrial customer buys. Of particular importance is the purchasing operation in customer firms. Not only is this a critical functional area in its own right, but it is also the major window through which the marketer can reach into the customer organization. As a general rule, the purchasing department is the greatest source of interaction between the marketer and the customer firm.

Purchasing by companies is a big business. A recent Gartner Group study (2000) shows that organizations spend 60% of their revenues on purchases, so a savings of only 2% on procurement would equate to a 1.2% contribution to the bottom line. Given the amount of money being spent, it is not surprising that purchasing operations in companies tend to be formalized and structured, and that purchasing professionals rely on fairly sophisticated methods for making buying decisions.

This chapter examines purchasing operations in commercial enterprises, including how this function tends to be organized, the procedures that guide its operations, and the tools and techniques used by purchasing professionals when deciding what to buy and from whom they should buy. The approaches and methods used will vary from company to company, so the discussion focuses on some of the more prevalent practices and trends. A number of excellent books on purchasing are available that provide a much more detailed treatment of the subject and nicely complement an industrial marketing text.

## Purchasing Procedures in a Company

Most of the customer organizations that a marketer will encounter have a set of formal purchasing procedures and documentation requirements. Given the amounts

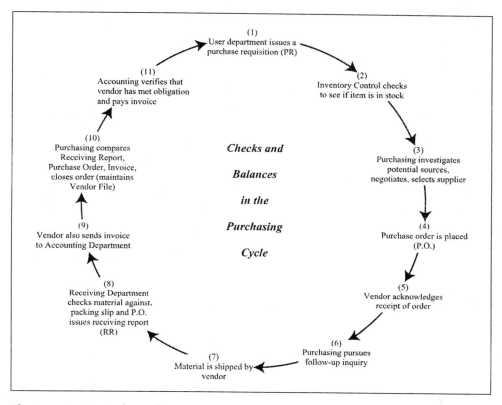

**Figure 2.1.** Typical Purchasing Cycle

spent on purchasing in the typical firm, such requirements create a system of checks and balances. It is critical for marketers to recognize and comply with these requirements. Some of them are described below and are illustrated in Figure 2.1.

Once a need has been identified for some product or service in the buying organization, often by a user department, that department will initiate a purchase requisition. Only authorized personnel can originate and sign off on such requisitions, which often are numbered to identify the originating department. The form must describe the needed item as specifically as possible and include information on the quantity required, when and where it is needed, and the account to be charged. Assuming that the purchase requisition has been properly filled out and approved, and that sufficient stocks are not already on hand, the next step is the issuance of a written purchase order—usually by the purchasing department. If the purchase is of something minor, the item may be obtained using the petty cash fund.

Before issuing a purchase order for a more substantial purchase, the buying organization will investigate potential sources, negotiate with suppliers or solicit bids, establish price-related terms, and select a supplier. The buyer may maintain a list of approved suppliers for certain items.

The purchase order will provide the company name as well as the name and signature of the purchasing individual who is acting as agent. The order will specify the quantity, item description, and terms of purchase—including discounts, free on board (F.O.B.) points (specifying the transportation vehicle and place of origin, as well as who pays the freight charges), date of order, and desired delivery date. For many products, including catalog items, an item number or code is required. Terms and conditions (e.g., those governing quality approval, cancellation clauses, or price changes) will often be preprinted on the purchase order.

The purchase order represents a formal offer and is the first step toward establishing a legal contract between buyer and seller. Upon receipt of this form, the vendor will acknowledge acceptance of the order, the second ingredient for a legal contract. This acceptance can involve immediate shipment of the requested goods, the return of an approved copy of the purchase order, the return of an acknowledgment form sent by the buyer along with the purchase order, or the completion of a standard acceptance form designed and used by the vendor. The vendor can alter the terms of the purchase order by writing in changes on whatever acceptance form is used. This counteroffer now must be accepted by the buying organization.

After sending out the purchase order, the purchasing department will follow up to ensure that the contractual relationship has been established, to check the status of the order, and to expedite production and delivery. Also, if the vendor has subcontracted any part of the order, the buyer may want to monitor the progress of these subcontracts.

Upon shipment of the order from the vendor, the receiving department will examine incoming materials and prepare a receiving report. Responsibility for inspection typically will rest within either the purchasing or the production department. The vendor's invoice is audited for accuracy and compared with the purchase order and the receiving report. This auditing function usually is performed by the accounting department, but sometimes by the purchasing department. The invoice is paid, at a time that depends on the discounts offered by the vendor. In some cases, invoices are prepaid (i.e., before delivery) to take advantage of vendor incentives. The last step in the process is order closing, which involves consolidating the documentation and correspondence pertaining to a given order in a closed-order file for future reference.

Much of the paperwork involved in this process (called the *purchasing cycle*) is replaceable by computerized communication systems. In fact, for routine and repetitive purchases, a computer interface between buyer and seller organizations can eliminate the need for human interaction. New technologies can dramatically reduce order and delivery time as well as decrease errors in accounting and control.

## How Companies Organize the Purchasing Operation

The purchasing process used by a particular organization will depend, in large part, on how the purchasing operation is set up. Where is the purchasing function located within the organizational structure? Is it centralized or decentralized? Is it a stand-alone function, or does purchasing report to some other function? How much authority and responsibility does purchasing have? Does management view it as a strategic function or more as an operational activity? Answers to these questions will vary considerably among customer organizations.

Although each department or functional area in a firm could conceivably handle its own purchasing needs, this approach generally is viewed as inefficient. As a result, a formal purchasing or procurement function is established in most industrial firms, with responsibility given to this department for making commitments in the name of the company for the materials, tools, supplies, and services needed by all user departments. The purchasing department is, in a sense, an intermediary between these user departments and vendors.

The major tasks facing the purchasing department can include identifying and evaluating sources of supply, negotiating prices and terms, establishing the purchase contract, ensuring that delivery arrangements are compatible with production scheduling, expediting orders, handling returns of unacceptable merchandise, establishing vendor files, and maintaining ongoing relationships with suppliers. The department is further charged with monitoring changes in markets, prices, and regulations.

Traditionally, purchasing was not a top-level function in the organizational structure. Rather, purchasing activities have been subordinate to the manufacturing or operations function. Over time, however, companies have moved toward the establishment of purchasing as a distinct functional area on the same level as production, marketing, finance, and R&D. The head of purchasing is often a vice president or other senior-level executive. The enhanced role and status of purchasing have developed for a number of reasons. For most industrial firms, more than 50% of sales revenue is spent on purchases. Combine this fact with inflationary cost trends, raw material shortages, high financing costs, and intense competitive pressures, and it is not surprising that increased attention is devoted to achieving efficiency and effectiveness in purchasing operations. Not only is purchasing a potential source of major material cost savings, but it is also a contributor to the operational efficiency of the organization. Purchasing is an important source of value and can significantly affect the firm's competitive position in the marketplace.

The organization of the purchasing department might resemble the structure found in Figure 2.2, which is appropriate for a medium-sized company with a centralized department located at a single site. Companies with multiple sites may maintain a single centralized purchasing department, may add local purchasing officers at each location, or may completely decentralize purchasing, with fairly autonomous departments at each site. The numerous structural alternatives available each have different implications for the industrial marketer.

As shown in Figure 2.2, the purchasing department can include a considerable amount of specialized expertise. For example, buyers may concentrate in particular product categories, and the department can include members whose sole function is to write orders or to work with vendors to expedite production and delivery. Staff assistants may be employed to perform studies on ways in which a purchased product's

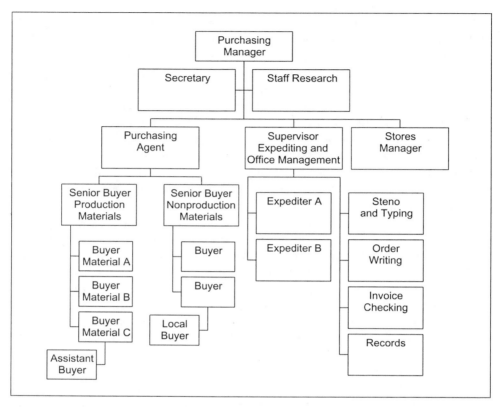

**Figure 2.2.** What a Purchasing Department Looks Like in a Mid-Sized Company

costs can be reduced, to assess economic trends, or to evaluate and forecast conditions in various commodity markets.

In recent years, the procurement function has been integrated into what has been labeled the *materials management concept*—a systems approach to managing the total materials flow in an organization. The flow begins with the purchase of materials and ends with the delivery of finished product to a warehouse, ready to be marketed. Activities such as receiving, incoming inspection, stores, materials handling, production planning and control, inventory management (raw materials, goods in process, finished goods), inbound and outbound traffic management, shipping, warehousing, and customer service are integrated into a materials management division (Figure 2.3). The three functions that are integrated, then, are buying, storage, and movement. Often the manager of this department is a vice president, and professional purchasing managers can use this position to enhance their influence and control within the organization. The materials management concept has been adopted by some service organizations as well as a large number of manufacturing companies.

The major benefit of this concept is the coordination that can be achieved within the materials area. In the absence of such an approach, decisions on purchasing (what to purchase, how much, when), inventory, or shipping may be made in isola-

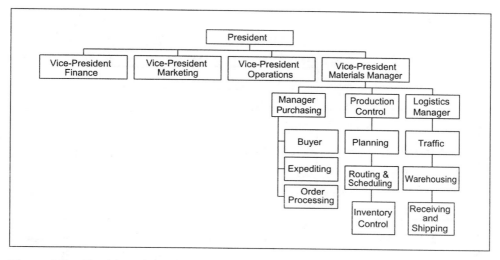

**Figure 2.3.** The Materials Management Organizational Structure

tion. Consider the example of a purchasing agent who buys larger quantities than currently required so as to negotiate a favorable price. The savings may be illusory if this purchase creates storage problems resulting from insufficient warehousing capacity, or when the costs of managing this inventory (e.g., costs of space, capital investment, taxes, obsolescence, and deterioration) exceed the apparent price savings. The materials management concept is intended specifically to address such problems. Also, better coordination is possible in satisfying the material needs of other functional areas in the organization.

The marketer trying to sell a product to a company organized around a materials management philosophy should recognize that the buyer is likely to assess the product from a total materials perspective. Although a purchasing agent may be attracted by a lower price, a materials manager may be willing to pay more for a product that offers greater use value in terms of storage, installation, maintenance, servicing, and disposal costs.

## The Changing Role of the Purchasing Professional

Procurement professionals still continue to spend considerable time negotiating prices and processing purchase orders despite relatively high levels of automation in most purchasing departments. The purchaser's role in an organization has changed, however, over the past decade. For instance, one study found a shift from purchasers spending 70% of their time on paper pushing and 30% on vendor management to 80% on vendor management and 20% on paper pushing (Forrester Research, 1998).

Today, purchasing professionals tend to define their jobs as being less clerical and more strategic, technical, and team oriented, with greater levels of responsibility. Cut-

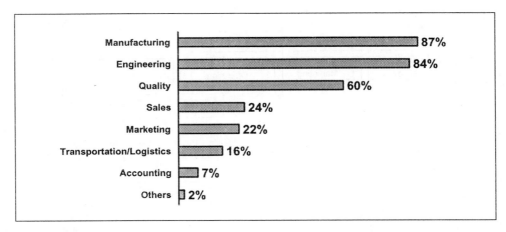

**Figure 2.4.** What Internal Functions Do Purchasing People Most Often Team With?

SOURCE: "OEM Buying Survey—Part 2: Buyers Get New Roles but Keep Old Tasks." *Purchasing*, 12 (July 16, 1998), Minahan.

ting costs and improving purchasing efficiency are now the more important considerations on the job. This trend is expected to continue as the role of a purchaser evolves to incorporate more strategic, vendor-related activities. In addition, purchasers are getting more involved in product design and development, supplier quality improvement, and supply chain management.

Purchasing professionals participate on cross-functional teams with manufacturing, engineering, quality assurance, marketing, and sales professionals (see Figure 2.4). A team of members with varied skills and experiences increases the probability that the company will make sourcing decisions that maximize value to the firm. A supplier's efforts must reflect this team concept rather than simply targeting the purchasing manager or the purchasing department. Successful marketers find that more active involvement with the buying organization becomes a necessity. They must be able to deliver better quality, service, and delivery at lower costs. Some creative marketers even try to get the buyer to include a representative from the selling firm on cross-functional teams.

In addition, larger firms have seen the need to increase the technical ability of their purchasing and supply management employees. According to John Poss, a senior buyer for Marotta Scientific Controls Inc.[1], as products become more sophisticated, firms may require a technical degree for employees holding a purchasing position.

To compete, those in purchasing want to ensure that their supplier's performance is as good as or better than the performance of their competitors' suppliers. Consequently, changes in the purchasing function are directed toward maintaining a network of capable suppliers who are competent to meet standards in quality, delivery, cost reduction, and technological advancements.

# Key Tools Used by Those Involved in Purchasing Decisions

Successful marketing practices will reflect the concepts and tools used by customer organizations to evaluate and manage the products they buy. Three of the most important of these purchasing tools are life-cycle costing, value analysis, and time-based buying strategies.

## Life-Cycle Costing

As our discussion of materials management has suggested, products can cost more than just the initial purchase price. Delivery, installation, plant modification, training, maintenance, and servicing are among the costs that can be incurred over a long period of time for certain products. The marketer will find it helpful to consider the useful economic life of a product to a particular customer, then to determine all the costs that will be incurred during that time period—the *life-cycle* costs of the product.

Three categories of life-cycle costs must be added together: initial cost (i.e., purchase price), start-up costs, and postpurchase costs. The *purchase price* is defined as the total dollar amount paid to a vendor for an item, including freight costs, insurance, and any technical training provided by the supplier for a fee. *Start-up costs* are initial costs that are not paid to the vendor from whom the product was purchased but that must be incurred to make the product operational or usable. These costs are either paid to other suppliers or absorbed by the customer. Examples include the costs of modifying physical facilities, meeting power requirements, or establishing the temperature control necessary to satisfy product requirements, as well as lost production time during installation or any training not provided by the product vendor. *Postpurchase costs* are generated to keep the product in working condition after it has been put into use. Such ongoing expenditures as repair, servicing, financing costs, power consumption, inventory costs, and space requirements related to the usage of the item represent postpurchase costs. To get a complete picture of a product's total cost over its useful life, the purchaser may also want to subtract the salvage value from the total of the initial, start-up, and postpurchase costs. *Salvage value* is the amount that can be recovered when the item is disposed of.

The calculation of life-cycle costs can be difficult, requiring technical expertise and insight. The expected life of a product must be estimated and reasonable judgments made regarding expected product performance, wear and tear, and use requirements. Past experience and value analysis studies can be useful here. Costs incurred over a number of years must be discounted and expressed in present value terms. To do so, a reasonable discount rate must be determined.

Life-cycle costing can have important meaning to the marketer. If company A's product has lower start-up and postpurchase costs than does company B's competing product, other things being equal, company A is delivering more economic value to the customer (EVC). This value factor can be a major source of competitive advantage. Furthermore, the company providing more EVC has a justification for charging a higher price.

## Value Analysis

Another purchasing tool having important implications for the industrial marketer is *value analysis* (also called value engineering, value control, or value assurance). It was developed by General Electric during World War II as an approach to cost reduction in a period of material shortages. Value, in this context, is defined as "the relative cost of providing a necessary function or service at the desired time and place with the essential quality" (Fram, 1974, p. 2).

*Value analysis* is the organized study of a product after it has been developed, aimed at identifying costs that do not add to the reliability or to the quality of the item and at determining whether the product can somehow be improved while achieving cost reductions. The components of an end product are analyzed in detail to determine whether they can be redesigned, standardized, or manufactured by a less expensive means of production (see the Business Marketing Capsule for examples). A key point in value analysis is that although cost reduction seems to be the main focus, maintaining quality, satisfactory functional performance, and customer satisfaction are critical. The analysis consists, then, of an appraisal of cost-benefit trade-offs.

After careful assessment of a product's design, it is not unusual to find that 80% of the total cost is attributable to 20% of its component parts and materials. Because of the pressures on purchasing departments to save money without sacrificing quality, purchasers often look for substitute products or product components that will deliver the same value at lower cost. This approach provides an opportunity for the marketing organization that can produce functionally identical products more efficiently.

Although there are various approaches to value analysis, some of the key questions that must be addressed are listed in Table 2.1. To conduct the actual analysis, the value analysis team will proceed through five stages: information, speculation, analysis, execution, and reporting. These stages, taken together, constitute a *job plan*. In the information stage, the concern is with describing the product, its cost, and its functions. Information is gathered regarding the materials used in manufacturing the product, the production process, the vendor's true costs, and what makes the product work. The speculation stage involves creative thought regarding how the product and its functions can be altered. Ideas such as substituting new materials or parts, reversing procedures, combining procedures, eliminating features that are not functional, and reducing or increasing product size are all results of speculative brainstorming sessions among the members of the value analysis team. The feasibility and cost of these ideas are evaluated in the analysis or judgment stage. Some proposals involve detailed testing, such as replacing a critical component with an untried substitute. Others are more straightforward, such as eliminating gloss paint on an interior machine part where paint may not be necessary. In the execution stage, the

## BUSINESS MARKETING CAPSULE

### *Value Analysis at Work*

The objective of value analysis (VA) is to reach equal or greater efficiency at a lower cost. Although cost reduction appears to be the principal focus, it is crucial to maintain quality, adequate performance, and customer satisfaction.

To be competitive, manufacturers have to first locate unnecessary costs, then get rid of them without impairing their products' use or value. Effective VA can be very rewarding—lower costs, better products, and higher profits.

Implementation of VA programs can be beneficial for the firm. The following real-life examples confirm this.

◆ An insulator costing $4.56 was originally porcelain, and leaded extra heavy. Now molded from polyester and glass, it is lighter and virtually indestructible, and its cost fell to $3.25.

◆ Packing material from incoming shipments was reused to pack outgoing shipments. Savings amounted to $676,024.

◆ Weights mounted on a rotor ring were curved to match the ring curve, but this proved to be unnecessary. Using a straight piece, the cost dropped from $.40 to $.04.

◆ Bottles of shampoo for distributors were formerly packed in plain chipboard cartons. By changing to a six-pack holder similar to that used in the beverage industry, more than $100,000 was saved in the first year.

◆ An exhaust manifold in an air compressor was originally a cast-iron part that required several machine steps. Switching to a powder metal process allowed four machine steps to be reduced to one. Savings were $50,000 per year.

◆ A casting was redesigned, resulting in material, freight, and machinery savings of $167,700 during the first year.

◆ The cost of engine valve guides was trimmed by 71% by switching from a casting process to powdered metals. First-year savings amounted to $65,000 on a volume of about 100,000 pieces per year; in addition, lead times were greatly reduced.

◆ A large equipment manufacturer saved $18 for each $1 spent on VA efforts on more than 2,000 projects simply by using a permanent, four-person committee to head up its program and keep it moving.

◆ The cost of a special spring was reduced by more than half. Savings were projected to be more than $250,000 in the first year.

VA programs obviously have great potential benefit for a firm. In fact, of the top 20 Japanese industrial firms, 17 have VA executives at the vice presidential level. Hitachi has 250 people in VA within materials management. Their efforts saved 5%—or $500 million—of the company's $10 billion operations in 1 year. Mazda has a group VE (value engineering) program that incorporated a team

*continued on the next page*

R&D concept to obtain high-quality, highly cost efficient cars. The Japanese are so interested in the VA concept that they instituted an award called the "Miles Award." It is named after Jerry B. Miles, of the General Electric Corporation, who originated the VA concept in the United States.

SOURCE: Adapted from various sources, including Vincent G. Reuter, "What Good Are Value Analysis Programs?," *Business Horizons*, 29 (March/April 1996), pp. 73-79.

proposals for change and evidence of their utility must be sold to management. Resistance to change of any sort, especially change regarding how a job is performed, is not unusual. A useful strategy is to include on the value analysis team those individuals thought to be most resistant. Finally, those who are involved in the reporting stage are concerned with implementing and following through on the changes. Success depends on organizational commitment to value analysis as a philosophy.

The value analysis team will consist of a group of functional experts and may have representatives from purchasing, design engineering, product engineering, accounting, and marketing, among others. The industrial salesperson often plays a role by providing data and technical assistance. The team approach is critical both in achieving a creative environment and in soliciting organizational resources and support for the value analysis effort.

Although this work can be performed at any time before or after a product is purchased, value analysis is especially relied on in the maturity stage of a product's life cycle, or when technologies change. Usually by this time, competitors have entered the market with less expensive replicas, while the original producer is attempting to solidify and maintain market share. Moreover, after a product has been on the market several years, customer organizations have seen what works and what does not, and they are more likely to pursue cost-saving measures.

Industrial marketers will find that it pays to be proactive when it comes to customer value analysis programs. Astute marketers may want to develop their own programs or get involved directly with those of customer organizations. The marketer who pays close attention to customer value analysis programs can also find such studies to be a valuable source of new product ideas. Marketers also may benefit from performing a type of value analysis on competitors' products in which they effectively take apart those products to see how they are made and why they are made that way, a process called *reverse engineering*.

## Time-Based Buying Strategies

The industrial marketer should be cognizant of the various objectives and strategies that underlie the way in which an organization buys. Traditional approaches to purchasing involve strategies that consider current usage or volume requirements as well as existing and anticipated market conditions. Depending on how these factors

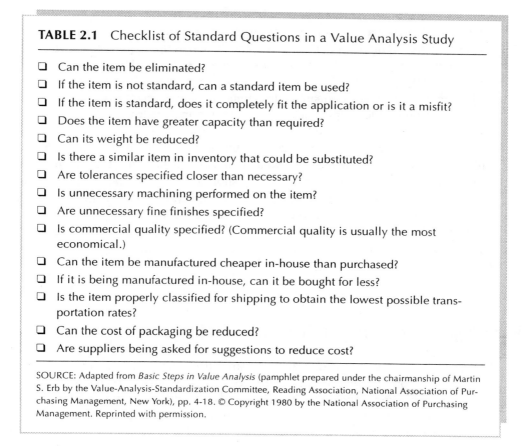

**TABLE 2.1** Checklist of Standard Questions in a Value Analysis Study

☐ Can the item be eliminated?

☐ If the item is not standard, can a standard item be used?

☐ If the item is standard, does it completely fit the application or is it a misfit?

☐ Does the item have greater capacity than required?

☐ Can its weight be reduced?

☐ Is there a similar item in inventory that could be substituted?

☐ Are tolerances specified closer than necessary?

☐ Is unnecessary machining performed on the item?

☐ Are unnecessary fine finishes specified?

☐ Is commercial quality specified? (Commercial quality is usually the most economical.)

☐ Can the item be manufactured cheaper in-house than purchased?

☐ If it is being manufactured in-house, can it be bought for less?

☐ Is the item properly classified for shipping to obtain the lowest possible transportation rates?

☐ Can the cost of packaging be reduced?

☐ Are suppliers being asked for suggestions to reduce cost?

SOURCE: Adapted from *Basic Steps in Value Analysis* (pamphlet prepared under the chairmanship of Martin S. Erb by the Value-Analysis-Standardization Committee, Reading Association, National Association of Purchasing Management, New York), pp. 4-18. © Copyright 1980 by the National Association of Purchasing Management. Reprinted with permission.

are viewed, the purchaser will usually use one of the following three types of buying strategies: speculative buying, forward buying, and hand-to-mouth buying (Dobler, Lee, & Burt, 1995). These strategies are time based; the length of time that coverage of needs is provided (number of days' supply kept in stock) is the variable that distinguishes each approach from the others.

With *speculative buying*, the organization purchases quantities of goods in excess of projected or foreseeable requirements. The expectation is that a large purchase at current market prices will, over time, generate a profit for the organization. This is appropriate during periods of prolonged inflation or when the market price drops temporarily because of excess supply or a short-term decline in demand. The purchasing profit should be realized as changing conditions drive market prices higher. Of course, the apparent savings to the buyer are somewhat offset by added inventory costs. There is a degree of risk involved in speculative buying. First, the organization's needs may change, such that the excess quantities purchased are never used. Although this excess conceivably could be sold, this alternative places additional demands on the buying organization. Second, prices may not move in the anticipated direction, or at least not as much as expected.

*Forward buying* also involves purchasing an amount of materials in excess of what is currently required, but not beyond anticipated future requirements. The need for what is being purchased can be clearly foreseen, so forward buying does not entail the risk found in speculative buying. Reasons to engage in forward buying might include taking advantage of quantity discounts or volume freight rates, providing security against unstable supply conditions, and buffering against unreliable transportation or delivery performance by vendors.

When the buyer purchases in quantities that just satisfy immediate operating requirements and that are smaller than what would usually be considered economical, *hand-to-mouth buying* is in operation. This short-term strategy is intended to minimize inventories when prices are falling, when engineering design changes are imminent, or when the firm is experiencing temporary cash flow problems.

Alternatively, the organization may establish an ongoing program with vendors in which ordering and delivery are tailored to daily production needs, commonly referred to as just-in-time purchasing, as discussed below.

# Technologies Are Changing the Way Companies Buy

The purchasing operations of many industrial firms are being revolutionized by modern technologies that help to reduce costs and greatly improve efficiency. A number of the key developments are discussed below, but the reader should keep in mind that the pace of technological change is quite rapid, with new tools becoming available all the time. The technologies described here tend to be computer based and share the common goal of helping companies operate on a "real-time basis," in which ordering, production, and distribution occur virtually simultaneously.

## Just-in-Time Inventory

There is a trend in purchasing toward minimizing inventories and away from an orientation where large inventories are seen as an asset to the firm. The aim is to create a situation where purchased materials and parts arrive at a user's location only as they are needed. Such an arrangement is commonly referred to as just-in-time (JIT) inventory. JIT approaches inventory as an "evil presence" that covers up problems and drives up costs, thereby keeping a company from being competitive. Ample inventories represent protection against human error, machine breakdowns, and defective parts; correspondingly, these inventories provide management with less incentive to eliminate production inefficiencies.

For JIT to be successful, the concept must be integrated into both the production and purchasing operations of the organization. The production control system will seek to keep work-in-progress and raw materials inventories to a minimum by scheduling delivery of the precise amount of materials or parts needed at each work station only as they are required. The production rate must be made fairly level or smooth, typically leading to smaller production lot sizes for each item and more frequent production setups.

At the same time, cooperative relationships with suppliers become a necessity. The establishment and maintenance of JIT requires companies to overcome the view that vendors and customers are adversaries. Instead, each must operate as an extension of the other. The emphasis has to be on mutual efforts to reduce costs and a sharing of the resulting savings. Substantial resource investments must be made by both parties, ultimately causing them to become more dependent on one another.

The purchasing department must persuade suppliers to deliver small quantities of needed items as they are demanded—which may necessitate deliveries on a daily, or even more frequent, basis. Delivery schedules must be extremely reliable, lead times for ordering must be very short, and deliveries can contain few, if any, defective items. Communication between the organizations must be intensive, with both parties sharing detailed proprietary data, such as cost figures, sales projections, and production schedules. Correspondingly, the buyer will often sign long-term purchasing contracts with vendors and order a wider variety of products from a smaller pool of suppliers.

Such radical changes in organizational roles and responsibilities suggest that special care must be exercised when buyers select potential relationship partners. Individuals in charge of supplier selection must objectively evaluate candidates in terms of performance capabilities, both current and potential. Criteria commonly used in the selection process include the supplier's product quality, financial strength and stability, technological capability, location, delivery capability, service responsiveness, management attitude and philosophy, and compatibility with the buyer organization. Not surprisingly, many companies encounter serious obstacles when attempting to move to a JIT environment. As summarized in Table 2.2, difficulties arise both inside the purchasing organization and in relationships with vendors. Of the obstacles cited, poor supplier support and inadequate commitment from top management are the most serious.

Where these obstacles have been avoided or surmounted, the results can be dramatic. JIT can lead to reduced purchasing costs, reduced inventory costs, faster response to product design changes, fewer delivery delays and production slowdowns, simplified receiving, fewer inspections, and more efficient administrative procedures because of a reduction in the number of suppliers required. Furthermore, JIT can enable the buying organization to improve product quality. Some of the key ways that this is possible include the following:

◆ Small lot purchases enable fast detection and correction of defects

◆ Suppliers become more quality conscious because JIT encourages buyers to evaluate and select them on the basis of quality

**TABLE 2.2**  Problems Commonly Associated With Just-in-Time Implementation

| Problems | Causes | Recommendations |
| --- | --- | --- |
| Lack of support from suppliers | 1. Perceptions that benefits accrue only to the buying organization<br>2. Tendency of buyers to stimulate competition among suppliers<br>3. Strain JIT places on suppliers through constant buyer scrutiny | 1. Educate and train suppliers on the purpose of JIT<br>2. Establish long-term relationships |
| Lack of top management support | 1. Preoccupation with short-term profitability and existing markets<br>2. Management skepticism concerning suitability of JIT to the firm | 1. Visits to companies using JIT, attendance at workshops or seminars on the subject<br>2. Highlight positive JIT results experienced by other firms to sell the concept to managers |
| Low product quality from vendors | 1. Inadequate experience on the part of the buyer in managing suppliers<br>2. Past manufacturing philosophies that permitted acceptance of an excessive percentage of defects in incoming material shipments | 1. Develop and use a supplier certificate program<br>2. Use a supplier plan audit program |
| Lack of employee readiness and support | 1. Resistance to a change of habits<br>2. Fear of job loss<br>3. Increased pressure and potential frustration | 1. Long-term, continuing JIT purchasing training<br>2. Educate employees on importance of JIT to company and personal well-being |
| Lack of support from carrier companies | 1. Absence of long-term relationships that provide for unique services or highly structured delivery schedules from transportation companies | 1. Reduce the number of carriers used<br>2. Purchase transportation from contracted carrier<br>3. Develop and implement an electronic data interchange network |

| | | 4. Develop a climate that fosters interorganizational integration |
|---|---|---|
| Lack of engineering support | 1. Inadequate interaction between design engineering and purchasing personnel | 1. Develop a climate that fosters interorganizational integration |
| Lack of communication | 1. Conflicts in the interests and goals of the personnel in material management, manufacturing quality control, transportation, and other key functional departments | 1. Development of systems and/or procedures that foster close cooperation and communication of purchasing with all other functional departments |

SOURCE: Adapted from "Just-in-Time Purchasing Problems and Solutions," *Journal of Purchasing and Materials Management*, 22 (Summer), 11A-15A, Ansari and Modarress. © Copyright 1986 by *Journal of Purchasing and Materials Management*.

◈ Vendors increasingly have to certify their quality, reducing need for receiving inspections by the buyer

◈ Use of single sources leads to frequent on-site visits by technical people from vendor organizations and thus a better understanding of the customer's quality requirements

◈ The fact that only essential product characteristics are fully specified gives suppliers more discretion in product design and manufacturing methods, which results in specifications that are more (consistently) attainable

◈ Because commitment to the vendor is long term, the vendor can afford to make longer-term investments to meet quality requirements

◈ Reduced paperwork frees up purchasing people to monitor quality and push for quality enhancements

American companies began to implement JIT largely in response to the inroads made into domestic markets by efficient Japanese competitors. JIT is a principal reason why Toyota Motor Company[2] could import all its raw materials, produce a quality car, ship it 7,000 miles, and still have a cost advantage over its American competitors of up to $1,500. U.S. companies are now realizing the same kinds of benefits. Omark Industries, a diversified corporation based in Portland, Oregon, saved an estimated $7 million in inventory carrying costs in 1 year. Its system is called ZIPS (zero inventory production system). Westinghouse Corporation[3] was able to slash the number of freight carrier companies it relies on from 200 to 14 after adopting JIT, leading to better service at lower cost. A much smaller firm, T. D. Shea Manufacturing of Troy, Michigan, which sells automotive plastic products, uses a similar system called Nick-of-Time. The Harley-Davidson Motor Company's[4] engine plant in Milwaukee,

Wisconsin, calls its version of the system MAN, for material-as-needed. Using JIT, A. P. Parts, of Toledo, Ohio, was able to reduce finished good (exhaust systems) inventory by 32%, eliminate 460,000 square feet in warehouse space, and consolidate two plants.

General Motors integrated the just-in-time concept into the production plan for the highly successful Saturn automobile. Using advanced production management techniques, the company achieved savings of about $2,000 in costs per car manufactured. To illustrate where production approaches are moving, consider the following transaction. A customer (either by going to a dealership or from his or her home computer) specifies the exact set of options desired on a yet-to-be-manufactured car. These data are entered on a computer terminal at the dealer location and sent electronically to the Saturn automobile plant. From there, computer messages are sent to Goodyear Tire and Rubber[5] (ordering four tires), to Champion (six spark plugs), to PPG Industries[6] (one windshield), and so on. The suppliers make these parts when ordered, maintaining virtually zero inventory, and deliver them immediately. The car is, in effect, made to order on the assembly line. It is delivered to the customer within a week of the order.

A comparison between JIT buying firms and non-JIT buying firms suggests a difference in the operations, organization, and performance of the purchasing department. JIT buying firms are likely to monitor profitability, costs, and productivity levels. They intensively evaluate supplier performance on price, delivery, and manufacturing capacity. In developing purchasing strategies, the use of cross-functional teams including specialists in materials handling, market research, and transportation scheduling is more extensively employed by JIT buying firms as compared to non-JIT buying firms. Altogether, a JIT buying firm's inventory costs are generally lower and market performance higher than those of a non-JIT buying firm. JIT requires that buyers pay close attention to their supplier base, viewing suppliers as an extension of the company's own operations. To meet customer demands of shorter lead time and delivery time, the supplier has to have a JIT philosophy that will minimize inventory costs and increase efficiency.

## Materials Requirement Planning

Materials requirement planning (MRP) is an important approach to the systematic determination of current and foreseeable needs for materials and parts. Although the concept has been around for a while, new software and network developments have greatly enhanced what companies can do with MRP. On the basis of sales forecasts and minimum desired inventory levels, the MRP technique performs the detailed calculations necessary to translate these projections into precise order, delivery, and inventory schedules. Numerous planning tools are incorporated, such as economic order quantity (EOQ) models, probability theory for establishing safety stocks, and statistical demand forecasting.

Consider how useful MRP can be to a buying organization. Assume that the organization buys some item (call it Item X), which it uses in a variety of its own products.

Demand levels for each of these products differ and are changing all the time. Previously, the buyer had to maintain sizable stocks of Item X to meet production needs for all of its products. Even then, the company might find itself occasionally out of stock, especially with any unusual swings in demand for particular products. The adoption of MRP changes all of this, as every change in demand for each of its own products is immediately reflected in the inventory and production plan for all the items purchased, including Item X. Adjustments can be made quickly in orders for items at every stage in the production process.

The typical MRP system consists of three key informational inputs: a master production schedule, a bill of materials, and an inventory record file. The *production schedule* indicates week-to-week output of finished products over the planning time horizon. A *bill of materials* identifies the materials needed to manufacture an item at each stage in its production process. The *inventory record file* monitors an item's current inventory balance on hand, the timing and sizing of outstanding orders for that item, the necessary lead time involved, and any related planning information. Working backward from these information sources, the MRP system spells out precise material needs for a given period of operation.

A well-known example involves the Steelcase Corporation,[7] a large manufacturer of office furniture. The company developed and installed its MRP system over a 2-year period. Once in place, the system was controlling the flow of 35,000 items supplied by 600 vendors. It reduced vendor past-due shipments from 35 to 3.2%. The number of items in short supply dropped from an average of 33 to 4. More important, sales grew by 59% while the purchased parts inventory rose by only 12%. Separately, the need to expedite orders, a costly activity, decreased significantly, allowing purchasing personnel to allocate more time to other cost reduction programs. The net result was annual cost savings in purchasing of almost $5 million.

MRP is not without its drawbacks. The technique is less applicable for purchases that require long order lead times, involve large volume buying, and are irregular or infrequent. A trade-off is involved between the benefits of reduced inventory carrying costs and the burdens of more complicated operating challenges and higher acquisition costs.

As MRP is adopted by more organizations, the buyer-seller relationship is affected, as is the job of the marketer. MRP serves to coordinate buying practices in the areas of specifications, design, annual requirements, sources, quality, and price. When customer organizations use MRP, the marketer will most likely find key purchase decision makers to be involved with the MRP function. Such customers are also likely to be more open to vendors who are interested in developing long-term planning programs for material needs.

## Electronic Data Interchange and the Internet

Another technological advance that continues to change purchasing operations dramatically is *electronic data interchange* (EDI). With EDI, the buying and selling organizations are linked directly by computer and can electronically transmit information back and forth with no personal contact. It becomes possible to transmit documents such as purchase orders and invoices between two companies or across a network of companies. With the wide dissemination of the microcomputer, recent advances in communications software, and the availability of third-party providers, EDI has become feasible even for many smaller firms. Third-party systems (called *value added networks* or VANs) involve an intermediary who takes the output from one company's computer, translates it to an accepted EDI format and protocol, and communicates the output to another firm's computer. As these formats and protocols have been made more uniform, it has become easier to process transactions between diverse industries. Directories are available listing both the companies using EDI and the third-party providers.

EDI networks permit both the buyer and the seller to obtain and generate much more timely information, improve data accuracy, reduce paperwork, and eliminate staff. Buyers are able to quickly obtain and compare price quotes, determine whether the supplier has an item in stock, process a purchase order, follow up on the status of orders in process, and give the seller information or changes in scheduling requirements or service needs. Letters and correspondence can be sent and received virtually instantaneously. These benefits and related drawbacks associated with EDI adoption are summarized in Table 2.3.

In industries in which EDI is currently in use, selling organizations must either adopt the technology or risk losing the market to competitors. Because electronic order transfer makes the buyer's job easier, he or she will be more likely to work with vendors who accept orders electronically. Some customer organizations have actually taken the lead and imposed change on vendors. The U.S. automotive industry represents a case in point.

The Internet is having a major impact on the use of EDI by firms. Internet-based electronic data interchange can eliminate the need for the traditional third-party value-added network (VAN). Estimates vary widely, with experts suggesting that anywhere from 25% to 80% of EDI transactions will be delivered over the Internet by 2003 (International Data Corporation, 2000). The advantage of the traditional third-party providers is the service and support they give the client, such as tracking a lost customer order, and their ability to meet very strict time constraints in terms of order fulfillment. The Internet can be much less expensive than third-party providers and represents the potential to do a lot more electronically. Firms are looking for the ability to manage supply chains and relationships among a collection of companies, negotiate deals, achieve real-time information exchange, and coordinate vendor-managed inventories, among other activities. Over time, it appears that EDI will be subsumed into the broader field of electronic commerce. Smaller firms or those with low trading volume have been the biggest initial users of Web-based EDI. Meanwhile, many third-party providers are augmenting their services with Internet-based capability. Other firms are developing mechanisms for traditional EDI networks to link with Internet-based systems, exchanging product and ordering information back and forth.

Implementation of EDI has also changed the marketing function. If the buying and selling organization are linked electronically, the salesperson does less order taking and spends less time negotiating prices. The firm can generate greater sales vol-

**TABLE 2.3**  Electronic Data Interchange

| Advantages | Disadvantages |
|---|---|
| 1. Fewer paper documents | 1. Network charges |
| 2. Reduced mail expense | 2. Hardware purchase price or costs |
| 3. Less file space and fewer file cabinets | 3. System maintenance costs |
| 4. Reduced inventory | 4. Line transmission charges |
| 5. Reduced purchase order cost | 5. File costs (i.e., cost of data storage) |
| 6. Reduced telephone expense | 6. License and translation costs |
| 7. Improves the timeliness and accuracy of information | 7. Data input errors |
| 8. Forces discipline in order processing system | 8. MIS support required |
| 9. Fosters buyer-seller relationship | 9. Education and training costs |
| 10. Reduces need to expedite orders | 10. Supplier support required |
| 11. Reduces time spent with incorrect or lost orders | 11. Salesperson is without copy of order |
| 12. Encourages information sharing | |
| 13. Allows buyer to monitor order status | |
| 14. Elimination of pickup of purchase order | |
| 15. Reduces interaction time with salespeople regarding orders | |

ume with fewer salespeople. Because customers have immediate information on the status of an order, marketers must provide higher service levels in the form of faster order turnaround and reduced lead time. EDI also represents a potential source of marketing intelligence. It allows the selling organization to track customers, order quantities, purchase frequencies, and prices over time. Such data can be valuable in analyzing markets, planning, and forecasting.

## Web-Based Procurement

The World Wide Web (WWW) and the Internet have the potential to radically change the procurement process. The WWW gives buyers a quick, low-cost medium to get data on suppliers and their offerings. On-line purchasing and electronic catalogs provide access to remotely stored information at any time. Search engines can assist buyers in finding information about particular vendors. Electronic catalogs consisting of Web-based pages represent an effective and efficient way to sell a wide range of goods and services via a graphical interface. Emerging technology makes it possible to enhance the look and feel of one's offerings through graphical and multimedia elements, to add value through background information, and to support the buyer's search processes, provide customer support, facilitate order processing, and obtain feedback from customers. These systems can assist buyers in improving their performance and selecting vendors more wisely by keeping track of their inventory levels and status of purchase orders.

Corporate globalization and ease of use of the Internet are some of the reasons why companies are turning to procurement via the Internet. Among the other perceived advantages of Internet procurement are

- 24-hour, 7-day-a-week availability

- Ease of finding products

- Speed in accessing a wide variety of products

- Accuracy in ordering

- Ability to adapt the interface to meet a company's specific requirements

- Ease of access to the WWW

- Possibility of two-way interactive communication on a real-time basis

- Ability to maintain electronic records of transactions and transaction status

- Streamlining of customers' existing purchasing relationships

- Reduction in operating costs

Forrester Research (1998) has identified three models for on-line procurement: catalog, auction, and bid. *Catalog-based procurement* involves one buyer and one seller at a time. This is the largest segment of the Internet procurement market, accounting for 60% of the $8 billion market. Noted companies such as Cisco Systems,[8] Dell Computers, and National Semiconductors[9] are using catalogs to sell products to corporate buyers, resellers, and distributors via the Web. *Auction-based procurement* involves an on-line event at which buyers compete with one another by offering various prices for a product or service from one or more sellers. A vendor can then decide to accept a particular offer from a customer. Many industrial companies are testing this model based on its success in the business-to-consumer (B2C) market (e.g., with airline tickets). *Bid-based procurement* help buyers of industrial products find the best possible suppliers and then make those suppliers bid for business. FreeMarkets Online,[10] a Pittsburgh-based Internet bidding service, invites suppliers to participate in the on-line bidding event, which takes place over a 4- to 6-hour period. Suppliers, without disclosing their identity, submit their bids to businesses and respond with lower and lower bids as they see their rivals undercut their prices. The result is an average saving of 17% in procurement costs. The customer roster of FreeMarkets includes companies such as Caterpillar, General Motors, Procter & Gamble,[11] and Whirlpool.[12]

On-line procurement benefits buyers by helping them achieve lower prices and save time by excluding the hassles of lengthy negotiations with suppliers. It also ex-

**TABLE 2.4**   Examples of Enterprise Resource Planning at Work

◆ Owens Corning's insulation group expected to reduce its material and supply inventories by 25% by implementing an ERP system.

◆ Analog Devices, a semiconductor maker in Massachusetts, consolidated its warehouses and created a worldwide order processing system through systems applications and products (SAP). This enables Analog to share the same onscreen information worldwide and thus ship products more efficiently and more cheaply. The company's worldwide operations are supported by SAP's ability to automatically calculate exchange rates and translate foreign languages.

◆ By installing a $25 million ERP system, Microsoft is expected to produce a common procurement system worldwide that could save the company $12 million a year in early-payment discounts.

◆ Before implementing ERP, employees at Warren Petroleum, a Chevron subsidiary, were writing purchase orders and invoices by hand and mailing them back and forth to the home office for processing. The system integration brought about by SAP has enabled them to cut the time for processing orders and retrieving information on order status from about a week to minutes.

pands the buyer's available pool of potential suppliers and force suppliers to be more efficient in making proposals to customers. For the vendor, on-line systems permit the sales force a crack at businesses they may have been pitching unsuccessfully for years. It also introduces a new type of "middleman" into the buyer-seller relationship, namely the on-line technology supplier, such as FreeMarkets, who makes money from both the small fees paid by the buyers and the larger sales commissions paid by suppliers.

## Enterprise Resource Planning

Enterprise Resource Planning (ERP) is a software-based system that facilitates the flow of information within an organization and ties together all the basic processes of the business—from taking orders to monitoring inventory levels to balancing books. According to a Booz Allen & Hamilton (1998) study, more than 70% of the *Fortune* 1000 companies had either begun implementing an ERP system or were planning to do so over the next few years. SAP,[13] Oracle,[14] PeopleSoft,[15] J. D. Edwards,[16] and Baan[17] are five providers that control two-thirds of the ERP software market. SAP, based in Germany, is the dominant leader, with 31% of the ERP market. Demand has been strong, with ERP providers earning $10 billion in 1997 from 20,000 companies worldwide, and license revenues were expected to grow at a 36% compound annual growth rate through 2001 (Trunick, 1999).

The appeal of such an integrated system for big companies is clear (see Table 2.4). As the company sales force enters an order on the computer, the transaction is reflected through the entire company. The inventory lists are updated and the suppliers are informed automatically, worldwide. The transaction even updates manufacturing schedules, enabling salespeople to promise delivery dates and managers to assess the effects of the decision on productivity and supply chain management. For purchasing, ERP systems can tie together inventory, order processing, and procurement systems worldwide. Companies can streamline their requisition and direct procurement processes and cut the overall cost of procurement.

Furthermore, ERP can lead to supplier integration, which allows purchasing professionals to reduce procurement cycle time and paper pushing. Correspondingly, they are able to spend more time on strategic sourcing and agreement negotiations. Buyers are tempted to reduce the number of suppliers and are demanding greater control of supplier performance to achieve greater economies through their purchasing operations. A developed ERP system contributes to their ability to draw more comprehensive and in-depth product and price comparisons.

There is also a downside to ERP systems. First of all, they take a long time to implement. Chevron Oil[18] started installing full ERP solutions in 1992, and the system was not up and running at all major sites until 1998. Many firms are therefore implementing ERP systems in stages, department by department. These systems may also require companies to convert data, slightly modify business processes, and overhaul networking infrastructure. ERP systems also come with a significant price tag and a low return on investment (ROI). It is not unusual for big companies to pay as much as $50,000 to $75,000 per user. Chevron spent nearly $160 million implementing solutions over a period of 5 years. Although many companies have decided that today's global and highly competitive business environment demands this type of investment, others question whether ERP systems can do all that they promise to do. The complexities of the operations within many companies can be quite difficult to capture.

## Additional Implications of Trends in Purchasing for the Marketer

These developments inside purchasing organizations will lead to a wide range of changes in how industrial marketing is performed. As buying is accomplished in a more strategic manner, so too will the vendor's marketing approach have to become more strategic. The primary focal points in the years to come will be a much stronger customer orientation, increased flexibility of operations, and the deployment of information technology. The future will bring more supply chain integration and increased emphasis on time-based strategies, the reduction of transaction costs, and value maximization for customers.

Successful marketers will be those who can develop closer, longer-term relationships with customer organizations. The foremost task confronting the industrial marketer will be to establish and maintain a sense of trust and loyalty with buying organizations. Firms will strive to create "seamless" linkages between seller and buyer organizations. At the same time, many of the more lethargic, reactive, and less efficient firms, as well as those with more limited product offerings, may find that they are unable to compete in an environment where customers

- Strive to increase profit potential through more effective purchasing
- Investigate suppliers much more thoroughly, in a more sophisticated manner, and on an ongoing basis
- Develop strategic business alliances with world-class supplier partners
- Consolidate their purchases to achieve economies, including purchasing through centralized buying organizations
- Stress one-stop shopping, with multiple purchasing needs met by a given supplier
- Reduce the size of the supplier pool
- Flatten their own purchasing and supply management organizations and rely on horizontal, self-managed teams

In addition, marketers are likely to discover that power relationships between buyer and sellers will shift in the direction of the buyer. There will be a greater emphasis on product simplification, quality, and the tailoring of products to customer requirements. Costs to supplier organizations are likely to rise, specifically because they will have to invest more in each customer relationship. These cost increases will not simply be passed on to customers in the form of higher prices, so profit margins may be affected. Prices themselves should remain relatively stable. Competition will be based less on price and more on competencies in creating unique and continually enhanced sources of value for the buyer. Vendor attributes may receive greater attention in marketing programs than do product attributes. The salesperson's role will change as that person becomes more of an innovator, consultant, and source of customer service. Distribution channels will get shorter, with much higher logistical service levels.

## Summary

The focus in this chapter has been on the formal purchasing operations inside customer organizations. These operations can be characterized in terms of the policies and procedures governing buying decisions, the manner in which purchasing is organized, and the tools and techniques used by purchasing professionals when dealing with selling organizations.

Organizations must purchase hundreds, even thousands, of items annually. These purchases account for more than half of the revenues generated in a typical company. To better manage and control these expenditures, most organizations attempt to formalize their purchasing processes. A number of procedural steps must be followed when ordering, acquiring, and paying for a product or service, and different paperwork comes into play at the various steps. In addition, six or more internal departments may get involved before the formal purchase is completed. Examples of key documents that must be completed include the purchase requisition, purchase order, traveling requisition, bill of materials, receiving report, and inspection report.

As the purchasing function has risen in importance within organizations, new types of organizational structures have been employed. Purchasing was traditionally subordinate to production or operations, but some firms have made the head of purchasing a senior executive-level position. Some have gone further, embracing the materials management concept, in which activities such as purchasing, materials handling, inventory, shipping, and receiving are integrated into a single function, resulting in much-enhanced coordination and control.

Organizations rely on a variety of analytical tools when evaluating vendors. Life-cycle costing is one example; it involves assessing a purchase in terms of all the costs the buying organization will incur over the usable life of a product. Another tool is value analysis, a detailed study of purchased items to find ways in which they could be redesigned to lower cost, improve quality, or both, or possibly be eliminated. Organizations will also use time-based buying strategies, including hand-to-mouth, forward, and speculative buying, to realize cost savings or greater returns from their purchasing operations.

Finally, new technologies are changing not only the way organizations purchase but also their relationships with vendors. Perhaps the most widely known of these advances is just-in-time inventory management. Others include materials requirement planning, electronic data interchange, distribution resource planning, enterprise resource planning, and Web-based procurement. Although these differ markedly and each has unique implications for the marketer, all employ computer technology to reduce lead times, eliminate unnecessary stock, and radically improve organizational efficiency.

An awareness of the procedures, structures, and technologies employed by buyers is vital if marketers are to penetrate customer organizations successfully. Moreover, sellers must adapt themselves to the operations of their customers to build relationships that will endure over time. In Chapter 3, we will turn to a more in-depth examination of organizational buying behavior.

# Notes

1. www.marotta.com
2. www.toyota.com
3. www.westinghouse.com
4. www.harleydavidson.com

5. www.goodyear.com
6. www.ppg.com
7. www.steelcase.com
8. www.cisco.com
9. www.national.com
10. www.freemarkets.com
11. www.pg.com
12. www.whirlpool.com
13. www.sap.com
14. www.oracle.com
15. www.peoplesoft.com
16. www.jdedwards.com
17. www.baan.com
18. www.chevron.com

# Questions

1. Consider the formal purchasing procedures summarized in Figure 2.1. Why would buying organizations involve so many different departments in the process of making a transaction? What are some possible implications for the selling organization?

2. McDonnell Douglas, manufacturer of the F-15 fighter jet, is one of the primary purchasers of Pratt and Whitney (P & W) turbines. P & W has discovered a new lightweight metal to use in construction of turbines. The new metal is considerably more durable than available materials. Discuss the purchasing-related concepts discussed in this chapter that might come into play as McDonnell Douglas decides whether to purchase turbines made of this new metal.

3. Purchasing agents are increasingly a highly professional, well-trained group of specialists. How should this professionalization of purchasing be reflected in the marketing and sales efforts of vendors?

4. Evaluate the following statement: "The industrial firm is threatened when its customers start performing value analysis studies, and it should discourage organizations from instituting such programs."

5. Explain why a customer that is especially cost conscious might select the product with the highest list price over the one with the lowest price.

6. Consider the concepts of hand-to-mouth, forward, and speculative buying. From the perspective of a publisher of weekly industrial journals and magazines, what are the advantages and disadvantages of each, if you were purchasing the paper used in your publications?

7.  Technographica is a major and rapidly growing marketer of business software for a wide variety of applications, including desktop publishing, accounting, and word processing. The demand for such software tends to fluctuate because of new computer technologies, which are continually being introduced. Assume that your firm does all the packaging for Technographica software. How would your firm benefit from the establishment of a materials requirement planning system? What information would you desire from Technographica? What are some of the problems that might be encountered?

8.  Thomson Corporation supplies ball bearings to customers according to customer specifications. It is attempting to develop just-in-time relationships with virtually its entire current customer base. How might both parties benefit from this move? What are some of the potential problems that might arise?

9.  Customer organizations make purchase decisions by evaluating the performance of vendors on particular product attributes. If a customer has adopted the materials management concept, how might this affect the attributes it emphasizes when evaluating vendors?

10. Discuss the advantages and disadvantages of an electronic data interchange system. How would these apply if you were a component parts supplier to Nissan Industrial Equipment Company, which manufactures forklifts on a custom order basis? How might the roles of buyer and seller in this situation differ from their traditional roles?

# CHAPTER 3

# How Organizations Make Buying Decisions

*Those who believe that customers will respond to the product
or service offered as long as it is backed with sufficient selling
firepower are making a dangerous assumption.*
—J. F. Engel and R. D. Blackwell

## Key Concepts

Buyer rationality

Buygrid

Buying center

Buying process

Buystages

Dyadic perspective

External publics

Information search

Interfunctional involvement

Internal publics

Modified rebuy purchase

New task purchase

Purchase involvement level

Straight rebuy purchase

Tactics of lateral relationships

Vendor attributes

Weighted-attribute approach

## Learning Objectives

1. Understand the need to build all marketing programs around customers and their needs.

2. Appreciate the technical, commercial, and behavioral complexities involved when marketing to organizations.

3. Recognize unique aspects of the industrial buying process, and recognize factors that affect whether decisions are more rational, more political, or more emotional.

4. Explain buying as a process and identify the major stages and activities in that process.

5. Grasp the buying center concept and perspectives on how to identify key role players in the buying decision.

## Marketing Starts With a Customer

One of the most serious, and yet common, mistakes made by marketing practitioners is to develop creative marketing programs consisting of innovative products, exciting promotional efforts, and expensive distribution arrangements, while demonstrating little or no knowledge of the buyer to whom the program is directed. Without a thorough understanding of who buys, why they buy, when they buy, where they buy, and how they buy, the marketer is greatly increasing the likelihood of market failure and wasted resources—and is, in effect, becoming a gambler. There are many "better mousetraps" in the proverbial junkpile of failed products and abandoned corporate visions.

This problem is especially critical for industrial companies, where technical experts and production or operations managers typically are quite influential in marketing decision making. Moreover, the person in charge of marketing may well be a repositioned engineer; under such circumstances, it is important that market-related decisions reflect more than just technological capabilities and product design specifications. The people making decisions about product characteristics, market segmentation, prices, distribution channels, sales management, advertising, and sales promotion are likely to be much more successful when they think and act from the customer's point of view.

The marketer, in the final analysis, is responsible for delivering value to customers. Value is not a tangible or absolute thing; it is perceived in the mind of the buyer. For example, AT&T could sell designer telephones to offices for much more than a standard black telephone because the customer perceived a marked difference in the value of the two products, not because the standard phone was all that much cheaper to produce. The value transmitted to customers transcends the physical product itself. Value may be enhanced through product packaging, support services, delivery reliability, warranties, customer training, special features, and even a strong vendor reputation, among other attributes. Furthermore, the attributes on which one group of customers places high value may be of little or no importance to another group of buyers.

All of this points to a need to begin marketing efforts with the customer, not with the product. Consider the advice offered many years ago by Tucker (1974), who encouraged marketers to study customers the way marine biologists approach fish, rather than the way fishermen approach fish. Fishermen care only about catching as many fish as possible. Alternatively, marine biologists seek to understand and predict the behavior of fish. Like the marine biologist, the marketer must become intimately familiar with customers, understanding why they respond in different ways, what their needs are under different conditions, and how to foster an ongoing relationship that will yield long-term returns.

An obsession with satisfying customers needs is the essence of the marketing concept. One might argue that buyers are not completely aware of their needs and must be assisted in understanding what to buy, and why. This premise is only partially true. Certainly, a customer did not invent the personal computer, nor did marketing research lead to its invention. For the personal computer to become a successful innovation, however, entrepreneurs had to be able to match technological capabilities and production requirements with marketplace needs. Ultimately, the entrepreneur had to ensure that the product represented value to the customer and that it could be produced, promoted, and distributed at a price commensurate with that value. Companies like Dell and Compaq surpassed IBM and Apple[1] not because they were technically stronger but because they had a better understanding of where the customer was going.

Actually, it is not unusual in industrial markets for customers to be important sources of new product ideas. In many instances, the customer has identified a problem with his organization's product or production process and requests help from a salesperson who is there to sell something else. Alternatively, it is sometimes the customer who may see how, with slight modifications, the marketer's product could be used in entirely new applications, opening up new market opportunities.

## Selling to Organizations

Chapter 1 emphasized that the most distinctive aspect of industrial marketing is that the *customer* is an *organization*. Selling to organizations is very different from selling to consumers. Organizations can be quite complex, and they have both a *social* and an *economic* dimension. There is a significant social dimension to all organizations because they are made up of people—individuals and groups who must work together. These individuals frequently have differing backgrounds, personalities, attitudes, and motivations and they rely on a variety of approaches to problem solving. At the same time, organizations ultimately exist to provide an economic function, that is, to provide some good or service. Whether an organization is commercial, governmental, or nonprofit, survival depends on successful completion of a mission and objectives. The behavior of the individuals (including buying behavior) within the organization must directly or indirectly contribute to the mission and objectives.

When organizations purchase things, both social and economic dimensions come into play. When selling to organizations, one is dealing with various individuals. These individuals are at work, reacting to some formal measurement and reward system, and are attempting to achieve both personal and professional goals. They may be from any number of departments, not just the purchasing department. In many cases, a purchasing decision may reflect the interactions of a number of individuals working with or through one another over time. As such, the decision might be characterized by personal agendas, conflict, compromise, and coalitions.

From an economic standpoint, the goods and services an organization purchases are likely to directly affect the day-to-day operations and economic health of the enterprise. As discussed in Chapter 1, industrial products are either used to make other products (foundation goods), become part of other goods (entering goods), or are used to support the ongoing operations of an enterprise (facilitating goods). Given the direct impact on operations and the fact that all organizations have limited resources, a bad purchasing decision can lead to interruptions or stoppages in operations, reductions in product quality, slowdown in distribution, dissatisfied end customers, and wasted resources. As a result, costs may rise, sales and net cash flow decline, and profits suffer.

Because of the potentially critical impact of buying decisions on organizational performance, purchases are often characterized by formal contractual relationships, considerable search and negotiation, a lengthy buying process, multiple sourcing, and long-term loyalty to a given source. These characteristics of industrial buying enable the purchaser to reduce the risk of making an incorrect decision. In fact, both social and economic aspects of organizational life have a bearing on how the risk inherent in a purchase is dealt with, an issue that will be discussed later in this chapter.

One of the most distinct features of selling in business-to-business markets is the smaller absolute number of customers to be reached, compared with those found in mass consumer markets. This concentrated customer base increases the relative dependence of the industrial marketer on each customer account. For many purchases, this dependence requires the marketer to consider the distinctive needs of each potential customer and to stress personalized communication. Moreover, as we shall explore in Chapter 4, a smaller potential customer base suggests the need for the marketer to foster long-term relationships with customers.

## Technical, Commercial, and Behavioral Complexities

Because both the buyer and the seller are organizations, purchase decision making represents a process that has the potential to become very complex. To obtain a truer picture of how organizations buy, let us consider three types of complexities that can be found in the typical buying organization: technical, commercial, and behavioral.

*Technical complexities* refer to the characteristics of the products and services being purchased, as well as to the ways in which they are applied or used by the customer. Technical product and service characteristics have a greater impact on buying decisions, as a rule, than does any other single factor. Unfortunately, these characteristics are not always easy to evaluate or understand. With rapidly changing technologies, shorter product life cycles (hence, rapid product obsolescence), and the myriad buying decisions an organization must make, the need to completely understand and evaluate the technical qualities of every vendor's products and services is an imposing task. Moreover, when designing a company's offerings, managers frequently must make an array of trade-off decisions regarding technical specifications. For example, quality or precision may be sacrificed for performance speed, or a trade-off might be made among product durability, flexibility, and cost. From the buyer's perspective, these trade-offs are often difficult to discern and quantify precisely. This is why value analysis (see Chapter 2) increasingly is used as a purchasing tool. The difficulties posed by the technical nature of industrial products are further affected by the source of product specifications. Products can be buyer-specified (typically by technical personnel in the buying organization) or supplier-specified. The buying process may take longer to conclude, with more people involved, when specifications are buyer-specified.

A second major dimension of industrial buying is the *commercial complexity* of the negotiations between the buyer and seller organizations. Agreement must be reached not only on the product and price but also on payment terms, discounts, warranties, customer service, delivery arrangements and timing, and handling of returns, among other issues. These negotiations are complicated by a number of factors, among them the legal complications when negotiating purchase contracts. The contract formalizes the responsibilities of buyer and seller, and it provides a fairly precise statement of what is expected of both parties. A written contract also limits the likelihood of misrepresentation or fraud on the part of buyers or sellers. Preparing such a formal and precise statement can require extensive and complex negotiations. Problem areas include concerns over product liability and nonperformance of contractual terms. The courts are predisposed to place complete liability on the vendor for damages incurred by the customer in the use or misuse of the vendor's product. Given changes in inflation, the cost of money, transportation costs, and the availability of key resources, vendors can sometimes find themselves worse off economically if they fulfill the terms of an earlier agreed-upon contract than if they do not.

Negotiations are also greatly affected by the relative power positions of the buyer and seller—power positions that determine the types and extent of concessions made by either party. Dynamic changes in the environments of organizations can significantly alter these power positions and make it more difficult to define power relationships. For example, a sharp increase in interest rates can make a buyer more dependent on a vendor for financing, thereby enhancing that vendor's position in future negotiations. Turbulent change makes it more difficult for the industrial marketer to discern which concessions are of greater importance to the buyer and in which areas to make compromises.

Overall, the complexity of commercial negotiations will vary with the characteristics and complexity of the product or service, the dollar value and volume of the purchase, the types of support services that must accompany the sale, the existence of reciprocity between buyer and seller, the number of parties involved in the commercial and contractual relationships, and the characteristics of each party. The trend is toward greater complexity, leading purchasing professionals to seek specialized training in negotiation and in the legal aspects of the sales contract.

The third important aspect of industrial buying concerns the *behavioral complexities* that take place inside the buying organization. The buying process may involve not only negotiation with the seller but also extensive negotiation among individuals and departments within the buying organization. Purchasing is a problem-solving activity—the buyer is purchasing something so as to solve a problem. Furthermore, the purchase decision may actually represent a number of decisions by the buyer. Such decisions concern not only what to buy, and from whom, but also how to pay for it, what technical specifications are to be met, whether to lease instead of buy, which information sources to rely upon, when to require delivery, how much inventory to maintain, and how total requirements should be divided among the vendors selected (see Figure 3.1).

The way these questions are answered affects on many people in the buying organization. As a result, a number of individuals are likely to get involved as the organization works its way through these decisions. These individuals can bring highly disparate points of view regarding what is best for the organization. Each of them becomes a "stakeholder" and is likely to work to achieve the decision outcomes that most benefit him or her. This means that there can be considerable conflict and that individuals may rely on any number of tactics to try to influence the company's buying decisions. Thus, the interactions among these stakeholders become a complicating factor in industrial buying. As with any behavioral process, the more people involved, the more complex the interactions. Furthermore, the greater the technical and commercial complexities, the greater the behavioral complexities.

## The Industrial Marketer's Lament: Who Buys?

Consider the plight of the marketer who sends a salesperson to call on an organizational customer, perhaps a new account. The first and foremost problem for both the marketer and the salesperson is to determine where they should target their efforts inside the client organization. Who makes the buying decisions? Which individual (or group of individuals) is the true customer? The marketer must figure out where to concentrate company resources to support the sales effort, while the salesperson must determine whom to call on.

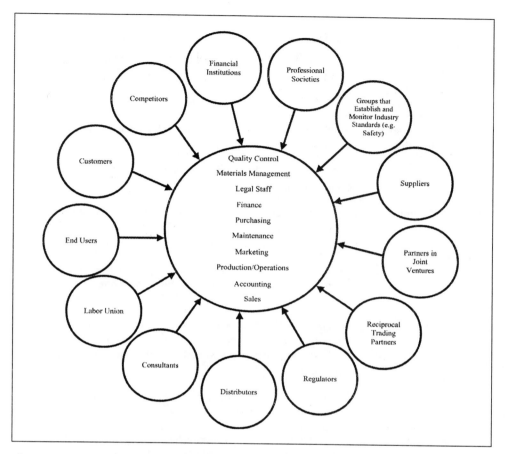

**Figure 3.1.** Internal and External Stakeholders in Organizational Buying Decisions

As discussed in Chapter 2, most organizations have a person or department charged with purchasing or procurement. It might seem logical, then, for the salesperson to first go to that person or department. Unfortunately, those persons responsible for the purchasing task frequently have only limited authority to actually make buying decisions. If not on the purchasing department, where does the marketer focus?

As a case in point, recall the importance of the technical characteristics of many industrial products. The concern for precise design specifications, and for compatibility with existing equipment and capabilities, may well lead those in R&D, quality control, product development, or production to get involved in the buying decision process. In addition, the relative cost of many purchases may encourage those in financial management to monitor or influence purchase decisions. Furthermore, when the items an organization is purchasing have direct impacts on the products or services it sells, marketers or salespeople in the buying organization have a stake and may get involved in the buying process. Table 3.1 provides examples of these and

**TABLE 3.1**  Functional Areas Frequently Involved in Purchase Decisions and Their Primary Concerns When a Vendor Is Selected

| Examples of Functional Areas | Key Concerns in Purchase Decision Making |
|---|---|
| Design and Development Engineering | Name reputation of vendor; ability of vendors to meet design specifications |
| Production | Delivery and reliability of purchases such that interruption of production schedules is minimized |
| Sales/Marketing | Impact of purchased items on marketability of the company's products |
| Maintenance | Degree to which purchased items are compatible with existing facilities and equipment; maintenance services offered by vendor; installation arrangements offered by vendor |
| Finance/Accounting | Effects of purchases on cash flow, balance sheet, and income statement positions; variances in costs of materials over estimates; feasibility of make-or-buy and lease options over outright purchasing |
| Purchasing | Obtaining lowest possible price at acceptable quality levels; maintaining good relations with vendors |
| Quality Control | Assurance that purchased items meet prescribed specifications and tolerances, governmental regulations, and customer requirements |

other functional areas to be considered in determining the identity of the industrial buyer.

The implication is that any number of specific individuals or departments might actually make a purchase decision, and a number of individuals can be expected to play a role. Although the purchasing department would seem to be the most obvious participant, it may be primarily responsible only for order processing, negotiation, value analysis, sourcing, expediting, and vendor relationships. Actual buying decisions frequently are made elsewhere. At the same time, the marketer cannot afford to ignore the purchasing department. Purchasing agents may not always be authorized to select a vendor, but they often can ensure that a particular vendor *does not* get selected. The purchasing department is also an important source of information to the marketer regarding (a) the identity of key decision makers, (b) the product and vendor attributes of greatest importance to these decision makers, (c) ways in which a salesperson can get access to the decision makers, and (d) company policies and procedures that govern purchasing.

# The Concept of the Buying Center

Trying to sort out the various people involved in the buying decision is one of the marketer's greatest challenges. In a sense, marketers must become jugglers, in some instances, balancing the different needs and interests of all those people in the customer organization who get involved in some way. One of the most useful tools for bringing a degree of order to this confusing maze is called the *buying center*. It is defined as all the individuals and groups participating in the buying decision process who have interdependent goals and share common risks. (Note: the buying center is sometimes referred to as the *decision-making unit* or DMU.)

At its most basic level, the buying center views purchasing decision making in terms of a set of roles that must be played. Individual participants are assigned to six primary roles that collectively enable the organization to accomplish the buying task. These roles are defined as follows.

- **Initiator:** first recognizes a need, opportunity, or problem that potentially could be resolved with a purchase. This person effectively defines the buying situation.

- **Buyer:** is responsible (but may have limited authority) for selecting vendors and consummating the purchase. Responsibilities may include vendor evaluation, solicitation of bids, negotiation, preparation of purchase orders and contracts, order processing, and expediting.

- **User:** will make on-the-job use of the product or service to be purchased. Users also tend to have limited authority and often also play the role of initiator. They can get involved in specifying minimum performance requirements that a product must meet.

- **Influencer:** does not make specific product or vendor choices but significantly influences the type of decision made. An influencer may affect the decision process by imposing task-related (quality, performance, price), procedural (company rules, policies and procedures), and/or political constraints that limit the number of acceptable alternatives.

- **Decider:** the actual maker of the buying decision. This person may not have the formal charge to make the decision in question but does so as a function of his or her power and influence in the particular product area under question. As a result, this can be the most critical, and yet most difficult to identify, member of the buying center.

- **Gatekeeper:** controls the types and flows of information regarding products and suppliers received by other members of the buying center when making a particular purchase decision. Also provides information to salespeople and other representatives of the vendor organization. The gatekeeper can determine which promotional materials and vendor information reach key influencers and whether salespeople are given access to the appropriate buying center members.

For many routine purchase decisions, most or all of the roles in the buying center could be filled by one or two individuals. Alternatively, for a more complex decision, a different person could fill each role, each representing a different department

### BUSINESS MARKETING CAPSULE

## Getting Past the Gatekeeper

When the buying center includes senior executives, the marketer is likely to have difficulties gaining access to those individuals. It is not uncommon, in such circumstances, to rely on direct mail as a communications vehicle, especially in the early stages of the customer buying process. Unfortunately, much of this direct mail never gets into the hands of the executive.

Surveys suggest that almost all secretaries or personal assistants act as gatekeepers, throwing out approximately one fourth of the promotional mailings that reach their desks. Executive secretaries of industrial manufacturing firms report that top managers receive an average of 20 promotion-related mailings a day, and this does not include e-mail messages from outside. Only about half of those mailings ever reach the executives' desks. Their secretaries follow up on another 1% of the mailings themselves, and roughly 24% get rerouted to other departments.

Some of the factors that help promotional pieces pass inspection include eye-catching colors, a professional presentation, and clearly expressed copy. Enclosing the salesperson's business card and using an executive's correct name and title also include the chances of being read.

Mail most likely to be thrown away includes card packs and sweepstakes promotions. Like all people, secretaries get especially annoyed by outdated or incorrect addresses.

within the company. Often, more than one person fills a given role. Thus, if the company were purchasing simple mechanical pencils, the purchasing agent might play most or all of the roles. If the same firm were selecting an advertising agency, a team from marketing might play most of the roles, but the company president may make the actual decision. Then again, if the company was purchasing a packaging design for a temperature-sensitive product line, the initiator could be an R&D engineer, the user a production manager, the buyer a purchasing agent, the influencer a quality assurance inspector, the decider a project manager, and the gatekeeper a sales manager. It is also likely that more than one person could fill any of the roles. There might be three or four influencers, and the decider role could actually be the majority vote of a committee.

Unfortunately, it is difficult to stereotype the buying center roles in terms of which individuals or departments will get involved. One might expect to find the user in operations or production, and the gatekeeper in the purchasing department, but such generalizations do not hold up across a wide range of purchase decisions. Buying center membership tends to be specific to products and companies. Industrial buying is a dynamic process that resists attempts at simplification.

Whenever two or more individuals fulfill the roles in the buying center, purchasing becomes, in effect, a *group decision process*. This is frequently the case. Early studies

**TABLE 3.2** Scale for Measuring a Person's Influence in the Buying Center

1. How much weight did others involved in the buying decision give to his or her opinions?
2. How much impact did he or she have on the thinking of the other participants?
3. To what extent did he or she influence the criteria used for making the final decision?
4. How much effect did his or her involvement in the purchasing process have on how the various options were rated?
5. To what extent did he or she influence others into adopting certain positions about the various options?
6. How much change did he or she induce in the preferences of other participants?
7. To what extent did others go along with his or her suggestions?
8. To what extent did his or her participation influence the decision eventually reached?
9. To what extent did the final decision reflect his or her views?

NOTE: Items are scored on a 5-point scale ranging from *very small* to *very large*.

SOURCE: Adapted from "Measuring Multiple Buying Influences," *Industrial Marketing Management,* 17 (August 1988), pp. 197-204, Kohli and Zaltman. © Copyright 1988 by *Industrial Marketing Management.*

of industrial buying behavior reported the average size of the buying center to range from 1.5 (Patchen, 1974) and 3.74 (Lynn, 1987) to 5.5 (Laczniak, 1979) and between 8.9 and 11.9 (Weigand, 1966). In an examination of 21 different industries, Spekman and Stern (1979) found buying centers averaging anywhere between 3.0 and 8.0 members.

We can conclude, then, that most buying decisions represent group behavior. In some instances, there is a formal buying group that meets regularly to evaluate options and make decisions. More often, though, it is an ad hoc or informal group that does not actually convene. Instead, the members communicate with one another directly and indirectly, formally and informally, over time. Each role member has certain goals and objectives that are shared with others in the buying center, but he or she can also have goals that conflict with the needs of the others. Each is attempting to perform a job task within the confines of departmental and organizational policies, procedures, and employee evaluation systems.

Two significant problems arise concerning members of the buying center. The first has to do with identifying exactly who is filling each role—which can be a fairly challenging feat in some purchase decisions. The most logical approach may be to utilize some variation of the snowball sampling technique. This technique involves contacting someone in the customer organization (often a purchasing agent or receptionist) and asking for names of three or four key people involved in a particular buying decision. Each of these people is, in turn, contacted and asked for a similar list of names. The process is continued until a list of names is generated that is fairly consistent among respondents. Table 3.2 provides an illustration of the types of questions that might be asked to determine a given person's influence in the buying process.

Keep in mind that identifying buying center members is not the same thing as determining the identity of the principal decision maker. In many instances, finding the source of the key buying influence may be a highly complex, if not impossible, task. The marketer may find it more productive to try and figure out who influences which tasks, then work with each individual based on the role he or she plays.

The second, and more difficult, problem is to develop an understanding of the interactions and relationships that occur among the buying center participants over the time period that a company makes a buying decision, and from decision to decision. Product and vendor choices are heavily dependent upon the expectations, power positions, coalitions or alliances, and approaches to conflict resolution relied upon by those in the buying center.

## Are the Decisions Made by Buying Centers "Rational"?

Economists assume, in their models of marketplace behavior, perfect rationality on the part of customers. In technical terms, they assume that customers maximize the marginal utility gained per dollar spent on each and every purchase. This assumption is unrealistic and typically does not apply to the way organizations or individuals make their purchase decisions. This is an important issue, as it explains why the company with the best product, best price, and best customer support is not necessarily the vendor that gets selected.

If customers are not perfectly rational, then how rational are they? One might be tempted to assume that buyers of industrial goods are much more rational in their purchase decisions than are buyers of consumer goods. Is this assumption accurate? First, buyers of consumer goods demonstrate a high degree of rationality in decisions regarding many types of product areas, despite strong social or emotional influences. Second, as we shall see, industrial buyers often make decisions that are just as influenced by social and emotional factors, and that may seem suboptimal to the rational observer.

By contrast, greater rationality on the industrial side might be expected for a number of reasons: the products being purchased are for use in the daily operations and functioning of the buying organization, the people doing the buying are being evaluated and rewarded based on the quality of the decisions they make, and organizational buyers are professionals. Moreover, management frequently imposes a formal structure on the buying process that might include a specific set of steps to be followed, criteria to be used in evaluating vendors, stipulations regarding the number of bids to be taken, and provisions requiring various approval signatures on the purchase requisition.

Organizational buying decisions nevertheless are made by people subject to some of the same emotional and social factors that influence them as consumers. Especially where the performance of the available products or vendors is not perceived to differ all that much, the buyer may be influenced by a range of factors that are not related to economic rationality. Examples include the influence of personal friend-ships with salespeople, personal dislike of certain vendors, personal favors granted by some suppliers, or the social influence of peers not involved in the transaction but who urge that a given vendor be used or another be boycotted.

Further evidence of the emotional and political influences on buying behavior can be found in the classic work of Strauss (see Table 3.3), who explored the kinds of tactics employed by purchasing agents to influence buying decision outcomes. He concluded that reliance on such tactics suggests that purchasing agents are con-cerned with personal needs and departmental objectives that are not always directly related to, and may occasionally conflict with, organizational goals and objectives. The purchase decision maker may be tempted to favor the use of vendors or products (or decide not to purchase a product) when that action makes him or her look good or enables him or her to achieve desired formal or informal rewards. Such self-serving behavior may come at the expense of long-term organizational welfare.

Ernest Dichter, a well-known advertising and marketing consultant, called it a common fallacy to believe that someone trying to solve a technical problem can somehow overcome ordinary emotions and act coldly and mechanistically (see also Wolter, Bacon, Duhan, & Wilson, 1989). In a popular critique (Dichter, 1973), he noted that "although (the industrial buyer) studies specifications, prices and quality much more than the consumer, when we dig a little bit deeper, we find that he is gov-erned by just as many emotions as the average housewife. He, too, suffers from illu-sions and is much more embarrassed to admit the often irrationality of his behavior" (p. 41). Dichter goes on to explain how, for example, engineers can be subtle, com-plex, sensitive, contradictory, and inconsistent, and how they frequently hold an ex-alted image of themselves and who they ought to be. He points to the engineer who has strong prejudices about the strength of aluminum as compared with steel or cast iron. Another example is the technical person who refuses to accept that a seemingly documented fact has become obsolete because of some new development. As a re-sult, the marketer may find it effective to create an illusion of rationality while playing on the same (and sometimes subconscious) irrational and emotional factors found in consumer buying.

We have also noted that industrial buying involves multiple individuals and is es-sentially a group process. Any group is likely to contain some degree of potential conflict. As a case in point, consider the conflicts that typically arise among a group of students working on an industrial marketing case. In a buying context, an examina-tion of the respective interests of the group members identified in Table 3.1 suggests a strong potential for conflict. For example, those in purchasing are concerned with cost savings, which may conflict with the design engineers' desire to establish extremely tight technical specifications, or with production management's demand for rapid de-livery. If, in fact, conflict is present, the rationality of organizational buying becomes dependent on the rationality of the tactics used in the conflict resolution process. As we shall see, this process has the potential to become quite political in nature.

Just as social or emotional factors can produce less than optimal purchasing behavior, so can an overly conservative orientation toward buying. Purchases that

**TABLE 3.3** Strauss's Tactics of Lateral Relationships

George Strauss, in a classic study of organizational behavior, interviewed a large number of purchasing agents in industrial organizations. Noting that those in purchasing frequently do not play a major role in buying decisions, he sought to determine whether or not they tried to enhance their role and, if so, the approaches they used. Not only did Strauss find concerted attempts on the part of purchasing agents to increase their influence, but he was also able to identify their specific techniques, which he called "tactics of lateral relationships." He used this label because such tactics were frequently directed at those in functional areas or departments at approximately the same horizontal level in the organizational hierarchy.

An excerpt from Strauss's work provides examples of the five types of gamesmanship tactics. In this scenario, the purchasing department is trying to counteract a demand from another department for immediate delivery of some product, when immediate delivery is costly and not really needed.

1. **Rule-oriented tactics**
   a. Appeal to some common authority to direct that this requisition be revised or withdrawn.
   b. Refer to some rule (assuming one exists) that provides for longer lead times.
   c. Require the scheduling department to state in writing why quick delivery is required.
   d. Require the requisitioning department to consent to having its budget charged with the extra costs (such as air freight) required to get quick delivery.

2. **Rule-evading tactics**
   a. Go through the motions of complying with the request, but with no expectation of getting delivery on time.
   b. Exceed formal authority and ignore the requisition altogether.

3. **Personal-political tactics**
   a. Rely on friendships to induce the scheduling department to modify the requisition.
   b. Rely on favors, past and future, to accomplish the same result.
   c. Work through political allies in other departments.

4. **Educational tactics**
   a. Use direct persuasion; that is, try to persuade the scheduling department that its requisition is unreasonable.
   b. Use what might be called indirect persuasion to help the scheduling department see the problem from the purchasing department's point of view (ask the scheduler to sit in and observe the difficulty in getting the vendor to agree to quick delivery).

5. **Organizational-interactional tactics**
   a. Seek to change the interaction pattern; for example, have the scheduling department check with the purchasing department as to the possibility of getting quick delivery before it makes a requisition.
   b. Seek to take over other responsibilities, for example, to subordinate scheduling to purchasing in an integrated materials department.

SOURCE: Excerpted from "Tactics of Lateral Relationships: The Purchasing Agent," *Administrative Science Quarterly*, 7 (September, 1962), p. 166, G. Strauss. © Copyright 1962 by *Administrative Science Quarterly*. Reprinted with permission.

involve large sums of money, or that include critical items used in the operations of the buying organization, represent a significant amount of risk. Those responsible for decision making may want to minimize the chance of making wrong decisions and thus take a more conservative approach to selecting new products and services. For example, when confronted with an excellent new product at an attractive price, but from a relatively unknown supplier, there may be a tendency to retain the status quo, or to stay with existing vendors and familiar products.

It is impossible to resolve conclusively the question "Is industrial buying rational?" or even "Is industrial buying more rational than consumer buying?" The formal and informal constraints placed on the buying process by the organization would seem to impose a kind of rationality not always found in consumer buying; however, it is rationality defined by the behavior of individual employees and subject to their own perceived self-interest.

The issue of rationality can be restated as a concern with the *quality* of purchase decision making. It is a subject that warrants further attention. Specifically, what are the explanatory factors that underlie making a *good* rather than a *mediocre* buying decision? To address this issue, let us look at industrial buying as a logical process.

## Buying as a Process: The Buystages

One of the most simple, yet far-reaching, insights into buying behavior is that it is actually a *process*—much more than the physical act of exchanging goods or services for an agreement to pay for them. There is a logical sequence of stages that collectively result in product and vendor choices. A number of purchasing-related decisions have to be made in each stage (see Table 3.4 for examples). These stages take place over time, frequently over months or years.

Approaches to defining buying processes generally include five generic steps. First, a need is recognized. Second, information is sought. Third, products are evaluated. Fourth, a purchase decision is made. Fifth, there is some kind of postpurchase evaluation. This general framework applies to both consumer and industrial buying.

Robinson, Faris, and Wind (1967) took these generic steps and tailored them to the industrial buying process by developing a set of eight sequential steps called *buystages*. These include the following:

1. Anticipation or recognition of a problem (need) and a general solution,

2. Determination of characteristics and quantity of needed item,

3. Description of characteristics and quantity of needed item,

4. Search for and qualification of potential sources,

5. Acquisition and analysis of proposals,

6. Evaluation of proposals and selection of supplier(s),

**TABLE 3.4** Twenty Potential Decisions Facing the Industrial Buyer

1. Is the need or problem pressing enough that it must be acted on now? If not, how long can action be deferred?
2. What types of products or services could conceivably be used to solve our need or problem?
3. Should we make the item ourselves?
4. Must a new product be designed, or has a vendor already developed an acceptable product?
5. Should a value analysis be performed?
6. What is the highest price we can afford to pay?
7. What trade-offs are we prepared to make between price and other product/vendor attributes?
8. Which information sources will we rely upon?
9. How many vendors should be considered?
10. Which attributes will be stressed in evaluating vendors?
11. Should bids be solicited?
12. Should the item be leased or purchased outright?
13. How far can a given vendor be pushed in negotiations? On what issues will that vendor bend the most?
14. How much inventory should a vendor be willing to keep on hand?
15. Should we split our order among several vendors?
16. Is a long-term contract in our interest?
17. What contractual guarantees will we require?
18. How shall we establish our order routine?
19. After the purchase, how will vendor performance be evaluated?
20. How will we deal with inadequate product or vendor performance?

7. Selection of an order routine, and
8. Performance feedback and evaluation.

In the first stage, someone in the buying organization becomes aware of a need. This could be an internal problem that is not being adequately addressed, or it could be an opportunity to do something new, different, or better. This recognition of a need or problem can originate in any number of places. A sampling of points of initiation for industrial purchase decisions might include the following:

◆ A computerized inventory monitoring system automatically delivers a signal that it is time to reorder

◆ Production personnel recognize that plant machines are producing an inordinate number of defective items

- R&D engineers encounter the need for a customized solution to a technical problem in developing some new product

- The purchasing department determines that a particular vendor is becoming less dependable, has limited capacity to meet growing needs, or will soon be bought out by a competitor

- The sales department receives a number of customer complaints regarding some component within the company's product

- Management anticipates new government regulations that will limit the organization's ability to use certain materials

The person who begins the buying process by identifying a need is not necessarily the one who ultimately decides what, if anything, will be purchased to satisfy that need. Nevertheless, the marketer should recognize where and why the buying process was initiated. Among other things, this knowledge will provide a more complete understanding of the context within which the customer need exists.

Furthermore, the industrial marketer can act as the initiator of the process. That is, the marketer helps the customer recognize a need. Industrial marketing frequently is characterized more by marketers seeking out customers than by customers seeking out vendors. The marketer might create a demand for some products by emphasizing some new capability, the opportunity for cost savings, more dependability in terms of supply availability, or higher quality. The perception of a need can be created by raising doubts in the buyer's mind whether or not he or she is paying too much for existing products, staying current with the opportunities presented by the latest technologies, or keeping abreast of the innovations being adopted by competitors.

The second and third buystages are closely related. In the second, members of the buying organization identify potential solutions to the needs recognized in the first buystage. Thus, they establish the types of products or services that conceivably could resolve the perceived problem. They may look internally or externally for solutions, and they frequently rely on alternatives that historically have been successful. When the problem is novel, of course, the only reference point may be a competitor's experiences. The marketer can play a key role in this stage by getting buyers to see solutions that otherwise might not be considered. That is, the marketer can help broaden the buyers' field of vision and suggest creative approaches to problem solving.

Once a general solution has been established, the organization translates its needs into a more precise statement of the specific characteristics and quantity required of some product or service. Through this process of formally describing product characteristics, needs can be better communicated to others in the organization, as well as to potential vendors. At this stage, product specifications are established— specifications that can range from a statement of the minimum cleaning power required of an industrial detergent or the copy quality and run-length capability of a copier to detailed blueprints describing some key components or exact temperature tolerances for a machine tool.

The decisions made in the second and third buystages can prejudice what happens throughout the remaining stages of the process. Product requirements or specifications can be, and frequently are, written so that only one or two particular vendors can readily satisfy them. That is, the description of needs is tailored to products that well-known and favored vendors are currently offering or easily could be offering. This preclusion creates problems for the marketer whose products would readily fulfill the buyer's needs but do not meet the precise specifications.

The message for the marketer, to this point, is that the marketing effort must begin early in the buying process. In some instances, the marketer is not only able to help the buyer recognize a need but also can try to get the buyer to specify product requirements in a way that clearly includes, and possibly favors, his or her company's offerings.

Because the establishment of requirements can be instrumental in determining what is eventually purchased and from whom, a number of stakeholders within the buying organization get involved at this stage in the process. The marketer is well advised to identify these stakeholders, their respective positions, and their objectives. It is not unusual, for example, to find key influencers attempting to set technical specifications or tolerances more conservatively than necessary, primarily as a risk-avoidance strategy. The intelligent salesperson may be able to counter such a strategy by directly communicating with those who are influential during this stage.

Once the buying organization has a firm idea of what it wants, a source of supply must be located. Thus, the organization is actually making two key decisions: (a) to buy a particular type of product and (b) to buy from a particular vendor. Unaware marketers conceivably could be in the ironic position of having convinced a buyer to purchase a product, only to have that customer select some other source of supply.

The fourth buystage involves searching for, and qualifying, acceptable vendors. Using obtainable information sources, the buyer may first identify the universe of available suppliers, then reduce this number to some subset of vendors who can meet the established quality and quantity requirements. This subset is called the buyer's *evoked set* and consists of vendors the buyer actually considers in making a final purchase choice.

In putting together this pool of potential vendors, the company often begins with internal files. The purchasing department will often maintain a cross-referenced index of vendors, orders, prices, and contracts. Many firms, and especially larger ones, rely on some sort of approved vendor list (AVL) when selecting suppliers. Sales calls, word of mouth, catalogs, industrial directories, trade shows, trade journal advertising, and other key sources also will be relied on for vendor information. The first problem for a marketer is to ensure that the buying organization is aware that his or her firm has a product offering in the area under consideration. Then, the marketer must ensure that his or her firm satisfies the vendor evaluation criteria used by the buyer.

A good product may not be enough to get a vendor included in the buyer's evoked set. A supplier who has an excellent product but an unstable labor force or unreliable delivery capabilities, or is inflexible in adapting to the buyer's needs, or constantly tries to hard-sell or oversell the buyer, may be more trouble than the buyer cares to tolerate. The critical nature of many industrial purchases suggests that the relationship between buyer and seller is akin to a marriage. As a result, the buyer will sometimes evaluate a vendor's production facilities, quality assurance program, financial health, service and delivery record, and even the quality of its management.

In the fifth buystage, after the field of suppliers is narrowed to an acceptable group of qualifying vendors, the buying organization acquires and evaluates specific proposals and/or alternatives. A proposal can take the form of a formal bid, a price quote from a salesperson, or a listing of products, prices, and terms in a catalog or directory. It is in this fifth stage that the process of negotiation with vendors over price, inventory levels, contract dates, delivery requirements, warranties, trade-in policies, and so forth receives the sharpest focus. For many routine purchases, or those with which the organization has past experience, buystages four and five are indistinguishable. That is, they occur simultaneously and become a single stage. For these types of purchases, the information needs of the buyer are relatively low.

The buyer may still be negotiating with selected suppliers, or requesting new bids, as he or she evaluates proposals and makes final supplier choices (buystage six). The actual selection of the source—or, more typically, sources—of supply may also involve considerable negotiation within the buying organization among stakeholders with conflicting interests. The individuals involved in the decision often place different importance weights on various supplier attributes and have differing perceptions of how well each vendor can perform on a given attribute.

The buying organization may attempt to quantify the selection process and rely on formal rules for making a choice. For example, decision makers may evaluate each vendor on a set of agreed-upon attributes, then opt to select those that exceed the minimum required standards on all attributes. Alternatively, they may choose the vendors whose performance is best on the most attributes. A number of such decision rules are possible.

A very practical approach for deciding which vendor should be selected is illustrated in Table 3.5. There, each vendor is evaluated on each attribute, using a rating scale. For the sake of example, a 100 percentage point scale is used to evaluate vendor Z, where .00 equals very poor performance, .50 equals medium performance, and 1.00 equals outstanding performance. The results are in column A. Then the importance of each attribute is established, this time by dividing 100 percentage points across the attributes. A higher percentage is given to *the* most important attributes (e.g., .00, of no importance; .50, moderately important; and 1.00, extremely important). These totals are put in column B, which must add up to 100 percent. Next, the evaluation scores for each attribute (column A) are multiplied by the importance weights (column B), and the results are summed. The outcome is a score for vendor Z. The process is repeated for other vendors, and those receiving the highest scores receive the organization's business.

Having decided what to buy and from whom to buy it, the buyer then resolves how much is to be bought from each vendor and how frequently orders will be placed and should be filled. The levels of inventory to be kept are agreed upon. In ad-

**TABLE 3.5** A Weighted-Attribute Approach to Evaluating a Particular Vendor

| Attribute | (A)<br>Assessment<br>of Vendor<br>Z's Capabilities | (B)<br>Weighting<br>Importance<br>Rating | Vendor Z's<br>Overall Rating<br>(A × B) |
|---|---|---|---|
| Delivery | .4 | .25 | .10 |
| Product quality | .8 | .30 | .24 |
| Price | .4 | .15 | .06 |
| Flexibility | .2 | .10 | .02 |
| Service capability | .6 | .20 | .12 |
| | | 1.00 | **.54** |

dition, the parties agree on the procedures for placing orders, taking delivery, making returns, and monitoring and expediting the process. This is buystage seven, and it is principally concerned with working out the mechanics of the exchange.

Although the relationship with a vendor usually lasts beyond the initial purchase, especially given how involved the choice process can be, loyalty is not automatic. Buystage eight involves the generation of feedback and the ongoing evaluation of each supplier. This evaluation can be formal in nature, such as a repeat of the method presented in buystage 6, especially with first-time purchases and untried vendors. At this point, however, the customer may be evaluating such things as the investment value of the purchased item, its ability to generate additional sales revenue, satisfaction of user departments, and the quality of the seller's training programs and aftersale service.

Poor performance by a supplier or a product is not likely to go unnoticed, as it will probably affect the job performance of someone in the buying organization. Most often this will be the product user. In addition, individuals involved with the buying decision who had reservations about the vendor selected by the organization are especially attuned to negative feedback regarding that vendor. When such feedback is not properly channeled, it may lead to frustration and harbored feelings of resentment regarding a vendor. These negative attitudes may surface much later, in the context of a completely different purchase decision.

For the marketer, the implication of the postpurchase stage is simple yet vital: Marketing *does not end with the sale*. In fact, the crucial importance of ongoing relationships with customers suggests that the marketing effort is really never over. The marketer not only must continue to promote the advantages of a product to key members of the buying center but also must monitor the feedback and evaluation process that occurs in the customer organization. Measurement by the marketer of user satisfaction levels and complaints is critical to ongoing success. Problems can be corrected before too much damage is done. In fact, quick response to customer problems can lead to even stronger buyer-seller ties; it also can provide an opportunity to identify new or changing customer needs.

This discussion is not meant to suggest that the process is the same for all products. Actually, with different products, the length of each stage will vary, and some stages will be omitted. For example, when purchasing routine items such as cleaning supplies, the organization may simply be loyal to its current supplier, automatically reordering without reevaluating needs or acquiring proposals from vendors. Alternatively, in a study of the purchase of intensive-care monitoring equipment by hospitals, Laczniak (1979) was able to find only four clearly identifiable stages: (a) the identification of needs, (b) the establishment of purchase objectives, (c) the identification and evaluation of buying alternatives, and (d) final deliberations and selection of supplier. Abratt (1986) found that six stages were involved when companies purchase high-tech laboratory instruments. Morris and Schindehutte (1999) identified five distinct stages over 18 months when trauma centers buy high-end medical imaging equipment.

Some of the stages in the process may take place simultaneously, rather than sequentially. The organization may be involved in describing the characteristics of the needed item (buystage 3) at the same time it searches for vendors (buystage 4). In addition, the process can be iterative, where the results of later stages lead the organization to return to and modify earlier-stage decisions. In acquiring proposals (buystage 5), for example, the buyer may find that the capabilities and requirements of vendors make it necessary that specifications be rewritten (buystage 3) or that the organization's needs have changed (buystage 2). Additionally, the entire process can be terminated at any one of the stages.

To better understand both the nature of the buying process for industrial products and services and the potential marketing implications, it is worth considering different types of buying situations, or scenarios.

# Buying Scenarios

As we have noted, the actual stages involved in the buying process and the kinds of activities that take place in each stage vary with the type of product or service being purchased. More specifically, the stages depend on the characteristics of the buying problem facing the organization. For example, the purchasing process might differ based on the amount of money being spent or on the perceived riskiness of the decision.

Understanding differences in how the buying process works is easier if we consider some of the more common types of buying situations. The problem is to determine the significant characteristics or criteria that differentiate various types of buying situations. One popular approach is to classify buying scenarios based on (a) the newness of the purchasing problem and amount of relevant past experience the company has with a given product or service, (b) the amount and type of information needed by those who influence the buying decision, and (c) the number of alternatives receiving consideration (Anderson, Chu, & Weitz, 1987; Robinson et al., 1967).

Using these criteria, three types of buying situations, or *buyclasses*, can be identified: straight rebuy, modified rebuy, and new task purchases.

A *straight rebuy* situation is one in which the organization has purchased an item in the past and probably will simply reorder it from the source of supply currently being used. This is a routine decision involving low levels of perceived risk and low information needs. Decision choice criteria have previously been established and evaluated. Given this, few people tend to get involved in these decisions. Little or no search and evaluation effort takes place on the part of the buyer, generally because it was performed on some previous occasion.

The *modified rebuy* scenario takes place when the organization has some past experience purchasing the item in question, but some aspect of the buying task has changed. For example, the technical people in the buying organization may have slightly modified the required product specifications, the marketing department may be asking for some new product feature not included on the originally purchased item, the purchasing department may be under pressure to find better prices, or production personnel are asking for improved service and better delivery. Based on experience, the decision criteria for selecting products and vendors may also have been changed. People in the buying organization are more informed now, so they may have a better understanding of particular product attributes or vendor capabilities. Experience may also mean their expectations toward vendors have changed. As a result, some effort is put toward searching for additional product and vendor information. Suppliers are reappraised, and some new ones could be considered. The buyer may also want to engage in new negotiations over particular aspects of the purchase.

With a *new task purchase*, the organization is buying the item for the first time. Generally, the need to buy is initiated by the occurrence of some problem or need not previously encountered within the organization, or by a management decision to deal with a recurring task in a markedly different way. The organization may have decided to purchase its first computer network, hire its first advertising agency, or employ a firm to steam clean machines that were previously manually cleaned by company employees. Because of the relative lack of previous experience with the product area, the information needs of the organization are considerable. The vendor identification, evaluation, and selection process is more involved here than in the other buying scenarios. New task decisions, which hold greater risk, are likely to take longer and involve more people.

## Linking the Buying Process, the Buying Center, and Buying Scenarios

The real value in the three buying concepts introduced up to this point can be found by examining the ways in which they are related to one another. First, consider how the buying process relates to the buying scenarios. Combining the stages

**TABLE 3.6**  Marketing Implications of Customer Involvement Levels in Buying Decisions

Cynthia Webster examined customer involvement levels when purchasing three different kinds of professional (financial, informational, promotional) services. She found that buyers exhibited a medium level of involvement for straight rebuy and modified rebuy decisions and a high level of involvement for new task decisions. A number of marketing implications can be drawn from customer involvement levels, as summarized below.

| *Level of Involvement* | *Buyer Characteristics* | *Marketing Suggestions* |
|---|---|---|
| *High involvement* <br> ◆ Informational and promotional services in the modified rebuy situation <br> ◆ Financial, informational, and promotional services in the new task-purchasing situation | ◆ Consider a number of attributes when comparing vendors <br> ◆ Likely to search for considerable information <br> ◆ Receptive to promotional messages <br> ◆ Will expend considerable effort in evaluating information <br> ◆ Will carefully evaluate the merits and weaknesses of the service <br> ◆ Likely to find new vendors acceptable <br> ◆ Loyal behavior is likely after initial decision <br> ◆ Rely heavily on word-of-mouth communications | ◆ Promotional messages should reach a number of people in the buying center (via direct mail advertising, trade journal advertising, etc.) <br> ◆ Concentrate on personal sales presentations <br> ◆ Focus on the quality of the argument presented in communications <br> ◆ Communications should be extremely informative (i.e., focus on copy) <br> ◆ Provide information on the services available as well as on the provider(s) <br> ◆ Need to identify and focus on opinion leaders |
| *Medium involvement* <br> ◆ Financial, informational, and promotional services in the straight rebuy situation <br> ◆ Promotional services in the modified rebuy situation | ◆ Will engage in limited information search <br> ◆ Buying process is passive <br> ◆ Receptive to many more communication messages <br> ◆ Little evaluation of alternative providers | ◆ Messages should focus on the attention-getting attribute <br> ◆ Decrease length of copy and increase emphasis placed on symbolism and illustrations <br> ◆ Place emphasis on sales promotion tactics (e.g., price discounts) |

*continued on the next page*

**TABLE 3.6** Continued

| Level of Involvement | Buyer Characteristics | Marketing Suggestions |
|---|---|---|
| | ◆ Relatively little commitment to suppliers<br>◆ Likely to find several providers acceptable<br>◆ Less likely to be vendor loyal | ◆ Continuously promote to maintain awareness and interest |

SOURCE: Adapted from "Industrial Buyers' Level of Involvement With Services," *Marketing Theory and Applications* (proceedings from 1990 American Marketing Association Winter Educator's Conference), pp. 69-74, Webster. © Copyright 1990 by American Management Association.

of the buying process with the types or classes of buying situations produces a matrix or grid, as shown in Table 3.7. This *buygrid* has important strategic implications for marketing.

As the buying process evolves, a number of decisions are being made (see Table 3.4), and the number of viable options open to the buying organization is effectively being reduced. In other words, the combined effect of the formal (and informal) decisions made during the buying process is to eliminate some product options and vendors and to create a growing commitment toward others. The vendor who gets involved too late in the buying process may never really have a chance, especially in the new task situation. Alternatively, with a straight rebuy, many of the decisions have been made in the past and are, in effect, automatically renewed.

For items purchased on a repeat basis, the goal of the marketer should be to create a straight rebuy situation where his or her company is the specified vendor. Once this is achieved, the marketer's focus will be on the latter stages in the buying process. Because buyers in this situation know what they want and are not typically seeking new information or proposals, the marketer concentrates on the negotiation, order routine, and evaluation stages. By contrast, where a straight rebuy exists but the marketer is currently not the vendor (an out-supplier), the goal is to identify potential areas of buyer dissatisfaction, possibly creating dissonance. In this manner, the marketer is attempting to change the buying situation into a modified rebuy.

Now, let us bring the buying center back into the discussion. The composition of the buying center, specifically the number and types of individuals involved, is likely to differ based on the stage in the buying process and the type of buying scenario in question. The influence of a given individual may vary depending on whether the organization is trying to determine its needs or, alternatively, is evaluating different vendors. Because numerous decisions are made during the buying process (see Table 3.4), the actual decider could change depending on the decision. Different types of information needs over the stages suggest that the gatekeeper role could also change hands.

**TABLE 3.7**  Buygrid Framework for Industrial Buying Situations

| | Buyclasses | | |
|---|---|---|---|
| *Buystages* | *New Task* | *Modified Rebuy* | *Straight Rebuy* |
| 1. Anticipation or recognition of a problem (need) and a general solution | | | |
| 2. Determination of characteristics and quantity of needed item | | | |
| 3. Description of characteristics and quantity of needed item | | | |
| 4. Search for and qualification of potential sources | | | |
| 5. Acquisition and analysis of proposals | | | |
| 6. Evaluation of proposals and selection of supplier(s) | | | |
| 7. Selection of an order routine | | | |
| 8. Performance feedback and evaluation | | | |

SOURCE: *Industrial Buying and Creative Marketing*, p. 23, Robinson, Faris, and Wind. © Copyright 1967 by Allyn & Bacon, Inc. Reprinted with permission.

Furthermore, more people might be involved in the early stages of the process, especially for a new task purchase. Similarly, engineers and production/operations managers might play the major role in the early stages of the new task and modified rebuy scenarios, and the purchasing department may be less of a factor. In one study it was found that purchasing personnel exerted less influence in the early stages of purchases involving more technical products with which the organization had little past experience (Giunipero, 1984). Conversely, the purchasing department may be of key importance throughout the stages of a straight rebuy decision. As a generalization, it is not unusual to find a dominant role played by engineers in product selection and by purchasing agents in vendor selection.

The manner in which final decisions are arrived at can also be expected to vary as changes occur in the number of people involved and in the functional areas having the strongest influence. Different product and vendor attributes will be stressed, the amount of conflict will vary, and the ways in which trade-off decisions are made will change, depending on the stage and class in the buygrid.

The marketer, in turn, must tailor the product, price, distribution, and promotional programs to the requirements of the different cells in the buygrid. As a result, the relative emphasis on price versus delivery reliability, on trade journal advertising versus direct mail, or on an in-house sales force versus manufacturer's representatives will depend on who is involved in the purchasing process. This can be expected to change with the stage and class in the buygrid. For example, the use of middlemen, such as industrial distributors, may be less effective in the early stages of a new task purchase than in a straight rebuy scenario. The marketing message in a modified rebuy situation may focus more on comparisons of product and company performance relative to that of the competition. Personal selling can become more important than other forms of communication as the buyer moves closer to making an actual purchase decision for both new task and modified rebuy purchases. Direct mail might be quite effective in reinforcing buyers during the evaluation stage of a straight rebuy decision. Caution must be exercised in generalizing across products and customers, but the buygrid and buying center remain important foundations around which marketers can begin to organize their efforts.

## Advanced Perspectives on the Buying Center

In a sense, the successful marketer lives in the buying centers of organizations. He or she keeps a finger on the pulse of what is happening among the key influencers, deciders, gatekeepers, and others. Because of its critical importance, researchers have attempted to gain richer insights into the workings of the buying center. They have explored it from the vantage point of structure, power, risk, problem-solving, and rewards.

## Structural Perspective

Because the buying center is not usually a formal group, its structure is not formally established by the organization. Instead, its structure is defined by communication linkages among the participants. By studying who communicated with whom in a variety of different buying situations, Johnston and Bonoma (1981) discovered that a structure started to emerge. They concluded that the buying center structure can be characterized in terms of the following factors:

- **Vertical involvement:** the number of levels in the organizational hierarchy that get involved. Different decisions will involve individuals as high up as the president or CEO, or as low as clerical workers.

- **Lateral involvement:** the number of departments, functional areas, or divisions within the organization that play a part in the buying decision. Does one department make the decision in isolation, or do a number of them get involved?

◆ **Absolute size:** the total number of people involved. More than one person can get involved from a given hierarchical level or functional area in the organization, so this number can be different from the total for vertical and lateral involvement.

◆ **Connectedness:** the extent to which the members of the buying center directly communicate with one another regarding the purchase decision. Some members will receive extensive communication from others in the buying center, while others are fairly isolated, receiving infrequent communication.

◆ **Centrality of purchasing:** the extent to which much of the communication within the organization regarding a purchase decision flows through the purchasing department.

Each of these dimensions has important implications for the marketer. If more vertical levels are involved, those at the higher levels are likely to exert a disproportionate influence on final purchase decisions, whether they intend to or not. The involvement of higher-level management is likely to be greater for larger dollar purchases and for purchases of capital equipment and critical entering goods. Greater lateral involvement suggests that the buying process will be less formal and probably involve more conflict. This is especially the case where departments have differing goals in purchase decisions. Absolute size is of concern because the buying process becomes more complex and lasts longer as more people get involved. It becomes more difficult for the marketer to reach all those involved in the decision process, or to tailor the marketing program to each member of the buying center. For various reasons, the industrial salesperson does not personally reach more than half of those involved. Connectedness is also of importance, in that a lack of much direct communication among decision participants means that the marketer's message may have to be communicated separately to each individual, and some people are just not reached. In addition, connectedness provides insights into the identity of the central players. Finally, the centrality of the purchasing department is especially relevant because the marketer's initial customer contact is often made through the purchasing department. Purchasing can help (or hinder) the ability of the marketer to understand the buying process in an organization and to know where to concentrate his or her efforts.

## Power Perspective

Knowing the members of the buying center is not enough. The marketer must determine the identity of the key influencer and the decider. A person's ability to influence or make buying decisions is a reflection of that person's power in the organization. In many, cases, however, power is situation specific—that is, a given person can have more or less power to influence things depending on the situation. In the case of organizational buying, it may depend on the type of purchase, the time pressure involved, the perceived risk of making a wrong decision, the number of alternatives to be considered, and a variety of other factors.

Where do members of the buying center get their power? French and Ravens (1959) have identified a number of power bases that apply whenever people interact in a social context, including any sort of group or organization setting. These bases include

- **Reward power:** Ability to influence others comes from the fact that you control the monetary, social, political, or psychological rewards they desire.

- **Coercive power:** Influence comes from the ability to penalize or punish those who do not cooperate.

- **Referent power:** Others comply with your wishes because they think highly of you. This attraction is based on personality, charisma, and persuasive ability.

- **Expert power:** Influence is rooted in one's expertise regarding the issue under question. A person achieves power because others perceive that he or she knows more than anyone else about the problem at hand.

- **Legitimate power:** Influence is based on one's formal position or title. The group or organization has formally granted the individual authority in some decision area.

These can be applied readily to the buying center. *Legitimate power* and *reward power* bases become especially relevant when higher-level managers are members of the buying center (i.e., more hierarchical involvement). Such managers may have formal power to determine buying decision outcomes. The managers may also control the rewards and evaluations of those in the buying center, leading to compliant behavior on the part of individuals when it comes to evaluating a product or vendor. Some members may achieve reward power (e.g., the purchasing department) because of their ability to perform favors for members of the buying center. *Coercive power* might be displayed when a buying center member, seeking the compliance of others regarding a buying decision, makes life more difficult for those who choose to disagree with that member. For example, the purchasing department could exert some coercive influence by making others follow rigorous requisition procedures, including a detailed written justification of each and every item requested. *Referent power* can be held by any potential member of the buying center, as long as that person has a personal following, attractiveness, or persuasiveness when it comes to managerial decision making. *Expert power* can be especially important in new task purchases, as well as in some modified rebuy situations. Engineers can achieve influence in the buying center because of their technical expertise regarding product specifications and performance capabilities. Production managers often have expertise regarding product applications in the production process. Purchasing agents provide expertise concerning vendors and their performance capabilities.

These bases of power suggest that things may not be as they appear in the organizational buying decision process. A given individual may have the formal authority for purchase decisions (i.e., legitimate power), but the actual decider is some other person who holds expert or reward power. Also, the bases of power are not mutually exclusive. A buying center member may have legitimate power, with this position achieved as a result of his or her expertise. This legitimate power base may also provide the ability to reward others.

Some important implications can be drawn for the marketer when analyzing power in the buying center. Tom Bonoma (1982) suggests the following:

1. Those with less power must frequently rely on persuasion and argument to influence the more powerful regarding company needs, product attributes, vendor capabilities, or some other purchasing-related issue.

2. When a buying center member raises questions about the opinions or abilities of another member, it is frequently an indication that the person being criticized is an important source of power in the buying center.

3. Those who hold the greatest power will tend to be the members who receive the bulk of information and communications that are exchanged concerning a buying decision.

4. The most powerful buying center members are not the most easily identified or most talkative members of their groups. Powerful individuals often send others to meetings in their place, knowing that no final decision will be made without their approval.

5. No correlation exists between the functional area of a manager and power in the buying center. The power of a functional area varies depending on the organization and the product being purchased.

6. Power and formal authority in buying decisions are not necessarily the same thing.

Bonoma proposes a step-by-step process for assessing power in the buying center. The first step is to identify the members of the buying center and attempt to identify the base of power on which each is likely to rely. Then, the strength of each of the power positions is evaluated, as well as the primary motives each of the more influential members has in making the buying decision. Next, the specific product and vendor attributes of greatest importance to each of the key buying center members are established. The perceptions of each of the key influentials regarding the marketer's product, company, and personnel (e.g., salespeople, technical support staff) are then determined. Once all these data have been placed into the matrix, the marketer is in a stronger position to design a set of marketing and communication approaches tailored to the key influencers in the buying process.

## Risk Perspective

Buying can be viewed as an activity filled with risks and uncertainties, and purchase decision processes as risk-reducing behavior. Using this perspective, the person or department best able to cope with relevant risks should have greater influence in deciding what is bought, in what quantity, from whom, and based on what criteria. There are actually two major dimensions that combine to determine the overall amount of risk in a buying decision (Peter & Ryan, 1976). The first is the probability of loss due to a bad decision. How likely is it that the organization will experience some economic loss if the wrong choice is made? The second is the amount of loss that could result from an incorrect decision. When the probability of loss is taken times the magnitude of loss, the result is a potential measure of the total purchasing risk.

Purchasing situations vary, however, in the problems they pose for the buying organization. There are at least seven major types of purchasing problem areas: those related to the supplier, the product, the customer, price, finance, legalities, and regulations. These problem areas can be related to the two major dimensions of risk; that is, within each of these problem areas one can talk about the likelihood of loss and the magnitude of loss. One type of risk concerns price. How likely is it that the organization is paying too high a price, and what is the potential loss the organization will suffer from paying too high a price? Total risk, then, would involve the combination of all these problem areas.

Influence within the buying center may stem from a person's ability to cope with (lessen) the risks involved in the buying task. When the risk of each of the problem areas is low, the purchasing department may be the primary source of influence. Correspondingly, senior management may play the major role when the risk of each type of problem is high. The question becomes, what happens between these two extremes? We might expect production or engineering personnel to be more influential when the buying decision is characterized by problems concerning technical aspects of the product. The same may be the case when the principal area of concern is the compatibility of the product with existing equipment. If the possibility of adverse reaction by customers to the use of some purchased component most characterizes the buying decision, the sales or marketing department becomes a key source of influence. Where there are legal or regulatory problems, the legal staff should play a larger role. Influence may rest with finance accounting personnel when there are concerns regarding payment arrangements, make-or-buy decisions, leasing questions, or additional capital needs. The ability of purchasing managers to solve problems of delivery or supplier reliability may enhance their influence when the firm is threatened with potential loss due to such problems. Lastly, purchasing situations involving risk resulting from problems related to employee safety or environmental damage should engender greater involvement and influence on the part of senior management.

Risk can also be related to the purchasing tactics used by the buying organization (Webster, 1984). When members of the buying center are uncertain about product or vendor performance, more suppliers will be contacted, multiple sources and shorter-term contracts will be used, and ability to meet specifications becomes a critical buying attribute. When buying center members are uncertain about the organization's needs or anticipate adverse reactions from others to a given buying decision, more people probably will be involved in the buying decision. Consequently, the process will take longer, more information will be sought, the quality attribute will be stressed, and source loyalty will be relied on.

Buying risk is also related to the structure of the buying center. Spekman and Stern (1979) suggest that buying centers that are more rigid and bureaucratic are less effective in dealing with uncertainties in the buying process, but more effective when uncertainties are minimal. A more flexible structure enables the buying center members to better cope with and reduce uncertainties. When the risk or uncertainty in a buying decision is great, the buying center might be expected to be more decentralized, to involve less formal assignment of specific individuals to roles or tasks, to be less reliant on rules and procedures, and to encourage greater participation in decision making.

Risk is something the marketer may try to influence. For example, when the marketer is the in-supplier, his or her efforts will focus on reducing perceived uncertainties. The out-supplier, alternatively, will try to heighten the perceived uncertainty to the point where personnel in the buying center are willing to consider new alternatives.

## Problem-Solving Perspective

An alternative perspective is to view purchasing as problem-solving behavior. Most industrial products will fall into four categories on the basis of problems likely to be encountered should the product be purchased:

- **Routine order products:** These are items ordered and used on a regular basis. These products present no anticipated problems regarding usage or performance, and they contain little risk (e.g., office supplies).

- **Procedural problem products:** The overriding concern with these items is in how to use the product. To successfully adopt the product, some amount of learning must take place, perhaps through formal training (e.g., a word processor to replace typewriters).

- **Performance problem products:** These are items for which there is serious concern about whether the product can successfully meet the user's needs. Questions are raised whether the product can perform at the level required and if it will be compatible with existing equipment and resources (e.g., machinery using new technology).

- **Political problem products:** Internal political problems arise when the purchase of an item will take resources away from other areas in the organization (e.g., high-priced items) or when the product being purchased will be used by different departments, or individuals, with conflicting needs (e.g., a computer software package).

It is likely that reliability of supply and price will be the important attributes when purchasing routine order products. In addition, current suppliers are favored in this situation (i.e., source loyalty). With procedural problem products, attributes that ease the learning problem become salient, such as technical service provided, ease of product operation or use, and training offered by the supplier. For performance problem products, the key attributes are those that assist the buyer in judging how well the product and vendor will be able to do the job. Examples include product reliability data, technical service offered, and the flexibility of the supplier in meeting the specific needs of the customer. Finally, if a purchase decision poses a serious political problem for an organization, the buying center will stress performance on those attributes that must be accomplished regardless of who in the organization will be using the item. By favoring attributes that are commonly recognized as important by all departments or functional areas involved, conflicts within the buying center are minimized.

Depending on the product under consideration, then, different attributes will be stressed. More important, a useful approach to understanding buyer behavior is to determine the nature of the problem the buyer is trying to solve. The marketer should focus on the key problem-sufferers and on positioning his or her product as a solution to the problem that is most salient to these individuals.

## Reward Perspective

The individual members of a buying center often demonstrate significant differences in terms of what is important to them when the company makes buying decisions. These potential conflicts can be explained, at least in part, by considering the motivation of each person in the buying center. Individuals in the buying center are pursuing their self-interests within the constraints imposed by the organization. Because organizational buying behavior is work behavior, the way people act when making buying decisions is influenced by the way in which they are evaluated and rewarded by the organization. Those involved in purchasing can be expected to behave in a way that maximizes their records of achievement in accordance with the ways they are measured (Corey, 1991).

When individuals become part of the buying center, they bring to it the values and objectives that they live with in their jobs every day. Their priorities are likely to reflect the performance measures and rewards applied to them by the organization. People are evaluated and rewarded differently depending on their job or the department in the firm where they work. As a result, purchasing agents may be rewarded for saving the company money, while operations managers are evaluated based on the number of clients served, average client waiting time, and number of client complaints. Someone in finance might be evaluated on the basis of the company's return on investment or cash flow position, while the marketing manager is measured based on whether sales and market share objectives are met.

It is also important to recognize that the actions of any one member of the buying center can affect the evaluation and rewards received by other members. For example, while purchasing agents may be rewarded for saving the firm money, their ability to do so may be limited severely by the manner in which engineers set technical product specifications, or by demands from finance that the company lease instead of buy. Rewards to production personnel for meeting certain production quotas may be reduced because the purchasing department saved money by using a less than dependable source of supply. The tendency to compromise in terms of buying decisions may actually be an attempt to ensure that a number of different people achieve satisfactory outcomes in terms of their own priorities.

Why do purchasing agents (or engineers or product managers) push for certain product attributes, or argue for particular products or vendors, when faced with a purchase decision? What determines how strongly they emphasize a given position? With whom will they form alliances or coalitions to influence the decision outcome?

The reward perspective suggests that the answer to all these questions is rooted in the evaluation and reward systems each of these individuals faces. A hypothetical purchase might find purchasing agents pushing for products and vendors with lower prices, while R&D engineers stress brand name and quality attributes and the production manager emphasizes the vendor's delivery and inventory capabilities. In each case, the attribute being stressed relates to the ability of the individual to perform successfully in the eyes of those who evaluate and reward that person. Members of the buying center bring to it their respective department's view of reality. Overall, the system of measurements and rewards becomes a major source of potential conflict in buying decisions.

To see reward systems in action, consider the classic example of the marketer who established list prices well below those of the competitors but gave small quantity discounts. Although all the competitors charged higher prices, they provided substantial discounts. When it came to buying decisions, customers tended to favor the competitors, despite the price disadvantage. As it turns out, purchasing agents could not care less about the marketer's low prices. These purchasing agents were being evaluated and rewarded based on the price concessions they obtained during negotiations, rather than on the actual price paid.

# A Comprehensive Model of Forces Affecting What Happens in the Buying Center

Much can happen inside a buying center. There can be considerable conflict or a strong spirit of cooperation. Alliances and coalitions can form, or a single person may dominate. Decisions can be made in a systematic, rational, and deliberate fashion, and decision makers can be methodical and well informed. They can also be emotional, disorganized, political, autocratic, hurried, and arbitrary, among many other possibilities.

What happens inside the buying center is the result of a wide array of influences. Frederick Webster and Jerry Wind (1967) attempted to build a comprehensive model that captured all these influences. For simplicity, we can group these influences into (a) those deriving from the external environment, (b) those related to the buying organization, and (c) those tied to the specific individuals who happen to get involved in a particular decision (see Figure 3.2).

The *external environment* includes general conditions (e.g., technology developments, the economy) and interest groups outside the buying organization that directly or indirectly influence the purchasing process. For example, financial institutions may regulate the inventory policies of the customer, the number of supply sources it uses, and its make-or-buy (or lease) decisions. Similarly, government agencies can affect buyer behavior through tax policies, safety and environmental regulations, and fair trade policies, among others. The capabilities of the buyer's distributors can also influence what is bought and in what quantities. In addition, when the

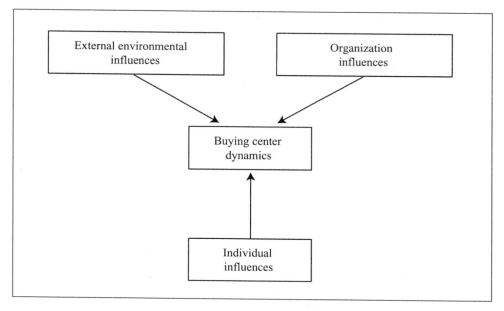

**Figure 3.2.** A Model of the Major Forces Affecting What Happens in the Buying Center

customer is engaged in reciprocal trading arrangements, its trading partners can have an impact on how much of a given item is bought from each qualifying vendor. Partners in joint ventures might have a similar impact, given the mutual stake they have in good purchasing practices.

In some product areas, formal bodies establish standards governing technical specifications or safety requirements for purchased items (e.g., the National Electrical Manufacturers Association). Additionally, some of those individuals involved in purchase decisions belong to professional societies or associations that offer guidelines for buying behavior (e.g., the National Association of Purchasing Management[2] or the American Institute of Electrical and Electronics Engineers).

A customer's buying patterns are also influenced by the purchasing practices of its competitors—especially in highly competitive industries where alertness to new product offerings can create a marketplace advantage. Furthermore, purchasing decisions in a customer organization are significantly affected by that organization's own customers. The influence of customers' customers can determine the establishment of product specifications, the selection of component parts, or even the choosing of vendors. For example, if a customer sells to the government, that customer may be required to direct some of its purchases to minority vendors.

Finally, suppliers themselves affect buying behavior. A given customer buys from a number of vendors, any one of whom can directly or indirectly affect how that customer buys a certain product. For example, if one vendor begins a value analysis or inventory management program with a customer, that customer may place demands on other vendors for similar programs.

The buying center is also strongly affected by the larger *organization within which it operates*. Important organizational factors in purchasing decisions include (a) company goals and objectives, (b) the structure of the company, (c) policies and procedures, and (d) available resources. For instance, if the company has goals and objectives that emphasize quality, or cost reduction, or quick customer response times, these can directly affect what it buys and from whom. Perhaps the most significant aspect of company structure is the extent to which the organization is more centralized or decentralized. This is a question of whether all decisions are made in one central location, usually at a fairly high level in the company, or decision making is delegated to people and units at lower levels and those located at facilities or branches away from the head office. Decentralized structures allow for more flexibility in purchasing, looser authority relationships between buyers and users, and more involvement (often informal) from people outside the purchasing department. Structure can also determine who in the buying center has what information.

Policies and procedures can determine how systematic the purchasing process is, the rules that are followed, and ultimately how bureaucratic the decision process becomes. They will also frequently address such issues as gifts or entertainment from vendors, the number of vendors that must be considered, how a vendor becomes qualified, and minimum performance expectations of any vendor. Examples of company resources that affect buying include the company's net assets, cash flow, technologies, product lines, inventories, and the capabilities of personnel. Significant resource constraints force a company to be much more conservative in what it buys and from whom, and they put the company in a less powerful negotiating position. Resources affect decisions on inventory levels, order sizes, financing of purchases, and integration of the latest purchasing technologies.

It is also important to consider the characteristics of the *individual participants* in the buying process. How risk oriented is each of the key role players? How competitive or aggressive are they? What experiences do they have, especially with the products and vendors in question? How technically oriented are they? Do they bring a more structured approach to decision making? How do they see themselves getting ahead? With whom inside the organization do they have things in common? It is by considering questions such as these that the marketer is able not only to determine what attributes or benefits to emphasize to whom, but also to identify ways to make the lives of key participants easier and/or help them look good in the organization.

# Summary

The marketer faces a distinct challenge when selling to organizations because industrial customers frequently have complex needs and a relatively complex buying decision process. The marketer must not only determine what to sell and how it can best be sold, but also to whom it should be sold within the customer organization.

Any number of individuals, representing a variety of areas within the firm, can get involved in organizational buying decisions. These individuals are motivated by needs and goals that are both personal and organizational. Because some degree of conflict may exist among these needs and goals, industrial buying decisions have a social or behavioral dimension. As a result, these decisions are often less than perfectly rational.

The industrial buying process evolves through a series of stages that begins with the recognition of a need and ends with a postpurchase evaluation process that affects subsequent buying decisions. Along the way, a number of key decisions are made regarding product and vendor choices. The nature of this process will vary depending on the type of buying situation, and particularly depending on the product or service being purchased and on the buyer's past experiences in this product or service area. Three types of buying situations were introduced: straight rebuy, modified rebuy, and new task.

The effectiveness of various marketing approaches depends on the stage of the buying process and the type of buying situation in question. The marketer is a problem solver, tailoring product and vendor attribute bundles to the perceived requirements of organizational customers. Marketing efforts should begin early in the buying process and endure well beyond the close of the sale.

A key tool for understanding the way organizations buy is the buying center, which was described in terms of a set of critical roles that individuals play as the company moves through the stages of the buying process: initiator, buyer, user, influencer, decider, and gatekeeper. Five different perspectives were presented to help the marketer determine who is likely to fill a given role and for unraveling some of the complexities that take place within the buying center. Linkages were established between the buying center, the buying process, and types of buying situations. Finally, a comprehensive framework was provided to summarize the major forces that affect organizational buying decisions.

In this chapter, we have explored the people and processes inside the customer firm. We probed into the behavioral complexities that take place as the organization attempts to make buying decisions. A number of factors, however, make it vital that marketers go beyond getting customers to buy their products and services. The great challenge of industrial marketing in the 21st century is one of relationship building, a subject to which we now turn.

# Notes

1. www.apple.com
2. www.napm.org

# Questions

1. Pick an industrial product and identify examples of technical, commercial, and behavioral complexities that are likely to come into play when marketing that product.

2. Assume you are selling valves for use in heating, ventilating, and air conditioning (hvac) systems. Your primary market consists of older buildings in which your valves could be installed (retrofitted) into the existing hvac system. If you are thinking about focusing your efforts on public school systems, how will you go about determining the key decision maker?

3. Cite five reasons why you might expect industrial buying to be more rational than consumer buying. What are some reasons industrial buying might not be all that rational?

4. Let's say you were the marketer of a new industrial product that was clearly superior in quality to the products of all the existing competitors and was priced slightly lower. Furthermore, you offered better delivery terms and a better warranty, and you could produce as many units as a customer desired. Why might a company never buy your product? Assume that it has a need for the product and currently purchase from one of your competitors.

5. How are the stages of the buying process likely to differ when selecting an advertising agency for the first time, compared to rehiring or replacing the advertising agency a company has been using for 3 years? Which stage is likely to last the longest in each of these two buying situations?

6. If you were developing a model, based on the eight buystages, of the way a customer or group of customers purchases your product, what specific questions would you answer about each state?

7. What are the differences between the buying center concept and a formal committee that has been assigned the task of selecting a vendor?

8. Assume you were the purchasing manager for the Brunswick Corporation, Bowling Division, and were involved in purchasing plastics, castings, wood, and rubber for pins and balls, electronic instrumentation for pinsetters, and related items. What are some of the risks involved in your firm's purchasing decisions? What are some possible implications for buying center behavior?

9. Consider the purchasing operations of a middle-sized furniture manufacturer based in Ontario, Canada. Under what conditions and for what kinds of purchases is there likely to be more vertical involvement in the buying decision process? When would there be more lateral involvement?

10. Explain the following statement: "To capitalize on individual characteristics, the marketer may try to ensure that key influencers see his or her product as ensuring their own successful task performance." Provide an example of how this might be done.

11. How does the presence of coalitions or alliances within the buying center affect the job of the marketer? How do coalitions affect the industrial salesperson's task?

12. If you were selling the same product to two companies, of which one had a centralized buying operation and the other had a decentralized buying operation at each of five plant locations, would you approach both in the same way? Discuss.

# CHAPTER 4

# Building Customer Relationships

*Long-term profit equals revenue from continuously happy
customer relationships minus cost . . . market creation and
relationship-building should replace marketing gimmicks as the
mainstay of achieving a thoroughly customer-obsessed firm.*
—Tom Peters

## Key Concepts

Alliances
Buyer-seller dyad
Customer equity
In-supplier
Internal marketing
Lifetime value
Non-retrievable investments
Normative variables
Out-supplier
Relational variables

Relationship management program
Relationship marketing
Social actor variables
Social structural variables
Source loyalty
Strategic partnerships
Transactional marketing
Types of loyalties
Types of relationships

## Learning Objectives

1. Identify specific ways in which the marketer's approach to the customer and the market is changing.

2. Explore trends in the types of performance variables for which marketers are held accountable.

3. Develop an understanding of source loyalty and the reason customers remain loyal to vendors.

4. Examine the concept of relationship marketing in theory and practice.

5. Recognize the need to treat different accounts in different ways.

6. Describe a logical framework for managing customer relationships.

## Introduction: Relationship Marketing

Marketing is in transition. Conventional marketing practices are being cast aside. The changes are ongoing; in fact, continuous change may be a permanent state of affairs. Just a few years ago, the core problem in many organizations was to move from thinking of marketing as selling to approaching marketing as a set of value-creating activities that are captured in the marketing mix. Today, the problem is much more complicated. Organizations must make fundamental decisions regarding how to approach different market segments and individual customers. The conventional wisdom is that the marketer is no longer interested in making a sale or achieving a transaction, but instead must focus on relationship marketing. The reality, however, is even more complex. In this chapter, we explore and attempt to make sense of the changes that are occurring in how buyers and sellers interact with one another.

## An Evolutionary Perspective: Part 1

Companies can have great products, attractive prices, and superb employees, but they have nothing without a customer. No company can survive without making sales to customers, and this is the fundamental task assigned to the marketing function. The objective must be to achieve profitable transactions over time, and this can mean making a sale to a given company at a given point in time, or it can mean much more. For instance, it may mean building a long-term relationship with a specific account, such that the customer places all of its orders with the same vendor for the next 10 years. Alternatively, it may mean making occasional sales to a wide

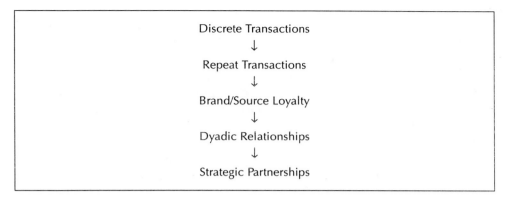

**Figure 4.1.** Evolution of the Marketer's Approach to the Customer

| Stimulus | → | Object | → | Response |
|---|---|---|---|---|
| Industrial Marketer (4 Ps) | | Customer | | Buying Behavior |

**Figure 4.2.** The Stimulus-Response Model Applied to Marketing

number of different customers. The reality is that a range of possibilities exist in terms of how the marketer approaches the marketplace.

The flow chart in Figure 4.1 summarizes five different types of approaches relied upon by marketers when dealing with customers. It is an evolutionary perspective, in that it captures the pattern in which marketing practice has developed over time. As we shall see, however, companies can simultaneously operate at a number of points in the diagram, depending on the market, segment, and particular customer in question.

The historical focus in marketing was on the transaction. In essence, a transactional focus stresses doing what is necessary to make a sale happen. This approach is somewhat analogous to a fisherman attempting to catch fish. The fisherman relies on experience, personal skills, and selecting an appropriate lure and the right type of bait to catch as many fish as possible. Transactional marketing can vary in terms of how proactive and aggressive versus reactive and passive the company and its representatives are; however, it typically relies on a stimulus-response approach and a shorter-term time horizon, much like that of our fisherman as he tries to stimulate the fish to respond to the lure and bait. Furthermore, this approach entails a one-way flow of activities from the marketer to the prospective customer, as pictured in Figure 4.2.

A step beyond the simple transaction is the repeat transaction, in which the marketer attempts to reinforce buyers so that they simply reorder from the same vendor whenever they have a need. The more a marketer can make this a routine, automatic, or conditioned response on the part of the buyer, the better. Marketers look for ways to "lock the customer in" or to create disincentives for customers to consider alternative sources of supply. A frequent flier program is an example of a program aimed at encouraging repeat transactions by travelers. So, too, is a cumulative volume discount program, where price per unit drops based on how much the customer purchases over time.

Source loyalty is more than repeat buying behavior. There is an attitudinal component as well as a behavioral component to loyalty. This means that a buyer tends to repurchase from the same vendor not because he or she is locked in or believe he or she has no real option, but by choice. The buyer is, in effect, biased toward a particular vendor and will make an effort to make most or all of his or her purchases from that vendor on an ongoing basis. Although the buyer may listen to presentations from out-suppliers, the situation is usually one where the out-supplier has to offer a product or service of much superior value or at a significantly lower cost to regain a place at the purchase table. Because of its importance, the complexities involved in creating and managing customer loyalty are elaborated on in the next section of this chapter.

Clearly, the most prevalent trend today is toward "relationship marketing." As we shall see later in this chapter, relationship marketing is not well understood by many managers, and companies are engaging in a wide array of practices under the generic banner of relationship marketing. At the root of a relationship approach is the abandonment of the unidirectional, stimulus-response approach described above. The buyer is not viewed as an object responding to a set of stimuli controlled by the marketer. Rather, a "dyadic" perspective is adopted. A dyad is a unit consisting of two members or, in this case, of two organizations. Each member affects and is affected by the other, and a complete appreciation for what is taking place requires that both be considered simultaneously. Both parties to any transaction are seeking certain attributes. The seller is trying to satisfy specific objectives through the buyer, while the buyer is doing the same in regard to the seller. Both have expectations, and the exchange between the two involves products, services, money, knowledge, information, and social interaction (see Figure 4.3). Each dyadic relationship is likely to have its own distinct nature. Furthermore, dyadic relationships tend to evolve and become more personal over time. That is, they move beyond formal discussions of task-related product and vendor performance variables, to informal social interaction and personal friendships. In the process, long-term buyer-seller arrangements are established, with both parties investing in the ongoing development of a mutually beneficial relationship.

In some instances, companies move beyond relationships and form strategic partnerships. A partnership involves the buyer and seller working together on some major initiative. For instance, they may jointly create a new product or collaborate on the development of a new technology. Together they might enter and develop a new market that neither has been in before. The creation of a new just-in-time inventory program or an electronic supply chain management network that links all the loca-

| Industrial Marketer | ←——→ | Industrial Customer |
|---|---|---|
| Goals: Sell Products/Services, Stabilize Demand, Grow, etc. | | Goals: Control Costs, Maintain Quality, Grow, etc. |
| Expectations Toward Customers | | Expectations Toward Vendors |
| Selling Experiences | | Buying Experiences |
| Variety of Resources | | Variety of Resources |
| Products/Services | | Needs and Requirements |
| Prices | | Willingness and Ability to Buy |
| Marketing Programs | | Perceived Alternative Sources of Supply |
| Expertise | | Expertise |
| Employee Motivations | | Employee Motivations |
| Other Partners | | Other Partners |
| Operating Constraints | | Operating Constraints |
| Competitive Pressures | | Competitive Pressures |

**Figure 4.3.** The Two Sides of the Buyer-Seller Dyad

tions of the buyer and the seller are also examples of partnerships. Shared risks and resources are defining characteristics of partnerships.

## An Evolutionary Perspective: Part 2

As companies move from transactional marketing to relationships and partnerships, a change also occurs in the objectives of the marketer. Marketers strive to accomplish a wide array of objectives, ranging from the profit contribution from a given market segment, to numbers of bids won, to awareness levels achieved among key buying influencers. It is worth examining the overarching concern of those in marketing, or the performance variables for which they are held most accountable. Again, there has been an evolution, as seen in Figure 4.4.

Consistent with the transactional focus and the fact that sales are the lifeblood of any company, the traditional concern of marketers has been to generate sales or "close the deal." A sales orientation tends to be somewhat short-sighted, as the company becomes more preoccupied with the tactics necessary to make a transaction happen than with considering the total value proposition as it relates to the customer over time.

Subsequently, driven by competitive pressures, as well as by the desire to achieve volume production economies, the concern of many marketers moved to achieving a certain share of the total market. Maintaining and increasing one's market share leads to a greater emphasis on customer retention, which means repeat business and cus-

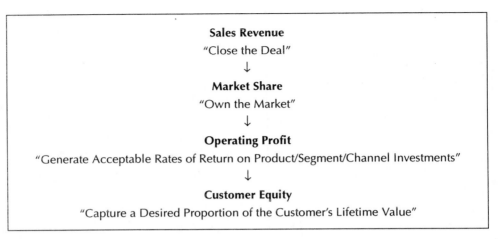

**Figure 4.4.** Changes in the Objectives of the Industrial Marketer

tomer loyalty. This orientation was reinforced by published empirical evidence suggesting a positive, statistically significant relationship between market share and profitability. Many examples were found, however, where the most profitable company in an industry was not the market share leader. In some instances, the cost of additional market share exceeds the benefit. Furthermore, markets today are continually redefining themselves, and firms are finding that competition is coming from nontraditional sources, making market share less meaningful as a performance indicator.

As companies become more strategic in their marketing operations, they tend to move beyond sales and market share to an emphasis on profitability. Thus, marketers begin to focus on margins achieved and on generating profitable sales over time. Efforts and resources are allocated based on which products, market segments, territories, and distribution channels generate the greatest rate of return. Similarly, bonuses and commissions are tied to multiple measures of profit performance.

In an industrial market, not only are markets concentrated, but the typical company also finds that the largest proportion of its profits come from a relatively small number of customer accounts. This tendency reinforces the importance of relationship building. It also leads firms to examine the profitability of individual accounts. Customer profitability is an important issue, but it is not sufficiently comprehensive. The profitability of a given account can vary depending not only on what the customer buys, and at what prices, but in what quantities, at what times, and with what type of customer support and servicing requirements. Furthermore, profitability can be enhanced when the buyer moves to a sole source relationship with the vendor and/or works with the vendor to incorporate technologies such as just-in-time (JIT) inventorying and electronic data interchange (EDI) (see Chapter 2). Profitability can also be enhanced when the marketer becomes intimately involved with the customer organization, so that he or she is continually identifying new needs and opportunities for value creation.

Recognition of these ways to improve the profitability of a given account has led some companies to prioritize a concept called customer equity and the related notion of *customer lifetime value*. Simply put, *lifetime value* refers to the total amount a customer will spend on a given product category over a strategically meaningful time period (e.g., the next 10-12 years). Customer *equity* refers to the proportion of the customer's total expenditures that the marketer seeks to capture. By placing a value on customer equity, the marketer knows what the customer is "worth" and, correspondingly, how much the firm can invest in marketing efforts directed toward the customer. The marketer also starts to modify the product/service mix to better reflect the customer's evolving requirements over time.

One implication of this discussion is that the ability to engage in successful relationship marketing requires that firms change the types of objectives that they are setting. Developing meaningful relationships with customers is unlikely if the firm is preoccupied with sales and market share. Relationships are facilitated when the measure of marketing performance is long-term customer profitability and customer equity.

## Source Loyalty as an Outcome of Buyer Behavior

Because buying decisions are normally negotiated compromises, once a vendor is selected, there is a strong tendency for the customer to remain with that vendor. In spite of the fact that the customer has viable alternatives, source loyalty emerges. This loyalty is particularly evident when the time comes for the customer to make additional buying decisions, because considering a new vendor only reawakens or heightens previous conflicts. As noted earlier, loyalty implies an attitudinal predisposition or preference to favor a particular supplier. Loyalty can also be a risk-avoidance strategy, in that some purchasers feel safer remaining with an established or a known source of supply.

The creation of a source loyal relationship is equivalent to converting the buying situation into a straight rebuy, where the marketer is the in-supplier. If this is the most favorable position the marketer can be in (especially where he or she is the sole source provider), the most unfavorable position involves a source loyalty relationship where the marketer is the out-supplier. Breaking into an established loyal relationship is extremely difficult. For these reasons, loyalty is a buying outcome that warrants considerable attention from buyers and sellers alike.

In trying to understand source loyalty, it is imperative for marketers to determine "loyalty to what?" Buyer loyalty or commitment can be to a technology, a product category, a particular brand, a vendor, or a person. Figure 4.5 illustrates possible buyer loyalties when purchasing telecommunications equipment. The industry has moved from an analog to a digital technology in manufacturing communications switches for the telephone systems used by organizations. Switches are the systems that control the ways in which telephones are linked together within an office, building, or set of buildings. They provide for such features as intercom, multibutton telephones, speed

**Figure 4.5.** Different Types of Loyalties an Industrial Customer Might Demonstrate

dialing, call forwarding, and hold capabilities. One of the major benefits of digital technology is the ability to transmit both voice and data over the same line. While attractive, this is not a benefit required by all customers.

Customers therefore have many options: They can remain loyal to the old technology, become advocates for the new, or be indifferent. A customer can also be loyal to a particular product category. For example, the telephone system in an office building can be designed around a private branch exchange (PBX), an electronic key system, or a central-office switch based at the local telephone company. Alternatively, the customer can be a strong proponent of a particular brand of PBX, such as the System 75, manufactured by AT&T, or the loyalty may be to AT&T itself, perhaps because of the company's reputation or service policies. Another possibility is that loyalty is not to the product or vendor, but instead to a salesperson, such as Mr. Jones. If Jones went to work for another company, the customer might then switch to the products of the new company.

Loyalty to a vendor or source, where it exists, is often divided. Industrial buyers are concerned that they will be vulnerable if they are reliant on a sole source supplier. For many goods, the buying organization cannot afford the risk of relying on one vendor for all its needs. Thus, loyalty does not necessarily mean that the customer buys all its requirements from the vendor or buys from the vendor every time they are in the market. As firms have adopted emerging purchasing and manufacturing technologies (see Chapter 2) in areas such as just-in-time, materials requirement planning, and electronic data interchange, it makes more sense for them to pursue undivided loyalty. The trend over the past 15 years has been for industrial companies to reduce the number of suppliers to a few and forge closer and longer lasting relationships with them. Stated differently, marketers are finding that both the strength of customer loyalties and the reasons for loyalty are changing.

Unfortunately, relatively little is known about the strength of loyalties in industrial markets, as limited research has been conducted in this area. It is probably correct to conclude that industrial loyalties take longer to establish, last longer, and are more difficult to dissolve than consumer relationships. Also, source loyalty is more likely to occur when the seller becomes involved with the buyer in setting product specifications during the early stages of product development. A critical question concerns the reasons that a customer chooses to remain loyal to a vendor. Jerry Wind (1970) conducted one of the most insightful studies in this area, discovering that loyalties were due to four overriding factors:

◆ Task concerns—Customer is loyal because the supplier is superior on traditional variables such as quality, delivery, service, or price

◆ Organizational concerns—Tendency to be loyal to a source because there are no complaints from user departments, because an alternative source would save only a small amount of money, or because the value of the order is very small

◆ Work simplification concerns—Customer is loyal because it makes things easier and involves less effort

◆ Attitudes toward source—Loyalty exists because of favorable personal attitudes toward the selling organization and its people

Wind's findings are important both to the marketer trying to build a relationship with a current account and the marketer trying to break into an existing relationship. As the in-supplier, the marketer must be wary of becoming complacent, taking the customer for granted, or taking advantage of his or her company's position in a source loyal relationship. Even a marketer who conscientiously manages customer relationships can lose part or all of an account if the wrong variables are emphasized. Thus, the marketer may stress keeping prices stable while users inside the customer organization have become more concerned with innovations in terms of product and vendor capabilities.

When the marketer is the out-supplier, the ultimate objective is to change customer behavior. The real problem, however, is that loyalty can be based on strongly held attitudes and beliefs. Marketers should focus on the specific reasons that the buyer decides to stay true to existing sources and on identifying ways to undermine or work around these reasons. Simply providing the buyer with reasons to switch suppliers is seldom a successful strategy. If the loyalty is due to organizational concerns as opposed to work simplification concerns, this suggests very different approaches to undoing current loyalties and breaking into the relationship.

# What Is Relationship Marketing?

Over the past decade, industrial companies have begun adopting a different approach to the way they interact with other members of the value-added chain. This new orientation has, at various times, been called relationship marketing, working partnerships, symbiotic marketing, strategic alliances, strategic partnerships, co-marketing alliances, channel partnerships, supplier partnerships, and real-time relationships. For our purposes, we will refer to these novel approaches to customers as *relationship marketing*.

The move in this direction has taken place for a number of reasons. Two of the most important ones are (a) the recognition by companies that sustaining a competitive advantage in the global economy increasingly requires them to become trusted participants within a network or set of strategic alliances (Morgan & Hunt, 1994) and (b) the availability of programmable technology—especially information technology—that allows companies to produce precise customized products or services that are manufactured to meet each customer's needs (McKenna, 1995).

This relationship approach, however, is not entirely "new" for industrial companies. One can argue that successful industrial firms have always tried to form long-term relationships with their best customers. Perhaps the change is really one of arranging the marketing function so that it is a "holistic process" (Aijo, 1996). It is also evident that the term *relationship marketing* has many meanings, depending upon whom you ask, and is practiced in many different ways by industrial firms.

There is no single, commonly accepted definition of relationship marketing. Examples of some of the prevalent perspectives include the following:

- The establishment of strong, lasting ties with individual accounts

- Earning the position of preferred supplier by developing trust with key accounts over a period of time

- Establishing, developing, and maintaining successful relational exchange

- The formation of long-term buyer-seller relationships through the creation of structural and social bonds between the companies

- Developing close interactions with selected customers, suppliers, and competitors for value creation through cooperative and collaborative efforts

- An asymmetrical and personalized marketing process that takes place in the long run, results in some bilateral benefits, and rests on an in-depth understanding of customer needs and characteristics

In an attempt to synthesize the various perspectives, we will rely on the following definition:

> *Relationship marketing* is a strategic orientation adopted by both the buyer and seller organizations that represents a commitment to long-term, mutually beneficial collaboration.

Another way of explaining relationship marketing is through the statement "Our competitors sell boxes, but we sell solutions." This type of approach is much more than aggressive selling or increasing the firm's attention to customer service. Companies that have adopted and practiced relationship marketing carefully select clients that can be satisfied at a profit. Through consistent positive actions, the supplier and customer learn to trust one another. Each party believes the other will not take advantage of them, and each attempts to make all encounters "win-win" situations. Dependency, and hence vulnerability, of both parties increases. Information is freely shared between companies, and collaborative efforts are made to solve problems before they occur whenever possible. As a result of the relationship, each party benefits. Aspects of relationship marketing can also be found in the Japanese channel system known as *keiretsu* (Berkowitz, Kerin, Hartley, & Rudelius, 1997).

In relationship marketing, the marketer's goal is to continually delight the customer. Although many industrial companies have traditionally tried to establish long-term relationships with their larger customers, few have adopted a formal marketing program to make this happen. To gain a better insight about this concept, let us say that two customers, Sky Airlines and Northeast Airlines, have a problem with an instrument on their 747s. A supplier that follows a nonrelationship approach might handle the problem in this way. First, Sky Airlines would have to call the main number of the supplier and request assistance through customer service. Most likely, if Sky was not aware if the part was under warranty, the customer service representative would instruct Sky to return the part (at Sky's expense) for rework or replacement. A new instrument would be sent out by overnight shipping, probably at Sky's expense. Once the instrument was repaired, it would be shipped back to Sky with a repair bill, possibly with no explanation for the failure or why the part was being returned.

Contrast this experience with what happened to Northeast Airlines when its instrument failed. Northeast sent a message electronically to the supplier explaining which instrument had broken. The manufacturer immediately shipped, at its expense, a replacement part. When the part arrived the next morning, a maintenance specialist from the supplier was waiting to assist in replacing of the instrument. The defective instrument was collected by the specialist and shipped to the factory, where it was analyzed to determine the cause of failure. Once this was accomplished, the supplier communicated electronically the cause of the failure and the design changes taken to ensure that this failure would not occur in the future. Finally, Northeast's maintenance supervisor received a phone call from her supplier counterpart apologizing for the incident and thanking her for using the supplier's components. Given these two scenarios, which supplier would you prefer to continue to do business with—the one who sold you a part or the one who provided a solution to your problem?

To create this kind of relationship marketing with its customers, the vendor must first practice internal marketing. *Internal marketing* is based on the notion that a company must focus on its employees before successful marketing programs can be delivered to customers. This focus includes employee development through proper recruiting, training, continuous communication, and administrative systems

## BUSINESS MARKETING CAPSULE

### Relationship Marketing in Action

Picture the manufacturing plant of a company that produces more than $51 million in electronics equipment each year. Imagine hundreds of employees and millions of dollars in expensive production machinery. All of this probably requires a facility with significant square footage and an elaborate organizational structure.

Then consider Novellus Systems Inc., a maker of semiconductor equipment. You can count the production workers on your fingers, and you have three fingers left over. Yet this is not an automated Japanese factory with robots laboring in the dark. In fact, there are no robots here, only seven gowned and booted human beings.

Robert Graham, president of 6-year-old Novellus Systems Inc., chuckles at a visitor's mystification. "How did we produce $51 million in shipments last year with only seven people? Simple. We buy completed, tested modules from our vendors. We don't allow them in here until a week before they will be used. In a week and a half, our seven people can put together an $800,000 or $900,000 machine."

Like the new chip companies, semiconductor equipment manufacturers such as Novellus are setting up long-term relationships with suppliers, relying on partners for all but a couple of key modules in the production process. But building and maintaining the necessary relationships is a demanding managerial art. Vendors must first be qualified and, as Graham puts it, trained. "We look at a shop and see what kind of equipment is in it. We look to be sure they're solvent. We ask if they'll do special things for us. A welding company Novellus wanted to work with did high-quality work but did not know how to test for vacuum tightness. We bought them a vacuum tester and showed them how to use it."

When a problem crops up at a vendor's shop, that problem is by definition Novellus's. A laser weld on a part was uneven, and the vendor complained that he couldn't seem to solve the problem. Novellus engineers paid him a visit and ended up buying $10,000 worth of tooling to solve the problem. If a supplier needs financial help to ensure just-in-time delivery, Novellus provides it. "We'll buy the invention, and sell it back to them," says Graham. "They don't pay until a finished product is delivered."

Novellus's incredible production figures, $365,000 to $380,000 in sales per employee, reflect the extension of the company's boundaries into supplier's shops. If the productivity figure is partly illusory, the bottom line is not, with an after-tax earning of 22%. "And that's in a competitive industry," says Graham, "that's supposed to be sick."

SOURCE: Adapted from "Factory of the Future," *Inc.*, 12 (August, 1990), p. 72, Case. © Copyright 1990 by *Inc.*

(Berkowitz et al., 1997). Regardless of what the company sells, internal marketing strives to convert all the people and systems of the firm into a "service organization." In fact, it has been argued that as relationship marketing is adopted, the distinction between service and physical goods industries is blurred (Aijo, 1996).

## Myths and Realities of Relationship Marketing in Practice

An apparent myth is that marketing today *is* relationship marketing, particularly in industrial markets. A so-called paradigm shift is said to have occurred in terms of how vendors approach their customers. The move is away from adversarial buyer-seller transactions and toward collaboration as buyers downsize their supplier base and sellers adopt "one-to-one" marketing programs where the marketing mix is tailored to the individual account.

But is this truly the case, and are marketers really doing anything new? The answer appears to be a qualified "Yes." Given the lengthy nature of the customer buying process, the multiple decision participants, the often technical nature of what is being sold, and the fact that the customer base is relatively concentrated, industrial marketers have long recognized the need to focus less on the transaction and more on encouraging repeat business and building source loyalty. Accordingly, the norm in industrial markets has been to concentrate on customer retention through ongoing interaction and follow-up, aftersale servicing, and supplier flexibility. Although this falls short of a true relationship approach (as described above), the general concept of relationship marketing is widely embraced by most industrial marketers.

In practice, marketers tend to "talk the talk" but do not necessarily "walk the walk." Few marketers currently emphasize the necessary level of commitment to true relationship development. Furthermore, many customers make even less of a commitment to forming close relationships with their suppliers. It may be that customers do not want a relationship with only one supplier or their level of trust is insufficient to enter into a long-term agreement (Morris, Brunyee, & Page, 1998).

A move toward more involved relationships may be under way, but the changes to date appear to be more in attitudes than in behaviors. This movement can be seen, in part, by considering the issues on which managers tend to agree. One study (Morris et al., 1998) found that industrial marketers believe that relationships are strategically important, take time to form, and represent a long-term involvement with the customer. Furthermore, relationships depend on a high level of personal interaction, trust, and the need to meet mutual expectations. There also appears to be a growing recognition on the part of managers that relationship marketing may require firms to customize their product/service offerings for individual customers and to adapt the selling firm's logistical arrangements to reflect unique customer requirements.

In spite of such beliefs, organizational realities find that companies are following a more conservative approach and that much of what they are doing is tactical rather than strategic. Morris et al. (1998) have identified a number of shortcomings in the approaches being employed by marketers:

**Locking the customer in:** The motivation of many marketers in forming relationships is less one of mutual investment and benefit over time and more one of securing as much of the customer's business for as long as possible. The outcome of successful relationship marketing is that customers will want to purchase from a supplier that is interested in their well-being because of the benefits each party receives from the relationship. Rather than locking the customer in, each party enters a mutually beneficial or "win-win" relationship.

**Informality:** Firms approach relationships more informally, with little in the way of structural agreements, formal goal setting, or establishment of mutual mechanisms for measuring performance satisfaction. Likewise, it is important for two firms that enter a relationship to share information, establish mutual goals, and performance measures in order to determine quality and value. These steps are formal and require time, effort, and a willingness to nurture the relationship by both parties involved.

**Nonfinancial investments:** Marketers are more likely to invest time and effort into customer communications, and less likely to change capital equipment, operating processes, personnel, or technologies to reflect the customer's requirements. Principal out-of-pocket costs incurred are related to product features and logistics. Firms must pay more than lip service to relationship marketing. This includes purchase of capital equipment and modifying manufacturing and logistical procedures to better satisfy the customer.

**Avoiding dependency:** Relationships are a source of competitive advantage today, but so is flexibility. Suppliers appear to want closer linkages with customers, while keeping their options open. They also do not let the customer "too far" into their own operations. Relationship marketing implies that suppliers and customers work in concert to be successful. Mistrust and apprehension about sharing proprietary information is certain to preclude establishing a true and lasting relationship between suppliers and customers.

**Unilateral efforts:** Evidence indicates that selling organizations are doing more to initiate and sustain relationships, including higher levels of investment and adaptation, than are the buying organizations. Relationship marketing occurs between members of a dyad. If a customer does not want to enter into a close relationship with its supplier, then it will not happen. Suppliers must carefully choose who could benefit from a closer relationship and then must realize that this relationship will develop only over a long period of time after both parties come to believe they can depend upon one another and that a closer relationship will result in increased benefits for all.

**Limited opportunity cost:** Marketers do not view relationships as limiting their ability to work with other clients or to pursue new business opportunities. If a company follows a true relationship marketing course, however, then clients are chosen carefully and not all customers are viewed as being worthwhile partners. Not all customers or opportunities, therefore, can or should be pursued in the name of relationship marketing.

**One size fits all:** Firms do not define different types of relationships for different categories of customers. Rather, they seem to have a general notion of a relationship that applies to those key accounts with whom they have been dealing for some time. Firms must organize their accounts, perhaps into key, promising, small, and other categories. Many firms, such as AT&T, have determined that some accounts will receive different levels of service and rates than other accounts. This strategy requires careful thought to ensure that key accounts are maintained and that unprofitable accounts are encouraged to seek another supplier.

In short, then, relationships in practice are currently more than simple customer retention programs but less than full-fledged collaborative partnerships. They do not appear to be approached systematically, involve little in the way of formal investments in individual accounts, and have resulted in only modest infrastructure change (e.g., in policies, systems, organizational design) on either seller or buyer sides.

The apparent gap between relationship theory and practice is due to a number of factors. The first of these is a simple lack of knowledge and experience regarding how to manage relationships, including the types and amounts of investments to make, information to share, and linkages to establish. The customer organization likely suffers from a similar lack of knowledge, so both parties are experimenting and learning as they go. Implementing relationship marketing may also be resisted because it requires that each party provide support, respect privacy and preserve confidences, and be tolerant of other friendships (Fournier, Dobscha, & Glen, 1998). If the customer feels the supplier is using confidential information to take advantage of the situation or is not tolerant of other suppliers, then a true relationship will not ensue. Firms must also realize that relationship marketing is not appropriate for all customers or in all situations.

## Types and Degrees of Relationships

A key question confronting the marketer involves determining which customers warrant a relationship approach (Cannon & Perreault, 1994; Wilson, 1996). We believe the goal of the industrial marketer is *not* to establish relationships with every customer. Many companies discover that they are investing considerable financial and nonfinancial resources trying to form relationships with unwilling and/or inappropriate customers. What becomes important is the need to recognize that not all customers need to be treated in the same way. Some accounts warrant significant investment and customization of marketing efforts, but others do not.

Another way of thinking about it is that there are degrees of relationships, where some are very deep and intimate and others are more shallow and short term. Olsen and Ellram (1997) found that relationship strength differs based on such things as the volume of purchases, the frequency of contacts between people in the buyer and seller organizations, the extent of collaboration in product development, and

## BUSINESS MARKETING CAPSULE

### *Do Customers Want a Relationship With Suppliers?*

Is relationship marketing the beginning of a beautiful friendship or the onset of customers feeling firms are stalking them? Firms relish acquiring information about customers, possess numerous tools to acquire these facts, and want to raise customer satisfaction levels. Given all the attention lavished on customers, then why are satisfaction rates in the United States at an all-time low?

Relationship marketing is neither to blame nor the answer for this dilemma. In theory, relationship marketing is a powerful tool, but in reality, it can be irritating to customers. Unless firms come to understand how they are misusing relationship marketing, the concept may realize a premature and untimely death.

Firms ask consumers to participate in one-to-one relationships that result in untenable demands and trivial and useless marketing efforts. Customers also perceive that they are constantly asked to provide feedback while receiving nothing in return. Firms want personal knowledge and opinions from customers but offer little in exchange.

All relationships involve loyalty, trust, intimacy, and respect, but customers often feel the opposite when dealing in the marketplace. They experience a loss of control, vulnerability, and stress. Firms need to realize that intimacy and vulnerability are related. To understand how to gain trust and attain intimacy with customers, firms need to understand consumers' mind-sets by using such tools as ethnography and phenomenology. Relationship marketing, in its present form, has not brought customers closer to firms. For firms to move relationship marketing back on track, they will need to understand what is important in consumers' lives—not just what products they buy.

SOURCE: "Preventing the Premature Death of Relationship Marketing," *Harvard Business Review* (January-February, 1998), Fournier, Dobscha, and Glen. © Copyright 1998 by *Harvard Business Review*.

the technological and physical distance between the two organizations (see Table 4.1).

Before attempting to establish a long-term relationship, the marketer needs to examine such variables as the amount of value the supplier adds to the buyer's product, operating risk, homogeneity of supply and demand requirements, and respective power positions. Then, all the customers in the firm's customer base need to be put into categories or groups. After a thorough analysis, and consistent with our earlier discussion, firms should classify their customers as on-off transactions, repeat transactions, source loyal accounts, relationships, or strategic partnerships.

**On-off (or one-off) transactions:** The customer contacts the supplier when something is needed, often seeking to purchase for the lowest price and/or fastest delivery. There is little or no source loyalty in this form of relationship. The marketer makes no unique investment in the account.

---

**TABLE 4.1** Factors Describing the Strengths of Relationships

**Economic factors**
- Volume or dollar value of purchases
- Importance of buyer to supplier
- Exit costs

**Character of exchange relationship**
- Types of exchange
- Level and number of personal contacts
- Number of other partners
- Duration of the exchange relationship

**Cooperation between buyer and supplier**
- Cooperation in development
- Technical cooperation
- Integration of management

**Distance between buyer and supplier**
- Social distance
- Cultural distance
- Technological distance
- Time distance
- Geographic distance

---

SOURCE: Adapted from "A Portfolio Approach to Supplier Relationships," *Industrial Marketing Management*, 26 (March, 1997), Olsen and Ellram. © Copyright 1997 by *Industrial Marketing Management*.

**Repeat transactions:** Customers purchase on a repeat basis but will purchase from another supplier when conditions warrant this type of action. There is little loyalty, with the buyer using the vendor principally because of price or convenience. The marketer may develop incentives for repeat buyers to reorder, and these are offered to all buyers.

**Source loyal accounts:** The supplier is expected to provide products and service necessary to satisfy the customer. The customer is loyal to the supplier and, in all but the most extreme circumstances, will not purchase from a competitor. A medium amount of loyalty is present in both buyer and seller. The marketer will frequently develop a loyalty program for these types of customers. Loyal customers receive more sales and service attention, and the company will make an effort to respond to special requests from the account.

**Relationships:** The customer and supplier share information and seek to make each interaction a "win-win" encounter. Each party believes it is in its best interest to cooperate with the other. There is a high level of loyalty exhibited by both parties. The marketer tailors the marketing mix to the account and looks for unique ways to create value for the account. A formal program is put in place for working with the account, often involving close interaction between representatives from both sides.

**Strategic partnerships:** Partnership between manufacturers and occupants within a supply chain that leverage the core competencies of each firm. The supply complex is completely redefined and reengineered from the concept to the consumer. Processes between the firms are matched, and infrastructures are developed on both sides to accommodate interactions. The two firms pursue new strategic initiatives together.

A firm may find itself simultaneously pursuing adversarial, competitive, cooperative, and partnering/networking approaches, depending on the category into which a customer falls. This strategic maze of transactions/relationships is easier described than implemented. It is apparent that firms need better guidance regarding how to discriminate among customers in their client base in terms of levels of investments, customization, and intimacy.

## Basic Considerations in Managing Relationships

A beginning point in trying to adopt a relationship perspective is to consider the major variables operating within a buyer-seller dyad. The workings and outcomes of any buyer-seller dyad are guided by relational variables, social structural variables, social actor variables, and normative variables. Table 4.2 highlights some of the key questions that marketers should attempt to answer in each of these four areas.

*Relational variables* concern how the two organizations are related to one another from an overall standpoint. What are their respective needs and capabilities? Both parties need each other or are dependent upon one another. The question concerns who needs whom the most. In times of critical shortages of a key raw material or component part, the buyer may be more dependent; when demand is down and the economy is recessionary, the seller may be more dependent. Examining the relative power positions can suggest insights into the negotiating tactics and flexibility of each party.

*Social structural variables* focus on the positions, in their respective organizations, of the actors involved in the industrial transaction. For example, a newly hired and inexperienced salesperson calling on a vice president for purchasing represents a buying situation in which a sizable social structural gap exists between the parties. Similarly, a salesperson with little or no technical background who must deal with an R&D engineer will encounter a similar social structural gap. There can be both horizontal and vertical gaps between the social positions of the actors in the dyad. Some companies deal with such gaps with job titles, such as "senior market manager" instead of "salesperson," but the more appropriate approach may be to get individuals at higher levels and in different functional areas involved in augmenting the salesperson's efforts. Many industrial firms today handle this problem by forming sales teams comprising members from all functional areas.

*Social actor variables* relate to the traits of the individuals themselves—age, sex, educational background, charisma, expertise, personality, communication style, and

**TABLE 4.2**   Questions for Marketers to Address About a Relationship

| Characteristics of the Buyer-Seller Dyad | Relevant Questions for the Marketer |
| --- | --- |
| Organizational relationships | 1. How dependent are we on this customer?<br>2. How dependent are they on us?<br>3. What are the sources of our respective dependencies?<br>4. What are the implications of the power balance (or imbalance) for negotiation strategies?<br>5. Where are the major sources of conflict between us?<br>6. What are the buyer's unique needs and capabilities? What are the seller's unique needs and capabilities? |
| Structure of the players | 1. How centralized and formalized is the buying process? Does our marketing approach reflect this degree of centralization and formalization?<br>2. At what level in the organizational hierarchy are key buying decision makers?<br>3. What functional areas play a key role in buying decisions?<br>4. What is the level, title, and functional background of our sales representatives and others within our firm who deal with the customer?<br>5. Are differences in the structural or status positions of buyer and seller representatives significant enough to affect decision outcomes? |
| Characteristics of the people involved | 1. What are the demographic and personality characteristics of key members of the decision-making process in the buying organization? What is their experience level? What is their history of rewards?<br>2. What are the demographic and personality characteristics of our sales representative? What is his or her experience level?<br>3. To what extent are seller and buyer representatives similar or dissimilar?<br>4. In what areas are they similar or dissimilar, and how might this relationship affect their interactions? |
| Roles, norms, and rules of the game | 1. Are there certain rules of the game or unwritten norms that determine acceptable tactics and unacceptable tactics on the part of the seller and buyer?<br>2. What are our expectations of the roles that representatives of the buying organization are to fill in their dealing with us?<br>3. What are their expectations of our sales representative, in terms of his or her actions and authority? What about their expectations of other employees of our organization?<br>4. Are there differences between our perceptions and their perceptions of roles and norms? |

other characteristics. The social actors here include all the key people interacting on both sides of the relationship. Some companies attempt to hire salespeople with characteristics that are similar to those of their customers. Others might work on the theory that opposites attract, then hire individuals with distinctive traits that make them more interesting to individuals making buying decisions. The best solution for social actor variable problems is to hire sales personnel who can adapt to different situations and individuals.

Finally, *normative variables* include the rules of the game, the norms, the accepted practices, and the role expectations of those involved in the buyer-seller dyad. Representatives of both the buyer and seller organizations typically have specific expectations concerning how the other party will behave throughout the buying process. Unofficial rules exist that are understood by each party. Frustrations and anxieties are less likely to arise when both parties agree on those rules. For example, purchasing agents may consider it highly inappropriate to attempt to play vendors off of one another in price negotiations. Thus, they may expect vendors to offer their best feasible price rather than cut their bids only after finding what the competition is charging. There may also be norms for conducting negotiations, deciding when price is to be mentioned, setting protocol to follow in calling on various individuals in the buyer (or seller) organization, determining how frequently to call on an account, and so forth.

Beyond this, the movement to relationships introduces a new way of thinking and a new vocabulary. Terms like trust, power symmetry, non-retrievable investments, and connectedness become relevant for describing what is taking place between the two parties. Table 4.3 defines a number of these terms.

Successful relationship marketing also has a financial dimension. The marketer has to consider the costs and benefits involved in working with a particular account. Calculating rates of return on investments made in customers is a complex and sometimes impossible undertaking. Many of these investments are nonfinancial and difficult to quantify. In addition, there may not be a direct, one-to-one relationship between expenditures and returns, and relationships can deliver benefits that are also not easy to quantify. Industrial customers "offer value" in terms of such benefits as stable orders, image enhancement, and technology sharing that must be considered in the overall equation.

An alternative approach is to project the lifetime value of a customer, then to discount the value so as to express it in present value terms. The result can then be compared to the projected expenditures or investments made in the customer account. There are complications here as well, such as in determining what is a realistic time period over which to estimate lifetime value.

A final consideration concerns the strategic implications of relationships for the firm's competitive position. The argument can be made that relationships are especially critical in a rapidly changing, hostile, and complex environment, because they provide a kind of competitive buffer. Under such conditions, however, it is also important for organizations to be maximally flexible, opportunistic, and able to move quickly in the marketplace. Relationships can develop to a point where they limit the

**TABLE 4.3** Key Terms Used to Characterize Relationships

**Adaptation:** the extent to which adjustments must be made by buyer and/or seller to process, products, or procedures specific to the exchange partner

**Asset specificity (non-retrievable investments):** the extent to which either party is required to make relationship-specific/non-retrievable investments

**Commitment:** an enduring desire to make maximum effort to maintain the relationship

**Complexity of the transaction:** the complexity of the products, processes, contractual terms, and human interactions

**Comparison levels of alternatives:** the costs and benefits associated with working with an alternative seller or buyer

**Connectedness between transactions:** how critical or, alternatively, nonexistent is the interdependence between a set of transactions over time

**Cooperation/cooperative norms:** reflect the attitudes, expectations, and behaviors the parties have about working jointly to achieve common and individual goals

**Duration of transactions:** the extent to which the exchange continues over a period of time

**Frequency of transactions:** this varies from single or occasional to virtually continuous

**Information exchange:** the willingness to openly share information that may be useful to both parties

**Intensity or extent of interdependence:** degree to which either party has requirements of the other that are not immediately available from alternative sources

**Legal bonds:** detailed and binding contractual agreements that specify the obligations and roles of both parties

**Mutual goals:** strategic and operational outcomes (financial, technical, competitive) from the relationship sought jointly by the parties

**Operational linkages/structural bonds:** formal, systematic, and structural interfirm ties that contribute to each firm's business operations, such as shared warehousing

**Performance measurement:** measurement of either party's satisfaction with the performance of the other, often measured on a number of tangible and intangible dimensions

**Performance uncertainty:** environmental change makes it difficult for either party to determine in advance how it wishes the other to behave

**Power symmetry or asymmetry of the roles:** extent to which relationships are either equal or unequal, where one party may be dominant or submissive

**Shared technology:** linkages that are established between the parties in terms of information, communications, manufacturing, logistical, and other technologies

**Social bonds:** personal ties that develop between or among members of the buying and selling organizations

**Trust:** confidence in an exchange partner's reliability and integrity

**Valence of the relationship:** relationships can be classified along a continuum ranging from those who are cooperative and friendly to those who are competitive and hostile

**Value extraction:** determination of who receives which benefits deriving from the relationship

SOURCE: Reprinted from "Relationship Marketing in Practice," *Industrial Marketing Management*, 27, no. 4 (July, 1998), p. 362, Morris, Brunyee, and Page. © Copyright 1998 by *Industrial Marketing Management*. Reprinted with permission.

vendor's flexibility and increase the vendor's vulnerability. Ironically, the relationship can enhance the customer's flexibility while limiting that of the selling organization. That is, customers can use relationships to create flexibility for themselves by leveraging the vendor's resources and shifting the inventory burden to the seller.

## Creating a Relationship Management Program

Marketers also need guidance on how to actually implement a relationship marketing program. There is no one right way, and it should always be kept in mind that each relationship is unique and will require the marketer to modify his or her general approach. At the same time, it is helpful to have a general framework for managing relationships. Below is an eight-step framework that can be adapted easily to different types of customer situations.

**Step 1:** Establish criteria and select potential partner

**Step 2:** Define the purpose of the relationship

**Step 3:** Set the boundaries

**Step 4:** Establish expectations

**Step 5:** Formulate performance goals

**Step 6:** Establish communication channels

**Step 7:** Create value

**Step 8:** Measure performance

In applying this framework, consider the case of a major sugar company whose customer base includes 180 firms involved in making soft drinks, fruit juices, candies, cookies, and jams. The company has decided to establish a relationship management program with a large fruit juice manufacturer. This customer was selected after a rigorous review that led to the classification of all 180 customers into three categories; 10 of them are candidates for formal relationships. Partner selection was accomplished by relying on a number of key criteria:

- The risk of losing the account is high
- The customer is one of the top 20 accounts in terms of annual sugar consumption
- The customer is receptive to relationship formation
- Opportunities exist for improvement in relationships with the account
- A match exists between the cultures of the two organizations
- Potential exists for mutual benefit to the two parties

❖ There is scope for adding service benefits

❖ Competitive position is medium to strong in this customer's market

Once the partner was selected and agreed to participate in a relationship program, the sugar company established a formal "relationship charter" with the customer. The two parties first agreed on the purpose of the relationship. From the sugar vendor's perspective, the purpose was threefold: to keep the account, to discourage the account from reducing its sugar requirements (e.g., by using substitutes for sugar such as glucose), and to find ways to increase the customer's sugar consumption. From the customer's vantage point, the purpose was to obtain a partner who could understand the role of sugar in the juice manufacturing process and handle all aspects of the sugar element in the product. Thus, it wanted a partner that not only took responsibility for sugar before it arrived at the customer's warehouse but also provided advice, support, and service all the way through the customer's manufacturing operation. Related to the purpose of the relationship, both parties identified expected benefits. Examples included transactional efficiency, price/production stability, optimal capacity planning, improved customer responsiveness, increase in brand usage, establishment of databases, increased juice production efficiencies, and opportunities to engage in joint promotional efforts.

The two parties then established boundaries for the relationship. This involved determining the issues that were and were not on the table for discussion. Examples of issues on the table included quality assurance for the sugar, new product development, terms of sale, logistical arrangements, rebates on juice exports, confidentiality in terms of information shared between the organizations, communication between the organizations, and all transaction contact points. Issues that it was agreed were not on the table included the base price of sugar, payment due dates, and policies related to syrup sales (which the sugar company also sold).

The buyer and seller must also appreciate the expectations each has of the other. For instance, the buyer made it clear that it did not want to find out that other customers were getting a better deal on sugar than it was, that it would receive adequate warning of price increases, that it would be kept abreast of developments affecting sugar supply, and that it would get better conformance to quality specifications and quicker response to customer problems. The seller made clear its expectations in the areas of information confidentiality, accurate forecasting of the buyer's sugar requirements, accurate data on actual volumes of sugar purchased, and cooperation in developing and testing new sugar variants.

Performance goals were then set for both parties. For the sugar company, standards were agreed to with regard to product quality specifications, delivery times, billing/invoicing/order cycles, total "all-in" cost of the sugar, technical support, sales representative knowledge, responsiveness to questions or complaints, and an overall customer satisfaction rating. For the juice manufacturer, standards were set in terms of growth in sugar volumes purchased, accuracy of forecasts, timely supply of information, timely payment, order placement, materials handling, and ease of doing business.

Attention was then devoted to ongoing communications between the two parties. A distinction was drawn between administrative communications (order placement, invoicing, forecasts), marketing communications (sales calls, mill visits, social get-togethers), and technical communications (production problems, quality problems, new product requirements). Lines of communication were established in terms of who was expected to communicate with whom in each of these areas. This process was facilitated by having the two parties map all the points of contact between the two organizations and identify the personnel involved on both sides at each point of contact. Attention was also devoted to dispute resolution and how it would be handled at different levels. To manage the ongoing relationship, each side identified a four-person team, and it was agreed that the two teams would meet regularly to review how things were going.

The buyer and seller also examined areas where each of them would need to make investments of time, money, and other resources. A number of value creation projects were identified and prioritized, and representatives from the respective organizations were assigned to work on the particular projects. Three projects were agreed to for the current year. These included formation of a joint value analysis team to identify ways to cut costs and improve quality, creation of a team to find a quick way to change from providing one-ton bags of sugar to bulk delivery, and establishment of a team to look at issues related to glucose substitution as well as the way in which sugar would be mentioned on the fruit juice labels.

Finally, each party regularly evaluated the other. It was agreed that this would be done annually and that data would be tracked and shared on performance in each of the areas for which a goal was set. The overall ratings of each party would be based on a survey of a number of people in the buying organization and a number of people in the sugar company. Evaluation forms were prepared and agreed to for both organizations.

The framework presented here is but one of many ways in which a relationship program can be established. A key characteristic of any approach to relationships is flexibility. Marketers will find that buyers vary widely in terms of how much time and effort they are willing or able to dedicate to these efforts. Furthermore, the relationship can be expected to evolve, such that the buyer, for example, initially may not be willing to do much about the issues of greatest concern to the marketer, but with time becomes more willing to put those issues on the table. At the same time, it is vital that the spirit of a relationship be established up front, such that what evolves is not a one-way street. Too often, buyers view relationships in terms of how much the marketer can give up without any reciprocation from the buying organization.

## Summary

Marketing is a field experiencing significant change. Nowhere is that change more evident than in the ways marketers approach customers. An environment where change occurs rapidly and competitive pressures are intense means that companies must rethink the role of the customer. That is, a focus on relationships must replace the old transactional focus. Marketing becomes more intense and more one-to-one, with greater customization of the marketing mix and higher investment levels in individual accounts.

The extent to which managers understand relationships remains in the formative stages. While many embrace the concept, relationship marketing has a variety of different practical meanings and applications. Studies indicate that marketing managers are pursuing a go-slow approach, and this caution may reflect a true understanding of marketplace realities. That is, it may be that management practice does not lag behind management concepts, but instead that the normative theoretical prescriptions—like relationship marketing—are often overstated. Although it seems reasonable to conclude that long-term relationships are now a growing fixture in industrial markets, movement beyond the experimental approaches being used by companies requires much more time to solve the inherent problems discussed in this chapter.

Firms wishing to pursue a relationship marketing approach should consider the following recommendations. First, determine your competitive advantage(s) and the type(s) of companies that would benefit from these competencies. Second, work diligently to gain trust by demonstrating that the customer will benefit from a closer relationship with your firm. Third, gain intimate knowledge of the goals, needs, and concerns of the customer. Fourth, share information about markets, technology, and manufacturing processes that are beneficial to the buyer. It may be necessary to assign people from your firm to the manufacturing or headquarters of your partner. Fifth, try to make as many encounters as possible win-win relationships. Sixth, compute the overall value of your partner and base your actions on the actual and/or potential value of the relationship.

Finally, firms should not expect to form a relationship with every customer. All relationships are not profitable, and you cannot afford to offer special conditions to all your customers. In a given period, you will have many different types of customers that range from transactional to relationship oriented. The bottom line is to behave toward your customer or supplier in a way that maximizes the benefit for both parties.

# Questions

1. First Rate Disposal, a new manufacturer of disposal systems for small and medium-sized manufacturing firms, is attempting to capture business from its leading competitor, Waste Management, Inc. Identify some approaches that First Rate might employ for overcoming customer loyalties to Waste Management. Keep in mind the different types of loyalties that exist.

2. What is the difference between segmented marketing and one-to-one marketing? If you had an Internet-based service that registers company Web pages with

all the relevant search engines, which of these approaches to marketing would make more sense?

3. Explain the concept of customer equity as it might apply to and be used by a marketer of customized uniforms designed and then rented to airlines, auto repair shops, restaurants, and an array of other businesses.

4. Industrial customers are often good sources of new product and service ideas. Why is this the case? In building a relationship, what are some ways in which the marketer can systematically tap customer ideas for new products and services?

5. The terms *relationship marketing* and *partnership marketing* have been coined to describe an emphasis on cooperation over conflict when dealing with customers. Consider the relationship between Timex, a leading watchmaker, and one of its suppliers of watchbands. What does *relationship marketing* mean in this case? What are the potential benefits and costs from the perspective of the watchband manufacturer?

6. The dyadic perspective is based on the assumption that industrial transactions represent a two-way process, and that both parties seek attributes and both have impacts on the other. What does this mean? Provide some specific examples of ways in which the vendor affects the customer and ways in which the customer affects the vendor.

7. Explain how the same trucking company might have a relationship program with certain accounts, treat others as loyal repeat business, and treat still others as "one-off" or occasional accounts.

8. Assume that you are in a media buying company and are initiating a formal relationship marketing program with advertisers. Many companies use media buying services based solely on whoever charges the lowest commissions and can get the best buys. You are trying to establish criteria for selecting customers who will serve as relationship partners. What sort of specific criteria might you employ?

9. Why do you think some industrial companies are hesitant to implement relationship marketing programs that involve mutual investments, interdependency, and the other key elements of a true relationship?

10. Although the things a customer might expect from the vendor in a relationship might be fairly apparent, identify some things that the vendor might expect from the customer. That is, what would a "good" customer be or do, if the vendor were rating different customers?

# CHAPTER 5

# Segmentation and Targeting of Business Markets

*An organization that decides to operate in some market . . . recognizes*
*that it normally cannot serve all the customers in that market.*
—P. Kotler

## Key Concepts

Concentrated marketing
Contribution analysis
Cost-benefit analysis
Coverage ratio
Homogeneity
Intermediate bases
Macro bases
Marginal analysis
Market segmentation
Micro bases
Nested approach

One-to-one marketing
Primary product specialization ratio
Productivity analysis
Resource allocation
Sales response curve
Segment evaluative criteria
Segmentation process
Submarket or segment
Target marketing
Undifferentiated marketing

## Learning Objectives

1. Establish the role of market segmentation in marketing planning and as a marketing strategy.

2. Describe a process approach for using market segmentation and targeting.

3. Establish useful criteria for evaluating segmentation as a practice, for evaluating specific bases of segmentation, and for allocating resources to target segments.

4. Identify bases for segmenting industrial markets.

5. Propose a cost-benefit/nested approach to market segmentation.

## The Need for Focus in Marketing

Once they have defined the markets they plan to serve, managers must determine if it is realistic to go after the entire market, or whether instead to focus on subsets or smaller parts. From a strategic standpoint, nothing the marketer does is more critical than effective segmentation of the marketplace and targeting of the firm's efforts. A *market segment* is a group of existing or potential customers sharing some common characteristic that is relevant in explaining (or predicting) their response to a company's marketing programs. The process the marketer goes through in identifying such groups is *market segmentation*.

On an intuitive level, segmentation is easy to comprehend and usually represents clear advantages for the company using it. The concept of market segmentation and targeting is illustrated in Figure 5.1.

As suggested in Figure 5.1, a market can be envisioned as an accumulation of numerous submarkets. For instance, a tire manufacturer realizes that there are several different types of industrial tire buyers. These buyers vary greatly in their characteristics and needs. Some tire buyers are automobile manufacturers that wish to buy large quantities of passenger tires. Others include transportation companies that wish to buy tires for 18-wheel tractor-trailers. Yet another category of buyers would be construction companies that are seeking tires for large equipment such as earthmovers and dump trucks. Discount stores, independent garages, and even some drugstores engaged in scrambled merchandising are prospective subsegments of the total industrial tire market. Consequently, the tire manufacturer has several alternative strategies available to segment its markets. For example, it may concentrate all of its efforts on one single submarket, such as major domestic automobile manufacturers. In this case, the tire manufacturer must have a strong conviction that it understands the purchasing decision characteristics of automobile manufacturers and can beat the competition on most of the key attributes necessary to gain long-term contracts.

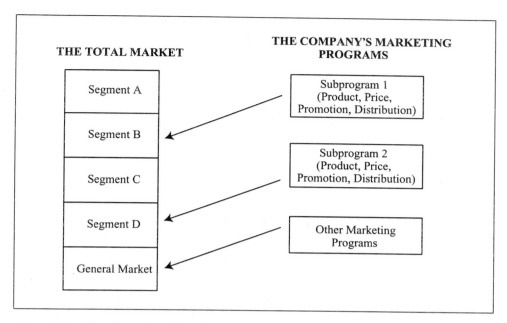

**Figure 5.1.** The Concept of Market Segmentation

In contrast, an alternative strategy would be to expand the tire product line so that several segments are targeted, each with its own unique marketing mix. In addition to a strategy aimed at domestic automobile manufacturers, the tire manufacturer would also have different and distinct marketing mixes aimed at construction companies, discount retail stores, and other target submarkets.

# The Process of Segmentation

Our tire manufacturer example illustrates the basics of market segmentation. *Segmentation* involves the identification of submarkets or segments within the total market, the decision on which one (or ones) to pursue, and the design of individualized marketing mixes for the chosen market segments. These activities can be envisioned as a six-step process, as illustrated in Figure 5.2. Let us examine each of these steps in more detail.

## Identify Relevant Market Segmentation Bases

The beginning point of market segmentation is an inspection of the total market, with an eye toward different ways in which it might conceivably be broken down.

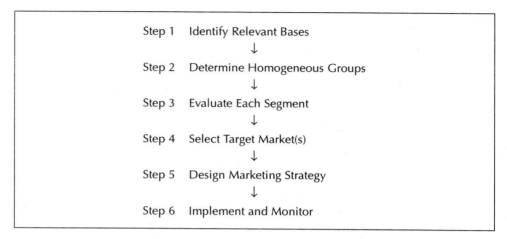

Step 1    Identify Relevant Bases
↓
Step 2    Determine Homogeneous Groups
↓
Step 3    Evaluate Each Segment
↓
Step 4    Select Target Market(s)
↓
Step 5    Design Marketing Strategy
↓
Step 6    Implement and Monitor

**Figure 5.2.** Procedure for Segmenting Markets

Discussions of buyer behavior and the general nature of industrial markets in previous chapters included numerous characteristics useful in grouping customers or prospects or both. A few of the possibilities include

1. Company size (e.g., under 1,000 employees),

2. Company location (e.g., large urban areas),

3. Type of industry (e.g., NAICS code),

4. Technology used (e.g., analog versus digital),

5. Ordering policies (e.g., frequency or size of purchases),

6. Product application (e.g., different uses of the same product),

7. Benefits sought (e.g., durability, accuracy, cost savings, expectations of service quality), and

8. Buying center characteristics (e.g., background of key decision maker).

As a point of comparison, consumer goods markets are often segmented based on demographic characteristics of purchasers and/or their reasons for buying. For instance, the large number of brands and types of soft drinks can be seen as evidence of the extensive number of ways in which that consumer market has been segmented. Numerous subgroupings of consumers are identifiable in terms of age, sex, consumption capacity, levels of sweetness desired, and concerns for sugar or caffeine content. Conceptually, there are no differences between industrial and consumer market segmentation at this step, but the characteristics (or bases) used to segment the market vary greatly.

## Determine Homogeneous Groupings

Once potential bases for segmentation have been identified, the next step is to apply those bases. Members of the total market are grouped into submarkets such that there is *homogeneity* among the members of the submarket. Homogeneity is the key word in segmentation. It refers to similarities or commonalities among the members of the subgroup that set group members apart in some way from members of other subgroups. A critical point, however, is that these commonly shared characteristics must relate to the buyer's susceptibility to differing marketing programs. Although this point may seem somewhat confusing, it simply means that a good segment includes a group of organizations with a shared characteristic (e.g., company size measured in terms of employees) and that this characteristic (or base) must be related to the way in which these companies purchase the product or service in question. So, if size is used, companies in a given size category must be homogeneous in terms of how, when, where, what, or why they buy. If companies with more than 1,000 employees tend to purchase in much larger quantities, or more frequently, or to place more emphasis on quality when making a purchase than do companies in other size categories, then size might be a good variable to use in segmenting the market. Marketing programs can be tailored to reflect such differences in buyer needs or behaviors. Another way to think about his point is to view company size as a *descriptor* of the segments and to view the tendency of organizations of a given size to purchase in a certain manner as the underlying source of marketing opportunity.

Among the many bases available for segmenting industrial markets, the most commonly used are company size, geographic location, and NAICS categories. These may be popular only because they are easier to use and data usually are readily available on markets broken down in such ways. The appropriateness of a given basis for segmentation *depends on the product or service in question.* Unless organizations of a given size, geographic locale, or NAICS category have homogeneous needs or buyer behaviors with respect to their particular product or service sold by the marketer, segmenting in this way may be a waste of time and money.

## Evaluate the Attractiveness of Each Market Segment

Having selected potential segments that appear to have homogeneous needs or buying behaviors, the marketer sets about evaluating the segments. Evaluation of segments is done in the light of the company's financial, market, and technology objectives. For now, attractiveness will be equated with long-run profitability of the market segment (this issue will be expanded on later in the chapter). Using marketing research and forecasting techniques, judgments can be made about the total size of each segment and, depending on the level of marketing effort applied, the likely market share to be gained in each segment. These judgments can be translated into estimates of long-run profits. Segments can then be ranked on their relative attractiveness.

## Select Target Segment(s)

Now the marketer has to decide which segment(s) the firm is going to go after. That is, over the next 1 to 2 years (or whatever the firm's planning horizon), into which segments will the firm invest resources? Segments are selected and prioritized in terms of how much time (e.g., sales force time), effort (e.g., effort at customer service), and money (e.g., money for promotional incentives or special delivery efforts) will be devoted to them. Evaluation will reflect the firm's objectives, which typically stress profitability; however, segments can be selected based on other criteria, such as sales volume, the ease of penetrating them, or the image enhancement that might come from serving the accounts in that segment.

Once a market segment is selected for targeting, additional market research may be conducted to better understand that segment's unique characteristics. Patterns in buying behavior within individual segments might be explored in more depth. Furthermore, analysis would be devoted to assessing the strengths and weaknesses of competitors in the chosen segments, so as to identify areas of competitive opportunity for the firm.

## Align the Marketing Strategy With Market Segment(s)

A frequent mistake made by industrial firms is to design general marketing programs intended to reach and appeal to all customers. Such an approach typically fails unless the product is unique in comparison with competitive offerings, the market is relatively small, and customer needs are fairly standardized or homogeneous throughout the market. For example, IBM historically was successful in pursuing the overall market for some standardized computer products, in part because it offered superior customer service. Market segmentation and targeting, on the other hand, involve designing individualized marketing programs that cater to the distinct needs or problems of subgroups within the entire market. Thus, a computer company that focuses on the distinct computer needs of hospitals and medical facilities in its product design, price, promotional efforts, and distribution system would be pursuing a segmentation and targeting strategy.

A segmentation approach makes sense only if there are subgroups of customer organizations in the market whose distinct needs or buying behaviors can be reflected in the firm's marketing programs. Otherwise, one common approach to the market is appropriate. Consider another example. A company sells security alarm systems and segments the market for these systems based on the average unit value of the merchandise in a customer firm's inventory. Assume the company has divided the market into organizations with very high inventory value, those with moderately valued inventory, and those having inventory of low unit value. The company is considering focusing its efforts on the first two segments.

Further analysis suggests that firms with inventory of high unit value are much less price conscious when it comes to security systems than the other groups, and they tend to hire consultants to recommend alarm systems. Organizations in the moderate unit value group, alternatively, appear to rely much more heavily on word-of-mouth referrals in evaluating security systems than do the other groups, and they tend to be very conscious of brand names. These differences suggest a number of ways in which the marketing mix can be designed to better meet the needs of each segment. The design of the company's product line, as well as its pricing programs, advertising appeals, and personal selling efforts, can be made to reflect such major differences.

## Implement and Monitor

The final stage of the market segmentation process involves the actual implementation of the custom-tailored marketing program and careful monitoring of the reactions of prospective customers and competitors in the market segment. The monitoring system should not only look at market share and other competitive dynamics within the market segment but also periodically assess the underlying bases used to identify and uniquely characterize that market segment. Better bases may emerge over time or become apparent after the company has had significant experience with the market segments. Also, some segments do not remain stable; customers move into and out of the segment.

The alarm system manufacturer, for instance, might find that the buyer behavior of companies with inventory of moderate unit value is becoming more and more like that of companies with high-value inventory, or the manufacturer may find that the physical location of a customer's facilities is becoming a more important factor than inventory value in explaining how customers buy alarm systems. Furthermore, new segments may be emerging, such as companies requiring mobile alarm systems.

## Degrees of Segmentation

One of the distinctive characteristics of segmentation in industrial markets is the greater precision that is possible in a company's segmentation efforts. At one extreme, the marketer can approach the entire market as a whole and not use segmentation at all. This approach is equivalent to treating the entire market as one big segment and is called *undifferentiated marketing*. At the other extreme, every customer could be treated as a distinct segment, with specific programs tailored to its needs. When one, or relatively few, organizations are given sole attention, this approach is termed *concentrated marketing* or *one-to-one marketing*. Between these two extremes, numerous options exist in terms of the size and scope of the marketer's segmentation efforts in various product-market areas. A number of segments could be pursued with a number of marketing mixes. Figure 5.3 illustrates these possibilities.

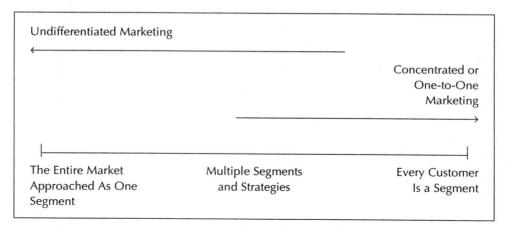

**Figure 5.3.** Strategic Options Possible Through Segmentation

With undifferentiated marketing, the company seeks to compete on a broad basis, with all customers assumed to be reasonably similar. A fixed product line is developed with standardized pricing, promotion, and distribution channels geared to what the company thinks are the needs of the typical customer or the vast majority in the market. With a concentrated marketing approach, the company channels its resources toward winning and building a relationship with a single company or segment. The marketing effort would be intense and the stakes obviously high, as the firm becomes more dependent on individual accounts.

The choice of any one of these approaches is constrained by two considerations. First is the question of the number of identifiable and meaningful segments. If the customer market is dominated by a variety of organizations that do not fall readily into any logical subgroupings, or if the market itself is not large, then segmentation is not feasible. Second, if the company has limited resources, it may be forced to focus on a concentrated approach; that is, it may not be able to afford the costs involved in tailoring the marketing mix to a number of different segments or in competing for the entire undifferentiated market.

## What Segmentation Does for the Industrial Marketer

With conscientious application of the six-step process described above, segmentation can provide the marketer with a number of benefits. Perhaps the most important of these benefits is improved *efficiency* in the use of the firm's marketing resources. The so-called 80:20 rule suggests that, in most markets, 20% of the prospects will generate 80% of any sales that materialize. When a company identifies specific target markets, it does not waste time and resources attempting to find, understand, and capture accounts that do not have a real need for the product, are less profitable, or are otherwise unattractive. With undifferentiated marketing, the company is reaching many organizations that are not really viable prospects in terms of their willingness and ability to buy.

Undifferentiated marketing can also lead the firm to spread its limited resources too thinly. Some refer to this issue in terms of a "shotgun" versus a "rifle" approach. Failure to segment and target is like firing a shotgun, with the shot sprayed far and wide and much of it wasted. Well-targeted marketing is like firing a rifle, where (assuming the target is hit) the intended customer group is "hit" cleanly and efficiently.

In addition to efficiency, market segmentation enables the marketer to be more *effective*. The firm is able to reap the benefits of specialization. Target marketing allows the firm to specialize by matching its skills or capabilities to the unique needs, wants, and problems of the market segments selected. Granted, specialization requires extra investment and will often result in higher unit costs; however, the result is a marketing program that is more customized and therefore one to which customers are likely to be more responsive.

The application of market segmentation also helps pinpoint specific customer prospects. This benefit is particularly relevant to the industrial market arena in which a market segment may, in fact, comprise only one or a very small number of potential buyers. Market segmentation in this case would help to reveal those prospects who reside in specific segments. The firm's marketing intelligence system can then begin to create a database on these particular prospects, and insights can be gained by examining data files of other customers that are in the same market segment.

Finally, the adoption of market segmentation helps the company identify and exploit the weaknesses of its relevant competitors. By studying prospective buyers in selected segments, the company can simultaneously become aware of the competitive environment and knowledgeable about the capabilities of competitors who are also targeting that particular segment.

## Making Decisions About Market Segmentation and Targeting

In evaluating the entire range of possibilities illustrated in Figure 5.3, a company must first decide whether segmentation is a useful practice that will serve company goals. If segmentation is deemed useful, the company must then evaluate market segments in terms of their relative attractiveness. Following this, the company must determine precisely how much marketing effort to allocate to each of the targeted market segments. Let us consider some criteria and related considerations when making each of these three sets of decisions.

### Criteria for the Usefulness of Market Segmentation

The initial question the firm must ask itself is whether the practice of market segmentation is useful and will serve its needs. To make this assessment, the company must address four points.

1. *Does market segmentation fit the firm's basic marketing strategy?* Some companies will not entertain the practice of market segmentation because it is inconsistent with their basic approaches to marketing. A company may have employed undifferentiated marketing as its basic approach in the past and has no desire to consider changing something that has been successful. Senior management may be unreceptive to the perceived risks involved in changing the marketing strategy, or the resource base of the firm may be so limited that it cannot respond, even if attractive market segments are identified. Resistance also arises when the company has managed to link itself with one or two large buyers and has a guaranteed purchasing arrangement for the long term. Here, the company may be complacent, or the single buyer may be adamant about its suppliers not selling to competitors.

2. *Does homogeneity exist within the total market?* For market segmentation to take place, companies grouped together must be similar in their underlying needs and buying behaviors and must be dissimilar from other groups. Just because companies are located in a particular part of the country does not mean that they have common needs or buying behaviors. Such commonalities are often difficult to identify with market research, and sometimes they are not clearly evident until the marketer has spent some time serving various firms in the market. If a company cannot identify commonalities for subgroups of buyers, the application of market segmentation will be futile.

3. *Are the segments measurable?* Even if subgroupings can be identified, there is the question of measuring the various market segments. Before target groups can be selected, the number of firms in the segment, their sales potential, and related descriptors need to be determined. Although secondary information often is available to help in this regard, there are cases where measurement remains troublesome. For instance, if prospects are privately owned companies, the amount of public information will be minimal. Decision makers within prospective companies may be reluctant to divulge information to interviewers in a marketing research study seeking to determine the size of the various segments. Certain descriptive characteristics such as the structure or orientation (e.g., innovativeness) of buying organizations may not lend themselves to easy measurement. Alternatively, the uncertainty of future circumstances may be so great that whatever indicators of size and profitability can be estimated for the present, it may be too risky to project them into the future.

4. *Are the market segments accessible?* Accessibility refers to the degree to which a market segment can be reached through a unique marketing program. It may be that the company's sales force, channels of distribution, or promotional capabilities will not reach certain segments, such as those in rural areas or those with highly decentralized buying operations. In some cases, customers can be reached only at unacceptably high cost. A different example of accessibility problems involves the bid listing practices of many federal, regional, and municipal governments. To gain access to the list and thereby be invited to make a bid on major projects, a vendor must qualify to the satisfaction of the government office. This qualification may require

## BUSINESS MARKETING CAPSULE

### *Targeting Customer Needs to Beat the Competition*

How can a small entrepreneurial company outflank multimillion-dollar marketing researchers in selling data-driven technology? It is happening in space management, a key area in manufacturer-retailer relations. Marketware, a Cambridge, Massachusetts, offshoot of a marketing consultancy called Package Perfect Ltd., has taken the lead in selling computerized planogram systems—the technology that drives space management—to the hardlines industry.

In doing so, the 2-year-old firm has surpassed systems marketed by Information Resources Inc. (IRI), Chicago, and Nielsen Marketing Research, Northbrook, Illinois. IRI's Apollo system and Nielsen's Spaceman still dominate the supermarket industry, where most automated planogram systems are found, but the giants have lost momentum to Marketware in hardlines.

Planogramming is a dry term for a tedious but essential retailing function: organizing merchandise on a store's shelves and display areas. Automating the planogram process relieves the trace of manually arranging products on a shelf, drawing a schematic of the final design, and taking a picture of the display so employees who ultimately stock the shelves have a map.

Computerization also opens the door to greater use of scanner data in deciding what products to carry and how many shelf facings to give them. That dimension lured Nielsen and IRI into the market by way of acquisitions.

Space management makes talk about manufacturer-trade partnerships come alive. Vendors and retailers share sales and replenishment data to create planograms tailored to the demographic in individual stores. Shelf facings are determined by item-movement data.

"It makes everyone honest," users say. If a hot item needs more shelf space, space management shows that. If a product isn't carrying its weight, the deficiency is quickly exposed.

The basic package costs about $40,000, but when computer hardware, training, and consulting are added, first-year costs range from $150,000 to $250,000, according to expert estimates. Studies show that despite high costs and the fact that the systems are not particularly easy to use, payback usually occurs in a year. The standing joke in the supermarket business, however, is that more systems are sitting on shelves than managing them. This set the stage for development of Pegman by Steven Kirschner, founder of Marketware.

"The other systems have us beat in sophistication," he said. "We have 16 financial variables, they have more than 100. But they don't have the ability to customize financial reports to emulate the way a company does business. Our system has that flexibility."

*continued*

"Pegman does fewer things than the others, but that isn't all bad, and it's priced right," said Ted Gladson, president of a self-named planogram service bureau in Lisle, Illinois, which has used Apollo, Spaceman, and AccuSPACE. "About 95% of what the other systems do isn't used on a day-to-day basis."

"Pegman has a lot to offer the hardlines industry," said Steve Gordon, a consultant with Marketmax, a Boston-area firm that sells inventory management systems. "It's not just an inexpensive product, it's an extremely good product tailored specifically for that industry."

SOURCE: Adapted from "Small Firm's Niche Strategy Topples Planogram Biggies," *Marketing News* (January 8, 1990), p. 40, Barry. © Copyright 1990 by *Marketing News*.

bonding of the company and employees, submission of financial records, or demonstrated expertise in certain areas.

## Criteria for the Selection of Target Markets

If the four questions above can be answered in the affirmative, the next set of criteria involves the selection segments to be targeted. Here, five different issues must be addressed.

1. *Does the target market fit the company's image and experience?* The targeting of a market segment must be aligned with the total corporate image. Generally, companies attempt to have an integrated and consistent image across all their activities; therefore, a target market that is not consistent with the image will be eliminated from consideration. Take, for example, the case of a computer manufacturer that attempts to move into the consumer goods market. Firmly established in the industrial market as a manufacturer and marketer of high-quality business machines, the company tries to penetrate a market segment that was inconsistent with its previous experience and marketing know-how. Movement into this market segment with a new computer product means that the company has to establish new channels of distribution, develop an entirely different perspective when it comes to communicating to households and prospective buyers, engage in discount pricing and retail-level consumer goods pricing wars, and ensure that the product is designed so that a child, literally, could use it. This is a surefire recipe for failure.

2. *Will the segment be responsive?* Responsiveness is the extent to which companies within a segment are susceptible to the vendor's marketing programs. If prospective customer organizations cannot be influenced by marketing stimuli (e.g., product features, a price deal, or a promotional program), then these programs are wasted on them. Lack of responsiveness can occur where managers are strongly committed to established ways of doing things and are closed to considering new alternatives. It can also happen when a prospective customer has little or no leeway to

consider the marketer's programs because of limited resources (including time), or because of regulations and procedures that must be observed (e.g., in government purchasing).

3. *Will the segment be substantial over time?* The issue here is the size of the segment not only in terms of the number of potential accounts but also in usage rate of the product or service by these accounts over time. Some segments have considerable potential over a long period of time. Others may become saturated or mature fairly quickly, after which growth will be very slow and opportunities limited. Segments may lose their attractiveness or meaningfulness as changes take place in the underlying needs or buying behaviors of organizations. In the industrial market, substantiality is an extremely critical consideration, as technological breakthroughs can render meaningless a given approach to segmentation. For instance, voice-activated and computer-driven telephone systems could rapidly undermine the traditional telephone market, making traditional approaches to segmentation of this market obsolete.

4. *Can the company be competitive in the target segment?* The key to marketing success is competitive advantage. Consequently, although a market segment may fit the company's image and seem substantial, it may be that the competitive circumstances dictate dropping it from consideration at this time. 3M[1] may be so dominant in certain adhesives markets that few companies choose to venture into these markets, even though certain segments may be very attractive on other dimensions. Alternatively, despite NCR's[2] dominance in selling point-of-sale cash register systems to retailers, a competitor specializing in the distinct sales transaction needs of, say, very small clothing stores may be able to establish a beachhead in the industry. The company must be able to demonstrate that it has the relative strengths necessary to maintain a competitive advantage over a reasonable length of time within a particular segment (or niche).

5. *Is the target market profitable?* Profitability is the underlying consideration in most marketing decisions. Consequently, profitability and the maintenance of profitability over time are prime considerations in the selection of a target market. Some segments have lots of accounts, and these accounts may purchase significant amounts of the product or service, but to get these accounts the firm must cut its margins too dramatically. In addition, to maintain a competitive edge, the costs (e.g., promotion, distribution, product development) of serving the firms in this segment may be so high as to make rates of return unacceptable.

## Criteria for the Allocation of Resources

Marketers struggle with the question of how much marketing effort to put into each of the targeted segments, and the tendency is to make these decisions in a fairly arbitrary manner. This problem is referred to as the *allocation of resources*. Two ma-

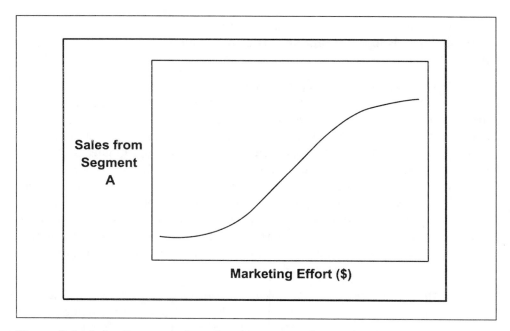

**Figure 5.4.** Sales Response Function for a Particular Market Segment

jor considerations should be kept in mind when making this determination. The first pertains to quantitative, and primarily financial, criteria for the allocation of resources, while the second pertains to qualitative, and primarily strategic, considerations.

With regard to the financial criteria, the marketer might want to employ either productivity analysis or contribution analysis (or both). Each is a measure of return from the segment. Because the marketer is allocating resources to segments, he or she requires some rate of return on that investment over a specified time period.

*Productivity analysis* theoretically is the most appealing, but it also is the most difficult to implement on a practical basis. Here, resources are allocated on the basis of marginal return, or how much a segment will generate in sales revenues or profits if the company invests an incremental amount (say, another $1,000) in marketing efforts directed at that segment. This return is reflected in a sales response function for each segment, such as that presented in Figure 5.4. The curve that is generated reflects the relationship between sales (or profits) and marketing effort. Different segments will respond differently to a given level of marketing effort, so the marketing program is envisioned as a resource budget that is allocated in an optimal fashion across key market segments.

Use of productivity analysis presents certain problems. Very few marketers have the good fortune to be able to work with sales response curves of sufficient precision. Measurement problems include the fact that the relationship typically is curvilinear rather than a straight line. Furthermore, typically there is a time lag between when marketing efforts are made and when returns are realized. These lags can vary, and precisely estimating them can be difficult.

The second method of resource allocation, *contribution analysis,* goes a step further and considers the expected revenues and costs incurred in producing and selling to a particular segment. The company's costs are grouped into three categories: variable, direct fixed, and indirect fixed. *Variable costs* are those expenses that change in direct proportion to the number of units produced and/or sold (e.g., direct labor, raw materials). *Direct fixed costs* include expenses that stay constant regardless of production or sales volume but that are traceable to a particular market segment (e.g., advertisements targeted just to that segment, a sales office to serve that segment). *Indirect fixed costs* also stay constant regardless of volume and include all the remaining fixed costs of the firm, none of which is related to a particular segment (e.g., depreciation on the manufacturing facility).

The total contribution from a particular segment is equal to revenue generated in that segment minus both the variable costs and direct fixed costs associated with the sales made in that segment. Given estimates of these costs as well as the anticipated revenues from units sold at the expected price, it is possible to identify the contribution margin dollars associated with any one sale. This knowledge leads to estimates of break-even points and levels of profit (or loss) given certain projected unit sales targets.

The following example will illustrate the use of contribution analysis in target market decisions. A desk manufacturer has identified three possible target markets. One is schools, where low bidders are awarded the contract. Another is small businesses, where moderate prices and quality are desired, and the third is banks, where senior executives desire high quality and prestige brand names. The estimated prices, unit volume, variable costs, and direct fixed costs needed to perform contribution analysis are illustrated in Table 5.1. Note that indirect fixed costs are not allocated to the segments, as most allocation schemes are arbitrary, serving only to distort the picture. Instead, the marketer gets a clear sense of how well each segment would pull its own weight and contribute to overall profitability.

The numbers in Table 5.1 point out the desirability of targeting small businesses and the danger of seeking to market to schools. Even though the total number of units expected to be sold to schools (1,000) exceeds those anticipated to be sold to small businesses (750), the desk manufacturer would be able to cover the variable costs of production but would come up short in terms of covering the direct fixed costs associated with selling to schools. At the same time, the luxury desks for bankers, which have a greater contribution per unit sold, would derive less total contribution because of lower total unit sales, but this target market is still more attractive than is the school desk segment.

In sum, the *quantitative* approaches for determining the amount of marketing effort to allocate to target segments are based on revenue and profitability assessments. The basic method must consider the size of the market segment, the share or portion of the market anticipated to be captured by the marketer, growth trends of the market segment, and any cost efficiencies that the marketer believes can be achieved. These inputs can be translated into estimates for a given segment of the return or contribution per unit sold.

**TABLE 5.1** Contribution Analysis for Three Segments Being Considered by a Desk Manufacturer

| Market Segment | Schools | Small Businesses | Banks |
|---|---:|---:|---:|
| Price per desk (P) | $1,000 | $1,500 | $2,000 |
| Projected unit sales | × 1,000 | × 750 | × 500 |
| Total revenue | $1,000,000 | $1,125,000 | $1,000,000 |
| Variable costs per unit | | | |
|   Raw materials | $500 | $700 | $1,000 |
|   Labor | $300 | $400 | $500 |
|   Sales commission | $100 | $100 | $150 |
| Variable cost per unit (VC) | $900 | $1,250 | $1,700 |
| Projected unit sales | × 1,000 | × 750 | × 500 |
|   Total variable costs | $900,000 | $937,500 | $850,000 |
| Total revenue | $1,000,000 | $1,125,000 | $1,000,000 |
| Total variable costs | − $900,000 | − $937,500 | − $850,000 |
| Variable contribution | $100,000 | $187,500 | $150,000 |
|   Direct fixed costs | − $110,000 | − $150,000 | − $130,000 |
| Total segment contribution | ($10,000) | $37,500 | $20,000 |
| Contribution per unit sold (P − VC) | $100 | $250 | $300 |

It is also important to consider qualitative or strategic benefit issues when selecting and investing in market segments. One qualitative dimension that might compel a company to move into a certain market segment would be the image benefits that are achieved by the corporation as a whole. For example, General Motors[3] operates a coach division that manufactures buses sold to public and private schools. In comparison with other market segments served by General Motors, this market segment is minuscule. In addition, there are substantial dangers of product safety criticisms from the public. Nevertheless, General Motors has decided to maintain its presence in this market so as to maintain the qualitative image benefits gained.

Another qualitative reason for selecting a target market is to insulate the company from competition. Very small marketers often select market segments that have been ignored or otherwise overlooked by larger competitors; they do so to minimize their presence in the eyes of their larger competitors and to survive in quieter competitive circumstances. In addition, a segment might seem attractive because it enables the seller to gain access to the technologies used by customer firms or to learn more about the nature of a particular business.

Finally, there is the issue of control. All companies seek to exercise control over their operations. Loss of control occurs because of volatility in demand, instability in market share, or loss of important components in their operations such as raw material sources, personnel, or distributors. Thus, although a market segment may not be

**TABLE 5.2**  Analysis of a Market Segment Cost Benefit

| *Sample Benefits* | *Sample Costs* |
| --- | --- |
| Estimated revenues | Product modification costs |
| Enhanced image | Transportation |
| Volume purchases | Marketing research |
| Referrals—pass-along sales | Selling effort required |
| Access to customer's technology | Discounts provided |
| | Distribution channel costs |
| | Promotion expenditures |
| | Inventory costs |
| | Small order lot size costs |
| | Opportunity costs (e.g., tied-up production capacity) |

the most attractive in terms of profitability and other quantitative measures, it may provide a means of gaining more certainty of control over sales and operations, and therefore be an attractive business arena.

## An Additional Perspective: Cost-Benefit Analysis

In applying these criteria to evaluate a particular segment, the marketer is basically attempting to identify what will be gained from focusing on the segment, and at what cost. Given this premise, it often is a good idea to perform a formal analysis on each segment to determine the specific costs and benefits associated with tailoring the firm's marketing programs to the requirements of a particular segment.

Table 5.2 provides a demonstration of how the possible costs and benefits associated with a potential segment can be examined. A number of evaluative criteria, including image, accessibility, measurability, fit with resources, competitive advantage, and longevity, have been considered in identifying these costs and benefits. For example, if the segment is not easily accessible, or if competition is well entrenched, expenditures for selling, distribution, and promotion are likely to be exorbitant.

Not only should benefits exceed costs, but the company also should prioritize segments based on the size of their net benefits. To quantify all costs and benefits, the marketer may have to make some subjective estimates. As a case in point, the value to a company of receiving access to a given technology or of benefiting from a segment's image has to be evaluated subjectively. Where actual dollar figures cannot be determined, an alternative approach might be to develop a rating form, including high (a value of 3), medium (2), and low (1) on each benefit or cost. Totals could then be determined, resulting in an overall score for the segment.

# Strategic Approaches to Segmenting Industrial Markets

As we have seen, market segmentation begins with the identification of relevant bases for breaking down the market. A base is a characteristic of a firm such as company size or price sensitivity. After consideration of all the possible bases of segmentation, they can be grouped logically. Let us consider one such grouping approach, then expand this perspective into something called the "nested" approach.

## The Macro and Micro Approach

Different levels of segmentation bases are available to the industrial marketer. A creative method for segmenting any industrial market is to first identify subgroups that share common *macro characteristics* and to select target segments from among these subgroups. Rather than stopping at this point, though, the marketer then breaks down these so-called macro segments into subgroups that share common *micro characteristics*. In this manner, the marketer goes through a two-step process.

Macro-segmentation involves dividing the market into subgroups based on overall characteristics of customer organizations. Examples include their size, usage rate of the product or service being sold, the application made of the product or service, the industry or NAICS category to which they belong, company structure, geographic location, the end market they serve, and whether the marketer's product represents a new or repeat purchase to them.

Macro bases share the distinctive feature of being relatively easy to use because data are readily available for identifying the organizations that belong to a particular macro segment. Such information usually can be obtained from secondary data sources.

Micro bases for segmentation pertain to characteristics of the decision-making process and the buying structure within customer organizations. These include such factors as the perceived importance of the purchase, the relative importance of specific product or vendor attributes, attitudes toward vendors, decision rules used in selecting vendors, the structure of the buying center, the amount of influence held by key departments in the buying center, and demographics and personality characteristics of key members of the buying center.

Micro bases can have many more direct marketing implications than do macro bases. The fact that a customer resides in a particular geographic region or is in a certain industry can provide some general guidance in developing the marketing mix for a specific product. Much greater insight can be obtained, however, by knowing how buying decisions are made or how much influence design engineers wield in comparison to purchasing managers. These micro bases relate more directly to a particular purchasing decision.

At the same time, characteristics of micro segments can be more difficult to identify because information on these characteristics usually is not readily available. This

**TABLE 5.3**  Information Collected by Companies for Segmentation Purposes

In a study of the segmentation practices of industrial firms engaged in export trade, Shuster and Bodkin found many of them routinely gather both macro- and micro-segmentation data. The authors concluded that in the space of just 10 years, there had been a significant move from collecting only macro-segmentation data to a strong emphasis on gathering information released to both types of segmentation. Listed below are the percentages of companies that collect data on potential customers in each of 17 different areas.

| Category | Percentage of Companies Collecting This Type of Information |
|---|---|
| *Macro-segmentation–related* | |
| Size of company | 51 |
| Geographic location | 61 |
| Usage rates | 45 |
| Buying strategy | 43 |
| SIC code (now NAICS code) | 29 |
| Financial information | 6 |
| End market | 49 |
| Buying situation | 31 |
| Decision-making stage | 41 |
| *Micro-segmentation–related* | |
| Buying criteria | 51 |
| Sources of conflict | 29 |
| Buying units | 35 |
| Importance of purchase | 45 |
| Attitudes toward purchase | 55 |
| Organizational innovativeness | 29 |
| Personal characteristics | 41 |
| Other | 8 |

SOURCE: "Market Segmentation Practices of Exporting Companies," *Industrial Marketing Management,* 16, no. 2 (March), p. 101, Shuster and Bodkin. © Copyright 1987 by *Industrial Marketing Management.* Reprinted with permission.

means that primary data may have to be collected, or at the very least, extensive knowledge of the internal operations of prospective customers must be developed. Some of this knowledge can be obtained from sales representatives or others who call on the firm. Despite these difficulties, it appears that companies are devoting increasing effort toward gathering information related to micro segmentation (see Table 5.3).

| Benefits Sought by Potential Buyers | Hardware Buyers | Brand Buyers | People Buyers | One-Stop Shoppers |
|---|---|---|---|---|
| Speed of operation | 0 | 0 | 0 | 0 |
| Operator ease of operation | 0 | 0 | + | 0 |
| Aesthetic aspects | 0 | 0 | 0 | 0 |
| Compatibility with present system | 0 | 0 | 0 | 0 |
| Service | 0 | 0 | 0 | 0 |
| Delivery speed | + | 0 | 0 | 0 |
| Absolute price | + | 0 | 0 | 0 |
| Price flexibility | + | 0 | 0 | − |
| Support software | 0 | 0 | 0 | + |
| Broad line equipment | 0 | 0 | 0 | + |
| Manufacturer image | 0 | + | 0 | 0 |
| Manufacturer stability | 0 | 0 | 0 | 0 |
| Competence of sales personnel | − | 0 | + | 0 |
| Reliability of operation | 0 | 0 | 0 | 0 |

SOURCE: Adapted from *Benefit Segmentation: An Industrial Application* (Report No. 82-110), p. 21, Moriarty and Reibstein. © Copyright 1982 by Marketing Science Institute.

NOTE: + = Attribute significantly more important to this segment, − = attribute significantly less important to this segment, 0 = insignificant attribute.

**Figure 5.5.** Micro-Segmentation in the Data Terminals Market

To illustrate the value of micro segmentation, consider a highly illustrative study performed on the data terminals market (Moriarty & Reibstein, 1982; see also Sinclair & Stalling, 1990). The study focused on the relative importance of specific attributes in the organization's buying decisions. As Figure 5.5 illustrates, the research identified 14 different product attributes or benefits sought by buyers of data terminals. Further analysis resulted in the discovery of four market segments. One, the "hardware buyers," was concerned with delivery speed and comparative price but unconcerned with sales competence of vendors. Another segment, the "brand buyers," relied on the manufacturer's image much more than the other segments. The "people buyers" centered their concerns around the interpersonal aspects of the sale and of terminal operation, with more desire for competent vendor sales personnel plus ease of equipment operation. Finally, the "one-stop shoppers" tended to seek a complete package from a single vendor and consequently identified the breadth of the vendor's product line and software support as primary benefits. Interestingly, this segment exhibited lower price sensitivity than the others.

Taking the findings of this type of study one step further, we can see the marketing strategy implications of the distinctive benefit characteristics of each segment. To target the hardware buyers, a company would emphasize low price and rapid delivery. Less emphasis would be placed on training of sales personnel, which would help reduce costs, and these cost savings could be passed on in the form of lower prices. The brand buyer segment, on the other hand, would need to be approached with a complete corporate image-building strategy. Well-known and respected vendors would be front-runners in the minds of these prospects. A completely different strategy would be appropriate for the "people buyers" segment. For these prospective purchasers, the marketer would stress the interpersonal relationship between sales personnel and decisions makers in the target company. Also, product design implications are apparent from the desire for ease of operation; consequently, the terminal should be engineered to be maximally friendly. Finally, the one-stop shoppers segment consists of decision makers who seek to purchase complete systems from single vendors and would respond to package proposals of hardware, software, installation, training, and other support even if they are priced somewhat high.

When macro-segmentation is used with micro-segmentation, the result can be improvement in both the effectiveness of marketing programs and the efficiency of resource usage. If the target market consists of companies in a particular industry category (a macro base) whose key decisions makers are very price conscious (a micro base), then marketing programs can be customized accordingly. Care must be taken, however, that the costs of serving such a narrowly defined audience do not exceed the benefits.

The marketer may not always perceive that there are clear advantages to be gained from focusing on micro segments. He or she may stop after identifying macro segments, especially if this produces segments that are thought to be sufficiently well defined in the light of the company's marketing resources. Let's now look at a more comprehensive approach.

## Intermediate Bases: The Nested Approach

In a ground-breaking contribution, Bonoma and Shapiro (1984) expanded the use of macro- and micro-segmentation into what is called the *nested* approach. This method assumes a hierarchical structure of segmentation bases that move from very broad or general bases to very narrow and specific bases. Rather than a two-step process, the nested approach allows up to five steps. An illustration can be found in Figure 5.6. There, macro bases are in the outermost boxes (e.g., company size), with micro characteristics in the innermost boxes (e.g., personal characteristics of members of the buying center).

The figure further suggests that a number of *intermediate* segmentation bases, such as situational factors or the general purchasing approach of the firm, lie between these two extremes. Situational factors could include the urgency of the purchase of the specific application of the purchased product. The purchasing approach might be the degree of formal structure in the customer's purchasing operations, general purchasing policies of the organization, or the decision criteria used to make a vendor or product choice.

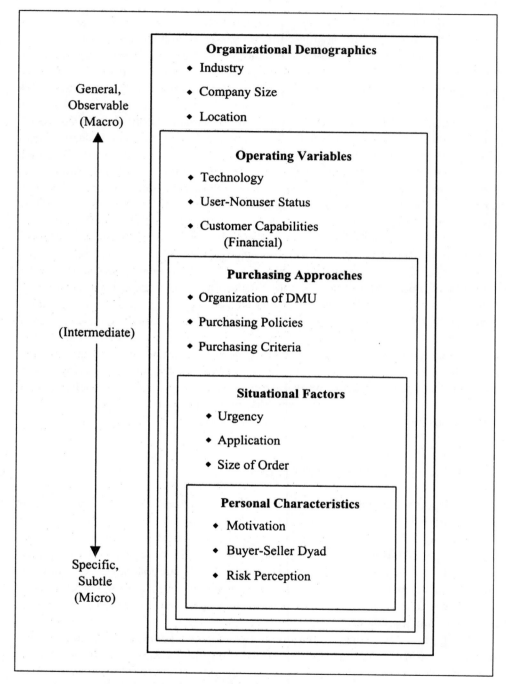

**Figure 5.6.** "Nesting" the Potential Bases for Segmentation

SOURCE: *Segmenting the Industrial Market*, p. 10, Bonoma and Shapiro. © Copyright 1983 by Lexington Books, D. C. Heath and Company.

As one moves from very macro through intermediate and then to micro bases, each subsequent (and more specific) segmentation base is contained within the one that preceded it. That is, the more specific customer characteristics are nested inside the broader situational or organizational characteristics. The end result is a very practical segmentation framework within which one can find virtually any imaginable base for breaking down an industrial market.

To implement the nested approach, let us look at an example. A firm selling mail equipment (e.g., postage meters, weighing scales) to organizations may first segment the market based on broad organizational characteristics, such as company size. It may decide to focus only on companies with 1,000 or more employees. Rather than stop there and focus on all such companies, the firm then further segments the market based on operating characteristics, such as whether the company has a mail department. Focusing only on those with a mail department, the firm goes one step further and pinpoints only those companies that emphasize low price as a key attribute in the purchase decision, and so on. The marketer can move through all five nests if he or she wants that much specialization or can stop at any point. Also, any one level could be skipped over, such as where the marketer starts with purchasing approaches, then goes to personal characteristics.

The nested approach suggests that segmentation can involve multiple stages. Kalafatis and Cheston (1997) have provided evidence from the pharmaceutical industry to suggest that 15% of firms rely on a one-stage segmentation process, 26% use two stages, and 31% rely on a three-stage process. Furthermore, they found that macro types of variables (e.g., end use or product application) were most prevalent at the initial stage, whereas usage variables (e.g., purchase volume, company size) became important at a second stage and micro variables (e.g., price sensitivity, benefits sought) became important in the third stage.

## Putting It All Together: A Dynamic Cost-Benefit/Nested Approach

Let us take the nested approach one step further and reintroduce the need to evaluate segmentation decisions using particular criteria. The end result is a comprehensive model for making segmentation decisions. As illustrated in Figure 5.7, the proposed decision model combines nested segmentation with cost-benefit analysis.

Using this model, segmentation strategy is developed around three questions, each of which involves cost-benefit analysis. First, the industrial marketer must pose the question of whether market segmentation makes sense: Do the benefits of trying to identify market segments exceed the cost? The answer requires a return to the four basic questions posed earlier in the chapter. That is, are segments measurable, accessible, and sufficiently homogeneous, and do they fit the marketing approach of the firm? If the evaluation of these criteria turns out to be negative, market segmentation at this level is not useful.

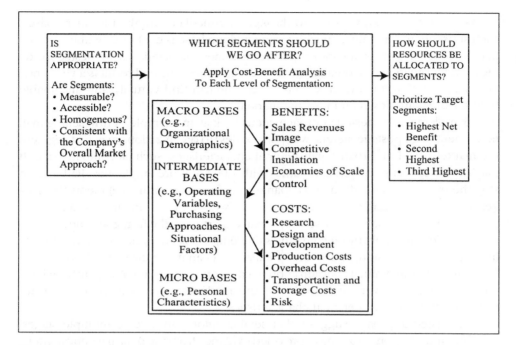

**Figure 5.7.** A Dynamic Cost-Benefit/Nested Approach to Industrial Market Segmentation

If the assessment of all four criteria is positive, the next question concerns which types of segments to pursue. Again, a set of criteria is evaluated from a cost-benefit perspective. These criteria, you will recall, include fit with company image, responsiveness, substantiality, competitive advantage, and profitability. You will also recall that the cost-benefit analysis at this stage includes judgmental considerations (e.g., revenues and profits). The analysis progresses systematically from the evaluation of macro-segmentation bases through intermediate bases to the evaluation of micro-segmentation bases.

The third question involves ways in which marketing resources should be allocated across the market segments that have been selected. The various segments will require differing amounts and types of resources. The marketer determines the investment to be made in each segment, again on a cost-benefit basis. Relevant tools at this stage include marginal analysis, average analysis, and contribution analysis.

Figure 5.8 illustrates how a company marketing a point-of-purchase electronic scanning system might apply the cost-benefit/nested techniques. Electronic scanning systems use infrared sensors to detect the product codes imprinted on merchandise and ring them up automatically at the checkout counter. Simultaneously, the system maintains accounting records of inventory sold, prices charged, taxes, and other details of transactions. In this example, we will assume that the company involved is new to the industry, is just entering this market, and is quite small—but has a dependable product.

| Macro-Segmentation Bases | Cost-Benefit Analysis |
|---|---|
| Type of retailer | |
|     Catalog sales | Too few catalog sales retailers |
|     Discount chain | Too many independents |
|     Independents | **Selection: Discounters** |
| Size of company | |
|     Very small | Very small, too costly |
|     Medium | Large, too competitive |
|     Large | **Selection: Medium** |
| | |
| **Intermediate-Segmentation Bases** | |
| Current system | |
|     Manual | Manual inconsistent |
|     Automated | Automated, already has system |
|     Mixed | **Selection: Mixed** |
| Capabilities | |
|     Programming expenses | System is turnkey |
|     No ability | **Selection: No ability** |
| | |
| **Micro-Segmentation Bases** | |
| System benefits | |
|     Inventory control | Limited capacity for inventory control |
|     Accounting primarily | **Selection: Accounting primarily** |
| Decision criteria | |
|     Compatibility | Vendor is start-up; unknown |
|     Vendor reputation | **Selection: Compatibility** |

**Figure 5.8.** Application of the Dynamic Cost-Benefit/Nested Segmentation Approach to a Point-of-Purchase Software Package Vendor

Macro-segmentation could begin with general designations such as those indicated in Figure 5.8. Actually, preliminary segmentation has already taken place, because the company has developed a retailer software package; consequently, lack of compatibility automatically excluded wholesalers, manufacturers, and other such companies. Three types of retail companies are noted as candidates: independents, catalog sales companies, and discount chains. These segments have been selected for their high volumes of business, which are consistent with needs for automatic scanning rather than manual cash register operations. Review of secondary information reveals that there is a multitude of independent retailers, and targeting them would take more resources than the software company has available. By contrast, too few catalog companies exist to warrant the cost of targeting them. The selection, then, is to target discount retail chains.

Next, the size of retail chain is considered. Again, secondary information might reveal three categories: very small single-city chains, medium-size regional chains, and large national chains. Cost-benefit analysis is used to resolve this stage. Because of the need to demonstrate the system, plus the installation requirements if purchased, the small chains are eliminated because of excessive cost. At the other extreme, the competitive environment for the large chains is recognized as intense, requiring extensive sales and promotion expenditures, so this segment is eliminated. The decision is to target regional discount retail chains, where the sales and competitive environment benefits exceed costs.

Intermediate segmentation bases (e.g., retailers having point-of-purchase systems already in place) might be considered next. Some prospective retailers may have resisted switching to computer-driven systems and still have manual checkouts. Others might have modern scanning systems. In the latter case, penetration will be difficult because competitors have already won the accounts. In the former case, significant resistance to new technology seems evident, and marketing efforts to change old ways might be unsuccessful. The target group, then, becomes those that have mixed systems—discounters that have computerized their personnel or inventory control systems but still have many operations that have not been converted.

Further intermediate segmentation can be accomplished by determining the internal software programming capabilities of these discount retailers with mixed manual and automated systems. Past experience may have revealed that the more responsive prospects are those who wish a turnkey system, for which the vendor installs the system and guarantees its satisfactory operation without requiring a programmer in the retailer's organization to serve a support function. In other words, the greatest likelihood of a positive response from this group makes it a more appealing target from a cost-benefit standpoint.

Then, micro-segmentation can come into play. The focus now becomes specific benefits sought and decision criteria employed by the buyer. For example, one segment may desire essentially an accounting records system because it already has a satisfactory inventory control system that is compatible with the marketer's current system. Another subgroup may desire a point-of-purchase system that can provide an on-line linkage to bank networks, so that checks and credit cards can be approved immediately. Attempting to provide the networking capability benefit might require extensive redesign and debugging, but the cost of that effort may not exceed the projected revenues from the segment. Finally, marketing research or informal discussions with prospects could uncover two more decision criteria: the consideration of a point-of-purchase system that fits or does not fit into the computer system already in place, and sensitivity to the vendor's reputation. Here, because the marketing company is new and relatively unknown, it should select retailers who are less concerned about company reputation. Also, if the software is compatible with the computer hardware already in the retailer's possession, it would be more efficient to target this segment.

# Summary

This chapter has introduced the concept of market segmentation as an approach to industrial markets. Although segmentation is not appropriate in some cases, it is often a means to achieve efficiencies and specialization in the firm's marketing efforts. To use this strategic tool effectively, the marketer should follow a systematic process in which segments are carefully identified, evaluated, selected, targeted with marketing programs, and monitored.

When using segmentation, the marketer must evaluate three key decision areas:

1. As a general practice, is segmentation realistic for our firm?

2. Which bases of segmentation are most appropriate, given our resources?

3. How should the firm's marketing resources be allocated to specific segments?

A set of evaluative criteria was presented for use in addressing each of these decision areas.

Although a number of approaches for segmenting industrial markets exist, two closely related techniques were emphasized: macro-/micro-segmentation and nested segmentation. The chapter argued for the use of a nested approach in which cost-benefit analysis is integrated at each step in the segmentation process.

Overall, segmentation is an underused practice in industrial firms. In practice, segmentation is applied unevenly and, in some cases, has been completely ignored by members of the industrial market. All too often, companies enter the market with no specific target group in mind. Then, much later, when they have determined who appears to be purchasing their product or service, they argue that this was how they segmented the market. In this sense, segmentation becomes a post hoc justification for an unplanned result.

In sum, practitioners of industrial market segmentation should observe a number of cautions as they adopt this valuable tool:

1. Industrial marketers must first decide on the appropriateness of market segmentation before attempting to implement it.

2. Segmentation should be considered an ongoing process and, to the extent possible, be built into a company's marketing intelligence system.

3. Market segmentation should balance the firm's total information needs with budgets and other constraints.

4. Micro-segmentation bases should be geared toward customer needs and requirements.

5. Strategic implications of the application of market segmentation must, at a minimum, consider economic aspects; even better, they should embody a cost-benefit frame of reference.

## Notes

1. www.3m.com
2. www.ncr.com/
3. www.gm.com/

## Questions

1. The president of Pilgrim Manufacturing Company, a maker of refrigeration units such as those commonly found in supermarkets, firmly believes his market consists of all potential buyers of the company's product line. You are the new marketing manger at Pilgrim. Present an argument for introducing market segmentation and targeting, where Pilgrim focuses on particular market segments.

2. Yage Corporation, a producer of safety nets for use in high-rise construction, is planning to introduce an improved polyurethane-coated nylon net to the construction industry. Consider the continuum illustrated in Figure 5.3. Which makes more sense for Yage: relying more on undifferentiated marketing or more on concentrated marketing?

3. "If the product being sold is virtually a commodity, such as motor oil, muriatic acid, copper wire, or computer paper, segmentation of the market really makes little sense." Present an argument agreeing or disagreeing with this statement.

4. Identify two products for which segmenting the market would be a mistake, and explain why segmentation has little to offer in those cases.

5. Gorman Machine Tool concentrates its sales and marketing efforts on large companies (more than 3,000 employees) using the logic that these firms represent much greater sales potential. Why might size be a poor basis for market segmentation?

6. Corwin Commercial Paints finds that its sales are growing slowly, but profits are declining. How might an ineffective market segmentation program cause this problem?

7. "Segmentation is not only a decision regarding which customers to pursue but also a decision on which ones not to pursue." Explain. Do you agree or disagree?

8. You sell temperature control devices for use in appliances such as refrigerators, air conditioners, and clothes dryers. Identify a market segment and some of the potential costs and benefits that would be involved if you targeted that particular segment.

9. Evaluate the homogeneity, accessibility, substantiality, responsiveness, and sustainability of banks as a market segment for a company that sells marketing research and advertising services.

10. South Hampton Manufacturing Co., a producer of small portable gasoline generators, introduced two new models into its product line last year. The two new models—DC40000 and DS4800—were sold to two major market segments, construction companies and the military. Given below are the cost and revenue figures for 1991.

| | DC-4000 | DS-4800 |
|---|---|---|
| Selling price per unit | $40.00 | $20.00 |
| Sales volume in units: | | |
|     Construction sales | 6,000 | 8,000 |
|     Military sales | 4,000 | 13,000 |
| Direct variable manufacturing cost/unit | $20.00 | $9.00 |
| Variable selling costs/unit | $2.00 | $1.50 |

Fixed costs related to construction sales were $5,000 and those for military sales were $5,400. Other fixed expenses for the firm amounted to $12,000.

a. Perform a contribution analysis by product.

b. Perform a contribution analysis by market segment.

11. When using the nested approach to segmenting a market, why would you not want to stop at organizational demographics? That is, why might you first select key demographic bases, such as geographic location, to focus on, but then segment further, by focusing only on companies within a geographic region that use a particular purchasing approach? Alternatively, why might you skip over organizational demographics and go directly to operating variables or situational factors?

# CHAPTER 6

# Industrial Marketing Research and Intelligence

*A decision is the action an executive must take when he has*
*information so incomplete that the answer does not suggest itself.*
—Admiral A. W. Radford

## Key Concepts

Database

Decision support system (DSS)

Decision-making uncertainty

Experimentation

External secondary data

Hypothesis

Internal secondary data

Marketing intelligence system (MIS)

Marketing research process

Model

Observation

Primary data

Reliability

Research design

Sampling strategy

SIC system

Survey method

Unit of analysis

Validity

Value of information

## Learning Objectives

1. Appreciate the role of marketing information as a tool for reducing uncertainty in decision making.

2. Recognize the benefits, limitations, and major applications of marketing research.

3. Describe a process approach to industrial marketing research and identify distinctive challenges in performing research on organizations.

4. Understand the evolution from marketing research to marketing intelligence to decision support systems.

5. Identify sources of and limitations to the use of secondary information sources, including the SIC and NAICS systems.

## The Role of Research in Marketing Decisions

In earlier chapters, we examined the complexities involved when selling to organizations. Added to the difficulties of understanding buyers and their changing needs is the unpredictability of competitor actions and reactions, along with rapidly changing technologies and turbulent economic developments. The industrial marketer attempts to make strategic decisions and tactical moves in an environment filled with uncertainties.

The best means for reducing uncertainty is to develop better information. Without quality information, the marketing decision process becomes little more than guesswork. The formal activities for generating this information constitute industrial marketing research, the objective of which is to obtain the best available intelligence given constraints on available time and cost. Essentially, marketing research is responsible for supplying the facts, estimates, expert opinions, interpretations, and/or recommendations needed by managers to understand the marketing environment and to make informed decisions.

As products and services move through their life cycles, a multitude of decisions must be made, modified, abandoned, or otherwise reconsidered across all areas of marketing. Unfortunately, marketing managers never have all the relevant facts for making decisions in such areas as segmentation and targeting, formulation of overall marketing strategies, design of the marketing mix, establishment of marketing budgets, and selection of marketing personnel. They must deal with dynamic, threatening, and complex change in their external environments. At the same time, marketing decisions cannot be delayed long enough to conduct exhaustive information searches. Even if they could, the cost of getting the relevant information can be prohibitive.

To demonstrate the role of marketing research, consider the following example. A distributor of business supplies is considering expanding its warehouse facilities by 30%. The impetus for the decision has come from a series of customer complaints about stockouts that the company experienced in the last year. Given only this piece of information, the company might rush headlong into capital outlays to expand its warehouse and to purchase additional materials handling equipment; however, the decision would be made under a great deal of uncertainty. This uncertainty concerns the actions of competitors, the business activity level of customers, the effect of stockouts on current customers, and the ultimate result of the capital outlay on the company's financial position.

In a relatively short period of time, marketing research could provide information that would help to clarify some of these issues. For example, the future business activity level of the target market can be judged by looking at the predictions of business analysts who have studied the industry over the past several years. The actions of competitors can be predicted by looking at their annual reports to determine financial reserves and current warehouse capacity. The attitudes of key customers can be evaluated by making telephone calls to purchasing agents, asking about the impact of missing shipping deadlines. In short, industrial marketing research activities can provide data input on a number of questions in the marketing manager's mind and can help reduce the uncertainty in the decision-making process. Then, the marketing manager will have more confidence in his or her assessment of what will happen if the expansion decision is or is not implemented.

Even with the aid of good research, however, the manager is always faced with imperfect information. Research always contains a certain degree of error. Part of the error is due to the time pressures placed on the research function, part is due to the unpredictability of the industrial marketing environment, and part is due to the less-than-perfect tools that the marketing researcher uses. Inadequately trained personnel are another potential source of errors. Fortunately, a judicious marketing researcher can minimize the amount of error that is introduced into the decision-making process. Decisions concerning obtaining marketing research information involve trade-offs between the amount of uncertainty the research eliminates and the amount of erroneous new information it introduces into the process.

# When Not to Do Research

Although marketers tend to view research as inherently worthwhile, there are times when this is not the case. At least five situations exist in which research will make little or no contribution to the decision-making process. The first instance is when the research has already effectively been done and additional information gathering represents duplication of effort. Too often, managers are oblivious to or ignorant of work that already has been done. Second, when the marketing decision has already been made, research has no effect other than to slow down implementation or otherwise add costs without gains. Unfortunately, some managers request research as a means of stroking their egos, or as artificial reinforcement after they have made decisions, rather than as a means of resolving uncertainty regarding the decisions themselves. Alternatively, some managers solicit research to prove their points or support their positions. This situation produces a clash of manager subjectivity with research objectivity. Under these circumstances, no changes in marketing decisions are likely regardless of the results, for if the findings conflicted with the manager's position, they probably would be ignored or discounted.

Another case of questionable need for research is when the manager fails to understand the scope of the research task and is unwilling to expend sufficient money to obtain the necessary information. Here, shortcuts and financial limitations will place restrictions not only on the reliability of the research but also on the generalizability of the results. This means the findings may not be able to be extended beyond the study to the marketplace in general. If the manager is unwilling to pay for what is needed to properly address the problem at hand, it may be better to spend no money at all on research rather than to compromise the integrity of the measurement process.

A slightly different but equally adverse situation is when a manager needs research inputs but does not have experienced employees and is unwilling to enlist the aid of marketing research specialists. Managers tend to underestimate the complexities of research and the skills necessary to do it properly. Research assignments are given to inexperienced staff members, or the manager will personally conduct the project. When there is minimal comprehension of the research process, the research effort is often wasted.

Finally, in all research undertakings, the manager must be firmly convinced that the expected results will reduce the uncertainty enough to warrant the cost of doing the research. No marketing decisions are made with complete certainty, but intelligent marketing decision makers weigh the cost of doing research against the value of reducing the uncertainty by some expected amount. The decision maker combines the known costs of research activities, including time and energy, and compares these costs to the expected gains from having a better understanding of key variables that affect the decision being made.

## Major Responsibility Areas of Marketing Research

What is the focus of industrial marketing research? Virtually any decision area in which the marketing manager requires more or better information inputs is a likely candidate for a marketing research project; the list of potential projects is endless. To bring some order to this state of affairs, we can group the major areas where research is conducted into the following categories: estimation of market potential, analysis of market share and customer equity, determination of market characteristics and attitudes, analysis of company sales data, forecasting, studies of business trends, determination of how new products or services will be accepted, analysis of competitors, and determination of appropriate sales quotas and territories.

## Estimation of Market Potential

One of the most critical decision inputs needed by industrial marketing managers is the sales and the profit potential of various market opportunities. The marketing research function is responsible for clarifying the magnitude and future growth prospects of specific markets. This information helps the marketer determine which markets to enter and exit, as well as how resources should be allocated among given markets.

## Market Share and Customer Equity Analysis

Marketing exists in a world of dynamic competition, and marketing research is assigned the responsibility of determining the relative proportion of the total market that a firm can hope to attain. Historical market share distributions are balanced against anticipated future competitive actions. The entrance and exit of competitors, the market's reactions to changes in marketing strategies and tactics, and the persistence of loyalty to industrial suppliers all go into estimating the share of the market for any product in a firm's line. Actual market share, once determined, provides a benchmark against which to compare objectives and future performance.

Perhaps even more significant is the need to estimate customer lifetime value, or the total amount a customer will spend on a product category over 10 to 15 years. Using this information, the company can set a goal for the proportion of this value that it estimates it will be able to capture. The resulting number, called customer equity, becomes a guideline for how much the firm should invest in getting, growing, and keeping the account.

## Determination of Market Characteristics and Attitudes

Marketing research must supply data on the salient characteristics of markets and customers. The nature of the purchase decision-making process, the identities of key role players in the buying organization, the importance of product and company attributes, the size of purchases, and the various specifications that must be matched in proposals or bids are all part of the market characteristics that the industrial marketing manager must understand to compete effectively. Other areas of investigation include the firm's image in certain markets and satisfaction levels among various segments of the market.

## Analysis of Company Sales Data

Breakdowns of sales, cost, and profit figures by product line, individual products, territory, customer segments, salesperson, and distributor type are all necessary for the industrial marketing manager to have a complete picture of what is happening, where, and possibly why. These analyses are helpful in determining where the company is making money, detecting profit contribution differences, isolating high and low producers, and otherwise alerting the manager to emerging problems and potential.

## Forecasting

Predictions must be made of strength of the economy, the future actions of competitors, the anticipated purchasing level of customers, and conditions of supply and demand. Short-term forecasts are also inputs to production planning and to intermediate-range forecasts (1 to 3 years) that define potential opportunities or threats. Long-range strategic planning is facilitated by forecasts of market conditions and the business environment over periods of 3 to 5 or more years. Trends in the economy, shifts in the business cycle, changes in the international environment, the pattern of growth in markets, and the possible impacts of technological change are all inputs to the long-term forecasts used in strategic planning. Industrial firms cannot set realistic goals or properly define their mission without expectations concerning the future business environment. Similarly, long-term forecasts are critical for decisions regarding product line changes, distribution channel changes, plant expansion, and capital requirements.

## Studies of Key Business Trends

The dependence of industrial firms on derived demand necessitates special-purpose studies of industries, technologies, and demographic shifts. For instance, computer component producers must have an understanding of the speed at which the market will adopt interconnected personal communication systems (linking e-mail, cellular telephones, and pagers); building supply companies must have an appreciation of shifting population patterns and their consequences on business and household construction; and financial institutions must anticipate the rise and fall of certain industries to plan to meet their short- and long-term financing needs. The typical industrial firm is affected by trends in a variety of different industries.

## New Product and Service Acceptance and Potential

New products and services have become the lifeblood of industrial firms. The identification of new product/service concepts and their development into tangible products or services involves substantial resource commitment and financial risk. Marketing researchers are assigned the responsibility of determining whether a need exists in the market and assessing the "diffusion rate" for the proposed new product. For instance, how quickly will companies adopt the new product, and to what extent will they replace the old? Industrial marketing research must assess the size of the new product's market when the new product exists only in prototype form.

## Competitor Analysis

Marketing planning relies heavily on knowledge of the strengths and weaknesses of competitors and their products. This task has become more complex because competition today often arises from unexpected sources. Marketing researchers often are called upon to investigate customer reactions to competitors' products and to identify effective substitutes. Alternatively, the opinions of the sales force or of distributors often are obtained to identify weaknesses in competitors' marketing programs. Furthermore, it is important that the marketer attempt to anticipate how competitors will respond to various moves a company might make.

## Determination of Sales Quotas and Territories

Vital to the management of the sales force or the coordination of middlemen is information that breaks down market potential and expected market share into geographic designations and, further, specifies the level of sales that can be expected under certain market conditions. Territories must be examined to design equitable workloads for salespeople, quotas must be established to communicate performance expectations, and actual sales levels must be compared with quotas and potential to evaluate performance.

As can be seen from the brief descriptions accompanying each of these responsibility areas, marketing managers—no matter who they are targeting—require a diverse mix of timely and accurate information to make intelligent decisions. Regardless of the type of information sought, however, a common set of tools, methods, and managerial frameworks are helpful when addressing a given research question. Market research should be approached as a step-by-step process.

# Marketing Research as a Process

Let us turn to the issue of how marketing research is conducted. To appreciate the inherent complexities involved and the many decisions that must be made along the way, it is vital that research be approached as a logical process that provides a means for deriving reliable and valid data. Figure 6.1 presents a series of interrelated steps in the process. Survey research, which is relied on extensively in

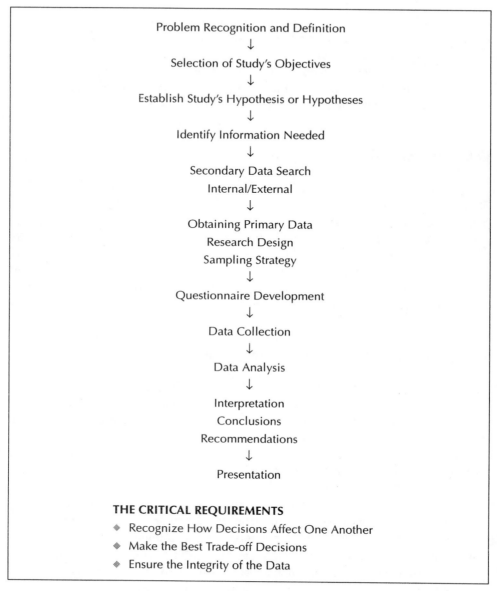

Problem Recognition and Definition
↓
Selection of Study's Objectives
↓
Establish Study's Hypothesis or Hypotheses
↓
Identify Information Needed
↓
Secondary Data Search
Internal/External
↓
Obtaining Primary Data
Research Design
Sampling Strategy
↓
Questionnaire Development
↓
Data Collection
↓
Data Analysis
↓
Interpretation
Conclusions
Recommendations
↓
Presentation

**THE CRITICAL REQUIREMENTS**

❖ Recognize How Decisions Affect One Another
❖ Make the Best Trade-off Decisions
❖ Ensure the Integrity of the Data

**Figure 6.1.** The Industrial Marketing Research Process

industrial marketing research, will be used to illustrate the issues that arise and the decisions that confront the researcher. To better appreciate the process, some important introductory comments may be helpful.

First, any research project is made up of a highly interdependent set of decisions. The decisions made at each step in the process depicted in Figure 6.1 depend on previous steps and have implications for subsequent steps. This point can be illustrated as follows. Assume that a major medical insurance provider such as Blue Cross-Blue

Shield[1] perceives a trend among its corporate accounts to drop their medical coverage and turn to self-insurance. Thus, medical insurance premiums are put into a company-controlled fund rather than paid to Blue Cross-Blue Shield or one of its competitors. To gain a better understanding of the gravity of this trend, marketing research could be applied in a number of ways. Let's examine two approaches and see how early decisions (e.g., how the problem is defined and the objectives are set for the study) affect subsequent decisions.

One approach would be to interview former customers to determine the sources of their dissatisfaction with the Blue Cross-Blue Shield corporate medical insurance plans. Research would concentrate on plan administration—claims processing, payment options, plan supplements, and specific coverage provisions. Telephone calls could be made to a few former key accounts in the search for some common themes regarding dissatisfaction. The sample size would be small, and the questions would be quite general to permit the respondents to elaborate on their frustrations and reason for dropping the coverage.

A different approach might involve determining whether the medical insurance industry as a whole was experiencing the same problem. In this instance, a much broader research plan would be implemented, with information collected from several different types of companies, in surveys of current customers as well as customers of competitors. Information would also be gathered on medical costs to acquire a feel for upward or downward trends in the prices of medical services providers. Consequently, the sample would be much larger, and the questions more precise, to facilitate tabulation and comparisons among various company types. With this alternative, the findings might determine an industrywide phenomenon rather than a company-specific shortcoming.

The second introductory point to be made is that the constraints of time, budget, and energy placed on the process force the marketer to make trade-offs between certain decisions. For example, the ideal survey would include information from every possible respondent—that is, a census. The time and monetary costs for a census, however, normally place it out of practical reach. Similarly, it is desirable to let respondents elaborate on their answers to the various questions, but practical limitations to data analysis often preclude this luxury and force the use of a standardized questionnaire. Personal interviews are frequently the most desirable form of data collection, but the necessities of travel and appointment setting sometimes make this method infeasible, leading the marketing researcher to use a mail questionnaire or telephone interview. In other words, more substantive information would be acquired from fewer respondents through personal interviews, and less elaborate information would be gained from more respondents in a telephone survey. Marketing survey designers often find that they must make similar trade-off decisions between the amount of information, the quality of the information, the sample size, the time horizon, analysis techniques, and other factors in such a way as to generate relevant information subject to reasonable and manageable error.

Finally, the marketing research function is responsible for ensuring the accuracy or integrity of the information. The two key concerns here are reliability and validity.

*Reliability* is the degree to which the measures used in the research (e.g., questions in a survey) generate similar results over time and across situations. A measure is unreliable if it does not produce consistent results across respondents and under differing circumstances. Unreliability may arise because some respondents are confused about the question, are ambivalent or uncertain about their answers, or unintentionally give different answers because of a lack of interest or motivation. Reliability, then, is a concern with random error.

By contrast, *validity* is a concern with whether the research measures what it purports to measure and thus is free of systematic error. Respondents may intentionally misrepresent their opinions, the sample may not be representative, interviewers may be biased in recording answers, data analyses may be inappropriate, or the interpretations of the results may be systematically erroneous. In addition, researchers may not measure what they intended to measure. Quesitons may be misunderstood by respondents or evoke answers that the researchers did not intend. Regardless of the origin of the validity or reliability problem, either one destroys the integrity of the findings. Marketers must constantly scrutinize their survey designs with an eye to both systematic and random error.

## Describing the Steps in the Process

To demonstrate in more detail what takes place in the steps or stages in the research process presented in Figure 6.1, it may help to go through each stage as it applies to a research project. Our example will use a firm attempting to make a market expansion decision.

### Problem Recognition and Definition

The problem definition stage involves specifying the managerial decision that has to be made. Assume that an environmental services company specializing in the disposal of industrial wastes sees an opportunity in the increasing scrutiny the government is giving local chemical and other plants regarding the disposal of their waste products. More stringent regulations are being instituted at all levels of government. Consequently, the waste disposal industry has grown rapidly in terms of total volume as well as the number of competitors. Normally, the environmental services company contracts with production facilities to carry away solid and liquid waste products that have been sealed in large metal drums. Occasionally, however, the client plants experience spillages, pipe ruptures, or containment tank failures that result in large pools of dangerous liquid waste that need to be cleaned up with special equipment. Consequently, the environmental services company is considering the purchase of one or more vacuum trucks that would clean up caustic liquids quickly and efficiently. The approximate cost of a single truck is $180,000. Would the market support the investment?

This example illustrates how the recognition and definition stage involves the sensing of changes in the environment (government regulation, competitive intensity, and market demand) and translating them into possible marketing actions to capitalize on opportunities or avoid threats. It also points out the uncertainty involved with solving the problem.

## Specify the Study Objectives

Research objectives are, quite simply, a statement of what the researcher wants to measure. They follow from the problem definition. In the example, the objectives included measuring (a) the incidence of liquid waste spillage in target market plants (i.e., behaviors), (b) whether prospective customers are inclined to attempt to clean the spill themselves or call in an outside service (i.e., their behavioral intentions), and (c) which industrial waste disposal companies they might call in (i.e., their preferences). Also, it was decided that the information should be gathered within 60 days so that any decision to purchase equipment could be funded in the budget for the next year.

This step should result in a crystallization of the problem into specific information needs and a time frame. Usually, the allowable budget is specified here as well. The interactive nature of the marketing research process can be seen in the example: If the time frame had been longer, activities such as intensive study of the competitors, in-depth interviews of several prospective customers, or more expensive steps might have been considered.

## Establish the Study Hypotheses

A hypothesis is a statement of what a study is expected to reveal. Studies should be designed in a manner that allows for hypotheses to be accepted or rejected, depending on the facts uncovered. The key hypothesis of this study was that firms in the target market that experienced liquid waste spillage would be inclined to call in outside specialists who were familiar with the regulatory factors and who could clean up and efficiently dispose of the liquid waste. In short, if the environmental services company bought the vacuum truck, demand within the target market would be sufficient to justify the investment. Based on general observations, management anticipated some level of demand for the truck, but the uncertainty concerned how much. Other, more specific hypotheses might be developed regarding the specific characteristics of companies that would most want such a service.

## Identify Information Needed

The information sought was specified as follows. For the incidence of spillage, it was necessary to determine the historical frequency and the amounts, as well as estimates of future spillage amounts. For internal versus external cleanup, it was important to determine what equipment prospective customer organizations owned or expected to purchase during the next few years to facilitate internal cleanup. For competitors, the perceived level of customer satisfaction with currently available toxic waste cleanup and transport services had to be determined. It is important that the information sought constituted a small and concise set. This example illustrates the effects of the three constraints (budget, time, and resources) placed on the research process. The research project director and the decision makers engaged in lengthy discussions to agree on the precise set of questions to address in the study.

## Secondary Data Search

Secondary data is information that has already been collected, such as that available in government reports, trade association studies, past marketing research studies, or internal company data files. Primary data, then, is new information generated by the marketing researcher to address a particular problem. In the case of the environmental services company, secondary sources were appraised to determine whether the required information already existed in some form or could be estimated from existing date. Although some general statistics were available on the incidence of spillage, no information could be found in the other two areas. Thus, primary data had to be collected.

## Develop the Research Design, Including the Sampling Strategy

With the information needs specified above and the operating constraints, it was determined that a cross-sectional survey involving personal interviews was the appropriate research design. Based on the company's familiarity with clients, it was concluded that approximately 60 chemical plants and other waste-producing facilities were located in the target area. Purchasing agents were defined to be the relevant contact point for each plant, because arrangements for the transport service companies generally were made through these agents. Because of the urgency of spill cleanup needs, the purchase decision process was often concentrated on one person, so it was assumed that the purchasing agent would have the primary decision-making responsibility. Interactions and trade-offs in the research process are illustrated well in this stage. The target sample was constrained to include companies familiar to the industrial waste disposal company. Similarly, only purchasing agents were to be interviewed despite the knowledge that other managers would have some input in the decision to use or not use the vacuum truck service.

## Determine the Method of Data Collection

Again, time and budget constraints posed problems for determining the best way to gather information from a sufficiently large and representative sample. Ultimately, a telephone survey was selected as the appropriate mode of data collection. Purchasing agents have busy schedules, and it might be difficult to schedule appointments for on-site interviews. In addition, the purchasing agents do a great deal of their business over the telephone and would be comfortable with this mode of questioning. Finally, the telephone interview approach was selected because a single interview might require several callbacks to find the purchasing agent in the office and with sufficient time to answer the questions without interruption. The vacuum truck service would have to be described verbally to the respondent—an important trade-off necessitated by using the telephone as the data collection method. Personal interviewers might have carried pictures (perhaps even videotapes) of the service. Supporting the decision to rely on a telephone approach was the belief that the respondents would be familiar with the nature of the service in question and could envision it sufficiently to guarantee the integrity of their reactions over the telephone.

## Develop the Questionnaire

A questionnaire was then developed. This took three iterations, with much consultation among various managers at the environmental services company. The relevant managers reviewed the questions for proper terminology and appropriate response categories, and the research project leader guarded against the use of leading questions and maintained proper disguise of the sponsor of the survey. This stage further illustrates an interaction between the steps in the survey and underlines the concern for integrity. Terminology that addressed technical issues but made sense to the respondents was inserted in certain questions to enhance respondents' understanding. Telephone interviewing limited the complexity and variety of response scales the interviewer could use for each question on the survey.

## Collect Data

A local telephone interview service was used to gather data. This service was selected because of the expertise of its professional interviewers, who had gained the reputation of being persistent yet polite in securing executive interviews. From the 60 targeted companies in the market area, a total of 49 completed interviews were collected in a 2-week period. The interviewers were instructed to contact the purchasing agent at the respondent plant, identify themselves as professional interviewers working on a marketing research project for an industrial waste company, and explain the general purposes of the survey. At no time during the survey was the client environmental services company identified to the purchasing agent. Similarly, agents were

## BUSINESS MARKETING CAPSULE

### *TeleFocus—An Alternative to Traditional Focus Groups in Industrial Markets*

Unlike their counterparts in consumer marketing, industrial market researchers often struggle to draw participants to focus groups.

It is relatively easy to set up sessions with consumers at local shopping malls, but because a typical focus group lasts 2 or more hours, business customers are reluctant to take the time to participate. In locales where customers or distributors compete with one another, they might decline invitations because they fear revealing competitive secrets.

To boost participation, some marketers have turned to TeleFocus groups, which involve conference calling participants in different locales. A call typically runs approximately an hour and a half. A moderator orchestrates the call while the client listens.

A typical group costs about $3,000. The costs vary, however, depending on the financial incentives for participants and the amount of prospect screening done by the client. The firm usually recruits participants from a list the client has provided.

TeleFocus eliminates the travel costs that occur when customers are geographically dispersed. Because they save travel expenses and time for a client's marketing executives, TeleFocus groups cost anywhere from one third to one fourth less than traditional focus groups.

Holding a focus group over the phone can also enhance group dynamics. For example, if a group consists of executives in a single locale who know each other, they may not speak freely. A perceived hierarchy or pecking order may cause some participants to refrain from commenting. Because TeleFocus participants do not meet in person and are spread out geographically, they are noticeably more candid.

TeleFocus is also an excellent way to test product concepts quickly and to identify user needs. For example, this technique has been used to gauge customer responses to published reports on new products.

TeleFocus is also used to get initial customer impressions about product concepts. In essence, it produces immediate reactions to products currently in development or still on the drawing boards.

Despite their inherent advantages, TeleFocus groups do not fit with every research project. Generally, they are not very effective when it is necessary to watch respondents interact with products. Correspondingly, TeleFocus groups are not effective when it is necessary for participants to view slides, videotapes, pictures, or other types of graphic materials. For some projects, though, it is possible to send ads or other print materials to participants for their review, either before or during group sessions.

On the whole, TeleFocus groups provide a cost-efficient and effective alternative to the traditional in-person focus group.

SOURCE: Adapted from "Advanced Research Finds a New Market," *Business Marketing*, 743 (March, 1989), p. 56, Eisenhart.

assured of confidentiality of their responses and anonymity with regard to their opinions. The interviewers were instructed to call back as many times as necessary to obtain a completed interview—or a refusal.

Employment of a professional interview service incurred expense, but the objectives of reliability and validity were paramount in this decision. The interviewers administered the questions identically among respondents. Moreover, they were trained to sense when the respondent was interrupted by important business, and to suspend the interview temporarily and to set an appointment to call back and complete it. Also justifying the additional cost were the benefits of a higher response rate, confidentiality assurances to encourage truthful responses, and overall professionalism.

## Analyze Data

The completed questionnaires were turned over to the marketing research department, and tabulation of the data was performed through a series of steps that involved transforming (coding) the raw responses into computer input, then scrutinizing the accuracy of this transformation, and then computing means, percentages, and other descriptive statistics to acquire a picture of the respondents' opinions. Further analysis was then performed to test the proposed hypotheses. Computer analysis was performed quickly and efficiently, and at a minimum cost, using a personal computer and an inexpensive statistical software package.

## Interpret Data and Present Results

Approximately half of the respondents indicated a present or possible future need for a wet materials cleanup and transport service. From these, the most commonly estimated volume was in the 100-barrel-per-month range. The results further indicated that the company was the most preferred waste transport service among 30% of the companies surveyed, and it was mentioned as the second choice by an additional 25% of the respondent companies. Thus, the environmental services company could anticipate being the first choice of approximately 15% of the companies in this market and that about 12% would select it as their second choice. Further analysis revealed that the respondents indicated a high level of general satisfaction with their current supplier of industrial waste transport service but were least satisfied with their suppliers' rates and personnel. The purchasing agents indicated that they would evaluate suppliers based on the following set of priorities: competitive rates, technical expertise, dependable and reliable service, and the ability to meet legal requirements.

This information was then used in a comparison of potential revenues against the total cost of purchasing and operating a vacuum truck in the target market area. Comparisons of the estimated revenues under various scenarios (best case, worst case, most likely case) revealed that the environmental services company would at least break even on the venture in the worst case and could realize a return of investment of more than 20% in the best case. Given these findings, the decision was made to purchase a truck and begin marketing the company's new service. In the marketing program, the environmental services company set prices at or just below the rates of its competitors. Communication programs stressed the technical expertise of the company's personnel as well as the company's long history of successful industrial waste disposal in compliance with legal restraints.

This description of an industrial marketing survey demonstrates the several steps and safeguards that should be followed to derive valid information on the industrial marketplace from primary data sources. Keep in mind that, throughout the research process, the overriding objective is to acquire the most accurate information possible within the established budget and time constraints.

## Industrial Marketing Research Is Different

Conducting marketing research in industrial markets poses its own distinct challenges. Consider the types of research conducted by industrial versus consumer marketers. All firms, regardless of market orientation, must do research to support basic marketing mix decisions. Consequently, forecasts and other special-purpose studies devoted to sensing opportunities in the marketplace, as well as assessments of the company performance, are relied on by both types of companies. New product acceptance research is also very prevalent in both markets. Major differences in the types of studies conducted are attributable to differences in the strategic importance of certain marketing variables. Thus, whereas consumer firms in general do more market research than industrial firms, they are especially more likely to pursue advertising research, test markets, customer panels, and research activities that tap the consumer psyche and lifestyle. For their part, industrial firms allocate more effort than consumer firms to ongoing testing of existing products and to research on packaging design.

The first chapter of this book noted three critical distinguishing characteristics of industrial markets. These considerations help to explain the ways in which marketing research is different. The first of the three is the technical nature of many products. In the industrial market, there is substantial need for an understanding of production technology, service support, and the special technical background of prospective buyers. For example, a chemicals company might be interested in learning why sales for an industrial catalytic agent have declined. Proper research requires an understanding of the chemical compounds involved and the conditions, such as temperature, pressure, and time of the chemical reactions where the catalyst is used. It would necessitate an understanding of the degree of volatility of chemicals and the by-products of chemical reactions. Transportation and storage aspects would need to be studied. Conditions of supply and demand for raw material ingredients would be examined along with the buying process for the catalyst. In short, several fairly technical factors would be studied by the marketing researcher to ensure that the survey was custom-tailored to the problem.

The second point of difference between industrial goods and consumer goods is that industrial products directly affect the operations and economic health of buyers/users. For example, a cleaning service company may not realize that its clients value scrupulously clean customer-contact areas as an important component of company image. Research might reveal that clients would pay a little more for meticulous cleaning of these areas. In other words, clients would see the cleaning service as an investment in image enhancement, not as a low-bid commodity purchase. Another example might involve a financial institution that buys an automated teller machine network. If the machines are unfriendly, too slow, or subject to downtime, the banks' customers may think about changing to a more responsive system at another bank. For example, research done for Diebold Corporation,[2] which manufactures ATMs, must take into consideration not only the banks but also the users of the ATM.

The third, and most important, difference is that the customer is an organization consisting or people trying to do their jobs. That is, the unit of analysis becomes the organization, not the individual. Because more people get involved in the buying process in organizations, and because they have diverse perspectives, the researcher often must survey multiple individuals to capture the organization accurately. The complexities of the buying process often make it difficult to be sure feedback has been obtained from the correct people. Two key individuals in the buying organization might have diametrically opposed views on the same research question.

The implications of these differences can be seen by reexamining the stages of the research process (see Table 6.1). For example, instead of markets with hundreds of thousands (or more) consumers, industrial markets tend to be characterized by hundreds (or fewer) of target companies. Often, extensive secondary data exist on these companies. Personal interviews with managers often must be performed, as opposed to random household telephone surveys or large mailings of questionnaires. Subjects are people at work who may be inaccessible or may not have time to participate in elaborate research projects. As a result, samples may be biased in favor of the opinions of purchasing agents, who are more frequent participants. The seriousness of the sampling problem has produced some creative methods of data collection (see the Business Marketing Capsule on page 166).

Furthermore, when collecting information from two or three respondents in a single target company, their input may have to be weighted in some fashion to reflect the different level of influence each respondent has in the buying decision process.

**TABLE 6.1** How Aspects of the Survey Process Can Differ in Consumer Versus Industrial Marketing Research

| Marketing Research Decision Area | Consumer Research | Industrial Research |
|---|---|---|
| Universe/population | Large—often numbers in the millions | Small—limited often to a few hundred |
| Respondent accessibility | Fairly easy—interviews at home, by mail, or by phone | Difficult—people are at work and are busy |
| Respondent cooperation | Becoming more difficult, but plenty to select from | Of major concern—will resist unless they see direct value |
| Sample size | Can be as large as is required | Usually very small |
| Respondent definitions | Fairly simple—users are usually purchasers | More difficult—purchasers not always users, others involved, often technically oriented |
| Unit of analysis | The individual or household | The organization |
| Interviewers | Fairly easily trained—they are consumers themselves | Difficult to train; must have expertise; the sales force can sometimes be used |
| Study costs | Key determinants are sample and incidence of target group members in the population | Critical elements are time and study complexity (e.g., multiple respondents per firm) |

Interviewers must be trained in the technical terminology and the proper approach to conducting personal interviews, often with managers from different backgrounds. The sales force is sometimes used to collect data in industrial marketing research projects and may require training. Furthermore, even though sample sizes tend to be smaller in industrial research, surveys may take a longer time to complete and cost more in total. Finally, small sample sizes and sizable differences among organizations place severe limitations on the ability to perform statistical analysis as well as on the generalizability of study results to other organizations.

Industrial and consumer marketing research are different because the sources of information and the techniques applied to tap those sources vary considerably. The types of research also differ because of variances in the strategic importance of marketing variables and because the underlying dynamics of industrial markets are driven by factors different from those driving consumer markets. Both types are identical, however, in their roles of providing accurate information to help reduce the uncertainty in the marketing manager's daily decision deliberations. Although industrial marketers historically performed less research than consumer goods marketers, this is changing. Furthermore, some industrial firms are finding ways to utilize research tools that have proven effective in consumer markets (see Table 6.2).

---

**TABLE 6.2**   Use of Consumer Goods Research Tools by Industrial Marketers

---

As business-to-business marketers become more market driven, they not only are spending more on marketing research but also are increasingly adopting the proven tools and techniques of consumer goods marketers. Some patterns include the following.

◆ Although industrial marketing research is generally less sophisticated than that found in consumer goods marketing, it is becoming more sophisticated.

◆ Industrial companies are more likely to use consumer product research tools if they operate in consumer product–like markets. Examples of such markets include computer software, telecommunications, office automation equipment, and financial services. These firms are also more likely to have in-house research units.

◆ Firms that sell to a few large customers in narrowly defined markets are more likely to rely on their sales forces for market intelligence.

◆ Industrial marketers tend to rely more on qualitative data than do consumer goods marketers. Leading qualitative tools are focus groups and one-on-one interviews.

◆ Intercept interviews at trade shows have grown in popularity in recent years.

◆ Trade-off or conjoint analysis, a consumer goods research tool that indicates how much customers would give up one product attribute to get another, has achieved widespread usage by industrial marketers.

---

SOURCE: Adapted from "Advanced Research Finds a New Market," *Business Marketing*, 743 (March, 1989), Eisenhart. © Copyright 1989 by *Business Marketing*.

## From Marketing Research to Marketing Intelligence

Up to this point in our discussion, research has been considered as an isolated activity undertaken to address a specific managerial problem. Unfortunately, managers often feel that an occasional marketing research project is sufficient to take care of the firm's total marketing information needs. A more strategic perspective requires that firms move toward a more comprehensive concept of marketing intelligence, of which marketing research is one part. For purposes of comparison, consider research to be a single activity in the marketing decision-making process, with marketing intelligence operating throughout the decision-making process. Figure 6.2 illustrates steps in marketing decision making together with two quite different views of the role of information gathering.

As Figure 6.2 demonstrates, the narrow view relegates marketing research to a periodic data-gathering and analysis role. For instance, if a company is considering a change in its customer service policies, the alternatives might be to (a) increase the amount of service, (b) decrease the amount of service, or (c) maintain service at its current level. If a primary objective of the company is to maintain customer loyalty, a marketing research study would be undertaken to determine the impact of each of

| Steps in the Marketing Decision Process | The Narrow View: Research as a One-Shot Activity | The Full View: Intelligence as an Ongoing Activity |
|---|---|---|
| → Recognition of problems and opportunities/ problem definition | — | External environmental monitoring<br>Assessment of internal performance measures |
| ↓ | | |
| Selection of problems to solve | — | Impact analysis |
| ↓ | | |
| Generation of alternatives | — | Feasibility studies |
| ↓ | | |
| Data gathering | Data gathering | Data gathering |
| ↓ | | |
| Evaluation and choice of course of action | Analysis and interpretation of data to address a specific problem | Profitability analysis<br>Payoff analysis<br>Acceptance analysis |
| ↓ | | |
| Implementation | — | — |
| ↓ | | |
| Control | — | Performance studies |
| ↓ | | |
| └→ Evaluation | — | Comparative studies<br>Marketing audits |

**Figure 6.2.** Research Versus Intelligence

those alternatives on customer propensity to shift to other suppliers. If the information acquired revealed that increased service levels would increase the loyalty factor, and furthermore that the increased service level would be cost justifiable, the decision would favor that alternative.

Industrial marketing intelligence, alternatively, is an enlightened view of the role of information-collection activities in the management process. Using the same managerial issue, data for service levels, costs, and customer satisfaction might be tracked routinely from month to month. The firm is able to determine quickly the ratio of costs to service levels and the ratio of costs to customer satisfaction levels. Investments in service levels can then be adjusted periodically. A much better feel is obtained for how these variables interact over time. Furthermore, because intelligence is gathered on an ongoing basis, the firm can regularly monitor the customer service efforts of competitors and changes in the buying behaviors of customers. In this manner, new customer service opportunities can be identified.

*Intelligence* is a term with roots in the military. The role of intelligence activities in a military context is to provide a continuous flow of information for use in developing strategies and tactics—both for winning the war and for keeping the peace. These activities can be defensive or offensive in nature, focusing on information relevant for maintaining current position or for making inroads into an adversary's position. A wide variety of informational inputs is collected, covering everything from identifying strengths and weaknesses of the opposition to uncovering untapped strategic opportunities. The information must be updated constantly, with regular reports provided to the senior military staff.

The parallels to a firm's marketing information needs are unmistakable. Marketers require the same continuous flow of information. Although some of this data can be obtained with periodic marketing research studies, a more systematic and ongoing information gathering process is needed.

A *marketing intelligence system* (MIS) can be defined as an interrelated set of specialists, procedures, hardware, and software that accumulates, stores, interprets, and disseminates (usually in report form) raw data on the external and internal marketing environments. Its purpose is to provide relevant, accurate, and otherwise valuable information to marketing decision makers on a timely and ongoing basis.

As indicated in Figure 6.2, the marketing intelligence system serves as a partner to the industrial marketing manager. The MIS provides information that helps the manager recognize problems and opportunities. It monitors the environment and provides information on shifts in the economy, changes in the regulatory system, competitors' actions and policy changes, technological breakthroughs, the emergence of new market segments, and more. At the same time, the MIS maintains constant vigilance on critical internal performance measures such as sales, market share, quota attainment, distributor accounts retained, stock levels, or service visits.

The industrial marketing manager is also concerned with generating alternative courses of action for capitalizing on opportunities or solving problems. Here, the MIS can perform feasibility studies that assess the appropriateness, cost, and viability of each alternative. The evaluation and selection of a course of action is assisted through profitability analysis, payoff analysis, and other studies that help to evaluate the attractiveness of various alternatives. Once the course of action is selected, the implementation stage takes place. This stage is the only one where the MIS has no active role, because it is a support function. Once implementation is effected, however, the MIS monitors performance measures used to gauge whether the course of action selected is generating sufficient sales or market share. Finally, overall evaluation of the decision-making process is assisted through the MIS through such tools as periodic marketing audits.

## Steps in Establishing and Operating an MIS

A marketing intelligence system must be planned and tailored to the unique information needs of the particular industrial marketing firm. The steps involved in de-

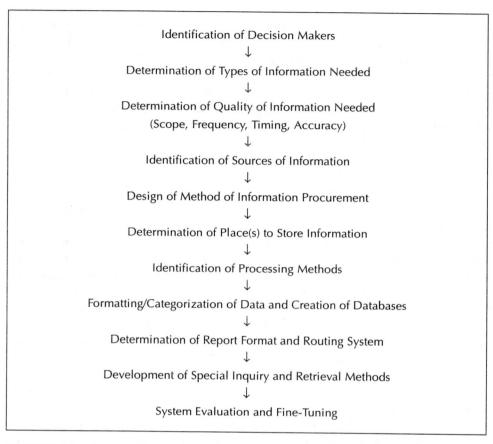

**FIGURE 6.3.** Steps in the Design and Refinement of a Marketing Intelligence System

veloping and fine-tuning an MIS are illustrated in Figure 6.3. We start by identifying the marketing decision makers in the company. Product managers, sales managers, advertising managers, strategic planners—in fact, all members of the organization who have marketing decision responsibilities—are identified. Next, the information needs of these individuals are specified with special concern for the quality, scope, frequency, and timing of information required for them to operate effectively and efficiently. Then, the available sources of information must be determined, and methods of obtaining the information from these sources must be identified and/or designed. The storage place(s) for information that flows into the company must be identified and maintained. The raw data inputs must be translated or grouped into categories that are meaningful in marketing analysis, such as expenses that are described as *variable* or *fixed*, or as *direct* or *indirect*. Methods of reporting information to executives must be established, and the format and routing system designed. Special-purpose access and retrieval methods must be provided. Finally, the marketing intelligence system itself is evaluated and fine-tuned.

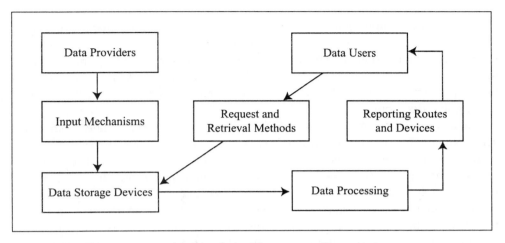

**Figure 6.4.** Components of a Simple Marketing Intelligence System

The actual component parts in a marketing intelligence system can be seen in Figure 6.4. The heart of an MIS is a centralized database—raw information that has been gathered, processed, recorded, and summarized. The database is usually organized into separate files, such as a customer file, a competitor file, a territory file, a product performance file, and a marketing activity file. Dedicated files can be set up for each marketing research project undertaken. The design of the database constitutes the basic structure of the MIS, which can range from very crude to elegant. Data in these areas, and others, is gathered from internal (e.g., the sales force, accounting records) and external (e.g., government publications, competitor catalogs) sources. These sources are labeled *data providers* in Figure 6.4.

The raw information is edited into usable form, then entered into a storage device—at the simplest level, manual files kept in a cabinet. A sophisticated system might involve a comprehensive database on a central computer network that can be accessed from a series of remote terminals. Between these two is the storage of data on disks for use on a personal computer, or on the computer's hard drive. The method used to input the data will vary depending on the amount and complexity of the information as well as the type of storage device. The input mechanism could range from a member of the marketing department simply keying in data, to the marketing analyst downloading data files stored in the company's central computer or data warehouse. The input process is continual because files are updated constantly.

Once in place, the MIS can be accessed to provide assistance in marketing analysis and planning. Basically, data users generate an information request. The desired information is then retrieved from the storage device, often simply by calling up a file on the computer terminal and having it printed out. Before retrieving the data, however, it may first be necessary to perform some manipulations or tabulations on the stored data. This is the *data processing* component. Tabulations may involve constructing averages or dividing one column of numbers by another.

The standard output of an MIS is a set of reports that are generated for management at periodic intervals. These might include a weekly sales activity report, a monthly report on profitability by product line, a competitor activity report, or a quarterly advertising effectiveness report. The MIS exists to satisfy both irregular information requests when particular problems or issues arise and regular information needs for ongoing decisions.

Take, for instance, the MIS that operates inside Alto Business Machines Company. This company manufactures and sells business machines such as duplicating equipment, copy machines, and dictaphones to a wide variety of companies. The decision makers who have constant needs for marketing intelligence information are the president, the vice-president of marketing, and the sales manager. Obviously, there are similarities and differences in the information needs of these managers. The sales manager requires specific breakdowns on salespeople, territories, and products. The marketing vice president is more concerned with market share statistics, competitors' strategies, and the performance of product lines. The president tends to look at the long term and identify areas of economic, political, and technological opportunity and threat.

Over time, the MIS at Alto has evolved to become an integral part of the daily operations of the company. Both formal and informal company policies support its use. Salespeople are required to submit monthly reports that detail their activities: calls, expenses, sales invoices, account prospects, and observations of market conditions. Service representatives submit reports of service calls, types of problems solved, and ages and configurations of machines repaired. Trade association reports, business periodicals, and financial analysts' observations are scrutinized. Periodic telephone calls are made to major customers to gain insight into their expected business activity changes and intentions to purchase equipment. Analysts abstract business trends and population shifts, execute market share studies, collect literature from competitors, and attend trade shows to research new products and technology.

All this data is systematized into reports, which are issued at regular intervals and in the form required by the manager involved. For instance, the sales manager is given trend line analysis of individual salesperson performance, along with comparisons with past performance. The sales manager also produces sales activity reports for the sales force that help salespeople to better manage their own territories. The marketing vice president receives a summary of product line sales and profit performance with detailed breakdowns included. In addition, a newsletter is issued to highlight national trends, competitors' product introductions, and other observations of the industry. The system will also satisfy occasional data requests, such as an inquiry from the marketing vice president regarding the number of new accounts generated during the past 6 months, compared with the preceding 6-month period.

## From Intelligence to Decision Support

Although an MIS provides a systematic approach for collecting, storing, and disseminating marketing information, its end product is primarily reports. In practice, the MIS is designed and used for routine marketing decisions. As marketing managers develop their skills and knowledge base, and as marketing decisions grow in complexity, information needs exceed the capabilities of an MIS. It becomes appropriate, then, to move to a decision support system (DSS), which is the logical extension of an MIS. Again, just as periodic marketing research was part of the MIS, the MIS is part of a DSS.

An MIS is used in a regular, planned, and anticipated manner, often to generate standardized reports, but a DSS is concerned with unstructured problem solving and decision making. In other words, where an MIS is designed to complement the step-by-step nature of the formal decision-making process, a DSS is designed for the manager who breaks out of the routine and casts imagination and personal creativity into the formula. Thus, the DSS is broader in content and capable of accommodating "what if?" types of inquiries. It must have the flexibility to respond to unusual requests as well as provide the structure for the routine inquiries and reports relied on by the bulk of the company's managers.

Users of an MIS are concerned primarily with retrieval questions. They want a system that is capable of quickly retrieving a piece of information, such as quarterly revenue in territory A or average gross margin on sales of product X. But the manager who asks questions that require various types of analysis (often nonroutine) on stored data may be better served with a DSS. Such nonroutine questions might include "How much did the competition's 10% price cut affect our sales of product X?" or "How much will the replacement of distributors with our own direct sales force affect profitability?"

A decision support system comprises data, statistics, models, and optimization, as illustrated in Figure 6.5. The *database* is similar to that provided through the MIS. *Statistics* are simple tools for manipulating the data. A number of complex multivariate statistical tools exist, but managers more often are concerned with simple correlations and basic ratios, frequency distributions, and descriptive statistics such as averages, ranges, and standard deviations. *Models* are attempts to examine relationships between or among variables; they could be based on the marketer's own hypotheses regarding how these variables are related. For example, models might be developed concerning the relationship between price charged and product sales (i.e., elasticity) or between advertising expenditures and the cost of a sales call. *Optimization* refers to the development of a set of decision rules for determining the best alternative from a set of alternatives. The DSS may, for example, rank-order sales territories based on the total contribution as a percentage of sales. Linear programming models might be used to determine the optimal level of sales support required.

Decision support systems are playing a growing role in marketing decision making, especially on the creative side of marketing strategy formulation. Some of the driving forces include the greater accountability that is being demanded of marketing functions, the increased focus by companies on total quality management via cross-functional teams that include marketing, the growing involvement of marketing in new product development activities, the increasing use of electronic data interchange (see Chapter 2), efforts to achieve greater coordination in the supply chain, and attempts to establish strategic alliances with customers.

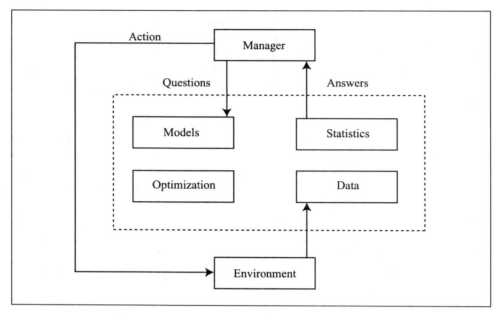

**Figure 6.5.** Elements of a Decision Support System

SOURCE: Reprinted with permission from *Journal of Marketing*, published by the American Marketing Association, J.D.C. Little, "Decision Support Systems for Marketing Managers," *Journal of Marketing*, 43 (Summer, 1979), p. 10.

Development of DSS capability in industrial firms is being aided by the growing availability of syndicated market databases and the availability of more sophisticated modeling tools. Although it is difficult to quantify the returns from investing in a DSS, firms are finding that they are able to consider a greater number of decision alternatives, generate solutions more quickly, improve the sophistication of their marketing analysis, and reduce costs by enabling management to allocate resources to products and markets more efficiently.

## The Use of Secondary Data Sources in Industrial Marketing Intelligence

Marketing intelligence, when organized around an MIS or a DSS, provides a living information system that greatly facilitates marketing decision making. If designed, implemented, and maintained properly, the intelligence system can become a significant competitive advantage for the company itself. Other companies might not have knowledge of marketplace events and trends that is as current. They may lack detailed profiles of the history of the marketplace and the performance of competitors under various marketplace conditions. In short, these systems serve to reduce the uncertainty level of marketing managers as they wrestle with marketing decisions.

A well-designed intelligence system is likely to rely heavily on secondary data sources. Industrial marketing situations are especially amenable to the use of secondary data because of its availability and the earlier-mentioned problems in collecting primary data. Normally, for example, it is possible to quickly identify a number of government reports, industry association studies, articles in trade magazines, or company publications that might provide timely information in a variety of decision-making situations. Typically, secondary data sources are divided into two basic types: internal and external.

## Internal Secondary Data Sources

Managers are often surprised to learn how many marketing insights can be obtained from data that already exist within the company—information the company collects and maintains as a normal part of its operations. For instance, sales records, salespeople's reports, annual reports, technical analyses, notes and memos from product evaluation teams, past marketing research reports, financial records—all the documentation maintained in the company's files—constitute the internal secondary information pool. Because the data are in raw form, difficulty arises in finding specific pieces of information. They are invariably mixed in among a wide array of other data. The value of a good marketing intelligence system is readily apparent in this case. If the MIS can accommodate inquiries and conduct searches of key words or other identifiers, the retrieval process will be much faster and more complete.

## External Secondary Data Sources

Data sources that are considered external are those that originate outside the company. The list of possible sources is almost limitless. Some examples in the United States include the following.

- *General business indices.* These cross-reference articles on various business topics. These include the *Business Periodicals Index, ABI-Inform, Public Affairs Information Service Bulletin, Social Sciences Citation Index*, and *The Wall Street Journal Index*.

- *Government sources.* The U. S. government publishes a number of census[3] and other documents that which are used extensively by industrial marketing researchers. Examples include the *Census of Business, Census of Manufactures, Census of Retail Trade*, and *Census of Wholesale Trade*. In addition, the U.S. government publishes a number of general information secondary sources, including the *County and City Data Book, Statistical Abstract of the United States*, and *Congressional District Data Book*. Finally, the various departments in the U.S. government publish their own business data sources, such as the *Business Conditions Digest, County Business Patterns, Economic Indicators, Economic Report of the President, Federal Reserve Bulletin, Handbook of*

*Basic Economic Statistics, Monthly Labor Review, Survey of Current Business, U.S. Industrial Outlook,* and *U.S. Occupational Outlook.*

◆ *Commercial sources.* Numerous publications are distributed by members of the private sector. Examples include the *Annual Survey of U.S. Business Plans for New Plants and Equipment, Predicasts, InfoAccess, Market Guide, Sales and Marketing Management's* annual surveys, *Standard Corporation Descriptions,* the *Survey of Buying Power,* and the *Thomas Register of American Manufacturers.*

There are also literally thousands of on-line databases that the marketer can access, and the list is rapidly growing. Many of these are of high quality, and a number are quite specialized. On-line databases allow the marketer to perform rapid searches to identify the available information in virtually any area. For instance, these searches can produce bibliographies on specific business topics (e.g., current uses of robotics in industry, techniques for evaluating trade show effectiveness, or uses of discounts when setting industrial prices). They can also provide actual data on employment or shipments in a particular industry, financial information on specific companies, or current economic statistics. To use these services, the marketer may need to pay an hourly computer access charge for the amount of connect time required to complete the information search. Some of the major database producers and distributors are Dow Jones News Retrieval (Dow Jones Inc.[4]), The Source (*Reader's Digest*[5]), Disclosure II (Disclosure, Inc.[6]), Predicasts PROMPT (Predicasts, Inc.), LEXIS/NEXIS[7] (Mead Data Central), FIND/SVP[8] (FIND/SVP Co.), ORBIT (Questel Orbit[9]), and DIALOG[10] (Information Services Division, Lockheed Corp.).

## Secondary Data, the SIC System, and the NAICS System

The ability of industrial firms to conduct marketing research and gather intelligence has been greatly enhanced by the development of the Standard Industrial Classification (SIC) system, which was recently superseded by the North American Industry Classification System or NAICS (pronounced "nakes"). Let's first consider the SIC system, because it provides the foundation and many data sources are still in this format. SIC codes are numbers, consisting of up to seven digits, that represent different types of economic activity. Establishments are assigned to an SIC code based on the major type of economic activity in which they are involved. Note that because one company might operate a number of different establishments, it would receive a code number for each of its establishments based on the primary product produced at the location. The primary product is defined as the one with which the largest amount of company activity is associated. This is based on either the amount of value being added to the end product, total sales of the item, or shipments of the item.

The numbering system is hierarchical in nature: The more digits included in a particular SIC code, the more descriptive that code becomes. Each of the digits has a

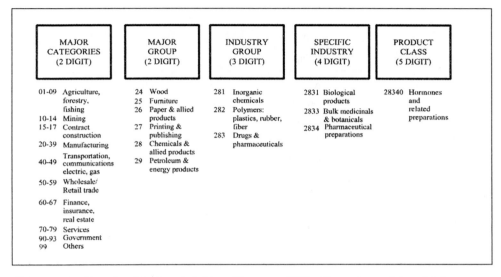

**Figure 6.6.** Standard Industrial Classification (SIC): Overview of the Digit System

meaning. In a given seven-digit code, the first two digits refer to the *major category* of economic activity. There are 10 major categories, as illustrated in column 1 of Figure 6.6. For example, all manufacturing activity falls between SIC 20 and SIC 39. Each category is made up of major groups, so SIC 20, 21, 22, 23, and 24 are *major groups* within the manufacturing area. SIC 28 is the major group that consists of companies that make chemicals and allied products (see the second column of Figure 6.6).

If a third digit is added, the code refers to a *group*. SIC 283, for example, is the group representing companies that make drugs and pharmaceuticals (see column 3 of Figure 6.6). With the addition of a fourth digit, the code now represents a *specific industry*. Many of the available secondary data are organized by four-digit SIC code. Using our example, SIC 2834 includes those establishments involved in pharmaceuticals (see column 4). The inclusion of a fifth digit allows for *product classes*, and the sixth and seventh digits represent *specific products* (see columns 5, 6, and 7).

Using SIC data, the marketer confronted with a research question regarding the nature and size of the opportunities in a particular market can find a wealth of information regarding the number, location, size of shipments, number of employees, geographic concentration, and number of large establishments. Sources of this information include the *Census of Manufactures*, the *U.S. Industrial Outlook*, and the *Survey of Current Business*, among many others. With these data, the marketer can begin to estimate market potential and to make targeting decisions. Marketing programs can be developed, and resources allocated, based on the needs and potential of this market.

For the all the value produced by the SIC code system, rapid changes in the global economy have resulted in growing criticism. A principal problem is the overemphasis on manufacturing and the underrepresentation of many new service industries. In

**TABLE 6.3** Major Sectors in the NAICS System

| Two-Digit Sector Code | Sector |
| --- | --- |
| 11 | Agriculture, forestry, fishing, and hunting |
| 21 | Mining |
| 22 | Utilities |
| 23 | Construction |
| 31-33 | Manufacturing |
| 42 | Wholesale trade |
| 44-45 | Retail trade |
| 48-49 | Transportation and warehousing |
| 51 | Information |
| 52 | Finance and insurance |
| 53 | Real estate and rental and leasing |
| 54 | Professional, scientific, and technical services |
| 55 | Management of companies and enterprises |
| 56 | Administrative and support, waste management and remediation services |
| 61 | Educational services |
| 62 | Health care and social assistance |
| 71 | Arts, entertainment, and recreation |
| 72 | Accommodation and food services |
| 81 | Other services |
| 92 | Public administration |

1997, the U.S. government announced the introduction of a flexible new industry classification system called the North American Industry Classification System, or NAICS. As NAICS replaces the SIC system, it will facilitate more informed economic and trade policies and permit better decision making by business users. NAICS is jointly compiled by the Economic Classification Policy Committee of the U.S. Office of Management and Budget, Statistics Canada, and Mexico's Instituto Nacional de Estadistica, Geografia e Informacion. The new system will provide common industry definitions that cover the economies of the three NAFTA partners, allowing reports done by the Mexican, Canadian, and U.S. governments to share a common code language for easier comparisons of international trade, industrial production, labor costs, and other statistics.

The characteristic that most distinguishes the NAICS system from SIC codes is that NAICS focuses on processes rather than products. NAICS, therefore, contains new industry sectors, such as "information," which include publishing industries, software and data publishing, broadcasting, and other businesses that produce information.

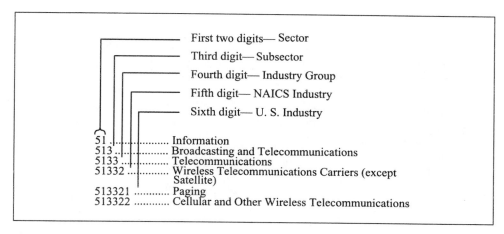

**Figure 6.7.** The Structure of the NAICS System

Erected on a production-oriented conceptual framework, the NAICS configures the entire field of economic activities to 20 sectors, as compared to 10 divisions in the old SIC system. Also included are 359 new industries that mirror businesses in the modern economy.

The structure of NAICS is hierarchical, much like that of the SIC code. The first two digits of the structure designate the NAICS sectors, representing general categories of economic activity. The NAICS sectors and their two-digit codes are shown in Table 6.3.

The NAICS uses a six-digit coding system to identify particular industries and their placement in this hierarchical structure of the classification system. Figure 6.7 provides an example of how the NAICS system represents a particular industry by a number code. A zero as the sixth digit generally indicates that the NAICS industry and the U.S. industry are the same.

The transition from SIC to NAICS involves a major change in the way that industrial statistics will be categorized and reported in years to come. Some of these changes totally redefine industries. For example, the SIC code for "eating places" is 5812, with no distinction between caterers, restaurants, hamburger stands, and tea rooms. The NAICS system will break the food services into well-defined categories to help researchers (see Figure 6.8). Furthermore, the NAICS system is scheduled to be revised every 5 years by the three nations to keep pace with changing business conditions, emerging businesses, and information needs.

# Problems With Secondary Data

External secondary data pose a basic dilemma for the marketer: Although these secondary data are readily available, are extensive, and often contain information

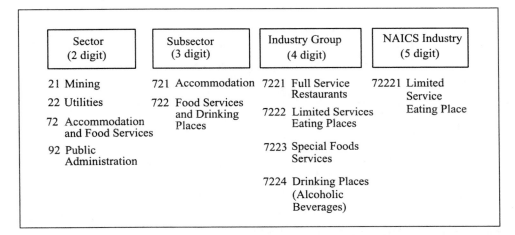

**Figure 6.8.** A Look at Eating Establishments Using the NAICS System

in encapsulated form, they must always be scrutinized for applicability and accuracy. Figure 6.9 illustrates the series of steps a manager should follow in assessing the usefulness of secondary data sources. Two levels of scrutiny are needed. First, the fundamental purpose of the secondary data is inspected to determine whether it varies from the basic objectives of the problem under consideration. For instance, there may be a mismatch in the comparison of populations under study, timeliness of the data, or units and classifications used in measurement.

If there is a consistent fit between the secondary data objectives and the problem being investigated, the second level of analysis focuses on problems in the accuracy of the data reported in the secondary data source. For example, the original sources of information may have been misquoted or misrepresented. It is possible that the methods of data collection or reporting have distorted the information as it was reported, or reservations regarding the accuracy of the data may be sufficiently strong to disallow its use, regardless of how inexpensive the secondary data is.

The detailed process for scrutinizing secondary data is another example of the balancing act between the value of information and its inherent error. Because the data were collected by a third party for a purpose other than the current research project, steps must be taken to ensure that the information fits the circumstances. If the fit is poor, the error factor will outweigh the accessibility and low cost of the data.

## Trends in Industrial Marketing Research

What lies in the future for industrial marketing research and marketing intelligence systems? With respect to information management capabilities, the most profound change in corporate marketing departments is the move to computer-driven operations. With every passing day, personal and other workstation computers penetrate

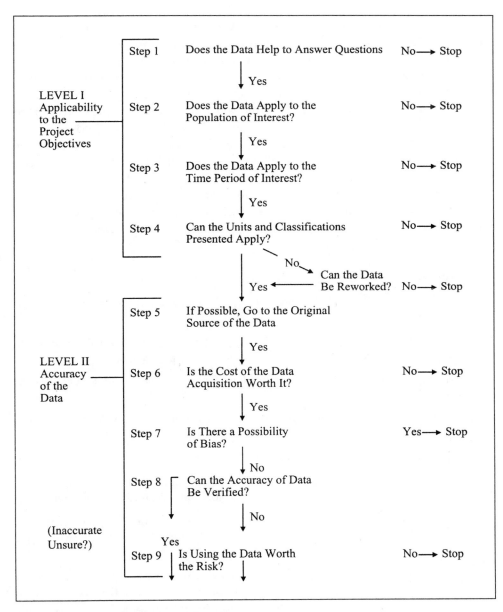

**Figure 6.9.** Evaluating Secondary Data

deeper into marketing analysis and decision making. Because these computers are the hardware of decision support systems, increasingly more marketing management decisions are made with more and better information than ever before. Software packages and internally programmed data analysis packages are well along in terms of adoption by industrial marketing firms.

The availability of information is being revolutionized by the Internet. Any topic can be searched quickly, with a wide array of facts, figures, and sources identifiable through search engines. Similarly, more and better Internet-based and dial-up databases are appearing every year, offering a wide array of information in various forms. Many of these databases are becoming very specialized in terms of SIC/NAICS codes.

Finally, the training and mind-sets of industrial marketing managers have shifted to computer-maintained and computer-manipulated data as well as information inquiries and retrieval. Given these developments, one can only expect that marketing research, and especially marketing intelligence systems, will become integral to marketing decision making in the coming years.

Continuing developments in research tools and methods hold promise for the conduct of industrial marketing research. Some of the developments are in areas where breakthroughs in industrial marketing research can have a significant effect on marketing strategy. Examples include

- Availability of extremely powerful yet easy-to-use statistical packages for use on PCs
- Continued development of sophisticated yet economical-to-apply models and measures of market potential
- Development of comprehensive methodologies for surveys of those in the buying center, such as sociograms, key informant studies, or Delphi techniques
- Development of simulation-based procedures for allocating expenses to segments and territories
- Development of commonly agreed-on performance measures for marketing investment and productivity
- Application of special-purpose measuring devices and analysis to study customers' preferences
- Continued studies of product portfolio strategy for product/market strategy formulation
- Industrywide and interindustry studies of the sales, cost, and profit impact of marketing strategy, market and industry structure, and product and product life-cycle characteristics
- Systematic research into organizational buying behavior with special emphasis on (a) coping with and anticipating environmental discontinuities, (b) research on the buying decision center, (c) information processing of organizational buyers, and (d) the buyer-seller interface
- Developments in market segment identification and assessment

In sum, the area of industrial marketing intelligence will fill a bigger role in the planning and implementation of industrial marketing strategy than in past years. Although the acceptance level among managers of the importance of marketing research and intelligence activities has risen considerably, the years to come will witness rapidly growing expectations of what these activities ought to be contributing. Managers not only will grow in their dependency on marketing intelligence but also will demand more sophistication in the timeliness, modeling capability, analytical power, flexibility, creativity, and comprehensiveness of both the people and the support systems involved in marketing research and intelligence.

# Summary

This chapter has emphasized the need for *quality* information when making marketing decisions. Information represents a means for reducing the uncertainty that surrounds most of the decision alternatives confronting industrial marketers. For this reason, information has value. Marketers, when considering whether or not to spend resources on information gathering, need to compare this value to the costs of data acquisition.

One of the most important sources of information is marketing research, and a wide variety of subject areas fall within its domain. No matter which decision area or research task is being addressed, research involves a systematic process. Managing research as a process provides direction for the research effort and helps to ensure that research dollars are spent in the most effective manner. In the absence of a systematic approach, the marketer often ends up performing research that is unnecessary, incomplete, or inconclusive.

The distinctive challenges in conducting industrial marketing research were discussed as they relate to the stages of the research process. Most of the difficulties concern the problem of conducting research when the subject, or unit of analysis, is an organization rather than an individual consumer. The individual stages of the research process were demonstrated with an example.

Companies tend to approach the marketing research process as an activity they rely on only when a significant problem or opportunity arises. Managers, however, require a broad spectrum of information on a continuous basis. Marketing intelligence was introduced as the concept that meets this need. A marketing intelligence system (MIS) is an ongoing mechanism for gathering, recording, storing, and analyzing all forms of marketing-related information. Marketing research is one component of the MIS. The output of an MIS is usually a series of weekly, monthly, quarterly, and/or annual reports to management. The reports include information in areas such as product and territory profitability, sales force performance, advertising effectiveness, customer satisfaction, and competitor activities.

One step beyond the MIS is the decision support system, or DSS. The DSS allows the manager to ask nonroutine, *what if?* kinds of questions. The focus is on building marketing models, statistically manipulating the data in an MIS, and developing marketing decision rules.

As industrial firms grow in their appreciation for the importance of marketing and invest more heavily in the marketing function, their expectations for marketing intelligence will also grow. Decision support is increasingly prevalent in nonmarketing areas, such as finance and production. The implication is that those in marketing must be conversant in designing and working with databases, model building, statistical analysis, and a variety of computer software packages.

Finally, the chapter expanded on the use of secondary data when gathering marketing intelligence. A few of the more commonly used secondary sources were identified, including on-line database services. An introduction was also provided to the SIC system and the new NAICS system. Limitations of secondary data were highlighted through the use of a step-by-step procedure for evaluating data sources.

## Notes

1. www.bcbsm.com/
2. www.diebold.com/
3. www.census.gov/
4. www.dowjones.com/
5. www.readersdigest.com/
6. www.disclosure.com/
7. www.lexis-nexis.com
8. www.findsvp.com
9. www.questel.orbit.com
10. www.dialog.com

## Questions

1. You are a member of the strategy development team at One-Step, Ltd., a British manufacturer of high-quality film development equipment. You have operations in the United States, and your firm is considering entering the Canadian and Mexican markets with its top-selling line of equipment. Discuss some of the uncertainties surrounding the decision to enter the new markets and the role marketing research can serve to reduce the uncertainty. How would you use cost-benefit analysis to determine whether the value of the research information exceeded its costs?

2. "Industrial firms have relatively few buyers, so it is easier for those buyers to know the problems and needs of the market accurately and early than it is for buyers in consumer product firms." Do you agree or disagree?

3. Identify examples of situations in which you would argue that industrial marketing research should not be performed, in spite of a desire by senior management to conduct a market survey.

4. How does the statement of a research objective influence decisions made at subsequent stages in the research process?

5. Provide examples of some of the trade-off decisions made during the marketing research process. How do decisions made at one stage influence decisions made in subsequent stages?

6. What are the limitations of mail surveys in industrial marketing research? Describe an industrial marketing research problem that would lend itself to a mail survey.

7. Assume you work for an industrial firm involved in selling direct mail lists to companies. What are the pros and cons of establishing your own marketing research department or team, rather than hiring an outside firm to perform your research?

8. As a marketer, what skills do you need to effectively develop and use a decision support system? Assume that you have a computer expert to take care of any computer software or hardware you might require.

9. Identify a number of possible "what if"–type questions an industrial marketer might attempt to address using a decision support system. Then, using one of these questions, identify the data requirements and cite an example of a model (for example, a model linking some marketing variable to some measure of market performance) that might be helpful.

10. Which of the nine responsibility areas of marketing research identified in the chapter would tend to require primary data collection, and which could be accomplished principally with secondary data? In which areas might SIC data be useful?

# CHAPTER 7

# Strategy and the Industrial Marketer

*The nature of business is to make your own product obsolete. If we
don't do it ourselves, we know our competitors will do it for us.*
—Akio Morita, Sony Corporation

## Key Concepts

| | |
|---|---|
| Business screen | Selective demand strategy |
| Differentiation | Strategic business units (SBUs) |
| Economies of scale | Strategic marketing |
| Experience curve | Strategic orientation |
| Focus strategy | Strategic planning process |
| Primary demand strategy | Strategy |
| Product life cycle | Tactic |
| Product portfolio | Technology life cycle |
| Product positioning | Types of strategies |

## Learning Objectives

1. Appreciate the nature and importance of marketing strategies versus tactics, and provide examples of types of strategies.

2. Understand the meaning and importance of a strategic orientation, and differentiate strategic marketing from marketing management.

3. Describe a systematic planning process for identifying opportunities and developing industrial marketing strategies.

4. Learn to apply a number of conceptual tools for planning marketing strategies and tactics.

## The Concept of Strategy

A common theme throughout this book is that the environments in which companies operate are rapidly changing, and the successful firm is the one that can most effectively anticipate and manage developments in its external environment. To do so, the firm has to be able to recognize and interpret opportunities in the environment and then capitalize on these opportunities in a timely fashion. *This capability is the essence of strategic management.* In this chapter we will take a number of views on strategy, but essentially these perspectives can be placed in two categories. The first is that strategy can be consciously thought out and planned, and that a range of strategic tools can be used to aid the strategic planning process. The second, somewhat more controversial and less certain, questions whether organizations can consciously plan strategy—it is this perspective that will close the chapter. We will also question whether in fact marketing and strategy are different issues. The astute reader will recognize that reality is somewhere in between the two extreme perspectives.

*Strategy* can be defined in a variety of ways, some of which derive from its traditional use in a military context. Basically, a strategy is a statement regarding what the company wants to be and how it plans to get there. Others see strategy as a way of thinking that strives to ensure the long-term prosperity of the firm. A more practical view is that strategy consists of a coordinated sequence of moves over time, one that allows for contingencies. None of these perspectives is wrong. Strategies are based on clearly defined objectives, they take a comprehensive approach to the organization's problems, they adopt a longer-term time horizon, and they are flexible. For the purposes of this discussion, however, strategy will be defined broadly as "the specification of overall policies and programs for achieving company objectives, including allocation of resources and organization structure." Strategy is an attempt to match the advantages of the firm to its environment.

Companies can develop strategies at a number of different levels, ranging from overall corporate strategies to strategies for individual products and markets. Strategies may be formally planned, simply evolve over time with changing circumstances, or occur haphazardly. In any case, a strategy generally exists, whether recognized by management or not. In fact, managers are sometimes hard put to describe the corporate strategy currently in use.

Our concern is mainly with marketing strategies, which must be logically consistent with overall corporate strategies. That is, marketing strategies must fit with corporate efforts in such areas as finance, personnel, technology, and operations. From a strategic standpoint, marketing focuses on questions regarding what the company sells (i.e., the product or service mix), to whom it sells (i.e., the targeted segments), and how it sells (i.e., pricing, the promotional mix, distribution). Accordingly, marketing strategy is a specification of the organization's target markets, with a related marketing mix to satisfy each distinct market. It is an attempt to create competitive advantage in each targeted segment.

A good marketing strategy has certain characteristics. First, it serves to coordinate the marketing activities of the firm. In other words, there is a sense of some overall theme that sets the tone of the strategy. This theme might be high quality, low price, or custom-tailored service. Regardless of which theme is selected, the coordination requirement means that some marketing activities will be subordinated to others to achieve the mix that best satisfies targeted customers. Consider, for instance, an armored car service that picks up receipts and cash and delivers them to a central bank. The cars are bulky, unattractive, slow, and energy-inefficient, but they provide protection and deter wrongdoers.

Second, a marketing strategy should respond to current and anticipated future market conditions. The marketing function is responsible for sensing opportunities or threats in the environment and must plan accordingly. Marketing is the only business function that interfaces with all facets of the environment, and formal monitoring systems are often established to track technological, economic, political, or even social changes that might affect the company's operations. Such tracking can lead to decisions to avoid certain markets, experiment with untried technologies, hire employees with expertise the company does not have, explore alternative forms of customer communication or distribution, and many others that ensure the longer-term growth of the business.

Third, a marketing strategy must solve customers' problems. Here, the importance of buyer behavior analysis becomes evident. All marketing decisions must include an understanding of, and assumptions regarding, the needs of prospective customers. Consequently, industrial marketing firms take pains to study the purchasing criteria used by buyers, the individuals involved in buying decisions, and specific requirements of members of individual target markets.

Fourth, the strategy should enable the firm to best the competition. A marketing strategy invariably is pitted against the marketing strategy of competitors, and current as well as prospective customers are usually well aware of alternative sources of supply. In some instances, the choice of one vendor over another is based on a single criterion, such as when the low-price bidder is rewarded with a contract. In many other cases, however, a number of considerations are involved, and the competitors are compared on quality, delivery, reputation, service, and other marketing characteristics, as well as price. Consequently, a marketing strategy must begin with the target customers' needs and then assess how well the competitors' marketing efforts suit these needs. If there are areas where a company can achieve a unique competitive advantage in the eyes of prospective customers, this advantage increases the number of reasons for customers to select that company over its rivals.

Finally, there is the need for strategy to contribute to the company's financial success. Here, the overall financial well-being of the company across a relevant planning horizon is emphasized. Rather than a concentration on profit maximization in the definition of strategy, the focus is on contribution to a number of financial objectives. Companies frequently have minimum required rates of return on investment (or hurdle rates) that are expected from different products and services in their product lines. At the same time, management will establish certain cash flow stipulations. To be of use, the marketing strategy must reflect and be directly tied to individual product goals as well as to the company's overall financial objectives.

## Strategies Versus Tactics

Companies frequently fail to adopt a strategic perspective at either the corporate or the marketing level. Rather, they rely entirely on a tactical approach and often do not see the difference between a strategy and a tactic. *Tactics* are short-term, action-oriented moves that seek to achieve a fairly narrow, immediate goal. They are sometimes called *action plans*. Generally, a series of tactics coordinated over time is required to constitute a strategy.

To use a soccer analogy, a *strategy* is an overall scheme for winning the game. A tactic is a specific approach to marking the opposition's key striker, so that this player's effectiveness is minimized. This is not, however, the main purpose of the game; the team must also outscore the opposition before game time runs out (the objective!). In soccer, football, basketball, or any other sport, as in business, there are always going to be future games to play, and new sets of strategies and tactics to develop.

A sharper distinction between strategies and tactics can be drawn by considering a business example. A company that sells process control instruments is deciding how best to market one of its products. Under consideration is either an expenditure of $12,000 for advertising in a trade journal or a 5% price reduction. Note that both of these are tactics. Assuming there is no strategy currently in place, management has little guidance as to which tactic to pursue, except past experience. Perhaps neither tactic is appropriate. Furthermore, the effectiveness of either of these tactics may be limited if it is not part of an overall plan. Conflicts and/or duplication of effort may exist between these tactics and other actions of the firm. Also, once in place, these tactics limit the options available to the marketer in future months. Such obstacles are over-come when the tactics are part of a coherent strategy.

The real question to be addressed by this manager when considering these two tactical moves should be this: "What exactly is the firm trying to accomplish?" Four different possibilities come to mind, although others do exist:

1. Attracting new users to the marketplace.

2. Increasing usage rates among current customers.

3. Taking customers away from competitors.

4. Preventing competitors from taking our customers.

The first two could be referred to as primary demand strategies, because both fo-cus on untapped market potential. The other two are called selective demand strate-gies, because they focus on redistributing existing market share. These two strategies will be revisited in the next section.

The important conclusion here, however, is that the price cut and the advertising expenditure might be pursued as part of any number of strategies. That is, the firm could be using them to accomplish any one of the four strategic possibilities. The rea-sons for choosing a particular tactic can vary widely, then, depending on the strategy in question. If managers fail to step back from the situation long enough to develop and update strategies, they are destined to jump from tactic to tactic with little sense of whether the organization's best interests are being served.

## Types of Marketing Strategies

A single marketing strategy is usually not developed for the entire company, espe-cially in larger organizations. Similarly, separate strategies are not developed for each and every product. It makes sense to design strategies around *strategic busi-ness units* (SBUs). An SBU consists of a product or product line that is fairly unre-lated to other lines or products in terms of customers, competitors, prices, cross-elasticities, or other market-related characteristics. Products with shared technolo-gies, production processes, or costs could also constitute an SBU because such commonalities can have implications for marketing strategy. A single SBU could be a particular division or product line but could also cross over divisions or lines. A company, or one of its divisions, can have any number of SBUs, each of which re-quires its own strategy.

There is, however, no one right strategy for a particular SBU. From the long list of possible strategies, any number of quite different approaches could be effective at a particular point in time. The challenge is to find a strategy that profitably matches company strengths to environmental conditions. The major limitations are the mar-

**TABLE 7.1** Characteristics of Good Strategies

A good strategy should have certain characteristics. Once a strategy is on the drawing board, the marketer can look systematically for flaws or areas for improvement, using the following six criteria provided by George Day.

◈ *Suitability.* Is the proposed strategy consistent with the foreseeable environmental threats and opportunities? Does the strategy exploit or enhance a current competitive advantage, or create a new source of advantage?

◈ *Validity.* Are the key assumptions about environmental trends and the outcomes of the strategy realistic? Are the assumptions based on reliable and valid information?

◈ *Consistency.* Are the basic elements of the strategy consistent with each other and with the objectives being pursued?

◈ *Feasibility.* Is the strategy appropriate to the available resources? Are the basic elements and premises of the strategy understandable and acceptable to the operating managers who will have the responsibility for implementation?

◈ *Vulnerability.* To what extent are projected outcomes dependent on data or assumptions of dubious quality and origin? Are the risks of failure acceptable? Are there adequate contingency plans for coping with these risks? Can the decision be reversed in the future? How long will it take? What are the consequences?

◈ *Potential rewards.* Are the projected outcomes satisfactory in the light of the provisional objectives for the business? Are the adjustments to the objectives acceptable to the stakeholders?

SOURCE: This table is based on the work of noted Wharton marketing strategy professor George S. Day: *Strategic Market Planning: The Pursuit of Competitive Advantage*, p. 152. © Copyright 1984 by West Publishing Co. Reprinted with permission.

Readers interested in Day's ideas should consult his other books, among them *The Market Driven Organization: Understanding, Attracting, and Keeping Valuable Customers* (1999) and *Market Driven Strategy: Processes for Creating Value* (1999).

keter's creativity and resources. Table 7.1 provides a set of characteristics that are useful in evaluating the merits of any one strategy.

Some major categories of strategies are helpful in trying to sort out the many possibilities. Let us examine three ways in which marketing strategies can be classified. A very general approach is to distinguish between an emphasis on new versus existing products/services, and new versus existing markets. This distinction produces four categories of strategies, as illustrated in the top portion of Figure 7.1. Where the firm goes after existing or current markets with existing products/services, a *market penetration* strategy is being used. Basically, the firm is trying to continue doing what it has been doing, only better. *Market development* is taking current product/service programs into new markets, and it centers on market selection and targeting. When new product/service programs (such as new versions of a product, line extensions, or flanker products) are introduced into existing markets, the strategy is termed *prod-*

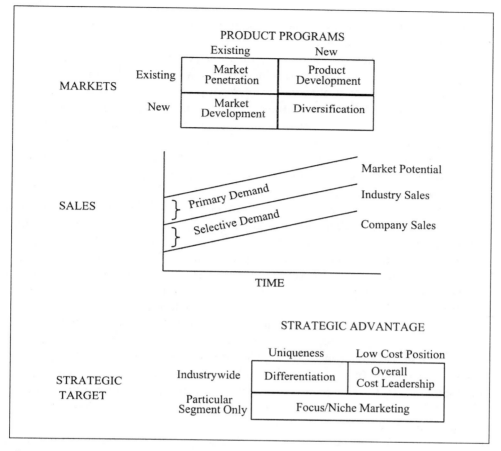

**Figure 7.1.** Three Approaches to Classifying Strategies

*uct development.* Finally, a company going after new markets with new product/service programs is *diversifying.*

Another way to classify strategies is based on the distinction between primary and selective demand. These types of demand are illustrated in the diagram in the middle of Figure 7.1. When the strategy seeks to close the gap between estimated market potential and current industry sales (called a *primary gap*), this is a *primary demand* strategy. Primary demand has two components. Both the number of users and the usage rate per customer can be increased by focusing on either the willingness or the ability of customers to buy. *Selective demand* involves the gap between current industry sales and current company sales. Strategies aimed at closing this gap, or at least keeping the gap constant, are *selective demand* strategies. These strategies can be offensive (taking market share from competitors) or defensive (maintaining current customers).

A third set of strategies is based on the work of Michael Porter (1980). He claims that virtually all strategies fall within one of three generic categories: overall cost leadership, differentiation, and focus (Figure 7.1, bottom). *Cost leadership* is an attempt by the company to have the lowest cost position in the industry; that is, to produce the particular product or service at the lowest delivered cost. The theme is efficiency in all facets of operations (production, administration, sales, distribution). By lowering costs and being efficient, the company generally hopes to be the price leader, setting the trend for other firms to follow; in more stable markets, it may simply enjoy better margins. In many more traditional manufacturing markets, cost leadership is often achieved by taking advantage of economies of scale and the experience curve, strategic concepts to be discussed later in this chapter. Cost reductions often come from high-volume production, so the firm pursues strategic actions to maximize market size and share.

When a firm cannot be the cost leader in a market, it has to make its product or service different from others in some way that matters to customers, and for which customers are prepared to pay. *Differentiation* also finds the company going after the entire marketplace, but now the goal is to be perceived as somehow different, or unique, compared to firms producing competing products or services. Companies may differentiate themselves or their products or services based on quality, depth and breadth of product selection, customer service, features, distribution, technological leadership, warranties, and any number of other factors. The marketing mix is used to emphasize this uniqueness. The key to this strategy is that customers must perceive significant differences among competitors on a particular factor, and the factor must be meaningful to customers. Note that differentiation requires an investment of resources and so may come at the expense of the firm's cost position—it costs money to make the product or service changes, pay for the advertising, or invest in distribution that differentiation demands.

Unlike cost leadership and differentiation, a *focus* (or *niche*) marketing strategy does not seek to capture as much of the entire market as possible. Instead, this is a segmentation and targeting strategy in which the firm specializes in meeting the needs of a particular niche of customers (e.g., the military, the hotel industry, rapid-growth firms, firms with fewer than 100 employees). Through specialization, the company is able to tailor products or services to the exact requirements of a group of customers and can completely penetrate that segment. A focus strategy may be achieved either through differentiation or the low-cost position, but only with the segment(s) in question.

Note that some companies try to pursue aspects of all three of these for the same product area, which usually leads to an unclear direction that Porter calls "stuck in the middle." However, could a company pursue market penetration, primary demand, and differentiation at the same time, for different products? The answer is yes. For instance, Hewlett-Packard[1] might possibly be a cost leader in computer printers, be a differentiated player in notebook computers, and employ a focused, differentiated strategy in laboratory measuring equipment.

Finally, let us consider all three of the general strategy frameworks presented in Figure 7.1 together. These three frameworks are not independent, so it is possible that the same company could simultaneously be pursuing a strategy from each framework. As a case in point, consider a company that is trying to pursue a selective demand strategy (e.g., capture customers from competitors) and does so by developing new services (a product development strategy) and differentiating these new services based on technical leadership.

## Strategic Marketing Management

More important than the development of individual strategies is the need for industrial marketers to adopt a strategic orientation when approaching the opportunities and challenges confronting the firm. A strategic orientation emphasizes the continuous search for competitive advantage. Management's attention is focused on identifying and understanding changes in key success factors, the requirements of market segments, and the nature of competitor strategies. There is also a recognition that the company's marketing interests can best be served by working closely with personnel in the operations, finance, and research and development departments. For example, by working with operations, the marketer can influence the inventory and servicing policies of the firm. By working with finance, the likelihood is greater that the marketer can get funding for strategies, as opposed to individual tactics. Cooperation with R&D can produce a greater role for marketing in developing product and service innovations.

Those who adopt a strategic orientation understand that goals for all products and markets are not the same. Rather than attempt to maximize profit from each product or service area in which the firm is involved, the strategic view is that different products serve varying roles. Some products are in dynamic growth markets requiring greater investment, as well as warranting higher sales and profit expectations. Others are new and need time to get established. Still others have been around some time producing very stable returns, but with slow growth. There also are products that generate meager financial results but that serve an important role in filling out the product line or in helping to support sales of other products in the line.

Strategic marketing, because of its concern with the longer-term considerations, with the bigger picture, and with interfunctional cooperation, is quite different from traditional marketing management. The latter concentrates on day-to-day decisions regarding the elements of the marketing mix and tends to rely on reactive approaches to problems as they arise.

## The Strategic Planning Process

An ability to plan effectively is a vital ingredient in strategic marketing. Regardless of a company's size, or whether it is selling a product or a service, planning must be approached as an ongoing activity. Shorter-term (quarterly, annual) and longer-

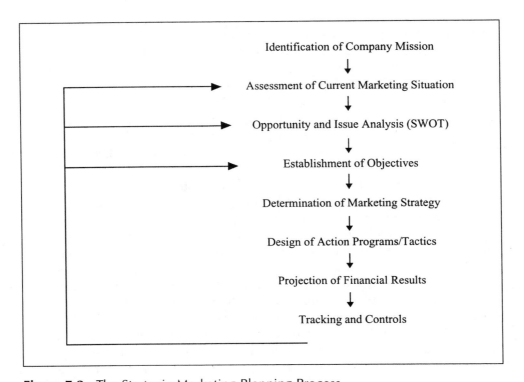

**Figure 7.2.** The Strategic Marketing Planning Process

SOURCE: Adapted from *Marketing Management: Millennium Edition*, chap. 3, Kotler. © Copyright 2000 by Prentice-Hall.

term market plans are increasingly seen as a necessity. Strategic planning can be defined as a getting the right people, issues, and information together on a timely schedule in order to make decisions that commit cash, people, and other resources to market positioning assignments extending beyond the current operating period. Marketing strategies follow from a logical, step-by-step planning process. This process is illustrated in Figure 7.2.

The beginning point is a company mission statement, which seeks to answer the question "What business are we in?" This mission statement is a long-run vision of what the organization intends to be. The statement should be reflective of the organization's past accomplishments and current distinctive competencies, and it should focus on generic marketplace needs. That is, the company should define itself not in terms of products or technologies, but in terms of needs. This definition serves to provide direction to all areas of the company, while leaving room for managers to capitalize on new opportunities. The mission statement for an office equipment manufacturer might be "to help solve administrative, scientific, and human problems in companies." A company like CNN[2] might define its mission as "providing instant information, anytime, from anywhere." Cisco Systems defines itself as "the company that provides the backbone of the Internet" and, in the process, says CEO John Chambers, he wants Cisco to become "one of the most influential companies in history" ("Cisco Systems: The Dogfood Danger," 2000, p. 66).

The core of the planning process is a detailed situation analysis that seeks to generate a database of relevant background information on the industry, company, product, market, competition, distribution system, and macro environment. Information is not just collected and organized, though. The data must be interpreted using insight, and managerial implications must be drawn. This planning activity can be divided into internal and external analyses. The internal section examines key aspects of the company and its products, including benefits offered, available resources, distinctive competencies, cross-product elasticities, a critique of current marketing mix programs, and a review of financial performance. The external section looks at everything outside the company. This overview would include an examination of industry trends, estimations of market size and growth rates, an assessment of customer needs and buying processes, an analysis of market segments, a determination of competitor strengths and weaknesses, a determination of competitors' apparent strategies, an evaluation of suppliers and distributors, and characteristics of the economic, technological, regulatory, and social environments.

With a good situation analysis in hand, the marketing planner performs an opportunity and issue analysis. This involves attempting to identify (a) company strengths and weaknesses (from the internal analysis), (b) major opportunities and threats facing the firm in a particular product market area (from the external analysis), and (c) notable issues that must be addressed. This process is often called a "SWOT" (Strengths, Weaknesses, Opportunities, Threats) analysis. In a sense, the planner is drawing summary conclusions from the information uncovered in the situation analysis. The ability to do this effectively depends on a marketer's analytical skills, insightfulness, and, most important, objectivity.

The determination of objectives comes next. Objectives (and strategies) should follow from a matching of strengths and weaknesses to opportunities and threats, as illustrated in Figure 7.3. Objectives are then established for overall financial performance as well as marketing performance. Financial objectives are set in such areas as cash flow and profitability. Marketing objectives can include sales levels, market share, penetration levels for various market segments, customer awareness or attitude levels, growth in distribution, and average price charged. Objectives should be challenging and involve "stretch," but they must also be achievable. They must be measurable and consistent with one another.

Strategy follows from objectives, and tactics from strategy. A good idea is to formulate an overall strategy statement, then break it down into statements regarding the target market, positioning, marketing research, and elements of the marketing mix. Tactics are the set of strategy implementation moves the marketer will make over the planning period. The discussion of tactics should include an explanation of dollar expenditures and the proposed timing of each action.

Strategic planning allows the marketer to judge systematically the relative merits of the various options open to him or her at a given point in time. This evaluation is illustrated in Table 7.2. A company that sells air filtration systems is considering chang-

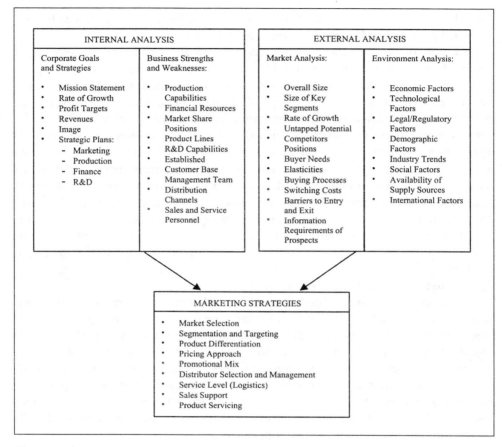

| INTERNAL ANALYSIS | | EXTERNAL ANALYSIS | |
|---|---|---|---|
| Corporate Goals and Strategies | Business Strengths and Weaknesses: | Market Analysis: | Environment Analysis: |
| • Mission Statement<br>• Rate of Growth<br>• Profit Targets<br>• Revenues<br>• Image<br>• Strategic Plans:<br> – Marketing<br> – Production<br> – Finance<br> – R&D | • Production Capabilities<br>• Financial Resources<br>• Market Share Positions<br>• Product Lines<br>• R&D Capabilities<br>• Established Customer Base<br>• Management Team<br>• Distribution Channels<br>• Sales and Service Personnel | • Overall Size<br>• Size of Key Segments<br>• Rate of Growth<br>• Untapped Potential<br>• Competitors Positions<br>• Buyer Needs<br>• Elasticities<br>• Buying Processes<br>• Switching Costs<br>• Barriers to Entry and Exit<br>• Information Requirements of Prospects | • Economic Factors<br>• Technological Factors<br>• Legal/Regulatory Factors<br>• Demographic Factors<br>• Industry Trends<br>• Social Factors<br>• Availability of Supply Sources<br>• International Factors |

MARKETING STRATEGIES

• Market Selection
• Segmentation and Targeting
• Product Differentiation
• Pricing Approach
• Promotional Mix
• Distributor Selection and Management
• Service Level (Logistics)
• Sales Support
• Product Servicing

**Figure 7.3.** Strategy as an Outcome of Planning

ing its price, reengineering its current product/process, or developing an entirely new product process. The planning framework used by this firm stresses the comparative assessment of each alternative, using six measures. Table 7.2 summarizes the conclusions drawn by management after a detailed situation analysis.

Strategies and tactics are likely to affect both revenues and expenses. It is appropriate, then, to perform a break-even analysis to determine the required level of sales needed to cover any proposed expenditures and to reach goals. Also worth constructing is a projection of what the income statement will look like at the end of the planning period, should the strategies and tactics be implemented.

The marketer then needs to establish benchmarks to compare actual against planned performance over the course of the planning period. This activity is called *tracking* or *control*. Benchmarks are set for key operating and performance variables at a number of stopping points (e.g., quarterly, monthly) over the planning horizon. Where there are positive or negative performance discrepancies, these data can be used as inputs to modify objectives, strategies, or tactics after they have been implemented.

**TABLE 7.2** Application of Planning Criteria to the Evolution of Decision Alternatives

| Planning Factors | Price Change | Reengineering of Existing Product or Process | New Product Development or Major Process Change |
|---|---|---|---|
| Longer-term market impact | Low | Moderate | High |
| Investment necessary | Low | Moderate | High |
| Risk | Low | Moderate | Moderate-High |
| Ability to implement on timely basis | High | Moderate | Low |
| Ease of competitive response | High | Moderate | Low |
| Likelihood of similar competitive response | High | High | Low |

## A Case Example of the Need for Strategic Planning

As a means of further exploring the strategic marketing planning process, consider an example involving business insurance. Insurance Associates (IA),[3] located in the southeast of England, marketed specialized policies to professionals. These insurance policies covered office equipment and provided liability coverage, except for malpractice. IA, an agent for a number of national insurance suppliers such as Commercial General Union[4] and Legal & General,[5] employed about 40 people, including the managing director, the sales manager, and a product specialist. For the past several years, IA had prospered by targeting two "affinity groups"—medical doctors and dentists. The company had the formal endorsement of professional associations of both groups.

The managing director of IA, a dedicated student of the industry, perceived important changes in the market and an upward drift in the rate structures of insurance suppliers. In particular, many companies and associations were changing agencies, and some had turned to self-insurance, dropping insurance policies and funding their own insurance internally to avoid rising insurance premium costs.

Membership of the dental association's insurance committee had changed recently and now seemed to have a majority in favor of IA's major competitor—Malcolm Norman and Partners (MNP).[6] Anticipating this change in circumstances, IA had commissioned a marketing research study to determine the importance of the association's endorsement in the insurance decision process of dentists. Simultaneously, IA undertook a search for other professional associations that were rethinking their insurance endorsements. This situation analysis revealed that most dentists seemed to be concerned about insurance rates but were less influenced by the association endorsement. Insurance industry analysis revealed that the major provider companies, including those represented by IA and MNP, were contemplating substantial premium increases in the coming year.

The strategic planning scene was now defined. Threats were evident in the loss of the association endorsement and the encroachment of MNP on IA's territory. In fact, MNP was lobbying intensely with the dental association's insurance committee to persuade the members to drop IA and endorse MNP. Part of MNP's strategy included offering rates lower than IA's current fees. A further threat was the probable premium hikes by insurance providers, which both IA and MNP would be forced to pass on to the dentists. Unusual as this seemed, MNP apparently was unaware of the rate hikes planned by its insurance suppliers. In the meantime, two important opportunities were identified. Both the law association and architects' associations were shopping for office insurance providers.

To fight MNP for the dental association endorsement seemed ill advised. IA did offer token resistance by making presentations to the insurance committee and protesting its lack of consideration for IA's long service to the association in favor of MNP's price advantage. Part of this resistance was to divert MNP from the realization that rates were going up, given the firm's apparent ignorance of the industry's plans.

Both long-run and short-run objectives were designed by IA's management team in the light of the opportunities and threats analysis. For the long run, IA's success would depend on its ability to spread itself across more target markets and thus minimize the impact of adverse circumstances such as those that had come about in the dental association. In fact, a 5-year goal of entering new markets was agreed upon, so that no one customer group would represent more than 20% of the company's profit stream. Ideally, IA would add a new target market customer group each year.

For the short-run planning horizon of 1 year, IA sought to shift its emphasis away from the dental association and toward the more attractive of its possible targets, the law association and the architects' association. At a minimum, IA needed to add new business from the law association equal to its anticipated losses of dentists, or roughly 75 clients, based on survey estimates. The sales manager assumed responsibility for reporting monthly business losses and gains from each target market and making updated projections for the end of the year as a means of monitoring the progress toward this objective. The management team agreed to watch the monthly figures carefully and to adjust plans and tactics if the projections suggested that the performance objective would not be achieved.

At the same time, plans were laid to "open up the bar." An advertising agency was employed to design a campaign for lawyer-oriented periodicals, as well as one in magazines and journals targeted at the architectural profession. Negotiations were begun with insurance company suppliers to allow IA to represent them to legal client prospects and registered architects. A portable sales presentation booth was purchased for IA to set up at the law association's next annual meeting and at the annual conference of the Royal Society of Architecture (RSA).

Ultimately, the dental association's insurance committee dropped IA's endorsement in favor of MNP. About one fifth of IA's dentist accounts gravitated to MNP in the first 6 months. When MNP announced the rate increases, the flow of lost accounts stopped. The law association opted to not endorse any company, but IA's promotional efforts proved successful in attracting a number of lawyers' offices to IA's services. The RSA did not give IA sole endorsement, but it added the firm to its "preferred" list. The exhibition at the annual conference was successful; enough architects were signed up to make up for the loss in dentists. In the meantime, chartered accountants were being targeted as next year's focus in IA's diversification program.

## Pitfalls of Strategic Planning

Despite the many advantages of the strategic planning process, planning can actually inhibit successful marketing performance. The reasons are threefold: poor planning motivation, poor planning ability, and unanticipated environmental change.

The first issue has to do with the purpose or goals of planning. Marketing plans are sometimes done for all the wrong reasons and, correspondingly, in all the wrong ways. For example, the plan is done to prove a point, or to support a decision that already has been made. In reality, a plan is meant to be a comprehensive assimilation and interpretation of the available information, followed by an objective determination of the goals, strategies, and action programs that represent the most opportune path for the organization to follow. In other cases, a plan is prepared as a defensive strategy. If things do not work out as the manager expected, the plan is pulled out to serve as a rationalization. Otherwise, the document is never really used. Many companies have volumes of planning documents that do little more than collect dust on shelves. Plans are also sometimes prepared simply to impress others, such as senior management, creditors, or suppliers. There is no real intent to live by the plan or to use the plan as a blueprint.

The second issue concerns inept planners. Planning is both art and science. Those involved must have a detailed knowledge of analytical concepts, tools, and techniques, but a large measure of creativity and insight is also required. This insight includes an ability to see products and markets in a way that others do not. Also critical is an ability to estimate reliable figures in key decision areas based on data sources that are diverse, incomplete, and often inconsistent. The underlying logic of market planning is lost on many decision makers. This logic, though, can produce the margin of difference between market failure and success. General Dwight D. Eisenhower once said that "plans are nothing, planning is everything." The focus, then, is as much on the planning process as on the end result, the written planning document.

A marketing plan is a road map. The planner is building a case, the outcome of which is a set of strategies and a program for implementation and control. As a logical argument, the plan requires the same kinds of structure a good manager applies to rational decision making. Many planners *begin* with a set of judgments regarding product positioning, segmentation, pricing, promotional programs, and so on. This approach is the biggest mistake the planner can make: the management equivalent of putting the cart before the horse. The backbone of a good marketing plan is a detailed analysis of an organization's current situation, on which logical marketing mix decisions can be based. Some of the leading causes of weak market performance involve problem areas that should be addressed in a good situation analysis.

The final issue involves the rate of change in the environment. Change is what most creates the need for strategic planning. A plan is an attempt to see the future and to incorporate it into current thinking. An important requirement, then, is that a plan be flexible and allow for contingencies once it is implemented. One approach is to include optimistic, expected, and pessimistic views.

The importance of marketing plans in operational decision making will only continue to grow, especially as environments become more turbulent and firms improve their abilities in data collection and data management. To be effective, though, putting together a plan must become more than a once-a-year activity. Planning is a continual process involving constant updating, modification of figures, changes in assumptions, and revision of forecasts. It actually becomes a large part of what managers do for a living!

# Conceptual Planning Tools

In strategic planning, marketers have increasingly relied on a variety of conceptual tools. Included among these are product life cycles, product portfolios, experience curves, economies of scale mappings, and technology life cycles. Before describing each of these, it should be pointed out that these are only tools that can aid planning. Managers still have to make decisions. In the hands of the astute, thinking marketer, these tools can enable keener insights, more creative deductions, and ultimately, better planning. Alternatively, when used poorly and unthinkingly, they may simply speed the company down the path to inept, ineffective, and sometimes foolhardy decisions.

## Product Life Cycle

The *product life cycle* (PLC) is perhaps the most widely known of marketing tools and is a focal point of marketing planning. Although there are drawbacks to its use, the PLC is popular because of its intuitive appeal and its direct implications for marketing strategy. Put simply, the PLC plots the sales volume and profit curves for a product class or category (e.g., conventional chest X-ray machines, a particular category of jet aircraft engine) over time. The sales volume trend is generally shown as an S-shaped curve, as found in Figure 7.4.

Take, as an example, the market experience of cellular or mobile telephones. These telephones were first carried by professionals and salespeople who were in the field but who had to be both contactable and able to make calls conveniently while out of the office and on the move. Prior to the advent of cellular telephone technology, these people had to call in frequently to find out who had called them or what tasks needed to be performed immediately, or to rely on pocket pagers. Like-

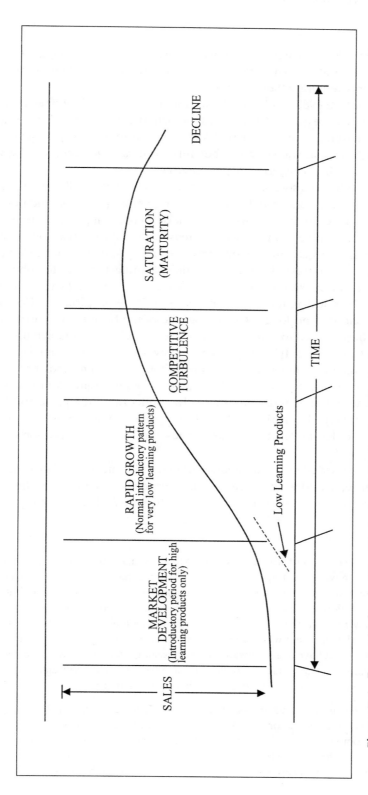

**Figure 7.4.** Dynamic Competitive Strategy and the Product Life Cycle

207

wise, doctors' telephone exchanges tracked down physicians through the many telephone number locations where they might be found, to update them on emergencies or other events requiring their attention.

During the late 1980s and early 1990s, the first cellular telephones appeared on the scene. They were quite bulky, had a short battery life and limited range, and were subject to interference and other problems; they were also very expensive. Initial adoption of these units was slow, but their relative advantage over the old system was very appealing. Gradually, sales began to grow.

Technical advances such as miniaturization, longer battery life, and the rapid expansion of networks rendered the cellular phones more attractive, and prices began to fall with volume production. As sales took off, more companies entered the market, further stimulating demand with increased promotion, availability, and price competition. In many cases the phone was given away free in exchange for a contract to utilize the service for a given period of time. Manufacturers of the phones began to develop and offer extended services as well as to make modifications to the product itself, such as adding Internet connections and internal modems. Nowadays the cellular telephone is no longer the prerogative of the business-to-business market; consumers have rushed to take up the product for their own personal use as well. It appears that sales velocity is beginning to slow and the market might be leveling out. As this happens, fewer potential new adopters remain, and these prospects might be more resistant to change than earlier adopters. Some companies may begin to exit the industry, and there is already a squeeze on the profits of those who remain. Eventually, the market will reach the point at which most sales will be replacement of older models of cellular phones, with a small proportion of first-time buyers.

The PLC is divided into five stages: market development, rapid growth, competitive turbulence, maturity, and decline. Other versions of the PLC use different names and/or a different number of stages, but these five are fairly descriptive of industrial products.

◆ *Market development* is a period during which the marketer is attempting to encourage trial of a new product by customers, in effect creating demand. Unanticipated product problems are being worked out, and the company may be adding distributors. Profits and cash flow are usually negative. This stage can be lengthy (i.e., slow sales growth) for new products that involve considerable learning on the part of users. Conversely, market development will normally be short (i.e., fast takeoff in sales) for low learning products that have a clear advantage over existing alternatives. Because many new industrial products are fairly complex and involve a more complicated buying process, this stage will tend to be longer than that for consumer products.

◆ The *rapid growth* stage finds sales increasing *at an increasing rate* from period to period. Customers are adopting the new product in large numbers just to maintain their own competitiveness. The marketer is attempting to establish and solidify a loyal customer base and strong brand preference. The product is expanded into a product line. Production may be approaching capacity with accumulating back orders. Competitors are showing up with new features and improved versions of the original product that appeal to certain benefit and user segments. Profits are now being realized and are growing.

❖ In the *competitive turbulence* stage, sales continue to increase, but at a *decreasing* rate. Competitors have established a firm foothold in the market, and market leadership may be up for grabs. At the same time, this tends to be a shakeout period for many of the marginal competitors. The marketer is attempting to differentiate his or her product(s) while uncovering untapped market segments. Attention is being focused on keeping the established customer base satisfied, giving them little reason to switch suppliers. Unit profits begin to decline, and total profits generally peak out.

❖ At the *maturity*, or saturation, stage, sales begin to level off, and the strategic posture becomes more defensive. The competitive environment stabilizes and is usually characterized as oligopolistic. As new prospects become fewer and fewer, marketers may attempt to stimulate existing customers to increase product usage and find new applications for the product. Even so, the opportunities of the revenue side are limited, especially given the downward pressure on prices. The pressure is due to the slowdown in sales and the fact that customers may increasingly see little difference between the offerings of the various vendors. This reaction is especially pertinent when selling component parts and materials to customers whose own products are becoming mature; often, these are customers with whom a long-term relationship has been established. Limited revenue possibilities lead to a focus on the cost side of the profit equation. Management looks for efficiencies in production and distribution. Profits are stable or falling, and net cash flow peaks out.

❖ *Decline* tends to proceed fairly rapidly for industrial products, as new technologies or technological applications make an established product obsolete. Competitors are dropping out. Customers have little choice but to abandon such a product in order to maintain their own competitiveness. A few customers usually continue to depend on the product, though, and their demand may be relatively inelastic. The marketer has a number of options. An obvious choice is elimination, but even that choice presents a timing question. Alternatively, promotion and sales support could be cut while price is maintained to get whatever profit can be milked from the market. Or, the price could be cut and the product could be used to support sales of other products of the company.

Although the S-shaped product life-cycle curve is straightforward, in reality the curve is not smooth and is different for virtually every product. Models are available of standard curves for products having certain basic characteristics, but research in this area has not progressed very far. Another major problem involves determining current position in the life cycle. Where an industry or product is (in terms of the stages of sales growth) may be difficult to determine until that industry or product has been there for a while. A slowdown in sales may not mean maturity has arrived; instead, this trend may be caused by a relatively temporary fluctuation in the environment.

Generally, product life cycles are shorter for industrial products than for most consumer products, with the exception of fads. Furthermore, industrial product life cycles are getting shorter because of rapid changes in technology and the information systems that are available to companies and customers. Not too many years back, a life cycle of 40 years for some capital goods, such as huge machine presses, was not unusual. Now, even these major items are maturing much more rapidly, sometimes in only a few years.

The message of the product life cycle is that no product lasts forever. Sales potential and profitability change over time; strategies for product, price, promotion, and distribution must be modified to reflect these changing conditions. To be useful, however, the life cycle must be more than a plot of sales over time. The marketer needs to track changes in costs, cash flow, unit profitability, market structure, competitor activities, and customer needs in each major stage of product evolution. Also, the life cycle is not a deterministic function; that is, the marketer is in a position to affect the shape and duration of the PLC through the marketing strategies and tactics pursued by the firm. Just as a company needs to incorporate the impact of company actions and expenditures into its own sales forecast, these activities should influence how the marketer interprets the PLC.

## Product Portfolios

The product lines of industrial companies will include products at various stages of their life cycles. This diversity is logical and can be quite effective if strategically managed. Earlier, this chapter introduced the SBU concept, a way in which products can be grouped for strategy development purposes. Each SBU, and each product, has a role in contributing to overall objectives. Each may have different prospects for growth and profitability; therefore, it is useful to consider the set of products or SBUs as a *portfolio*.

Portfolio thinking is prevalent in the field of finance, where a portfolio is defined as a combination of assets. Financial managers attempt to select an optimal set of financial assets (e.g., stocks and bonds) that will produce the highest rate of return at an acceptable level of risk. Some assets will be more risky, others less so. Some will generate immediate or steady growth, while others will provide long-term returns. As funds are generated from a given asset, they can be reinvested to support other parts of the portfolio.

The decision to develop a particular product or business area represents a type of investment for a company. It makes sense, then, to examine the firm's portfolio of products and services. To design a portfolio, management must have criteria by which products can be classified. As mentioned above, the financial world uses risk and rate of return. These attributes probably will not suffice, as marketers need criteria that reflect the competitive marketplace.

Some years ago, the Boston Consulting Group[7] developed a type of product portfolio called the *growth-share matrix*. Products or businesses are classified according to the industry growth rate (a proxy for the PLC) and a product's relative market share. Figure 7.5 demonstrates the growth-share matrix. Products or businesses are classified within one of the four cells, based on management's assessment of their growth prospects and market performance to date. Depending on where products fit

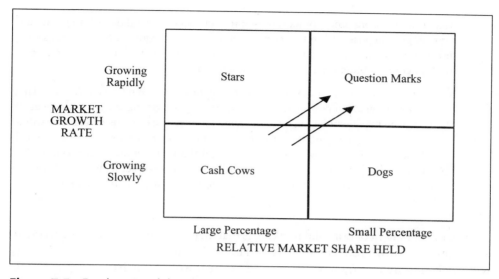

**Figure 7.5.** Product Portfolio Grid

SOURCE: "Strategy and the Business Portfolio," *Long Range Planning*, 10, 1 (February, 1977), p. 11, Hedley.
© Copyright 1977 by *Long Range Planning*. Reprinted with permission.

in the portfolio, management can determine which are the best investments, which provide the best cash flow potential, and which might be candidates for elimination. For simplicity, the cells have been given easily remembered descriptive names.

◈ A *cash cow* is a product with high relative market share (compared to the leading competitor) in a slow-growth industry. The name is appropriate, because these products generate considerable positive net cash flows for the SBU or company—literally, they can be "milked for cash." These are generally well-established products in the competitive turbulence or maturity stages of the PLC. Strategies tend to emphasize defending market share while maintaining a market leadership position. Because of their advantageous market positions, cash cows do not require heavy investments in R&D, market research, and promotion. Excess cash can be redistributed to support other products in the portfolio, especially stars or question marks. This is a point of some controversy, however, as cash cows often have considerable remaining profit opportunity and market staying power. In such cases, they may warrant heavier investment.

◈ *Stars* are potential cash cows but have yet to achieve a strong net cash flow. These products have a strong market position in a dynamic growth market. Although profitable, they require substantial investment because the competition is intense (hence the frequently negative cash flow). Many firms are attracted by rapid growth prospects, and the battle typically is over new customers and new product applications.

◈ A product is classified as a *question mark* if it is doing poorly in a rapidly growing industry. Profit margins are anemic, but the investment required to remain competitive is sizable. If management is not willing to invest either the excess cash from other products or money from other sources, these products become candidates for elimination. Another growth possibility is to increase market share by acquiring competitors and/or distributors. An alternative option would be a segmentation and niching strategy, with the firm concentrating on a specific customer group.

❖ A large percentage of the products on the market qualify as *dogs* ("*Die or Grow*"). They have relatively small market share, and their industry is growing at a slow rate, if at all. The company may be breaking even or losing money. The obvious conclusion would be to get rid of such apparent losers, through either sale or licensing (both of which provide additional sources of cash), or by outright abandonment. There are other roles, however, for dog products. They can be used to support complementary products that fit in other cells, or costs can be cut back while management harvests the remaining profit potential.

The major benefit of portfolio thinking is that management is encouraged to move away from a narrow product mentality and toward considering the roles of products within a larger strategic framework. Also, effective use of resources across products is emphasized. However, it is not clear that growth rate and market share are the most appropriate criteria, particularly in an era of relationship marketing that emphasizes building the equity in the customer relationship, or so-called share of customer thinking (see Berthon, Hulbert, and Pitt, 1999). An alternative version of the portfolio that addresses this concern is called the *business screen*.

## Business Screens

The screen is a more elaborate portfolio developed by General Electric. The concept replaces industry growth with industry attractiveness, and market share with business strengths. The underlying logic is that firms should choose to compete in attractive markets and where their resources allow them to be strong competitors. Consistent with the strategic planning model, internal strengths are being matched to external opportunities. The classification grid uses a three-by-three matrix, permitting an "average" category. Figure 7.6 provides an example of the business screen, with sample industry attractiveness factors and business strengths. Each circle is a distinct product or SBU; the size of the circle represents market size. The pie-shaped area within each circle identifies the firm's market share.

The three cells in the upper left-hand corner of Figure 7.6 contain opportunities in which the firm should invest resources with an eye toward long-term growth. The diagonal cells, moving from top right to bottom left, are equivalent to question mark products in the growth-share matrix. These receive a medium priority in terms of investment. The strategy is to maintain position and selectively focus the firm's profit-seeking efforts. The remaining cells in the lower right-hand corner contain products that are equivalent to dogs, where the industry is not all that attractive and the company has few real strengths with which to capitalize on the market.

The position of a product, a line, or an SBU in the business screen can be quantified. The firm first determines importance weights for each of the factors on the

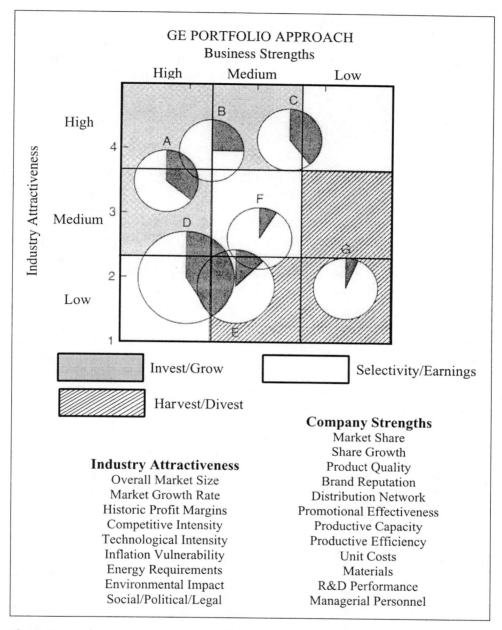

**Figure 7.6.** The General Electric Business Screen

SOURCE: Adapted from *Business Policy and Strategic Management*, p. 166, Glueck. © Copyright 1980 by McGraw-Hill. Adapted with permission.

industry attractiveness dimension of the screen. Only those factors thought to be strategically relevant are used. These weights should add up to 1.0. Then, products are evaluated on each of the weighted factors, using a five-point rating scale. The importance weights are multiplied by the evaluation scores. The results are then added to-gether across the factors to determine an overall score for the industry attractiveness dimension. This process is then repeated for the company strengths dimension. In this manner, the marketer arrives at a product's position within the screen.

## Alternative Portfolio Approaches

It should be increasingly apparent that a planning matrix could be developed with any number of cells, using a wide range of evaluative criteria. This flexibility not only is possible but is a positive feature of portfolio thinking. The particular approach used depends on a firm's resources, market, competitive position, and goals. At the same time, the usefulness of a portfolio depends on its relative simplicity. As more variables and dimensions are added, collecting and organizing the data necessary for properly classifying types of products becomes significantly more difficult.

A sample alternative portfolio approach is provided in Figure 7.7. Here, strategies are developed around a firm's competitive position in a given product area and the product's position in the life cycle. The *market leader* generally is the firm that either is largest, has the biggest market share, or has the most favorable cost position. *Challengers* and *followers* are runners-up in terms of market share. The challenger is aggressively attempting to overtake the leader, while the follower is satisfied with the status quo. Followers may achieve satisfactory returns by imitating the successful programs of leaders and challengers. *Marginal competitors* are barely holding on to a piece of the market. A policy of specializing on a segment or niche may prove profitable for marginal types of firms.

The portfolio in Figure 7.7 encourages management to determine objectively what its competitive position has been, as well as the competitive posture it is capable of assuming. Different objectives, strategies, and resource allocations are appropriate depending on this competitive posture. Subsequent modifications must be made in these areas as a product moves through the life cycle.

## Experience Curves and Economies of Scale

The next planning tool, the *experience curve*, attempts to find strategic marketing advantages in a company's production and cost control systems. The basic idea is that the more times a person performs an activity, the better the performance. As more efficient ways are learned to get the job done (i.e., through division of the job into particular tasks and through learning over time of better techniques and shortcuts in terms of those tasks), unit production costs fall. Workers can produce more in less time, and material usage declines as waste and mistakes are eliminated. All the while, quality is improving. This notion of producing better-quality products at lower costs is the strategic basis for many of the industrial inroads made by the Japanese into world markets.

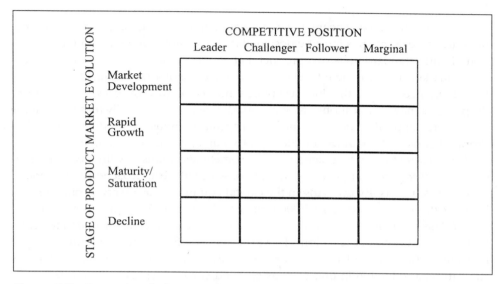

**Figure 7.7.** Example of Alternative Portfolio Approach

An experience curve is a plot of the relationship between unit costs and *cumulative* volume (as opposed to absolute volume in a given time period, which would produce an average cost curve). Numerous studies have shown that unit costs fall a fixed percentage each time cumulative volume doubles. This fixed percentage ranges as high as 20% to 35% for many industrial and high-tech products. The cost savings come primarily from lower variable production costs (e.g., direct labor and materials) but can also take the form of lower selling and distribution costs. Purchasing and inventory costs can also be reduced, especially if just-in-time systems are adopted.

One means to take advantage of the experience curve is through product standardization. By reducing the number of options available with a product and by modularizing components, a company can more quickly move out to the right on the curve.

Although the experience concept applies especially to continuous process manufacturing situations and to capital-intensive heavy industries, its application to service industries and products with short life cycles is unclear. Furthermore, its strategic implications for firms operating in information-intensive industries is doubtful—the fixed costs of producing a piece of software, for example, may be huge, but the variable costs are almost irrelevant. The very first copy of Windows 95®, for example, cost Microsoft[8] many hundreds of millions of dollars to produce; the second copy, a few cents. Also, unlike purely physical goods, information-intensive products are not scarce in the economic sense. Although a firm like Microsoft might sell a copy of Windows NT to a company to run its network, Microsoft still "has" the product. The economics of these phenomena will certainly have an impact on the way many business-to-business marketers think about strategy. (For a good discussion of these issues, see Kelly, 1998.)

To benefit from the concept, the experience curve must be managed over a product's life cycle. Strategies must be designed that will allow for large-volume production of fairly standard units of a product. Penetration strategies that emphasize capturing market share can be effective if competitive conditions permit. One lesson of the experience curve is that industry price tends to follow costs down. As this price drop occurs, new applications of the product become economically feasible, leading to even greater proliferation. The integrated circuit, an industrial product whose costs dropped about 28% with each doubling of volume, is a good example.

*Economies of scale* is a related concept sometimes confused with the experience curve. For discussion purposes, economies of scale will be approached as a phenomenon of fixed costs. By investing in the capital equipment necessary to operate on a larger scale of operation (e.g., 5,000 units per day versus 50), unit costs can be reduced. This point may seem confusing, because costs are increasing due to the capital investment (i.e., depreciation); however, this is a fixed total. As more units are now able to be produced, the fixed total is spread over this higher output. The net result can be a reduction in unit costs as all fixed costs are spread or allocated.

Consider a firm that sold marketing research services and performed a lot of mass mailings. A mailing can be broken down into a number of tasks, including letter signing, folding, stuffing into envelopes, sealing, stamping, affixing an address label, and bundling. Assume that management employs three laborers, each performing all these tasks. Output is initially 300 letters per hour. At an hourly wage rate of $5, the labor cost per letter is $.05. With time, however, workers become more dexterous and develop systems and techniques for breaking the task down and getting jobs done more efficiently. Output per worker increases appreciably. The experience effect finds unit costs falling with each doubling of accumulated output, as labor time per letter is reduced. Wastage of materials (letters, envelopes, and stamps) is also reduced. Both labor and materials are variable costs. At the same time, finished letter quality goes up. This scenario happens only in a work environment that encourages and rewards learning.

Staying with the same example, assume that management purchases machines to perform all these tasks. One employee is paid $10 an hour to run the equipment and move materials from machine to machine. The total investment is $20,000, depreciated over 5 years. Machines are operated about 1,600 hours per year. There is also a cost of about $2 per hour to run the machines (i.e., for electricity, lubricants, and maintenance). Output per hour is now 9,000 letters. Unit costs per letter (excluding materials) drop all the way to $.0016 due to the economies brought on by large-scale production. The fixed costs are higher but are being spread over many more units.

## Technology Life Cycles

Just as products evolve through some sort of a life cycle, so do the technologies that generate these products (Ford & Ryan, 1981). When a new technology is first discovered, it represents a scientific breakthrough. At this point, the commercial appli-

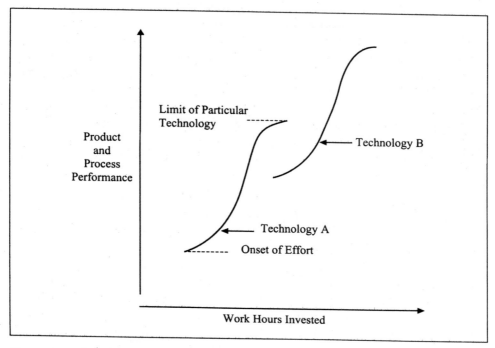

**Figure 7.8.** Two Technology Life Cycles

SOURCE: "A Call for Vision in Managing Technology," *McKinsey Quarterly* (Summer, 1982), Foster. Originally appeared in "A Call for Vision in Managing Technology," *Business Week*, no. 2740 (May 24, 1982), pp. 24-28, 33. © Copyright 1982 by *Business Week*.

cations of the technology may not be apparent. Alternatively, the technology may have several potential applications, some of which remain fairly vague (e.g., we think it might have some application in surgery). Some technologies never actually result in practical commercial applications, usually because the projected costs prove to be enormous. If the investment is made, and if the technology is successfully embodied in a new product, then the PLC concept comes into play.

Next, design engineers come up with product modifications and possible applications of the technology to other product areas. Licensing the technologies to other manufacturers is considered. Then, there may be a kind of takeoff, with significant growth in the number of new applications. The technology eventually matures, although modifications and improvements are being made. At this point, the firm might consider selling the technology. The application opportunities are becoming limited, and it may make sense to focus on transferring the technology to less-developed countries. Finally, the technology becomes degraded, having been fully exploited, and new technologies have been developed.

The suggestion is that technologies evolve through the same type of S-curve as that for products, as illustrated in Figure 7.8. Here, technology A is developed and eventually begins to mature. By the time it does, technology B has begun to generate product applications superior to those from technology A.

Industrial marketing managers would be wise to monitor technology life cycles. They drive product life cycles and can influence the rate at which a product moves through the PLC. Customers of the industrial marketer who benefit from consciously seeking ways to achieve and maintain an advantage over their competitors are more likely to consider novel solutions to their needs that have been developed from new technologies. As a result, the technology life cycle can serve as an early warning system for marketing managers, forecasting the impending maturity and decline of their own products (Shanklin & Ryans, 1987). By contrast, sales volume, which is the focus of the PLC, tends to be a lagging indicator of a product's maturation.

## Alternative Perspectives on Strategy and Marketing

Thus far, this chapter has explored many of the core concepts and tools in strategy as they apply to the industrial marketer. It may also be worthwhile to consider different perspectives on these issues that have begun to emerge. This is done in an effort to provide the reader with a more complete picture, not to suggest that one perspective is wrong and the other right. As with most important questions in life, there is probably no one right answer, and the astute reader will realize that the truth probably lies somewhere in between.

### Is Strategy Really a Conscious, Rational, Planned Activity?

The logic as presented up to this point is that every organization must have a strategy and that it is the task of management (especially top management) to formulate and oversee the implementation of that strategy. An organization without a strategy is like a ship without a rudder: directionless and sure to founder in a sea of growing turbulence. Strategy typically is conceived of as a set of rational techniques for managing organizations in changing environments, and, although things may deviate at times from this ideal, strategies are generated in a logical and systematic fashion.

Some observers have questioned the notion of strategy as a taken-for-granted, unquestioned resource for directing where companies go (e.g., Mintzberg, 1994). Some argue that strategy is not independent of the actions or practices that it is frequently drawn upon to explain or justify. In a sense, those involved with creating a strategy may be creating or overemphasizing the very problems the selected strategy is designed to address. Thus, strategy, rather than being a response to preexisting problems, is actively involved in the creation, or redefinition, of problems in advance of offering itself as a solution to them (Knights & Morgan, 1991, p. 270).

The practice of strategy may have at least four less conscious consequences. These include the following.

1. Strategy is not so much rational as a process of rationalization: It renders the world explainable. The vagaries of the market, competitors, and one's own organization's success and failure are explainable through strategy.

2. Strategy legitimizes managerial hierarchies and inequalities in terms of income and work conditions: After all, it is top management who brings the skill of strategy formulation to organizations, without which they are doomed to failure (according to strategic theory).

3. Strategy engenders managers with a feeling of power and control: They have their destinies, at least in part, in their own hands. It also provides a sense of meaning: Through strategy, life avoids the existential crisis of the "meaningless void."

4. Strategy enhances an organization's image to the outside world: By practicing strategy, organizations and their management are seen as rational, purposeful, and thus worthy of trust and investment. From this perspective, strategy has overtones of formal religion.

Apparent shortcomings in how strategy may work in companies have not gone unnoticed, and indeed some observers argue that strategic decisions are not *made*, they are *realized*. Management comes to realize what the larger strategic direction of the firm is by piecing together the actions, developments, and resource allocations of the firm over time. The common thread that runs through the concepts of "muddling through" "emergent strategy," and "logical incrementalism" (Mintzberg & McHugh, 1985), is that when we talk about strategic decision making, there is not really any deciding going on.

## Is Strategic Planning Different Because of New, Emerging Forces?

The traditional view of strategy in organizations has been that it is possible to understand fully the environment in which the organization functions, and therefore to plan accordingly for the firm's future. This view might be acceptable when the environment changes slowly and the future is reasonably predictable; however, in recent years some observers (e.g., Downes & Mui, 1998) have noted that the environment is changing so swiftly that it is not possible to plan strategically for the future. The changes that occur rapidly are not so much in the political or legal, economic, or social and cultural environment—they emerge as the result of phenomenal changes in technology and the effects these have on society.

If one were to study the occurrence of inventions in history, one phenomenon is particularly prominent—the rate at which technological change occurs over time. During the Middle Ages, for example, significant innovations appeared at a very slow rate—sometimes as infrequently as 200 or 300 years apart. During the time of the Renaissance, new technologies appeared slightly more rapidly—for example, the invention of movable type by Gutenberg. During the time of the Industrial Revolution, inventions began to emerge far more frequently, roughly at the rate of one every 5 or 10 years. Entering the 20th century, innovations began to surface once every 2 years, or indeed every year.

The kinds of innovations that we are talking about are not simple improvements; rather, we are referring to what have become known as "killer applications" (Downes & Mui, 1998). A killer application, or "killer app," is not merely an innovation that improves the way something is done. It is not even something that changes a market or an industry—a killer application is one that changes the way society works and functions. The motor car was a "killer app" because it did not just simply replace horse-drawn carriages or change the way people traveled—it changed the way we live, shop, work, and spend our leisure time. In the past 10 or 15 years, we have seen killer applications appear at the rate of more than one a year. Strategy that attempts to plan 5 years ahead is thus befuddled by the fact that society and the way the world works may indeed change at the rate of one or two killer applications a year. The more traditional strategic planning models are less effective at dealing with the kind of strategic planning problems caused by killer applications and rapid technological changes.

We may need a new perspective on the emerging forces that affect strategy and the way organizations deal with the future. One possibility is that we consider five new forces that will affect the way the business-to-business environment works. These are Moore's Law, Metcalfe's Law, Coasian economics, the flock of birds phenomenon, and the fish tank phenomenon.

## Moore's Law

In 1965, an engineer at Fairchild Semiconductor[9] named Gordon Moore noted that the number of transistors on a chip doubled every 18 to 24 months (see the Business Marketing Capsule). A corollary to "Moore's Law," as that observation came to be known, is that the speed of microprocessors, at a constant cost, also doubles every 18 to 24 months. Moore's Law has held up for more than 30 years. It worked in 1969 when Moore's start-up, Intel Corp.,[10] put its first processor chip—the 4-bit, 104-KHz 4004—into a Japanese calculator. It still works for Intel's more current 32-bit, 450-MHz Pentium II processor, which has 7.5 million transistors and is 233,000 times as fast as the 2,300-transistor 4004. Intel planned a 100-million-transistor chip for the market in 2001 and a 1-billion-transistor powerhouse performing at 100,000 MIPS in 2011. For users, it has been a fast, fun, and mostly free ride, but can it last? Although observers have been saying for decades that exponential gains in chip performance would slow in a few years, experts today generally agree that Moore's Law will continue to govern the industry for another 10 years, at least.

The implications of Moore's Law are that computing power becomes ever faster and ever cheaper. This means not only that just about everyone can therefore have affordable access to powerful computing but also that the power of computers can be built into devices other than computers themselves. Already, computers are used in

## BUSINESS MARKETING CAPSULE

### Moore's Law—Recent Developments

Moore's Law does face two other formidable sets of laws: those of physics and economics. A mind-numbing variety of things get exponentially harder as the density of circuits on a silicon wafer increases. The Semiconductor Industry Association's (SIA) 1997 Technology Roadmap identified a number of "grand challenges" as the width of individual circuits on a semiconductor chip shrinks from today's 250 nanometers (or billionths of a meter) to 100 nanometers in 2006, four product cycles later. One hundred nanometers is seen as a particularly challenging hurdle because conventional manufacturing techniques begin to fail as chip features approach that size. It isn't just making the chips that's getting more difficult—as Intel discovered in 1994 when an obscure flaw in its then-new Pentium processor triggered a firestorm of bad publicity that cost the company $475 million. Modern chips are so complex that it's impossible, as a practical matter, to test them exhaustively. Increasingly, chip makers rely on incomplete testing combined with statistical analysis. The same methods are used to test very complex software, such as operating systems—but for whatever reason, users who are willing to put up with software bugs are intolerant of flaws in hardware. At the present rate of improvement in test equipment, the factory yield of good chips will plummet from 90% today to an unacceptable 52% in 2012. At that point, it will cost more to test chips than to make them, the SIA says. Chip makers are hustling to improve testing equipment—and are extremely reluctant to discuss the matter, which they see as vital to their future competitiveness.

Although the cost of a chip on a per-transistor or per-unit-of-performance basis continues to fall smartly, it masks a grim reality for chip makers: A fabrication plant costs about $2 billion today, and the price is expected to zoom to $10 billion—more than a nuclear power plant—as circuit widths shrink below 100 nanometers. Significantly, "scaling" isn't one of the SIA's grand challenges. "Affordable scaling" is. Indeed, the industry's progress may eventually be slowed by a lack of capital, says James T. Clemens, head of very large-scale integration research at Bell Laboratories, the Murray Hill, N.J., research and development arm of Lucent Technologies, Inc. "Social and financial issues, not technical issues, may ultimately limit the widespread application of advanced [sub-100 nanometers] integrated circuit technology," he says. As an analogy, Clemens points to the airline industry, which knows how to routinely fly passengers faster than sound but, due to the cost and technical complexity, doesn't do it. "A lot of people are worried about cost," says John Shen, a professor of electrical and computer engineering at Carnegie Mellon University in Pittsburgh. "You see more and more companies bailing out."

*continued*

Transistors are etched onto silicon by optical lithography, a process by which ultraviolet light is beamed through a mask to print a pattern of interconnecting lines on a chemically sensitive surface. The conventional approaches that work at 250 nanometers probably can be refined to etch features as small as 130 nanometers: 400 atoms wide, which is one thousandth as thin as a human hair. But at 100 nanometers and below, where the wavelength of light exceeds the size of the smallest features, entirely new methods will be needed. An Intel-led consortium is working on "extreme ultraviolet" lithography, which uses xenon gas to produce wavelengths down to 10 nanometers. An approach favored by IBM uses X rays with a wavelength of 5 nanometers. Meanwhile, Lucent is developing lithography that uses a beam of electrons. These and other alternatives are complex, costly, and still unproven.

Continued progress in processor speeds will require better ways of designing and making chips, but the biggest obstacles to higher performance may currently lie just off the chip: in the motherboard and in the logic that connects the chip to cache memory, graphics ports, and other things. "We do not have the design or manufacturing capabilities in those off-chip structures to keep up with the rapid growth in processor clock speeds," says Bruce Shriver, a consultant in Ossining, N.Y., and a computer science professor at the University of Tromso in Norway. "Unless the design and implementation capabilities in those areas catch up, they will be a critical limiting point." But Albert Yu, general manager of Intel's Microprocessor Products Group, says Shriver is worried about a "very temporary problem." Increasingly, off-chip units such as cache will become integrated onto the processor chip, allowing them to work at the same high frequencies as the processor and eliminating the bus between them, he says. In just the past few months, a number of promising announcements have come out of U.S. research labs: Last month, IBM began shipping 400-MHz PowerPC chips that use copper wiring instead of the conventional aluminum, which doesn't perform as well but is easier to manufacture. As circuits shrink, the performance and cost advantages of copper grow. IBM announced last month that it could boost transistor switching speeds 25% to 35% by putting an insulating layer of silicon dioxide—called "silicon-on-insulator"—between the transistor and its silicon substrate. Refinements of the technology, which reduces distortion and current drain, could push feature widths down to 50 nanometers, IBM says. In February, a graduate student research team at the University of Texas, working with the industry consortium Sematech, printed 80-nanometer features (one-third the size of today's) on a semiconductor wafer. Remarkably, the tiny features were produced with conventional deep ultraviolet light. The advance was due to a special etched-quartz mask developed by DuPont Photomasks, Inc., in Round Rock, Texas. None of these is the breakthrough that will buy another decade for Moore's Law, but they illustrate the kinds of advances that chip away at the brick wall toward which Moore's Law is habitually said to be headed. Says Carnegie Mellon's Shen, "We've always said there's this wall out there, but when you get closer to it, it sort of fades away or gets pushed back." Many hands make light work.

Ultimately, users don't care about transistor counts, clock speeds, or even MIPS. They care how much real work their computers get done. One way to make the processor do more work is to move some of the work from hardware to software. Today's microprocessors are able to achieve "superscalar" performance by executing several instructions simultaneously. Intel's Pentium II—which can execute up to five instructions at a time—predicts the flow of a program through several branches by looking ahead in the program. It analyzes program flow and schedules execution in the most efficient sequence. It also executes instructions "speculatively"—before they are needed—and holds the results in suspense until the predicted branches are confirmed. But there's a law of diminishing returns for this technique because the chip must devote more and more of its circuitry to management of the complex processes. Now an old concept—the very long instruction word (VLIW) processor—is making a comeback, notably in the new 64-bit Merced chip, part of the Explicitly Parallel Instruction Computing (EPIC) family of processors being developed by Intel and Hewlett-Packard Co. VLIW counts on the compiler, and to some extent the programmer, to specify where parallel execution of code is possible, relieving the processor of that burden. VLIW has some pitfalls, says Carnegie Mellon University's chip expert John Shen. "Merced is hoping that, by moving the work to the compiler, you can make your hardware very clean and fast," he says. But complexity in software traditionally has been harder to manage than complexity in hardware, he says, and it takes longer to develop new compilers than new microprocessors. Intel senior vice president Albert Yu won't reveal how EPIC works, but he says labeling it a VLIW architecture is a "misinterpretation." Rather, he says, "We rely on the compiler to do a lot of stuff." Bruce Shriver, co-author of a new electronics book, *The Anatomy of a High-Performance Microprocessor*, says improvements in hardware-based branch prediction algorithms will allow superscalar processors to execute a dozen or more instructions simultaneously, twice what is possible today. He says compilers will be created that do a better job of optimizing code for more efficient execution.

SOURCE: Gary Anthes, IDG.net homepage, on www.cnn.com, October, 1998.

products as diverse as vehicles, surgical equipment, and elevators, enabling these machines to operate more efficiently, predictably, and safely. In the not too distant future we can expect to see computer chips in disposable products such as packaging as the costs continue to decline.

### Metcalfe's Law

How useful is a piece of technology? The answer depends entirely on how many other users of the technology there are and on how easily they can be interconnected. For example, one telephone is relatively useless, a few telephones have limited value, and a million telephones create a vast network. These effects are known as *Metcalfe's Law*. Robert Metcalfe, founder of 3COM Corporation[11] and the designer of the robust Ethernet protocol for computer networks, observed that new technologies are valuable only if many people use them. Specifically, the usefulness or utility of the network equals the square of the number of users, a function known as Metcalfe's Law. The more people who use software, a network, a particular standard, a game, or a book, the more valuable it becomes and the more new users it will attract, increasing both its utility and the speed of its adoption by still more users. The Internet is perhaps the best illustration of Metcalfe's Law. Although it began in the 1960s, it was only in the mid to late 1990s that it gained momentum. As more users joined the medium, it became more useful to even more users, thus accelerating its growth. Now its potential to spread new ideas, products, and services is awesome.

### Coasian Economics

Nobel Prize winner in economics Ronald Coase made a discovery about market behavior that he published in a 1937 article titled "The Nature of the Firm" (Coase, 1937). Transaction costs are basically inefficiencies in the market that arguably should be added to the price of a product or service. Table 7.3 notes six basic types of transaction costs and shows how technologies such as the World Wide Web can affect them. Transaction cost economics gives us a way of explaining which activities a firm will choose to perform itself and which it will rely on the market to perform. For example, transaction cost economics is a useful way to explain the outsourcing decisions that many firms face—for example, whether the firm should do its own cleaning or pay someone else to do this. Also consider communication technology. The effect of communication technology in the past has been to increase the size of firms. Communication technology permits transaction costs to be lowered to the extent that firms are able to subsume many activities within themselves. This has enabled multinational corporations such as General Motors,[12] Siemens,[13] and Unilever[14] to operate as very large entities across continents, essentially managed from a head office. What is overlooked is that the effect of technologies, accelerated by Moore's Law and Metcalfe's Law, will be to reduce the costs of the market itself. As the market becomes more efficient, the size of firms might be considerably reduced. A very tricky strategic issue indeed!

### The Flock of Birds Phenomenon

A feature of the new communication technologies of the late 1990s was that, in many cases, these technologies did not "belong" to any one institution, nor were they controlled by any particular authority. Some have referred to this as the "flock of birds

**TABLE 7.3**   Type of Transaction Costs and How the World Wide Web Affects Them

| Types of Transaction Costs | Examples of How the World Wide Web Can Reduce Them |
| --- | --- |
| Search costs (finding buyers, sellers) | Reduce time and effort in finding products, services, and potential suppliers. Example: A collector of tin soldiers wishes to identify sources for collection worldwide. Search engines and comparison sites will find these using the search term "tin soldier." |
| Information costs (learning) | Example: A customer wishes to learn more about digital cameras and what is available before purchasing. He or she previously would have had to read magazines, talk to knowledgeable individuals, and visit stores but can now access company and product information easily and at no cost, obtain comparative product information, and access suppliers on the Web. |
| Bargaining costs (transacting, communicating, negotiating) | Time normally taken by the customer to negotiate can now be used for other purposes as intelligent agents transact and negotiate on the customer's behalf. On-line bidding systems can achieve similar results. Example: General Electric in 1996 purchased $1Bn from 1,400 suppliers over the Internet, and there is evidence of a substantial increase since. Significantly, the bidding process for the firm has been cut from 21 days to 10. |
| Decision costs | The cost of deciding in favor of Supplier A vs. Supplier B, or Product A vs. Product B. The Web makes information available on suppliers (off their own or comparative Web sites) and products and services. Example: Travel Web sites allow customers to compare hotels and destinations online. |
| Policing costs (monitoring cheating) | Previously, customers had to wait to receive statements and accounts, then to check on paper for correctness. Example: On-line banking facilitates allowing customers to check statements in real time. Chat lines frequently alert participants to good and bad buys as well as potential product and supplier problems. Example: The flaw in Intel's Pentium chip was communicated extensively over the Internet. |
| Enforcement costs (remedying) | When a problem exists with a supplier, how does the customer enforce contractual rights? In the real world, this would require legal assistance. Publicizing the infringement of rights would be difficult and expensive. Chat lines and bulletin boards offer easy and inexpensive revenge, if not monetary reimbursement. |

phenomenon." When one observes a flock of birds flying in formation, or a school of fish swimming in a distinct pattern, one is tempted to speculate whether there is or could be a "head fish" or a "bird in charge." Naturalists will explain that flocking is a natural phenomenon and that there is indeed no "head" fish or bird in charge. The network in effect becomes the processor. We have been conditioned to seek a controlling body or authority for most of the phenomena that we experience in life. This could be a large firm, a government body, or a ruling institution. In the case of many of the phenomena of the late 1990s such as the Internet and the World Wide Web, there is indeed no one in charge. These are great mechanisms for democracy but are also anarchic, and society may have to develop new ways to deal with these liberating effects.

### The Fish Tank Phenomenon

Moore's Law and Metcalfe's Law combine to give individuals inexpensive and easy access to new media such as the Internet. This means that anyone can set up a Web site and, theoretically at least, be seen by the world. As a result, many have noticed the so-called fish tank phenomenon. There is an immense amount of junk on the Internet—such as sites that show a video camera perched on top of a coffee percolator or someone's tropical fish tank. It is tempting to suggest that perhaps the Internet should be left to large organizations so that we may enjoy the creative capability and resources of these institutions. When we think about which is more profound, however—the resources of large corporations or the creative ability of millions of individuals—the power of the fish tank phenomenon becomes apparent. Although large organizations may have the resources to produce large and rich Web sites, the creative potential of millions of individuals working in different parts of the world will indeed be more significant. There may be an enormous amount of junk out there, millions of individuals trying to show us their fish tanks, but there will also be creativity of unlimited potential. This means that many firms may find themselves threatened by small start-ups that were previously unable to gain access to the market. No longer will it be good enough to merely observe one's close and known competitors. In the future, the competitors could be anyone and anywhere.

## Are Corporate Strategy and Marketing Becoming One and the Same?

Perhaps the most profound impact of the environmental turbulence companies face today is the manner in which it is changing the nature of relationships between organizations and their external publics, and most notably, their customers. Webster (1992) has argued persuasively that customer relationships are increasingly the key strategic resource of any business. Moreover, without customers, strategy does not really matter. From a business-to-business marketing perspective, this argument obviously makes a lot of sense.

As things are evolving, marketing begins to transcend all the elements of strategy in a firm. McKenna (1991) notes, "Marketing today is not a function; it is a way of doing business. . . . [It] has to be all-pervasive, part of everyone's job description, from the receptionists to the board of directors" (p. 65). His thinking resonates with the marketing concept as discussed in Chapter 1. It is possible that marketing and corporate strategy are becoming one and the same. Consider three perspectives on what strategy means for a company, and the corresponding implications for how marketing operates in the company.

◆ With the first perspective, strategy is a process of matching internal strengths and weaknesses to external opportunities and threats. Product/market choices are a key outcome. Marketing becomes the set of decisions (the 4 Ps) for accomplishing this by specifying how the firm will compete in its chosen markets.

◆ In the second perspective, strategy is approached as the result of interactions among key forces operating within an industry, especially the intensity of rivalry among competitors. Strategies can be formally developed or may emerge over time, but they are concerned with the ongoing quest for competitive advantage based on the firm's position within its industry. Moreover, a set of generic strategies is identified. Marketing becomes a major vehicle for turning generic strategies into reality. Identification of sources of differentiation, segmentation of markets, establishing bases for product positioning, and targeting of the firm's resources become critical marketing concerns.

◆ A third perspective finds strategy and marketing beginning to converge as environmental turbulence and chaos become defining forces for the firm. New forms of business organization begin to appear. Customer relationships are recognized as the most vital strategic resource of the firm. Strategy is a process of flexibly adapting to accelerating environmental change, and for capitalizing on the firm's distinctive competencies within defined market niches, or indeed the "ultimate market of one" (Blattberg & Deighton, 1996). The focus is on "leveraging" and "stretching" the organization in terms of marketplace aspirations (Hamel & Prahalad, 1993). Entrepreneurship is emphasized (see Chapter 8) as the firm seeks to create and capture new markets while leading customers with a steady stream of innovative new offerings. The role of the industrial marketer becomes negotiating mutually beneficial relationships with customers, investing in projects that heighten the dependence of buyer and seller on one another, jointly exploring new technologies, sharing resources, and developing new products and markets together. Traditional market segmentation may even disappear as an option as the individual firm is addressed. Value-based relationships with suppliers and distributors are also key responsibilities. Marketing measures of performance (e.g., customer satisfaction, loyalty, and share of the customer rather than share of the market) begin to be regarded as accurate indicators of the strategic health of the firm.

Elements of all three perspectives can be found in companies today, but the clear trend appears to be toward the third perspective.

## Implications for the Marketing Professional

Where does all of this leave the traditional marketing department in the industrial firm and the specialists that reside therein? One suggestion is that there will be no need for these units in 10 or 20 years—they "self-destruct" as everyone in the firm assumes responsibility for marketing (Bonoma, 1990). Just as the pyramid-shaped, hierarchical organization is becoming obsolete, so too may most functional departments, especially marketing, become artifacts. In their place may be flexible teams and partnerships consisting of individuals of varied backgrounds and representing multiple organizations. Members will flow into and out of these groups as conditions require, and the groups themselves will form and dissolve in accord with the life of a product concept or a market niche. The only constant will be customer relationships, and the organization as a whole will continually put together novel packages of resources to grow these relationships and to capitalize on new opportunities.

The need for specialized knowledge, such as market research or customer service training, will remain, but the so-called specialists of today may find themselves out of place if their abilities and knowledge are not broadened. Organizations likely will contract out for many such services as they attempt to better leverage their resources. Thus, today's specialists will have to develop a wide range of skills related to assessing and satisfying the needs of customers, suppliers, and distributors. Today's industrial marketer will have to become a champion of innovation whose ongoing charge is to make the firm's current offerings obsolete while creating entirely new market niches. He or she will have to be comfortable with multiple technologies, speed as strategy, and extensive customization in the marketplace.

Marketing, particularly in the business-to-business sphere, will become more "complicated" in the years to come. These complications will occur in the sense that formula-based approaches to the marketing mix will give way to more qualitative, subjective approaches. One has only to consider the complexities involved in tailoring products to diverse user requirements, in setting value-based prices instead of relying on cost-plus formulas, and in evaluating employees based on their performance at relationship building rather than in meeting sales quotas.

Such a conceptualization of marketing as a boundary-less activity is much closer to the essence of the marketing concept as espoused almost 40 years ago. Under this conceptualization, marketing becomes strategy, and strategy becomes an approach for bringing the customer inside the company. It is consistent with McKenna's (1991) claim that "marketing is everything."

## Summary

This chapter began by introducing the concept of strategy, with a specific focus on marketing strategy. Marketing strategy is a specification of the target markets a company is after and the related marketing mix intended to satisfy each distinct market. The next few chapters will elaborate on each of the elements in the marketing mix. A marketing strategy serves to coordinate marketing activities in a manner that reflects current and anticipated future market conditions, and it addresses customer problems to provide a distinctive competitive advantage—all done in a manner that contributes to the organization's financial objectives. A distinction is drawn between strategy and marketing tactics, the actions and expenditures used to implement a strategy.

Industrial firms not only need to build their marketing efforts around coherent strategies but also need to adopt a strategic marketing perspective. Here, the managerial orientation is toward environmental analysis, a longer time frame, and cooperation among the major strategic areas of the firm in designing marketing strategies. Products are seen as playing different roles, making different contributions to the overall performance of a company.

Recognizing the large variety of potential strategies open to the industrial marketer, methods of grouping or classifying strategies were presented. These included strategies aimed at new/existing products and new/existing markets, primary versus selective demand strategies, and Porter's three generic strategies. Although such classification schemes provide direction, it is important to keep in mind that strategy development is a creative process on which few limits should be placed.

The chapter next provided a planning framework within which industrial marketing strategies can be developed. Marketing planning involves projecting the future and determining the courses of action that will best achieve marketing objectives. Toward this end, strategic planning should not be a once-a-year activity. Rather, planning should be an interactive, continuous process in which assumptions are tested, performance deviations are analyzed, and strategies are modified. Strategic planning is a philosophy as much as an activity. Viewed in this way, proper motivation and skills are prerequisites.

A number of conceptual tools can be useful in successful planning. Among these tools are the product life cycle, product portfolios, the experience curve, and technology life cycles. Each of these was explained, with implications drawn for the determination of strategy.

Strategic thinking and planning has become a must for the industrial firm. The competitive environment is changing at a pace unlike that at any time in the history of commercial enterprise. Dynamic, threatening change creates uncertainty; strategic planning is a vehicle for understanding and coping with a complex, turbulent world. In fact, the most successful firms in any industry are almost always the ones doing more and better strategic planning. They use planning to manage and control their futures, creating change rather than simply responding to it.

Marketing and strategy are both changing in fundamental ways—indeed some, authors are questioning whether it is possible and feasible to plan as formally as organizations have done in the past. These perspectives were also considered in this chapter, including a view of five new forces that may shape the environment of the business-to-business marketer in the future. The chapter concluded with a discussion of the possibility that marketing and strategy may indeed converge in the firm of the future.

# Notes

1. www.hp.com/
2. www.cnn.com/
3. www.insurance-assoc.com/

4. www.cgu-insurance.net/
5. www.landg.com/
6. www.mnp.com/
7. www.bcg.com/
8. www.microsoft.com/
9. www.fairchildsemi.com/
10. www.intel.com/
11. www.3com.com/
12. www.gm.com/
13. www.siemens.com/
14. www.unilever.com/

# Questions

1. A medium-sized firm that provides temporary employees to companies on an as-needed basis has traditionally relied on a short-term, reactive approach in managing its marketing-related activities. Why is it important for this company to adopt a strategic orientation? How would such a strategic orientation affect the way in which the firm approaches and carries out the marketing function?

2. Identify an example of a marketing tactic. Demonstrate how that same tactic could be part of two different types of marketing strategies. Explain the different purposes the tactic might serve in each of the strategies.

3. How might a firm be pursuing primary and selective demand strategies at the same time and for the same product? Assume the company is NCR and the product is electronic cash registers.

4. All-Pro Chemical produces a line of fertilizers used in home gardening applications. The company recently announced the successful development of a new fertilizer, to be called Ultragrow, that has been shown to increase fruit tree output by 25%. Consequently, inquiries from fruit growers have been overwhelming, and demand is expected to be very strong. Demonstrate how each of the strategy frameworks presented in Figure 7.1 might be applied to guide All-Pro's initial marketing efforts.

5. In the strategic marketing planning model presented in this chapter, why are objectives established in the middle of the process, instead of at the beginning?

6. What are some potential dangers in placing too much emphasis on market share gains as the objective when designing and implementing marketing programs?

7. What kinds of information would you need to estimate the experience curve for a new product? Can you have economies of scale without the experience curve effect?

8.  How would you expect your sales, costs, cash flow, unit profits, customer demand, and competition to change in moving from the growth stage to the maturity stage if you were a manufacturer of automated teller machines sold to financial institutions?

9.  Walker Wire Corporation manufactures copper wire for use in electrical cords. A number of companies compete with Walker, and each produces an almost identical product line. Given this apparent homogeneity in what is being sold, what are some ways in which Walker might differentiate its product offerings?

10.  Would portfolio thinking be useful in developing marketing strategies for a small company that sells video production services (e.g., for television commercials, training films, industrial films, convention support) but also sells and leases video equipment (e.g. monitors, cameras, recorders) as well as video accessories (e.g., cables, switchers, tripods, carts, tapes, jacks, and plugs)?

11.  You manufacture deadbolt locks and sell them to businesses of all types. Your product line consists of 67 different lock models, all made of steel and operating mechanically. How would an understanding of technology life cycles be useful in strategic planning for your firm?

# CHAPTER 8

# Innovation, Entrepreneurship, and the Business Marketer

*Think revolution, not evolution.*
—Richard Sullivan, Home Depot

*The computer revolution is now more than 50 years old . . .*
*but what's coming makes what's here look Neolithic.*
—Tom Peters

## Key Concepts

| | |
|---|---|
| Barriers to product success | Market launch |
| Brainstorming | Market merit |
| Cannibalism | Operational merit |
| Categories of adopters | Proactiveness |
| Concept testing | Product failure categories |
| Continuous innovation | Product testing |
| Discontinuous innovation | Profitability analysis |
| Dynamically continuous innovation | Screening criteria |
| Embodiment merit | Strategic window |
| Imitation strategy | Structures for innovation |
| Innovation charter | Synergy |
| Innovation diffusion process | Technical feasibility analysis |
| Intrapreneurship | Test marketing |
| Inventive merit | Venture team |

## Learning Objectives

1. Establish the importance of innovative activities in industrial firms and identify major types of innovation.

2. Determine major reasons for new product/service success and failure.

3. Explain the concept of a product/service innovation charter and the need for a strategy in the innovation area.

4. Describe a process for developing new products and services, and outline the role of marketing during the stages of the process.

5. Identify ways to structure organizations to encourage innovation, and emphasize the need for marketing departments to be a source of corporate entrepreneurship.

## The Importance of Innovation

The marketing concept (Chapter 1) dictates that long-term profitability can be achieved only if a company identifies and stays in touch with the needs, wants, and problems of the market. Furthermore, the company must develop products and/or services that address these needs, wants, and problems better than competitors' offerings. Maintaining this competitive advantage involves fighting a never-ending war. Battles may be won or lost, but the war continues—because needs, wants, and problems change, and so do the competitors. As a result, product and service innovation must be a normal, ongoing activity within the industrial firm.

The primary markets of a company can expand or contract, or markets may become more segmented or fragmented, requiring multiple products where one or two were adequate before. Financial conditions change, forcing customers to restructure their purchasing criteria. Such developments might force customers to gravitate toward, or away from, the vendors on whom they currently rely. At the same time, a company's raw material sources may become scarce or more expensive. New technologies may be adopted that make the firm's operations more efficient. Competitors may introduce advances that make a company's products obsolete. These are very common developments in companies today, and each of them initiates the need for new product and service development (see Table 8.1 for a more complete list). Without a steady flow of new products and services, industrial companies invite their own demise. In fact, market leaders are increasingly finding that *30-40% of their revenues come from products that did not exist 3 years ago*. The same is likely to be true 3 years from now.

This is not to say that any given company must be producing breakthrough innovations. In some cases, it may be profitable to innovate incrementally, or to adopt an

**TABLE 8.1** Factors That Initiate the Need for New Product and Service Development

Companies generally are motivated to develop new products by one or more of the following interrelated factors:

1. The perceived inability to achieve final goals of profit and earnings per share with the existing product line
2. The desire to maintain an established rate of sales growth
3. Moves by competitors to develop new products or reposition existing products
4. Management recognition that the product life cycle of an existing product is reaching maturity
5. Rapid changes in technology, placing pressure on management to innovate as competitors develop the new technology
6. Major inventions that open entirely new markets and create opportunities for a number of new products
7. Government regulation or deregulation, forcing firms to consider new products or product changes in compliance with the current regulatory environment
8. Major changes in the cost or availability of key raw materials
9. Changes in customer demographics that cause changes in their wants or needs
10. Requests from customers who have encountered a particular problem or need
11. Identification of a new product opportunity by a supplier, who then induces the manufacturer to pursue the opportunity

SOURCE: Adapted from *Entrepreneurial Intensity*, p. 30, Morris. © Copyright 1998 by Quorum Books. Adapted by permission.

imitation strategy, following the lead of others into a new product or technology. Whatever the approach, the firm must continuously stay abreast of innovative opportunities, or management will find the company slowly losing the capacity to adapt to changing market conditions.

This chapter examines various types of innovation activity and the risks associated with new product, service, and process development. The position is taken that marketing not only must be intimately involved in innovation but also should serve as an important vehicle for achieving an entrepreneurial orientation in companies.

# Types of Innovation Opportunities

The word *innovation* brings to mind dramatic new products and services that create entirely new markets and change the way customers satisfy their needs. Although a major breakthrough is sometimes the case, most new product activity takes the form of improvements to existing items or extensions of the current product/

| Product or service that is new to the world |
| --- |
| Product or service that is new to the country or market |
| New product or service line (new to the company) |
| Addition to a company's existing product or service line |
| Product/service improvement or revision, including addition of new feature, option, or capability |
| New application of existing product or service, including application to a new market segment |
| Repositioning of an existing product or service |
| Process improvements that lead to customer value creation, productivity enhancement, and/or cost reduction:<br>◈ New administrative system or procedure<br>◈ New production method<br>◈ New marketing or sales approach<br>◈ New customer support program<br>◈ New distribution or support method<br>◈ New logistical approach<br>◈ New financing method<br>◈ New pricing approach<br>◈ New purchasing technique<br>◈ New organizational form or structure |

**Figure 8.1.** A Continuum of New Product Opportunities

service line. In fact, it is helpful to recognize that different degrees of innovation are possible. A distinction can be drawn between a discontinuous innovation, a dynamically continuous innovation, a continuous innovation, and imitation (Robertson, 1967).

A *discontinuous* innovation is fairly revolutionary and has a disruptive impact on established buyer behavior patterns. These types of products or services address needs that previously have gone unmet (e.g., the first airplane or the integrated circuit) or change the way in which customers satisfy a need (e.g., facsimile machines). *Dynamically continuous* innovations, alternatively, generally do not alter established ways of satisfying a need but do have some disruptive effects. Examples include the electric typewriter and the cellular telephone, when each was introduced. *Continuous* innovations are the most common type, and they have little or no disrup-

**TABLE 8.2**  Characteristics of Different Types of Innovation Activity

| Category | Risk | Potential Return | Investment Required | Number of People Involved | Level of Management Approval | Development Cycle |
|---|---|---|---|---|---|---|
| New to the world | High | High | Major | 20-35 | Board level | 3-4 years |
| New to country or market | High | High | Major | 10-15 | Board level | 2-4 years |
| New product line | Moderate | High | Major | 10-15 | Board or senior executive level | 1-3 years |
| Extension of existing line | Moderate | Moderate | Moderate | 5-6 | Business unit level | 18 months |
| Product revision | Low | Moderate | Low | 3-5 | Product manager | 6-12 months |
| Product support innovation | Low | Low | Low | 1-3 | Functional manager | 3-6 months |

tive effect. Existing products or services are improved incrementally. New features may be added, or quality may be increased. The risk to the buyer, as well as the marketer, is usually lower for these types of products and services, but the long-term profit potential is also lower. Finally, *imitation* involves simply replicating someone else's innovation. When 3M successfully introduced Post-it Notes some years ago, a number of competitors followed suit with virtually identical notepads.

Figure 8.1 provides a more complete breakdown of innovation opportunities. Here, a continuum of innovation activity is presented, ranging from entirely new-to-the-world products and new lines on one end, to repositioning efforts, significant cost reductions, and major process improvements on the other. What becomes apparent is the amount of room for innovation beyond that involved in major technological breakthroughs. Different kinds of innovation are appropriate, depending on the company in question and its current circumstances. Also, a firm may be pursuing efforts in a number of the areas along this continuum at the same time. Marketers should also be aware of the tremendous potential in the area of process (as opposed to product) innovation. Finding new ways to price, promote, sell, distribute, bill customers, or manage logistics and customer service can be just as innovative and have just as much impact as a new or improved product.

The risks involved and the resources necessary to engage in the different types of innovation will vary widely (see Table 8.2). Clearly, whereas an adept value analysis team with a modest budget may be able to create cost savings in production or distribution, much more funding would be needed to develop a new product line for the

**TABLE 8.3** Fourteen Dilemmas of Innovation

1. Innovation is about the unknown. Management is about control. How do you control the unknown?

2. Innovation is about breaking the rules. People who break rules don't last long in organizations.

3. Successful innovation tends to occur when there are constraints, routines, and deadlines. There is a need for both freedom and discipline, and the issue is one of balance.

4. An innovation succeeds because it addresses customer needs, yet when you ask customers about their needs, many do not know or cannot describe them to you except in very general terms.

5. Innovating is risky. Not innovating can be more risky.

6. Innovation can be revolutionary or evolutionary. The costs, risks, and returns of both types differ, and the two require different structures and management styles.

7. A company that innovates frequently makes its own products obsolete when there was still profit potential in those products.

8. Innovation requires supporting infrastructure to be successful, and the existing infrastructure is often inadequate. These infrastructure needs may not become apparent, however, until after the innovation is developed.

9. Although innovation is more technically complex and costly today, the majority of breakthrough innovation comes not from large companies or corporate R&D labs with sizable budgets but from individual inventors and entrepreneurs.

10. People who design innovations typically seek to perfect their new product or service, making it the best possible, but the marketplace wants it to be "good enough," not "perfect." The additional time and money necessary to make the innovation the "best possible" may drive up prices beyond what the customer will pay and result in missed "windows of opportunity."

11. Technology-driven innovation leads to dramatic new products that prove to be "better mousetraps nobody wants." Customer-driven innovation leads to minor modifications to existing products or "me too" products meeting a competitive brick wall.

12. Although typically associated with genius or brilliance, innovation is more often a function of persistence.

13. Although innovation is associated with breaking the rules of the game (e.g, 3M), it frequently entails playing an entirely different game (e.g. Starbucks, Dell).

14. Being first to market is not consistently associated with success, and being second or third is not consistently associated with failure.

company. In the same vein, companies often will find that they must create different organizational structures to match the type of innovation they are encouraging. This point will be elaborated on later in the chapter. The role of marketing also varies along the innovation continuum, and this changing role is another area to be expanded on later.

## Innovation Dilemmas and Risks

Understanding how innovation works is difficult. It is inherently a messy process; tends to require incredible persistence; has the occasional "aha!" moments surrounded by long and tedious research, analysis, and experimentation; and can be very frustrating. Once an innovation has been developed, there may be tremendous resistance to it within the very company where it was developed. Those who attempt to make innovation happen find it to be an activity filled with dilemmas that do not lend themselves to simple resolution. Table 8.3 summarizes a number of these dilemmas, each of which is elaborated upon throughout the remainder of this chapter.

External forces (e.g., diminishing opportunity streams; short decision windows; turbulence in the technological, economic, regulatory, and competitive environments) are making innovation a necessity in virtually every industrial firm. It is not simply an issue of developing more new products, services, and processes, but one of developing them faster, getting them to market faster, and replacing them faster with even newer innovations. Achieving this kind of continuous innovation requires that firms *not* try to perfect each new product or service, adding an array of technical "bells and whistles" and trying to ensure that each will be a major improvement and successful in the market. Instead, innovations must be designed to be "good enough," reflecting the trade-offs customers make when buying a new product, and without a lot of costs engineered into a new product or service that customers find no value in or for which they are unwilling to pay. Furthermore, as companies come to recognize that large research laboratories or R&D departments are not always the most productive source of successful innovations, they are attempting to encourage pockets of innovation throughout the organization. Phrases such as "skunk works" have become popularized to describe teams or individuals who, on their own initiative, work in isolation (or on the side), pursuing ideas or projects that have yet to be approved or assigned formal budgets.

Despite what has been said up to this point, there is a tendency within industrial firms to actually resist innovation. It is natural in companies to resist any kind of change, especially if the change means learning new ways of doing things, or if it might take resources away from existing product and service programs. In addition, failure rates for new products are quite high, and substantial funds can be spend on products that never get past design, development, and test marketing. As a result, product and service innovation sometimes seems to present a kind of Catch-22: Innovation is vital to the survival of the modern industrial firm, yet the high costs and uncertain market reaction associated with an innovation can cause the same failure the company was attempting to avoid.

What are the effects of new product failure on a company? First is the obvious danger of negative financial and economic effects on the company. New product innovation requires the application of cash, fixed assets, people, and other scarce resources. If the effort fails, the overall profit performance of the firm is affected. A string of product failures could cause a company to become insolvent. Furthermore, any product failure only serves to increase the returns required from the next innovation.

A more subtle type of danger is the effect of failure on company image. Current and prospective customers who see new products fail generalize these observations to their image of the company. A succession of new product failures will have a negative impact on customer assessments of the ability of the company to deliver satisfactory products. At the same time, stockholders and other investors may begin to lose faith in the ability of senior management and specialists in the firm to perform their jobs adequately.

Another area of concern could be described as the psychological well-being of the company. Just as a series of product successes builds pride among company personnel, a string of failures erodes their faith in the organization. Salespeople, for instance, might become reluctant to push new products on trusted customers, or they may begin to doubt their company's claims of product superiority over the products of leading competitors. Also, personnel retention becomes an issue where product failures are not managed and held to a reasonably low level. Loss of personnel, particularly salespeople and senior managers, results in more than the loss of bodies. Investments in training, product and market knowledge, and perhaps even company secrets may be lost.

Even where innovation produces market success, there are potential dangers. A new product, once introduced, can absorb substantial amounts of company resources, leaving fewer dollars to support research or the promotion and distribution of existing products. The sales force and/or distributors have less time to support those existing products.

Management's time is also diluted, especially given the high visibility of innovation efforts. Distraction of managerial time is especially serious where new products or services are either very successful or very unsuccessful. With very successful products, the company usually has not established new organizational structures to accommodate the growth of these products, resulting in greater demands on management. With unsuccessful new products, a hesitancy to admit failure finds management preoccupied with correcting problems and improving results. Meanwhile, internal pressures to perform continue to mount.

A new product that represents a significant technological improvement can also speed the decline of the existing product line. Cannibalism, whereby new products take sales away from existing ones, becomes a problem. In addition, new products significantly different from those traditionally sold by the company can dilute or alter the company's image or position in the marketplace. Successful new products may also absorb a sizable portion of the firm's production capacity, resulting in more stockouts and longer delivery lead times for existing products.

Beyond putting pressure on existing products and services, innovations that really take off in the marketplace cause significant cash flow problems in their own right. The escalating costs of inventory and receivables can produce a negative cash flow, despite impressive sales growth. Although there is likely to be a payoff down the road, severe financial pressures develop in the interim.

## Why Do New Industrial Products and Services Fail?

Although the word *failure* is not widely used or acknowledged in many companies, a surprisingly high number of new products and services do not achieve management's minimum performance objectives in the marketplace. Some years ago, a Booz Allen & Hamilton study (1968) found that less than 15% of all products introduced became commercial successes. Subsequently, Crawford and di Benedetto (1999) concluded that 20 to 25% of new industrial products fail, while the failure rate for consumer products is between 30 and 35%. Cooper (1993) claims that the overall success rate is only about 59%. Furthermore, even where new industrial products initially succeed, rapid technological change shortens their life cycles. Success frequently is short-lived.

How can the probability of success be improved? A first step is to identify the underlying causes of failure. In a landmark attempt to address this issue, Calantone and Cooper (1977) examined a wide variety of industrial product winners and losers. They found that the product failures could be grouped into six basic categories.

1. *The better mousetrap no one wanted* (28% of failures). These products, despite being unique in certain ways, did not satisfy the needs of many potential customers and were ignored by the bulk of the market. Typically, the company overestimated market penetration. There were usually no other obstacles to the product. Technical problems were minimal, the competitive environment was not intense, the selling effort usually was adequate, and there were no problems in the timing of the product introduction. This type of failure often results from technical R&D efforts that are not guided by marketing research or other inputs from sales and marketing personnel.

2. *The me-too product meeting a competitive brick wall* (24% of failures). In these failures, the product was very similar to products already on the market. The imitative product met customers' needs but faced intense competition from entrenched firms with established market shares and a loyal customer base. In essence, these limitations lacked a significant differential advantage and were not welcomed by the marketplace. Such noninnovative new products are commonplace because management sees them as having low risk.

3. *Competitive one-upsmanship* (13% of failures). New products falling into this category might be described as orphans of the new product development process. They often received insufficient market analysis, internal development, or market launch support. Consequently, once in the market, they were one-upped or copied by competitors who

## BUSINESS MARKETING CAPSULE

### *Failure of a Better Mousetrap*

Introduce a unique product especially designed to satisfy the needs of a well-defined customer segment, and sales will respond positively, right? Not necessarily.

Hewlett-Packard Co. thought it had the perfect marketing strategy: Focus on the millions of U.S. salespeople who weave their way across the corporate countryside. Attack that market with a computing tool explicitly suited to its needs and desires: long battery life, ruggedness, and light weight. The ultimate weapon was Hewlett-Packard's Portable Plus.

"Think about the sales environment," said Rick Baker, then the marketing manager for Hewlett-Packard's Personal Computer Division, in mid-1987. "All day you are in and out of customer locations—booting the laptop up, interrupting operations, shutting down, maybe 10 or 15 times a day. So you'd like a product that's very well adapted to this start/stop, constant-interruptions environment. With the Portable Plus's electronic disk drive, you can stop whatever you've been doing, close up the box, and never have to worry about off-loading files. With the Plus's continuous built-in memory, files stay intact, even when the machine is suddenly turned off."

Ironically, it was the electronic disk drive, representing the major source of innovation, that caused the Plus's failure in the marketplace. As with most products, there are trade-offs involved in design and development. "The Portable Plus is not PC compatible. The electronic disk drive means you cannot run your floppy software or files," acknowledged Mr. Baker.

Research at Hewlett-Packard had indicated that the Plus would be quite popular with sales reps and sales managers. With the Plus's unique configuration—ruggedness and idiot-proof file storage—the company hoped for good sales in a segment where it would not have direct competition.

Things didn't quite work out that way. "It's fair to say that the Portable Plus's reception by the marketplace has not been all we expected it to be," says Terry Eastham, portables manager. "The absence of PC compatibility was a negative factor. You'd go in to talk with sales managers and, based on user features, you would have the sale made. But data processing managers of the major corporations we had targeted voted very, very strongly for a PC-compatible machine. Their question was, in the long-term view of overall corporate data processing, what's it going to cost to support this non-PC compatible enclave of computing?"

"Hewlett-Packard made some bad strategic decisions in the laptop arena," adds Steve Hess, director of the microcomputer group for Creative Strategic Research International. "It had the potential to be a winner, but it forgot about

*continued*

industry standardization. Even if end-users would end up never wanting to run their floppy software, they still wanted the option to be able to run it. When you deviate from the standards, people get leery. Hewlett-Packard simply alienated the market."

*Source:* Adapted from "Hewlett-Packard Misfires Its Marketing Weapon," *Business Marketing,* 74 (January, 1989), p. 56, McCarthy. © Copyright 1989 by *Business Marketing.* Adapted with permission.

had done their marketing homework. Although the market clearly appreciated the products, their producers were beaten to the marketing punch by competitors.

4. *Environmental ignorance* (7% of failures). Products in this category were plagued by a variety of deficiencies, beginning with the planning process and carrying through to implementation and launch. Product development and/or introduction did not reflect the changing requirements of the technical, regulatory, competitive, economic, or customer environments.

5. *The technological dog product* (15% of failures). These products simply did not do the job; they did not perform in the manner expected by the marketplace. Interestingly, the companies marketing these products often clearly understood what their customers wanted in product design but were unable to deliver. As a consequence, the product was labeled a dog.

6. *The price crunch* (13% of failures). For this group of products, the market price was not commensurate with the value that customers felt the product contained. Price must be a reflection of value, and value is perceived in the minds of the customers. Too often, when new products are introduced, management expects to recover the costs of design, development, and introduction too quickly. These costs should be recovered over the life cycle. Also, companies preoccupied with costs often will expect new products to immediately cover a sizable amount of corporate overhead.

Usually, a number of specific underlying causes of failure can be identified. The company may not possess, or may not allocate, resources sufficient to ensure product success. These resources include financial support, engineering skills, R&D expertise, marketing research efforts, production capabilities, and selling activities. Evidence suggests that companies tend to spend much more on technical activities, while many critical marketing activities receive little attention and even fewer funds.

Even if the company possesses and spends the resources, product development may be performed in an inept or deficient manner. Internal incompetence can produce poor technical assessments, loose screening criteria, inflated estimates of market potential, inaccurate financial analysis, and weak quality control standards in production. Failure can also be traced to a host of marketing-related errors. Marketers often show bias in their marketing research efforts, both in underestimating customer loyalties to current vendors or customer switching costs and in inaccurately assessing the strengths of products already on the market. It is easy to misinterpret the reasons for a competitor's success. Furthermore, new product introduction can be too early or too late for the market, or it may not be coordinated with the timing of marketing efforts such as promotional programs or distribution channels. Also, the elements of the marketing mix can be inconsistent with one another. In short, then, new product failure is a multidimensional problem facing most industrial organizations.

## Dimensions of Success

Successful innovation in the industrial marketplace appears to be contingent on a few key conditions (see Figure 8.2). The ground-breaking work in this area has been done by Robert Cooper, who, in one of his key studies (1979), compared 102 new product successes with 93 failures. He determined that the most important success factors are product uniqueness and superiority in the market. This finding underlines the need for companies to identify a truly unique product and a meaningful differential competitive advantage. Success also appears to be directly linked to the company's knowledge of the marketplace and its proficiency in marketing activities (i.e., selling, distribution, and promotion). In other words, companies that have a firm understanding of the needs, wants, and characteristics of target customers, and are able to translate this knowledge into appropriate marketing actions, tend to achieve positive marketplace results. One implication is that when developing new products, it may be more appropriate to emphasize markets with which the company is familiar and avoid completely new markets. Success also requires certain technical capabilities. Specifically, the company must be proficient in both technical engineering and production, and it should be able to achieve synergy between the two.

In addition to these keys to successful new products, Figure 8.2 identifies certain facilitators of success. Among them are the availability of sufficient marketing resources (money, people) and the managerial skills to manage those resources, a strong marketing communication and launch effort, and a large, growing market with a clear need.

On the other side of the coin, Cooper notes some significant barriers to success. The most important barrier involves the need for a vendor's product both to be perceived as offering an economic advantage to the customer and to be priced competitively. Problems in this area most typically can be traced to a high cost structure on the part of the manufacturer, especially in new product areas where the firm has little experience. Success is also more difficult in markets characterized by numerous product introductions in short periods of time. Under such circumstances, the level of uncertainty and the aggressiveness of competitor actions suggest that any new product is in jeopardy. Another barrier to success concerns the attitudes and preferences of potential customers who are already well satisfied with entrenched competitors, and where source loyalty is fairly well established. In such cases, even products that are of higher quality and lower price can be resisted or ignored in the marketplace.

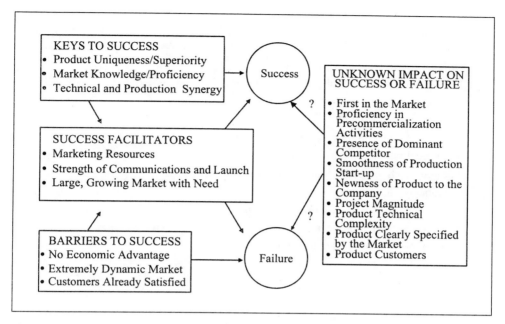

**Figure 8.2.** Factors Affecting the Success or Failure of a New Product

SOURCE: Adapted from "The Dimensions of Industrial New Product Success and Failure," *Journal of Marketing, 43* (Summer, 1979), pp. 101-102, Cooper. © Copyright 1979 by the American Marketing Association. Adapted with permission.

In Figure 8.2, the box to the far right includes a number of factors whose impact on product success or failure remains unclear and continues to be debated. For example, being the first company to introduce a new product, having a smooth production start-up, or pushing products that are more technically simple does not necessarily increase or decrease the chances for success.

## The Need for Strategy: An Innovation Charter

Recognizing the opportunities and dangers posed by new products and services, management must take positive steps to improve the probability that innovative efforts will be successful. Toward this end, there is a need for industrial companies to develop a specific strategy for innovation, sometimes referred to as the firm's innovation charter (Crawford & di Benedetto, 1999). Innovation is like any other significant activity in companies: If plans, objectives, and strategies are not formulated in this area, it is unlikely that much will happen, and certainly not much will happen on a consistent basis. By formulating an innovation strategy or charter, management is forced to think through, and make formal decisions regarding, a number of issues that otherwise might be overlooked (see Table 8.4).

**TABLE 8.4** Major Decision Areas to be Addressed in the Innovation Charter

A. Nature of new products developed
   1. Degree and nature of the product differential advantage sought
   2. Product innovativeness
   3. Product quality level
   4. Product concentration versus diversification
   5. Product type (e.g., customization)
B. Nature of technology (production and development used)
   1. Concentrated versus diversified technology
   2. Technology fit or synergy with the firm
   3. Maturity of technology (e.g., state-of-the-art versus old technology)
C. Types of new product markets sought
   1. Market size, growth, and potential
   2. Competitive situation
   3. Stage of the product life cycle
   4. Marketing synergy with the firm
   5. Market newness to the firm
D. Orientation and nature of the new product program
   1. Whether the program is defensive or offensive
   2. Internal versus external sources of new product ideas
   3. Technical versus market orientation of the program
   4. Whether the R&D effort is pure or applied
   5. Risk level of projects
   6. Magnitude of spending

SOURCE: Adapted from *New Products Management*, pp. 59-71, Crawford and di Benedetto. © Copyright 1999 by Irwin Publishing.

Major decisions areas include the characteristics of new products and services to be focused on, the types of technologies to be developed, the nature of the markets for which new products and services are to be developed, and the kind of development program to be relied on. In making decisions in these areas, the company must make three overarching decisions: (a) how conservative or innovative new product and service efforts will be, (b) how offensive (proactive) or defensive (reactive) they will be, and (c) how much these efforts will reflect synergy or diversification. *Innovativeness* concerns the degree to which a new product or service is a complete departure from existing offerings, relies on state-of-the-art technologies, or is a high-risk venture. *Offensiveness* (*proactiveness*) concerns the extent to which a company takes the aggressive lead in developing new products or markets. *Synergy* is the consistency or compatibility of new products and services with the company's current product/services mix and resources.

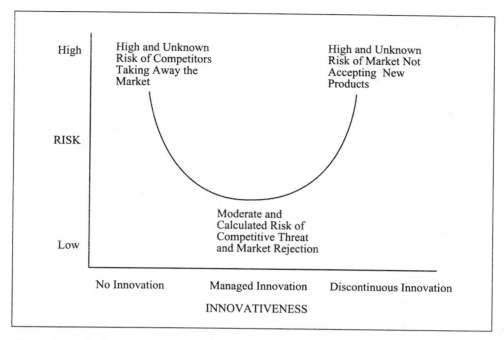

**Figure 8.3.** To Innovate or Not: The Curvilinear Risk Function

The innovation charter will determine the amount of emphasis placed on the development of new products and services within the company's total marketing effort. At one extreme, a company may opt for no innovation whatsoever. Management may simply emphasize existing offerings and devote no resources to sensing marketplace changes or meeting competitors' new products and services. At the opposite extreme, a company may seek to be the innovation leader in an industry, providing a steady and continuous flow of major improvements and entirely new innovations. Such major breakthroughs hold the lure of tapping sizable profit opportunities. Between these two endpoints is an intermediate position where new products and services are balanced against existing ones and development activity emphasizes product modifications, revisions, line extensions, and occasionally a new item or line. Thus, the firm has a "portfolio of innovation activity" with a number of projects under way at a given point in time. Furthermore, the firm seeks to vary (and balance) the levels of risk, potential return, time of return (short versus long term), amount of learning, technological sophistication, and related variables across this innovation portfolio.

Figure 8.3 illustrates different innovation orientations as they relate to the amount of risk the company assumes. As can be seen, risk is high both when the company ignores new product and service opportunities and when it pursues truly innovative opportunities. Companies that do not innovate are faced with higher risk of market and technology shifts that go unperceived and are capitalized on by competitors. Unless a company has a strong customer franchise and enjoys stable market demand assumed to last for long periods of time, market share will be lost to proactive competitors. At the same time, those firms that engage in extensive innovation are often moving into uncharted waters. Consequently, there is a high risk of market failure through improper market analysis, mismatch of technology to market needs, or inadequate design of marketing programs. These companies also may find themselves inundated with product and service launches and in real danger of being unable to devote sufficient time, energy, and other resources to all these projects. In the middle of the continuum, risks are moderate and success rates are the highest. This position, however, is not necessarily the one that generates the most profitable new products and services.

The key conclusion to be drawn is that innovative activity must be managed. In fact, the most successful innovators are often not the firms spending the most on R&D and product launches. Instead, they are the companies that manage innovation as an integral and everyday aspect of the strategy and structure of the organization. Some of the characteristics of companies that are consistently successful innovators include the following (Rothwell, 1980):

1. Organizational commitment to continuous innovation,

2. Innovation as a corporationwide task,

3. Attention to marketing, user needs, and aftersale servicing in product/service development,

4. Effective design and development work,

5. Good internal and external communication, and

6. Management skills and professionalism.

The beginning point, however, is to recognize that innovation consists of a variety of activities that must be organized into a logical process. Let us now examine the stages of this process and the role of marketing over these stages.

## Product/Service Innovation as a Process: The Role of Marketing

*Management* implies planned, controlled, and predictable activities, whereas *innovation* is often unplanned, uncontrollable, and unpredictable. The terms *management* and *innovation*, however, are not necessarily contradictory. As a creative process, innovation requires direction and a certain amount of control. Otherwise, money is wasted, projects are not coordinated and often are not completed, and efforts are duplicated. The end result can be a variety of impressive technical innovations for which there is no market.

The new product or service development process usually does not evolve in a neat, orderly fashion. Its complexity is demonstrated in Figure 8.4. After the fact, when people are recounting what happened in developing an innovation, it seems far smoother and systematic than it actually was. Innovations never happen as

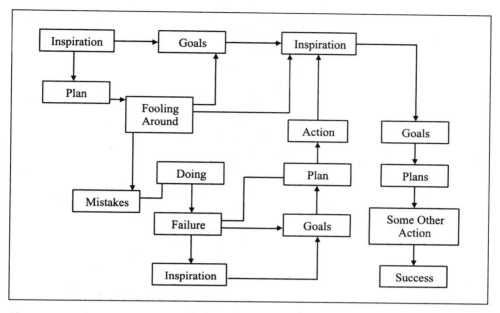

**Figure 8.4.** How Innovation Actually Works

SOURCE: Reprinted with permission of the publisher. From *Intrapreneuring in Action: A Handbook for Business Innovation,* © Copyright 2000 by G. Pinchot and R. Pellman. Berrett-Koehler Publishers, Inc., San Francisco, CA. All rights reserved. 1-800-929-2929.

planned because no one can accurately plan something that is truly new. Some have referred to the management of innovation as "controlled chaos"; nevertheless, there are some key steps that generally must be accomplished to produce a commercially successful new product. These are outlined in Figure 8.5. The process itself is never as linear as suggested in Figure 8.5, a point to which we shall return. Also, keep in mind that ideas are being discarded all along the way. Each stage, from idea generation through market testing, represents a go/no go decision. As a result, only one of every 100 new product or service ideas might actually get to the market. Furthermore, activities performed in the early stages in the process—especially initial screening, preliminary market assessment, and technical feasibility analysis—are the most critical for new product success and tend to be the most weakly handled (Cooper, 1988). Let us briefly examine what takes place at each stage and the role that marketing should play.

## Idea Generation and Screening

The ideas for new products and services come from a variety of sources. R&D engineers often discover the potential for a new product by exploring new and established technologies or by examining new patents. Production managers identify opportunities for product improvement, modifications, or cost reductions based on their understanding of current and alternative production techniques. Those in mar-

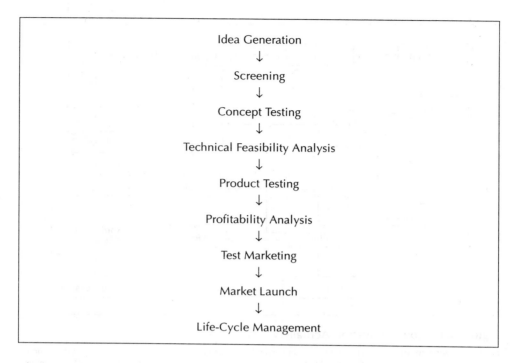

**Figure 8.5.** A More Formal New Product Development Process

keting and sales generate new product ideas through their formal and informal interactions with customers, distributors, and others. To the extent possible, competitors' R&D strategies (including expenditures) and market testing efforts should be monitored. Customers are an especially important source of new product ideas in industrial markets, as they are likely to do extensive analysis of their own problems and needs, often coming up with ideas for technical solutions. Customers, however, are not in a position to actually develop the products to meet those needs.

Managers and employees not involved with new products are also a vital source of creative thinking. Companies will institute suggestion boxes, incentive programs, and other formal efforts to reward employees who present viable ideas for new innovations. For such programs to be effective, however, careful attention must be given to submitted suggestions. Employees become skeptical of these programs if the focus is simply to ignore ideas or find out what is wrong with them, rather than finding ways to make the ideas work.

Brainstorming sessions involving key personnel also can be useful. People with different backgrounds are assembled after having a few days to think about a particular customer problem or market opportunity. They try to generate as many ideas as possible, worrying more about quantity than about quality. Criticism of ideas is not permitted; the group tries to build on ideas rather than attacking them. Often, trying to address a problem using a frame of reference that no one has thought of before or

**TABLE 8.5** Checklist for Selecting New Product Ideas

*Fit with the company*
- ❑ Equipment necessary
- ❑ Production knowledge and personnel necessary
- ❑ Raw materials availability
- ❑ Relation to present product lines
- ❑ Effects on sales of present products
- ❑ Relation to present distribution channels
- ❑ Quality/price relationship
- ❑ Salability and promotability
- ❑ Fit with company culture and image
- ❑ Impact on development of other projects

*Fit with the market*
- ❑ Numbers of potential users and uses
- ❑ Extent to which customers would be new or current
- ❑ Growth rates of users and usage
- ❑ Breadth of market
- ❑ Extent to which customers perceive a need
- ❑ Extent to which customers currently are satisfied
- ❑ Learning required of new users
- ❑ Similarity/dissimilarity to current products on market
- ❑ Number and aggressiveness of direct and indirect competitors
- ❑ Barriers to market entry
- ❑ Seasonal and cyclical nature of demand
- ❑ Time before product becomes obsolete

that initially seems a bit outlandish can produce innovative solutions. Once the session is over, raw ideas are categorized, evaluated, and tested.

The largest number of new ideas is discarded during the screening stage. The company applies a set of evaluative criteria to the ideas and rates each one. This evaluation includes a determination of how well the idea fits with the company and how well it fits with the market. Specifically, evaluation answers such questions as Does the firm have the internal resources to turn the idea into a commercially successful product? Will the product be consistent with the current strengths and strategies of the firm? and What is the growth potential of the market? Examples of screening criteria are listed in Table 8.5.

The more radical a technical innovation seems, the more difficult the evaluation process becomes. In such cases, it is useful to investigate four considerations regarding the product concept: (a) inventive merit, (b) embodiment merit, (c) operational merit, and (d) market merit.

*Inventive merit* is the degree to which the innovative concept relieves or avoids major constraints in the existing way of solving a problem or need, thus advancing the scientific state of the art. *Embodiment merit* is the assessed value of the physical form given to an inventive concept. Having come up with a technological advance, the concern now becomes turning the concept into a physical product. The form the product takes must reflect user requirements while offering as many enhancements as possible. *Operational merit* pertains to the effect of an innovation on a company's existing business practices. This merit is derived from eliminating or superseding certain business operations, such as eliminating required service support or reducing required inventory levels. *Market merit* refers to the revenue opportunities provided by the innovation. Revenue opportunities can be substantial where innovations are clearly more attractive to customers than existing competitive offerings. Of course there are trade-offs among these four sources of merit; for example, the form of the product may dilute the value of the inventive concept. Note that the first two forms are related primarily to the technical potency of the innovation; the second two are more concerned with the business advantage provided by the new product. (For an insightful discussion of this, see White and Graham, 1978.)

## Concept Testing

Those ideas that survive initial screening must undergo further scrutiny through concept testing. At this point, the company is often working with only a hypothetical product and is often considering a number of different versions. A concept test provides initial reaction from customers regarding their intentions and probabilities of purchasing the different versions of a product, should it be developed. This test usually is carried out through individual interviews with key decision makers and users in prospective customer organizations, and occasionally with focus groups. When test results are combined with estimations of awareness and distribution coverage, management has a tool for generating an initial sales forecast. A determination can also be made of the benefit segments most likely to buy the product. In addition to soliciting customers' basic responses to the product concept, marketers usually ask which aspects customers like and dislike, how the product is similar to or different from products currently in use, if they see any potential usage problems, and for suggested improvements.

## Technical Feasibility Analysis and Product Testing

The remaining product concepts, now fairly well defined around some core benefit, must be transformed into a physical product and undergo performance testing.

*Technical feasibility analysis* involves identifying the technical requirements for designing and producing the product. Despite an enthusiastic response by the market, the company may be unable to translate the product concept into a finished product at a reasonable cost. Management must determine if this can be done and must estimate the R&D spending necessary to overcome all the technical constraints. The required investment in plant and equipment is also estimated, together with the unit cost of production. The more specific the data generated from concept testing, the more precise these estimates can be.

Assuming that technical obstacles can be surmounted at a reasonable cost, a physical product is engineered. This may be a prototype, although prototypes are sometimes developed for use in concept testing. Design engineers conceive different versions of the product, based on the many trade-off decisions that must be made among product attributes. For example, there may be a trade-off between speed of performance and product safety, or between heat resistance and ease of use. Whatever trade-offs ultimately are made, the core benefit is critical and must not be sacrificed.

With *technical product testing,* the innovation is subjected to a thorough examination of tolerances and performance capabilities. Close scrutiny is given to differences in product reliability or performance under differing conditions, such as light/heavy or frequent/infrequent usage, extremely cold temperatures, or unusual power surges and outages. Companies may be asked to use the product in their businesses and to draw comparisons with competing products. Such tests will enable management to establish maintenance schedules and service requirements, as well as to determine any improper applications of the product, which are to be avoided.

Marketing plays two key roles at this stage. First, technical staff involved in product design will often overengineer a product, seeking to achieve performance standards or capabilities that go beyond what a customer wants or is willing to pay for. Thus, marketing provides insights regarding the trade-offs in product performance on key attributes that the customer is willing is to accept. Second, marketing provides inputs regarding the way in which the customer is likely to actually use the product, as opposed to the way the engineers would like the product to be used. Customers typically use products in ways never intended, or in work conditions that differ from those the designers had in mind. When they do so, and when the product subsequently malfunctions or does not perform up to expectations, it becomes the liability of the seller, not the buyer.

For those products that perform successfully in the areas of technical feasibility analysis and product testing, the product tests also become a valuable source of information for establishing the initial pricing, promotion, and distribution strategies. Estimates of production and user costs will influence price. Technical reports can be included with promotional materials. Personal sales calls and advertising should be build around the attribute bundle included in the final product. Sales training will emphasize technical product considerations, as will the design of the initial distribution channel.

## Profitability Analysis

Products that successfully pass a detailed technical examination will not necessarily be profitable. To determine profit potential, projected net cash flows (net revenues minus actual expenditures) must be estimated for the company's planning time horizon and compared to the initial investment in the product. Industrial firms tend to evaluate new products over some predetermined time period, such as 3 to 5 years.

Because of the time value of money (i.e., the many other things the firm could be doing with its resources if this new product were not developed), companies generally expect that the sum of the projected net cash flows for the time period will exceed the initial investment and provide some minimum rate of return. This rate of return should reflect a number of factors, including the opportunity cost of the project, the riskiness of the project, company objectives, and expected inflation. Firms will sometimes use their current cost of capital as a minimum rate of return.

Two logical questions result from this analysis. First, how long will each project take to repay its initial investment? Second, which project(s) will exceed the minimum required rate of return over the planning horizon? Given the limited resources of most organizations, not all the projects expected to be profitable can be pursued. Projects have to be prioritized on the basis of their payback period and overall rate of return.

*Cannibalism* is a related issue that should be incorporated into this financial analysis. New product sales come from new customers attracted to the market, from competitors' customers, and from the firms' existing customer base. If the new product is taking sales away from other products in the firm's product line, this generally means that customers see the new product as a substitute for something they already purchase from the same firm. The key point here is that failure to take cannibalism into account means that revenues from the new product are being overstated. Subtracting the cannibalism effect from the new product revenues results in a more accurate estimate of the product's financial performance.

## Test Marketing

The company now has an innovation that management believes will meet or exceed objectives, and which is consistent with resources. Rather than introduce the product to the entire market simultaneously, the company may limit initial sales to a smaller geographic area. This is called a test market and should be similar to the entire market in terms of the types of customers, their buying processes, and their needs in this product area.

Test marketing is a means of limiting risk, especially when product acceptance is uncertain, sales projections are difficult to estimate, or the costs of a full-scale launch are quite high. Through test markets, the firm is able to better match prices, promotional efforts, and other marketing decision variables with marketplace requirements. The firm is testing the elements that make up the rest of the marketing mix, not simply the product.

Conversely, test markets are expensive and can take a long time to evaluate. They are unrealistic for products with long buying cycles, those with short life cycles, and those with a relatively small customer base. In addition, a test market can tip the company's hand to competitors and should be avoided when beating the competition to the market is crucial. This caution is especially appropriate for easily imitated innovations. Also, competitors are often able to distort test results by accelerating or decelerating their marketing programs within the test market. Because of this possibility, results must be very carefully scrutinized, with an allowance for any unusual or atypical developments during the time period of the test.

## Market Launch and Life-Cycle Management

The full-scale introduction of a new product is truly a team effort. Marketing, production, distribution, selling, and service must be closely coordinated. Timing is critical for each of these activities and should be well synchronized. The acquisition and start-up of the production process, including purchases of machinery and components, has to be accomplished early enough to ensure that bugs can be worked out of the system and that costs can be controlled within acceptable variances. Starting too early, however, can produce costly inventories with the related carrying costs. Starting too late is even more troublesome, because customer back orders accumulate and goodwill is lost. Growth to capacity of production will maximize benefits subsequently derived from the experience curve and economies of scale.

Not only must production be synchronized with sales efforts, but distribution channels also must be in place to capitalize on the market opportunity. Resources are wasted if promotional efforts have been effective in creating awareness among target customers but trained distributors are not in place or there is no follow-up sales call. In some instances, initial promotional efforts may be moderate to ensure that demand can be well-served as it materializes.

Timing of the launch itself is another critical decision area. Marketers refer to the concept of the *strategic window* to describe an optimal time period within which a product or market opportunity can be taken advantage of. Premature introduction (before the window is open) usually fails because the market does not yet perceive a need. Late introduction takes place after the window is closed, when competitors are well entrenched, loyalties are established, or distribution channels are saturated. Determining the window of opportunity early in the product development process is therefore important.

An important, but somewhat overlooked, marketing activity in product/service development is the manner in which the firm announces a new item to the marketplace. These announcements should be based on formal objectives, such as (a) preempting the competition by encouraging buyers to await the firm's new product rather than purchase available offerings, (b) communicating plans for a retaliatory move against a competitor, (c) testing a competitor's reaction, (d) reassuring customers and creating a stable image for the company, and (e) repositioning the firm in a particular industry (Rabino & Moore, 1989). The announcement process is likely to include a variety of both formal and informal messages targeted to different audiences (e.g., customer groups, shareholders, competitors, trade associations, industry observers) at different points in time. Some of these messages may precede actual product/service introduction by up to a year or more. Although there is no set rule, the process frequently will begin after the new product/service has been tested internally (sometimes called *alpha testing*) and before or during testing at customer locations (*beta testing*).

The considerable uncertainty surrounding a new product launch suggests the need for a preestablished tracking program. Specific market performance milestones should be in place to identify trouble spots early. Assumptions must be monitored regarding market price sensitivity, customer purchase intentions, and competitor response. The key elements are feedback and flexibility. An immense amount can be learned in the early days of the market launch. Effective feedback can result in alterations or fine-tuning of product features, distribution strategy, prices, or the design of the selling effort—but only if the company is receptive to learning and flexible in responding to change. Often, whole new opportunities are uncovered that were not envisioned during product development.

For those products that subsequently achieve commercial success, the managerial focus becomes life-cycle management. The product life-cycle concept, introduced in the preceding chapter, is directly related to the innovation diffusion process. *Diffusion* refers to the pattern innovations follow as they are adopted by customers in the marketplace. Keep in mind that different customers will adopt an innovation at different times. Marketers want to manage, or at least influence, the diffusion of a new product to the extent possible.

The innovation diffusion process is illustrated in Figure 8.6, which plots a distribution of the number of customers adopting a new product over time, expressed as a percentage of all potential adopters of the product. Studies of the diffusion process suggest that adoption demonstrates a fairly normal distribution over time. As a result, customers can be placed into categories based on how long they wait to try a new product, relative to other customers. These categories are innovators, early adopters, the early majority, the late majority, and the laggards.

Rather than go after all potential adopters of an innovation, marketers are better served to first focus on innovators and, especially, early adopters. These are the organizations that tend to be more innovative and more willing to try something new. Once these organizations experience success with an innovation, they influence the other categories of adopters through word of mouth and example. The task, then, is to identify the characteristics of organizations more likely to fall into these first two categories. Unfortunately, innovators and early adopters vary depending on the type of new product in question and a number of situational factors. For instance, one might find that early adoption of a new computer product is more likely among companies that are larger and that have more experience with computers. Adoption of the product might be linked to decision makers with more education, buying center members with experience in a variety of jobs, and those with more self-confidence.

Although the adoption curve is bell shaped, or fairly normal, the length of time a new product takes to diffuse from the first adopter through complete market penetra-

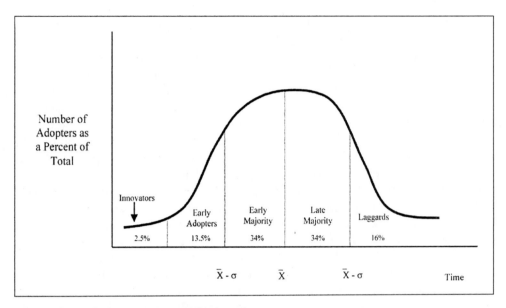

**Figure 8.6.** The Innovation Diffusion Curve

tion will vary. This time period could be a matter of months (e.g., for a new airplane safety device that the Federal Aviation Authority has mandated for inclusion in all new aircraft) or a number of years (e.g., for a highly effective chemical additive for use in textiles and industrial detergents that is potentially toxic under certain circumstances).

The speed at which an innovation will move through the diffusion process is strongly affected by its relative advantage, compatibility, complexity, divisibility, and communicability. *Relative advantage* is the degree to which customers perceive a new product to be superior to those currently in use. *Compatibility* refers to how consistent a new product is with existing customer attitudes and behavior. *Complexity* is the degree of difficulty customers will have in understanding or using the innovation. *Divisibility* concerns whether the product can be tried on a limited basis. *Communicability* is the ease with which information regarding an innovation can be communicated to users. The greater the relative advantage, compatibility, divisibility, and communicability—and the less the complexity—the more rapidly a new product will diffuse into the marketplace.

## The Process Is Not Linear

In practice, new product and service projects do not simply move from step to step in the linear fashion presented in Figure 8.5. Steps tend to overlap or may be taken out of order, and it is not unusual to get to one stage and find out certain things that force the innovation team to return to an earlier stage. A very important issue concerns the need to match the structure of the process to the selection of the team members who will be expected to work on a particular project.

An alternative perspective can be found in the "stage-gate process" (Cooper, 1996). This process involves some broad stages, each consisting of a number of activities occurring in parallel. Thus, idea generation, screening, and concept refinement may take place in tandem. A cross-functional team is put together, with the members bringing different backgrounds and perspectives to the major stages. The entrance to each stage is a gate. These gates control the process and serve as quality control and go/kill/hold/recycle checkpoints. The stage-gate process requires completion of each stage before the project can pass through a gate to the next phase of development.

Yet another perspective is to view the process as being circular, with a champion and a core team driving the project. The team is augmented by people with expertise in specific areas as the project unfolds. Within the circle are four continuous planning cycles (or loops). Figure 8.7 provides an illustration. The first loop is concerned with capturing market value and addresses the question "Does the customer care?" The second loop establishes the value of the proposed new product to the firm and addresses the question "Do we care?" The third loop focuses on putting together a solution that will be a winner and addresses the question "Can we beat the competition?" The fourth loop applies project/process planning to address the question "Can we make it happen?" Each loop contains an evaluation screen that includes criteria for assessing success potential of the new product as well as the effectiveness of the team. The core team is augmented by specialists in the different loops, such as marketing researchers to explore customer reactions to a concept in Loop 1 and financial analysts to estimate the profit opportunity in Loop 2. As the team progresses through each loop, it continually returns to a center circle that represents the value proposition created in the form of a new product. As a function of ongoing learning and adaptation, this circle, or the total value proposition, should steadily get larger. Alternatively, if over time the team is certain that the value added cannot reach the required level and there is no possibility of removing the constraints in the time available, the project is dropped or shelved. If shelved, the conditions for removing it from the shelf are clearly specified.

## Organizing for Innovation

The discussion above highlights the value of cross-functional teams, but there are many ways in which companies structure themselves for innovation purposes. Structure refers to the way in which a company divides its work into distinct tasks (i.e., marketing, finance) and achieves coordination among those tasks. It includes such issues as the number of levels in an organization's hierarchy, the span of control of managers, the amount of autonomy given to individuals, and decisions regarding who reports to whom. In terms of innovation, structure includes the assignment of responsibility and authority for new products to specific departments and personnel.

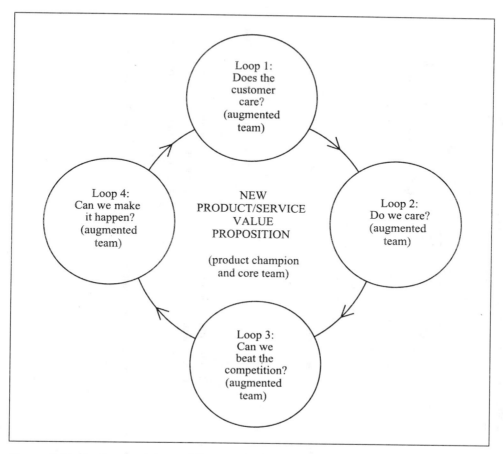

**Figure 8.7.** A Circular View of the Innovation Process

There is no one best way to organize for innovation; however, it appears that the effectiveness of different structural approaches depends on the type of innovative activity undertaken. Table 8.6 summarizes a number of the approaches that have been tried by firms. Each organizational structure has unique advantages and potential problems.

Many large divisionalized firms have consolidated new product activities in a *new product division*. Such a division tends to be large and self-sufficient, serving all the new product needs of other divisions. This form seems best suited to large firms with continuing new product demand and similar products across divisions. It has a number of advantages. Coordination and control of new product activities is centralized. Top management attention and resource allocation necessary for a long-term commitment are more likely. The division serves as a base of operations and source of rewards for creative and entrepreneurial personalities. As for disadvantages, a division may encounter problems of coordination with other divisions at points of contact such as the transfer of new products to ongoing operations. Because of the scale and

**TABLE 8.6** New Product Development Organizational Structure Alternatives: Advantages and Disadvantages

| Type of Organizational Structure | Description | Advantage(s) | Disadvantage(s) |
|---|---|---|---|
| New product division | ◆ Large and self-sufficient division | ◆ Centralized coordination and control<br>◆ Top management attention ensured<br>◆ Resources adequate<br>◆ Long-term commitment | ◆ Coordination with other divisions<br>◆ Inflexibility due to size<br>◆ Opportunity for vested interests |
| New product department | ◆ Department within division | ◆ Specialization<br>◆ Integration of efforts | ◆ Fewer resources<br>◆ Less authority |
| New product manager | ◆ One manager who is responsible for a new product | ◆ Simplicity | ◆ Can overwhelm one manager<br>◆ Cooperation from others difficult to achieve |
| Product or brand manager | ◆ New product responsibility added to normal duties | ◆ Best for line extensions or modifications | ◆ Not suited to truly innovative products<br>◆ Manager torn between regular and new product duties |
| New product committee | ◆ Standing committee with diverse representation | ◆ Several functional areas involved | ◆ Dilutes responsibility across members |

| | | | |
|---|---|---|---|
| Task forces | New product department set up on a temporary basis | Tap specialized managers on full-time basis | Unpopular with heads of departments who lose the managers |
| Ad hoc committee | Temporary matrix task force | Tap specialized managers on part-time basis | Multiple demands placed on group members |
| Venture team | Internal as well as external personnel used | Brings in outsiders' expertise | May acquire resources greater than the worth of the project |
| Outside suppliers | Contract with another company to develop | Utilizes specialists for independent work | Can be costly<br>Coordination and control problems |
| Multiple organization forms | Use of hybrid forms depending on the nature of the project | Form designed to fit needs of the project | Difficulties in managing, coordinating, and evaluating the efforts of several unique structural forms |

SOURCE: Adapted from "The Implications of Structure for New Product Success," *Proceedings*, Annual Meetings of the Southern Management Association, p. 238, Bennett, Calantone, and Morris. © Copyright 1985 by the Southern Management Association. Adapted with permission.

permanence of such a division, the firm risks the perennial problems of inflexibility, vested interests, and resistance to shifts of resources.

A more common form is the *new product department*. This structure appears well suited to any firm with continuing demand for new products. A divisionalized firm may have a number of such departments that report either to senior management or to one of the functional areas (typically marketing or R&D). A department can be staffed with functional specialists or entirely with new product specialists, who draw on functional areas for expertise as needed. Generalizing about the departmental form is difficult because of the diversity of personnel included, functions served, and reporting relationships. A department is likely to have some benefits of specialization in common with a division, but typically with fewer resources and less power. Innovative efforts may be undermined if the department's primary role is to integrate efforts of functional departments unless it has full power to control those functions. If the department is attached to, or identifies with, a particular function, resistance may be encountered from others.

Some firms vest responsibility in a *new or special products manager* (in essence a one-person new products department) who reports to a corporate, divisional, or functional executive and coordinates all new product activities. A divisionalized firm may have one such position for each division. This one-person department appears to be a rather rare approach because it is an imposing task for one manager to integrate disparate functions and activities in a firm of any size, particularly when cooperation must be engendered by personal influence rather than formal authority.

*Product or brand managers* in many firms are given some new product development responsibilities, in addition to responsibility for existing products. This approach appears to be effective when the desired new products are line extensions or minor modifications of existing products for familiar markets. It generally presupposes that the product or brand manager will be directly involved only in selected phases of the product development process. There appear to be two major drawbacks to this approach. First, product managers are rarely suitable for the development of truly innovative products that are beyond their current product and market expertise. Second, given the short-term orientation and time pressures characteristic of this position, combining current and new product responsibility in a single position may result in the neglect of even minor innovations whenever day-to-day operations make demands on the manager's attention.

Standing *new product committees* have been used as essentially part-time new product departments. These committees typically are staffed with representatives of different functional departments and coordinate all phases of the development process (in contrast to senior management review committees, which typically only authorize and oversee projects). This form may be effective for a smaller firm lacking the resources to support a full-time new product unit (especially when demand for new products is sporadic) and may also be used by a large firm concerned about avoiding the potential duplication when full-time specialists (engineers, market researchers) are housed in both functional and new product departments. The main weakness in the committee approach is that no single individual has full-time responsibility for new products. As a result, commitment can become diluted, and problems that do not fit neatly into any member's area of responsibility can be neglected.

Firms whose new product needs are sporadic and tend to involve significant departures from existing products may develop a *task force*, essentially a temporary new product department, to coordinate particular projects. These units draw specialized personnel from functional departments on a full-time basis for the duration of the project, after which the members return to their home departments. The task force is likely to be unpopular with heads of functional departments who are asked to sacrifice key personnel needed to support current operations.

A related alternative is the *ad hoc committee*, which has the temporary nature of a task force and the part-time nature of the standing new product committee. Functional specialists assigned to an ad hoc committee on a part-time basis for the duration of a project are often supervised on a matrix basis, in that they report simultaneously to a functional manager and project director. Although this structure may be suited to the needs and resources of a small firm, it has the major disadvantage of placing multiple demands on committee personnel.

In some cases, a *venture team* will be formed to develop a product that is beyond the product/market expertise of the existing organization. This form is similar to a task force in that some personnel will be drawn from existing departments and the team will operate only during the particular project. A venture team, however, often recruits personnel from outside the firm, and if the project is successful the team typically forms the nucleus of a division or spin-off business. The venture concept is an extreme form of matrix structure in which full authority is given to the team leader. The teams typically are full-time during their period of operation, independent from the rest of the firm, able to circumvent existing policy, and concerned with a single project. Such projects focus on high-risk, highly uncertain, and highly important products that are disruptive to regular company operations. This form is most common in large industrial firms. The burgeoning literature on venture teams appears out of proportion to the actual extent of their use.

Some small firms that lack formal new product units nevertheless succeed in developing new products by making use of *outside suppliers*. These suppliers have proliferated to the point where every phase of product development can now be contracted out for specialized attention. This approach can be costly and difficult to coordinate and control; however, it is a relatively cost-effective way for a firm of any size to take short-term advantage of external expertise until internal resources can be developed.

*Multiple organizational forms* for new product development are used by a large and increasing number of firms. It would seem sensible for a firm not to become wedded to a single organizational form, but rather to develop a hybrid or combination of forms appropriate to its own circumstances and the types of products being developed. Large firms frequently have brand managers working on line extensions while one or more task forces simultaneously coordinate radical innovations and outside suppliers are used for specialized development services. Reliable estimates of the proportions of firms using various combinations are difficult to obtain because of continuous structural change in dynamic firms and the temporary nature of some of the forms in question. The trend, however, appears to be toward such customized structures.

Companies have experimented with new structures essentially on a trial-and-error basis. There is still much to be learned about what works and why, and only a few concrete conclusions have been drawn. It appears, for instance, that higher success rates are achieved by new product development efforts either headed by marketing personnel or including strong marketing representation from start to finish. Also, team efforts tend to outperform one- or two-person shows and more cumbersome organizational structures.

## The Marketing–R&D Interface

The critical element in any new product development project is the dialogue between marketing personnel and technical personnel (i.e., engineers, chemists, food scientists, medical technologists, software programmers, and others, depending on the industry). These technical people may or may not actually be in a research and development department, but for our purposes, we shall refer to them as R&D personnel. Without proper direction, little is accomplished through innovation. R&D managers are often unacquainted with basic management principles. They frequently are not delegated sufficient authority but are overstretched in terms of accountability. Marketers can play a major role in providing direction. Years ago, Bogaty (1974) suggested, tongue in cheek, that the probability of commercial success with an innovation is inversely proportional to the square of the distance between marketing and technical people. His insight remains true today. R&D needs marketing to decipher increasingly complex customer demands, and marketing depends on R&D for a flow of genuinely new products, especially given the dynamics of competition and the pressures of inflation, resource shortages, and government regulation. There is, nevertheless, evidence that the relationship between these two functional areas is often either poor or nonexistent.

Marketers and R&D people have completely different orientations, at least in part because of the ways they are evaluated and rewarded. Marketers may see company actions in terms of specific products, sales quotas, competitive position, or, ideally, long-term customer satisfaction. Alternatively, the frame of reference for technical researchers might be a specific project, the development of a particular technology, the quest for the perfect product, or the need to exhaust but not exceed a research budget. R&D personnel reason from vision and scientific judgment, often putting forth plans enveloped in technical jargon, hope, and uncertainty. Theirs is an orientation shared by few others in the firm.

The implication of these differing orientations for the marketer is that he or she must have a solid grasp of the technologies, the perspectives, and the limitations of other functional areas in the firm, particularly R&D. He or she must develop an

**TABLE 8.7**  Areas Requiring R&D/Marketing Integration

A. Marketing is involved with R&D in
  1. Setting new product goals and priorities
  2. Preparing R&D's budget proposals
  3. Establishing product development schedules
  4. Generating new product ideas
  5. Screening new product ideas
  6. Finding commercial applications of R&D's new product ideas/technologies
B. Marketing provides information to R&D on
  1. Customer requirements of new products
  2. Regulatory and legal restrictions on product performance and design
  3. Test-marketing results
  4. Feedback from customers regarding product performance on a regular basis
  5. Competitor strategies
C. R&D is involved with marketing in
  1. Preparing marketing's budget proposal
  2. Screening new product ideas
  3. Modifying products according to marketing's recommendations
  4. Developing new products according to market need
  5. Designing communication strategies for the customers of new products
  6. Designing user and service manuals
  7. Training users of new products
  8. Analyzing customer needs

SOURCE: Reprinted from "R&D and Marketing Dialogue in High-Tech Firms," *Industrial Marketing Management*, 14, p. 293, Gupta, Raj, and Wilemon. © Copyright 1985 by Elsevier Science Publishing Co., Inc. Reprinted with permission.

understanding of the unique orientations and decision-making techniques used by research personnel.

Cooperation between marketing and R&D is vital throughout the stages of the product development process. Table 8.7 outlines some of the areas where the efforts of these two groups should be integrated, and Figure 8.8 demonstrates this integration over the stages of the product development process. Note in this figure that the stages of the process have been grouped into three major phases. Commitment to this cooperation by *both* parties in each phase tends to distinguish successful from unsuccessful new product programs. Senior management must promote such integration, perhaps by establishing joint reward systems for R&D and marketing personnel.

The importance of the R&D and marketing departments sharing the blame for product failures should be emphasized. Companies—particularly the marketers within them—often use the lack of innovation as a scapegoat for their own poor performance but are not supportive of technologically new products when they do

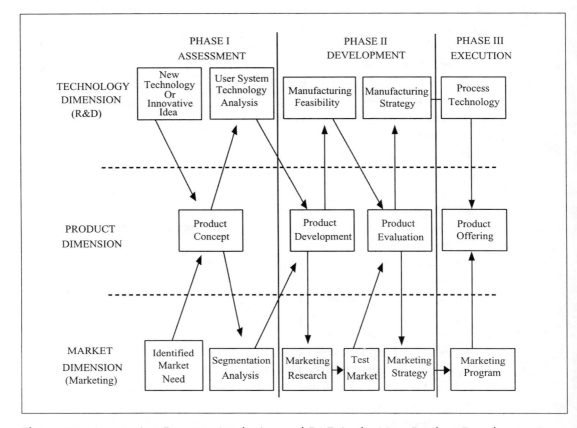

**Figure 8.8.** Interaction Between Marketing and R&D in the New Product Development Process

SOURCE: Adapted from "A Systems Approach for Developing High Technology Products," *Industrial Marketing Management* (November, 1982), p. 257, Miaoulis and LaPlaca. © Copyright 1982 by Elsevier Science Publishing Co., Inc. Adapted with permission.

arrive. Even where the innovative resources of the firm have been directed toward a legitimate market need, marketers may become a barrier to new product success. They sometimes worry excessively about protecting current products, distribution channels, sales territories, and customer relationships from the unsettling threat of change. Despite verbal support for innovation, marketers may find security in the status quo or support only minor product changes. The result is an antagonistic, mutually suspicious relationship that involves confrontation rather than cooperation, with each party blaming the other for failure.

## Corporate Entrepreneurship and Marketing

For a variety of reasons, innovation in industrial companies often is stifled. Over time, internal resistance has led to a loss of competitive position in the marketplace on the part of many firms. The severity of this problem in recent years has produced a call for *corporate entrepreneurship*, which refers to "the pursuit of opportunity by companies without regard to resources currently controlled (Stevenson, Roberts, Grousbeck, & Bhide, 1999, p. 4). This concept is also called "intrapreneurship" to distinguish it from the new start-up venture pursued by the individual entrepreneur.

Corporate entrepreneurship has three major dimensions—proactiveness, risk taking, and innovativeness. Proactiveness is the opposite of reactiveness. An emphasis is placed on trying bold new ideas and ways of doing things, seizing growth opportunities, and aggressiveness in dealing with competitors. Risk taking in this context is a willingness to pursue ideas now, despite inherent uncertainties. This risk is calculated and managed, and it represents a moderate likelihood of significant loss. Innovativeness is an emphasis on a continuous flow of new products/services, changes in methods of production, and/or delivery, as well as a search for unusual and novel solutions to problems.

A growing set of concepts and tools is available for encouraging corporate entrepreneurship in industrial firms. A complete discussion of these is beyond the scope of this book, but some of the major ones tend to focus on organization structure, resource allocation, reward systems, and company culture. In general, more decentralized and flatter (fewer hierarchical levels) structures are encouraged to allow for greater flexibility in responding to the environment. These structures also permit more interfunctional communication. Planning and staff functions should be made as lean as possible. Specific resources should be made available to those who develop innovative ideas and are willing to see them through to commercialization, regardless of the obstacles to be overcome. Reward systems must be designed to encourage people to develop and try new ideas, to foster cooperation among functional areas, and to emphasize long-term results. Although success should be rewarded, failure should not be punished; otherwise, the disincentives of a fear of failure may be outweigh the lure of success. Most major successes have come only after a string of failed efforts.

Those in marketing can play a central role in fostering corporate entrepreneurship. Unfortunately, marketers often work within a set of well-established (by experience) rules of thumb. These helpful guidelines cover decisions regarding how to price, what to spend on advertising, ways to motivate distributors, and so on. Examples include "maintain advertising at 4% of sales" or "cut prices if the proposal-to-order ratio goes above four." These rules can become very counterproductive, however, if market conditions change or if the company modifies its overall strategic direction.

Thomas Bonoma of the Harvard Business School argues that when conditions are changing, companies need *marketing subversives*—managers who challenge old practices and bend company rules. Such improvisation might include circumventing normal communications channels to ensure customers that are talking to production people, or ignoring the official budget by bootlegging resources to support products and markets ignored by senior management. Subversives, finding the formal corporate reporting process too general and slow, tend to uncover ways to obtain their own profit and performance measures for products, segments, salespeople, or distributors. They form networks to generate support for issues in which they believe. Bonoma (1986) summarizes one marketer's philosophy as follows: "Look, if I followed the rules around here, my brand would fail. I do what it takes, which is usually a little bit of creative rule breaking followed by begging for forgiveness when I get caught. As long as I've got the numbers, the boss will be pretty flexible" (p. 115).

This book repeatedly has stressed marketing's role as the keeper of the organization's customer orientation. Marketing can also take the lead in fostering an organization's entrepreneurial orientation. Murray explains:

> Of all the areas of technical and professional expertise, within the firm, marketing is uniquely equipped and indeed should feel uniquely responsible for analyzing environmental evolution and translating its observations into recommendations for the redesign of the corporate resource base and its product-market portfolio. (quoted in Morris, 1998, p. 149)

Companies today must learn new and different ways to compete. Creativity and innovativeness are necessary not only in promotional activities but also in finding profit opportunities through new products, lines, features, distribution arrangements, services, and customer segments. Because environmental change has become a way of life, marketers must provide direction in managing that change by continually redefining the product and market context within which the organization operates. In fact, there is some evidence that marketing departments in the more entrepreneurial firms tend to be key sources of direction in terms of innovation and tend to affect the strategic direction of such firms significantly (Morris, Schindehutte, & Zahra, in press).

The skills of those in marketing need to reflect the entrepreneurial dimensions of proactiveness, innovation, and risk taking. Marketers must have the insights necessary not only to find and understand customers but also to further translate developments in the technological, economic, social, regulatory, and competitive environments into commercially viable products and service concepts. One possible approach is to make the marketing department a profit center, with specific objectives for new products and markets.

## Summary

This chapter has focused on innovation as a marketing-oriented activity within industrial companies. New products and services are the lifeblood of the organization, especially in today's competitive environment, yet a sizable percentage of new product efforts fail. These failures create a dilemma for the managers of industrial firms: They cannot afford the loss in competitive position that results from not innovating, but they also are not eager to risk the losses that come with product failure.

To better understand this dilemma, six major categories of new product failures were examined. Underlying most of these would seem to be the lack of a marketing orientation among those responsible for new product innovation. Common causes of failure include developing technically advanced products for which there is little perceived need, underestimating current customer loyalties, underestimating the strength of competitors' responses to new products, pricing at a level inconsistent with perceived value, and misinterpreting environmental change. Each of these is traceable to an underemphasis on marketing activities and a tendency to give those with marketing responsibility an insignificant role in decision making regarding new products.

Product success appears to be directly associated with a firm's ability to link superior technical capabilities to an in-depth understanding of the marketplace. Successful innovations are those that achieve a differential competitive advantage based on their uniqueness and superiority. Doing so implies a thorough understanding of the needs, wants, and problems of target customers and an ability to translate these into marketing actions.

Innovation as an activity does not lend itself to tight managerial control, bureaucratic structure, or overly constraining policies and procedures. It often occurs in a haphazard fashion, and it requires an environment that encourages risk taking and creativity. At the same time, projects cannot be pursued blindly, without managerial direction or financial control. Overall direction can be achieved by developing an innovation charter, which is an explicit corporate strategy for new products and services. Direction can also be accomplished by identifying the major stages or steps involved in the product development process, and by establishing goals and performance criteria for each stage. Eight major stages were presented, although alternative versions of the process exist. The stages will generally overlap, with those individuals involved sometimes going back and forth among them.

Perhaps the most important responsibility of senior management during the innovation process involves facilitating interfunctional cooperation among R&D, production, marketing, finance, and other specialties. The chapter placed special emphasis on the interface between marketing and R&D. Areas where cooperation is critical were identified, as were inherent conflicts between these two areas.

Management must also ensure that the company is properly organized for innovation. A variety of different structural approaches exist, 10 of which were evaluated. The most appropriate structure appears to depend on the type of innovative activity the company is trying to pursue. As a result, structure should follow from the innovation charter.

For their part, marketing personnel often resist innovation, focusing their creative energies on support activities for existing products and emphasizing minor product improvements or line extensions. These are types of innovative activity, but they have a more short-term payoff and leave the firm vulnerable over time. Most fundamentally, marketing departments in industrial firms need to adopt an entrepreneurial orientation. This orientation is a proactive, innovative, and calculated risk-taking approach to translating environmental developments into profitable new product and market opportunities. Marketers must adopt a longer-term perspective on both customer satisfaction and profitability. New approaches to deciphering present and future needs must be adopted, matching them to technological possibilities. Marketers must, in short, redefine the rules regarding how, where, and when to compete.

# Questions

1.  Assume that your company manufactures and sells cardboard boxes in a variety of sizes and designs. What might be some of the specific factors that create the need for innovation in your firm?

2.  Why must firms selling industrial services innovate as much as or more than those selling industrial products?

3.  Provide examples of continuous, dynamically continuous, and discontinuous innovations in the industrial market. What are some process innovations within a firm that might have marketing implications?

4.  Gosat Corp., a manufacturer of mobile electronics equipment, has just added a new mobile tracking system to its product line. The new technology allows transportation and shipping companies to keep track of their fleets of trucks via satellite. The system tracks as many as 25 variables for each vehicle that is in the field. Identify the major causes of failure of industrial products and discuss how each might lead to the demise of Gosat's new tracking system.

5.  The most common type of product failure in industrial markets is the better mousetrap nobody wanted. Explain what this type of failure means. Why do you think it is so prevalent in industrial firms? How can this problem area be avoided?

6.  Identify possible roles for the marketing department of an industrial firm at each stage in the new product development process. Assume that the firm makes paint spraying equipment and is attempting to develop a new type of portable spray gun that uses a paint cartridge, is programmable, and requires no outside power source.

7.  What is the purpose of an innovation charter? What would be the key issues or areas addressed in an innovation charter for a company that develops and markets computer accounting software to small and medium-sized businesses?

8.  There appears to be no relationship between being first to the market with a new product innovation and the likelihood of product success or the likelihood of failure. What are some possible reasons for this?

9. Consider a company that makes handheld portable radios and is working to develop a powerful, but very small, new mobile radio (e.g., for use in utility trucks, police cars, or corporate vehicles). Identify some of the major areas in which marketing, R&D, and manufacturing might have conflicts with one another during the new product development process.

10. Why are different types of organizational structures required for major new product innovation, compared to minor product improvements or cost reductions?

11. "Marketing is the home for the entrepreneurial process in industrial organizations." Do you agree or disagree? Why?

# CHAPTER 9

# Marketing Industrial Products and Services

*The greatest thing to be achieved in advertising, in my opinion, is*
*believability, and nothing is more believable than the product itself.*
—Leo Burnett

*There is no such thing as a commodity.*
—T. Levitt

## Key Concepts

Augmented product

Breadth, depth, and length

Characteristics of a product

Characteristics of a service

Contribution margin income statement

Core product

Delivery quality

Items, lines, and mixes

Perceptual mapping

Positioning

Product quality

Product/service strategy

Quality

Service delivery

Service marketing

Service operations

Support quality

Tangible product

## Learning Objectives

1. Appreciate the central role of the product or service within the industrial marketing mix.

2. Understand the variable nature of products and services and present frameworks for creatively identifying sources of variability.

3. Comprehend the unique characteristics of industrial products and services, as well as their similarities, and be able to draw implications.

4. Recognize the critical role of quality and quality improvement when managing products and services.

5. Be able to specify and apply the major considerations in formulating product/service strategy, including decisions regarding product/service deletion.

## The Central Role of "Product/Service" in Marketing Programs

The most important marketing decisions in any firm concern the nature of the products and services to be sold. Although managers devote considerable attention to determining the prices to be charged, how to promote a product or service, and the appropriate distribution channels, the product or service lies at the heart of a firm's marketing strategy. It is the primary vehicle for delivering the benefits sought by target markets. Stated differently, the product or service lies at the heart of the industrial marketing mix, whereas price, promotion, and distribution are the supporting elements of the mix.

Product strategy in business-to-business markets usually requires more time to design and execute than pricing or promotion, and indeed more than distribution. Product strategies necessitate a great amount of effort in planning, development, and implementation. For instance, a medical technology firm may spend years coming up with the idea, agreeing on the design, and actually developing a machine that will deliver high-resolution photographs of internal organs. Such machines enhance the ability of physicians to diagnose patients' symptoms without performing exploratory surgery or exposing them to potentially harmful drugs. By contrast, in only a matter of months or weeks, the price, promotion, and distribution strategies designed to support this product can be decided on and implemented. The machine itself is the most tangible and permanent aspect of the marketing mix. It remains with the customer for a longer period of time and ultimately determines whether the user is satisfied.

The product or service offering also defines or determines the quality position of a firm, the customer groups it is able to serve, and the competitors with which it must be concerned. Furthermore, distribution and logistical arrangements are directly related to the characteristics of what is being sold. In addition, a firm's ongoing cost structure and financial needs are strongly influenced by the design, production, and delivery requirements of its products or services.

Unfortunately, practitioners and students of marketing often downplay the product or service itself and place much more emphasis on innovative advertising and selling programs. In business-to-business markets, this is a serious problem, because industrial products and services can be technical in nature, the customer often has specific performance expectations, and the technical competency of customers frequently is high. Marketers must understand how a product or service works, and why. Furthermore, marketers must learn to recognize the creative ways in which products and services can be modified to meet a given customer's requirements. Otherwise, they will be less able to identify unmet customer needs in a given area or to communicate with those in other parts of the company (especially technical people) regarding marketplace opportunities.

There is also a tendency in marketing to regard products as being different from services, and therefore to approach them in different ways. Thus, Caterpillar sells earthmoving and construction equipment and might regard itself as being a "product" firm. Federal Express[1] would be a services marketer, as it is not providing customers with some tangible item but instead is moving their packages and documents from one place to another.

Not surprisingly, considerable attention has been devoted to distinguishing the characteristics that products possess that make them different from services. We will discuss these distinguishing characteristics, as they have some important implications for the industrial marketer. It is unlikely, however, that business customers make these same fine distinctions. They might in reality be purchasing "solutions to problems," "need satisfaction," "experiences," or "performances." Also, customers expect the products they purchase from Caterpillar to come with a range of excellent services. Federal Express, while delivering a service, uses packaging, aircraft, vehicles, handling equipment, computers, and employs people, in identifiable uniforms, who also produce physical documentation.

# What Is a Product?

This might seem like an obvious question. The answer can vary significantly, however, depending on whether it comes from the person who makes the item or the person who is buying the item. The design engineer or production manager at the selling firm might see the product as a set of physical characteristics, ingredients, components, dimensions, design tolerances, and technical features that result from a formal design and development process (see Chapter 8 for a description of this process). That is, they see the product in terms of how it was made.

From a marketing standpoint, however, the product is defined in terms of what it does for the customer. Customers are less concerned with particular physical

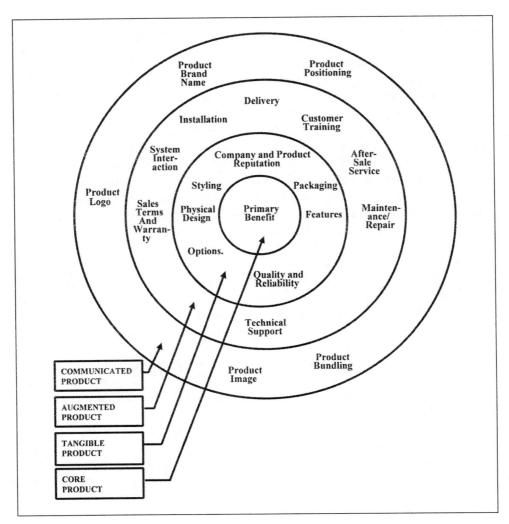

**Figure 9.1.** Communicated, Augmented, Tangible, and Core Product Concepts

features, ingredients, or components and more concerned with solving a problem or need. They do not really care about the seller's state-of-the-art equipment, modern facilities, or intricate processes. Accordingly, a product should be thought of as a *bundle of problem-solving attributes* or a package of benefits.

Approached in this manner, the product consists of much more than the physical item itself. If company A and company B are selling identical versions of the same product but company B provides superior aftersale service or a better warranty agreement, company B is really selling a different product. This distinction led Levitt (1991) to suggest that even the most standard or commodity-like products (copper wire, grains, primary metals, screwdrivers) can be differentiated in the marketplace.

A useful framework for recognizing the many dimensions of a product is illustrated in Figure 9.1. Here, products are defined at four levels: the core product, the tangible product, the augmented product, and the communicated product (see Levitt, 1991). At the *core,* or most basic level, the product is defined in terms of the primary benefit sought by a customer. Consider the example of Rolls Royce jet aircraft engines, which power a large proportion of the world's jet aircraft fleet, including many Boeing 767s. The core benefit for such a product might be superb power and reliability.

The *tangible* product refers to any and all aspects of the physical product itself. At this level, products can be distinguished by quality levels, features, options, styling, colors, and packaging. Again using jet engines, a distinctive feature (power-to-weight ratio) can produce, in the customer's view, an entirely different product.

The tangible offering can then be *augmented* by a variety of support services, including installation, delivery, credit, warranties, advice, training, and postsale servicing. Rolls Royce is able to provide worldwide servicing, maintenance, and replacement backup for its engines, thus minimizing the downtime airlines will experience if their aircraft are powered by Rolls Royce. Such services or benefits are an integral part of the total value the customer is purchasing. This post-purchase support is an excellent example of a product dimension frequently ignored by managers. Product support covers anything that contributes to maximizing a customer's satisfaction after the sale, such as parts availability, equipment loans during downtimes, operator and maintenance training, serviceability engineering, and warranty performance. These programs must be flexible and require frequent modification. Customer needs for product support usually become more sophisticated as the product moves through the life cycle. Also, expectations regarding support will frequently vary by market segment. For example, the tolerable amount of downtime for a malfunctioning machine will differ depending on the type of customer and time of year (e.g., peak order time versus a period of slack demand).

The final level involves the *communicated* product, which includes the assignment of a brand name (can one get more prestigious than Rolls Royce?) to the product, the design of a logo or trademark to convey product identity, the manner in which the product is positioned, and ways in which the product is bundled with other products or services.

By relying on the four-circle framework presented in Figure 9.1, the marketer is better able to realize the creative potential of the product variable. The core, tangible, augmented, and communicated product concepts provide a road map for identifying the many ways a product can be changed or customized to reflect market conditions and the needs of individual customer segments. It is also interesting to note that moving toward an outside ring is not the only viable strategy—sometimes, business-to-business marketers can focus customers away from competitors' augmentation efforts by minimizing product/service differences and once more focus on the core product. For example, Tom's Tyres, a large Australian vendor of tires to truck and auto fleets, refers to the fact that it sells "those round, black things" in its advertising.

This framework can be used to successfully differentiate any product from those of competitors.

## Unique Characteristics of Industrial Products

When considering the nature of industrial products, it is easy to overgeneralize. There is, in fact, considerable diversity among the many products purchased by organizations. The category of goods labeled "industrial" includes everything from paper clips costing a few pennies and sold to almost all organizations, to multi-million-dollar generators sold by multinational firms such as Siemens and ASEA Brown-Boveri[2] to a small number of utility companies.

To gain a more complete picture of these products, it is worth considering some of their major underlying dimensions. Eight of these dimensions are illustrated in Figure 9.2. They include customization, complexity, unit cost, related system requirements, purchase volume, installation requirements, degree of completion, and rapidity of consumption. A large number of products exist at every point on each of the dimensions pictured in Figure 9.2, and many combinations are possible among the various dimensions. For instance, facsimile machines are fairly standardized, reasonably simple, relatively low cost, stand-alone, finished goods that are typically sold on a per-unit basis, come ready to use, and are consumed over a number of years. A communications network linking sales branches in a region can be characterized as a customized, somewhat complex, and fairly expensive system of finished products that requires installation, has a long life, and can be continually modified or updated.

Each of these product dimensions has implications for the development of marketing strategy and tactics. For instance, the more an item is customized, complex, part of a system, or of high unit cost, the greater the likelihood that distribution channels will be shorter, a technically qualified sales force will be employed, prices will be used to reflect quality, and a heavy emphasis will be placed on customer service. Products with low unit costs that are standardized, simple, ready to use, and consumed quickly frequently will be part of a broad line, will be sold through distributors, and will utilize price promotions while receiving higher expenditures for advertising. An emphasis on life-cycle costs is relevant only for those items consumed over a number of years; cross-product elasticities (a measure of how much sales of the product are affected by prices of other products) become especially important when selling unfinished goods, component parts, and products that are part of a system; and quantity discounts apply only for items likely to be purchased in volume in a specified time period. These are but a few of the potential implications of a product's underlying characteristics. Although there are no universal rules regarding how to market a product, a careful evaluation of its characteristics can yield valuable insights for pricing, promotion, and distribution decisions.

A large number of industrial firms sell both products and services, and many exclusively sell services. As discussed in Chapter 1, the growth rates for services as a

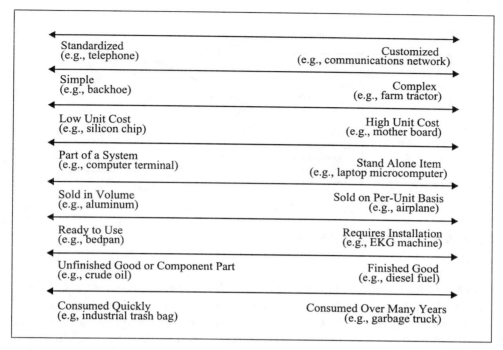

**Figure 9.2.** Underlying Characteristics of Industrial Products

whole have actually exceeded those for products in recent years. Services tend to differ in some significant ways from products and have distinct marketing requirements. Let us consider some of their characteristics and unique differences.

## What Is a Service?

Whereas a product is an object, device, or physical thing, a service is a deed, performance, or effort. As with products, every industrial service represents a bundle of need-satisfying attributes. These attributes are provided to a buyer through the "service experience." The term *experience* is used to connote all aspects of the person-to-person customer service interaction. In providing a particular need-satisfying experience to a customer, the marketer is said to be "delivering" a service.

The success of service providers hinges on their ability to manage three highly interrelated areas efficiently: service operations, service delivery, and service marketing. It is the interaction among these three areas that determines how much value a buying organization receives. Lovelock (1996, p. 22) refers to this as the "servuction" process (combining "service" and "production"), for in the production of service, marketing cannot operate in isolation from other functional departments, and indeed

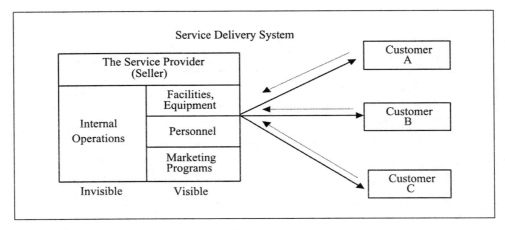

**Figure 9.3.** The Delivery of Industrial Services

from the firm's infrastructure. Thus, customers interact with personnel, see the service provider's facilities and equipment, and are exposed to its marketing programs.

Service operations can be broken down into those components that are visible to the customer and those not visible (see Figure 9.3). Some observers have referred to these areas as "front office" and "back office" (e.g. Schmenner, 1994). The visible components (or front office) include personnel, facilities and equipment (physical assets), and marketing programs to which customers are exposed. The invisible component (or back office) includes internal operations (e.g., administration, purchasing, accounting, computer operations, maintenance, employee training) that are responsible for managing and supporting the visible component, but to which the customer is not directly exposed.

The service delivery system is represented in Figure 9.3 by the visible components of the operating system plus the individual customers being serviced. Of concern here is the means by which services are actually being provided. This includes the specific people and equipment necessary for each job, the methods used, the procedures followed, the time involved, and the extent to which customers become part of the service. Also of importance is the manner by which the service is taken to the customer organization or the customer comes to the service organization. The arrows in Figure 9.3 (longer going to the customers than from the customers to the service provider) suggest that industrial services are more frequently taken to the customer. There are also services that are delivered on an "arms-length" basis, such as utilities or on-line data services.

Service marketing is a subcomponent of service operations and overlaps with service delivery. It includes all those activities that directly facilitate customer purchases from the firm. Although it can be argued that marketing is a companywide function in service organizations, the primary focus is on those activities that make customers aware of, and that influence their decision to buy, the vendor's services. Examples include advertising, sales calls, publicity, price schedules, billing, and facility tours.

Also common is the tendency to view contact personnel, the equipment used to deliver a service, and satisfied clients (i.e., the major components of the service delivery system) as potential marketing tools.

These areas can be brought together by examining the case of Roadway Corporation,[3] an independent trucking firm that hauls manufacturers' goods anywhere in the continental United States. Each shipment of goods represents a service experience. The attribute bundle might include large truck capacity, a temperature-controlled shipping environment, clean vehicles, well-trained and courteous drivers, on-time pickup and delivery, insurance of merchandise in transit, temporary storage facilities, and accurate billing.

In terms of service operations, the most visible items would be the trucks and drivers. Some of the key invisible areas might include vehicle maintenance, route scheduling, driver recruitment and training, payroll, and the purchasing or leasing of trucks. The service delivery system would involve processing customer orders, scheduling pickup times, assigning vehicles and drivers to a job, interactions between drivers and employees of the shipping and receiving organizations, customer billing, and temporary storage. Finally, the service marketing system might take the form of sales calls, advertisements in business publications, direct mail pieces, professional artwork on the trucks, price quotes, or a toll-free (800) number to handle customer information requests and complaints.

## Unique Characteristics of Industrial Services Versus Products

The opportunities available to the marketer of industrial services can be better understood by drawing two comparisons. First, we will assess the differences between industrial services and products. Second, the differences between industrial services and consumer services will be examined.

Industrial services can be distinguished from products in a number of significant ways. Included here are the fact that services (a) are intangible, (b) cannot be held in inventory, (c) are often consumed at the time of purchase, (d) frequently do not lend themselves to production economies, (e) more frequently must be customized to individual users, (f) tend to be consumed in irregular patterns, and (g) have a tendency to generate less customer loyalty. Of these, the most distinguishing characteristic is the intangible nature of services.

Services are intangible in the sense that they cannot be seen or touched. They have neither a visible physical form nor any clearly measurable physical characteristics. Hence, the buyer experiences the service but does not possess it. A public relations firm sells its expertise in raising the visibility and improving the image of a client firm. A janitorial service sells its ability to deliver a clean working environment to customer firms. In both instances, the client may be able to see the end results of having purchased the service (e.g., mentions of the company name in a respected trade journal, empty wastebaskets in an office); however, only the people and equipment used to deliver the service can be seen or touched, not the service itself. As a result, marketers will often try to "tangibilize the intangible," such as when the janitorial service presents the customer with a daily checklist of cleaning tasks accomplished or when Prudential Insurance[4] tells its customers they are getting "a piece of the Rock" when they purchase a policy from the firm.

Because they are intangible, services cannot be stored in inventory. They must be sold when produced, or produced when sold. This creates a problem in terms of matching supply to demand. If an hour of a CPA's time goes unused or a cargo ship sets sail with empty bays, neither of these services can be recovered (stored) and sold at a later date. They are lost forever. The marketer will strive to manage the relationship between supply and demand, such as with price incentives and intensified promotions during periods of low demand. Temporary employees and leased equipment might be employed in times of excess demand.

An additional characteristic of services is that they are often consumed when produced. A company offering computer training finds that its courses are attended (consumed) at the times they are offered. This tendency suggests that services are short-lived. At the same time, some services are consumed over months or years, such as those of a consultant on retainer, an insurance policy, and banking services.

Although many products can be standardized and mass produced, the same cannot be said for most services. This is because services are usually produced and consumed one at a time and frequently must be customized to the individual user. Furthermore, they are often labor-intensive (e.g., third-party cleanup crews in Exxon's 1989 oil spill). These characteristics make it difficult to achieve production economies or to take meaningful advantage of the experience curve (see Chapter 7). The firm that specializes in corporate law cannot really standardize or mass produce its legal offerings. Instead, its services must be tailored to the distinct needs of each client. Even janitorial services must be adapted to meet the cleaning requirements of each building or plant. Where firms *are* able to achieve standardization in service delivery (usually through process innovation), the profit opportunities can be considerable. Federal Express represents a prime example, with its overnight package delivery service.

Consumption of industrial services will also tend to demonstrate more erratic demand patterns and less vendor loyalty as compared with consumption of products. The intangible nature of services makes it more difficult for customers to evaluate their worth. As a result, service purchases may be evaluated more critically, decisions may be put off, experimentation may be more prevalent, and budgets for services may be the first to be cut in bad economic times. Although component parts, machine tools, and office supplies are purchased on a steady and routine basis, a corporation may vary considerably the amount and source of its purchases from advertising agencies, vehicle maintenance firms, management consultants, and even health care plan providers. This is not to say that long-term loyalties do not develop between service providers and customers. A company may rely on a trusted accounting firm or local machining shop for many years.

# Unique Characteristics of Industrial Services Versus Consumer Services

Industrial services also have a number of characteristics that differentiate them from services overall, and particularly from consumer services. Compared with these others, industrial services

- Tend to be non-convenience type services

- Are transportable

- Usually are brought to the customer

- Involve customer contact in delivery

- Are not as conducive to mass production or mass marketing

- Frequently do not involve the customer as an individual becoming part of the service; that is, the service is directed at things, not people

- Often involve expensive equipment but also tend to be people intensive, with an emphasis on people's capabilities, experience, and background

- Involve customers with more precise service-level expectations, which are more clearly communicated to the vendor

- Involve fairly formal buying process, with a heavy emphasis on the tangible evidence of the seller's ability to provide the service

- Involve somewhat longer-term, and more stable, relationships with vendors

- Demonstrate demand patterns that are somewhat more stable and predictable

Convenience services are those for which the customer is not willing to spend much effort in searching and comparing among alternative vendors. Industrial services are more non-convenience in nature, as they are more customized and have a direct impact on operations within the customer firm. Many are transportable and do not require that the customer come to the seller's place of business. Although the service provider usually must interact with employees of the purchasing organization, the service itself is often performed on facilities, equipment, and end products, as opposed to people. That is, unlike when a consumer gets a haircut, individuals within the buying organization frequently do not become part of the service. Exceptions would include management development programs and corporate travel.

Although some consumer services can be standardized, franchised, and mass marketed (e.g., Hyatt Legal Services[5]), the same is generally not true for industrial services. Also, machinery and equipment are often necessary to produce industrial services, some of which are quite expensive. The personnel involved in service delivery will often be technically qualified professionals within their field of expertise.

Organizational buyers can be expected to have fairly precise requirements or specifications for the services they purchase. In many cases, they have the option of satisfying their need for a particular service on an in-house basis and are especially apt to do so with frequently purchased services. The buying process will tend to be formalized, as with industrial products, with a number of bids or proposals given careful scrutiny. Buyers will look for tangible evidence of vendor performance capabilities, including references from other clients, examples of completed work, employee résumés, service guarantees, and on-site inspections of a vendor's facilities and equipment. Once established, buyers of industrial services are apt to demonstrate stronger loyalties to a vendor and to purchase in more predictable patterns when compared to buyers of many consumer services. After being selected, an industrial service provider comes to more intimately understand the distinct needs of a given client organization and can do a better job of tailoring aspects of the service to satisfy those needs.

## Selling Both Products and Services

Discussions of product versus service marketing seem to imply that there are "pure" products and "pure" services, and that the differences are clear cut. This is usually not the case. Many companies find that their offerings have both tangible and intangible aspects (see Figure 9.4). A commercial printing firm may sell graphic design, typesetting, and printing services but also produce a tangible four-color brochure for a client. Similarly, a software company that sells programming skills that solve a particular customer problem may also provide the customer with a tangible diskette containing the program.

The implication is that marketing programs must reflect degrees of tangibility. For instance, the more service-dominant the offering, the more the marketer may want to stress tangible evidence. Conversely, those with product-dominant offerings may find it worthwhile to emphasize intangible benefits.

An additional complication is that firms often market products that are relatively independent of one another. AT&T sells long-distance services but also electronic switches and personal computers. Managers in such companies are apt to become frustrated if they use traditional product marketing approaches to sell services, or vice versa. Alternatively, management may tend to emphasize one area over the other (e.g., products over services) depending on where their expertise lies. Some firms deal with this problem by organizing their efforts so that responsibility for products and services is assigned to separate managers. Although this separation is not always necessary, it reflects a recognition that product and service marketing do involve some fundamental differences.

This is not to say that products and services must be marketed separately. Not only should efforts in both areas be coordinated for consistency with the firm's overall marketing strategy, but creative efforts also can sometimes be made to market them together. The possible linkages can be seen by examining the efforts of a company that sells security services (e.g., night security guards, consultations regarding security procedures) as well as security products (e.g., alarms, locks, cameras, metal

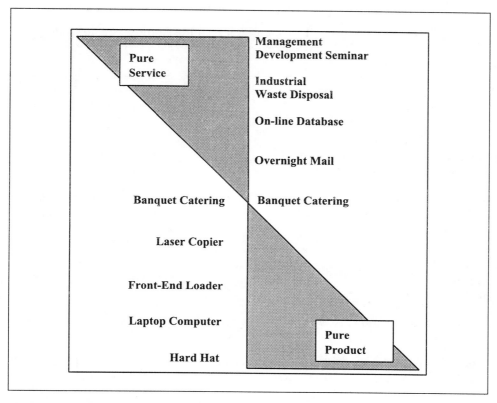

**Figure 9.4.** Service/Product Classification Based on Tangibility

detectors). Management might find it effective to give price breaks on products to those customers who use the firm's services, or to otherwise bundle products with services. The firm's security consultants can recommend procedures and systems that require the firm's products. Advertisements in trade journals might stress the fact that dependable security requires both people and equipment.

The ability to engage in such joint marketing programs depends on a number of considerations. Chief among these are the extent to which the products and services are marketed to the same customers and the same set of decision makers within buying organizations. Also important is the degree to which customers see the items as related, and especially complementary, to one another.

# Mixes, Lines, and Items

The task of product/service management is better understood by distinguishing among the overall product/service mix, product and service lines, and individual items (see Table 9.1). Companies do not, as a rule, seek to maximize profits on individual items or lines. Instead, they attempt to achieve desired profit, market share,

**TABLE 9.1**    Examples of Mixes, Lines, and Items in the Communications Industry

| Mixes | Lines | Items |
|---|---|---|
| Sharp business machines | Sharp personal computers | Sharp Model PC-4501 laptop computer |
| GTE communications | GTE Spacenet | GTE VSAT |
| AT&T telecommunications | AT&T office equipment | AT&T Model 35000 fax machine |
| Xerox document processing | Xerox photocopiers | Xerox Model 5046 mid-sized copier |
| Hewlett-Packard business machines | Hewlett-Packard printers | Hewlett-Packard jet series laser |
| Nokia mobile communications | Cellular telephones | Nokia 3210 cellular telephone |
| Toshiba information systems | Toshiba portable computers | Toshiba microtic cellular telephone |
| Western Digital disk controllers | Western Digital 3.5-inch disk drive | Western Digital SCSI320MB 3.5-inch disk drive |

sales, and cash flow objectives for the entire product or service mix. This mix is the total set of items and lines offered by the firm. For service businesses, the mix often consists of different bundles or packages of items.

Items can stand alone but more typically are part of a line. For example, companies carry low-, medium-, and high-quality versions of the same item. They also sell items that are complementary to one another or that are used in basically the same application (e.g., different kinds of building materials). A product or service line can be defined as a set of items related to one another by technology, production processes, cost structures, distribution requirements, or customer applications. Different companies in the same industry will not necessarily define their lines in the same way. One might place 10 items into a single line, while another may put the same 10 items into three different lines. Precise definitions depend on the organization's purpose in grouping items. The general aim is to facilitate sales while simplifying product planning, analysis, and control.

An item is any clearly unique offering sold to customers on a regular basis. From a product perspective, this definition includes all the dimensions highlighted in Figure 9.1. With services, it includes the intangible service, plus any tangible evidence of service delivery. Individual items often have distinct requirements demanding special attention from the marketer. Unless the firm sells only a single product or service, however, managing items in isolation is a mistake. This potential error was emphasized in the discussion of strategic business units and portfolio approaches to product management (see Chapter 7).

As we have seen, some products and services may be used to support sales of others. A computer company may find overall profitability enhanced if computers are sold at a price barely above their cost, but then a premium price is charged for accessories or software. A copier company may attempt to establish a solid base of customers with aggressive selling and discounting of copier equipment, but with the real goal of tapping the very profitable market for service after the sale.

If this same copier company sold a line of four copiers that vary in terms of features and quality, marketing actions that maximize revenues on one of the copiers may actually take sales away from the others. Furthermore, if some of the other copiers generate a higher gross margin per unit sold, overall corporate profitability may be harmed by this approach. Such drawbacks, however, may be worth enduring. Let's say that one of the copiers is only marginally profitable or causes significant cannibalism of the markets for the other three. The firms might find these costs are exceeded by the overall benefits gained from being perceived as a full-line supplier or from limiting competitor inroads.

In fact, marketers should regularly attempt to assess formally the relationships among the various items in the overall mix. When sales of one item affect those of others, the products or services are linked by cross-elasticity. Positive cross-elasticities occur when items are viewed by customers as substitutes for one another (e.g., a low-end version of a product for a mid-range version of the same product). Negative cross-elasticities suggest that the market sees the items as complements (e.g., a computer and a computer printer). Cross-elasticities can be identified by monitoring sales, prices, and marketing support for each item over a period of time.

## Breadth of the Mix, Length of the Lines, and Depth of the Items

After a product or service is first introduced, it is not unusual to add features, options, capabilities, and/or attributes. As the item moves further through its life cycle, a normal strategy is to expand the offering into an entire line of related items (products or services). Management's focus is now on the breadth, length, and depth within the product or service mix (see Figure 9.5).

Breadth is measured by the number of different lines carried by a firm. General Electric and 3M are examples of firms with extensive breadth. Managing breadth requires that attention is given to line consistency—the degree to which product lines are related in terms of technology, production or distribution requirements, and customers. Industrial organizations should be wary of spreading themselves too thin or getting into product areas that do not emphasize their distinctive competencies.

Length is the number of items in a given line. Lines can be overly shallow (too few alternatives) or overly deep (too many). A shallow line will appeal to fewer market

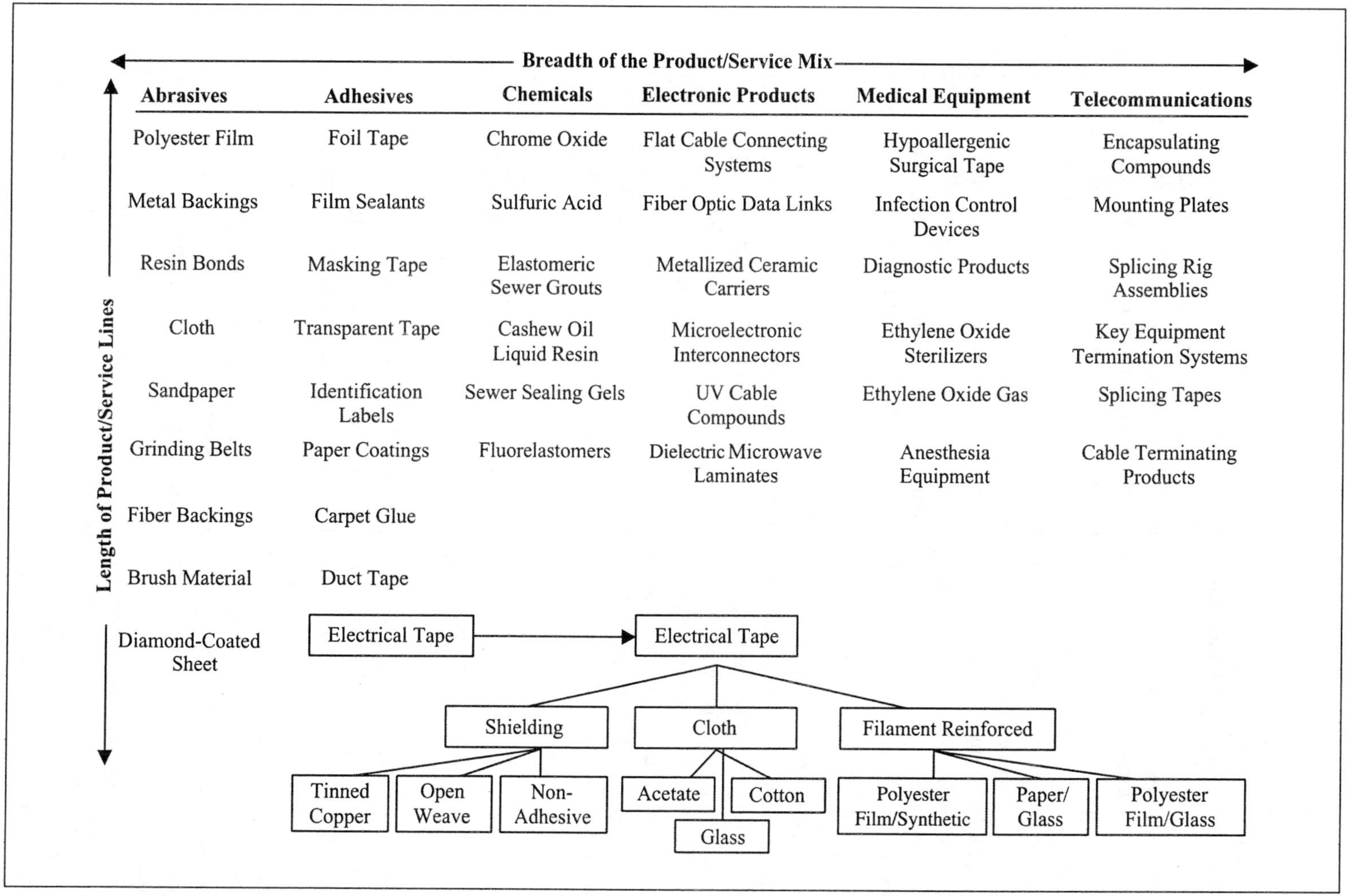

**Breadth of the Product/Service Mix** →

| Abrasives | Adhesives | Chemicals | Electronic Products | Medical Equipment | Telecommunications |
|---|---|---|---|---|---|
| Polyester Film | Foil Tape | Chrome Oxide | Flat Cable Connecting Systems | Hypoallergenic Surgical Tape | Encapsulating Compounds |
| Metal Backings | Film Sealants | Sulfuric Acid | Fiber Optic Data Links | Infection Control Devices | Mounting Plates |
| Resin Bonds | Masking Tape | Elastomeric Sewer Grouts | Metallized Ceramic Carriers | Diagnostic Products | Splicing Rig Assemblies |
| Cloth | Transparent Tape | Cashew Oil Liquid Resin | Microelectronic Interconnectors | Ethylene Oxide Sterilizers | Key Equipment Termination Systems |
| Sandpaper | Identification Labels | Sewer Sealing Gels | UV Cable Compounds | Ethylene Oxide Gas | Splicing Tapes |
| Grinding Belts | Paper Coatings | Fluorelastomers | Dielectric Microwave Laminates | Anesthesia Equipment | Cable Terminating Products |
| Fiber Backings | Carpet Glue | | | | |
| Brush Material | Duct Tape | | | | |
| Diamond-Coated Sheet | Electrical Tape | | | | |

↕ Length of Product/Service Lines

Depth example (Electrical Tape):

Electrical Tape →
- Shielding → Tinned Copper, Open Weave, Non-Adhesive
- Cloth → Acetate, Glass, Cotton
- Filament Reinforced → Polyester Film/Synthetic, Paper/Glass, Polyester Film/Glass

**Figure 9.5.** Breadth, Length, and Depth Applied to Minnesota Mining & Manufacturing (3M)

segments. Unit costs of each item may be relatively high. Also, with fewer items, a direct sales force may not be justifiable or affordable. As the line proliferates (gets deeper), however, cannibalism becomes a bigger problem. That is, customers have difficulty distinguishing among items in the line. Although the benefits of economies of scale can sometimes be realized with a deeper line, there is also a point of diseconomy. Also, deep lines can have so many individual items that some are likely to be ignored by the marketer and fail to receive sufficient sales support. Another possible result is customer confusion, with buyers finding themselves unable to keep abreast of all the items in a vendor's line.

Depth refers to how many variations are available for a particular item in a line. A product might come in three sizes, and with or without a special feature. A service might be varied in terms of the number of individual tasks performed for the customer. By adding depth, the marketer is better able to tailor a firm's offerings to individual customer groups.

Product/service strategy includes long-term considerations of breadth, length, and depth. Correspondingly, the strategies of most industrial firms can be characterized as one of the following: full line/all market, market specialist, line specialist, limited line specialist, single-item company, and special situation company (see Table 9.2 for examples). A full-line/all market company carries a group of related lines, each consisting of a fairly comprehensive set of items. The firm is attempting to satisfy the general needs of a wide range of customer segments in a broad product/service category. Market specialists concentrate their efforts on tailoring a set of items to satisfy the unique needs of a particular market or segment. Line specialists typically offer one line with considerable length and depth; selection within this line is more comprehensive than that found with other strategies. Limited line specialists concentrate on a subset of items within a line but may offer considerable depth for this subset. Single-item firms concentrate all their resources on a single product or service. The final category, special situation companies, includes those firms that tailor product or service solutions to the specifications or requirements of individual clients.

## Product/Service Strategy: The Importance of Quality

The single most important decision area in product/service management is that of quality. The level of quality provided in a product or service is its ultimate source of competitive advantage. Competitors may be able to match a change in price, promotion, or customer service quickly, but superior quality and ongoing quality improvements require considerable time and effort. In fact, there is an impressive body of support, both from academic literature (e.g., Cooper, 1995; Gale, 1985; Shetty, 1993) and from the managerial press (Juran, 1993; "Special Report: Quality," 1992; Waterman, 1987) for the finding that quality is positively and strongly related to company profitability and product/service success rates.

Traditional definitions of quality focus on how well an item meets or conforms to its design and delivery specifications. These specifications, however, are technical

**TABLE 9.2**  Corporate Product Strategies by Type of Strategy

| Type of Strategy | Example |
| --- | --- |
| Full line/all market | **General Electric** sells a full line of appliances, office equipment, and heavy machinery in a wide array of commercial, institutional, and governmental markets. |
| | **The Singer Company** sells a wide assortment of products in governmental and commercial markets, including flight simulators, navigation devices, and underwater fire control systems. |
| | **Hyundai** offers a wide variety of products and services ranging from ship-building to automobiles and high-tech electronics within commercial, institutional, and governmental markets. |
| Market specialist | **Kidder Peabody**, a brokerage that specializes in institutional clients, sells a line of financial services within select markets. |
| | **Buckeye Steel Castings** manufacturers and sells cast-steel products, such as couplings, in industrial markets. |
| | **H. K. Porter** distributes light industrial equipment (e.g., monkey wrenches, hydraulic jacks, and torque wrenches) to commercial and industrial markets. |
| Line specialist | **TRW** markets a complete line of valves for hearing, ventilating, and air-conditioning applications. |
| Limited line specialist | **Radius Manufacturers** sells monochrome displays and graphic engines for design, publishing, and engineering professionals. |
| | **3M** offers a single line maning perfusion system to heart care specialists. |
| Single-item company | **FLA Automated**, a fuel management company, monitors fuel consumption for trucking fleets. |
| Special situation company | **Environmental Risk Consultants**, a firm specializing in toxic-waste consulting, concentrates on environmental accidents and surveying property for evidence of contamination. |
| | **TRC Temporary Services**, a temporary employee provider, supplies employees for emergency and unusual staffing needs, as well as for periodic demand fluctuations. |
| | **Winzeler**, a custom molded gear manufacturer, produces and distributes customized gears to meet precise customer specifications. |

details that may or may not consider how well the product or service satisfies a customer's need. This problem led Groocock (1986) to define quality as the degree to which the relevant features and characteristics of a product/service satisfy all aspects of a customer's need, limited by the price and delivery the customer will accept.

This definition has a number of key points. First, quality is a comprehensive concept, referring to the totality of an item's features and characteristics, including all aspects of its performance and reliability. Second, quality exists in relationship to a customer's need. Third, comparisons of quality among items require that the items address the same needs. It is meaningless to compare the quality of the BIC pen to that of a Cross pen, given that they address different customer needs. Rather, the BIC pen would be compared to other inexpensive, disposable ballpoint pens. Also, the particular need in question is defined by the price and delivery requirements that a customer is willing to consider. This usually means that quality comparisons are made among directly competing products or services having roughly the same prices.

In the late 1980s and throughout the 1990s, organizations around the world began to devote more attention to quality and demand more with regard to it. Of great importance to business-to-business marketers was the fact that companies in many countries demanded that their suppliers comply with international standards. The best known of these is the so-called ISO-9000 protocol, originally developed by the Geneva-based International Standards Organization (ISO) for the members of the European Union. This standard has since gained prominence around the world as firms in countries as diverse as Australia, Brazil, Thailand, and South Africa not only aspire to it but realize that without it, many markets will be closed to them. The ISO-9000 standard requires firms to document their quality assurance procedures before they can gain certification. Many U.S. firms and organizations, including the Department of Defense, also demand ISO-9000 certification or similar standards from suppliers, and a number of major players, such as Xerox, have acquired the certification.

Many companies have departments whose sole responsibility is quality management. These departments often have such names as *quality control* or *quality assurance*. A more appropriate name would be *quality improvement*. Quality is a moving target, not a fixed level of performance. The best-run companies are engaged in a continuous quest to raise quality levels, regardless of what they produce (i.e., to conform better to customer needs, which are always changing). Furthermore, although there may be a department that sets standards and measures, quality must be the responsibility of all employees. With this in mind, let us examine unique aspects of product and service quality.

## Managing Product Quality

When producing and selling products, there are three major categories of quality: product quality, support quality, and delivery quality (Groocock, 1986). *Product quality* deals with a number of issues. First, how well do the product requirement specifications express the customer's need, and how well does the product design

**TABLE 9.3** Product- and Service-Related Quality and Departments With Prime Responsibility

| Main Categories | Subcategories | Responsibility for Improvement |
|---|---|---|
| Product quality | ◆ Accuracy of product requirement specifications and conformance of design to specifications | ◆ Marketing/design development |
| | ◆ Conformance of product to design at time of delivery | ◆ Purchasing/manufacturing |
| | ◆ Performance after delivery (e.g., reliability, maintainability, durability, safety) | ◆ Design development |
| Support quality | ◆ Customer design support | ◆ Design development |
| | ◆ Customer service at time of sale | ◆ Marketing |
| | ◆ Aftersales service | ◆ Marketing |
| | ◆ Assurance documentation | ◆ Quality |
| Delivery quality | ◆ Promised delivery schedules | ◆ Manufacturing/marketing |
| | ◆ Conformance to promised delivery | ◆ Manufacturing/purchasing |
| | ◆ Response to emergency delivery needs | ◆ Marketing/manufacturing |

conform to these requirements? Second, how well does the actual product conform to the design at the time it is manufactured? Third, how well does the product perform in terms of reliability, safety, durability, maintainability, and so forth, after it is purchased by the customer?

*Support quality* is a question of how well the organization conforms to customer needs for product-related service at the time of and after the sale. *Delivery quality* has to do with specifications regarding delivery schedules and promised times, as well as conformance to those times. Table 9.3 summarizes the main categories and subcategories of product, support, and delivery quality, and identifies the departments within a company most responsible for making quality improvements in each area.

Although its role in support and delivery quality may be more apparent, the marketing department can also serve a vital role in product quality improvement. Marketers must continually stay on top of customer needs, translating these needs into specific features and characteristics of products. Unfortunately, customers do not always know their needs, so marketers must be well acquainted with customers' operations and the problems they have in attempting to accomplish particular tasks. One way in which some successful industrial companies, such as Hewlett-Packard, achieve this is through customer visit programs, to learn about the problems facing customers, the way in which the company's products get used, their influence on the customer's operations, customers' requirements, and opportunities for further product improvements (Webster, 1994). A number of successful industrial marketers use this type of system for measuring customer satisfaction (McQuarrie, 1991). Another role for the marketer is to make quality comparisons between the firm's products and those of competitors on a routine basis. The judgments of company managers and employees are useful, but assessments should also be made of customer perceptions. Relative quality of competing products should be rated on a formal scale, such as *best in quality*, *joint-best* (two or more products that are equally superior), *average*, and *worse*. Associated with these responsibilities is the need to reassess continually the dimensions or components of quality, and their relative importance, from the buyer's vantage point.

Marketers must also strive to ensure that the quality being delivered is consistent with, or exceeds, the quality expectations of customers. A legitimate criticism directed at those in marketing and sales is that they encourage customers to have unrealistic quality expectations, and/or that their promises of features and capabilities make it difficult for the firm to deliver a given level of quality.

The efforts of marketers and all others concerned with quality must ultimately have some sort of focus or goal. A satisfied customer is certainly the preeminent goal. A second, and related, focal point is termed *quality costs*. These costs can be approached negatively (e.g., the costs that accrue to a firm from making defective products) or positively (e.g. the difference between actual production and selling costs and the cost if there were no defectives or chance of defectives). The advantage of the positive approach is that it stresses quality costs as a means to quality improvement. Examples of these costs include inspection and testing of purchased items and finished goods, costs to rework or scrap defective items, measurements of customer quality satisfaction, handling of customer complaints, training of employees on quality issues, and staffing of the quality department.

Operationally, firms need to identify and measure quality costs. Most of these will be variable costs. Specific goals can be set for these costs, perhaps as a percentage of sales. The ability to lower this ratio depends not on spending less on quality but instead on regularly introducing new quality improvement projects. That is, the best way to lower quality costs is by producing fewer defects.

# Managing Service Quality

Like product quality, service quality is concerned with conformance of the relevant service features and characteristics to customer needs. Arguably, service providers face a more difficult challenge in defining and managing quality levels when compared to product providers. This difficulty can be traced to the intangible, customized, and transportable nature of industrial services.

To measure service quality, firms must set formal service standards. Typical product quality standards, such as conformance to design specifications or the number of defective items produced, do not really apply. Standards can be identified, however, by focusing on the major components of the service experience, including the people and equipment used to deliver the service, as well as any supporting tangible evidence.

Services can be evaluated based on their *technical quality* and *functional quality* (Gronroos, 1983). Technical quality refers to *what* the customer receives, such as the audit report provided by a CPA firm or the transportation of goods provided by a trucking firm. Quality concerns here include the firm's general know-how, technical abilities of employees, ability to generate effective technical solutions to problems, physical equipment, and the computer support system, among others. Functional quality concentrates on *how* the customer receives a service, such as the professionalism of the accountant or the cleanliness of the truck. Management of functional quality emphasizes the attitudes and behaviors of those employees in contact with customers, the internal relationships between these and other employees, the appearance of personnel and equipment to which customers are exposed, the accessibility of the firm's services, and the maintenance of communication/contact with customers.

These two quality dimensions work in tandem. A well-trained accountant who is rude to customers and a fully equipped state-of-the-art truck that is routinely late with deliveries both represent quality problems. It does appear, though, that customers will sometimes excuse minor technical quality problems if functional quality is excellent.

The difficulties in measuring service quality often lead marketers to rely on subjective rather than objective evaluations. An objective measure might be a firm's percentage of on-time deliveries. Subjective measures usually rely on customer judgments, such as customer ratings of the courtesy of contact personnel. With many services, objective measures simply are not available. For instance, what are the objective indicators that measure the difference between a high-quality accounting audit and a medium-quality audit?

Relying on the customer's subjective perceptions of quality would not seem to be a problem, though, because customers are often directly involved in the delivery of the service experience. At the same time, customers may not have enough experience or exposure to assess technical quality accurately, so more emphasis is placed on measuring functional quality.

The most widely accepted approach to measuring service quality is based on the work of Parasuraman, Zeithaml, and Berry (1988). These authors define service quality as the "gap" between what a customer *expects* from an excellent service provider (e.g., a top-class industrial engineering services firm) and what the customer *perceives* he or she actually received from a particular service supplier, such as an industrial engineering services firm (e.g., Fluor Corporation[6]). If customer perceptions exceed expectations, then the service quality gap is positive, and the firm can be seen to be exceeding expectations by delivering service of a quality that delights the customer. Similarly, when expectations exceed perceptions, customers are receiving service of a quality that frustrates and dissatisfies them. Given the choice, they may not return to the service provider.

Parasuraman and his colleagues developed a scale to measure service quality called SERVQUAL (Parasuraman et al., 1988), and this has been used in a wide variety of settings, including business-to-business markets (e.g. Babakus & Boller, 1992). The SERVQUAL scale is based on 10 major dimensions of perceived quality, summarized in Table 9.4. Subsequent analysis suggested that these 10 dimensions could be collapsed into 5: tangibles, reliability/dependability, responsiveness to customers, assurance/confidence, and empathy with customers. In essence, the customer an-

**TABLE 9.4** Areas to Focus on When Measuring Service Quality

| Service Dimension | Examples of Evaluative Criteria |
|---|---|
| Tangibles | Appearance of physical facilities and personnel |
| Reliability | Performing service right the first time |
| Responsiveness | Willingness and ability to provide prompt service |
| Communication | Explaining service to customers in language they can understand |
| Credibility | Trustworthiness of customer-contact personnel |
| Security | Confidentiality of transactions |
| Competence | Knowledge and skill of customer-contact personnel |
| Courtesy | Friendliness of customer-contact personnel |
| Understanding/knowing customers | Making an effort to ascertain a customer's specific requirements |
| Access | Ease of contacting service firm by telephone |

SOURCE: Adapted from "SERVQUAL: A Multiple-Item Scale for Measuring Consumer Perceptions of Service Quality," *Journal of Retailing*, 64, 1, (Spring), pp. 12-40, Parasuraman, Zeithaml, and Berry. © Copyright 1988 by *Journal of Retailing*.

swers a series of questions in each of the five areas first in terms of their expectations, and then in terms of their perceptions of what was actually delivered. Gaps are computed in each of the five areas, and then overall.

Service quality expectations have also been found to be a useful variable for market segmentation in business-to-business markets. For example, one study using SERVQUAL in the mainframe software industry found significant differences in the service expectations of two segments labeled software "experts" and software "users" (Pitt, Morris, & Oosthuizen, 1996). Experts had high expectations only on reliability (that the software should be delivered on time, and that it should work as promised). Users, on the other hand, had highest expectation on the dimension of empathy—they wanted to be treated as individuals, in a personal way.

# Product/Service Strategy: The Concept of Positioning

An important consideration in product/service strategy concerns how the firm wants products or lines to be perceived by customers. This is called *positioning*. Products and services are positioned with respect to (a) perceptions regarding their underlying benefits and (b) perceptions regarding how they compare to competitive offerings. The marketer's task is to select those associations that are to be built upon (using the marketing mix) as well as those associations that are to be removed or de-emphasized.

Customer perceptions are key. The marketer must find out not only how the company is perceived by customers in a given product or service area but also how competitors are perceived. Market research studies in this area can provide managers with a rude awakening regarding their own assumptions. What they "know" about their products or services is often quite different from what customers believe. This is because customer perceptions are influenced by the consistent behavior of various vendors over time. Once in place, considerable effort is required to change these perceptions.

There are many ways to position a product, most of which involve the establishment of an explicit segmentation and targeting strategy. Some of the more popular methods include positioning by attribute (e.g., the most durable tractor), by price/quality (e.g., a low-budget manufacturer of network servers), by competitor (e.g., a new market entry compares itself with the market leader), by product application (e.g., a synthetic fiber for parachutes), by product user (e.g., computer software for hospitals), and by product class (e.g., door locks positioned as security devices).

There is a mistaken tendency to approach positioning as a promotional strategy. Certainly, promotional efforts can go a long way toward establishing, reinforcing, or changing an item's position—especially for consumer products and services. With industrial goods, product/service performance features, pricing arrangements, after-sale support, and the efforts of distributors can have a bigger impact on how items are perceived than does promotion. Remember that the product/service evaluation process used by industrial customers is much more detailed, and the buyer-seller relationship is often long term.

## Perceptual Mapping and Positioning

Positioning can be illustrated with the use of a perceptual map (see Figure 9.6). This is a pictorial representation of how a vendor or product/service is perceived by customers in comparison to other vendors or items. Although these maps can consist of any number of dimensions, a two-dimensional approach is easiest to work with. Each dimension represents an attribute of a vendor or product/service. Perceptual maps can be generated by statistical tools available with a number of computer programs, and they usually are based on customer data. Customers rank vendors or items on certain attributes or evaluate how similar or dissimilar different vendors or items are to one another.

Three significant pieces of information result from perceptual mapping. First, the marketer identifies the key attributes used by customers to distinguish among vendors or items. Second, the marketer determines how his or her product/service or firm is perceived with respect to these attributes. Third, the marketer is able to see the

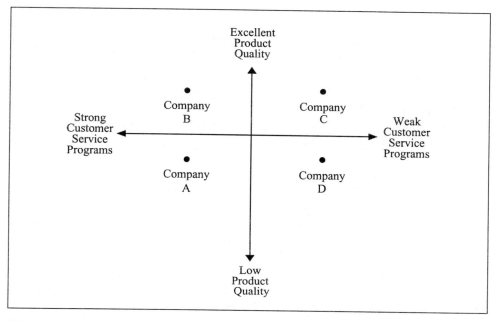

**Figure 9.6.** Two-Dimensional Perceptual Map of Vendors and Attributes in the Postal Equipment Industry

position of his or her product/service or firm relative to the competition. Note that maps can be used to demonstrate how the items in one company's product or service line are perceived relative to one another and to compare the perceptions of different types of purchase decision makers, such as engineers and purchasing agents.

The perceptual map presented in Figure 9.6 illustrates the positions of four manufacturers of postal equipment (e.g., postage meters, labeling equipment). The map indicates that product quality and customer service are the most salient attributes in this market. Customers perceive vendor A as offering excellent service, in absolute terms, and better service than any of the competitors. Vendor A's quality, however, is mediocre. Vendor C has the best quality but the worse service. Vendor B has the strongest combined performance on both attributes. Vendor D is perceived as low-quality, low-service vendor. This image may be intentional, as Vendor D may also be the low-price vendor. The point is to manage one's position purposefully, rather than assume that customers will perceive vendors or items correctly.

## Determining Product or Service Line Profitability

Earlier in this chapter, it was pointed out that companies should attempt to maximize profits not on individual items but on the entire product/service mix. This means having different goals and expectations for the various items being sold at any given time. The product portfolio concept (see Chapter 7) emphasizes that some items are heavier generators of cash, whereas others are heavier cash users. Strategies are often developed whereby items with lower margins or slower sales growth are priced and promoted in ways that support sales of higher-margin or faster-growth items.

The ability of marketers to develop realistic goals and creative strategies that take full advantage of the product/service mix requires that they have detailed knowledge of exactly where money is being made and lost. This means tracking the revenues, variable production/delivery/selling costs, and direct fixed costs for each product or service line and, where feasible, each item.

A useful tool in this regard is the contribution margin income statement. Here, revenues and expenses are broken out for each major item or line. Only those costs that are directly traceable to a given product or service category are applied. This includes an item's variable costs (e.g., labor, materials) and its direct fixed costs (e.g., depreciation on equipment used only to produce the item in question, advertising spent solely on the item, salaries for personnel who work solely on the item).

All remaining expenses are indirect fixed costs, so called because they cannot be tied directly to a particular product or service. These are costs that arguably would be incurred whether or not a particular item was being produced and sold (e.g., salaries of general management and staff personnel *not* assigned to a product or service). Correspondingly, they are not assigned or allocated to individual items; rather, they are put into a common category. Each product or service is evaluated to see how much it covers its own variable and direct fixed costs as well as how much it *contributes* to these common fixed costs. As a result, the marketer gets a truer picture of how much in revenues and expenses an item is actually generating, and how much it contributes to bottom-line profitability.

Table 9.5 provides an example of a contribution margin income statement for Advanced Audiovisual Systems, Inc. The statement summarizes profit performance for three lines: slide projectors, large-screen video projection machines, and overhead projectors. As can be seen, large-screen projectors generate the largest amount of revenue, and overhead projectors the lowest. By contrast, slide projectors produce the largest total contribution to indirect fixed costs and profit. Insights can also be gained by dividing the total product contribution for a line by the revenue from that line, producing a profitability index. These have been calculated in Table 9.5, and it appears that slide projectors are the top performer, followed closely by overheads, and then large-screen projectors. Thus, the top seller is the weakest profit performer.

Such contribution margin income statements should be a regular output of the marketing intelligence system discussed in Chapter 6. The ability to create these statements requires a conscientious effort and formal process for collecting and saving sales data by product. More difficult, but just as critical, is a system for grouping costs into direct and indirect fixed categories as they are incurred. This task is complicated by the fact that those in the company normally responsible for collecting and tabulating such data are in the accounting or finance areas. Their information needs differ from those of the marketer, so they may group revenues and costs in some other man-

**TABLE 9.5**  Contribution Margin Income Statement for Advanced
Audiovisual Systems, Inc.

|  | *Slide Projectors* | *Large-Screen Video Projectors* | *Overhead Projectors* | *Total* |
|---|---|---|---|---|
| Sales revenue | $5,390 | $6,115 | $4,598 | $16,103 |
| Variable costs: |  |  |  |  |
|     Manufacturing | 980 | 2,492 | 880 | 4,352 |
|     Selling | 147 | 165 | 154 | 466 |
|     Distribution | 98 | 66 | 88 | 252 |
|     Total | 1,225 | 2,723 | 1,122 | 5,070 |
| Variable contribution | 4,165 | 3,392 | 3,476 | 11,033 |
| Direct fixed costs | 450 | 720 | 590 | 1,760 |
| Total product contribution | 3,715 | 2,672 | 2,886 | 9,273 |
| Indirect fixed costs |  |  |  | 2,940 |
| Profit |  |  |  | 6,333 |
| Profitability index | 0.689 | 0.437 | 0.628 | 0.576 |

ner. Furthermore, because of their training and functional responsibilities, accounting and finance personnel usually are eager to allocate all fixed costs fully to units of a
product or service.

## Elimination of Products and Services

Discussion of the strategic management of industrial products and services should
not end without examining one of the marketer's most controversial decision areas:
when to drop a product/service line. This area is controversial because of the many
stakeholders in a company who are threatened by item elimination. Either their
jobs may be on the line, they are concerned about the effect of elimination on other
products/services, or they simply do not wish to be associated with the stigma of
failure. In terms of this last point, dropping an item need not be construed as failure. The product or service may simply have run its course in the life cycle. Better
opportunities may have come to the fore.

Little is known at present regarding the best time to delete an item. George
Avlonitis, who has done extensive work in the area of product elimination, finds that

**TABLE 9.6** Ten Leading Considerations in the Product or Service Deletion Decision

1. How will elimination affect the company's full-line policy?
2. Will the sales of other products/services be affected?
3. Are customer relationships going to be harmed?
4. Are substitute products/services available to satisfy customers?
5. Will the profitability of other items be affected by changes in allocation of production overhead? Selling overhead?
6. How will fixed and working capital be affected?
7. Is a new product or service available to replace the deletion candidate, and how much in the way of resources will be freed up to support the new product or service?
8. What are the likely competitive moves if the item is eliminated?
9. How will corporate image be affected by the elimination?
10. How will employees respond to the elimination?

SOURCE: Reprinted from G. Avlonitis, "Industrial Product Elimination: Major Factors to Consider," *Industrial Marketing Management*, 13, © Copyright 1984, p. 81. Reprinted with permission from Elsevier Science.

industrial marketers generally do not have a formalized procedure for making a deletion/retention decision. They do, however, tend to rely on a systematic set of considerations that they evaluate. Table 9.6 identifies the 10 leading factors taken into account by managers when evaluating candidates for deletion.

These considerations can be grouped into financial issues, marketing issues, released resource issues, and alternative opportunity issues. The preoccupation is frequently with financial issues, especially how the overhead being allocated to the deleted product will have to be reassigned to existing products and the subsequent impact on the profitability of these other items. Another financial issue involves the fixed and working capital invested in the product or service, and the return being generated on this capital.

Marketing issues are concerned with the effect dropping an item has on customers. Sales of other items may be hurt, or these other items may be expected to pick up the lost revenues resulting from deletion. Furthermore, the corporate image may suffer, and the overall product/service line strategy may be undermined. Released resource issues focus on how the human, physical, and financial resources assigned to an item will be affected by deletion. Will valuable employees be lost, or useful machinery be wasted? Management is further influenced by alternative opportunities that can be capitalized on should a product or service be dropped. Executive time, production capacity, dimension channels, and cash flow are freed up and can be reassigned to new products or services. The concern with alternative opportunities is especially great when management is faced with strong pressures from competitors.

The nature of these issues suggests that deletion decisions should involve representatives from the major organizational specialties: finance, production, marketing, and engineering. Purchasing is also a desirable participant, given this department's closeness to trends in the costs and availability of key materials, components, and product substitutes. It should always be kept in mind that product and service deletion/retention is a strategic decision area, meaning that deletion decisions must be consistent with the overall objectives and strategies of the firm.

# Summary

In this chapter we dealt with the first, and most important, element of the industrial marketing mix: the product or service offering of a firm. Products and services were defined as bundles of attributes that provide the ultimate source of value to a customer. Marketers can play a critical role in defining this attribute bundle and in tailoring it to reflect the distinct needs of individual market segments.

Products and services should be approached as variables that can be manipulated in a variety of ways. Managing the product element of the marketing mix involves manipulation of the core, tangible, and augmented dimensions of a product as it moves through the life cycle. With services, the marketer is managing aspects of the total service experience, which means manipulating service operations, service delivery, and service marketing.

Key differences between products and services were identified in the areas of tangibility, storability, time of consumption, production economies, customization, consumption patterns, and degrees of customer loyalty. Implications for marketing management were drawn from these differences. In addition, industrial products and services were shown to differ in many ways from their counterparts in consumer markets. It was also noted that considerable diversity exists among industrial products themselves, and among industrial services, such that one must be careful not to overgeneralize in either area.

Although single-item firms exist, most companies sell a line of products/services, and many offer a mix of various lines. Concepts of breadth (of the mix), length (of a line), and depth (of the items) were introduced to describe the decision alternatives confronting those responsible for designing a company's total portfolio of product/ service offerings. Product/service strategies built around considerations of breadth, length, and depth were summarized. These considerations also have important implications for the other elements in the marketing mix.

Of all the decisions in the area of product/service strategy, quality should be the overriding issue. That is, how much quality does the firm wish to provide, how can quality perceptions be influenced, and what programs must be put in place to ensure both quality control and ongoing quality improvement? Quality was defined in terms of conformance to a customer's need. In the product area, a distinction was made between product quality, support quality, and delivery quality. With services, both technical and functional quality were examined, and specific measurements of quality were discussed. The role of marketers in quality improvement was stressed, especially in measuring customer needs and willingness to pay for quality, assessing customer perceptions of current quality, evaluating competitor quality levels, influencing customer quality expectations, and identifying means of reducing quality costs.

Another significant and related aspect of product/service strategy is positioning. All products and services with which customers are familiar have a "position" in the marketplace. This may not be the position management intends, however, so all the elements of the marketing mix must be built carefully around an explicit positioning approach. The product/service map was introduced as a tool for understanding and implementing positioning efforts. Major types of positioning strategies were summarized.

Once such strategies are implemented, management must continually evaluate product and service line profitability. Measures of item and line performance are necessary for making realistic resource allocation decisions, specifically for determining how much emphasis different product or service areas should receive in ongoing marketing efforts. The contribution margin income statement was presented as an effective vehicle for gaining insights for these decisions.

We concluded with an examination of product/service deletion. Little is known about when to drop an item or how to determine the net effects of deletion on a company and its customers. Dropping an item clearly is not just a financial question. In fact, the manager must also consider marketing issues, released resource issues, and alternative opportunity issues. The need for firms to develop more formalized and systematic procedures for evaluating and deleting products and services was emphasized.

## Notes

1. fedex.com
2. www.abb.com/
3. www.roadway.com
4. www.prudential.com/
5. www.legalplans.com/
6. www.fluor.com/

## Questions

1. A product is more than a set of physical characteristics, design specifications, and component parts. Discuss an alternative way of conceptualizing products and provide an example using satellite dishes sold to corporations and hotels.

2.  Assume that you are selling banking services to corporate clients. What specific decisions must be made in terms of the service offering itself, as opposed to decisions about price, promotion, or distribution? Discuss the role of the service itself in formulating overall marketing strategy.

3.  When thinking of the underlying characteristics of a product, describe the major characteristics of a garbage dumpster. What implications do these particular characteristics have for the way in which the product is marketed?

4.  What are some ways in which industrial services differ from industrial products? Separately, think of three examples of industrial services. What are some ways in which these three services differ from one another in terms of key underlying characteristics?

5.  You are the marketing manager for an advertising agency. Describe the key aspects of the service operations, service delivery, and service marketing systems for a firm such as yours.

6.  For a firm selling direct mail services to corporations and nonprofit organizations, do you think it is possible to apply the experience curve and economies of scale concepts? What about a firm selling accounting services?

7.  Can a product or service line be too shallow? Can it be too deep? What sorts of problems arise in each case? Assume you are selling computer monitors.

8.  Explain the concept of positioning. What are some major ways a firm that sells microscopes could position itself? Select one positioning method and demonstrate how a perceptual map could be used to illustrate a firm's position relative to its competitors.

9.  Discuss major aspects of quality if you were a manufacturer of file cabinets. For this product, identify five ways in which the marketing department might affect quality.

10. AT&T manufactures pay telephones traditionally sold to local phone companies. The market for such telephones is relatively mature, with sales continuing to rise at a slow but steady rate. The deregulation of the telecommunications industry attracted many new competitors, providing lower-quality pay phones at a price well under that of AT&T. In addition, these pay telephones can now be purchased outright by stores, shopping centers, and office building owners, where before they were always owned and maintained by the local phone company. Discuss the alternatives that AT&T should consider if it were contemplating the deletion of pay telephones from its product line.

# CHAPTER 10

# A Creative Perspective on Industrial Pricing

*A man indicates by the price he offers for a good, the
importance he attaches to another unit of the good.*
—G. Stigler

## Key Concepts

Base-point pricing
Bid rigging
Cash discount
Closed bid
Collusion
Competitive bidding
Contribution analysis
Cost-plus pricing
Cross-elasticity
Demand elasticity
Economic value to the customer (EVC)
Financial lease
Gold-standard pricing
Hard benefit
Internet and pricing
Life-cycle costing
Margin distribution index
Negotiated pricing
Oligopoly
On-line auctions
Open bid
Operating lease
Opportunistic pricing

Parallel pricing
Parity pricing
Penetration pricing
Predatory pricing
Pressure pricing
Price discrimination
Price fixing
Price leadership
Probabilistic bidding
Profit-payoff matrix
Quantity discount
Reference product
Skimming pricing
Soft benefit
Standard cost analysis
Start-up cost
Target-return pricing
Trade discount
Transfer pricing
Value
Zone of price bargaining

## Learning Objectives

1. Recognize factors that complicate setting prices for industrial products and services as well as reasons marketers often fail to take full advantage of the price variable.

2. Approach price as a measure of value and be able to determine key sources of value.

3. Apply a four-part framework for determining the price of a product or service.

4. Appreciate how to establish competitive bids using probabilistic bidding.

5. Grasp the role of a number of special topics in industrial pricing, including discounts, leases, and transfer prices, and summarize key legal issues in pricing.

6. Understand how new marketing media such as the Internet and the World Wide Web are affecting pricing strategy, the forces they will exert on price, and the options that business-to-business marketers can exploit in the years to come.

The second element of the marketing mix to be addressed is the price variable. Among the marketing decision variables, price is unique in that it directly affects the organization's revenues and margins. Industrial pricing represents a challenging task that can be characterized as both an art and a science, and one that requires both creativity and flexibility. Creativity in pricing represents one of the untapped frontiers in marketing. In reality, pricing is a complex decision area that management too often tries to oversimplify.

Our theme in this chapter is that prices are a valuable marketing tool that can be used in a number of ways to accomplish a variety of objectives. We will examine the major concepts and tools available for managing industrial prices and present a framework for making pricing decisions. A series of specialized pricing topics are discussed, including price discrimination, discounts, bidding, leasing, and transfer pricing.

## Characteristics of Industrial Prices

Industrial prices have many distinguishing characteristics. First, the true price an industrial customer pays is often more than just the list price quoted by a salesperson or printed in a catalog. The actual price that must be paid often includes delivery and installation costs, discounts, training costs, trade-in allowances, two-for-one price deals, and financing costs, among others. Because the customer is likely to see a product's price in terms of the total cost to his organization, the marketer must also take such a comprehensive view.

Second, price is not an independent variable. Pricing interacts with product, promotion, and distribution strategies to achieve the firm's overall marketing objectives. For example, a high price can help convey a quality product image. A special price deal can be an integral part of the firm's promotional program. A trade discount can be an incentive for distributors to provide stronger support in pushing the company's products.

Third, prices for industrial goods cannot be set without considering other products that are complements or substitutes sold by the company. Cross-elasticities often exist, where the price of one item affects sales of other items. For example, the price a firm charges for its ink-jet printers may affect sales of its ink-jet cartridges. The same dependency exists between the price of a product and the prices of products sold by other companies if those products are used in conjunction with the firm's products.

Fourth, prices can be changed in numerous ways. Some of these are (a) changing the quantity of money or goods given up by a buyer, (b) changing the quantity of goods and services provided by the seller, (c) changing the premiums or discounts that are offered, (d) changing the time and place of payment, and (e) changing the time and place of transfer of ownership. As a result, pricing is often a more flexible decision area than, say, product or distribution. When the industrial firm decides on a price, it is in effect making a whole set of decisions regarding the time, form, quantity, and place of payment. Unfortunately, because price is relatively easy to change, managers may rely on short-run reasons in making hasty decisions that are harmful in the long run.

Fifth, industrial prices are often established through a process of competitive bidding, or tendering, on a project-by-project basis. As a result, the marketer may have to determine a price without knowing exactly what competitors are charging. Alternatively, where bidding is not used, prices frequently are resolved through a process of negotiation. The demands of the marketplace suggest that considerable flexibility is required in managing price negotiations and that the firm may need to delegate some pricing authority to the sales representative.

Sixth, industrial pricing is often characterized by an emphasis on fairness. When attempting to raise a price, the industrial marketer will often encounter experienced and fairly sophisticated buyers who are able to estimate the vendor's approximate production costs. These buyers expect price increases to be justifiable on the basis of either cost increases or product improvements, and not on the basis of whatever the traffic will bear.

Seventh, industrial prices are dramatically affected by a host of economic factors beyond the control of the firm. For example, if prices are not adjusted to reflect inflation rates, they may be over- or understated in real terms. This problem is especially critical for the marketer locked into a long-term contract with no price escalation clause. Fluctuations in interest rates affect the cost of money, which is an important component of price when goods are purchased on credit. Ups and downs in international rates of currency exchange undermine the effectiveness of a firm's pricing strategy, especially in increasingly global markets, in terms of both the firm's costs and its prices. Costs of key goods purchased from foreign suppliers can change significantly because of currency fluctuations. For goods sold abroad, a change in the exchange rate determines whether the marketer's price is competitive (high or low). The currency exchange problem is even more complex for companies selling goods in a number of different countries.

Unfortunately, the potential of the price variable is not fully realized in many industrial firms. It is not unusual in industrial companies for price decisions to be made by finance or operations personnel, rather than those in marketing. People in these other areas are oriented more toward achieving rates of return and covering costs than toward customer value or competitor actions. Too often, cost considerations play the predominant role in industrial pricing. Creative pricing is also neglected because of the relative importance of other (non–price-related) product attributes. For example, a customer may be so concerned with product quality or delivery reliability that pricing issues become secondary. The marketer, correspondingly, focuses on these other attributes.

## Price as a Measure of Value

The ultimate task of the industrial marketer is to deliver value to a customer. The price a customer is charged is both a determinant of and a reflection of the amount of value being received. Put more simply, price is a statement of value. A company can easily fail in the marketplace by charging an initial price that exceeds the value customers perceive in the product or service. This mistake often happens when the firm tries to recover its investment in R&D and related product development costs too rapidly or too early in the life cycle. Similarly, a price can be set so low that management is not taking full advantage of the profit potential of the item. The price is below the value customers associate with the good or service. Customers may, in fact, perceive the product to be somehow inferior because of its low price.

Value has two major dimensions, and the marketer considers both. First, value can be defined as the customer's *subjective* estimate of a product's capacity to satisfy a set of goals. In effect, the customer looks at it in terms of what they perceive they are getting divided by what they perceive they are paying. Different customers are not likely to perceive the value of a good in the same way. Consider the purchase of a small electric generator. The buyer with little generator experience may place more value on the product made by a vendor with a well-established reputation than the product made by a lesser-known supplier. Reputation is a product attribute for which he or she may be willing to pay a higher price. Another, more experienced, buyer may see these two alternatives as roughly equivalent and place equal values on each. An established reputation adds little value to the product in the case of the second buyer. In a similar vein, the value of a generator that provides energy savings to a company will vary depending on a number of company-specific factors. Some of these include the firm's total energy consumption, its current cash flow, and its relative concern with cost control.

Second, values for goods are determined *objectively* in the competitive marketplace. Based on the freely interacting forces of supply and demand, a market price is established. That is, the willingness and ability of a set of customers to buy and the willingness and ability of a set of suppliers to sell determine the value of a product at any point in time. From a marketing standpoint, value-based pricing is a means of efficiently allocating available supplies to customer groups. This value can be distorted, however, when the market operates inefficiently. In the absence of sufficient competition, or where regulatory constraints exist, the company may be charging a price that does not reflect its true value.

## Economic Value to the Customer

A value-related concept that is helpful when setting industrial prices is called *economic value to the customer* (EVC). Here, the focus is on purely economic sources of value. To understand EVC, we must return to a concept first introduced in Chapter 2, life-cycle costs. Included in life-cycle costs are all expenditures (initial price, start-up costs, postpurchase costs) incurred by a customer in using a product over its expected life, less any salvage value. The calculation of EVC for a product requires that the marketer is able to estimate the life-cycle costs of the best available substitute (also called a *reference product*).

Let's consider two products, A and B. Product A (the reference product) is currently sold for $100; it has estimated start-up costs of $50 and postpurchase costs of $80 over its useful life of 6 years. For simplicity, assume there is no salvage value, although this is rarely the case. Total life cycle costs are $230. Product B is a new competitor going after the same market as Product A and also has a useful life of 6 years. A successful product development effort has resulted in start-up costs for B of only $30, while its postpurchase costs are estimated at $60. Also assume that B has a desirable feature not found on Product A, for which customers appear willing to pay $20. This is called *incremental value*. The price of B has yet to be determined.

If one takes the life-cycle costs for the product currently being sold (A), subtracts the start-up and postpurchase costs of the new product (B), and then adds back any incremental value contained in B, the result is the economic value to the customer (EVC) of product B. In this case, EVC is $160. Another way to arrive at this figure is to take the price of the existing product and add the savings in start-up and postpurchase costs and the incremental value provided by the new product.

EVC provides a justification for charging a higher price than that currently charged for available substitutes. This can be seen in Figure 10.1, which presents an illustration of the EVC for product B. Subtracting the competitor's price ($100) from this EVC figure ($160) gives us $60, which is product B's competitive advantage. Let's say, how-

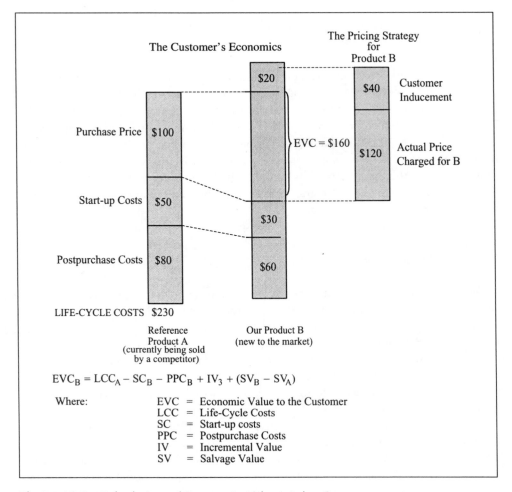

The Customer's Economics

The Pricing Strategy for Product B

$20

$40    Customer Inducement

Purchase Price   $100

EVC = $160

$120    Actual Price Charged for B

Start-up Costs   $50

$30

Postpurchase Costs   $80

$60

LIFE-CYCLE COSTS   $230

Reference
Product A
(currently being sold
by a competitor)

Our Product B
(new to the market)

$$EVC_B = LCC_A - SC_B - PPC_B + IV_3 + (SV_B - SV_A)$$

Where:

| | EVC | = | Economic Value to the Customer |
|---|---|---|---|
| | LCC | = | Life-Cycle Costs |
| | SC | = | Start-up costs |
| | PPC | = | Postpurchase Costs |
| | IV | = | Incremental Value |
| | SV | = | Salvage Value |

**Figure 10.1.** Calculation of Economic Value to the Customer

SOURCE: Reprinted with permission from "Value-Based Strategies for Industrial Products," *Business Horizons*, 24 (May-June 1981), p. 33, Forbis and Mehta. © Copyright 1981 by the Board of Trustees at Indiana University, Kelley School of Business.

NOTE: Value-based pricing still receives much attention today. See Stedman (2000) and Anderson and Narus (1998).

ever, that the price for B is set at $120. The difference between EVC and the actual price charged can be thought of as an inducement to the customer ($40, in this case).

Of course, getting the customer to see the advantages to be found in buying the higher-priced product requires a convincing sales effort. Many customers may not take such a long-term viewpoint. Life-cycle costs are estimates, based on an evaluation by the firm's technical product experts. Furthermore, because start-up and postpurchase costs are incurred over time, they must be discounted and expressed in present-value terms. Nevertheless, unlike other sources of value, estimates of economic value should be somewhat similar across companies using the product for the same purpose or application.

**Exhibit 10.1.**
What's It Worth: Questions to Guide the Establishment
of the Value of a Product/Service to a Customer

Q: How much money can customers save internally by using the product?

Q: Can the product help them increase sales or reach new customers themselves?

Q: Does the product give them a competitive advantage over their rivals?

Q: Does it improve the safety of the goods or equipment the customer manufactures?

Q: How much time can customers save by buying instead of building the product?

SOURCE: Adapted from "Value-Based Pricing," *Computerworld*, 34 (March 13) pp. 11, 58-63. © Copyright 2000 by *Computerworld*. Adapted with permission.

Knowledge of the value of the product or service to the industrial buyer can be extremely useful to the marketer. The relevant information for making these judgements, however, usually is not easy to obtain. The checklist in Exhibit 10.1 offers practical guidelines as to the kinds of questions that could be considered in determining customer value for pricing decisions.

## A Framework for Setting Industrial Prices

Industrial firms tend to manage prices in a fairly reactive and piecemeal fashion, with a heavy reliance on formula-based methods. To realize the true potential of the price variable, individual price decisions must be part of a larger program of action. Firms should develop what are called *strategic pricing programs*, which include four components: objectives, strategy, structure, and levels (tactics). Figure 10.2 provides an illustration of how these components fit together.

### The Role of Price Objectives

There is no one best price to charge for a given product. Once the need to set or change a price has been recognized, the manager must determine pricing objectives, or what he or she is trying to accomplish with this particular price. The answer might seem obvious: to make as much money as possible from the firm's products or services. This response, however, is too general and may not even be the case. In fact, companies can have a number of different pricing objectives.

Table 10.1 provides a partial listing of some of these objectives. The ones cited are not mutually exclusive, and some could be used in combination. For instance, using price to accomplish an image, such as that of premier quality provider, may also serve to maximize long-run profitability. By contrast, certain of these objectives conflict with one another. Charging low prices to discourage market entry may serve to irri-

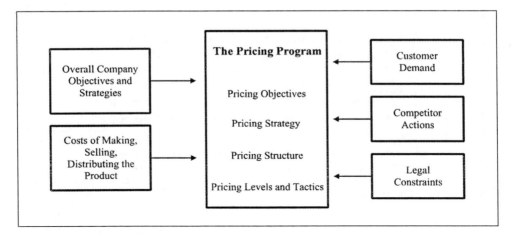

**Figure 10.2.** The Pricing Program and Its Determinants

tate middlemen and to detract from the desired image of the firm. In their attempts to compete effectively with Dell Computer's Web-based sales, the traditional marketers of PCs, such as Compaq, Hewlett-Packard, and IBM, have had to cut prices (reducing margins for both themselves and intermediaries) while at the same time being frustrated in their efforts to sell directly to customers because of the risk of antagonizing distributors.

## Establishing a Strategy

If objectives are the performance levels the manager wishes to achieve, then strategies represent comprehensive statements regarding how price will be used to accomplish the objectives. A pricing strategy provides a theme that guides all the firm's pricing decisions for a particular product line and a particular time period. Thus, it serves to coordinate all the pricing activities related to the product line.

To illustrate, the FMC fire apparatus division uses a pricing strategy that can be characterized as premium pricing for its fire trucks. High prices and margins are charged, with relatively lower volume expectations. The central theme is excellence. Price is used to reflect the highest quality levels, and the firm is careful not to compromise its image with overly aggressive price deals or discounts. The vignette below also illustrates the role of creativity in pricing strategy.

Marc Andreessen was a 22-year-old student at the National Center for Supercomputing at the University of Illinois toward the end of 1993, when he developed first Mosaic, and later (with Jim Clark) Netscape, two pieces of "browser" software. These software packages are used to "browse" or "surf" the World Wide Web, the multimedia platform on the Internet. The Internet is an interconnection of tens of thousands of public and private networks worldwide that provides more than 30 million users with access to information from around the globe. The price for Mosaic or

**TABLE 10.1** Possible Pricing Objectives

1. Target return on investment
2. Target market share
3. Maximize long-run profit
4. Maximize short-run profit
5. Sales growth
6. Stabilize the market
7. Convey a particular image
8. Desensitize customers to price
9. Be the price leader
10. Discourage entry by new competitors
11. Speed exit of marginal firms
12. Avoid government investigation and control
13. Maintain loyalty and sales support of middlemen
14. Avoid excessive demands from suppliers
15. Be regarded as fair by customers
16. Create interest and excitement for the item
17. Use price of one product to sell other products in the line
18. Discourage others from lowering prices
19. Quickly recover investment in product development
20. Encourage quick payment of accounts receivable
21. Generate volume so as to drive down costs

Netscape? Mosaic and Netscape were distributed *free of charge*, despite the fact that the software had very obvious value. Millions of individuals and organizations availed themselves of the free offer and quickly learned to use and love the software as the vehicle to access all manner of information and entertainment.

When Andreessen (as vice president of technology) started a company with Jim Clark (former chairman of Silicon Graphics[1]) as president in August, 1995, it was one of the hottest new listings in financial history. Netscape Communications Corporation[2] shares opened for trading at multiples of the offer price, despite the fact that the company had until that time not really "sold" a single product. Andreessen's personal wealth on the day of the listing was estimated to be in excess of $58 million.

Pricing strategies will generally fall into one of two groups: cost based and market based. *Cost-based* strategies usually rely on a formula in which costs are fully allocated to units of production, and a markup or rate of return is added to this total. *Market-based* approaches tend to focus either on the competition or customer demand, or both. Table 10.2 provides examples of specific pricing strategies.

Cost-based approaches are much more prevalent among industrial firms than are market approaches. This tendency is one of the great ironies of business and reflects

---

**TABLE 10.2** Two Major Types of Pricing Strategies

---

**Cost-Based Strategies**

◆ *Mark-up pricing*—variable and fixed costs per unit are estimated, and a standard markup is added. The markup frequently is either a percentage of sales or of costs.

◆ *Target return pricing*—variable and fixed costs per unit are estimated. A rate of return is then taken and multiplied by the amount of capital invested in the product; the result is divided by estimated sales. The resulting return per unit is added to unit costs to arrive at a price.

**Market-Based Strategies**

◆ *Floor pricing*—charging a price that just covers costs. Usually used just to maintain a presence in the market given the competitive environment.

◆ *Penetration pricing*—charging a price that is low relative to (a) the average price of major competitors and (b) what customers are accustomed to paying.

◆ *Parity pricing (going rate)*—charging a price that is roughly equivalent to the average price charged by the major competition.

◆ *Premium pricing (skimming)*—the price charged is intended to be high relative to (a) the average price of major competitors and (b) what customers are accustomed to paying.

◆ *Price leadership pricing*—usually involves a leading firm in the industry making fairly conservative price moves, subsequently followed by other firms in the industry. This limits price wars and leads to fairly stable market shares.

◆ *Stay out pricing*—the firm prices lower than demand conditions require so as to discourage market entry by new competitors.

◆ *Bundle pricing*—products or services are combined into sets or bundles, and a lower single price is charged for the bundle than would be the case if each item were sold separately.

◆ *Value-based pricing (differentials)*—different prices are set for different market segments based on the value each segment receives from the product or service.

◆ *Cross-benefit pricing*—prices are set at or below costs for one product in a product line, but relatively high for another item in the line that serves as a direct complement (e.g., certain brands of cameras and film).

---

a general level of naïveté among managers responsible for pricing decisions. Price must be a reflection of value; value and customer willingness to pay are market-based considerations. Costs, alternatively, frequently are unrelated to the amount customers are willing to pay; simply, in a vast number of cases, customers don't care what the product cost the manufacturer to make—they care what it is worth to them. The popularity of cost-based strategies reflects the fact that they are easy to implement and manage. In addition, setting a price that covers costs and generates a fixed profit margin makes intuitive sense to the typical manager.

The actual strategy chosen should be based on a careful evaluation of a number of key factors, both internal and external to the company. These will be described later

**TABLE 10.3**  Some Key Managerial Questions in Developing a Pricing Structure

1. Should a standard list price be charged for the product or service?
2. Should frequent or large customers be charged the same base price?
3. Can and should separate prices be charged for different aspects of the product/service?
4. How should the time of purchase affect the price charged a customer?
5. To what extent should the price charged be varied to reflect the cost of doing business with a particular customer?
6. Should customers who value the product more be charged a higher price than other customers?
7. What is the nature of any discounts to be offered to buyers?
8. When and where should title be taken by the buyer?
9. Is it realistic to offer a dual-rate structure, where the same customer has a choice between two pricing options for the same product or service?
10. Should the price structure involve a rental or leasing option?

in this chapter. The underlying philosophy, however, must be that every pricing consideration is examined from a customer perspective.

## Developing a Structure

Once a pricing strategy has been selected, the concern becomes implementation. Implementing a strategy requires that the manager develop a pricing structure and then a tactical plan.

The pricing structure is concerned with which aspects of each product or service will be priced, how prices will vary for different customers and products/services, and the time and conditions of payment. A number of managerial questions that should be addressed when establishing the pricing structure are identified in Table 10.3.

The most basic structure involves charging one standard price for a product or service, with no discounts or variations. This is relatively simple to administer and is easily understood by customers and middlemen. At the same time, customers and middlemen often feel they deserve price breaks or special concessions for a variety of reasons, and both may be eager to negotiate on price.

The biggest problem with such simple structures concerns their lack of flexibility as markets become more competitive and as new profit opportunities arise for the firm. Consider the case of a fire extinguisher company that charges relatively moderate list prices on its line of extinguishers. The firm is basically making a trade-off between the customers that perceive high value from these products and those that perceive lower value. That is, high valuation customers (e.g., building architects who rely on technical specs) would likely pay more than the firm is asking, while lower perceived value customers (construction firms) may purchase less of the product than would be the case at lower prices, because they are strongly cost driven. Management may hope, in the process, to maximize revenue.

Consider the ways in which flexibility could be added by altering the price structure. Revenue might be enhanced by giving construction firms a 10% price discount, especially if they generally fall into the group of customers with lower value perceptions value. Resources might be more completely used by charging less for certain extinguishers during low sales months, or a premium during peak months. The firm could offer 3-for-1 deals or some form of quantity incentive, or, alternatively, special "packages" might be put together for a single price, for example, when bidding on equipment for a large office building. To facilitate source loyalty, repeat buyers might be given price breaks based on cumulative purchases or might be told they can purchase on credit. The structural possibilities are virtually limitless if the manager is creative and knows his or her customers.

As competition in an industry intensifies, price generally moves in the direction of costs, while demand is increasingly saturated. Both developments have implications for price structure. First, any differences in the cost positions take on significance, as the price structure is modified to reflect a competitor's cost advantages or disadvantages. Second, competitors are apt to respond to market saturation with more aggressive market segmentation and targeting. The frequent result is price breaks for certain groups of customers.

Creative price structures are also critical for companies that do not sell a tangible product that can be inventoried indefinitely. This includes most service businesses as well as those that sell perishable goods or products with short life cycles. Airlines, shipping companies, freight forwarders, and consultants, for example, sell asset usage, not the asset itself. If a particular seat on a flight, space in a container, or consultant's skills are not purchased during a particular time period, revenue is lost forever. As a result, a large container shipping company such as the Anglo-Dutch company P&O NedLloyd[3] may vary price (or what the trade calls "rates") based on the distance to a destination, the popularity of that destination, the season, whether the customer is a regular patron, how far in advance the reservation is made, and whether or not the customer will accept a "no cancellation" penalty. Many of these structural approaches have proven effective in reducing the number of unfilled containers or container spaces on specific routes.

## Determining Price Levels and Related Tactics

Once established, strategies and structures may remain in place for a fairly long period of time. The day-to-day management of price focuses, alternatively, on setting specific price levels and employing periodic tactical pricing moves.

*Price levels* refer to the actual price charged for each product or service in the line, as well as the specific amount of any types of discounts offered. In determining exact levels, the manager's decisions must not only translate the firm's pricing strategy into specific numbers but also reflect a variety of practical considerations. Some of these issues include finding the acceptable range of price levels that convey the desired value perception, determining whether or not to charge odd prices (e.g., $199 instead of $200), ensuring that price gaps between items within the same line are wide enough to convey meaningful differences in the items, and setting prices to reflect tax considerations.

Levels may require frequent modification in response to changes in production costs, competitor tactics, and evolving market conditions. For instance, costs of a key raw material may increase, a leading competitor may unexpectedly lower prices on a selective basis, supply conditions may change because a competitor has overproduced, or demand sensitivity (elasticity) may change within the current price range.

The ability to manage price levels effectively is heavily dependent on the manager's sense of timing. Price changes must not come across as arbitrary. Customers should sense a degree of consistency and stability in the firm's price levels over time. They must be able to justify, in their own minds, paying prices that are higher or lower than was previously the case. Otherwise, the company winds up sending conflicting signals regarding the value of its products or services and thus undermining customer confidence.

Beyond levels themselves, periodic tactical moves can include rebates, 2-for-1 price deals, a liberal trade-in policy, or any other creative means of temporarily varying price. These tactics are generally promotional in nature and are usually part of special sales campaigns. They should be used with specific short-term objectives in mind, some of which may be communications related (e.g., creating product awareness, encouraging product trial). The pricing manager must ensure, however, that such tactics are consistent with the firm's overall pricing program.

## Putting Together the Pricing Program Components

The four components of an effective pricing program (strategy, structure, level, and tactics) are not independent and should not be approached in an isolated fashion. Rather, they must be closely coordinated, with each element providing direction to the next. Consider some examples. Assume a local truck rental company has entered the market positioning itself as a no-frills, low-cost provider. Price objectives are set with an emphasis on high volume and revenue, low unit profits, and using price to convey a bargain image. To implement these objectives, the company selects a penetration strategy, in which price is set low relative to competitor prices and customer expectations. Structure is designed to include a low price per day and unlimited mileage for each of three classes of trucks, with relatively small differences within each truck group. An even lower rate is offered to those who rent for 5 days or more at a time. Levels for the basic truck groups are established at $46.95, $69.95, and $85.75, respectively.

This pricing program may serve the company for a number of years. Pricing objectives and strategy may remain largely unchanged for an indefinite time period. Structure may require periodic modification, such as with the addition of a "frequent renter" program or special price deals for those who use the truck for particularly clean jobs or during certain seasons. Levels and tactics will require ongoing modification as competitor rates and tactics, production costs, and demand conditions fluctuate.

As a second example, a major manufacturer of quality copiers has found that unit costs have been falling; at the same time, competition has intensified and the product line has proliferated. Product life cycles have been getting shorter, as brief as 1 year for some models. In response, the firm has instituted an entirely new marketing strategy, of which price is a central component.

The pricing objective in this case involves maximizing annual profitability across the product and service line. The strategic focus is on selective demand, where sales result from replacements/additions sold to the existing customer base and from taking accounts away from competitors. The pricing strategy is parity pricing, with the firm attempting to charge base prices at or near the average competitive price. Structure is designed to be flexible, with salespeople given some leeway in arriving at a final price. This is especially the case on mature products and those with the lowest manufacturing costs. The actual intent is to use the structure to place machines, but then to sell customers a service contract, for which margins are considerably higher. In addition, significant discounts are provided to customers who purchase multiple machines. Finally, base price levels are established and adjusted monthly to reflect an index of the average prices of the three top-selling machines in each major product category. A discount of 20% is provided for each purchase of three or more units. Approached in this manner, price becomes an innovative variable with immense potential for affecting the strategic direction of the firm.

## The Underlying Determinants of Pricing Decisions

When putting together the firm's strategic pricing program, and subsequently managing the program over the stages of product or service life, the marketer continually evaluates a number of critical price determinants. Recent research by Noble and Gruca (1999) of a sample of 270 business-to-business pricing decision makers yielded some interesting results. More than 50% indicated that they used more than one pricing strategy in formulating their most recent pricing decision for a high-value industrial product sold in the United States. Results suggested that product line pricing strategies (bundling, complementary product, and customer value pricing) were more likely to be used by firms that sell substitute or complementary products. Cost-based pricing was more likely to be used in markets where demand is very difficult to estimate.

## Company Objectives/Strategies

Pricing programs must reflect the overall marketing strategies of the firm. A large number of marketing strategies are available to any firm (see Chapter 7). One example of a common strategy is differentiation, where the company attempts to create unique perceptions among customers of its product or service offering relative to the competition.

If a company was pursuing a differentiation strategy, how might the pricing program be designed to reinforce this strategy? As a general rule, successful differentiation allows the manager to charge somewhat higher margins than competitors, reflecting the higher value being delivered to customers. In addition, differentiation encourages brand loyalty, frequently making customers less price sensitive. Customers are likely to perceive fewer acceptable substitutes. The more salient the source of differentiation is to customers, the more brand loyal they are likely to be.

Another marketing strategy is targeting or niching. This involves focusing on a particular market segment, such as a certain type of user, a specific product application, or a single geographic region. Square-D Corporation[4] targets its "homeline" line of electrical distribution equipment to the low-end user, while Porter Paints[5] products are positioned solely to the professional painter. Using the Square-D example, price is set below that of conventional equipment to convey the idea that the buyer is getting a reliable but lower-quality product. This represents a good value for the money to a sizable segment of the market.

Inconsistencies between overall marketing strategy and the firm's pricing strategy frequently produce failure in the marketplace. The company that has positioned itself as a high-end or premium-quality provider but that then drops prices when confronted with competitive pressures is undermining its own market position, confusing customers, and giving away margins. Similarly, pricing strategies that focus on quickly recouping the initial investment in a product or service often result in prices that are too high given the firm's desired position in customer's minds.

## Examining Costs

The second determinant of a firm's pricing program is costs. They indicate what must be charged for a product to break even, or to achieve a certain rate of return. Even here, however, there are instances in which a firm will set price below the full cost of a product. Possible reasons for this include (a) maintaining the workforce and keeping facilities running during temporary periods of slack demand, (b) helping sales of other products in the line, (c) bidding low on an individual contract to establish a relation with a certain customer or a position in a particular market, (d) gaining experience, or (e) acquiring some new skill. In this section, two approaches to cost analysis for pricing are presented: standard cost analysis and contribution analysis.

## Standard Cost Analysis

A popular approach to assessing costs for the purpose of price setting is *target-return pricing*, a type of cost-plus pricing in which the manager attempts to establish a price for a product that will generate a predetermined rate of return on capital.

To set a price, the manager first must estimate the quantity or volume of the product to be produced during the next year, or the average annual volume over a number of years. This forecast becomes the cornerstone of the firm's pricing strategy, so its accuracy is critical. The estimate is called *standard volume*.

For a given standard volume, the manager determines what unit labor and material costs will be, then adds any other variable costs (e.g., sales commissions) to arrive at variable cost per unit. In addition, the total fixed costs are estimated for this range of production and then divided by standard volume to get fixed cost per unit. Fixed costs are allocated evenly across units of production for a given product. These variable cost and fixed cost estimates are called *standard costs*.

The desired level of profit per unit is added to these standard costs. This desired unit profit is determined by multiplying the required rate of return by the amount of capital, or operating assets, employed in producing and distributing the product and then dividing that total by standard volume. In summary, the price to be charged is equal to

$$P = DVC + FC/Q + rK/Q$$

where

P   = price
DVC = direct variable cost per unit
FC  = fixed cost
r   = desired rate of return
K   = capital employed
Q   = estimate of standard unit volume

So, assume that direct variable costs per unit are $8 and total fixed costs are $400,000. The company projects standard volume at 200,000 units. The product will require $1 million in capital. Further assuming a required rate of return of 20%, the formula will produce a price of $11 per unit.

In practice, industrial firms often use much more elaborate versions of the formula. Other factors built into the equation might include interest rates on debt, tax rates, or an inflation factor. Further complicating the calculation, costs frequently are not so easily placed into fixed and variable categories; they may be broken out and allocated in any number of ways for the purpose of the target-return formula.

The target-return approach to pricing has a number of limitations. If actual sales fall short of the standard volume estimate, then the only way to achieve the desired rate of return is to raise prices, which seems counterintuitive. This approach also can lead to what has been called the doom loop. Prices are raised and volume subsequently falls, causing unit costs to rise as scale economies are lost—whereupon the formula will force the marketer to raise price further, and so on.

In addition, wide fluctuations in demand create problems for firms using target-return pricing, as it becomes difficult to determine reliable standard volume estimates. These fluctuations may be due, in part, to competitor actions and may warrant a pricing response. AT&T provides an example. Prior to deregulation in the telecommunications industry and the company's forced divestiture of local telephone operating companies, demand for many of its products was fairly predictable. Most of this demand came from the operating companies, so it was captive. Target-return pricing worked fairly well in such a constrained and stable environment. In a less regulated and more competitive market, demand is more volatile, and inflexibility of target-return pricing results in prices that are too high for some products and too low for others.

Target-return prices are arrived at by fully allocating fixed costs to units of a product. The method used to allocate is arbitrary, regardless of how logical it may seem. In fact, alternative methods for allocating overhead can produce quite different prices. This allocation problem is especially apparent where a company produces a number of products with shared fixed costs, and these products vary in terms of how labor- or capital-intensive each is. Full-cost pricing also ignores the idea that products in different stages of their life cycles will not be equally profitable, or that companies may initially price low to generate volume that will, in turn, bring unit costs down.

### Contribution Analysis

When setting the price of a new product, the marketer often will find it useful to estimate the volume of sales necessary to either break even or achieve some level of profitability at different prices. The marketer who is considering a price cut wants to know how many more units must be sold to at least maintain the current level of revenue. If a price increase is under consideration, then the concern becomes the number of unit sales which can be lost before the firm is any worse off than in its current position.

"What must happen?" questions can be answered through contribution analysis. This analysis is based on the logic that a product first should be held accountable for those costs that are directly attributable to its production and distribution (i.e., direct costs). Then, assuming it generates enough revenue to cover these costs, any remaining revenue would be applied to indirect costs (i.e., costs that are not directly attributable to the product) and profits. To perform contribution analysis, the total variable costs for a product are subtracted from its total revenue. The difference is called the *variable contribution margin*. This margin can also be expressed on a per unit basis by taking the product's price and subtracting unit variable costs. Dividing contribution per unit into total fixed costs, the result is the number of units that must be sold to break even. If a profit of, say, $10,000 were desired, then this figure would be added to fixed costs before dividing by contribution per unit.

As a hypothetical example, consider Everlight Corporation, a manufacturer that develops a standard 72-inch fluorescent lamp that burns 800 usage hours longer and uses 10% less energy than available lamps. Primary customers would be factories, packing houses, assembly operations, and similar types of production facilities. The variable manufacturing costs incurred in producing the new lamp are estimated to average $6 per unit. A plant to manufacture the lamp would have to be built and equipped for, let's say, $7 million and depreciated over 7 years ($1 million per year). Administrative overhead is projected to be $200,000 annually, while sales and distribution expenses are estimated at $300,000 per year. Annual fixed costs therefore will be $1,500,000.

Assume that annual sales of fluorescent lamps of this particular type are 5 million units. Furthermore, assume that these sales are primarily accounted for by 10 major manufacturers, the 3 largest having 70% market share among them. The market leader currently charges its distributors $8 for lamps of this standard variety.

Everlight, as manufacturer of the new lamp, wants to evaluate the viability of various prices, initially assessing the feasibility of charging $9.00, $8.00, $7.50, or $7.00. These prices have been selected because of their proximity to competitor prices and to provide management with a starting point from which to assess costs using a contribution approach. If the contribution margin is calculated for each of the pricing alternatives, the results are as shown below.

| Price | $9.00 | $8.00 | $7.50 | $7.00 |
|---|---|---|---|---|
| Variable cost | –6.00 | –6.00 | –6.00 | –6.00 |
| Contribution margin | $3.00 | $2.00 | $1.50 | $1.00 |

The units and market share required to break even at each price can now be calculated.

| Price | Break-Even Units | Break-Even Market Share |
|---|---|---|
| $9.00 | $1,500,000/$3.00 = 500,000 | 500,000/5,000,000   = 10% |
| $8.00 | $1,500,000/$2.00 = 750,000 | 750,000/5,000,000   = 15% |
| $7.50 | $1,500,000/$1.50 = 1,000,000 | 1,000,000/5,000,000 = 20% |
| $7.00 | $1,500,000/$1.00 = 1,500,000 | 1,500,000/5,000,000 = 30% |

As can be seen, the new manufacturer will need to capture 15% of this market if the competitor's price is matched, just to break even. If a penetration pricing strategy is attempted, where the manufacturer attempts to attract attention and market share by going in below the current market price of $8.00, a price cut of only $.50 would require 20% share, and a cut of $1.00 would require 30% share. Given the competitive structure of this market, this goal might seem overly ambitious, especially if the competition is able to duplicate this innovation. Now, it might be argued that the 30% share is achievable given the superiority of the new lamp and, at such a relatively low price, that customers would be lining up to purchase it. If the lamp is that much better, however, then it is providing the customer with more value. A high price may be in order to convey this superior value.

At a price of $9, only 10% of the market must be captured to break even. Such an approach is closer to a premium or skimming strategy. The marketer may be trying to achieve a quality image then, or to go after a particular segment that is less price-sensitive. Or, the marketer may use the EVC concept to argue that he or she is actually saving money for the customer over the product's useful life.

The point is that cost analysis does provide some important insight into what price should be charged. This analysis must be considered, however, within the context of the objectives management is trying to achieve (e.g., market share, image, or profit). The final pricing decision depends further, however, on a detailed analysis of demand and competitive reaction.

## Assessing Demand

*Cost-Benefit Analysis.* Earlier, this chapter stressed that price should be a reflection of the value a customer is receiving from a product. Accordingly, the marketer must have a thorough understanding of the customer's usage of the item and the utility it provides. When assessing demand, it is helpful to perform an analysis of the benefits received and the costs incurred by the customer in purchasing and using the product.

In examining benefits, a distinction can be drawn between hard and soft benefits. *Hard* benefits refer to the physical attributes of the product, whereas *soft* benefits include service, training, warranties, delivery, company reputation, and other supporting elements that were referred to in Chapter 9 as the augmented product. It is generally easier to evaluate the customer's utility for hard benefits. A given customer will have specific requirements regarding such physical product characteristics as horsepower, production rate, durability, error rate, or performance tolerances. The marketer can calculate price-performance ratios if he or she divides the price in dollars by the benefit measured in units. For a copying machine, for example, the price-performance ratio might be dollars divided by copies produced per minute. Comparisons can then be drawn between the price-performance ratios of various competitors. Soft benefits are more difficult to assess. The relative importance of a warranty, for example, will vary widely from customer to customer, and even among those within the buying center in a given organization. At a minimum, the marketer should attempt to estimate the utility of the benefit by market segment.

In examining the cost side of the equation, the marketer wants to consider the complete range of expenses a customer will incur in purchasing and using the product in question. The marketer may need to go further, however, because the customer may be concerned about costs that would be incurred only if something went wrong. For example, in purchasing a piece of machinery, the customer may be concerned about what it would cost if the machinery became defective and the production process had to be shut down. The risk of such a development represents a real cost.

Having identified the important benefits and costs to the customer, the next step is to evaluate possible cost-benefit trade-offs. Customers who are willing to hold more inventory in return for slower delivery by a less expensive mode of transportation are trading off costs and benefits. A quantity discount may also provide the incentive to purchase larger stocks if the amount of the discount exceeds the costs of maintaining the inventory. Similarly, the decision to purchase an optional feature on some product should reflect the perception that the benefit received exceeds the total price paid.

*Elasticity of Demand.* Cost-benefit trade-offs that an industrial customer is willing and able to make will be reflected in that customer's price elasticity. *Elasticity* is a measure of the sensitivity of the customer's quantity demanded to changes in price; it is an important indicator to the marketer of the feasibility of various pricing alternatives.

The demand curve for most products normally has a negative slope, indicating that customers buy more at lower prices. To properly gauge this price-quantity relationship, the analyst must control any other variables that affect customer demand, such as the customer's own sales volume, customer preferences, the price of substitute goods, and customer expectations regarding inflation or product availability. Usually, a different demand curve exists for each market segment.

Elasticity is measured over some range of a demand curve, and it usually changes along the demand curve. Thus, demand may be fairly inelastic (or insensitive to changes in price) for a product within a given range of prices but may become elastic (or sensitive) once price exceeds some threshold level. Importantly, substitutes that would not have been considered in the lower price range become viable alternatives once price exceeds that threshold.

To determine elasticity, divide the percentage change in quantity (which results from a price increase or decrease) by the percentage change in price (which caused that increase or decrease in quantity demanded). If the percentage change in quantity exceeds the percentage change in price, demand is said to be *elastic*. If the percentage change in price exceeds the percentage change in quantity, demand is said to be *inelastic*. The flatter (closer to horizontal) the demand curve, the more elastic is demand. As the curve becomes steeper (more vertical), demand is becoming more inelastic.

Elasticity is an indicator of how price changes can be expected to affect total company revenues. Cutting prices will lead to a loss of revenue if demand is inelastic but to an increase in revenue if demand is elastic. Conversely, raising prices will result in higher revenues if demand is inelastic but lower revenues where demand is elastic.

Eight major factors determine how elastic a customer's demand will be:

◈ Availability of substitutes

◈ Extent to which the product in question is a necessity

◈ Relative dollar size of the purchase

◈ Extent of product differentiation

◈ Customer switching costs

◈ Ease of comparison (complexity)

◈ Existence of a third-party payer

◈ Tendency to associate price with quality

◈ When payment is due (i.e., time)

Demand for a product will tend to be more elastic in a situation where there are many substitutes, the item is not a necessity, or the item represents a sizable percentage of the customer's budget or spendable income. Also, when a product is not well differentiated from competitive products, has low switching costs, and is easy to compare to competitive offerings, demand will be more elastic. In addition, demand is more elastic if a third party is paying part of the price, when the customer does not tend to associate quality with price, and when a customer can finance a purchase or pay over a number of months. Demand tends to become more elastic over time as well. The most important factor—and fundamental to all of them—is the availability of substitutes, or the number of alternatives available to the customer for satisfying a given need.

The demand for many industrial products and services tends to be relatively inelastic. This is especially true where products and services are technically sophisticated, customized, or critical to the customer's operations. That is, they are necessity items with few available substitutes. There are, however, many exceptions. Industrial customers may demonstrate elastic demand for many routine-order purchases where competitor offerings are fairly undifferentiated. Demand elasticity tends to be situational, dependent on customer and marketplace circumstances at a given point in time.

The marketer is in a position to affect a customer's elasticity of demand. Ideally, it is beneficial to the marketer for customers to be relatively inelastic in their demand for his or her product. This inelastic demand can be achieved by convincing customers that there are few *acceptable* substitutes and that the product is a "must" item that they really should not be without (i.e., that they require to achieve a competitive advantage). Companies such as 3M, Microsoft, and Federal Express have successfully achieved this perception in establishing loyal customer "franchises" for their brand name products.

Marketers often will find that demand elasticities vary across market segments. Where variation exists among segments, there may be an economic justification for price differentials. That is, two different segments might be charged different prices, dependent on how elastic their respective demand functions are. The price variable may be more important to purchasers in one segment than to those in another. If large users are given a price break, for example, such a tactic would suggest not only that it is more economical to sell to large users but also that such customers are sensitive (elastic) to such price breaks. The evidence indicates that price discrimination is a widely used tactic in industrial markets (Morris, 1987).

Before leaving the concept of elasticity, it is worth noting that products also can have *cross-elasticities*, where the price of one product affects the demand for another product. The coefficient of cross-elasticity is defined as the percentage change in quantity demanded for product A divided by the percentage change in price for product B. This coefficient can vary from negative infinity to positive infinity. Where products are complements (e.g., electrical drills and drill bits; printers and cartridges), they will have negative cross-elasticities. Substitute commodities (e.g., delivery by truck rather than by train) have positive cross-elasticities. In making pricing decisions, then, it is worth evaluating other products in the line to determine positive or negative cross-elasticities. The marketer also wants to be wary of the effect that the prices charged by other companies have on his or her sales. Again, such cross-elasticities can be positive or negative.

Cross-elasticity analysis can be accomplished to some extent with informal observation, and its application to pricing is common for companies with large product lines. An office supply company provides an example. The typical office supply company has a set of clients who have standard reorder patterns for supplies. It also has another set that reorders more sporadically and may even shop among the various local office supply companies for better prices on specific items. Periodically, an aggressive supply house will run price specials on items in its line. If a 20% price savings was offered on printers, computer paper, and printer cartridges, the reduction would probably elicit a good response in terms of total unit sales; however, consideration of the cross-elasticities of demand would reveal that these are complementary products (paper and cartridges are normally bought along with printers), so it would actually be better to offer a special on printers and hold paper and cartridge prices at their normal levels, because the price incentive on the paper and cartridges would not be as important to the buyer of printers—once given an incentive to buy the printer, a customer will pay normal prices for the other items. In fact, it would be more advantageous to offer a discount based on repurchases of printer paper and ribbons over time and thereby convert the price-sensitive supplies buyers into more loyal customers.

## Analyzing the Competition

Industrial pricing policies that reflect company objectives, costs, and demand considerations can still be ineffective unless they also address the competitive environment. Given the complexity of the price variable, the importance of life-cycle costs, the role of discounts, and the many ways in which prices can be varied, it becomes crucial that competitor actions and reactions regarding pricing decisions be anticipated and continually monitored.

The purpose in examining competitor prices is not simply to ensure that the marketer is charging the same amount or less, although this goal tends to be emphasized in competitive bidding. Rather, the marketer is attempting to examine the value his or her product delivers to different customer groups in comparison to that provided by the competition. He or she must go one step further and anticipate ways in which a competitor will alter its pricing policies once the price is established.

Industrial markets tend to have an oligopolistic structure; that is, a relatively small number of firms have a disproportionate share of the market. *Fewness* is the name of the game; four or five companies may account for 80% to 90% of a given market. This economic concentration has a major impact on the pricing practices within the industry. Where markets are oligopolistic, the strategies pursued by companies are heavily interdependent; that is, whatever one firm does with its price is dependent on what other firms do, and its actions will also affect the decisions of those other firms. Often a price leader emerges. This firm sets the tone on price, and others follow. Although any number of firms can play the role of price leader, it is often the firm with the most favorable underlying cost position.

It has been suggested that an industrial firm in an oligopolistic market will pursue one of four strategic pricing options: pressure pricing, opportunistic pricing, gold-standard pricing, and negotiated pricing (Webster, 1984). The first two represent longer-term strategies over time, whereas the latter two are appropriate for short-term individual transactions *Pressure pricing* involves a market leader maintaining price at a fairly stable level regardless of fluctuations in demand, and managing price increases in a controlled manner. Competitors, facing prices kept stable during periods of demand upswing, are discouraged from entering the market. By contrast, *opportunistic pricing* involves raising a price as high as customer elasticity and goodwill permit, and similarly lowering it in accord with market forces. *Gold-standard pricing* is the short-run policy of quoting all customers the same price, regardless of specific circumstances. Alternatively, *negotiated pricing* involves tailoring the price charged to the individual customer or customer segment based on the demand elasticity of, and the nature of competitive alternatives available to, that particular type of customers. The marketer may find it effective to combine an overall longer-term strategy with a more specific short-term strategy. For example, the firm that relies on opportunistic pricing over time is likely to use negotiated pricing in dealing with a specific account.

With the completion of a detailed analysis of the competitive situation, the marketer has now moved through the major determinants of the strategic pricing program and is in a position to establish pricing positions. Note that the sequence started with overall objectives, then considered costs, demand, and finally, competition. These elements do not have to be approached in this particular order. Also, the relative emphasis placed on costs, competition, or demand considerations will differ depending on the pricing problem. Exhibit 10.2 shows how these components come together when considering a price change.

**Exhibit 10.2.**

Analysis of a Price Change

---

Jefferson Chemical produces a variety of specialty and commodity chemicals, including muriatic acid, for industrial use. Based on a decline in market share over the past year, the product line manager has proposed that the firm either cut price by 10% or increase sales and promotional support by $50,000. How would a marketer go about evaluating the price component of this manager's suggestions?

The first step would concern product and company objectives. What are the implications of the price cut for the image of our product? How will the price cut affect other products in the line? What is the profit goal associated with such a price cut? Much of the remaining analysis follows from objectives in these areas.

Assume the goal to be a 5% increase in profit and that this increase is the sole objective of concern. The next step would involve examining costs. A logical approach would be to determine the increase in sales needed to cover the lost unit revenue form the price cut (i.e., to break even on the price cut) plus the sales necessary to increase total contribution by 5%. This could be accomplished by determining the total amount of contribution dollars currently being generated by the product (before the price cut) and adding to this a 10% increase in contribution. This total figure would then be divided by the new contribution margin $(P - VC)$ that would result from the price cut. The result would be a required sales figure. Current sales would be subtracted from this figure, leaving the required sales increase.

The required increase would next be expressed as a percentage of current sales. Assume it to be 20%. This brings us to demand analysis. For the price reduction to stimulate demand this much, demand would have to be fairly elastic. Is this likely to be true? Based on experience and knowledge of the market, management must determine if customers are that price-sensitive. This analysis raises questions about the importance of price compared to other product attributes, the strength of existing customer loyalties, and the extent to which market potential (both users and usage rates) has already been reached.

Finally, even if the analysis up to this point indicates that the price cut makes sense, management must anticipate competitor reactions. How does our cost structure compare to theirs? How dependent on cash flows from this product are they? How well-established are their customer ties in this product area? Do they view this market as growing, mature, or declining? The answers to these questions will provide insight into whether or not competitors will match the price cut.

---

# Pricing Over the Life Cycle

The concept of the industrial product life cycle was introduced in Chapter 7. The marketer will rely on varying strategies as a product moves through the stages of its economic life; pricing strategy represents a case in point. Price is a key factor in each stage, but particularly in the introductory stage. For example, earlier in this chapter, a range of options was presented, with penetration (low) pricing at one end, parity (matching competition) pricing in the middle, and premium pricing or skimming (high) on the other end. The question of which to use must be addressed in the introductory stage of the life cycle.

This initial strategy places constraints on any subsequent pricing decisions. As an illustration, consider the marketer who uses a penetration strategy in anticipation of significant cost savings with large-volume production—then does not achieve such economies. Although a price increase may be desirable, the market may strongly resist such a change, for it has come to equate a certain amount of value with a given price. It is almost always easier to lower price than to raise price.

Also, the marketer does not necessarily set a single price for a product in each stage of its life. Different segments come into play in each stage, perhaps with differing demand elasticities. Charging a relatively high price initially may be related to an initial target segment that views the product as a necessity with few or no substitutes. As other segments enter the market, different pricing strategies can be tailored to their differing needs. One danger in introductory stage pricing is attempting to recoup too quickly any R&D expenditures incurred prior to introduction. These expenditures can be significant and place an undue burden on the new product. Their recovery, together with an acceptable rate of return, should be achieved over a product's life cycle.

A product in the growth stage typically is facing new competitive entries and the development of more specialized need segments. The benefits of scale economies and the experience curve, if any, are beginning to surface. A common market price begins to emerge in this stage, with the range of acceptable prices narrowing. The marketer is encountering downward pressure on prices, although this depends on the extent of product differentiation among competitors and the rate at which technological improvements are being made to the product. With maturity comes an increasingly saturated market and fairly well entrenched and aggressive competition. At the same time, competitors may see the product area as a cash generator, which they use to support newer, growth-stage products and services. The marketer focuses largely on repeat sales to established customers and on internal cost efficiencies. Competition is more heavily price based, although head-to-head price wars are likely to be dysfunctional. Under such circumstances, the marketer should probably attempt to maximize short-term direct product contribution to profit.

Market decline presents a number of pricing opportunities. For example, the marketer may raise price to take advantage of any remaining segments with inelastic demand. The spare parts business represents an example. Alternatively, the strategy might be to cut expenditures and leave the price alone, letting the product die a natural death. Another strategy might be to cut the price perhaps to the break-even level or lower and use the product as a loss leader to help sell complementary products in the line.

# Special Topics in Industrial Pricing

## Competitive Bidding

In many instances, a company's price takes the form of a competitive bid. Formal bidding is encountered most frequently when selling to the government and other public agencies and when selling non-standard materials or complex products made to buyer specification (usually at prices that exceed $300) to commercial enterprises. Job-shop companies and those making products with a long manufacturing cycle often will rely on a bidding process to secure business. Although government bidding generally awards the contract to the lowest bidder, this outcome is much less frequently the case for commercial bidding.

Commercial enterprises usually will solicit fewer bids and often will temper a given company's bid with an evaluation of that bidder's ability to meet quality, design, and delivery requirements. Alternatively, the invitation to submit bids (i.e., RFP or request for proposals) will have very precise quality and service specifications, and bidders may be asked to provide a performance bond with their bids. In addition, bidding can be either sealed or open. Sealed (or closed) bidding requires each potential vendor to submit a sealed written proposal, and typically all bids are opened and evaluated, and a decision rendered, at a prespecified point in time. The lowest bid usually will win. With open (or negotiated) bidding, offers are formally made, sometimes verbally, after which the buyer may provide feedback that prompts a vendor to adjust its bid. This method is, in a sense, a combination of bidding and negotiation. It is possible that competitive bidding may become a more prominent feature of the purchasing policies of many organizations in the future as a result of technological developments such as the Internet and the World Wide Web. For examples, one has only to look at the on-line purchasing efforts of such multinational companies as Caterpillar and General Electric.

The industrial marketer should consider a number of key criteria in determining whether to bid on a project (Dobler, Lee, & Burt, 1989). Some of these include the following:

1. Is the dollar value of the purchase large enough to warrant the expense involved in making a bid?

2. Are the specifications of the product or service precise, and can the cost of producing the product or service be estimated accurately?

3. How will getting the bid affect capacity utilization and our ability to serve other customers? Will it affect other products in our line?

4. How many potential bidders are there likely to be, and how eager are they to get this business?

5. How much time is available to put together an adequate bid and to have it considered by the customer?

Once the decision has been made to make a bid, a bidding strategy must be developed. One of the more popular approaches to competitive bidding, and one with a proven record of success, is probabilistic bidding. This technique assumes the price objective to be profit maximization. Also, the assumption is made that customers will select the lowest bid submitted. Three variables are focused on: the size of the bid, the expected profit if the bid wins, and the probability that the bid will win. A trade-off exists between bid amount or profit, on one hand, and the probability of winning, on the other. With probabilistic bidding, the marketer is objectively trying to identify the optimal trade-off.

The optimum bid, then, seeks to maximize the following basic equation:

$$E(X) = P(X)Z(X)$$

where

$X$ = dollar amount of the bid
$Z(X)$ = actual profit if the bid is accepted
$P(X)$ = probability of acceptance at this bid price
$E(X)$ = expected profit at this bid price

The most difficult task facing the marketer when using this formula is estimating the $P(X)$, the probability of a given bid being the lowest one submitted (the probability of winning). The ability to make this estimate depends on the marketer's experience in this market and with these competitors.

The marketer can use such experience to estimate data similar to that in Table 10.4. Determining actual probabilities would involve the following step-by-step process. For simplicity, assume the marketer is bidding against a single competitor.

❖ First, determine how much the competitor bid in the past on projects similar to the one being bid on (column 1, Table 10.4).

❖ Second, determine how much the marketer's own direct costs would have been to complete each of these projects (column 2).

❖ Third, express the competitor's bid on each of those projects as a percentage of the marketer's direct costs (column 3).

❖ Fourth, for each of the bids submitted by the competitor, count the number of times the bid was higher than this percentage of the marketer's estimated direct costs on a project (column 4). Looking at Project 14, for example, the competitor's bid was 149% of the marketer's direct cost on the job. Only five times did the competitor submit bids that were a higher percentage of the marketer's direct costs.

❖ Last, express this number as a proportion of all 20 bids (column 5). This proportion represents the probability of the marketer winning the bid if he or she bids less than a given percentage of his or her own direct costs.

**TABLE 10.4** Estimating Probabilities for Use by the Marketer in Competitive Bidding

| Project | Competitor's Bid | Marketer's Estimated Direct Cost | Competitor's Bid as a Percentage of the Marketer's Direct Cost | Number of Times Competitor Submitted a Bid Higher Than This Percentage of Direct Costs | Percent Higher (Probability of Underbidding if Marketer's Bid Is Less Than This Percentage of Direct Costs |
|---|---|---|---|---|---|
| 1 | 039,600 | 30,000 | 132 | 16 | 0.80 |
| 2 | 176,800 | 130,000 | 136 | 12 | 0.60 |
| 3 | 125,600 | 80,000 | 157 | 2 | 0.10 |
| 4 | 67,500 | 50,000 | 135 | 13 | 0.65 |
| 5 | 145,000 | 100,000 | 145 | 7 | 0.35 |
| 6 | 22,200 | 20,000 | 111 | 19 | 0.95 |
| 7 | 129,720 | 94,000 | 138 | 11 | 0.55 |
| 8 | 24,160 | 16,000 | 151 | 4 | 0.20 |
| 9 | 107,520 | 64,000 | 168 | 0 | 0.00 |
| 10 | 198,800 | 140,000 | 142 | 10 | 0.50 |
| 11 | 59,400 | 44,000 | 135 | 13 | 0.65 |
| 12 | 121,800 | 84,000 | 145 | 7 | 0.35 |
| 13 | 79,800 | 60,000 | 133 | 15 | 0.75 |
| 14 | 59,600 | 40,000 | 149 | 5 | 0.25 |
| 15 | 46,500 | 30,000 | 155 | 3 | 0.15 |
| 16 | 68,800 | 42,000 | 164 | 1 | 0.05 |
| 17 | 95,040 | 72,000 | 132 | 16 | 0.80 |
| 18 | 86,400 | 60,000 | 144 | 9 | 0.40 |
| 19 | 82,320 | 56,000 | 147 | 6 | 0.30 |
| 20 | 147,500 | 118,000 | 125 | 18 | 0.90 |

SOURCE: Adapted from "Probabilistic Bidding Models: A Synthesis," *Business Horizons*, 18 (April, 1975), pp. 69-70, Morse. © Copyright 1975 by *Business Horizons*.

NOTE: Competitive bidding using probabilistic models still continues to attract attention in the research and management literature. For a more recent application see McKim (1999).

So, let's say the marketer was considering submitting a bid on Project X (a new product) of $260,000 and that this bid is equal to 149% of his or her company's estimated direct costs on the project. If, in total, the competitor had submitted bids on similar projects 20 times in the past and 5 of those were at a price exceeding 149% of the marketer's estimated direct costs on the project, then the marketer has a 25% probability of winning bids on projects similar to Project X at this bid.

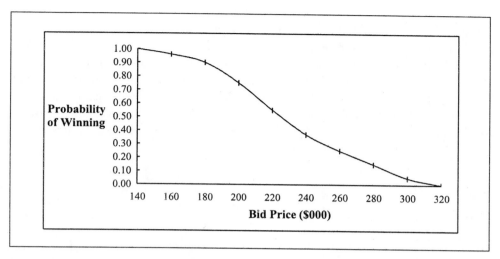

**Figure 10.3.** Estimated Probability of Thompson Underbidding the Competition

Finally, the marketer applies probabilities to each of the bid prices that he or she is considering for the actual bid. At each price, the expected profit is calculated using the formula provided about. Thus, at a bid price of $260,000, if costs are estimated to be $180,000, then profit is $80,000. If the estimated probability of winning at a price of $260,000 is 25%, then expected profit is $20,000 ($80,000 × .25). The marketer submits the bid that provides the highest *expected profit*.

Figure 10.3 is an illustration of a diagram that a marketing department might put together before making a bid. In Figure 10.3, the Thompson Corporation is bidding to provide computers to a chemical company for training new employees. Based on an evaluation of competitor positions and an assessment of historical bidding processes on similar jobs, the marketers attempt to relate the range of possible bid prices to the estimated probabilities of winning the bid. As can be seen in Figure 10.3, a bid of $140,000 has a 100% chance of winning, whereas a bid of $320,000 has a zero chance of winning.

Unfortunately, the marketer frequently either has no experience in a particular product market area or is unable to obtain reasonably accurate data concerning the previous bids of competitors or their costs. As a result, probabilities are estimated in a subjective manner, based on bidding and pricing experience, competitor analysis, market intelligence, management intuition, and related factors. Whether the decision is based on hard data regarding previous bids or on more subjective estimates, the objective is to detail the relationships between winning the bid and the range of possible bid prices.

The approach described here represents a more basic bidding model. Although this model and more complex ones do produce an ideal bid price, the decision maker must recognize that these are only tools to aid in the price decision. In practice, such bids are often further modified by managerial judgment. The models may be used to simply provide direction in bidding strategy.

Bids, once made, are also not always at a fixed price. When the supplier's costs are unstable and inflationary, a common approach to hedging risk is the use of escalator clauses. Here a fixed price bid is agreed upon, but the agreement allows for price increases if certain of the supplier's costs rise during the period of the contract. Such costs may be linked to economic indices, such as the wholesale price index. Changes in the index permit adjustments in certain cost estimates and the price charged.

## Price Negotiation

Although industrial goods and services are sometimes purchased at a standard or list price, the more typical scenario involves negotiation between buyer and seller. These negotiations can include any number of individuals and issues. They can be formal or informal, and last hours, weeks, or months. Negotiation is both art and science. The scientific aspect involves systematic approaches for resolving conflicts between two parties. The artistic side concerns interpersonal skills, the ability to convince and be convinced, and judgment regarding which ploys to use and when.

Both parties gain from a transaction. The customer acquires a need-solving product or service, and the vendor makes a sale. The possibility of mutual gain is what brings the buyer and seller together. The amount of gain realized by either party creates conflict that must be negotiated. This conflict occurs because the two parties find themselves competing for some of the same gains.

There is a tendency to approach the negotiation process as a *zero sum* game, in which one party's gains come completely at the expense of the other, in exact proportion. For example, if the seller gains revenue by negotiating 5% more in terms of the price charged, then the buyer experiences an expense to his or her organization's budget in the same amount.

It is frequently possible to turn the negotiations into a *positive sum* game. Creative thinking is the key. The seller focuses on finding options that hold merit for both parties. An example might be standing firm on the price increase but giving the customer a favorable cash and quantity discount structure or adding to the provisions of the warranty. Another possibility is a longer-term contract with the customer, guaranteeing that the price will not be raised during the period of the contract. The goal, then, is to increase the size of the pie, rather than merely competing for existing pieces of a fixed pie.

The best negotiation strategies are tailored to the buying situation at hand (Table 10.5). Underlying any negotiation is the set of risks and rewards confronting both buyer and seller representatives and their respective organizations. Before establishing a bargaining position, the risks and rewards faced by those on the other side should be calculated. These estimations require the seller to determine the best alternative available to the buying organization should no agreement be reached with the

**TABLE 10.5** Five Types of Negotiation Style

The negotiation styles of the parties play a critical role in the negotiation process. For instance, whether a seller is overtly aggressive or a buyer somewhat passive will affect the end outcome. Researchers have noted five distinct negotiation styles: accommodative, collaborative, competitive, sharing, and avoidant. Generally, collaborative, competitive, and sharing styles are most prevalent among industrial sellers and buyers. Each of these five styles is outlined below.

- *Avoidant*—The buyer or seller is indifferent to the concerns of the other party. This is a "withdrawal" style in which the buyer avoids a confrontation with the seller.
- *Collaborative*—The buyer or seller attempts to satisfy both his or her own concerns and the concerns of the other party fully. This is an integrative, problem-solving approach in which a party's main objective is the maximization of the joint gain of both parties.
- *Competitive*—The buyer or seller attempts to satisfy his or her own concerns fully at the expense of the other party's concerns. This is a win-lose or zero sum gain style, in which each party attempts to enhance his or her own position relative to the other.
- *Sharing*—The buyer or seller settles for the partial satisfaction of the concerns of both parties. This is a compromise approach in which one party attempts to split the difference with the other.
- *Accommodative*—The buyer or seller attempts to fully satisfy the concerns of the other party at the expense of his or her own concerns. This is a self-sacrificing style in which one party seeks a peaceful coexistence with the other.

SOURCE: Adapted from "Negotiation Styles of Industrial Buyers," *Industrial Marketing Management*, 15 (1986), Perdue, Day, and Michaels. © Copyright 1986 by *Industrial Marketing Management*.

seller's firm (Fisher & Ury, 1981); they also require an evaluation of a buying organization's resources and the motivations of its negotiating representative(s).

In formulating a negotiation strategy, the seller should seek to determine settlement ranges for both parties. A settlement range is the distance between a party's reservation, or walkaway, price and its initial offer (Figure 10.4). For the seller, the reservation price is the minimum acceptable price, while for the buyer it is the maximum acceptable price. These should reflect each side's assessment of the consequences of not coming to any agreement. As illustrated in Figure 10.4, if the seller's minimum is compared to the buyer's maximum, the difference is called the bargaining zone, or zone of agreement. The final price should fall in this zone. Also illustrated in Figure 10.4 are the buyer and seller aspiration levels, which often fall in between the opening offer and the reservation price.

When attempting to determine the buyer's opening position, it is important to recognize that these positions may be deliberately exaggerated for tactical purposes. If either the buyer or the seller position is too extreme, the negotiation may degenerate into a purely adversarial contest. Assuming that both parties have performed suffi-

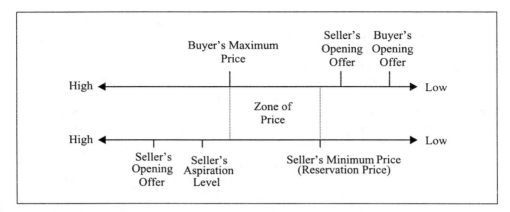

**Figure 10.4.** Defining the Bargaining Zone for Price Negotiation

cient background research, opening positions will be realistic, if not immediately optimal. There is an inherent dynamic in negotiation that motivates each party to expect movement in position from the other side. Sellers may tend to aim high and then switch discussions of price to other aspects, such as volume discounts.

Negotiation strategy should also reflect the structural characteristics of the relationship between the vendor and the buying organization. Let us briefly outline some of these characteristics, keeping in mind that each can have a direct impact on the ultimate outcome.

The extent to which the representatives of buyer and seller organizations are actually speaking for their respective organizations is a primary consideration. How much clout do these representatives have in terms of the issues under negotiation? Are there conflicts within the organizations on some of these issues? The degree of interdependence between the organizations is another consideration. How much does each need the other? The final agreement, if one is reached, is likely to be closer to the more dependent party's threshold level.

It should also be determined if the negotiation will be repetitive. That is, is it a one-time sale, or will there be frequent negotiations in the future? Repetitive bargaining usually finds the parties adopting a more cooperative stance. Separately, the marketer should evaluate the presence of any linkage effects—where a particular negotiation, and its outcome, are linked to other negotiations. Obstacles sometimes can be overcome by using linkages creatively.

Bargaining can be further characterized by the number of issues involved. Price is not always the central thrust; delivery guarantees, returns policies, the volume of goods purchased, quality standards, financing, and servicing arrangements are examples of items that may be on the agenda of the vendor or the customer. When multiple terms are involved, it is a real challenge to determine which trade-offs the other party will be inclined to make.

Next, the existence of time constraints should be noted. Optimal use of the time frame available can avert the disadvantages of hasty negotiation by one party. In addition, marketers need to assess how public the negotiation will be. In industrial markets, different terms are often worked out with various customer accounts. The ability to negotiate flexibly with any one account is affected by how much other customers will learn of the tactics used and final terms agreed on. Competitors are also in a position to benefit from learning a firm's negotiation strategy. Lastly, it is critical to determine if any norms exist that govern the kinds of negotiation tactics used by either party.

## The Role of Discounts and Incentives

The industrial marketing organization has at its disposal a variety of price concessions that it can offer a customer. These include prepaid freight, drop-shipping privileges, installment financing, postdating, liberal returns allowances, and rebate programs. Chief among these, at least in terms of use, is the structure of discounts provided to customers.

Three types of discounts are provided to industrial customers or to middlemen: cash, quantity, and trade. Cash discounts are given to encourage speedy payment of invoices. A cash discount might be quoted at 3/10, n 30, indicating the buyer will receive a 3% discount if the invoice is paid within 10 days; otherwise, the credit period until full payment is due extends to 30 days. Additional price incentives may be given for payment prior to receipt of goods or upon delivery.

Quantity discounts are also quite common in industrial markets, providing an incentive to buy in large dollar amounts or large unit amounts. The discount can also be cumulative or noncumulative. Cumulative quantity discounts allow the buyer to include a series of purchases over some prespecified time period in determining the size of the discount for which he or she qualifies. Noncumulative discounts apply only to a single purchase. These discounts frequently are applied not just to a single item but also to a set of products within the marketer's line.

Trade (or functional) discounts are provided to middlemen such as industrial distributors to encourage distributor support for the marketer's products. Discounts frequently are used to encourage the performance of specific functions, such as storage or warehousing, selling activities, transportation, and promotional efforts.

Discounts can result in significant savings off the list price. Consider the case of a manufacturer selling fire extinguishers to commercial firms and institutions through industrial distributors. Assume the discount structure includes terms of 2/10, n 30, plus a 10% incentive for orders of $500 or more and a trade discount of 30%. One of the manufacturer's middlemen, Hospital Distributors, Inc., has placed an order for four different types of extinguishers. The distributor will, in turn, sell them to hospitals and health care facilities. The list price for the total order comes to $1,860, as illustrated in Table 10.6. If the customer qualifies for all three discounts, the actual remittance comes to $1,148.36. This represents a 38% saving off the list price. Table 10.6 also illustrates the logical order in which the discounts would be taken. Those charged with setting prices should recognize, then, the potential price flexibility that

**TABLE 10.6** Application of Manufacturer's Discount Structure to Hospital Distributors, Inc.

The Hospital Distributors, Inc. order:

| | |
|---|---|
| 10 extinguishers at $45.00 each | $450.00 |
| 15 extinguishers at $24.00 each | 360.00 |
| 10 extinguishers at $60.00 each | 600.00 |
| 5 extinguishers at $90.00 each | 450.00 |
| **Total** | **$1,860.00** |

**Step 1: Apply quantity discount**

| | |
|---|---|
| Total order amount | $1,860.00 |
| Discount ($1,860.00 × .10) | 186.00 |
| *Net order amount* | *$1,674.00* |

**Step 2: Apply trade discount**

| | |
|---|---|
| Net order amount | $1,674.00 |
| Discount ($1,674.00 × .30) | 502.20 |
| *Amount due manufacturer* | *$1,171.80* |

**Step 3: Apply cash discount**

| | |
|---|---|
| Amount due manufacturer | $1,171.80 |
| Discount ($1,171.80 × .02) | 23.44 |
| *Actual (net) remittance* | *$1,148.36* |

SOURCE: Adapted from *Pricing: Making Profitable Decisions*, p. 171, Monroe. © Copyright 1990 by McGraw-Hill Book Co. Adapted with permission.

a competitive discount structure provides to both the marketer and the purchase decision maker.

Discounts can be used as inducements to all customers, or only to select accounts. They can be used just to attract new customers or to retain existing business. In addition, discounts do not have to be offered on all the products or services sold by a company. Certain items or bundles of items can be made more attractive with discounts, while others are sold only at list prices.

## Leasing

A sizable volume of industrial transactions involve a customer leasing a product rather than purchasing it outright. A lease is a contract by which the owner of an asset (the lessor) grants the right to use the asset for a given term to another party (the lessee) in return for a periodic payment of rent. To a customer, a leasing arrangement means avoiding the need to pay the cash purchase cost of the product or service, as well as avoiding any maintenance and operating expenses paid by the lessor. A lease also offers the buyer certain tax advantages and preserves the buyer's debt capacity. A lease also is a hedge against rapid product obsolescence, such as with information technology.

There are two major types of leases: financial or full-payment leases, and operating or service leases. A *financial lease* is a longer-term arrangement that is fully amortized over the term of the contract. Because the lease may cover the economic life of the product, the sum of the lease payments should exceed the price paid for the asset by the marketer (lessor). With such longer-term commitments, the buyer (lessee) is usually responsible for all operating expenses and any liabilities associated with product use. The buyer also may be given the option of purchasing the asset upon fulfilling the terms of the lease, and of applying a portion of the lease payments to the purchase. This type of lease might be used for a manufacturing facility, a major piece of operating equipment, or company trucks. An *operating lease* is for a shorter time period, is cancelable, and is not completely amortized. The marketer (lessor) assumes liability and responsibility for ownership expenses. Typically, there is no purchase option, and the lease price is higher than that of a financial lease for a comparable period of time. These leases are desirable for equipment or space that is needed only for a relatively short period of time—such as special plant cleaning equipment, temporary storage space, or an outdoor billboard.

A lease price will reflect a variety of factors, somewhat different from those used to price a product to be sold. In addition to the original cost of purchasing an item or its manufacturing cost, the marketer may want to consider the projected product life, the expected salvage or scrap value, investment tax credits and tax rates, inflation rates over the term of the lease, debt interest rates, servicing costs, and maintenance costs. Careful evaluation of these and other factors is necessary to establish a lease price that provides a reasonable rate of return over the product's useful economic life.

The marketer faces a problem in that a price must be determined not only for the lease but also for outright sale of the product. The lease-to-purchase price ratio becomes a strategic variable in that it indicates whether management wishes to encourage lease arrangements or outright sales. Although leasing may be attractive to customers, it places financial strains on the supplier. Cash flow is tied up, and inventories must be financed. As a result, higher lease prices relative to purchase prices may be established.

Lower relative lease prices might be offered, however, to encourage lease renewals or sales of other products in the line. The lessee may be encouraged to trade up to higher-quality products in the marketer's line by granting lease credits that can be applied to these other products. The marketer must consider implications of the lease price for the entire product mix.

## Transfer Pricing

Although price decisions generally are made for products to be sold to customer organizations, industrial companies also manufacture products that are used internally. In many cases, one division of a company will supply components and materials to another division. An internal price, called a transfer price, may be established for these items. This transfer price is the amount one division charges another division of the same company.

The division attempting to establish a transfer price is influenced by two key considerations. The first is a desire to ensure that the price covers manufacturing and delivery costs. The second is a desire for the transfer price to reflect the going market price for similar goods. In fact, the real problem often is that of determining whether to set the price based on production costs plus some markup, or to base it on going market prices. Market price is the average amount that other companies charge for the product. The transfer price should fall somewhere between production cost and market price. The issue becomes how much of the difference between cost and market price is credited to the supplying division and how much to the buying division. This allocation can create internal political problems, for the selling division would like as high a markup over cost as feasible, and the buying division would prefer as big a discount off the market price as possible. Some important strategic issues are involved, for the approach used to set transfer prices determines how much profit both the selling and the buying divisions will show. Transfer prices influence the selling division's amount of incentive to control or reduce cost; however, they also affect the ability of the buying division to price finished goods competitively in the marketplace. When transfer pricing is used, both divisions can be profit centers; if so, the transfer price will determine, in part, how profitable each division is.

One suggested approach to resolving the potential dilemmas is for the two divisions to engage in an annual (or periodic) negotiation process, the purpose of which is to agree on a *margin distribution index*. This index serves to allocate the margin between the supplying and buying division. For example, assume that the parties agree on an index of two, indicating that for every $2 of profit made by the supplying division, the buying division will receive a $1 discount from the market price. So, if the total cost to the supplying division is $7 dollars and the comparable market price is $10, the transfer price will be $9. The index itself remains constant, even if production costs or market prices change. The result is that the supplying division is given a financial incentive to be cost efficient, as the index permits a profit performance measure. The buying division is given the incentive to purchase internally, which also reduces purchasing and inventory costs.

Transfer pricing is important to the industrial marketer because of its effect on some of the major costs of the final product the company is attempting to market. Marketers in the buying division have a large stake in the transfer price and are likely to get involved in the negotiations with the supplying division. The marketer is also in a key position to provide information regarding going market prices charged for products that are manufactured internally.

In the international environment, transfer pricing assumes another dimension—that of the impact of the different corporate tax rates in different countries in which a multinational firm operates. For example, a computer manufacturer may assemble its monitors in Taiwan and the processing unit in Malaysia, and assembly, printing, and packaging may take place before the product is sold in Canada. Each of these countries taxes corporate profits at various rates. The question that therefore complicates transfer pricing is where the firm wishes to maximize its profits. Under these circumstances, different international divisions may sell products at cost, in order not to make a profit and thus avoid excessive tax, while an even more substantial profit is achieved in a country with a more favorable tax rate.

## The Future: Pricing and the World Wide Web

The emergence of the Internet and the World Wide Web is having and will continue to have a profound influence on industrial pricing strategy. Some of these effects will be negative in the sense that they will drive more and more products and services toward becoming commodities, and in doing so take away the marketer's freedom as a price maker. Markets and customers will make prices and force firms to "take" them. On the other hand, all is not doom and gloom, and the technologies will in many instances offer hitherto undreamed of opportunities to industrial marketers in the area of price. We now speculate briefly on these negative and positive forces.

### Force 1: Technology Facilitates Customer Search

Information search by customers is a fundamental step in all models of consumer and industrial buying behavior. Search is not without sacrifice in terms of money and, especially, time. A number of new technologies are emerging on the Internet that greatly facilitate search (see Bakos, 1997). The tools range from a simple facilitation of search, through more advanced proactive seeking, to the actual negotiation of deals on the customer's behalf. All, however, hold significant promise. These tools include

- Search engines (searches by key word(s) on the World Wide Web), for example Alta Vista[6] and Yahoo![7]

- Comparison sites (Web sites that enable comparisons of product/service category by attributes and price), for example Compare.Net (www.compare.net), a Web site that lists comparative product information and prices

- True bot (a piece of software that combs sites for prices each time a request is made), for example used by search engines Lycos[8] and Excite[9]

- Intelligent agent (a piece of agent that will seek out prices and features and negotiate on price for a purchase), for example Kasbah, a bot being developed by MIT that can negotiate based on price and time constraints that it is given

At the very least, tools such as search engines and comparison sites can reduce the customer's costs of finding potential suppliers and those of making product and price comparisons. More significantly, the more sophisticated tools such as true bots and agents will seek out lowest prices and even conduct negotiations for lower prices.

## Force 2: Customers Make, Rather Than Take, Prices

Suppliers tend to make prices while customers "take" them, with the obvious exception of the bidding or tendering situations already described in this chapter. Another exception would be auctions, but the proportion of goods purchased in this way has always tended to be rather small and has been mainly devoted to used goods. There are a number of instances on the World Wide Web where the opposite situation is now occurring. On-line auctions allow buyers to bid on a vast range of products as well as services such as airline tickets and hotel accommodation. Onsale.com[10] is a huge auction Web site that runs seven live auctions a week where buyers outbid one another for computer gear and electronics equipment. Onsale buys surplus or distressed goods from companies at fire sale prices so they can weather low bids. At a higher level of customer price making, Priceline.com[11] invites customers to name their price on products and services ranging from air tickets to hotel rooms and new vehicles. In the case of air tickets, for example, customers name the price they are willing to pay for a ticket to a destination. Priceline then contacts airlines electronically to see if the fare can be obtained at the named price or lower, then undertakes to return to the customer within an hour. Priceline's margin is the differential between the customer's offer price and the fare charged by the airline. Governments are also becoming very active in this type of on-line purchasing (see Business Marketing Capsule).

## Force 3: Customers Control Transactions

Caterpillar uses its Web site to invite bids on parts from pre-approved suppliers. Suppliers bid on-line over a specified period, and a contract is awarded to the lowest bidder. Negotiation time is reduced, and average savings on purchases are now 6% (Berthon, Pitt, Katsikeas, & Berthon, 1999). In this way, the customer has taken almost total control of the transaction, for it has become difficult for suppliers to compete on anything but price. There is little opportunity to differentiate products, engage in personal selling, or add service, as traditional marketing strategy would suggest suppliers do.

## Force 4: A Return to One-to-One Negotiation

The Internet will find buyers and sellers negotiating over the sale of many individual items. An article in *Business Week*[12] quotes Jerry Kaplan, founder of Onsale Inc., a

## BUSINESS MARKETING CAPSULE

### *On-Line Auctions Hit the Public Sector*

It was just a matter of time before an Internet-savvy state or local government became bold enough to get in on the cyberauction frenzy. After all, millions of Americans each day click on popular Web sites to buy everything from Beanie Babies to baseballs slugged by the likes of Mark McGwire and Sammy Sosa.

Pennsylvania stepped up to the plate this winter, locking in an agreement with FreeMarkets OnLine. The deal provides for a series of on-line auctions that the state's Department of General Services will use to buy simple commodities such as fuel and office furniture. By the time baseball's Spring training season rolls around, Pennsylvania and several of its vendors will have traded on-line to the tune of about $20 million.

Said Glenn Meakem, FreeMarkets's chief executive officer and cofounder, "You would have expected a state like California to do this since California is very progressive." It turns out that Pennsylvania's deal with Pittsburgh-based FreeMarkets is progressive for two reasons.

First, it's central to the state's economic development strategy. The announcement of the agreement was timed to coincide with some political posturing: Pennsylvania Gov. Tom Ridge is signaling that he will deliver a plan to put the state ahead in the race to build an electronic-commerce infrastructure. Second, and perhaps more important, the use of on-line auctions puts Pennsylvania at the forefront of modernizing government purchasing. It's also a sign of the times, another signal that government procurement is swiftly becoming more market-driven. But Pennsylvania is not the only state breaking free of confining procurement practices while still upholding fair and open contracting practices. That quest to break free is the driving force behind the Massachusetts-led electronic shopping mall, or E-Mall, another experiment that is pushing the procurement envelope.

Given the current climate, we're predicting that progressive government buying strategies will continue to open up on other fronts in the coming months. It's easy to see where this is heading. If a person can buy a $3 million baseball with the click of a mouse, why couldn't state officials bargain for computers in an on-line auction?

SOURCE: Jennifer Jones, IDG.net (on www.cnn.com), March 9, 1999. Originally published in civic.com. Reprinted with permission of FCW Government Technology Group.

Net auction site, as saying "The future of electronic commerce is an implicit one-to-one negotiation between buyer and seller." Kaplan continued, "You will get an individual spot price on everything" (Sager, 1998). As negotiation costs decrease significantly, it might be practical to have competitive bidding on a huge range of purchases, with a computer bidding against another computer on behalf of buyers and sellers.

## Force 5: Commoditization and Efficient Markets

The first goods to be bartered in electronic markets have been commodities. Price rather than product attributes, good selling, or warm advertising is the determining factor in a sale. When the commodity happens to be perishable—such as airline seats, fruit for canning or juice, or electricity—the Net is even more compelling: Suppliers have to get rid of their inventory fast or lose the sale. The problem on the World Wide Web is that when customers can easily compare prices and features, commoditization can also happen to some high-margin products. Strong brand or company names alone may not be enough to maintain premium prices.

## Counterforce 1: Using Differentiated Pricing All the Time

It is possible that a business-to-business marketer considering the forces discussed above may become pessimistic about the future of marketing strategy, especially concerning the flexibility of pricing possibilities. There are strategies, however, that managers may exploit that will allow them to make marketing more effective in a time of market efficiency.

The information age—and the advent of computer-controlled machine tools—lets customers have it both ways: customized and cheap, automated and personal. This deindustrialization of customer-driven economics has been termed mass customization (Pine, Peppers, & Rogers, 1995). The Web gives business-to-business marketers the opportunity to exploit a phenomenon that service providers such as airlines have long known: As discussed under price differentiation, the same product or service can have different values to different customers. The Web should allow the ultimate in price differentiation—by customizing the interaction with the customer, the marketer can differentiate price to the supreme extent that no two customers pay the same price.

## Counterforce 2: Using Customer Data to Optimize Pricing by Creating Customer Switching Barriers

The technology allows sellers to collect detailed data about customers' buying habits, preferences, and even spending limits, so they can tailor their products and prices to the individual buyer. Customers like this because it recognizes them as individuals and serves them better. For example, when one of the United Kingdom's largest building societies, the Woolwich, demutualized and became a bank, it chose Dell as its computer supplier. Dell constructed a special home page for Woolwich on its Web site so that the new bank could order all its computer requirements on-line. Individual purchasers within the company could customize and order their machines, based on a standard specification that had been constructed for it. Dell now keeps and manages a complete IT assets database for the Woolwich. Even individual branch managers are able to log on to the site, obtain information, specify and construct a computer, then order and pay for it from their own branch budget. This type of strategy in turn creates switching barriers for customers that competitors will find difficult to overcome by mere price alone. Although the customer may be able to purchase the product or service at a lower price on another Web site, that site will not have taken the time or effort to learn about the customer and so will not be able to serve the customer as well. In terms of economics, the customer will not actually be purchasing the same item.

## Counterforce 3: Using Technology to De-Menu Pricing

Most firms have resorted to "menu" or "list" pricing systems in the past to simplify the many problems caused by attempting to keeping price recorded and up to date. Pricing is not just about the Web—within firms there can be private networks, or "extranets," that link them with their suppliers and customers. These systems make it possible to get a precise handle on inventory, costs, and demand at any given moment—and to adjust prices instantly. Without automation, there is a significant cost associated with changing prices, known as the "menu cost." For firms with large product or service lines, as is typical of many industrial marketers, it used to take months for price adjustments to filter down to distributors, other intermediaries, and salespeople. Streamlined networks reduce menu cost and time to near zero, so there is no longer a really good excuse for not changing prices when they need to be changed.

## Counterforce 4: Being Much Better at Differentiation—Stage Experiences

The more like a commodity a product or service becomes, the easier it is for customers to make price comparisons and to buy based on price alone. Marketers have attempted to overcome this in the past by differentiating products by enhancing quality, adding features, and branding. When products reached a phase of parity, marketers entered the age of service and differentiated on the basis of customer service. In an era of increasing service parity, it is the staging of customer experiences that may be the ultimate and enduring differentiator (Pine & Gilmore, 1998). The Web provides a great theater for the staging of unique buyer experiences, whether aesthetic, entertaining, educational, or even escapist.

## Counterforce 5: Customers May Be Willing to Pay More Than You Thought

Marketers may make a big mistake by assuming that customers will expect and want to pay less on the Web than they do in conventional channels. Indeed, managers in many industries have a long record of assuming that customers underestimate the value of a product or service to them and would typically pay less for it if given the chance. The reality may be quite different. For instance, one study found that car resellers pay significantly more for used vehicles on on-line auctions than they would at their "real-world" equivalents (Watson, Zinkhan, & Pitt, 2000).

## Counterforce 6: Establishing Electronic Exchanges

Many firms, particularly those in business-to-business markets, may find it more effective to barter rather than to sell when prices are low. A number of electronic exchanges already have been established to enable firms to barter excess supplies of components or products that otherwise would have been sold for really low prices. In this way, the firm rids itself of excess stock and receives value in return in excess of the price that would have been realized. For example, Chicago-based FastParts Inc.[13] and FairMarket Inc.[14] in Woburn, Massachusetts, operate thriving exchanges where computer electronics companies swap excess parts. U.S. industries generate some $18 billion in excess inventory a year—around 10% of all finished goods, according to Anne Perlman, CEO of Moai Technologies Inc.,[15] a Net start-up that makes software for creating on-line bartering sites. She cites excess and obsolete equipment as a big and painful problem. Moai sells a $100,000-plus package to companies that want to run their own auctions to generate revenue from aging merchandise. The availability of off-the-shelf software packages from Moai and others should help jump-start more electronic exchanges.

## Counterforce 7: Maximizing Revenue, Not Price

Many managers overlook a basic economic opportunity—that in many instances it is better to maximize revenue rather than price. Airlines, for example, have perfected the science of yield management (Desiraju & Shugan, 1999), concocting complicated pricing schemes that not only defy customer comparison but also permit revenue maximization on a flight, despite the fact that the average fare might be lower. Many airlines are now using their Web sites to sell tickets on slow-to-fill or ready-to-leave flights, either on specials or on ticket auctions. They also make use of external services such as Priceline.com, wherein the customer in a real sense provides an "option" to both discern market conditions and sell last-minute capacity.

## Summary

Price is one of the more visible of marketing management decisions. It is also one of the most flexible. Traditional approaches have ignored the creative marketing potential of the price variable, however, and emphasized more simple cost-plus formulas. The key to creative pricing is to recognize that price is a statement of how much value has been provided to the customer. Value, however, is a subjective commodity, existing in the mind of the buyer. The task of the marketer, then, is to weigh the costs and benefits a customer receives from a product and compare them to available alternatives.

The chapter has presented a framework for establishing and managing industrial prices, consisting of four sets of decisions (price objectives, price strategy, price structure, and price tactics/levels) and four sets of determinants (objectives, costs, demand, and competition). Unique aspects of, and approaches to, each of these decision areas and determinants when selling to businesses were examined. In addition, a number of special pricing topics of relevance for industrial markets were addressed, including discounts, leasing, and transfer pricing. Each has important implications for the actual price that a customer is charged for a commodity.

Industrial pricing is likely to become more complex in the years to come. New forms and sources of competition, shorter life cycles, widely fluctuating rates of inflation, volatile interest and exchange rates, and the availability of alternative purchasing and payment schemes affect both the industrial buyer and the seller. Decision makers must become more sophisticated, not only to ensure they are charging an appropriate price but also (and increasingly) to recognize the potential of the price variable as a tool for product differentiation.

The impact of new technologies and media such as the Internet and the World Wide Web on pricing strategy will be especially interesting and challenging. On one hand, the effect may be to make marketing less effective by making markets more efficient. By facilitating search and lowering other transaction costs, the result may be a number of downward pressures on prices. On the other hand, creative marketers may find exciting new opportunities created for pricing in the new media.

# Notes

1. www.silicongraphics.com/
2. www.netscape.com/
3. www.PONL.com/
4. www.squared.com/
5. www.porters.com.au/
6. www.altavista.com/
7. www.yahoo.com/
8. www.lycos.com/
9. www.excite.com/
10. www.onsale.com/
11. www.priceline.com/
12. www.businessweek.com/
13. www.fastparts.com/
14. fairmarket.com
15. www.moai.com/

## Questions

1. What does it mean to say that price is a measure of value? What different sources of value might a hospital perceive in purchasing a new type of blood pressure machine that also measures a patient's pulse and temperature?

2. Trane Corporation manufactures and sells central air conditioning units to a wide variety of customers, including contractors and building owners. Discuss some of the ways in which Trane can vary the prices actually paid by customers, without changing list prices.

3. Toro and Caterpillar sell comparable tilling machines for use by small farming operations. Toro's is currently sold for $650, has an estimated start-up cost of $80, and has postpurchase costs of $175 over its useful life of 4 years. The salvage value is $75. Caterpillar's till has an estimated start-up cost of $50 and postpurchase costs of $125. Its salvage value is estimated at $100. Also, Caterpillar's tiller has an additional gear not found on Toro's machine, for which customers appear willing to pay $35. Using the model presented in Figure 10.1, can you determine the economic value to the customer of Caterpillar's tiller?

4. Why do you think cost-plus pricing approaches are so prevalent in industrial markets? How does this approach limit the marketer's flexibility? How is it possible that this approach could be costing the firm some potential profits?

5. Omega Tool produces a line of power tools, including sanders, saws, and electric impact wrenches. Cite examples of 10 different pricing objectives that might be relevant when establishing pricing strategy for Omega's line of portable hand drills, comprising three different models.

6. How does the presence or absence of a significant experience or learning effect (see Chapter 7 on experience curves) relate to industrial pricing programs? Specifically, how might it relate to the establishment of pricing objectives and to reliance on a penetration, parity, or premium pricing strategy?

7. You sell marketing research services to corporate clients. Cite 10 ways in which you might vary your pricing structure to take advantage of marketplace opportunities.

8. What are the determinants of demand elasticity? Using these determinants, evaluate the elasticity of demand for
   * A major canning company purchasing aluminum for its cans
   * A small regional airline purchasing aircraft maintenance services
   * A restaurant chain purchasing uniforms for its employees

9. "To increase your probabilities of winning bids, you should bid on as many projects as possible." Do you agree or disagree? Describe how you would estimate

your probabilities of winning bids at various price levels if you were an architectural firm bidding on a local hospital construction project.

10. Your company manufactures keyboards for computer terminals. What are the arguments for and against offering quantity discounts to your customers?

11. Why might it be easier to use price differentials (charging different customers different prices) when selling industrial services than when selling industrial products?

12. What information would you attempt to gather prior to going into a negotiating session over prices and related terms with a prospective customer? The customer is a regional cable television company, and you are attempting to sell it technical engineering services. Your services involve grounding all the company's installed cable lines in the local area.

13. How do you think the Internet might change the way in which pricing is accomplished for chemical products sold to companies over the next 5 to 10 years?

# CHAPTER 11

# Communications With Business Customers
## Engineering the Promotional Mix

*Those in the advertising industry have a vested interest in prolonging the myth that all advertising increases sales. It doesn't.*
—David Ogilvy

## Key Concepts

Advertising
ADVISOR studies
Budgeting methods
Buying process models
Catalogs
Communications objectives
Direct marketing
General business publications
Hierarchy of effects models
Horizontal publications
Industrial directories

Internet advertising
Personal selling
Promotional mix
Publicity
Sales promotion
Technical reports
Telemarketing
Trade shows
Vertical publications
Waste exposure

## Learning Objectives

1. Be able to identify the types of promotional vehicles relied upon by industrial marketers and the ways in which these promotional tools are used.

2. Recognize the need in industrial firms for a strategy that integrates a mix of promotional activities variables to accomplish a set of communication objectives.

3. Be able to relate promotional strategy to the way business customers make buying decisions.

4. Understand the role and limitations of advertising when selling industrial products and services.

5. Learn to apply a logical process for formulating industrial advertising programs.

6. Appreciate the importance of sales promotion in industrial marketing strategy and how sales promotion complements the personal selling effort.

## The Industrial Promotional Mix

Communication is the essence of marketing. Great marketing organizations constantly communicate with key audiences: customers, indirect users further down the channel, industrial middlemen, and the general public. They do not badger, irritate, or always try to sell something to these audiences. Instead, firms are engaged in an ongoing conversation or dialogue. Firms have a central message but realize they must continually adapt their communications to reflect the needs and problems of customers and others. It is important for managers to understand that a dialogue is a two-way conversation, and today's marketers recognize the need to continually listen to their customers, respond, and then listen some more.

Companies can communicate with business customers in numerous ways. Each means of communication is a promotional tool, and the way in which the marketer combines these tools is called the *promotional mix* or *blend*. For simplicity, the promotional mix is organized into four major components: personal selling, advertising, sales promotion, and publicity. These four areas include all the possible ways in which a marketer can communicate with a target audience.

*Personal selling*, usually the cornerstone of the industrial promotional effort, involves direct one-to-one contact with current and potential customers, either in person or by telephone. *Advertising*—a nonpersonal method of communication where a message is placed in a medium for a fee—has the capability to reach a larger number of potential buyers, users, influencers, deciders, and gatekeepers than does personal selling. *Sales promotion* is a "catch-all" category of sales support activities, including both personal and impersonal communication tactics. Trade shows, samples, premiums, rebates, trade-in allowances, calendars, and customer entertainment are examples. *Publicity* attempts to influence target groups without incurring direct costs. Publicity involves the release of company or product information to print or broadcast media with the hope that it will be disseminated. Although impersonal in nature, because the message appears to be news, publicity is often perceived as objective information by the target market.

Ultimately, promotional efforts serve the purpose of stimulating and maintaining demand for the firm's products and services. The key, however, is to manage the various promotional tools as a coordinated mix. This means that the individual forms of promotion are *blended together in a way that accomplishes the organization's communication goals over the stages of the customer's buying process.*

## How Industrial Promotion Differs

A promotional mix that works effectively for industrial products and services is usually quite different from that employed by the consumer marketer. This is due to the technical nature of industrial products, the smaller relative number of potential buyers, the geographical dispersion of customers, and the complex nature and length of the organizational buying process. Because of these characteristics, a strong personal sales effort is a vital ingredient in successfully communicating the technical merits of most industrial products and services. The salesperson plays a significant role in the negotiation process with key members of the buying center. This relationship, when managed effectively, can engender long-term source loyalty. Because of its critical importance in industrial marketing, personal selling is further examined in the next chapter.

Advertising, sales promotion, and publicity regularly play *supporting* roles in the industrial promotional mix. On their own, none of these promotional areas is normally sufficient to accomplish a sale. Rather, they support the general sales effort by generating customer interest, influencing customer attitudes, and reassuring customers after the sale that they have made the correct decision.

Advertising, when utilized in industrial markets, seldom relies on mass media vehicles such as television and radio. Not only are mass media expensive, but they also do not allow the marketer the opportunity to specifically target efforts toward different types of industrial customers. In addition, use of the mass media results in extensive wasted exposure, which drives up the cost per contact. As a result, the principal vehicle used in industrial advertising is print media, which include trade journals, general business publications, direct mail, industrial directories, and technical literature. The advertising message itself tends to be more factual, emphasizing functional product or service benefits, as opposed to more emotionally based messages.

Examples of key industrial promotional tools are presented in Table 11.1, while Figure 11.1 depicts how marketing dollars are allocated to these tools. The various promotional alternatives can be distinguished in terms of what each is capable of accomplishing, and how effectively. Figure 11.2 presents a partial illustration. The ex-

**TABLE 11.1** Types of Promotional Alternatives Available to the Industrial Marketer

**General business publications:** Large circulation magazines are aimed at a wide variety of markets and buying influences (e.g., *Fortune, Business Week, Forbes*).

**Trade publications—vertical and horizontal:** Vertical publications are directed toward a specific industry and its members (e.g., *Modern Plastics, Iron Age*). Horizontal publications are directed toward a specific task, function, or area of concentration, across multiple industries (e.g.. *Purchasing, Modern Materials Handling, Production Engineering, Electronic Design*).

**Industrial directories:** A compiled list of known suppliers within a large variety of product areas intended for use as a reference group for industrial buyers. There are general directories covering most industries, directories for individual states, and private directories (e.g., *Thomas Register*).

**Trade shows:** A trade show is a formal exhibition at which a supplier rents space to introduce and display its products and make sales. Competitors' products are also demonstrated at these exhibitions. Personal contacts with a large number of prospective and present customers in the industry can be established in a short period of time and in one location.

**Catalogs:** Printed material containing information describing a supplier's products, their applications, and other product specifications (e.g., price) distributed among organizational buying influences for use as a reference and buying guide. Catalogs often contain enough information so the buyer can purchase products directly.

**Direct mail:** Letters or brochures sent to selected buying influences to provide information—on a supplier and its products or services. This type of medium enables a marketer to relay personalized messages to these influences.

**Videos:** Films illustrating the use and benefits of a company's products or services. These are given to customer organizations for viewing in-house on a VCR.

**Technical reports:** Written, detailed descriptions of product design specifications and performance capabilities. Results of product testing are summarized, including data on quality and reliability.

**Web sites and the Internet:** Web sites can be a valuable source of vendor and product information, and they can be "hotlinked" to other sites that deal with aspects of a given customer need or product category. Advertisements can also be placed at common user locations on the World Wide Web.

**Samples:** Products given to certain customers on a trial basis for the purpose of promoting and demonstrating a supplier's product (e.g. electronic components, copier paper).

**Publicity:** A presentation of company and product information for which the marketer does not pay and does not control. These presentations appear in media (e.g., newspapers, trade journals) that can increase public awareness—and can develop a favorable image for an organization.

**Novelties:** Free gifts such as calendars, pens, and paperweights that are imprinted with a company's name and possibly an advertising message. These small, useful items are given to customers as a reminder of a supplier and its products or services.

**Telemarketing:** Using the telephone to find out about a prospect's interest in the company's products, to create an awareness or understanding of those products, and even to make a sales presentation or take an order.

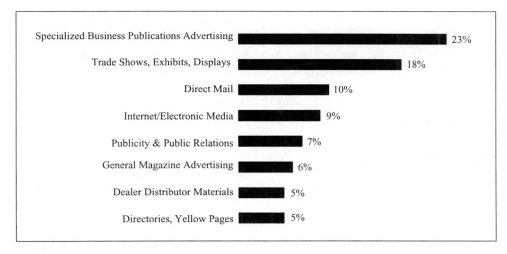

**Figure 11.1.** Selected Allocation of Marketing Dollars in Industrial Firms

SOURCE: Adapted from Cahners Advertising Research Report No. 510IE.

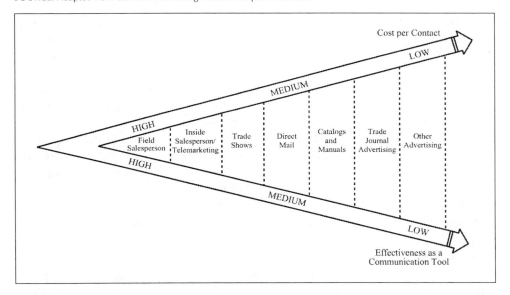

**Figure 11.2.** Comparing Components of the Industrial Promotion Mix on Cost and Performance

SOURCE: Adapted from *Industrial Marketing Management*, p. 222, Haas. © Copyright 1976 by Van Nostrand Reinhold.

tensiveness of the message and personal involvement possible with personal selling can be contrasted with the high cost per customer contact. By contrast, print advertising offers a brief message and lower buyer involvement, but the cost per contact can be quite low because of the number of people reached.

Industrial buying poses a number of specific complications for the promotional effort. Differences between individual customers and their needs can be significant enough to sometimes warrant a separate promotional effort tailored to each organization. Furthermore, because there are a number of potential decision participants from various functional areas within a given buying organization, each with a different background, a promotional effort that effectively communicates with one person may be ineffective with another. Even if two members of a buying center receive an identical message, they will likely process the message selectively to make it consistent with their own goals, values, and expectations. In addition, many participants in a company's buying decision are difficult to reach through promotional efforts, except at exorbitant cost.

To better understand the role of promotion in communicating with organizational customers, it is helpful to consider two buyer perspectives: a *micro* approach and a *macro* approach.

## Promotion and the Buyer: A Micro Approach

An individual involved in organizational buying goes through a cognitive process in selecting a particular vendor or product. An examination of the steps that take place inside the mind of a decision maker can shed some light on promotional strategy.

The buyer must first be made aware of the vendor and what product or service is being sold. Next, the buyer develops knowledge and understanding of the vendor or product, including technical characteristics, performance capabilities, and selling requirements. Following this, if the buyer is sufficiently interested in the vendor or product, favorable or unfavorable attitudes are developed. Favorable attitudes can then create a predisposition to buy from the vendor; such conviction or intention to buy may translate into an actual purchase if conditions are correct.

This process is called a *hierarchy of effects*. There are alternative versions of the hierarchy, but the basic idea is that the customer moves from cognition (or awareness), to affect (or attitude), to behavior. This sequence is normal for high-involvement purchases, including many industrial products and services. The marketer, through effective promotional programs, can affect the buyer's progress through the hierarchy. This movement can be accomplished by directing promotional efforts at specific stages, such as creating awareness, educating the buyer, or modifying attitudes.

A common error in promotion management is for the marketer to expect to see a direct relationship between expenditures for advertising or sales promotion and product sales. It may be more appropriate to examine the impact of such expenditures on customer awareness levels or on customer attitudes. Furthermore, a promotional effort that does an effective job of creating awareness may have little or no effect on the customer's understanding of the product, or on the amount of customer interest generated. The hierarchy of effects model, correspondingly, provides the marketer with some direction in the establishment of promotional objectives. Each stage in the hierarchy presents a distinct communications objective.

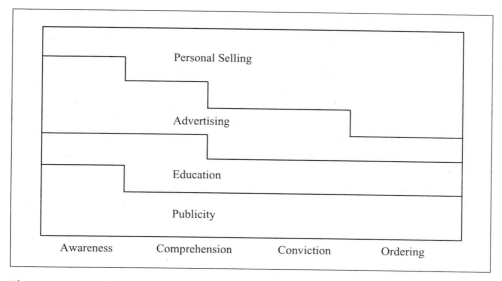

**Figure 11.3.** Relative Effectiveness of Four Promotional Tools at Different Stages of the Customer Buying Process

SOURCE: Adapted from *Marketing Management: Knowledge and Skills*, 4th ed., p. 132, Peter and Donnelly. © Copyright 1995 by Irwin. Reprinted with permission.

As demonstrated in Figure 11.3, the relative importance of the elements contained in a company's promotional mix change over each hierarchy of effects stage. Advertising and other nonpersonal forms of communication, which may be effective in creating awareness, have a smaller impact as the buyer moves toward conviction and actual purchase behavior. At the same time, the role of personal selling increases in importance and is paramount in achieving conviction and getting the customer to place an order.

## Promotion and the Buyer: A Macro Approach

Not only should the marketer consider how individual members of the buying center become aware and develop a preference, but he or she will also find it useful to take a more macro approach and examine the total buying process of the customer organization. As explained in Chapter 3, organizations move through a series of stages in making a buying decision, from first becoming aware of a problem or need, to determining the characteristics of an acceptable solution, seeking out information on products and vendors, evaluating alternatives, making a decision, and evaluating the decision after the fact.

Customers have particular information requirements in each of these stages, and the promotional mix should be designed to address these needs. Customer reliance on internal versus external information sources, on objective versus subjective sources, and on personal versus impersonal sources varies with each stage of the process. Also, the key role players in the buying decision change during each stage, suggesting that promotion directed at a particular stage should reflect the characteristics and goals of the relevant individuals.

Consider, for example, the need recognition or arousal stage for a product with which the customer has little or no purchasing experience. The task of the promotional effort might be to help the buying organization members see that they have an unmet need and to isolate that need. The target group might be senior management or current product users. Trade shows and advertisements in trade publications are often effective and efficient tools in accomplishing this task.

The same organization, once a need is clearly established, must express a way to satisfy that need in the form of a specific product or service. The characteristics of acceptable products or services next have to be determined and described. The marketer's communication task is to demonstrate how a particular product class meets a need and satisfies technical requirements; the focus is on the buying organization's technical expertise in the specific area of need. Catalogs, samples, and trade journal advertising may be appropriate, but the sales force must be involved to reduce the likelihood that decision makers in the buying organization will tailor the description of product requirements to the characteristics of a competitor's product.

When vendor evaluation is the concern, members of the buying organization are more susceptible to communications that demonstrate an established record of vendor and product performance. The marketer might be tempted to use comparative advertising (i.e., advertisements that draw comparisons with competitors) or even testimonials from satisfied customers. The evaluation process may be fairly formal, however, suggesting the need for a more persuasive, direct approach. Personal sales calls by the field sales force, technical reports, and favorable publicity may be more effective. The relevant target group may now be purchasing managers.

There is, in general, heavy concentration on personal selling in the middle and later stages of the buying process. In these stages, it is necessary to provide specific, detailed communications concerning the product and the vendor that are difficult to convey through impersonal forms of communication. These buy stages may involve an extensive negotiation process, the adaptation of a given product or service to the needs of a particular organization, or a discussion of the decision criteria used in evaluating proposals and making a final decision. All these situations usually require direct personal contact—by the company sales force—between the supplier and the buying organization.

In the postpurchase stage, the communication task is to reinforce the customer's decision, encouraging source loyalty and positive word-of-mouth publicity. The perception of negative discrepancies or "gaps" between customer expectations and actual experiences must be minimized. Inside salespeople and direct mail can also be helpful in maintaining customer satisfaction.

Implicit in this discussion is the assumption that marketers can affect the industrial buyer's decision through the source, time, and quality of information they provide.

## The Pitfalls of Global Advertising

Global companies are faced with a number of significant problems when attempting to develop a global communications program. First, should the advertisement be created at headquarters and then distributed to other countries, or should the ad be developed locally, where the nation's culture is better understood? Companies like Nike prefer standard ads developed at headquarters with slight modifications made to fit local market conditions. Conversely, Reebok prefers different localized advertisements that use different themes. Global firms may also be faced with legal restrictions on the type of advertisement selected. For example, Ireland bans television ads about pharmaceutical products.

The availability of media also differs from country to country. For instance, some countries restrict commercial air time to specified maximum periods of the day, while other nations like Norway and Saudi Arabia do not allow commercial messages to be broadcast on television. These restrictions limit the number of viewers of television ads.

However, technological changes, like satellite communications, permits global firms to advertise their products via cable and dish systems around the world. Satellite systems such as STAR, CNN, and BBC are available in many homes and business locations worldwide. This technological innovation reduces governmental control of the airways and results in greater exposure to global products for business consumers.

SOURCE: Adapted from *Marketing Management*, p. 614, Kotler. © Copyright 1997 by Prentice Hall.

Moriarty and Spekman (1984) found buyer reliance on inputs from personal and commercial information sources earlier in the buying process, on impersonal commercial sources during the search for alternative vendors stage, and on impersonal noncommercial sources in both the recognition and search stages.

Keep in mind, however, that there is no one right way to design promotional strategy. The overriding requirements of the marketer is to determine (a) which stages of the buying process are the *most* critical for the particular type of product and market segment in question and (b) which promotional tools can best communicate with the appropriate individuals in those stages. Not all purchases involve the same set of stages, and the length of the stages will depend on what is being sold and to whom. Also, the amount of information sought by the buyer will tend to be directly related to the amount of risk and conflict in the purchase decision. The challenge is to optimize the allocation of promotional expenditures to the key decision points in the buying process, while remaining within the budget constraints placed on these expenditures.

# Why Advertise?

Business-to-business advertising has generated considerable controversy over the years. Some people actually argue that advertising is a waste of money. As previously indicated, industrial advertising relies heavily upon print media because of the need to target specific industries, organizations, and individuals within those organizations with precise information. There are occasional uses of television or radio, but these media tend to be for products and services with broad-based markets and universal applications—such as copying machines, small computers, Internet services, and business insurance.

Print media are limited in their ability to convey technical product information to the appropriate members of the decision-making unit in sufficient quantity and detail and at the right time. An industrial advertisement cannot hope to address the multiplicity of questions and concerns that ultimately determine what is bought and from whom. The length of the buying process also makes it difficult to ascertain the effectiveness of advertising. Furthermore, experts report that people are overexposed daily to commercial advertising messages. After all, how many advertisements can a person be expected to remember when they are exposed to 270 messages a day? (See Figure 11.4.) As a result, some companies question the advisability of spending money on advertising and may advertise only because their competitors advertise.

Even given the points above, there are numerous valid reasons to advertise in industrial markets. First, advertising has an ability to extend beyond the salesperson and reach inaccessible or unknown members of the buying center who exert considerable influence on an organization's purchases. It has been estimated that, on average, salespeople do not reach half of those who fill an influential role in buying decisions. Some influencers are never identified, some will not or are unable to talk with the salesperson, and the salesperson may not have the resources to spend time with others. In addition, the salesperson may violate protocol and offend certain members of the buying center by meeting with others. A message placed in a trade journal read specifically by electrical engineers or in a publication that deals solely with school supply products may be noticed by otherwise unreached decision participants. Table 11.2 provides additional examples. The importance of advertising's ability to reach inside the buying center is further emphasized in research conducted by Cahners Publishing.[1] In a survey of industrial advertising managers, 55% indicated the need to reach two or more primary buying influences with their advertising message to get products specified and purchased (Cahners Advertising Research Report 551.9).

Advertising is also a tool for customer prospecting. Customer response can be encouraged by including a reply card, a toll-free telephone number, or simply an information-request e-mail address as part of an advertisement in a trade journal or business publication. By carefully scrutinizing the names of those who request product information, the marketer can generate a list of new sales prospects.

In addition to prospecting, advertising can provide the foundation for a salesperson's call by creating an awareness of vendor capabilities and providing general information about products and services. This approach is especially valid when selling

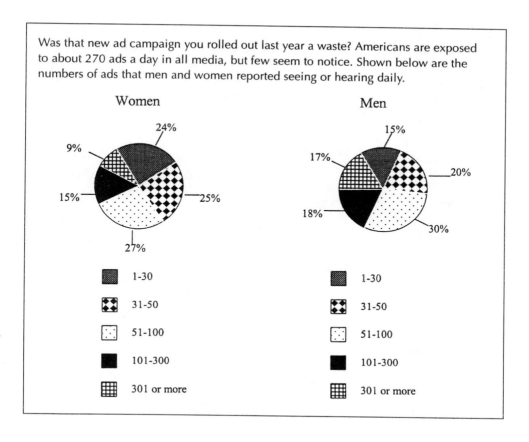

Was that new ad campaign you rolled out last year a waste? Americans are exposed to about 270 ads a day in all media, but few seem to notice. Shown below are the numbers of ads that men and women reported seeing or hearing daily.

products in categories that customers may not associate with the company's past history. Some of the preliminary questions of the buyer can be addressed. This is cogently demonstrated in the well known McGraw-Hill[2] man-in-the-chair advertisement, shown in Exhibit 11.1. McGraw-Hill is a leading publisher of trade magazines such as *Modern Plastics, Textile World, Aviation Week,*[3] and *Space Technology, Byte,*[4] and *Chemical Engineering.*[5] This message is directed toward sales and marketing managers, encouraging them to conduct more industrial advertising. It also emphasizes how an advertisement can lay the groundwork for the salesperson by addressing the kinds of questions being raised by the "dour" gentleman in the chair.

Properly directed, advertising can also help *reduce the average cost of sales calls.* Advertising designed to support the sales effort can bring down the selling cost per sales dollar generated. The significance of this finding cannot be understated. It suggests that advertising should be examined not only on its own merits but also within the context of the total promotional mix. The cautious marketer will recognize, however, that the effect of advertising depends on the frequency with which one advertises. It is possible to advertise too little as well as too much—a point discussed later in this chapter.

**TABLE 11.2**  How Trade Journals Can Be Used to Reach Target Groups

| If you are looking for engineers and professionals in | Look for them in these magazines |
|---|---|
| **Construction** | |
| Civil engineers | *ENR* |
| Architects | *Architectural Record* |
| Electrical engineers | *Electrical Construction & Maintenance* |
| **High tech** | |
| Aerospace/avionic mechanical engineers | *Aviation Week* and *Space Technology* |
| Computer scientists, engineers | *Byte* |
| Data systems, telecommunications | *Data Communications* |
| Electrical, electronic | *Electronics* |
| **Chemical science** | |
| Chemical engineers | *Chemical Engineering* |
| Management | *Chemical Week* |
| Plastics engineers | *Modern Plastics* |
| **Energy** | |
| Electrical/nuclear utility engineers | *Electrical World* |
| Electrical/power nuclear/mechanical | *Power* |
| **Mining** | |
| Coal mining, geological engineers | *Coal Age* |
| Mineral, mining, metallurgical | *Engineering & Mining Journal* |
| **Metalworking** | |
| Manufacturing engineers | *American Machinist & Automated Manufacturing* |
| Metallurgical engineers | *33 Metal Producing* |
| **Entry level** | |
| All engineering disciplines | *Graduating Engineer* |

NOTE: All the above magazines are published by McGraw-Hill.

Industrial advertising also represents a means for motivating and supporting sales intermediaries, such as industrial distributors. Most intermediaries sell multiple products, originating from a number of firms. Their loyalties are correspondingly mixed, and their strongest efforts are likely to be devoted to the manufacturer whose products are easiest to sell, who has the highest commission or margin, or with whom the

**Exhibit 11.1.**

McGraw-Hill's "Man-in-the-Chair" Advertisement

*I don't know who you are.*

*I don't know your company.*

*I don't know your company's product.*

*I don't know what your company stands for.*

*I don't know your company's customers.*

*I don't know your company's record.*

*I don't know your company's reputation.*

*Now what was it you wanted to sell me?*

**MORAL:** Sales start before your salesman calls—with business publication advertising.

**McGRAW-HILL MAGAZINES**

BUSINESS-PROFESSIONAL-TECHNICAL

Reprinted with permission of McGraw-Hill Publishing.

intermediary has the closest working relationship. Advertisements that directly or indirectly support a middleman's sales can contribute to the strength of the ongoing manufacturer-intermediary relationship.

In addition, derived demand can be stimulated through industrial advertising, by extending the firm's promotional focus to the customer's customer. Exhibit 11.2 provides an example. More often than not, the target is the ultimate user in the consumer market. For example, GD Searle and Co. advertises its NutraSweet[6] sugar substitute to final consumers, although the product is actually sold to food and beverage manufacturers. A different example can be found with the Ventron Division of Morton Thiokol, Inc., which makes an antibacterial product called Bio-Pruf. When floor mops are treated with the product, it can be used as a germ killer. Ventron promoted the prod-

**Exhibit 11.2.**
Who Is DuPont Trying to Reach With This Ad?
(An Example of Derived Demand)

# Times like this call for ultra-tough luggage of Cordura.

**It stands up to the rigors of travel without losing its good looks.**

You get there with style and aplomb when you travel with luggage made of DuPont CORDURA® nylon. It stays serviceable and good-looking, no matter what tortures it has to take. Here are some good reasons why.

Tests show CORDURA resists abrasion 3 times better than stan-dard nylon, 2 times better than ballistic nylon, and 1½ to 3 times better than vinyl. And it resists punctures and tears 5 times better than standard nylon, 3 times better than vinyl, and 2 times better than leather.

Lightweight luggage made of CORDURA comes in a wide variety of colors and styles - plain weaves, fancy weaves, and tweeds. It won't rot or mildew. And it's easy to clean and quick to dry.

Luggage made of CORDURA stands up to the rigors of travel like nothing else. Ask for it at leading department stores and luggage shops.

Reprinted with permission of DuPont Corporation.

uct directly to hospitals, recognizing their acute concern with sterile facilities. The hope is that hospitals will pressure mop manufacturers to add Bio-Pruf to their products. Such pull-through strategies are quite expensive and the results are often very difficult to measure, but they are being employed with greater frequency.

Another role for industrial advertising involves conveying the desired corporate image to target audiences (see Exhibit 11.3). A firm might run ads featuring the company name or logo, emphasizing an image it wishes to portray, rather than advertising specific products or services. For example, such ads might stress the firm's position as an innovative leader, that it is environmentally responsible, that the firm

**Exhibit 11.3.**
Advertisement Stressing the Product More Than the Company

---

# "Are Your Territories Costing You Business?"

**Introducing TerrAlign OptAlign™**

Automatically balance hundreds of territories.
Minimize driving time.
Improve customer coverage, retention, and share of business.
Reduce sales force turnover.
*Want to know more about the best way to balance your territories?*
Call TerrAlign.

**Before** OptAlign™

The two largest territories are each too large for one salesperson to cover. The salespeople working these territories are forced to neglect some customers and prospects, helping your competitors gain share at your expense.

The two smallest territories require less than twenty hours per week to cover. The salespeople working these territories are probably making hours of unproductive calls and struggling to meet quota. Territories that are too small waste valuable selling time and increase sales force turnover.

**After** OptAlign™

Within seconds, OptAlign automatically realigns the territories to give each salesperson a balanced territory *and* to minimize total driving time. Balanced territories help maximize your revenues and market share by giving every salesperson the right number of customers.

OptAlign gives you the power to produce dozens of what-if scenarios. Compare balancing territories on workload, market potential, or any other combination of variables in seconds, and find the best territories for your business.

# TerrAlign

---

stands behind its products, or that it is especially customer oriented. Image and credibility of the firm are quite important with industrial goods, for the customers are buying the company and its reputation as much as they are purchasing the company's products and services. Image advertising is also one way to keep the company's name before the public.

When used properly, advertising can play a significant role in the industrial marketer's overall communication program. Unfortunately, many industrial advertising programs generate unclear or even dismal results, typically because those managers who are responsible do not really understand why or how to employ advertising. To be consistently effective, advertising programs must be well planned, carefully executed, and constantly monitored.

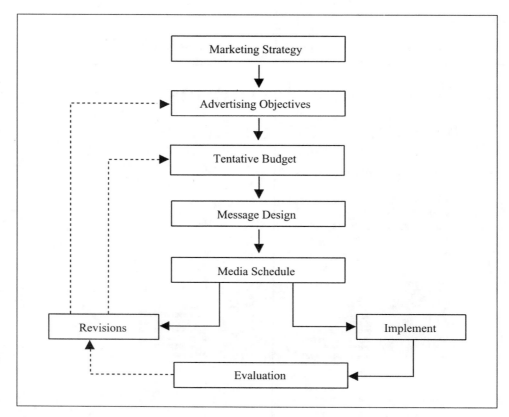

**Figure 11.5.** A Model for Managing the Advertising Program

SOURCE: Reprinted from *Marketing Management: Strategies and Programs* (7th ed.), p. 240. Guiltinan and Paul. © Copyright 1991 by McGraw-Hill. Reprinted with permission.

## Managing the Industrial Advertising Effort

The marketer should resist the temptation to manage advertising on a piecemeal basis, such as where each message and each media alternative is evaluated and decided upon individually or when advertising budgets are set in a vacuum. A strategic approach is needed, where individual decisions are coordinated as part of a larger plan to achieve specific communication objectives. A process model for planning, executing, and controlling advertising strategy is provided in Figure 11.5.

Industrial advertising should be positioned as an integral part of overall marketing strategy (e.g., product differentiation, niching, or market development). With a strategy in hand, the marketer then determines the communications necessary to implement that strategy. For example, if the firm were attempting to differentiate itself on the basis of service or product quality, then the communication requirement may be to change the beliefs of target groups about the capabilities of various vendors and their offerings. The next step is to determine the role that advertising can play most effectively in meeting these communication needs.

## Advertising Objectives

Having established the role of advertising, specific advertising objectives should be determined. Setting objectives is critical, both for directing the advertising program and for providing standards against which to gauge its effectiveness. For these reasons, it is important to state objectives in specific terms and, where possible, to quantify them. Advertising objectives can be stated in terms of sales or market share, and these measures are certainly quantifiable. As the discussions of the hierarchy of effects and the stages of the buying process suggest, however, advertising does not close sales. It is critical, therefore, to emphasize communication objectives. Some of these include creating specific awareness levels (e.g., increase awareness of our new self-cleaning feature among metallurgical engineers from 5% to 50%), changing attitudes about the application of the product form (e.g., a synthetic material used in producing tires can also be used in carpeting), changing beliefs about vendors and their products (e.g., repositioning ourselves as the premier service provider), or changing perceptions about the importance of product attributes (e.g., stressing life-cycle costs to the buyer who focuses only on initial cost). The goal of advertising also might be simply to remind the buyer to use a product or service, or to reassure the buyer after the purchase. Moreover, each of these objectives should be stated in terms of specific target audiences and the time that will elapse before measuring the outcome.

Glover, Hartley, and Patti (1989) developed an integrated advertising framework geared specifically for industrial markets. This structure outlines specific advertising objectives and various strategies associated with each. Table 11.3 presents a number of advertising objectives and strategies and their related characteristics. In a survey of the members of the Business/Professional Advertising Association, 82% of respondents indicated that their firm uses one of the advertising strategies stated in Table 11.3. The most frequent strategies employed were ones with moderate to high levels of persuasiveness. Less than half of the respondents, however, were able to correctly link their strategy to objectives. This suggests that industrial firms often fail to use advertising objectives as a guide for determining advertising strategies.

## Budget

The next step is to determine how much to spend. A number of methods exist for establishing an advertising budget, including percentage of sales, competitive parity, product profitability, productivity judgments, and product objectives. *Percentage of sales* involves setting the budget as a straight proportion of projected sales for the next year. For most industrial companies, advertising expense is a relatively small percentage of sales, often less than 1%, and of the total promotion budget, often about 10%. Figures for a select group of industries are shown in Table 11.4. Alternatively, some companies simply take the previous year's advertising expenditures and add a percentage increase based on the projected growth rate for sales in the coming year. These sales-based approaches tend to limit the marketer's flexibility in responding to marketplace demands, especially during periods of recession or aggressive

**TABLE 11.3**  Industrial Advertising Objectives and Correlated Strategies

| Objective | Strategy | Characteristics |
|---|---|---|
| Awareness | Corporate | Diffuse, long-term benefits. Low persuasion. |
| | Generic | Benefit offered by competition, no attempt to establish superiority. Informative, limited persuasion. |
| Knowledge | Preemptive | Benefit offered by competition, seeks to establish superiority. Informative, moderate persuasion. |
| Liking | Brand image | Concentrates on active benefits without reference to competition. Emotion, moderate persuasion. |
| Preference conviction | Positioning | Emphasis on differentiation relative to competition. High to moderate persuasion arises from placement in consumer's mind. |
| Purchase | Unique selling proposition | Concentrates on benefit not delivered by competition. High proposition persuasion. |
| | Direct appeals to action | Benefit delivery and incentives to act. High persuasion. |

SOURCE: Reprinted from Glover, Hartley, and Patti, "How Advertising Strategies Are Set," *Industrial Marketing Management*, 18, © Copyright 1989, p. 22, with permission from Elsevier Science.

competitor action. More fundamentally, this approach sets the advertising budget as a result of the organization's sales volume, rather than the sales volume being approached as a direct result of advertising efforts. These sales-based methods, however, are employed frequently because they are easy for managers to understand and implement.

*Competitive parity* involves matching the budget to the expenditures of your competitors. It assumes, unwisely, that the competitor is spending the correct amount or that equal advertising budgets will cancel one another out. Budgets set on the basis of *product* or *service profitability* reward financial performance but result in underinvestment in low-profit areas that could be made more profitable. *Productivity judgments* evaluate how effective different levels of expenditures are in accomplishing objectives; budgets are established based on a cost-benefit analysis. The *task and objectives* approach sets budgets in accordance with the specific goals established by management for individual products or lines. This method is the most advantageous because it has the capability to reflect the criteria (sales growth, competitor actions, profitability, and advertising effectiveness) emphasized by each of the other methods. This method, however, is also the most complex and time-consuming for determining advertising budgets.

**TABLE 11.4**  Advertising and Promotional Expenditures as a Percentage of Net Sales in Selected Industries

| Industry | Ad/Sales Ratio (1998) | Projected Growth Rate (1998-1999) |
|---|---|---|
| Office furniture | 0.8 | 11.2 |
| Periodicals | 7.0 | 1.5 |
| Chemicals and allied products | 1.9 | −1.6 |
| Industrial inorganic chemicals | 0.2 | −24.7 |
| Plastic and synthetic materials | 1.2 | 1.7 |
| Petroleum refining | 1.0 | 6.8 |
| Heating equipment and plumbing fixtures | 7.0 | −15.2 |
| Farm machinery and equipment | 1.0 | 4.9 |
| Metalworking machinery and equipment | 3.6 | −3.8 |
| Computing and office equipment | 1.9 | 8.8 |
| Refrigeration and service industry machines | 2.2 | 10.0 |
| Ophthalmic goods | 8.2 | 11.5 |

SOURCE: Adapted from *Advertising Ratios and Budgets* (esp. pp. 6-8), Schonfeld and Associates, Inc. © Copyright 1998 by Schonfeld and Associates, Inc.

One of the dangers in determining budgets is to "spend what we can afford." Although it is logical to ensure that the company or division should not spend money it does not have, what the company can afford in no way reflects the demands of competitive strategy. Ineffective advertising often can be blamed on the failure to spend enough money. For this reason, spending what one can afford can produce results that are little different from those produced by spending nothing at all.

Early research on advertising expenditures were published as the ADVISOR studies and sponsored by the Massachusetts Institute of Technology and the Association of National Advertisers (Lilien & Little, 1976). In two separate studies, the relationship between the marketing communications budget and various product and market characteristics were examined for 34 companies and 191 products. The analysis focused on three ratios: marketing budget to sales (M/S), advertising expenditures to the total marketing budget (A/M), and advertising expenditures to sales (A/S). The results of the two studies were quite similar. The M/S ratio averaged close to 7%, A/M was about 10%, and A/S approximated 0.7%.

It appears that industrial companies change their advertising and marketing budgets in response to a number of influences. One of these is the stage of the product's life cycle. Both the M/S and A/S ratios appear to decrease over a product's life, and both ratios are lower for products with larger market shares, suggesting economies of scale in the level of a company's marketing expenditures. These two ratios are positively related to growth in sales volume and growth in number of users. Products purchased more frequently apparently justify a higher A/M ratio. Alternatively, when a company relies on a relatively small number of customers for a disproportionate amount of its sales, the M/S and A/S ratios are lower, but A/M is unaffected or increases.

In terms of product characteristics, A/S rises with a product's uniqueness, quality, and identification with the company. Each of these is a means for differentiating products from those of competitors, and such differentiation is, in part, accomplished through strong advertising efforts. Also, companies that concentrate on customized products will spend less on marketing overall, and on advertising in particular. Marketing expenditures appear to be higher, as a percentage of sales, for more complex products and products whose characteristics and benefits are harder to communicate.

The CARR Reports, prepared by Cahners Publishing Co., provide additional insight into industrial advertising spending. Figure 11.6 illustrates the relationships between advertising levels and product standardization, product line breadth, quality, price, plant utilization, and purchase amounts.

## The Message

Although the actual message communicated through industrial advertising is limited only by the advertiser's creativity and budget, there are sound principles in developing good advertising. Ten rules have been proposed by the Copy Chasers, a group of anonymous advertising professionals who regularly critique industrial advertisements in *Business Marketing*. These rules are summarized in Table 11.5.

A common theme in the rules is the importance of understanding the customer. Advertisements that do not capture the reader's attention, involve the reader, reward the reader, or logically approach the reader on a personal basis are likely to be ineffective. The failure to understand customers and their buying criteria nevertheless is apparently a common malady afflicting industrial advertisers. It is easy to assume that industrial customers think and act just like the marketer. They seldom do.

The message communicated through industrial advertising should reflect two points concerning the customer: the typical buyer is fairly well informed and learned, and the customer seeks benefits and examines advertisements for information about those benefits. Because the audience is knowledgeable, the advertiser has to be especially wary of talking down to or patronizing customers in the advertising message. In addition, puffery and exaggerated claims will detract from advertisements directed at an industrial audience. The effectiveness of emotional claims is also subject to question under such circumstances.

Emotional appeals, directed at a person's feelings, values, and beliefs, can play a useful role in industrial advertising when carefully and professionally managed. Especially in copy written to influence technical people in the buying firm, creative appeals to their prejudices, ego, need for reinforcement, pride, and self-image help get through the psychological barriers the marketer faces in motivating these individuals to consider new alternatives. Positive emotional appeals stress the benefits and rewards to be gained from a product or service; negative appeals emphasize the

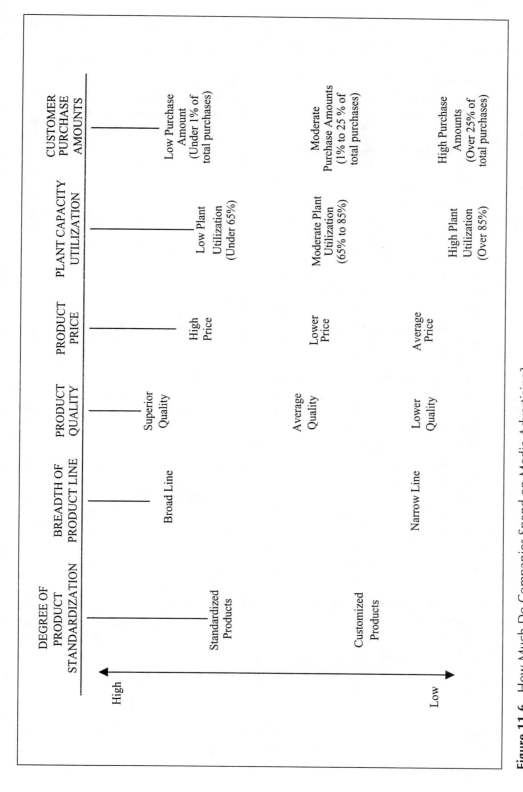

**Figure 11.6.** How Much Do Companies Spend on Media Advertising?

Developed from Cahners Advertising Research Reports Nos. 2100.01, 2100.04, 2100.06, 2100.07, 2100.08, 2100.09, and 2100.10.

**TABLE 11.5** What Makes Good Business/Industrial Advertising

1. **The successful ad has a high degree of visual magnetism.**

   A good industrial advertisement should capture the reader's attention so that a single component—either the picture, the headline, or the text—will dominate the area.

2. **The successful ad selects the right audience.**

   The reader's first glance at a picture or headline should let him know that the advertisement contains information that is related to his or her job interests.

3. **The successful ad invites the reader into the scene.**

   The advertisement should visualize, illuminate, and dramatize the selling proposition that will appeal to the reader's job type.

4. **The successful ad promises a reward.**

   A good advertisement should give the reader specific promises of benefits, whether explicit or implicit, positive or negative.

5. **The successful ad backs up the promise.**

   An advertisement must provide evidence to support the validity of the promise through a description of the product's characteristics, a competitive comparison, case histories, or testimonials.

6. **The successful ad presents the selling proposition in logical sequence.**

   The advertisement should be organized so that the reader is guided through the material in a sequence consistent with the logical development of the selling proposition.

7. **The successful ad talks "person to person."**

   The advertisement's copy should speak to the reader as an individual, in a friendly tone, and in terms of the reader's business. The writing style should be simple, using short words, short sentences, short paragraphs, active rather than passive voice, and no advertising clichés.

8. **Successful advertising is easy to read.**

   The advertisement's type should appear black on white, should stand clear of interference from other parts of the ad, and should not be more than half the width of the ad.

9. **Successful advertising emphasizes the service, not the source.**

   A good advertisement should make the reader want to buy or consider buying before telling him where to buy it.

10. **Successful advertising reflects the company's character.**

    The advertisement should favorably portray the company's personality and remain consistent over time and across the spectrum of corporate structure and product lines.

SOURCE: "The Copy Chasers Rules: What Makes Good Business/Industrial Advertising," *Industrial Marketing* (December 1982), pp. 51-52. © Copyright 1982 by Crain Communications, Inc.

undesirable consequence that might result from *not* using the item. In terms of the latter, companies might attempt to capitalize on the buyer's fears of failure, disapproval, competition, or economic loss. Exxon, for example, attempted to build on the buyer's fears by depicting the office automation systems market as exploding and revolutionary, with rapidly changing technologies and costs. An overemphasis on fear can backfire, however, for the anxiety it creates may be manifested in more negative feelings toward the advertiser.

In practice, rational messages are much more common in industrial ads than are emotional appeals. Cutler and Javalgi (1994) found a heavy emphasis on appeals to the buyer's concerns about quality, sales potential, and status. Rational messages present a factual and informative perspective on companies and their products or services. Emphasis is placed on logically conveying information regarding dependability, quality, durability, cost savings, and meeting technical requirements, among other areas. One study found that a rational advertising approach is most effective and that ads should show business buyers that a product will produce the desired benefits—quality, economy, value, and/or performance (Lohtia, Johnston, & Aab, 1995). Furthermore, when companies used a rational appeal, four areas tend to receive higher ratings from audiences: ad characteristics, reader's feelings, the selling proposition, and a positive effect on company's visibility.

That said, it is important to have creative, interesting copy and a vivid presentation of the main advertising theme. Some researchers suggest that buying center members look for technical information in copy, but others claim that engineers, managers, and purchasing agents differ in their relative concern with purely technical information (Bellizzi & Hite, 1986). Advertisers frequently err with messages that discuss product features but fail to devote attention to actual customer benefits. The advertiser who only highlights the physical characteristics and makeup of the product is forgetting that the customer is trying to solve a problem and is concerned primarily with how purchases from this vendor will benefit his or her organization.

A fundamental question when creating advertising copy concerns whether to place emphasis on the company name or to stress individual products and lines. Appeals that emphasize the company but make no mention of particular products are commonplace. The underlying rationale is that the customer is buying the company, not just a product. Company reputation, delivery reliability, service levels, and returns policies are often as important to the buyer as specific product characteristics.

There is also a distinction between corporate image (or institutional) advertising and business-to-business advertising that emphasizes the corporate name. The former is directed at the financial markets, the overall business community, the government, employees, and the general public. The latter is targeted at customers. William Marsteller (1984), of the public relations firm Burson-Marsteller, claims that "most (institutional advertising) is still vague and vacant, a teetering assemblage of platitudes resting on a meaningless slogan. Few people seem to be able to do it well" (p. 5). Nevertheless, companies are spending more on this type of advertising than ever before.

The argument for an emphasis on products and their trademarks has a number of legitimate bases as well. Copy that stresses the company, its logo, and perhaps a motto can be generalized and taken for granted by the reader, so that individual products receive little benefit. Also, when the product is pushed with institutional advertising, poor product performance or failure is likely to reflect more negatively on the company and its reputation. By contrast, featuring a product that performs well and becomes recognized can help build the company reputation.

Beyond the written copy, the physical characteristics of advertisements can be manipulated to accomplish communication objectives. McGraw-Hill has conducted research evaluating the relative impact of advertisements with different characteristics during the stages of the buying process (Donath, 1982). A large number of ads were rated to determine their respective abilities to establish contact, create awareness, arouse interest, build preference, or keep the customer sold. In *establishing contact*, for example, four-color ads with illustrations tended to be important, as did the use of bleed (running an illustration off one or more edges of the printed page). *Awareness* is generated by showing the product by itself and by including long copy (300 words or more), along with tables or charts. Techniques for *arousing interest* include featuring the product by itself, using toll-free telephone response numbers, and including three to five illustrations, as well as tables/charts. Four or more copy blocks help *build preference*. Long copy is good for *keeping customers sold*. Adopting these findings should be done with care, but they do suggest that all other things being equal, certain physical characteristics can make a difference.

Advertisement size and color have long been known to impact effectiveness (Hanssens & Weitz, 1980). Culture has been shown to affect colors utilized in industrial ads across countries. For example, blue is the masculine color in the United States, and red serves the same purpose in France. Black is the color of mourning in France and the United States, while purple is used in Venezuela. One study found that U.S. industrial firms employed greater numbers of black and white ads than those in France and Venezuela—especially service and insurance firms (Clarke & Honeycutt, 2000). Although black and white ads may communicate conservatism in business-to-business advertisements, another study pointed the out that conservatism may not be the correct strategy to follow in an emerging economy (Huang, 1993). The usage of women in advertisement content may increase reader recall, but this approach can "backfire" on the ad sponsor. In the United States today, the workplace is more diverse, which implies that ad sponsors must be careful not to negatively impact the credibility of the firm producing the advertisement (Reese, Whipple, & Courtney, 1987). It becomes apparent from the limited available evidence that content and colors evoke different feelings and perceptions across—and even within—cultures; therefore, multiple factors must be considered when planning industrial advertising campaigns.

## The Media Decision—Some Industrial Alternatives

Numerous media are available to the industrial advertiser. Major alternatives were identified in Table 11.1. The decision to rely upon a particular form of media must reflect the goals the marketer wishes to accomplish. These can include credibility,

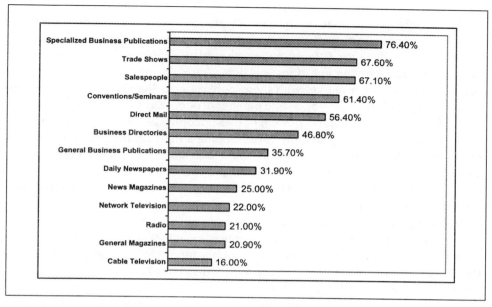

**Figure 11.7.** How Subscribers (Potential Buyers) Rate Different Information Sources With Regard to Usefulness

SOURCE: Adapted from Cahners Advertising Report No. 550.0.

timing, motivating the audience, imparting information, audience control, audience reach, and cost expended per contact. Figure 11.7 compares different media alternatives in terms of usefulness of the information imparted.

*General business publications, such as Forbes,*[7] *Fortune,*[8], *Business Week,* and inflight magazines, cover a broad range of subject areas and reach a wide variety of people in business. They also tend to have a superior editorial quality. This is a good type of media for advertising products and services with wide appeal to a large and geographically dispersed customer base. For example, office automation products such as personal computers, telecommunications equipment, and office equipment have become the most advertised items in general business publications in recent years. Also, a company such as an office supply distributor that is based and operates in a given geographic area will advertise in regional editions of these publications. General business publications are also a medium for institutional advertising, as they represent an effective vehicle for projecting a favorable corporate image to a broad-based audience and for keeping the business community aware of changes or new developments in the organization.

Advertisements are run in this medium to supplement other forms of more specific trade publication advertisements. General business publications may be read by upper levels of management who may not read specialized types of trade journals in their industry. This is a good medium for marketers to reach senior-level buying influences with messages of overall benefits for the organization (e.g., increased productivity or cost savings)—information that otherwise may not be conveyed through a sales call, advertisements in industry journals, or other types of promotional efforts.

Conversely, certain disadvantages exist with this type of publication. Advertising pages in the general business magazines cost up to 10 times the amount charged by an equivalent trade journal. Because they are read by individuals representing a multitude of occupations and industries, it is difficult for a marketer to define, and try to reach, a specific target market with these publications. Significant waste exposure generally results from exposing a large number of people in a variety of organizations to advertisements when only a portion of these people are potential customers. The marketer also might have difficulty in developing a message that will communicate effectively with a wide variety of markets and individuals, yet contain enough information to effectively stimulate interest in the product or service. Advertisements may not be detailed enough for potential customers to realize what a particular product or service can offer them.

*Trade journals*, or business papers, are more specific in nature and are directed toward a distinct industry, technology, organizational function, occupation, or other area of specialization. The readers of these publications have a special interest in the topics that pertain to their field. Because trade journals are read by individuals knowledgeable in their specialized areas, the advertisements contain more exact, detailed information that would help these individuals learn more about the product and its application and recognize a need for the product in their operations.

A marketer can acquire extensive data on trade publications from professional rating services and from some of the publications themselves, to determine which trade publications are read by those buying influences the marketer is targeting with the advertising (see Table 11.2). Using data compiled by rating services such as the Audit Bureau of Circulation, a marketer can learn how the readership for various publications is broken down into industries classified by NAICS (North American Industry Classification System) codes. The marketer can then match the target audience with the appropriate trade publications read by those individuals, selecting publications that will most effectively and efficiently accomplish the organization's promotional goals. A common error is to spread the company's advertising dollars over a wide variety of media rather than concentrating on publications that best reach likely buyers and influencers, and hitting them multiple times.

Trade publications are of two basic types: vertical and horizontal. Vertical publications contain articles and advertisements of interest to individuals in a specific industry. *Iron Age, Modern Plastics*, and *Chemical Week*[9] are good examples. *Modern Plastics* covers the subjects of management, engineering, machinery, and new materials within the plastics industry; *Chemical Week* discusses subjects such as the markets, technology, management, and research in the chemical industry.

Research indicates that 95.7% of purchasing influencers read the specialized business magazines serving their industry (Cahners Research Report No. 411.2). Many company personnel, from the top executives to the people on the shop floor, are likely to read these publications. It follows, then, that a marketer can reach a variety of buying influences in a specific industry by advertising in one or two of the publications serving that industry. For example, Bethlehem Steel[10] may advertise in automotive publications to reach purchasing agents and designers in the automobile industry with the description of Bethlehem's low-cost steel for car bumpers. Horizontal publications are directed to individuals who work in a particular technology, occupation, organizational function, or other area of specialization. Advertising in these publications does not limit a marketer to a particular industry but instead enables him or her to reach interested buying influences in a specialized area across industries. *Electronic Design, Modern Materials Handling, Robotics Age,* and *Assembly Engineering* are a few examples of horizontal publications. *Electronic Design* contains articles and advertisements that appeal to engineers and engineering managers in electronics worldwide. *Modern Materials Handling* examines the equipment, systems, trends, and management of the functions that relate to handling of inventories.

Trade publications are useful for directing specific, technical advertising messages about specialized products and services to buying influences in publications they are most likely to read and refer to for information. Marketers do not have to waste space providing general information because they can use more technical information that the readers of specific trade journals will comprehend and find useful in their decision making. Through advertising in these publications, marketers can often reach inaccessible and unknown buying influences who do not have direct personal contact with the salesperson—but who do read journals. This advertising is also a less costly form of promotion, because it reaches many prospective and present customers (both known and unknown, accessible and inaccessible) at a low cost per thousand members of the target market reached (i.e., CPM).

*Industrial directories,* or buyer's guides, are comprehensive listings of the current suppliers of a wide array of product types. Vendors can advertise in these publications in addition to their company listing—just as in the business-to-business Yellow Pages. General directories cover most industries, regional directories compile data for individual states or groups of states, and private directories limit their coverage to specific industries.

The *Thomas Register of American Manufacturers,*[11] one of the most widely known general directories, covers most industries and product areas listed under more than 40,000 headings. Suppliers are grouped by products or services and then broken down by state and city. A company's name, address, phone number, and value of its tangible assets are included in this directory. An extension of the *Thomas Register* is the *Thomas Register Catalog File,* also called the *Thomcat,* which contains the catalogs of various suppliers, listing them in alphabetical order, as opposed to product area. These catalogs describe and often illustrate the products and their applications.

State and county industrial directories provide information on the industries in their areas, classified by NAICS codes. For example, some state directories contain an economic overview of the state and list suppliers alphabetically, geographically by county and/or city, by NAICS codes, and by product group. These directories are usually published every 1 or 2 years.

Private directories, such as *Chemical Week Buyer's Guide,* are published annually and list suppliers in a specific area or industry. The *Chemical Week* directory is divided into two sections: (a) Chemicals, Raw Materials, and Specialties, and (b) Packaging, Shipping, and Bulk Containers. Suppliers are listed by product; they can submit technical data such as product line descriptions, formulas, and product applications, and they can buy advertisements or inserts in the directory.

Directories are purchased by industrial buyers to aid in finding vendors. Customers looking for a particular product refer to directories to determine the number of available suppliers and which ones to contact. Often, industrial buyers learn about the existence of suppliers that would otherwise never have been considered. When referring to directories, it has been estimated that 83% of users consult the manufacturer listings, 72% examine the advertisements, 53% take action by phoning or writing the manufacturer and 50% send in a reader service card (Cahners Research Report No. 450A). Most users keep the directory for more than 1 year, so advertisements in directories serve as continuous reminders of suppliers and products. Also, advertisements may supplement the listings, increasing the exposure of suppliers to potential buyers.

Some industrial marketers perceive certain disadvantages to advertising in industrial directories. They argue that both an advertisement and a listing by product group are duplication and unnecessary exposure. Because the various suppliers of that product are listed together, there is considerable competition within each product group. Directories are expensive, so certain industrial organizations may not purchase them or may rely on older editions. Another disadvantage is that a marketer cannot develop a specific message targeted at a defined audience, because the buying influences referring to these publications represent a broad range of industries and interests.

*Telemarketing* uses the telephone to perform certain marketing functions, including both advertising and personal selling. This often involves the use of a toll-free telephone number and/or a WATS (Wide Area Telephone Service) line. Telemarketing can be categorized as either incoming or outgoing. Incoming involves customer-originated telephone calls, while outgoing operations consist of calls that originate within the firm. The latter of the two forms represents the highest future growth potential for industrial firms.

This form of marketing communication is a personal way to handle customer complaints and inquiries, take orders, receive requests for customer service, and maintain personal contact with customers. Telemarketing provides the opportunity for an immediate response to a customer inquiry for additional information in catalogs or other literature, or a request for a salesperson to call. Instead of reader response cards found in advertisements in publications, an advertisement can contain a toll-free telephone number the customer can call.

Because of the high cost of a sales call, some organizations have replaced personal selling with telemarketing, supplemented with catalogs and other types of direct mail literature. Customers who purchase directly from catalogs can phone in their orders. If an organization uses personal selling, telemarketing can be used to identify prospects, answer questions, maintain contact between sales calls, and gain feedback from customers. Customers can be informed immediately of any situations that require their attention such as partial shipments, out-of-stock problems, or product performance problems. For a company using the WATS line, a 3-minute call used for tasks such as receiving customer inquiries or handling customer complaints costs very little.

Larger organizations may outsource incoming calls to an inquiry-handling company whose only job is to respond to calls on a toll-free line. The companies can take requests for literature and provide information such as names, phone numbers, and locations of dealers and representatives. New technical advancements in telecommunications, computers, electronic data interchange, and database management will aid in the development of telemarketing in the future. The company homepage on the World Wide Web (WWW) that provides such organizational information as catalogs, sale items, phone directory, and history of the company is only a first step toward integrated and interactive communications. These advancements will enable industrial suppliers to keep track of customer ordering patterns and inventory supply, as well as to direct personalized messages to selected individuals determined by their needs for a product or service. Catalogs and other forms of sales promotion are often included.

*Direct mail* is a flexible type of industrial promotion because marketers can control the content, the timing, and the target audience. Before a salesperson's visit, a letter can introduce and answer general questions about the salesperson, the company, and the product or service. Direct mail can serve as a way of personally maintaining continuous communication with industrial buying influences between sales calls or after the sale has been made. Remaining in contact with a buying organization also serves to remind customers about the supplier and can work to establish a favorable buyer-seller relationship. Letters and brochures can be sent to key individuals, some of whom a salesperson may be unable to call upon, to introduce and promote products, or services. In addition, direct mail can elicit customer feedback, serving as a form of market research.

The industrial marketer faces several problems using direct mail. Establishing and maintaining a mailing list of prospects may be a lengthy, complex task. In fact, the cost effectiveness of direct mail is directly related to the quality of the mailing list. Prospects need to be identified by their organization, position, and name. Mailing lists can be rented or purchased from commercial list houses, publishers of trade publications, and many professional societies (e.g., Society of Civil Engineers). They can be compiled from within the organization if a concerted effort is made to collect and update data files on past and current customers, customer inquiries, and contacts made at trade shows or through referrals. Often, salespeople are aware of present and prospective customers to whom direct mail should be addressed. In some cases, the mailing list may be too general or may not reach the prospects the organization needs to reach. In addition, a marketer must know the customer's location, organization, and other customer characteristics to design and individualize a message that directly addresses the customer's needs. This is complicated further if a supplier has multiple, diverse types of products or a long product line. Problems also exist for the marketer if the selected individuals who receive the mail disregard its content. Organizational buying influences receive many pieces of mail a day and may be too busy to read or refer them to others. Mailing product literature that is not read is both wasteful and expensive for the marketer.

## Evaluating Advertising

Management is sometimes skeptical about allocating sizable amounts for advertising industrial products and services because of the difficulty in determining whether or not those expenditures were well spent. Many managers have been heard to say: "I know that half of my advertising is wasted, but I don't know which half" (Bellizzi & Hite, 1986, p. 117). This problem has a number of causes.

When managers fail to set specific advertising objectives, they have no standard or guideline against which to compare the results of an advertising campaign. Whether they focus on sales, reach, customer awareness levels, attitude change, or some other indicator, objectives provide a basis for resource allocation and a means for control over those resources once they are allocated. Without such objectives, the industrial advertiser is virtually shooting in the dark.

In the absence of other goals, managers look for bottom-line results in terms of sales. Sales, however, are affected by a variety of external factors, including pricing policies, sales force efforts, competitor actions, and economic developments. It is difficult to control for these factors and isolate the impact of advertising on sales. In addition, although managers frequently look for a direct linear relationship between advertising and sales, the relationship is generally nonlinear, because diminishing returns set in at some point.

A related issue that poses difficulties for evaluation lies in estimating the time it takes for the advertising to have an impact. Rarely can an instantaneous impact be expected. Furthermore, for advertising to achieve results, the target audience usually must be exposed to the message more than once. The time lag between instituting an advertising program and realizing results can extend to a number of months or even longer.

Sales tend to be emphasized not only because of a concern with the bottom line but also because sales data are readily obtainable. The same reasoning lies behind the frequent reliance on circulation data for print media and attendance figures for trade shows as performance indicators. If not just sales, and in addition to overall objectives, what should an evaluation focus upon? Key areas for investigation include determining whether the target audience was reached, which media most effectively reached that audience, if the message registered with the target audience, and if the message had a favorable, unfavorable, or neutral bearing on the customers' predispositions toward the vendor and/or product.

If the firm emphasizes communication objectives, such as influencing customer awareness levels, comprehension, or perceptions, the evaluation process often requires the collection of data before and after an advertising program has been implemented. Surveys after the campaign, directed at a representative sample of those in the target audience, can be used to identify changes in audience predispositions relative to some benchmark. As valuable as this approach appears to be, it presents a number of measurement problems and can be expensive. Awareness, recall, attitude, and behavioral intention are difficult concepts to measure reliably. They are unobservable phenomena, subject to a variety of influences beyond the marketer's advertising effort.

In addition to communication effects, the marketer is concerned with measuring efficiency of the firm's advertising expenditures. Toward this end, it is useful to develop and monitor efficiency indicators such as advertising expense per sale, inquiries generated per advertisement (and how this varies by size), or advertising cost per person reached in the target audience. To measure any impact on sales force productivity, advertising effectiveness can be monitored by tracking the cost per sales call as advertising programs are varied. In this way, the focus is placed on advertising's role in the communication mix.

At the same time, performance evaluation should not focus simply on the effectiveness of the organization's media or message choices. Frequency of exposure is also an important area of concern, because it can be a major source of waste expenditures. As indicated previously, advertising run too few times can be as ineffective as advertising run too many times. Even if a single advertisement reaches all the members of its target audience, which is a highly unlikely outcome, the first exposure probably will not cognitively register with many of these individuals. Recipients block out the advertisement or are distracted by other stimuli. As a result, it often takes multiple exposures for an ad to be noticed and absorbed by the receiver. At some number of exposures, however, the advertising objective is accomplished and further exposures serve little purpose.

Evaluation should be an integral and ongoing component of the strategic approach to advertising management. The ability to evaluate can be greatly enhanced through the development of a strong database to assist in decision making. This is referred to as a marketing information system. As a case in point, Rank Xerox,[12] the European subsidiary of Xerox Corporation,[13] developed a computerized database marketing system that enables it to target promotional efforts directly to specific companies. This system contains such information as the machines a company is currently using, the products that will best satisfy that particular company's needs, inquiries received per product, and the medium used when making inquiries (response card or telephone call), to name a few.

# More on the Web

One of the hottest topics in business and the media today is electronic commerce, which encompasses the technologies of EDI (electronic data interchange), kiosks, electronic classified advertisements, and on-line services. The Internet and its graphical interface, the World Wide Web (WWW), are key components of an electronic commerce initiative that is playing an ever-increasing role in industrial promotion mix. Indeed, many industrial firms have brought a global edge to provincial businesses by advertising and communicating on the WWW (Honeycutt, Flaherty, & Benassi, 1998).

The Internet provides opportunities for an organization to enhance its business in a cost-effective and practical manner. That is, the Internet can be utilized to reach new markets, better serve customers, distribute products faster, solve customer problems, and communicate more efficiently with both customers and business partners. The Internet is an especially useful tool for dispensing information about one's company and/or products.

One of the unique aspects of the Internet is that it is appropriate for developing closer customer relationships. In addition to being viewed as a low-cost alternative to the fax, express mail, and other communications channels, the Internet enables employees—such as the sales force—to access vital information while being out of the office. Internet marketing, however, differs from traditional marketing. This medium requires a paradigm shift in thinking because marketing over the Internet is similar to traditional person-to-person networking where the quality of the information provided and the credibility of the organization making the offer are everything. This means that the company Web page must present the image desired by the firm and provide both current and correct information to the prospective customer.

Although the exact size is difficult to estimate, the growth rate of Internet users has doubled every year since the inception of the WWW in 1993. Approximately 51% of large companies and 25% of medium-sized companies are connected to the Internet, and the number of new WWW pages created on the Internet doubles every 2 months. The sheer magnitude of the Internet market and generally high income and education levels of its users appear to represent a potentially lucrative opportunity for industrial marketers, because many buyers believe that companies marketing via the Internet or WWW offer higher service quality than conventional firms.

Another noteworthy characteristic of today's Internet users is that they tend to hunger for information, yet they are highly resistant to traditional, aggressive advertising. That is, potential Internet customers do not like to receive "spam" or unwanted electronic solicitations and advertisements. To effectively utilize this medium, perceptive industrial advertisers have learned to behave more "low-key" by making their Web sites into value-added information services for consumers.

With the tremendous growth of on-line users, traffic congestion on the WWW has become a significant problem for some firms. Coupled with this is the plethora of information available on the Internet. As the amount of information accessible on the Internet increases, the more difficult it will become for potential customers to search efficiently for information. One recent method for navigating the Internet maze is Webcasting.

Although the Internet is a unique, interactive selling opportunity, many firms realize the potential only after discovering Internet customers are interested in their product offering. One of the promotional programs implemented by a welding firm was the adding of more items to its "Cyberspace Special" page. As the number of offerings increased, however, the welding firm realized the need to develop a user-

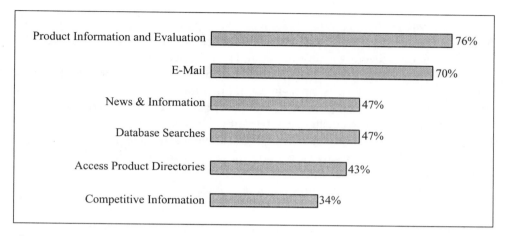

**Figure 11.8.** How Manufacturing Professionals Use the World Wide Web (percentage of respondents)

SOURCE: Adapted from Cahners Advertising Research Report No. 824.0A.

friendly way for its customers to access information and view the various Web pages. To address this need, industrial firms have developed a dual-purpose CD/Internet catalog. In addition to offering a user-friendly product information directory, customers should also be able to facilitate order entry by selecting an item and placing it into a "virtual shopping cart." One of the greatest advantages of offering an on-line catalog is the elimination of paper and postal costs.

To provide technical support assistance to Internet customers, some industrial firms offer newsletters that feature technical education, new processes, safety information, new product developments, and a question and answer forum. The newsletter is written approximately 6 to 12 times per year by specifically selected field employees. It is posted on the firm's Web site, where a free "subscription" and notification of a new edition can be electronically mailed to all interested subscribers. This superior customer service offering provides value to the customer and enhances residual business for the firm through education and increased marketplace exposure (Honeycutt et al., 1998).

## The Role of Sales Promotion

Sales promotion plays an even more essential function in the total communications mix than does advertising. As with advertising, it typically fills a supplemental and complementary role with the personal sales effort. Occasionally, though, sales promotion actually incorporates or replaces personal selling. Of the many sales promotion tools available to the industrial marketer, three are examined in this section: trade shows, catalogs, and technical reports.

*Trade shows* permit the formal exhibition of a supplier's products for the purpose of demonstrating, promoting, and ultimately selling these products. A show is an excellent forum for delivering a message to, and making personal contacts with, a large number of current and prospective customers at one location. The show-and-tell format is especially useful for customers in the information search and alternative evaluation stages of the buying process. For the exhibitor, the average cost per visitor (CVR) at trade shows is estimated at $90 (Herbig, O'Hara, & Palumbo, 1994). When exhibitors reach 70% or more of their potential audience, the average cost per visitor is reduced significantly. In any case, trade show costs are appreciably less than the cost of a cold personal sales call.

The specific uses of trade shows include the following.

1. Introduce and demonstrate product improvements, product applications, and new technological developments. Salespeople have the opportunity to demonstrate products that are too bulky or complex to demonstrate during a sales visit. Also, demonstrations can be made to a number of people at one time.

2. Build awareness of the supplier and its products among organizational buying influences previously inaccessible or unknown to the salespeople.

3. Make personal contacts with present and prospective (often unknown) customers, answer questions, provide company and product information, obtain feedback, discuss problems, generate leads, produce sales, and promote goodwill. Keep in mind that prospects come actively seeking information and have specifically set aside their own time to do so. Trade shows provide a medium for satisfying customer information needs more completely and immediately.

4. Remain competitive by participating in trade shows attended by the supplier's top competitors. This participation allows customers to compare products and suppliers to evaluate developments and trends in their industry.

5. Hire personnel and establish relations with new representatives and distributors. A successful appearance at a trade show can, for some products, make enough contacts, generate enough leads, and produce enough sales to make trade shows the focal point of an organization's promotional efforts (Green, 1985). Some firms report that as much as 25% of annual sales are generated from a single show.

To ensure that a show appearance is successful, the marketer should begin by establishing clear-cut objectives for using a trade show. Many exhibitors do not, and the frequent result is an unsuccessful show. Some considerations in setting trade show objectives include (a) the company's overall reason for exhibiting (e.g., establish contacts, make sales, project an image); (b) the target audience to be reached; (c) the relative advantages of national, regional, and local exhibiting; (d) the balance between efficiency (e.g., cost per person contacted) versus effectiveness (e.g., contacts made or sales gained at shows versus through other channels); (e) competitors' trade show strategies; and (f) the budget and projected cost ratio per sales lead obtained.

Proper selection of the trade shows in which to participate is also critical for success. The key is to determine which shows actually attract the target audience the organization is trying to reach. There are national, regional, and local trade shows from which to choose. Data are available in the form of surveys and audits on the attendance level of various shows, audience quality, and certain demographic characteristics of individuals who attend these shows. Exhibitors must insist upon good quantitative information about the quality of the attendees at trade show. Examples of sources of such reports include Exhibit Survey, Inc. and the Trade Show Bureau.

After selecting the show, the displays and literature to be utilized at the show must be developed. The display should be unique and interesting to selectively attract the attention of those with a real interest in the products on display. On average, 67% of those who visit an exhibit are actually interested in that company's type of product, 31% plan to buy that type of product, and 74% have some influence in the buying decision for it (Cox, 1985).

Four major types of exhibit techniques include static displays, attention-getters, audiovisual presentations, and live-product demonstrations. A *static display* features display areas for products but no demonstration. The emphasis is on salespeople working individually with prospects. *Attention-getters* include special performances (e.g., magic acts, celebrities) and contests meant to attract large crowds. *Audiovisual presentations* might include films, tapes, or computer screen displays and can involve multimedia presentations. Product applications can be demonstrated, detailed product information can be conveyed, and both the product and company can be dramatized. *Live product demonstrations* are quite effective and should be used where possible. Some suggest that these demonstrations last no longer than 10 to 12 minutes.

The single most important aspect of the show is the selection and training of booth personnel. Failure to make one-on-one contact with more than half of the potential audience is generally attributable to the people working the booth (Cox, 1985). The sales task is different from a personal sales call because the salesperson has much less time to establish the relationship and work the sale, and frequently knows little or nothing beforehand about a particular prospect.

It is also extremely important for the organization's marketing communications team to coordinate activities to enhance trade show effectiveness. This includes coordinating all marketing media in regard to content, timing, and audience (Kajewski, Yoon, & Young, 1993). Trade show visitors often have limited time and are confronted with a sizable number of exhibits, not all of which they plan to see. Marketers want to ensure that their exhibit is on the customer's must-see list. It is also important to advertise the occurrence of trade show exhibits for products that cannot be demonstrated during routine sales calls. Also, giveaways that visitors carry around the show after leaving an exhibit can be helpful. Direct mail or advertisements in trade publications can be used to contact key buying influences about a supplier's planned participation in a show and possibly of the products to be displayed or the theme of the display. During the show, advertisements sometimes will be placed by exhibitors in local media, including billboards. It is also common for trade show participants to move beyond the booth by hosting hospitality suites and banquets. In this way, the sales team is able to enhance rapport and establish relationships by meeting in a more relaxed environment. After the trade show, the supplier will follow up on contacts with prospective customers through letters, phone calls, or personal sales calls.

The effectiveness of the trade show can be determined by measuring the number of people who visited the supplier's display, the number of inquiries received at the show for more information or a sales call, and/or the amount of sales generated by the show. Also, a survey can be conducted of the show's visitors to determine the percentage that visited the exhibit, talked to a salesperson, and/or received literature. Such data should be examined in relation to the total potential audience at a show. These results can help the industrial marketer determine the effectiveness of the display in creating interest, making contacts, and generating sales. In addition, the marketer can use these results for planning which trade shows he or she will continue to participate in in the future.

Industrial companies can also benefit from trade shows, particularly in the global arena, by engaging in a number of nonselling activities during a show. Significant returns can be realized from information exchanges, relationship building, and assessments of channel partners at shows. Trade shows also permit the firm to stay abreast of technological developments, changes in the marketplace, and new competitor offerings. Shows are a quick, easy, and relatively inexpensive way to gather information (Sharland & Balogh, 1996). Many managers, however, fail to appreciate the utility of trade shows, so trade show budgets are often cut before advertising budgets or other marketing expenses. Poor management of this valuable resource diminishes the potentially sizable benefits.

Another popular form of sales promotion is printed *catalogs*. Catalogs contain information that describes the supplier's line of products, their applications, and other important product information, including price lists, warranties, and service requirements. Industrial buyers can use them as reference guides in selecting potential suppliers and products and in comparing a supplier's products against those of its competitors. Furthermore, catalogs can help user companies keep up with a supplier's new product introductions, improvements, and modifications. Companies with extensive product lines design their catalogs to contain just a brief summary of the most important information to be relayed to industrial buyers. An alternative to this would be to print a number of smaller catalogs for specific products or product groups and distribute them to individuals interested in those specific areas. With desktop publishing, a firm can produce customized versions of its catalog for different customers.

Catalogs can be distributed in a number of ways. They can be distributed by mail to a selected list of organizational buying influences or to those individuals who request more information on a supplier's products. Many industrial advertisements will contain an address or toll-free telephone number that can be used to request a catalog. It is also possible to go on-line and view product catalogs on the World Wide

Web. Salespeople can distribute catalogs to buying influences during sales calls or at trade shows. In addition, a supplier's catalog can be combined with the catalogs of other suppliers in industrial directories.

Other than salespeople themselves, catalogs are one of the few promotional alternatives that provide those in the buying center with specific, detailed information concerning a supplier's product line and prices. A catalog received prior to a salesperson's call can prestructure the visit by allowing the buyer to become familiar with the products and certain specifications and applications. After the sales call, a catalog can be referred to for answers to questions the buying-center member might have. Those influential members of the buying center who do not have direct contact with the salesperson may have access to catalogs. Often catalogs contain enough information, especially on standardized products that require little explanation, that an industrial buyer can purchase from them directly. For companies with extensive lines, the catalog may be the only way to keep customers informed of all the items the firm sells.

Catalogs can be an invaluable form of promotion if they are distributed to significant buying influences who can use them effectively. They can generate sales calls or even motivate sales themselves; consequently, poor distribution can result in lost sales opportunities. Buyers may rely heavily on catalogs for some purchasing decisions, ignoring suppliers whose catalogs are not available. At the same time, the considerable costs of planning, designing, printing, and dispersing the catalogs suggest that mailing lists be updated and maintained to ensure catalog delivery to the appropriate buying influences. Catalogs themselves must be updated frequently to reflect changes in the vendor's products or services and prices.

*Technical reports* are distributed by the supplier of a product and include specific, detailed product information. These reports describe the product, its applications, and its specifications in technical terms, to provide information necessary for technically qualified buying influences to see how the product can be used in their organization. The reports contain illustrations and diagrams that provide a detailed analysis of the product's composition and its functions. Technical reports usually detail results from product testing—including product performance and data such as product quality and reliability. Exhibit 11.4 typifies the use of such technical test results in a direct mail piece. These types of literature can be used in training people for production and maintenance work, because the reports describe the installation, use, repair, and servicing of the product.

Reports can be distributed through direct mail, during a salesperson's call, and at trade shows. Organizations often keep reports to refer to when making buying decisions, comparing a product against that of its competitors, and when repairing the product. Technical reports are useful to supplement the supplier's catalog. Catalogs usually provide general product information, but buyers more familiar with the complex nature of the product may find in technical reports the information they require to make buying decisions. Reports can also alert them to any possible problems in the installation, use, or maintenance of the product.

## Exhibit 11.4.
### Technical Test Results Used in a Direct Mail Program

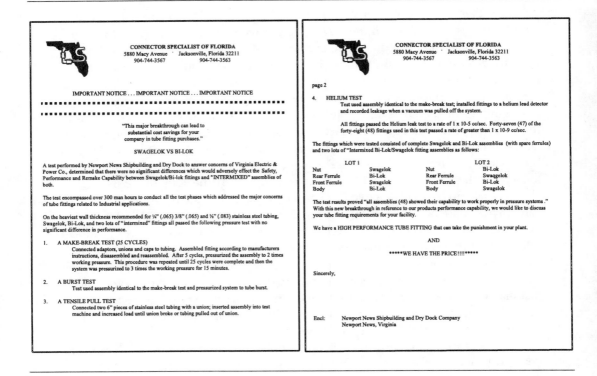

# The Role of Publicity and Public Relations

Publicity and public relations functions for companies operating in industrial markets represent a relatively inexpensive, high-credibility means of communicating with current and potential customers. The most common forms of publicity are the news release and the feature article. Other forms of publicity include press conferences, written or oral interviews, and speeches.

Creative marketers will get on a regular schedule where they send out publicity releases each month regarding new products and services, technology the company is working on, changes in the management team, key orders or contracts won, entry in new markets, findings of market research done by the firm, and a host of other developments. These are sent to a fixed list of trade journals, newspapers, conference and professional association newsletters, and trade associations.

It can also be quite effective to have members of the technical or marketing staff write articles that are submitted to trade magazines and/or for inclusion in conference programs or professional newsletters. Such articles usually address some technical or professional topic, outlining the company's experience in that topical area. Subtle mention is also made of positive aspects of the company's own products and capabilities. The key here is a soft sell that is hidden within the editorial content of the article.

Overall, publicity and public relations typically are used as a supplemental tool but make up an integral part of the overall communications plan. They serve a threefold purpose: (a) to inform customers about new products, services, and policies; (b) to generate inquires; and (c) to increase public awareness. In addition, publicity and public relations are used for industry recognition. Although publicity is often referred to as "free advertising," it should be remembered that there are hidden costs involved in obtaining publication space (e.g., preparation time, correspondence costs).

# Summary

This chapter focused on the advertising and sales promotion components of the industrial promotional mix, approaching them primarily as support activities supplementing the personal selling effort. It was argued that the role of promotion varies depending on the steps in the hierarchy of effects (a micro perspective) as well as the stages of the organizational buying process (a macro approach). Furthermore, differences between individual customers, their needs, and their buying decision processes can be so great as to warrant separate promotional efforts tailored to each organization or each market segment.

The controversy over the merits of advertising to industrial customers was examined, and some of the major reasons for advertising were established. These included reaching unknown or inaccessible buying decision makers, identifying new prospects, laying the groundwork for the sales call, supporting intermediaries, stimulating derived demand, and projecting a favorable corporate image to customers and other publics. Proper management of an industrial advertising program involves approaching it as an integral part of the firm's marketing strategy, with its own strategic framework. Starting with marketing strategy, the suggested approach included setting measurable objectives, establishing operational budgets, designing effective messages, selecting appropriate media, and evaluating performance. Issues, approaches, and findings in each of these decision areas were assessed. Emphasis was placed on the importance of reflecting the nature of the market and the needs of the customer throughout the process of conceptualizing and implementing the advertising program. The temptation to get so caught up in the appeal of various promotion techniques and alternatives often overshadows the basic need to provide product education to target groups.

The major media alternatives available to the industrial advertiser were described. These included general business publications, vertical and horizontal trade publications, industrial directories, telemarketing, direct mail, and the Internet. Advantages and disadvantages of each were identified in areas such as audience reach, ability to impart information, timing, flexibility, and cost per contact.

Finally, the chapter examined sales promotion and publicity, highlighting the uses of trade shows, technical reports, and catalogs. These tools serve to complement the personal sales effort and must be coordinated with advertising strategy. In some cases, they can be used to accomplish sales. Publicity was presented as an inexpensive source of highly credible communication.

As technology progresses, as product life cycles grow shorter, and as industrial buyers become more sophisticated and demanding, promotion and advertising must assume new dimensions. Advertising budgets are likely to grow, and advertising programs will become more aggressive. Companies increasingly will rely on an array of media to build recognition and position products. There will also be increased emphasis placed on evaluating promotion results, which will further the development of sound databases and up-to-date marketing information systems.

## Notes

1. www.cahners.com/
2. www.mcgraw-hill.com
3. www.aviationweek.com/
4. www.byte.com/
5. www.che.com/
6. www.nutrasweet.com/
7. www.forbes.com/
8. www.fortune.com/
9. www.chemweek.com/
10. www.bethsteel.com/
11. www.thomasregister.com/
12. www.rankxerox.com/
13. www.xerox.com/

## Questions

1. What is the industrial promotional mix? Why are personal selling, advertising, sales promotion, and publicity grouped together? Which of these receives the most emphasis in the typical business-to-business marketing firm? Which tends to receive the second most emphasis? Why?

2. Explain the hierarchy of effects. How might an understanding of this model be useful in designing the communications strategy for a company that manufacturers paper shredding machines?

3. "Marketing does not end with the sale, especially in industrial markets." Explain this statement. What kinds of communications activities might the marketer pursue in the postpurchase evaluation stage when selling business forms to corporations?

4. Unlike in consumer markets, the industrial customer does not come to the vendor, or "shop." Given this, what role does advertising fill in industrial markets?

5. Although setting communication objectives (as opposed to sales or profit objectives) would seem to make sense, such objectives are not very practical because they cannot be quantified or measured. Do you agree or disagree? Why?

6. You are the advertising coordinator at Gladstone Cordage, Inc., which makes and sells a complete line of braided and twisted rope and cordage. Last year you asked for and received a 25% increase in the advertising budget. Sales were largely unchanged, however, over the ensuing 12 months, and your boss feels the increased expenditure was wasted. Cite examples of alternative measures that might be used to demonstrate that the advertising was effective.

7. Freightway Transportation Company, a freight hauler serving most of the United States, sets its advertising budget for the coming year as a percentage of the projected sales for the year. Explain the advantages and disadvantages of this approach. How would you suggest Freightway determine the budget?

8. Why would you emphasize the company instead of its specific products in your trade journal advertising? Why would you stress a number of product lines instead of individual products? When might you place the emphasis on individual products instead of broader product lines, or instead of the company itself?

9. "It is generally a mistake to use emotional appeals (i.e., humor, fear, sex) in industrial advertisements." Do you agree or disagree? Why?

10. Six months ago, Fendt Engineering Corporation spent $40,000 to participate in its first major trade show. At the show, heavily attended by buyers and manages from the retailing industry, Fendt featured its new electronic cash register. Hardly anyone visited the company's exhibit at the show, and it does not appear that any orders were subsequently received as a direct result of the show. Identify five possible reasons for this apparent failure. Assume the product itself is a significant improvement over existing products and is priced competitively.

11. How might direct mail be used as a promotional tool during the stages of the buying process? Explain different possible uses of direct mail at each stage.

# CHAPTER 12

# The Changing Role of the Sales Force

*Sales and marketing are one! Your marketing vice presidents may
not like to accept this. Your sales vice presidents are probably too
indignant to join forces. But, for the good of your company, do it.*
—Nick Dibari

## Key Concepts

| | |
|---|---|
| Activity points | Prospecting |
| Buyer-seller dyad | Psychological testing |
| Call planning | Relational characteristics |
| Customer servicing | Roles and norms |
| Draw | Sales force structure |
| Expectancy model | Sales management |
| Incentive pay | Sales quota |
| Missionary selling | Selling aids |
| National account | Sliding scale commission |
| New prospect selling | Social actor characteristics |
| Order taker | Structural characteristics |
| Postsale stage | Technical selling |
| Preparation | Trade selling |
| Presentation | Workload method |

## Learning Objectives

1. Recognize the central role of personal selling in the promotional mix for industrial firms.

2. Appreciate the distinctive characteristics of personal selling in industrial markets.

3. Understand the dyadic perspective as it applies to sales force management in industrial markets and be able to draw implications from each dimension of the dyad.

4. Explain a logical process for managing the industrial sales effort.

5. Learn to apply a number of analytical tools and concepts that are useful in evaluating decision alternatives at each stage in the sales management process.

## Personal Selling Is the Cornerstone

Few industrial sales are closed solely as a result of advertising or sales promotion activities. Unlike most consumer purchases, the complexities of organizational buying often demand personal forms of communication—or personal selling—before, during, and after a purchase decision. Although the buyer in a consumer market frequently seeks out the supplier's product by visiting a particular store, the industrial seller normally seeks out the customer. The vendor's own sales force and/ or the selling efforts of intermediaries such as agents or distributors play the central role in the communications mix.

The sales force is the physical link between the selling and buying organizations. Not only do salespeople communicate information about the attributes of the vendor and its products or services to customers, but they also communicate information regarding customer problems or changing needs back to the vendor organization. In this manner, those in R&D, production, quality control, shipping, order processing, collections, and other key areas can adapt their operations to better serve the customer. Sales force inputs are critical in sales forecasting. In addition, the salesperson frequently serves to negotiate price and delivery terms, including discounts, return policies, shipment quantities and supplies, and transportation forms. Furthermore, the sales force often services customer accounts as well as providing demonstrations and training in the use of the vendor's products. In sum, an industrial salesperson can be characterized as playing at least four roles:

- ❖ Crusader for the company's cause

- ❖ Market researcher

- ❖ Negotiator

- ❖ Consultant or problem solver

Personal selling has been defined as an interpersonal communication process during which a seller uncovers and satisfies the needs of a buyer to the mutual, long-term benefit of both parties (Weitz, Castleberry, & Tanner, 1998). Selling is not manipulation. A salesperson can attempt to persuade, cajole, stimulate, encourage, and entice, but he or she cannot force customers to buy. This is especially true in industrial marketing, where the salesperson must behave professionally in all interactions with the client. If an industrial salesperson attempts to pressure or manipulate the buyer too forcefully, the outcome would almost certainly be a lost opportunity. Personal selling is important because it is a direct, immediate, and personalized form of communication, but one that requires an immediate response of some form from the buyer. In industrial markets, personal selling is a more expensive, but also a more effective, form of communication.

Industrial personal sales expenditures are frequently two to three times as high as those for consumer sales. These costs can be attributed to the technical nature of industrial products, the longer buying process, and the larger size of the buying center. Purchases often involve large dollar amounts for high volumes of products. Industrial customers are more involved with their purchases than the average consumer because the purchased items will directly affect the organization's operations, end products, and profits. Moreover, industrial buyers spend greater time, effort, and money making purchasing decisions than those in the consumer segment, and they are themselves technically qualified. Industrial markets also tend to be characterized by more direct, shorter channels, a situation that places increased responsibility on a vendor's own sales force (see Figure 12.1).

The average cost of a business-to-business sales call has risen from around $70 in the mid-1970s to more than $218 today ("What a Sales Call Costs," 1998), a rate of increase that has more than outpaced inflation. The rate of increase has slowed in recent years as companies have introduced efficiency measures into the sales management process. Computer technology and telemarketing have been major factors in cost control. It also appears that the cost per call is higher for companies with 10 or fewer salespeople and for those that sell directly rather than through distributors.

## Distinctive Requirements of Industrial Selling

If personal selling is the cornerstone of the marketing program, then it is important to appreciate the unique nature of industrial selling activities. Let us examine distinguishing characteristics of the selling task in three areas: the salesperson, selling aids, and the sales process.

### The Salesperson

Are industrial salespeople different from those who sell consumer goods and services? As a general statement, the training and skills required to successfully sell many

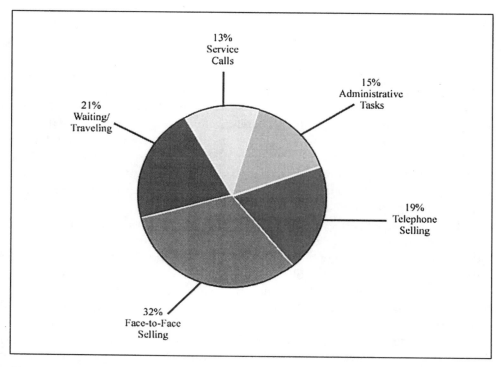

13%
Service
Calls

15%
Administrative
Tasks

21%
Waiting/
Traveling

19%
Telephone
Selling

32%
Face-to-Face
Selling

**Figure 12.1.** How Salespeople Spend Their Time

SOURCE: "1990 Survey of Selling Costs," *Sales and Marketing Management* (February 26, 1990), p. 81. © Copyright 1990 by *Sales and Marketing Management*.

industrial goods and services are distinctly different from those necessary for the consumer goods salesperson. Industrial selling requires a more technical background, usually obtained through a college education, corporate training, and/or practical experience. Many business-to-business sales representatives today also hold advanced degrees, such as the M.B.A. Salespeople must be able to communicate with a variety of people from many different backgrounds and orientations. They must be able to *speak the language* used in various functional areas (e.g., engineering, production, finance, purchasing) within the customer organization and adapt to a wide variety of selling situations. They often require the skills to build and harvest a long-term customer relationship. In addition, industrial salespersons must be able to effectively negotiate terms favorable to the supplier in a variety of business areas (e.g., payment terms, delivery, order quantities, returns, aftersale servicing).

It is just as important to recognize that there are different types of sales positions. One perspective is to define sales positions based on key activities performed, which produces five basic types of selling: trade selling, missionary selling, technical selling, new prospect selling, and customer servicing. These positions are not mutually exclusive; most sales jobs involve a mix of similar and different activities. Virtually all salespeople have jobs that entail some degree of selling, working with orders, servicing the product, information management, account servicing, conferences/

meetings, training, entertaining, travel, and partnering with distributors. Although a few "other" sales categories have been identified (such as order takers and trade servicers), let us focus on these five.

*Trade selling* is used when the vendor sells through intermediaries such as industrial distributors. The sales force works to ensure that distributors are supporting the company's marketing strategy and achieving its sales goals. Toward this end, salespeople call on distributors to explain how both they and the manufacturer will benefit from specific advertising, sales promotion, inventory, pricing, or product-assortment policies. The sales force also provides service to the distributor by assisting in such areas as product training, arranging financing, information requests, preparing job specifications and bids, expediting delivery, handling complaints, and processing goods the distributor may wish to return to the manufacturer. Occasionally, trade sellers supervise product installation and employee training at customer locations.

A *missionary salesperson* is one who goes through the selling process but does not actually close the sale. Rather, customers are called on and encouraged to purchase the vendor's products or services. The purchases are actually made from a distributor or products are ordered directly from the company. Missionary salespeople are primarily concerned with providing information about new or existing products and promoting goodwill. An example of a missionary salesperson is a pharmaceutical sales representative who calls on doctors.

*Technical selling* is one of the most common types of selling in industrial markets. A salesperson engaged in this type of selling has technical expertise and often holds a degree in either science or engineering. Frequently, however, such technical sales personnel have limited formal business training. Their focus is on providing customers with extensive technical information and advice, helping with product applications, and solving problems in the use or adaptation of the vendor's product to customer needs. Such technically qualified salespeople are often paid as much as 15% more than nontechnical salespeople and are likely to receive a larger portion of their earnings in the form of salary. One approach to technical selling is to form a *sales team*, which might consist of a nontechnical salesperson who makes the formal sales presentation, a financial expert, a production specialist, and the technical sales expert. This team approach allows the technical sales expert to concentrate on the product and its complex specifications and applications.

*New prospect selling* is what comes to mind when most people think of sales jobs. The focus is on the generation of new accounts, as opposed to increasing sales to existing accounts or supporting distributor sales. In new prospect selling, the salesperson makes "cold calls" on potential buyers or follows up on unsolicited inquiries and inquiries generated through other promotional efforts. The ability to penetrate new accounts, especially when they are buying from a competitor, typically requires highly developed selling skills.

The final type of selling position, *customer servicing*, involves activities that facilitate and complement the selling process. Here, the salesperson works directly with the end-user to ensure effective and satisfactory usage of the vendor's product. In such a role, he or she is a critical part of the relationship-building effort of the firm. Similar to the service function provided in trade selling to distributors, customer servicing includes handling complaints; assisting in training, installation, repair, and maintenance; and developing positive personal relationships. In addition, service reps will work trade shows and gather intelligence on customers and competitors. They are also frequently encouraged to sell supplies, service contracts, and product upgrades to customers.

## The Use of Selling Aids

When building a relationship with a particular customer, the industrial salesperson supplements regular calls with selling aids. These include small gifts, plant tours, business lunches, and other activities that are believed to support sales and maintain good standing with buyers.

Small gifts (e.g., paperweights, lighters, memo pads, rulers, inexpensive calculators, business card holders) may have the vendor's name on them and serve as a constant reminder to the prospect. Characteristics of effective gifts include usefulness, generality, permanence, conspicuousness, quality, tastefulness, and some apparent relationship between the gift and the vendor's product (Zinkhan & Vachris, 1984). Such small gifts generally are accepted, although a measure of tact is called for in their distribution. Many companies have policies that employees cannot accept substantial gifts from vendors. In recent years, the suppliers of these mainly inexpensive items have reported more than $4 billion in annual sales.

A buyer tour of the supplier's plant is another effective selling aid. Tours require the buyer to enter the seller's environment, as opposed to the norm in which the salesperson calls at the customer's location. A tour has the additional advantage of limiting the factors that may distract the prospect during a normal sales call, such as telephone calls or interruptions by other employees. This characteristic enhances the salesperson's ability to establish closer personal rapport. Finally, a plant tour educates the buyer about the vendor's people, production facilities, and quality control efforts. It also presents an opportunity to improve or solidify the buyer's image of the seller's product offering.

Entertainment activities also represent valuable tools for use by the industrial salesperson. Five of the more prevalent types of such activities include taking clients to lunch, for an evening meal, for a drink, or for leisure activities (e.g., professional sporting events or golf), as well as hosting parties for clients. These activities provide a neutral ground where the buyer and salesperson can discuss transactions or terms and become more personally acquainted. The business lunch is especially important. Compared to other entertainment options, a business lunch can be inexpensive.

## The Steps in Selling

The selling task is best accomplished by approaching it as a set of stages. In an industrial context, these stages have some distinctive characteristics. One perspective is to break the process into four major steps: prospecting, preparation, presentation, and postsale (see Table 12.1).

*Prospecting*, or identifying potential new accounts, is more involved than simply finding organizations that can use the vendor's product. The cost of a personal sales call is such that the sales manager must ensure that a given organization is a viable prospect. High customer switching costs, deep-seated loyalties to other vendors, small potential orders, excessive service level demands, and an inefficient location are but a few of the many reasons to avoid particular potential customers. Prospecting is conducted more today through telemarketing, referrals from current customers, and inquiries generated by information request cards, through toll-free telephone numbers included in print media advertisements, and at trade shows (see Table 12.2). Cold calls are also used, but they are an inefficient means for finding customers, given the type of product that is usually being sold and the manner in which industrial products are purchased.

An advance in the management of sales leads is the use of specialized software developed to qualify, or classify, prospective customers. Until qualified, leads are considered worthless to salespeople. The goal of qualification is to determine if the

**TABLE 12.1** The Personal Selling Process

**Prospecting**
> External sources
> Internal sources
> Personal contact
> Miscellaneous (e.g. trade shows/seminars)

**Preparation**
> Make appointment
> Investigate prospect's industry and market
> Prospect research (Web page/annual report)
> Determine approach/goals

**Presentation**

*Approach*
> Introduce yourself
> Compliment prospect
> Find common interests

*Presentation*
> Open discussion with questions
> Help prospect visualize offering
> Demonstrate product/service
> Discuss benefits to be gained

*Addressing concerns*
> Direct-response method
> Cost/benefit method
> Demonstration method
> "Yes, but" method
> Testimonial method

*Closing the sale*
> Direct close
> Summary close
> Minor point close
> Contract close

**Postsale Follow-Up**
> Customer training
> Reassure the customer
> Follow up all actions
> Billing concerns
> Adjustments/returns
> Installation maintenance
> Curiosity inquiries
> Relationship building interaction

**TABLE 12.2**  Where the Customers Are

A recent survey asked sales executives the question, "How would you rate the best prospecting techniques to find new customers?" Participants rated the viability of the following techniques by using a scale of 1 to 5, where 1 is *not important* and 5 is *very important*. The averages are shown below.

| Most Effective Techniques to Attract New Customers | Rating |
| --- | --- |
| Referrals | 4.8 |
| One-to-one marketing | 4.5 |
| Direct mail | 3.8 |
| Trade shows | 3.2 |
| Cold calls | 1.5 |

SOURCE: The Nierenberg Group and New York University's Management Institute. See Nierenberg (2000b).

prospective buyer is a key decision maker, if the buyer's needs fit the vendor's product, and if the buyer has the potential willingness and ability to buy. Whether the inquiry comes over the phone, via modem, or by mail (e.g., reader response cards), sophisticated lead processing systems are capable of significantly reducing qualifying time, sometimes to as little as 24 hours. These systems range in price from under $100 to more than $100,000. Top-notch systems are capable of identifying market trends, locating and developing profitable markets, enhancing sales forecast accuracy, and measuring media effectiveness.

*Preparation* for a sales call can involve extensive research. The salesperson wants to develop a feel for the nature of a customer organization's needs in a particular product or service area and the way in which that customer would apply the vendor's product. Research on an organization's buying process is equally important. The salesperson is attempting to determine which members of a prospective customer organization are influential in the salesperson's product area, as well as which ones are accessible. Furthermore, an effort should be made to determine which individuals cannot be ignored and which ones will require larger quantities of the salesperson's time. Personal information about these individuals is extremely useful.

In addition to identifying key personnel, the salesperson wants to become acquainted with the policies and procedures used by the prospective customer organization in purchase decision making, such as those governing the setting of specifications, bid solicitation, supplier selection, and rules that guide the behavior of purchasing agents (free lunches, gifts). Preparation for a sales call may be further enhanced by learning as much as possible about the organization, including the organization's history, which competitors it has purchased from previously, and current trends and common trade practices of the industry in which the customer operates.

## BUSINESS MARKETING CAPSULE

### Sales Force Certification

Salesforce certification programs were initiated to improve the professional image of both salespersons and sales managers. Two national organizations, the Sales and Marketing Executives-International (SME-I) and the National Association of Sales Persons (NASP), currently certify salespersons in the United States. The programs, which enforce similar standards, require proof that the applicant has acquired specific formal educational and practical sales experience, passed a written exam, provided references, and agreed to adhere to a stated code of ethics. The certified program objectives are to (a) maintain professionalism and expertise, (b) encourage self-improvement through continuing education, and (c) recognize professional expertise.

In a survey of sales and marketing managers, respondents reported that a certified salesperson was more credible (66%), that customers would purchase higher amounts and be more source loyal (38%), that certified salespersons should be hired over noncertified applicants (45%), and that certified applicants should receive higher pay (38%). The same managers did not feel that certified salespersons were more ethical (71%) or that they should receive faster promotion (68%).

Certification programs provide salespersons with a differential advantage: initial credibility. Managers can be assured that the certified salesperson possesses minimum qualifications for performing the job. Although certification provides the salesperson with initial credibility, sales and marketing managers prefer to reserve judgment about pay and promotion until they see the effects of certification in performance on the job. It is quite likely that buyers may also be initially impressed by certified salespersons, but the salesperson will have to work hard to meet the heightened expectations of the buyer!

SOURCE: Adapted from "Sales Force Certification," *Journal of Personal Selling and Sales Management*, 16 (3), pp. 59-65, Honeycutt, Attia, and D'Auria. © Copyright 1996 by the *Journal of Personal Selling & Sales Management*.

Major differences in the *presentation* itself include the probability that one presentation will not result in a sale. In fact, it takes 4 to 4.5 calls to close an average industrial sale (Cardozo & Shipp, 1987). Multiple presentations are necessary because of the lengthy buying decision process and because the content will have to be tailored to different members of the customer organization. It is also important to remember that the buyer in an industrial transaction is a professional and is likely to be wary of the salesperson who is too eager to close the sale, who tries to oversell the prospect, or who is unlikely to be around if problems develop when using the purchased item. Recent studies have found that trust between the buyer and seller is essential for forming long-lasting relations. That is, the presentation is an opportunity to communicate and learn what is necessary for a win-win situation. A salesperson who

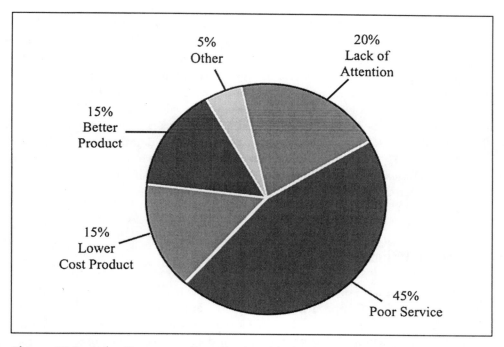

**Figure 12.2.** Why Customers Stop Buying: It's the Service, Not the Product or Price

SOURCE: *Eliminating Barriers to Service Excellence*, Carroll. © Copyright 1997 by The Forum Corporation.

tries to use high pressure to sell the buyer a product that is not needed or is inappropriate for the buying situation probably will not succeed. Some firms have investigated certification of their salespeople as one way to increase customer trust.

The *postsale* stage of the process is of special consequence for the industrial marketer. Once a sale is closed, the salesperson continues to work with the customer in such areas as installation, training, servicing, maintenance, and returns—attempting to establish and solidify a loyal relationship. The salesperson is now better informed regarding the customer's purchasing decision process and is in a position to reinforce key buying influences while establishing more personal relationships. He or she is alert to new opportunities that might arise with the account. The vital importance of postsale service can be seen in Figure 12.2.

## Sales Management Activities

Sales management refers to the planning, implementation, and control of personal contact activities designed to achieve the sales objectives of the firm. Industrial sales managers are concerned with recruiting, training, organizing, motivating, evaluating, and compensating the sales force.

These managerial activities must reflect a number of unique characteristics of the industrial marketplace. For example, recruiting and training efforts must stress the ability of an individual to communicate and negotiate over complex product benefits with different individuals from diverse backgrounds within a given organization. This diversity takes the form of a wide range of social and intellectual sophistication among the people involved. The organization of the sales force should reflect the fewer absolute number of customers, the time required to close a sale, and the specific activities each salesperson is required to perform, in addition to more traditional considerations. Motivation, evaluation, and compensation must reflect the dollar value of purchases, the extended buying process, and the desirability of establishing long-term buyer-seller relations, among other factors.

## A Two-Way or Relationship Perspective on Selling

A marketing transaction is never a one-way street. It is not simply the marketer using various tools and approaches to get the buyer to respond in the desired way. Rather, both parties to the transaction seek benefits, and both determine the outcome of the transaction. To properly understand and manage exchanges of industrial goods and services, the seller and the buyer should be examined together, because they affect one other. This is called the dyadic approach, where a dyad is a unit of two (see Chapter 4). The focus is on the dynamics that take place between the buyer and the seller rather than on examining buyer or seller activities in isolation.

Among all the elements contained in the marketing mix, the dyadic approach has its greatest usefulness when applied to personal selling—where the two-person or two-party interaction is most predominant. There are four key dimensions to a dyadic relationship: organizational relationships, structural positions of the players, characteristics of the people involved, and roles and rules of the game. These four interact to determine the outcomes of the industrial marketing exchange process. Table 12.3 provides examples of questions a sales manager might raise, based on the dimensions of the buyer-seller dyad. Let us now look at each of these dimensions in further detail.

### Organizational Relationships

As with any two-party relationship, the buyer-seller dyad can be characterized by the relative power positions of each party. Power is a function of dependency. The power that organization A has over organization B is a function of how dependent B is on A. Organization B's dependency is determined by how much it needs the resources controlled by organization A and how available these resources are from alternative sources. For example, if organization A manufactures a critical component

**TABLE 12.3**  Applying the Dyadic Perspective to Sales Management

| Characteristics of the Seller-Buyer Dyad | Relevant Sales Management Questions |
|---|---|
| Organizational relationships | 1. How dependent are we on this customer?<br>2. How dependent are they on us?<br>3. What are the sources of our respective dependencies?<br>4. What are the implications of the power balance (or imbalance) for negotiation strategies?<br>5. Where are the major sources of conflict between us? |
| Structural positions | 1. How centralized and formalized is the buying process? Does our sales approach reflect this degree of centralization and formalization?<br>2. At what level in the organizational hierarchy are key buying decision makers?<br>3. What functional areas play a key role in buying decisions?<br>4. What is the level, title, and functional background of our sales representative?<br>5. Are differences in the structural or status positions of buyer and seller representatives significant enough to affect decision outcomes? |
| Characteristics of the people involved | 1. What are the demographic and personality characteristics of members of the decision-making process in the buying organization? What is their experience level? What is their history of rewards?<br>2. What are the demographic and personality characteristics of our sales representative? What is his or her experience level?<br>3. To what extent are seller and buyer representatives similar or dissimilar?<br>4. In what areas are they similar or dissimilar, and how might this relationship affect their interactions? |
| Roles, norms, and rules of the game | 1. Are there certain rules of the game or unwritten norms that determine acceptable and unacceptable tactics on the part of the seller and buyer?<br>2. What are our expectations of the roles that representatives of the buying organization are to fill in their dealings with us?<br>3. What are their expectations of our sales representative in terms of his or her actions and authority?<br>4. Are there differences between our perceptions and their perceptions of roles and norms? |

part needed by organization B and has an exclusive patent preventing anyone else from making a similar component, then A's power (or B's dependency) is high. Power, however, is always a two-way street. Both parties involved in an industrial transaction need, or are dependent on, each other. The buyer needs a source of supply, and the seller needs a profitable sale. The real concern is with the power balance: Which party needs the other more?

Some other factors that determine power positions include reciprocity arrangements between buyer and seller (where each is buying from and selling to the other), supply shortages in a particular market, purchasing a disproportionate amount of one's total needs from a single supplier, selling a significant amount of one's total output to a single customer, the service level requirements of a just-in-time inventory arrangement, proximity to a particular supplier or buyer, and financial or physical plant constraints.

Power positions of the buyer and seller are likely to evolve and change over time. For example, a supply shortage may be a temporary phenomenon that enhances the position of the seller. Entry of a new competitor or changes in technology, however, may reduce the seller's bargaining position. A serious mistake can result from efforts to pursue sales tactics that reflect a current power advantage but fail to consider potential future changes in relative power positions.

In addition to power/dependency, relationship characteristics also include any conflicts between the organizational capabilities or requirements of the two parties. If the seller must have minimum orders of a certain amount, or the buyer requires a 2-year fixed price agreement, and these restrictions are at odds with the interests of the other party, the outcome of the exchange relationship is in serious jeopardy. It must be recognized that such conflicts affect the costs and benefits of each of the two organizations doing business with the other. The sales manager can best manage these conflicts by identifying costs and benefits to each party of various conflict resolution approaches, and by working toward those solutions that best serve the objective of establishing and maintaining a profitable and mutually beneficial dyadic relationship.

## Structural Positions of the Players in Their Organizations

The salesperson is not selling to an organization, but rather to specific representatives of an organization. The representatives hold formal positions in their organization, as well as both formal and informal positions in the purchasing decision process. A significant determinant of the seller-buyer interaction is the relative "horizontal gap" and "vertical gap" between the positions of the seller and buyer representatives in their respective organizations. A horizontal gap might exist where the salesperson is dealing with people from different functional areas that have very different backgrounds, such as a nontechnical sales rep interacting with a highly qualified engineer or finance expert. These different groups have distinct languages, goals, and values. Alternatively, where the salesperson is at a fairly junior level in the sales organization but is making a presentation to the chief of R&D or the senior VP for finance, a significant vertical gap exists. This second type of structural gap might be one reason some firms upgrade their sales representative's title to senior account executive or something equivalent. Status differences can undermine credibility and affect the nature of the interaction. The perception that the salesperson is able to simplify the buying task and save the buyer time and effort is directly a function of respective social structural positions.

Furthermore, the salesperson must determine the interdependencies among various representatives of the buying organization. How, for example, does the purchasing department interact with human resources, production, design engineering, and finance in arriving at a purchase decision? On the other side of the relationship, the buyer is looking beyond the salesperson at the set of interdependencies within the seller firm. How does the salesperson interact with personnel in production, design engineering, or finance to satisfy the buyer's requirements? A buyer is often searching for a salesperson who has influence within the vendor organization and who will be an advocate within the selling firm for the buyer's needs.

Another structural variable is the extent of formalization, centralization, standardization, and complexity in the customer's purchasing operation. More formalized, standardized, or centralized buying processes may limit the salesperson's flexibility. At the same time, these characteristics can simplify the salesperson's job of identifying decision makers and decision criteria.

The salesperson should, in addition, attempt to identify any differences between the customer's formal policies and structure and the manner in which things are actually done. For example, when selling the plastic connectors used in splicing together telephone lines, 3M found that the telephone companies often have formal policies of specifying approved vendors at the head office. It appears that the sales effort should, correspondingly, focus on the decision makers in the head office, yet 3M effectively penetrated this market by sending salespeople out to work with repairmen who were actually doing the splicing in the manholes. These users then routinely specified 3M in their requisitions, and the head office went along.

The dyadic perspective also suggests a need to design and structure the marketing and sales effort to reflect the buyer's requirements. The decisions to organize the sales force around products rather than markets, to employ or not employ team selling, to use sales engineers, or to have decentralized distribution points, among others, can be as important in determining the outcome of the dyadic relationship as are the policies and structure of the purchasing organization.

## Characteristics of the People Involved

An examination of the personal characteristics of the individuals who get involved on both sides of the transaction can also be helpful in understanding the dynamics of the relationship. Here, the focus is on the personalities, physical resources, personal goals and standards, and history of the seller and buyer representatives involved in the transaction. The outcomes of face-to-face contact depend not on the characteristics of either party alone but on how the two parties view and react to one another.

Interpersonal attraction between the salesperson and prospect can be an important ingredient in building relationships and making sales. One stream of thought is that people are attracted to those who are like themselves, so similarity between the sales force and prospects should be emphasized. Unfortunately, this is often impractical and, if employed, can be costly. The problem lies in determining (a) the types of buying situations in which similarity is important and (b) the dimension(s) on which the two parties should be similar. Certainly there are buying situations where the other dimensions of the dyad play an overriding role and characteristics of the people themselves are less important. In terms of the second problem, the ways in which buyer and seller might be similar are virtually limitless. A few examples include age, experience, educational background, lifestyle, race, gender, and personal goals. Also, there may be situations where the sales manager wants to emphasize differences between salesperson and prospect, based on the idea that opposites attract.

One implication is that the sales approach should be tailored to the audience, not limited to the canned presentations relied on by some companies. Ability to recognize the salient characteristics and personal needs of a prospect, and to empathize in terms of his or her own behavior, become important characteristics of the salesperson. Also, from a sales management vantage point, the industrial firm might attempt to hire salespeople with characteristics similar to those of major customer segments (e.g., a person with an agricultural background to sell farm machinery to farmer cooperatives). This approach becomes unrealistic where a company is selling to a widely diverse audience. Many sales managers have come to realize that an important skill needed by successful industrial salespersons is an ability to *adapt to the customer.*

Gender is a personal characteristic of salespeople that has received considerable attention in recent years. Women have encountered difficulties attempting to find sales positions for certain industrial products because of traditional biases that selling is a man's game, or that male buyers prefer to deal with male salespeople. Women continue to be underrepresented in the industrial sales force, constituting about 22% in the 1990 census (Siguaw & Honeycutt, 1995). Furthermore, about 80% of industrial buyers are male, and they often do not accept female salespeople as openly as they accept males. The business marketing capsule on gender differences highlights some of the areas in which women are perceived differently from men by industrial buyers. Such outmoded stereotypes ignore the growing pool of women with technical qualifications and selling skills equal or superior to those of their male counterparts, and they do not make economic sense. That is, performance is maximized when companies hire the best-qualified applicant.

## Roles and Rules of the Game

The fourth dimension of two-way relationships is concerned with the norms, laws, rules, or guidelines that govern the manner in which the sales force and repre-

## BUSINESS MARKETING CAPSULE

### *Are There Gender Differences?*

As women have entered industrial sales in significant numbers, many companies have devised separate selection, training, and motivation programs for women. In a survey of industrial salespersons who were members of the Association for Information and Image Management, some surprising results were reported. First, women reported a lower incidence of role conflict and role ambiguity than men. Second, there were no reported differences in self-assessed performance between men and women. Third, women reported they were more adaptive and market oriented than men.

Based upon these findings, it was recommended that sales managers should (a) consider women for additional sales positions, (b) not provide special considerations of training programs for women to socialize them into the industrial sales force, and (c) take actions to expunge existing stereotypes of women as being less effective sales force members. The study concluded that where differences were noted, women were found to be more favorable on those attributes.

SOURCE: Adapted from "An Examination of Gender Differences in Selling Behaviors and Job Attitudes," *Industrial Marketing Management*, 24 (February, 1995), pp. 45-52, Siguaw and Honeycutt. © Copyright 1995 by *Industrial Marketing Management*.

sentatives of the buying organization interact. Many of these so-called rules are not formal or written, but are simply understood. As a case in point, some purchasing agents may believe that playing different vendors off one another to gain a better price or delivery arrangement is an inappropriate tactic. In some circumstances, the vendor who engages in such behavior may be violating accepted norms in the industry and will find that vendors are actually less willing to cooperate. Another possible rule violation might involve the salesperson who circumvents the purchasing agent and attempts to sell directly to a production manager, or who is too eager to try and close a sale. Giving gifts, taking a prospect to lunch or for a drink, and giving parties for purchase decision makers represent other actions for which the buying and/or selling organizations may have stated or unstated policies.

The normative dimension is also concerned with what might be called "role definitions." People are filling a role when they act as a buyer or seller for their organization. Each party has certain expectations regarding the behavior of the other. The buyer who is purchasing a new truck is likely to open the hood and examine the motor, in spite of knowing very little about truck engines. People engage in this behavior because they perceive it to be part of their role as a buyer. More than likely, they think the salesperson expects them to act in this way. In the same vein, the industrial buyer may feel compelled to negotiate a slightly lower price, even if the quoted price is actually acceptable. The salesperson may feel that he or she has to be aggressive, or has to compliment the buyer, also because it is expected. Some relevant questions for the industrial salesperson include the following: What does the other party expect of me? What do I expect of myself? What do I expect of him or her? How might his or her own self-expectations differ from mine? By recognizing such dyadic complexities, the salesperson can more clearly understand his or her role in the exchange process.

Three role concepts are relevant here: role ambiguity, role consensus, and role fulfillment. *Role ambiguity* results from an unclear understanding of the specific responsibilities that constitute the role. This uncertainty can result when it is unclear how much authority a purchasing agent has in making a company's buying decision, or how much authority a salesperson has in negotiating a company's price or delivery terms. *Role consensus* refers to the degree to which buyer and seller representatives agree on their respective roles. *Role fulfillment* concerns how satisfied the buyer or seller representatives are with the way the other party fulfilled his or her role. Inadequate role consensus or role fulfillment can undermine the dyad and, under certain conditions, result in an end to the buyer-seller relationship.

## A Negotiated Social Process

The relative importance of each of the dimensions of the relationship will vary depending on the buying situation. Buyer and seller personal characteristics may be irrelevant because of the buyer's and seller's power relationship or their respective social structural positions. Conversely, in a given power dependency situation, buyer-seller similarity may assume even greater importance.

Combining these four dimensions provides a more complete picture of the dynamic and intricate nature of the buyer-seller relationship. As noted, it is a mistake to examine the customer organization in isolation. A real understanding of what happens when the sales force works with buyer representatives over the stages of the buying process requires that we consider both parties as they see and affect one another. The sales transaction ultimately becomes a "negotiated social process whereby people interact, explore their thoughts and feelings, exchange information, and perhaps evolve to new or novel positions and relationships" (Bonoma, Bagozzi, & Zaltman, 1978, p. 62).

## Managing the Industrial Sales Force

Let us now turn to a more detailed discussion of sales force management. Although the role of the sales manager varies from company to company, it is not unusual for sales managers to become involved in product innovation, research, strategic planning, budgeting, pricing, channel management, advertising and sales promotion, production, and plant location decisions. Some firms assign all marketing responsibility to the sales manager; however, the more traditional aspects of this position, and the focus points here, concern organizing, staffing, training, motivating, supporting, and evaluating the sales force.

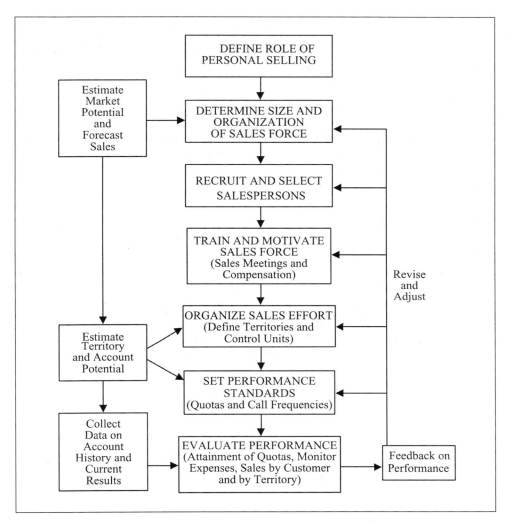

**Figure 12.3.** The Sales Management Process

SOURCE: *Sales Management*, p. 3, Dalrymple and Cron. © Copyright 1998 by John Wiley & Sons.

Figure 12.3 illustrates the sales management process, which begins with determining the role of personal selling. As discussed in the previous chapter, personal selling is part of the promotional mix, which is, in turn, a component of the marketing mix. The sales program must support the firm's strategic marketing plan. Sales objectives should be compatible with the organization's overall marketing objectives. The marketing plan will provide the sales manager with direction in attempting to define what the sales force should accomplish. Does the purpose lie in establishing new accounts, servicing current accounts, supporting distributors, or some other area? Are sales made apart from the sales force, or are salespeople the centerpiece of the promotional mix? To what extent should a company rely on intermediaries rather than its own sales force? With the answers to these questions in hand, the sales manager must then determine how many salespeople to employ and how they should be organized.

## Sales Force Size and Organization

The number of people that should constitute a company's sales force is affected by a number of issues, including the workload to be accomplished, the marginal productivity of one more salesperson, and the rate of turnover among the sales force. Let us examine how this decision might be approached by using a hypothetical example.

Consider the development of a new piece of computer equipment to monitor patients' vital signs during a hospital stay. The initial plan is to market the product to hospitals throughout Portugal. Assume that there are 300 hospitals within the country, of which 50 are large (400 or more beds). To effectively sell to large hospitals, it has been estimated that they must be called on at least once a month. The smaller facilities can be called on every 2 months. The average call consumes 2 hours, including travel and waiting time. The company estimates that the typical salesperson has about 1,330 hours available per year to make sales calls. This total is based on 190 days and 7 hours per day. Using these data estimates, the requisite size of the sales force is 4.06 (or about 4) people. The calculation is based on the following formula:

$$\frac{\text{Number of accounts (current and potential)} \times \text{Ideal call frequency per account} \times \text{Average call length}}{\text{Selling time available per salesperson}} = \text{Required number of people}$$

Or when using the numbers from the example:

$$\frac{(50 \text{ large accounts} \times 12 \text{ annual visits} \times 2 \text{ hours per visit}) + (350 \text{ small accounts} \times 6 \text{ annual visits} \times 2 \text{ hours per visit})}{190 \text{ days} \times 7 \text{ hours}} = \frac{5,400 \text{ hours}}{1,330 \text{ hours}} = 4(4.06) \text{ salespersons}$$

This workload method ignores the costs and profits involved and assumes a standard level of customer service for each category of customer (e.g., large and small hospitals). The sales manager can vary service levels by changing call frequency or call length for different types of customers.

A different method finds managers focusing on the marginal productivity of additions to the sales force. That is, in determining the size of the sales force, the manager attempts to estimate a response function for additional expenditures on personnel. As more salespeople are assigned to a territory, do sales increase by more than the cost? Are sales increasing at an increasing or decreasing rate with each additional salesperson? Historical data for company sales, sales per representative, and number of representatives can provide insights regarding the marginal productivity of each additional person. In practice, such productivity estimates can be difficult to calculate. The sales manager often must make assumptions based on his or her best judgment.

In addition, the sales manager will probably want to factor in the sales force turnover rate. Turnover results in lost sales, disaffected customers, termination costs, and additional expenditures to hire and train new people. The turnover rate is equal to the number of separations per year divided by the average size of the total sales force.

Hand in hand with the question of how many people to hire is the problem of organizing the sales force. Common approaches include organizing by task, product, customer type, geographic area, or some combination of these. For instance, if the sales manager wishes to ensure that critical marketing functions are performed well, it may be worthwhile to have different salespeople specialize in certain tasks. Individuals might be assigned to outside sales, inside sales, new account development, account maintenance, or distributor support. This type of allocation constitutes a functional structure and is appropriate when little diversity exists in the company's products or markets.

When the firm sells a mix of products with distinctive characteristics, user applications, and selling requirements (i.e., products with little in common), it may make sense to assign different salespeople to individual products or product groupings. Here, products receive individual attention, and those that are harder to sell or have lower margins are not ignored by the sales force. A problem arises, though, in that product-oriented structures tend to produce duplication of effort. If a customer is a potential user of a number of products, then several salespeople might call on this organization and/or send key decision makers overlapping sales promotion materials.

Alternatively, the sales manager often finds that the market includes customer groups with divergent needs. For example, the ways in which the marketer's products are used, the nature of the purchasing decision process, or the service level requirements of various customer groups may be sufficiently different to warrant assigning a number of salespeople to each customer category. The sales force might be divided, then, based on large versus small accounts, or according to governmental, institutional, and commercial accounts, or by customer SIC or NAICS code, among many other possibilities. In this manner, the sales manager can better serve the needs and requirements of a particular type of customer and can provide more timely service to these accounts. Specializing based on customer needs is especially relevant when selling in dynamic competitor and customer environments found in most industrial markets today.

Assignment of specific salespeople to national accounts (e.g., to Hilton Hotels or Unilever) is also commonly practiced. National accounts are both large and complex customers that are located at geographically dispersed buying points. They often have buying influences dispersed among various functional areas, as well as across various operating units within the company. The selling effort must, correspondingly, cut across multiple levels, functions, and operating units. Formal national account programs are often developed to support this part of the sales force.

Perhaps the most popular approach to organizing the sales force is the use of geographic territories. Salespeople are assigned to regions, trading areas, states, MSAs (metropolitan statistical areas), municipalities, or some other logical geographical breakdown. This method generates more intense coverage of a territory and promotes more efficiency in travel expenditures and time. Geographic structures can, at the same time, require more spending on overhead, including the cost of branch, district, and region managers. This type of coverage is useful, however, when selling industrial products in large national and international markets.

A combination territory structure can involve any or all of the above approaches. The company may have salespeople assigned to specific products (e.g. hydraulic pumps) or customer types (e.g., textile mills) within a given geographic locale (the northern half of Portugal). The combination approach allows the sales manager to realize the attributes of more than a single structural approach at one time. In this example, the benefits of both a product structure (i.e., emphasis on the unique characteristics of individual product groups) and a geographic structure (i.e., thorough market coverage) can be achieved.

## Recruiting and Selecting Salespeople

Sales force selection is both difficult and risky. A number of studies suggest that the majority of college graduates possess negative attitudes toward sales careers. Worse yet, relatively few college graduates consider a career in industrial sales (Honeycutt, Ford, Lupton, & Flaherty, 1999). Hiring high-quality salespeople, which normally involves a multistage screening process, is the most critical decision area facing the sales manager. The first step of the hiring process is to develop a job description and job qualifications based on a detailed analysis of what constitutes a given job. This description can vary considerably among different types of positions (e.g., order taker compared with technical sales representative). Establishing the job qualifications can be extremely difficult—further suggesting a need for sales managers to develop a clear definition of successful personal selling performance.

Managers, like most people, look for simple decision rules to aid in decision making when confronted with a difficult and recurring problem. The job of selecting individuals as company salespeople is just such a problem. As a result, over the years, companies have attempted to identify the characteristics of a successful salesperson and then look for potential employees who possess those characteristics. Psychological tests and other rating devices that attempt to measure and weight such factors as age, education, interests, longevity in other jobs, personality traits, past performance, and personal goals are often used to identify desirable prospects or to eliminate candidates who do not fit a minimum profile.

Such hiring tools have produced questionable results because of the difficulties in identifying and measuring the set of factors that indicate whether a person will be successful in a particular selling job. The complexities of human nature, combined with the considerable diversity among industrial products and buying organizations, raise serious questions about the ability of a single test to determine the characteristics of the best person for a job. Likewise, every sales position differs in some way from every other.

Where companies have been successful in this area, it is usually because they have tailored the tests or rating method to their industry, customer needs and expectations, and products or services. This tailoring requires the development of a fairly extensive database that includes information on a large number of variables for previously successful and unsuccessful salespeople. Even after developing a valid tool or methodology, there must be flexibility in interpreting how an individual is rated, or qualified candidates will slip through the cracks because they fail to meet a specific criterion. Sales managers must ensure that these characteristics predict success on the job, rather than using such tools to eliminate sales candidates against whom they are personally biased.

Effective hiring practices can also be aided by the creation of a database that monitors employment referrals. The sales manager will want to track sources of leads regarding potential employees (e.g., recruiting at colleges and other schools, job fairs, employment agencies, advertisements, recommendations from present employees, referrals from suppliers or customers). Data are kept on which leads resulted in new hires and the performance of these employees. In this fashion the manager develops intuition, based on the results of previous hires, concerning where to concentrate future recruiting efforts.

## Training the Sales Force

Once an individual has been selected to join the company's sales force, a variety of employee training issues must be addressed. Training represents one of the more expensive outlays in operating a company sales force. Depending on the type of sales position in question, the total training cost per recruit can range from $15,000 to $50,000, with average costs around $25,000. When effective training is not conducted, the outcome is often early termination or resignation. Turnover rates vary widely among industries, but retaining between 50 and 70% of new recruits beyond 2 years is considered good performance by many companies.

Lack of formal training can result in salesperson frustration and underachievement. New recruits, whether they have sales experience or not, require training to become socialized in the organization's way of doing things. It is also important that the expectations of the firm are clearly communicated, and the recruits must become effective at selling. In a good training program, the salesperson develops a knowledge of company operations and policies, products and product lines, the competition, the customer organization (needs, operations, buying processes), and the customer's product(s). One study reported that industrial firms devoted most of their training program to product knowledge (43%), followed by sales techniques (25%), market information (14%), company information (12%), and "other" information (2%) (Honeycutt, Howe, & Ingram, 1993). Time management (including call frequency,

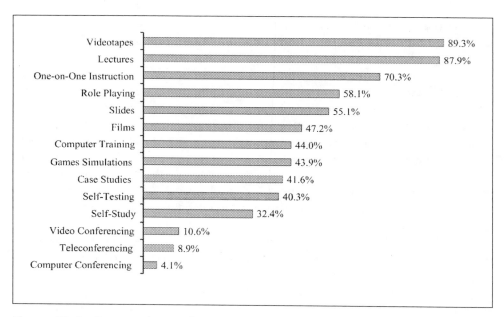

**Figure 12.4.** Commonly Used Training and Instructional Methods

SOURCE: "1990 Survey of Selling Costs," *Sales and Marketing Management* (February 26, 1990), p. 96. © Copyright 1990 by *Sales and Marketing Management*. Reprinted with permission.

duration, and scheduling) is another issue addressed in many of the better training programs.

Sales training can take place in a formal classroom atmosphere or in the field. In the classroom setting, the teaching methods often include lectures, role playing, demonstrations, and group discussion (see Figure 12.4). Field, or on-the-job (OJT), training alternatively provides the recruit with hands-on experience, where learning is achieved through observation and participation in actual selling situations. The initial classroom training for many industrial firms typically lasts either 1 or 2 weeks, while the average length of the sales training period in industrial firms is close to 4 months (Honeycutt et al., 1993). Continuous refresher training is also becoming necessary to keep the sales force abreast of policy changes or new products and applications, as well as to improve existing selling skills. To accomplish this, industrial firms use videotapes, audio tapes, brochures, web-based courses, and satellite broadcasts.

It is also extremely important to provide specialized training for sales personnel who are assigned to international positions. For example, should expatriate managers be provided with language and culture training? If so, to what level of expertise? Knowledgeable observers recommend that all global salespersons be trained about the culture in which they will work, how to sell in international settings, product and performance information, local market conditions, and company policies. To reduce early requests to return home, it may also be helpful to include the salesperson's family in culture and language training (Honeycutt & Ford, 1995).

**TABLE 12.4** Money Talks

When asked which factors would most likely convince men and women to continue working for their current employer, increased compensation was the clear front-runner.

|  | Men (%) | Women (%) |
|---|---|---|
| A raise | 40 | 47 |
| Improved benefits | 25 | 21 |
| More flexible schedule | 11 | 17 |
| Stock options | 12 | 5 |
| Better training | 5 | 5 |
| Don't know | 7 | 5 |

SOURCE: Market Facts for BridgeGatee (www.marketfacts.com/).

## Motivating the Sales Force

Although effective sales training can produce the skills and knowledge needed to succeed, a greater challenge (and many would argue the greatest challenge of all) concerns finding ways to produce highly motivated salespersons. A poorly motivated sales force member is costly to the firm in terms of unsatisfactory performance, excessive turnover, increased expenses, increased use of the sales manager's time, and negative impact on the morale of fellow employees.

Motivation, from a sales management perspective, represents an individual's desire or drive to perform the *specific* selling-related tasks that the manager deems necessary to accomplish the organization's sales objectives. Our interest in motivation is thus more accurately stated as a concern with a salesperson's drive to call on new versus existing accounts, to call more frequently, to perform customer service activities, or to provide managers with detailed customer feedback in the form of sales reports, among other forms of information.

One of the more practical approaches to explaining a salesperson's motivation is called the expectancy model (Porter & Lawler, 1968; Vroom, 1964). Simply stated, this model posits that motivation is determined by (a) how much a person perceives a direct relationship between the effort he or she puts forth and successful performance on the organization's measurement or evaluation system, (b) how much that person perceives a direct relationship between good performance and rewards, and (c) whether the organization is offering the correct rewards. The expectancy model is illustrated in Figure 12.5.

In an actual selling situation, the specific tasks on which the manager desires the salesperson to expend effort may include any of those mentioned above, and possibly others. Salespeople are often unclear, however, as to the priority they should assign to different tasks and exactly what is expected of them. The performance

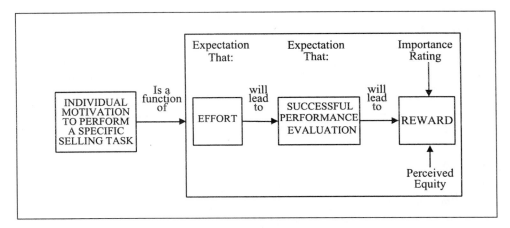

**Figure 12.5.** Expectancy Framework for Explaining Salesperson Motivation

measurement system refers to management's formal method of evaluating a salesperson's work output. This might be something as simple as a sales goal or quota, or as involved as a multiple-item rating scale subjectively completed by the manager. Rewards refer to the benefit or gain the employee receives in return for his or her work efforts. Rewards can be extrinsic or intrinsic, but the principal concern is with those rewards that managers control or can affect. Examples include regular pay, bonuses, job security, an expense account, a company car, a promotion, a particular territory, recognition (plaque, pat on the back), or even a nice office (although today many salespeople work from a "virtual office," relying on a laptop computer with a fax modem, cell phone, and beeper to allow them to conduct business from anywhere).

The flow diagram presented in Figure 12.5 helps identify some reasons a salesperson might *not* be motivated. The first linkage in the model is between effort and management's evaluation of performance. If the salesperson feels that the sales quota has been set unrealistically high and cannot be achieved, then he or she may be unmotivated. Or the salesperson working on a straight commission may be unmotivated to spend significant time on account servicing when the performance evaluation system stresses sales, not servicing. Alternatively, if the salesperson feels that the evaluation system is biased, providing the same evaluation regardless of the effort expended toward a particular task, then motivation concerning that task is unlikely. In addition, the task or the evaluation system may simply be too vague or ambiguous.

The second linkage in Figure 12.5 involves identifying reasons salespeople might not see a relationship between doing well on the performance evaluation system and receiving a reward. Managers often ask for one type of behavior but actually reward a different behavior. One possibility is the situation where the reward (perhaps a fixed salary) will be earned whether or not effort is put forth toward a particular task (e.g., calling on new accounts). The salesperson facing this circumstance has little motivation to spend a lot of time on new accounts. Another possibility would be the salesperson who perceives other ways to earn the reward (perhaps a bonus) rather than putting effort toward the task in question (again, calling on new accounts). Perhaps he or she feels that the bonus can be achieved by currying favor with the boss. Effort then is expended toward this activity rather than toward new account development.

Finally, even if the salesperson sees a link between effort and performance, as well as between performance and reward, he or she may be unmotivated because management is offering inappropriate rewards. That is, the rewards may be wrong in the sense that the salesperson does not attach much importance to them or because they are considered inequitable or unfair. The sales manager may be offering money in the form of a commission when the salesperson would much prefer to receive a better territory or a promotion. Or the manager may be offering a bonus, but the salesperson feels the amount of the bonus is not commensurate with the effort required, or with bonuses received by others for simpler tasks. Keep in mind that salespeople have economic needs, but they also have professional development, social, and ego needs, among others.

These instances are but a few of the many ways that sales force motivation can become a problem. Perhaps the most fundamental challenge of a good sales manager is ensuring that the salespeople sees a clear linkage between what is being asked of them, how they will be evaluated, and how they will be rewarded. The expectancy model suggests that considering the perceptions and needs of individual salespeople is a necessity. Ford, Churchill, and Walker (1985) have demonstrated, for instance, how the attractiveness of different rewards will vary significantly as a function of such demographic characteristics of the sales force as gender, family structure, financial situation, and educational level, as well as a variety of personality traits. Also, the needs of individuals change over time, so a reward that worked last year may be unsuccessful this year.

Managers cannot develop distinctive reward and measurement systems for each employee, but they can attempt to include enough flexibility in these systems to at least partially accommodate individual requirements. For example, many companies allow their sales force to select from a list of rewards with similar costs. The assumption that all salespeople are motivated by the same reward is likely to result in a high turnover rate for the sales manager (see Figure 12.6). The manager who relies on this assumption must determine whether turnover cost can be justified.

Motivation does not, however, always translate into performance. For instance, a motivated salesperson may lack the ability to do successfully what is being asked. This limitation further emphasizes the importance of the employee screening and selection process. By contrast, salespeople are sometimes unable to perform well because they do not understand the role management expects them to fill. Role conflict and role ambiguity are two possible reasons. *Role conflict* might occur, for example, because the territory sales manager directs the salesperson to concentrate on selling more, while the sales vice president tells the individual to spend more time working with current customers to uncover problems or untapped needs. *Role ambiguity* might occur because management fails to provide the salesperson with clear job responsibilities, specific goals, or proper training. As a result, the salesperson is unclear as to exactly what is, or is not, supposed to be done.

The following chart shows the percentage of adults who say they would be motivated to improve their work performance if their employer offered them one of these noncash rewards worth $1,000.

| | 1994 | | | 1996 | | | | | |
|---|---|---|---|---|---|---|---|---|---|
| | Salary ($000) | Incentive ($000) | Total | Salary ($000) | Salary Increase (%) | Incentive ($000) | Incentive Increase (%) | Total ($000) | Total Increase (%) |
| Top marketing executive | 74.3 | 22.5 | 96.8 | 100. | 35.4 | 33.2 | 47.6 | 133.0 | 38.2 |
| Top sales executive | 65.1 | 21.4 | 86.5 | 91.2 | 40.0 | 31.5 | 47.2 | 122.7 | 41.8 |
| Regional sales mgr | 51.6 | 16.6 | 68.2 | 69 | 33.7 | 23.3 | 40.4 | 92.3 | 35.8 |
| District sales mgr | 48.9 | 19.7 | 68.6 | 61.8 | 26.4 | 22.0 | 11.7 | 83.7 | 22.0 |
| Senior sales rep | 39.4 | 17.1 | 56.5 | 45.1 | 14.5 | 23.2 | 35.7 | 68.3 | 20.9 |
| Intermediate rep | 30.4 | 11.0 | 41.3 | 34.6 | 13.8 | 16.1 | 46.4 | 50.7 | 22.8 |
| Entry level sales rep | 24.2 | 7.7 | 31.9 | 28.8 | 19.0 | 10.9 | 41.6 | 39.8 | 24.7 |
| Nat'l major acct rep | 57.4 | 18.4 | 75.8 | 66.9 | 16.6 | 18.7 | 1.6 | 85.6 | 12.9 |
| National acct rep | 50.4 | 11.6 | 62.0 | 58.8 | 16.7 | 17.4 | 50.0 | 76.1 | 22.7 |
| Major (key) acct rep | 2.8 | 9.9 | 52.6 | 54.6 | 27.6 | 16.6 | 67.7 | 71.2 | 35.4 |

**Figure 12.6.** The Best Motivators

SOURCE: Americans on the Job: Part II, The Wirthlin Report—Current Trends in Public Opinion, 9, no. 1 (January), p. 4, Wirthlin Worldwide. © Copyright 1999 by Wirthlin Worldwide.

---

**TABLE 12.5**  Types of Compensation for Industrial Salespeople

---

**Straight salary**

Salespeople are paid a fixed income regardless of performance. Emphasis is placed on the quality of the sales transaction (e.g., customer service) rather than the quantity of transactions. This type of compensation is good for low-volume products or ones that involve a long buying process. Disadvantages to straight salary include a lack of incentives to generate new sales, the need for close managerial supervision, and high selling costs when business is down.

**Straight commission**

The salesperson is paid only a percentage of whatever he or she sells. This method provides a great incentive for salespeople to generate high sales, although nonselling tasks tend to be neglected. Salespeople have control over their income, do not require close supervision, and are weeded out if they are poor producers. Straight commission is good for homogeneous, undifferentiated products.

**Salary plus commission**

Salespeople are paid a base income and are given a percentage of their sales in addition. This method provides more of a balance between the security of a salary and the incentive to earn additional income through high sales. Salespeople can perform nonselling as well as selling tasks. Firms are adding customer service measures that must be met if commission is to be paid.

**Salary plus bonus**

Salespeople are paid a fixed income but are given a bonus periodically based on their level of performance. The bonus may be based on the individual salesperson's performance, on the performance of the sales force as a whole, or on the performance of a group of salespeople in a specific territory.

---

A distinction should be made between salesperson performance and salesperson satisfaction. One of the more controversial issues in employee management is whether satisfaction leads to good performance, or if good performance leads to worker satisfaction. This issue is important, for the answer indicates whether the sales manager should place more emphasis on making the employee happy or enhancing the employee's ability to be productive. Performance and satisfaction actually both affect each other, but it appears that performance is the antecedent condition. That is, the emphasis should not be on satisfying the sales force and then hoping for performance. Rather, the sales manager should focus on providing the support activities, goals, and structure that will better enable salespeople to do the job. Satisfaction will follow.

Clearly, one of the most potent tools the sales manager possesses to affect both motivation and performance is the organizational compensation system. A variety of reward alternatives are available; Table 12.5 summarizes some of the key options. Let us assess the relative effectiveness of these alternatives.

A *straight commission* system is especially effective at generating new sales. Quite simply, if the salesperson does not sell, he or she does not get paid. This system is advantageous for a company with limited resources, a new company attempting to increase its total sales, or a company experiencing a widespread downswing in sales, such as during a recession. Selling activity is all that is being encouraged, however, leaving the manager with little control over other sales force activities. A straight commission system can also cause sales force stress and burnout, encouraging turnover. Although straight commission systems require less direct supervision, they can be complex to administer. Complexities come into play when the company has a variety of commission rates on different products or customer types, or when a sliding scale is used, where the amount of commission on a particular sale depends on how much the salesperson has sold so far during the current operating period. Commissions, further, can be set as a percentage of sales or as a percentage of gross margin. Compensation based on gross margin encourages the salesperson to focus on the profitability of a sale. Unless these systems are delineated properly, however, salespeople can find them confusing.

A *straight salary* compensation plan provides the sales manager with the ability to exert more control over nonselling activities such as paperwork, customer feedback, customer servicing, and call planning. A salary-based plan involves more initial investment when the salesperson first starts out but can result in greater profits once the person is established and becomes a high producer. This plan provides the inexperienced salesperson time to establish contacts and a client base; it also gives the sales manager more freedom in changing the customers or territories to which a salesperson is assigned. Straight salary is generally easier to administer because the same amount is due each pay period, and it generally results in longer retention of employees.

A *mixed compensation* program, which contains elements of both salary and commission, represents the most popular reward system among industrial companies (see Table 12.6). This system combines the benefits of both forms of compensation and provides the sales manager with more flexibility in reflecting the needs of individual salespeople. The salesperson has the security of receiving a regular salary, which encourages him or her to devote effort toward engaging in nonselling activities, but also knows there is an incentive to achieve high levels of sales. The system can be quite expensive, because the company is guaranteeing a base salary for salespeople with few or no sales while also paying out potentially substantial commissions to the high achievers. The trade-off, however, may be higher levels of motivation.

Providing salespeople with a salary advance or "draw" is another approach to reducing the pressure of a straight commission program. This draw is generally deducted from future commissions. Draws are sometimes guaranteed, in which case the salesperson keeps the advance whether or not his commissions exceed that amount. Of course, constant failure to exceed the draw invites dismissal.

Incentive compensation is used by many companies as a supplement to the regular salary and/or commission system. Incentives take the form of cash bonuses, vacation trips, tickets and travel to major sporting events, home computers, stereo equipment, cellular phones, and even furs and jewelry. Incentives are generally given

TABLE 12.6  Cashing In: What People in Different Types of Sales-Related Positions Get Paid

| | 1994 | | | 1996 | | | | | |
|---|---|---|---|---|---|---|---|---|---|
| | Salary ($000) | Incentive ($000) | Total | Salary ($000) | Salary Increase (%) | Incentive ($000) | Incentive Increase (%) | Total ($000) | Total Increase (%) |
| Top marketing executive | 74.3 | 22.5 | 96.8 | 100.0 | 35.4 | 33.2 | 47.6% | 133.0 | 38.2 |
| Top sales executive | 65.1 | 21.4 | 86.5 | 91.2 | 40.0 | 31.5 | 47.2 | 122.7 | 41.8 |
| Regional sales manager | 51.6 | 16.6 | 68.2 | 69.0 | 33.7 | 23.3 | 40.4 | 92.3 | 35.8 |
| District sales manager | 48.9 | 19.7 | 68.6 | 61.8 | 26.4 | 22.0 | 11.7 | 83.7 | 22.0 |
| Senior sales rep | 39.4 | 17.1 | 56.5 | 45.1 | 14.5 | 23.2 | 35.7 | 68.3 | 20.9 |
| Intermediate rep | 30.4 | 11.0 | 41.3 | 34.6 | 13.8 | 16.1 | 46.4 | 50.7 | 22.8 |
| Entry level sales rep | 24.2 | 7.7 | 31.9 | 28.8 | 19.0 | 10.9 | 41.6 | 39.8 | 24.7 |
| National major account rep | 57.4 | 18.4 | 75.8 | 6.9 | 16.6 | 18.7 | 1.6 | 85.6 | 12.9 |
| National account rep | 50.4 | 11.6 | 62.0 | 58.8 | 16.7 | 17.4 | 50.0 | 76.1 | 22.7 |
| Major (key) account rep | 2.8 | 9.9 | 52.6 | 54.6 | 27.6 | 16.6 | 67.7 | 71.2 | 35.4 |

SOURCE: *Dartnell's 29th Sales Force Compensation Survey*, Dartnell Corporation. © Copyright 1997 by Dartnell Corporation.

**TABLE 12.7** Taking Stock of Compensation

Salespeople like to know how their compensation matches up to their colleagues. The numbers below reflect total cash compensation, including bonuses and commissions, paid for nine sales-related positions.

| Position | Salaries |
| --- | --- |
| Sales and marketing managers | $59,700-159,000 |
| Divisional or regional sales managers | $63,800-125,500 |
| District sales managers | $47,500-103,700 |
| Technical sales representatives | $38,400-63,900 |
| Key account representatives | $39,800-90,600 |
| Senior sales representative | $39,800-78,200 |
| Intermediate sales representative | $30,000-60,800 |
| Customer service/technical support | $28,900-58,800 |
| Junior sales representative | $26,600-50,400 |

SOURCE: *1997/98 Sales Compensation Report*, p. 23, Canadian Professional Sales Association. © Copyright 1998 by the Canadian Professional Sales Association.

based on a point system or sales contest, or simply for exceeding a quota. Point systems give the sales manager more flexibility to weight different factors, such as the rate of increase in a given person's sales, the type of customer to whom sales were made, or the percentage amount by which a person exceeded quota. Contests can be effective motivators and generators of sales; however, contests that are held too frequently, have unattainable goals, or do not clearly specify the terms for participating or winning will have little appeal and may demoralize salespeople. In addition, because contests often require direct competition among salespeople, the rivalry this competition engenders can be a plus but can also become dysfunctional and create added managerial problems.

Comparative data on different compensation levels by sales position are provided in Table 12.7. As can be seen, salary increases with experience and responsibility. Total salaries listed include salary, bonus, and commission.

## Allocating Sales Efforts

In addition to these issues of training and motivating the sales force, the sales manager must design efficient and profitable territories, then assign the sales force within those territories. This managerial task includes decisions regarding call frequency, as well as salesperson authority and responsibility. Note that these decisions are interdependent with the determinants of sales force size and organization, discussed earlier in this chapter.

When designing sales territories, the sales manager generally has a number of criteria in mind. Management seeks territories for which it is easy to estimate sales potential and that are simple to administer. The sales manager must also organize sales territories that minimize travel time and expense while providing equal sales potential and workload for the sales representatives. Accomplishing all these goals across the sales force is a tall order.

An initial step is to estimate market potential for current and prospective accounts in each product category, as well as the projected market share the company expects to achieve. This projection is sometimes done by region and metropolitan area, and sometimes for individual accounts. Accounts are then assigned to territories so that each has approximately equal potential. Problems arise, though, when a territory has more key accounts than another or is more geographically dispersed than another. Another problem is that the sales potentials of each territory may be equal, but the sales force workloads are not. One salesperson may require greater travel time or call frequency than another. An alternative approach might be to construct territories based on the number of sales calls required. Equalizing workload, however, can create discrepancies in sales potential.

The likelihood is that territories will not be equal on all criteria; some will be more desirable and others less desirable. This disparity causes difficulties in assigning salespeople to territories. Are the better territories given to the top performers or to the more senior employees? Are rookie salespeople assigned to weaker territories, where their mistakes will not be as costly? Should the compensation packages be adjusted to reflect differences in territory potential? These approaches to handling inequities among territories are but a few of the alternatives available.

Establishment of equitable sales territories is directly related to, and must be coordinated with, the allocation of sales force resources to accounts. Thus, the amount of sales effort warranted by different customers must be determined. Various computer models are available for this task. The models depend on the subjective estimates of salesperson ability, customer response to different levels of call frequency, and potential sales for customer groups. A major benefit is that the use of these models encourages managers and salespeople to discuss customers in sufficient depth to make such estimates. The output of the model is an actual sales revenue projection for each customer group (groups might include only one firm). Management can see how the sales response projected by the model varies from actual sales and make corrective modifications in the assignment of salespeople to customer groups (matching customer characteristics to salesperson abilities), in territory design (assigning customer groups to territories), or in call frequency.

Whether or not such formal models are used, sales call frequency is a valuable resource that must be carefully managed. Table 12.8 presents an approach in which estimates of total calls are based on account size, specific sales objectives, and unplanned calls.

It should also be apparent that extensive planning and analysis are vital ingredients in territory and account management. Major objectives should be to maximize the time and effort spent in face-to-face interaction with customers and to minimize

**TABLE 12.8** Estimating Total Required Calls

| Account Group | Number of Accounts | Regular Call Frequency | Additional Calls to Meet Program Objectives | Unplanned Calls | Total Calls |
|---|---|---|---|---|---|
| A | 90 | 24/yr | 3/yr | 3/yr | 2,700 |
| B | 200 | 10/yr | 2/yr | 2/yr | 2,800 |
| C | 600 | 6/yr | 0/yr | 0/yr | 3,600 |
| New | 100 | 0/yr | 2/yr | 0/yr | 200 |
| Total | | | | | 9,300 |

SOURCE: The Nierenberg Group and New York University's Management Institute. See Nierenberg (2000a).

the time and effort spent in activities such as traveling, waiting, and paperwork. Salespeople need a systematic plan for complete and efficient coverage of their territory. A computer can be a major asset in this area. As a case in point, Ori-Dri Corporation of America uses a PC-based system known as Sales Track. This system helps salespeople plan their work by organizing the many facets of the customer/prospect base: account number, name, address, ZIP code, telephone number, contacts, products, prices, and status of account. Sales Track allows the sales manager to analyze buyers' needs accurately, target marketing programs, and direct salespeople's efforts with a sales call analysis by category.

Organizing the sales effort also involves questions of authority and responsibility. How much of each should the sales manager delegate to individual salespeople? Call planning (i.e., research, account selection, scheduling, preparation of presentation) is an example. This activity is normally delegated to the salesperson, but sales managers want to have an impact on what is done in the field, and sales reps often are not well versed in structured, formal approaches to planning. These dilemmas also arise in other areas, including pricing authority, negotiation, sales forecasting, and customer feedback.

At the same time, computer technology is changing the fundamental nature of how these issues are addressed. A case in point is Westinghouse Electric Corporation's[1] system, called WesMark. It consists of three subsystems: order processing, electronic communications, and advanced negotiation. The order-processing system permits salespeople to enter new orders, check on the status of existing orders, or determine whether or not an item is in stock. With the electronic communications system, the salesperson finds it possible to perform a variety of communications-related activities. The system includes word processing for sending letters, an electronic filing system for information on customer accounts, the ability to work up spreadsheets, and an electronic mail system for sending or receiving information from the home office. Advanced negotiation is a module for developing price quotations for customers. For products that are built to customer specifications, the salesperson enters any special product features into the terminal and is provided with a quote. WesMark's strongest attribute, however, is that a salesperson can immediately switch from one subsystem to another. Using a laptop computer while out in the field, for example, the salesperson dials into the office and gets tied into the main computer network. He or she can check the mail, write a letter, and in the middle of composing the letter, check the status of an order. While sitting in a customer's office, he or she can place an order, and quotations can be worked up. Important customer information can be recorded, such as a reminder to send a particular piece of literature or to check on a particular problem the customer is encountering.

## Determining Performance Standards and Evaluating Salespeople

The final step in the sales management process involves sales force evaluation. The manager must ensure that sales goals and objectives are being met or that proper progress is being made toward their accomplishment. Standards are developed when setting objectives, so that the salesperson's actual performance can be compared to planned performance. Performance measures can be quantitative (e.g., dollar or unit sales) or qualitative (e.g., salesperson attitude), as well as input (e.g., number of calls made) or output (number of closed deals). The most common performance measure is the sales quota.

A quota provides the salesperson with a target to shoot for and gives management a source of control. It should be challenging but reflect realistic estimates of market potential and be achievable. When set too conservatively, quotas will not be a successful motivator, and they may lead to game playing and "sandbagging." Quotas can be based on dollar sales volume, unit sales, sales by type of account, gross margin, net profit, or activity points.

Activity points are given to salespeople for certain tasks, such as number of calls made, new accounts generated, missionary service provided, and so on. Involving sales representatives in the process of setting their own quotas is an excellent idea, as the reps can better understand why a given sales level is necessary and are more motivated to achieve goals they helped to establish.

Performance evaluation focuses not just on the salesperson, but also on territories, segments, individual customers, products, and average order size. Based on the outcome of performance evaluation, sales territories may need to be modified, certain customers may be dropped, or some segments may warrant heavier investment of sales resources.

Not surprisingly, sales managers and salespeople often have opposing views on the best ways to increase sales (see Figure 12.7). A survey of 979 salespeople and 242 sales managers in the United States and Canada revealed that salespeople linked increased sales with organizational factors (e.g., better market strategy, improved cus-

Sales managers and salespeople often have opposing views on the best ways to increase sales. A survey of 979 salespeople and 242 sales managers in the United States and Canada revealed that salespeople linked increased sales with organizational factors (e.g., better market strategy, improved customer service, more information from the company). Conversely, sales managers cited personal factors (improved selling skills) as the key to increasing sales volume.

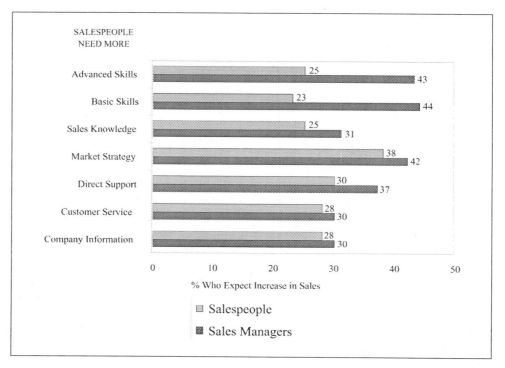

**Figure 12.7.** Differences Between Salespeople and Sales Managers on Ways to Increase Sales

SOURCE: "Salespeople and Sales Managers Disagree on How to Boost Sales," *Marketing Times* (July/August, 1990), p. 3. © Copyright 1990 by *Marketing Times*.

tomer service, more information from the company). Conversely, sales managers cited personal factors (improved selling skills) as the key to increasing sales volume ("Salespeople and Sales Managers Disagree," 1990).

## The Changing Role of the Salesperson

Given the many changes taking place in technologies, markets, and the supply chain, as well as the move toward relationship marketing by many firms, some have questioned whether the conventional salesperson is obsolete. Perhaps it is necessary to redefine what is meant by a salesperson.

Few, if any, industrial buyers need a salesperson as we commonly think of this role; they do not want to be sold, they want to purchase. Ultimately, they want a problem solver. Although this point may appear to be one of perspective, it is important to understand the emerging requirements for success in today's global, technology-driven marketplace. Industrial marketing organizations are finding that their futures depend on highly qualified personnel who can perform satisfactorily in diverse situations. From meeting with buyer executives, engineers, and finance managers, to solving technical problems for users inside buying organizations, the person representing the selling organization must be able to adapt quickly to new and challenging contexts. He or she must also be adept at computer usage, market analysis and forecasting, and project management. It is not enough to simply visit an industrial buyer as an advocate for the selling organization, trying to hawk what the company can make. Stated more simply, today's salesperson must be more than an order taker or an order getter. Today's buyers are looking for competent sales representatives who can help them achieve their goals while making a profit. This requires account managers who have a quality, formal education, excellent training by the company, and people with both the ability and authority to successfully navigate a fast-paced marketplace. A salesperson must be a "market maker," identifying new sources of value for customer organizations and then working with key people inside his or her own firm to deliver this value.

# Summary

This chapter examined the characteristics of the industrial salesperson, the sales task, and the sales management process. Personal selling plays the central role in the industrial promotion mix and represents the front line of the vendor's interaction with customers. There are similarities with retail selling, but the industrial sales process has many distinctive challenges. The industrial sales effort must reflect the technical nature of products or services and their applications, the conflicting needs and priorities of different buying center members, the lengthy buying process, and the low absolute number of customers. These circumstances tend to produce a more technically qualified sales force, different types of sales positions, heavier reliance on a variety of selling aids, more thorough research on a given account, more extensive negotiation, and stronger postsale account servicing.

The chapter introduced a general framework within which to approach the industrial selling task. This framework is built on the idea that the outcome of exchange relationships is determined by the needs, expectations, and behaviors of representatives from buying *and* selling organizations. Implications of four dimensions of the dyadic relationship (relational, social structural, social actor, and normative) were drawn for selling strategy in such areas as negotiation, sales force design, and sales approaches.

Detailed attention was devoted to the industrial sales management process. This process began with a determination of the role of personal selling, which follows from organizational objectives and the company's overall marketing plan. The sales force size and organization is then determined, salespeople are recruited and trained, motivational problems are addressed, territories are established, and salespeople and sales responsibilities are assigned. Finally, to assess the planning process, an ongoing evaluation process is applied to salespeople, products, customers, segments, and territories.

The importance of formal planning and analysis in modern industrial selling is an underlying theme of this chapter. One reason why highly successful salespeople do not always become successful sales managers rests with their inability to systematically assess customer and market requirements and match them with a properly recruited, trained, motivated, and organized sales force. Further, as the role of marketing takes on greater weight in industrial organizations, the need to integrate sales efforts with ongoing marketing strategies becomes even more paramount.

## Note

1. www.westinghouse.com/

## Questions

1. Why is personal selling usually the central ingredient in the industrial promotional mix? What are some specific ways in which the personal selling effort can be coordinated with advertising or sales promotion if you are selling database management services (e.g., databases on clients or prospects) to companies?

2. Identify a product or service situation in which it would be more appropriate to use

   ◆ Technical selling
   ◆ Missionary selling
   ◆ Trade selling
   ◆ New prospect selling

3. Tankline, Inc., a large manufacturer of stainless steel and plastic storage tanks for use in the chemical, paper, and petroleum industries, estimates that it costs the company $350,000 every time the company loses a salesperson. What do you think are the sources of these costs? Identify five of the leading types of costs and estimate the percentage of the total $350,000 you think each accounts for.

4. The similarity hypothesis suggests that the sales manager might want to hire salespeople who are similar to, or share characteristics with, the customer. What

are some of the difficulties encountered in attempting to implement this idea? Assume the sales manager is working for a company selling fiberglass to companies that manufacture boats.

5. What might be some of the differences in the four stages of the personal selling process (prospecting, preparation, presentation, and postsale) when selling various types of springs to manufacturers, compared with selling stocks and bonds to consumers? Assume the springs are a component part in the manufacturer's final product.

6. A company that sells credit report services to financial institutions in the eastern part of the United States is expanding its markets to include California. Describe the step-by-step approach you would use to determine how large a sales force the company will require in California.

7. You are attempting to design sales territories on a geographic basis. Your customers are schools of all types within the province of Quebec in Canada. Discuss some of the major difficulties you are likely to encounter and some of the conflicts that your decisions, whatever they are, are likely to create among members of the sales force.

8. Discuss the pros and cons of a compensation program that emphasizes salary compared with one emphasizing commission, if the company in question is selling (a) glass bottles and jars to current customers in the food industry, (b) laundry equipment (washers, dryers) to laundromats, (c) large computer mainframes to businesses and government organizations, or (d) audiovisual equipment to hotels, schools, and other businesses.

9. Your sales force is putting forth only nominal effort in support of a product that has recently been added to your product line. Using the expectancy theory of motivation, identify a number of reasons for their apparent lack of willingness to push the new product.

10. Which do you think is a more serious problem: setting sales quotas too low, or setting them too high? Explain your reasoning.

11. One of the controversial issues in sales management concerns the relationship between the performance of the salesperson and his or her job satisfaction. Specifically, some believe that high performance leads to satisfaction, whereas others argue that a satisfied worker will be a better performer. With which position do you agree? Why? What are the managerial implications?

# CHAPTER 13

# Distribution and the Value-Added Chain

*Competitive advantage is now about the relentless pursuit of speed,*
*stretch, and finding untapped sources of customer value.*
—Stan Davis

## Key Concepts

| | |
|---|---|
| Alliances | Logistics |
| Captive distribution | Manufacturer's agent |
| Channel evaluation | Middleman conflict |
| Contribution analysis | Middleman motivation |
| Direct distribution | Service level |
| Distribution channel | Single sourcing |
| Distribution strategy | Total cost concept |
| Distributor value | Value chain |
| Hidden costs | Vertical marketing system (VMS) |
| Indirect distribution | Weighted factor approach |
| Industrial distributors | |

## Learning Objectives

1. Recognize how the industrial distribution channel serves as a source of value within the overall marketing mix.

2. Understand the major distribution alternatives available to the industrial firm, including characteristics of the leading types of middlemen.

3. Appreciate the major sources of conflict in industrial channels and the need to manage the distribution function.

4. Be able to apply a process for developing and managing a distribution strategy over time.

5. Determine the marketing implications of the logistical decisions made by the firm and grasp key concepts for managing the logistics function from a marketing perspective.

## What Is a Distribution Channel?

A *distribution channel* is an interdependent network that creates value through the physical flow of goods and services and the transfer of ownership. The channel is made up of manufacturers, assemblers, middlemen (or intermediaries), and customers (see Figure 13.1 for an example of industrial marketing channels). It is the core part of the "value-added chain," which also includes all the suppliers to each company in the channel. Each member of the channel makes contributions to the total value package received by a final customer. Furthermore, each member of the channel affects the costs and effectiveness of the other members.

Distribution channels attempt to bridge the gap between the "production orientation" of a manufacturer and the "usage orientation" of a buyer. This bridging is accomplished through a variety of value-creating functions provided by members of the channel. Examples of such functions include transportation, storage, inventory, breaking bulk, sorting, creating assortments, financing, selling, promoting, market feedback, training, and service. Members of the channel form relationships with one another to ensure the successful accomplishment of these functions. For instance, a manufacturer with limited financial resources might depend on an industrial distributor to maintain large inventories or a manufacturer's representative to perform the sales job. These intermediaries, in turn, rely on the manufacturer for adequate supplies of a quality product. The effectiveness of a channel depends on the amounts of value added by members at each stage of the distribution chain.

Channel members are concerned with the flows of goods and services. Flow implies movement between and among members of a chain. Such flows involve not

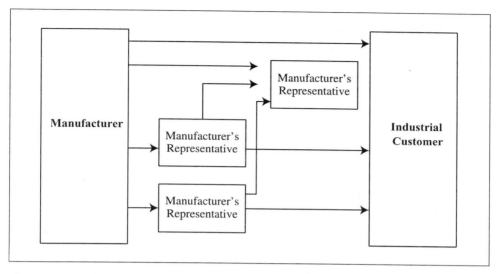

**Figure 13.1.** Illustration of Industrial Marketing Channels

only the physical movement of products but also the movement or assignment of risk, the transfer of title, financial flows, and the assignment of information through the chain. These flows are not in one direction but rather involve movement both up and down the chain. Information regarding product performance characteristics flows down the chain, and information regarding order quantities (demand) and market feedback flows up the chain.

Because of the interdependence among channel members and the critical importance of a well-managed set of flows, the marketer may want to view a channel of distribution as a system rather than as a set of individual parts. Firms often have to restructure their distribution chains to increase value and enhance their competitive position. The goal of a firm's *value chain,* which includes the distribution channel, is to provide the desired level of value to an end-user. Specifically, the objective is to provide goods to the right customers, in the right quantity, quality, time, and place. Doing so in a way that maximizes profit requires that all the parts of the channel operate as a well-oiled machine or system.

The value of a manufactured product is not normally the same as its value when placed in the hands of a customer. Channel members add value to the product by performing such functions as sorting, financing, storing, and servicing. In the same sense that manufacturing adds value to raw materials, distribution adds value to finished products. Of course, value is defined in the minds of those in the buying organization. A machine awaiting pickup 1,000 miles away, or a chemical available only in truckload quantities when just a few hundred gallons are needed, possesses less value to the buyer. Value is enhanced in these cases by having middlemen who make the machine available locally by holding it in inventory, or who repackage the chemical into smaller quantities.

## The Value of an Intermediary

The notion that intermediaries contribute value to a product may run counter to the popular view that middlemen do little more than drive up the cost of a product. When an advertiser claims to eliminate the middleman and pass the savings on to the customer, however, what is not clearly stated is that the middleman's functions are also being passed along to the customer. That is, to realize the promised savings, the customer may have to travel farther, buy in larger quantities, take responsibility for product assembly, or finance the purchase.

A distribution truism is that *you can eliminate the middleman, but you cannot eliminate the middleman's functions.* If a manufacturer decides not to use a distributor but instead deal directly with customers, functions such as personal selling, inventory maintenance, and aftersale service must still be provided. If the manufacturer assumes these functions, then its total costs will increase. In fact, an intermediary that specializes in certain distribution functions should be able to provide those functions at lower costs than the manufacturer and improve the efficiency of the channel in the process. Thus, rather than increasing costs, efficient value chain members improve service while reducing buyer costs.

The cost or margin that a channel member adds to a product's price should be commensurate with the value added by that member. Consider the value chain member who, by maintaining larger inventories, enables a customer to obtain a product at a more convenient time and place than is the case when purchasing directly from the manufacturer. The middleman can reasonably add a markup that reflects the added costs and customer benefits resulting from larger inventories. If a distributor establishes excessive margins in a competitive marketplace, that middleman will most likely be underpriced and replaced by competitors. Alternatively, higher margins encourage a manufacturer to assume the middleman's functions and profits.

## Distinctive Aspects of Business-to-Business Channels

Industrial channels are different from those established for consumer goods and services. Smaller numbers of customers, larger purchase quantities, often complex delivery requirements, and customer needs for technical support and service all lead to shorter and more direct channels of distribution (often involving no middlemen). Intermediaries, when utilized, are technically qualified and have a close relationship with the manufacturer. The types of intermediaries used with industrial goods and services also tend to differ. Instead of traditional wholesalers and retailers, the industrial marketer uses industrial distributors, manufacturers' agents, jobbers, or brokers to service the customer. Channels are also changing, with a move away from face-to-face transactions and increased reliance on E-commerce, as can be seen in Figure 13.2.

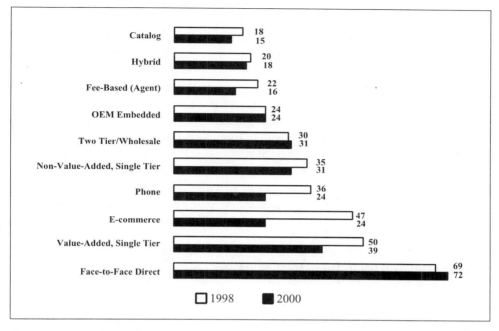

**Figure 13.2.** Channel Usage in 1998 and 2000

SOURCE: Adapted from "Tuning in to the Right Channel," *Sales and Marketing Management*, 152, no. 3 (March, 2000), pp. 67-70, Hochwald. © Copyright 2000 by *Sales and Marketing Management*.

At the same time, fewer channel alternatives are available to a given industrial marketer. For a particular product, there may be only one type of intermediary available in a given market area that possesses the technical, financial, and physical capabilities necessary to achieve the manufacturer's distribution objectives. Furthermore, there may only be two or three of that type of intermediary to select from in a particular market.

The four most prevalent approaches to distribution in industrial markets are selling directly to the customer, selling through the company's own sales force, selling through manufacturers' reps, or selling through industrial distributors. For large orders and when contracts exist, firms sell directly to one another. For example, steel orders may result from a direct call to the manufacturer that concludes with an order and shipment of the product. Increasingly, as we saw in Chapter 2, suppliers are online with customer organizations. Raw materials, parts, components, and subunits are supplied based on an "as needed" basis directly from the supplier.

A number of circumstances support the use of a direct sales force. When products generate sizable sales volume, are part of a broad product line, require a concentrated technical selling effort, involve a lengthy buying process, are relatively early in their life cycles, require extensive servicing, or are subject to occasional supply shortages, selling directly is more justifiable. Similarly, a geographically concentrated customer base justifies a direct selling approach.

The other two popular options represent indirect distribution, or the use of middlemen. Because of their prevalence in industrial markets, we will examine the nature and role of manufacturers' representatives and of industrial distributors in greater detail below.

Mixed systems (some combination of the above) are increasingly prevalent. They are effective when the company sells to customers or market segments that differ in their requirements or buying behavior, and again, when the company has resource constraints. The firm may use independent intermediaries to cover territories that the direct sales force cannot reach. Alternatively, the sales force might be used just for larger or major accounts. In some cases, the sales force may act in a missionary capacity or provide service and technical assistance, with the customer actually purchasing from a distributor. In other cases, distribution efforts are augmented by the Web.

## Types of Intermediaries in Industrial Markets

Channels for industrial goods and services can include a variety of different types of middlemen, and different names are applied to them depending on the country in which one is operating. The most common types include manufacturers' representatives, sales agents, industrial distributors, dealers, brokers, jobbers, and commission merchants. Each is characterized in Table 13.1. Let us look at the two most prevalent of these in more detail.

### Manufacturers' Representatives

The typical manufacturer's representative, or agent, operates an independently owned business. The organization (i.e., rep agency) normally has around 10 employees, has one to two offices, and represents from 5 to 15 manufacturer clients. The represented manufacturers are not direct competitors with one another but instead tend to sell related kinds of products (see also Table 13.2). The association between each manufacturer and the rep agency is generally long-term, lasting 10 or more years. An agent usually covers a large geographic territory and may serve more than 100 industrial customers.

The principal function of manufacturers' representatives is selling. That is, reps do not take title to the product, nor do they maintain inventories. Representatives are professional salespeople, normally possessing technical training or education, who have established contractual (agency) relationships with various manufacturers. The terms of sale are established by the manufacturer, although representatives may have limited authority to negotiate. Compensation comes in the form of straight commissions, which average about 6% in the United States. There is no fixed financial burden to the manufacturer because the representative is paid only when a sale is made. As a

**TABLE 13.1** Types of Industrial Middlemen

**Brokers**

Brokers bring together the buyer and seller to complete transactions that involve large quantities of products that are usually highly standardized or seasonal. The broker may represent either the buyer or the seller, but the relationship is short-term and often only a one-time arrangement. Brokers do not take title or possession of the goods and are paid on a commission basis.

**Commission merchants**

Commission merchants deal on a short-term basis with manufacturers of products sold in bulk (such as raw materials). They do not take possession of the materials. Commission merchants represent the manufacturer; they can negotiate prices and complete sales.

**Facilitators**

A facilitator is any party that improves the efficiency of the distribution process but does not take title or negotiate purchases or sales. Facilitators may provide financing/credit, market information, and grading/certification of the product, among other products and services.

**Industrial distributors**

Industrial distributors are local, independent sales organizations that take title and maintain inventories of specialized or diversified product lines, then resell these products at a margin above their cost. Distributors have long-term relationships with the manufacturers whose products they sell. In addition to selling, they also solicit new accounts, deliver products, offer credit terms, and sometimes provide assembly and repair services.

**Jobbers**

Jobbers represent manufacturers of products sold in bulk (such as raw materials) for which they take title but do not take possession. The relationship between jobbers and manufacturers is usually short-term.

**Manufacturers' representatives**

Manufacturers' representatives are independent salespeople who represent, on a long-term basis, a number of manufacturers whose products complement one another but are not competitive. The manufacturer's agent does not take title or possession of the products. These agents have expert knowledge on technical products and the markets for those products. They are paid on a commission basis.

**Sales agents**

Sales agents are independent salespeople who represent and are responsible for the entire marketing function of a single producer. Sales agents may design promotions, establish prices, determine distribution policies, and recommend marketing strategies for the producer.

**TABLE 13.2**  Criteria for Evaluating Potential Reps

Below is a helpful set of questions that manufacturers can utilize to screen potential rep firms.

1. Representative company information
   A. History
      i. What is your legal status: corporation, partnership, or a sole proprietorship?
      ii. How long have you been in business?
      iii. Please furnish a brief company history, resumes, brochure, and Web site address.
   B. Company growth and future plans
      i. Describe your firm's growth history.
      ii. Do you operate on a sales plan and budget?
      iii. What are your growth plans?
   C. Territory covered and market served
      i. What territory do you cover?
      ii. Please supply a map that describes your territory.
      iii. Will you consider deviations from this territory?
      iv. What do you consider to be your primary and secondary markets?
   D. Office facilities
      i. How many offices do you have, and what are their locations?
      ii. List all forms of communication capability.
      iii. What computer software do you employ?
   E. Warehousing
      i. Do you have a warehouse?
      ii. What is its size?
      iii. What items do you presently stock for resale?
   F. Personnel
      i. How many people are employed by your company?
      ii. How many are outside sales personnel?
      iii. How many are inside sales personnel?
      iv. Please provide resumes of all sales personnel.
   G. Management
      i. Who manages your firm?
      ii. What are their backgrounds?
      iii. How active is management in sales?
   H. Present lines represented
      i. Who are your current principals?
      ii. Are current products compatible with our products?
      iii. Is there any product that conflicts with our product line(s)?

I. Trade membership

    i. Is your firm a member in good standing of a trade organization?

    ii. Are you active in the local chapter?

    iii. To what other professional organizations does your firm belong?

J. Stock ownership

    i. Do you participate in stock ownership of any of your principals?

2. Marketing services

A. Quotations

    i. Do you write quotations?

    ii. Do you make proposals?

B. Sales forecasts

    i. Do you make sales forecasts?

    ii. How often?

    iii. Are forecasts initiated by you or the manufacturer?

C. Market surveys

    i. Do you conduct market surveys for your present manufacturers?

    ii. What compensation do you think is fair for conducting these surveys?

D. Sales management

    i. Do you provide periodic training to your sales force?

    ii. Does your sales compensation plan include customer satisfaction weights?

E. Sales performance

    i. How do you monitor sales performance?

    ii. Will you advise the manufacturer of performance, when requested?

    iii. Do you make monthly sales reports?

result, representatives are especially appropriate for small and medium-sized companies that do not have the resources to develop and maintain a direct sales force. This advantage is obvious when the substantial overhead costs (e.g., training costs, employee benefits) involved with fielding a company sales force are considered. As sales volume increases for reps, the cost advantage of straight commissions eventually disappears.

Conflict can occur between the manufacturer and the agent when sales revenues increase to the point where it is less expensive to establish and maintain a company sales force in a territory. In effect, once the manufacturer's representatives have built the accounts to a high level, they are replaced! This is a difficult but not uncommon occurrence in industrial marketing, as the manufacturer must maintain an efficient value chain system. To continue to employ a manufacturer's representative at higher total costs than can be paid to a company salesperson decreases the efficiency of the value chain. Most manufacturers' representatives understand this dilemma and many include a clause in their agreement with the manufacturer to smooth this process. Basically, the manufacturer must give the representative firm sufficient notice of the impending change, and there is often some form of financial compensation and/or sharing of commissions over a negotiated period of time.

Representatives provide the manufacturer with a means of entering untapped markets and with market coverage in geographic areas where the manufacturer could not deploy a company sales force (e.g., territories with low market potential or widely dispersed customers). Because of their extensive knowledge of customer needs and buying behavior in the covered geographic region, representatives offer the manufacturer immediate access to key customers and decision makers in the region. Establishing a sales force in a new market is both time-consuming and expensive, and rarely will an unfamiliar sales force gain such acceptance. Representatives often have, and work closely with, an established customer base. Their contacts have been established over a period of years, including when the representative was employed as a salesperson for a particular manufacturer.

A major concern of the manufacturer is the extensive control that is sacrificed when opting for representatives instead of a direct or company sales force. Because they represent a number of companies, the representatives' time is a scarce commodity for which each manufacturer competes. The manufacturer who provides higher commissions, better-quality products, a more personalized relationship, or stronger sales promotional support is encouraging a more concerted effort from the representative. Motivation of representatives can also be affected by the kind of year they are having or whether they believe the manufacturer plans to replace them with a direct sales force once the market is developed.

It is not unusual for manufacturers to want representatives to specialize in a particular product area more than they do at present. Additional concerns include the tendency for representatives to provide poor market feedback and aftersale servicing. As an independent salesperson, the representative may not spend sufficient time surveying problems that customers may have with the manufacturer's products, or in identifying new applications or unmet needs the products could fulfill. Similarly, the representative is paid to make sales and, as such, is not especially motivated to provide a quality service function after the sale, unless this action directly leads to further sales. Most intuitive salespersons realize, however, that overall performance—including aftersale service—will influence future sales orders. Qualified representatives do tend to provide good technical advice to customer organizations.

Viewed from the other side, the major concerns of the representative in selecting manufacturers to work with include product quality and reliability, support from the principal, acceptable commission rates, reputation and image of the principal, and product training provided by the principal. Of these, income-related concerns are paramount. The representative is concerned not only with the amount of income received but also with the likelihood that the manufacturer will remain a stable source of income over time. The representative seeks an ongoing relationship with the principal and is concerned that the products being sold will not soon become obsolete. The enthusiasm a representative demonstrates toward a particular product or product line is also greatly affected by the quality of his or her relationship with the manufacturer.

## BUSINESS MARKETING CAPSULE

### Saving a Relationship

Although the value chain is created to provide satisfied customers with the products and services they desire, managers should understand that unexpected problems and delays inevitably will occur. For managers, there are three important tips to remember for keeping valued customers, both before and after problems arise.

First, *find a way to compensate customers for their trouble.* That is, make amends through paying for losses, air freighting the component needed at no cost to the customer, or providing an additional free product or service. The bottom line is that the customer should feel good about the solution you provide.

Second, *employ top-quality salespersons who can perform during both good and not-so-good times.* This is extremely important because selling during good times is not as difficult as selling during troubled times.

Finally, *adopt and practice a customer-oriented attitude.* Firms that have reputations for treating customers fairly will retain customers regardless of most situations. In effect, customers are always right—even when they are wrong! By following these three tips, firms will greatly increase their chances of maintaining valued customers and value chain partners through all types of situations.

SOURCE: Adapted from "Saving a Relationship," *Sales and Marketing Management* (February, 1998), p. 57, Campbell. © Copyright 1998 by *Sales and Marketing Management.*

## Industrial Distributors

The second major type of intermediary is the industrial distributor, defined as a wholesaler who sells the majority of its goods and services to industrial, commercial, and institutional customers; the government; builders; and farmers. A distributor is an independently owned and operated merchant intermediary who takes title to products, keeps them in inventory, provides for delivery and frequently for credit, and may service products after the sale. Occasionally, a distributor will also become involved in manufacturing or product assembly.

There are two main categories of industrial distributors: general line and specialized. A general line distributor is much like an industrial supermarket store, carrying a wide array of differing products. As a rule, no single product category generates more than 49% of the organization's sales. In fact, the general line distributor may carry literally thousands of products either in inventory or through catalog sales. Specialized distributors, as the name implies, focus on a narrower range of related products, such as cutting tools. A trend toward specialization in recent years has found this type of distributor growing in size and numbers, while general line distributors have introduced specialized departments. A third type of distributor, the combination house, sells in both consumer and industrial markets.

A sizable portion of the assets of industrial distributors (as much as 90%) is accounted for by inventory and accounts receivable. Inventory averages about 15% of sales for both general line and specialty distributors. Correspondingly, there is a heavy reliance on short-term debt and retained earnings to meet these asset requirements. The firms themselves tend to be small, privately held organizations employing between 15 and 20 people. Many have a single warehouse. Sales average just over $2 million for both types of distributors, although some larger organizations annually exceed sales of $100 million. About 45% of the employees are salespeople, both outside and inside. An outside salesperson calls directly on customer accounts in person, whereas an inside salesperson sells via the telephone (i.e., telemarketing) or to customers who come to the distributor (i.e., counter sales). The outside sales force, which sells to larger customers, generates the bulk of company sales.

Many of these organizations are growing rapidly, and mergers among them are commonplace. Recent years have also witnessed a growth in distributor chains, some of which are regional or national in scope. Such chains have the advantage of deeper inventories, centralized warehousing, volume discount purchasing, multiple-brand coverage (providing the customer with greater choice), and even private labeling.

About 75% of the unit sales of industrial goods move through distributors, but this activity represents only 15 to 20% of the total dollar sales. In other words, distributors stock smaller-ticket items, such as machine parts, lubricants, fasteners, bearings, hand and power tools, small machinery and equipment, and even nuts and bolts. The average order size is under $300. The small percentage of dollar volume conducted through distributors is also due to the tendency of manufacturers to make direct sales to large customers, using distributors for small customers.

The principal functions provided by industrial distributors include selling, local market coverage, holding inventory, and providing credit. The inventory function is especially important because it represents a means for the manufacturer to spread risk. Distributors can also provide the manufacturer with valuable information regarding local market trends. Because of their proximity to customers, industrial distributors are relied upon to sell products for which rapid delivery and servicing is critical. Distributors are used most frequently for stocking standardized items that appeal to a large potential customer-base and that can be sold in small-quantity lots. Many of these products are routine-order or straight rebuy items.

Manufacturers can reduce distribution costs through the use of industrial distributors. Consider the case of AT&T, a major supplier of copper wire and cable for use in telephone systems. Serving the needs of small customers who purchase limited amounts of such commodity-like products, as well as small and medium-sized accounts in distant markets, may not be economical for the company sales organization. Rather than ignore such potential users, the company was able to efficiently reach large numbers of small accounts through distributors. In this manner, distributors support a market segmentation strategy. This permits the sales force to concentrate on larger accounts.

The key concern of the manufacturer in using industrial distributors is control, as was the case in employing manufacturers' representatives. The problem is more criti-

## BUSINESS MARKETING CAPSULE

### *When Is Channel Conflict Good?*

Channel conflict is one topic most marketing managers would prefer to avoid, especially in today's fast-paced marketplace. At Xerox General Markets Operation, the firm has moved away from a traditional channel of field sales reps pushing their product line to a channel that encompasses retailers, resellers, dealers, the Internet, and inside sales reps. A Xerox sales executive states that a multiple channel approach increases the level of channel conflict, but that firms like Xerox that do not aggressively embrace multiple channels for multiple product lines will be left behind.

Competition motivates resellers and field sales reps to work together and to offer added value for customers in the form of solutions to their problems. This channel conflict, however, must be properly managed or the market will become chaotic with price wars between supposed partners. Xerox has increased cooperation between channel partners by paying a commission on leads and referrals to other partners that result in sales. The bottom line is this: Instead of expecting channel members to "do the right thing," it is more important for sales and marketing managers to motivate channel members by providing the appropriate rewards.

SOURCE: Adapted from "When Channel Conflict Is Good," *Sales and Marketing Management* (April, 2000), p. 13, Cohen. © Copyright 2000 by *Sales and Marketing Management*.

cal with distributors, however, because they also carry competitors' product lines and because of the sheer number of products they carry. Some distributors are large, especially compared to the size of the manufacturer, which creates control problems. The manufacturer may actually need the distributor more than the distributor needs the manufacturer, particularly when dealing directly with the end-user is uneconomical for the manufacturer.

With distributors, the manufacturer loses some or all control over key variables, including sales effort, generation of new accounts, delivery reliability, service quality, returns policies, pricing, and customer feedback. Some of these variables, such as sales effort and service, require technical capabilities that the distributor may not have, and may resist developing or updating. Distributor responsibilities are nevertheless, if anything, increasing. Distributors' willingness to be cooperative depends on how easy they find the manufacturer to deal with, as well as the support and incentives the manufacturer provides. Also, some distributors are simply satisfied with the status quo. They have an established customer base, are achieving stable sales and profit levels, and are not especially motivated to develop new accounts.

Industrial marketers face a number of decisions in managing distributor relationships, many of which involve trade-offs. For example, if the manufacturer pushes the distributor to carry larger inventories of a given item, this probably means the distributor is less able or willing to carry or support all the items in the manufacturer's line. Another trade-off comes in the form of exclusivity agreements—a tactic used to motivate distributors. It involves offering the distributor an exclusive arrangement where no other intermediary is allowed to sell the manufacturer's line within the distributor's market area. The distributor, for its part, will carry only the manufacturer's line in a particular product category. The marketer is betting the arrangement will lead to more aggressive support from this exclusive distributor, in exchange for the lost potential sales from other intermediaries in the region.

When working with distributors, the industrial marketer should attempt to strike a balance between what is being given up and what is being gained. When manufacturers provide technical training programs, discounts, free merchandise, exclusive arrangements, or other incentives to the distributor, they should carefully evaluate what they receive in return. Does training result in better service and more complete market penetration? Do exclusive arrangements result in distributors carrying and supporting only the manufacturer's brand? It is not unusual for manufacturers to provide a missionary selling effort in support of distributor sales. In such circumstances, are distributors maintaining adequate stocks and providing timely delivery in support of these sales efforts? Distributors should be managed much the same as a direct sales force. All too often, manufacturers establish a relationship and then either take the distributor for granted or provide costly incentives from which they receive little benefit.

An illustration of how a firm might assess its investment in distributor training programs is seen in the case of Caterpillar, the large manufacturer of earthmoving equipment (Cavusgil, 1990). Caterpillar developed a dealer (distributor) training program known as the Sales Team Development System (STDS). To evaluate the effectiveness of STDS, Caterpillar compared those dealers who receive training with a randomly selected group of dealers who do not. The performance measures they observed included sales, net revenue per personal call, market share, lost sales, and impact on new product sales. In this fashion, Caterpillar was able to determine the overall benefit of its training program.

Motivation of distributors is the key. A popular approach is to provide direct incentives to the distributor's sales force, such as contests that offer prizes or bonuses. Many of these promotions are ineffective, however, because they are not well publicized, they are too complicated, too many occur at once, they do not support distributors' goals, they last either too long or not long enough, and they fail to reward the right people. These problems often arise because the manufacturer designs the incentive program without distributor input. Distributors handle thousands of products and, with so many incentives available, it is possible for salespeople to win prizes for unknown contests. Basic management theory tells us that when a salesperson is rewarded for unproductive behavior, the salesperson is likely to repeat that behavior.

Another frequent mistake is when a manufacturer offers one generic support program to all dealers. The most effective distributor support programs are tailored to different types of distributors. Beyond support programs, industrial distributors have a number of concerns about dealing with manufacturers. The more common problems confronting the modern industrial distributor are summarized in Table 13.3.

**TABLE 13.3** Common Problems Faced by Industrial Distributors

1. Intense price competition
2. Decreasing customer purchases
3. High interest rates
4. Late/irregular customer payments
5. Customers who switch for marginally lower prices
6. Increasing cost of field sales force
7. High overall labor costs
8. Hiring competent employees
9. Manufacturer's returns policies
10. Training new employees
11. Motivating inside sales force
12. Low manufacturer discounts
13. Dumping by distributors
14. Inventory monitoring
15. Keeping catalogs up to date
16. Setting prices
17. Slow delivery by suppliers
18. Data processing
19. Dumping by manufacturers
20. New competitors
21. Assigning field sales force
22. Maintaining current web site
23. Keeping up with technology

The problems perceived by both the manufacturer and the distributor point out the absolute need for effective communication between the two parties. The relationship is multifaceted, because the distributor plays myriad roles that include customer, partner, and employee. In industrial channels, success in one organization depends on the actions of the other.

## Conflict and the Channel of Distribution

The importance of *managing* channel relationships is rooted in differences in the objectives and needs of the different parties within the supply chain. These differences can lead to conflict among individual channel members, a fairly common occurrence. Conflict, in and of itself, is not necessarily a negative factor, unless it escalates to a dysfunctional level. When it does, the involved parties often refuse to

**TABLE 13.4**  Potential Conflicts Between the Interests of Manufacturers and Those of Industrial Intermediaries

| The **Manufacturer** May Prefer | The **Intermediary** May Prefer |
| --- | --- |
| Lower manufacturer inventories | Higher manufacturer inventories |
| Higher distributor inventories | Lower distributor inventories |
| Lower distributor margins | Higher distributor margins |
| Limited discounts to distributors | Generous manufacturer discounts |
| Lower promotional expenditures | Strong manufacturer promotional support |
| Well-trained field representatives | Salespeople in field, not in training |
| Restrictive returns policies | Liberal returns policies |
| Timely customer feedback from distributors | Salespeople who sell, not do market research |
| Continuous product improvements | Products that do not continually become obsolete |
| Product line extension | A limited assortment of the manufacturer's products |
| Sales to new accounts | Sales to existing accounts |
| Delivery by most cost-efficient means | Timely delivery |
| Sales support for its products over others | Sales of those products with highest margins and/or commissions |

recognize their mutual objectives. Alternatively, low levels of conflict might actually encourage competitiveness and creativity on the part of channel members.

The manufacturer and intermediary can, at times, find themselves at odds with one another in a number of areas. Table 13.4 demonstrates some of these. For example, manufacturers may complain about an intermediary who rarely calls on new accounts, carries the lines of competitors, is concerned only about making the sale, and returns a disproportionate amount of merchandise. The intermediary may be frustrated with low-quality products, continual new product introductions, slow deliveries, manufacturers who maintain the large accounts for themselves, and manufacturers who are distant and unconcerned about the intermediary's problems. In either case, the result can be arbitrary actions intended as retribution against the other party. The manufacturer may lessen support or terminate the relationship, and the intermediary may push the goods of other manufacturers.

Industrial marketers should be cognizant of existing and potential conflicts experienced by intermediaries, and it is important to continually monitor such conflicts. Conflict requires an outlet, or a means to constructively express itself. Otherwise, they will only escalate. This is one reason why an open and effective communication network between manufacturer and intermediary is critical. Regular meetings, site visits, a complaint telephone or e-mail interface, distributor councils, and surveys of intermediaries are some possible steps to enhance communication.

It is also important that channel members collectively look beyond their own parochial interests and recognize that the channel itself is a system. As a system, the channel consists of a set of interdependent players who combine to produce value. The success of the overall value chain, and that of the individual members, depends on how much value the members combine to deliver to end-users. Like parts of an engine, value chain members are mutually interdependent, and the system falters when any component performs its mission suboptimally.

Because the channel is made up of independent organizations, the systems perspective becomes meaningful only when purposefully adopted by managers. Relationships must become less adversarial, with channel members dealing with one another as partners. One approach is to develop the channel as a *vertical marketing system* (VMS). With a VMS, the marketer attempts to achieve technological, managerial, and promotional economies through the integration, coordination, and synchronization of efforts from points of production to points of final use by a customer (Kotler, 1997).

The coordination and control necessary to realize such economies in a VMS can be achieved through either ownership, legal contract, or economic power. When the coordination and control are achieved by buying out intermediaries (i.e., making them captive), a *corporate* VMS is established. If formal legal contracts are used to specify the roles and responsibilities of channel members, coordination and control are achieved through a *contractual* VMS. Alternatively, channel members sometimes cooperate with one another because of their economic dependency on one of the members, often the manufacturer. For example, intermediaries may find a disproportionate amount of their sales consists of one manufacturer's products, or they may find that customers are more receptive to them and the various products they sell because they represent a particular manufacturer. In such cases, the manufacturer is using economic power (e.g., the threat of dropping or providing poorer service to the middleman) to achieve coordination and control in an *administered* VMS.

## Designing and Managing Industrial Channel Strategy

The design and implementation of channel strategy, like pricing or promotional strategy, is an ongoing process. A common mistake made by industrial marketers is to decide on a type of intermediary, select specific firms of this type to serve as intermediaries, and conclude that distribution strategy is set (see Table 13.5). Recog-

---

**TABLE 13.5**  Six Steps to a Sound Channel Strategy

---

*Step 1: Understand how customers buy*
The balance of power has shifted to the customer, who can gather information on the Internet and compare offerings quickly and efficiently. Ensure that your offering is centered on the customer rather than the product. Surveys and customer research will help you understand how customers currently buy and how they would prefer to buy from you.

*Step 2: Include your sales goals*
What are your sales goals? This will allow you to understand which channel(s) can support the sales volume you desire.

*Step 3: Evaluate your core competency*
Can your company satisfy customers' requirements? If not, then what type of partners are required to gain these competencies?

*Step 4: Be prepared to move into the market*
Today's channels require a call center, Web site, channel partners, and field presence. Otherwise, you are reducing your growth potential. Many of today's firms have designed multiple channels to serve the customer.

*Step 5: Segment your market*
Divide your market by such buying patterns as likes, wants, and needs, then place these on the left side of a sheet of paper. On the right side of the paper list your current customers. In the middle of the paper, place your channels to market. These channels should include the Web, catalogs, telemarketing, direct salespersons, and distributors, among others.

*Step 6: Remember the influencers*
Don't forget to target the parties who influence your target customers, which can include consultants, engineers, or other experts. It may be necessary to create a second channel to communicate with these highly influential parties.

---

SOURCE: Adapted from "The Channels to Watch," *Sales and Marketing Management*, 150, no. 3 (March, 1998), pp. 54-56, Rasmusson. © Copyright 1998 by *Sales and Marketing Management*.

---

nition that the environment is fluid is critical to any type of channel strategy. As market conditions change, so too must the strategy. Distribution is one area where change is being thrust on companies, and no company is immune.

Let us consider channel strategy in terms of three stages. An initial distribution strategy must first be formulated, based on a variety of considerations. As changes occur in the product and market environment, it then becomes necessary to make changes in the original distribution strategy. Change is often difficult to bring about, though, because a number of forces resist such change. New strategies eventually emerge that reflect compromises based on these forces.

## Considerations in Formulating the Initial Distribution Strategy

Designing a distribution channel involves decisions concerning whether to sell directly or use intermediaries, which intermediaries to use, whether to use multiple channels, whether to supplement intermediaries with a direct sales force, how long (number of levels) the channel should be, and where to concentrate the company's channel efforts. For example, the design options considered by a manufacturer of air-conditioning equipment could include direct sales to large buyers such as hotel chains, manufacturers' reps in certain regions, industrial distributors for small accounts, manufacturers' reps who sell to contract installers who then sell to end-users, distributors who sell to dealers and contractors who sell to end-users, other variants, and all the above. The selected options will reflect the manufacturer's needs in such areas as inventory, credit, customer service, and transportation.

The beginning point in channel design is the determination of *distribution objectives*. These objectives include not only sales, profits, and market share, but also market coverage, channel control, channel cost of sales effort, service level, and company image. A sample objective might be to make one's product available to 200 plants in certain targeted industries located within a specified geographical area within an average of 3 days. Objectives help to guide decisions regarding intermediaries. For example, manufacturers desiring extensive market coverage may not want to establish exclusive arrangements with distributors. An image-conscious firm known for high quality and customer service may consider a direct sales force as the only way to maintain control over that image. Likewise, a firm concerned with cost reduction may find it best to supplement its sales force with manufacturers' representatives.

The distribution objectives a company establishes, together with the eventual distribution strategy selected, should be based on a careful analysis of the current market situation. Key considerations include buyer characteristics, the product, the competition, the available channels, and the legal environment.

The buyer has a major effect on distribution strategy. When there are few buyers and they are geographically concentrated, direct distribution is most efficient. Other buyer-related concerns, which often vary by market segment, include frequency of purchase, quantity purchased, and whether the product is purchased as a stand-alone item or bundled with related items. In addition, buyer information requirements are relevant. These needs are a function of buyers' past experience with this product category. Organizational demographics, such as whether purchasing is centralized or decentralized, also have implications for the selection of intermediaries.

Product characteristics that influence distribution include technical complexity, unit value in relation to bulk, life-cycle stage, and perishability. Complex products that require a technically qualified salesperson may eliminate industrial distributors as a viable option. Alternatively, products that do not require sorting can often be handled efficiently through jobbers. Beyond the product itself, the depth and breadth of the product line influence distribution choices. A broad line can be an argument for selling directly. In this case, the company salesperson is able to provide for a number of the customer's needs—thus justifying the cost of using a sales force. With a deeper line, exclusive arrangements with distributors are more likely to pay off.

The industrial marketer cannot afford to ignore the distribution strategy employed by competitors, even if they differ in their objectives, because distribution is a source of competitive advantage. For example, the competitor's distribution strategy can produce economies that result in cost advantages. Another potential result is more immediate delivery, which leads to a service advantage. Or, a customer operating in multiple markets may be loyal to a competitor only because that competitor has more complete market coverage. An analysis of the competitor's distribution strategy is also useful in identifying weaknesses (e.g., slow delivery or distributors with mixed loyalties) that the industrial marketer is able to exploit. Hyundai Electronics of America[1] was able to exploit this strategy successfully in entering the U.S. microcomputer market with a low-priced PC sold directly to dealers.

A major constraining factor in industrial distribution is the number of channels available and the functions that available intermediaries are willing and able to provide. Often, not only are few alternatives available for a particular product, but those channels can also be saturated. Consider the case of Japanese personal computer manufacturers attempting to enter the U.S. business computer market. Existing channels were sufficiently saturated with competitors, which significantly raised the costs of market entry. In assessing available channels, the marketer should try to match the functions required by buyers with the functions provided by the various intermediaries. If financial and physical constraints require that the burden of inventory is shared with intermediaries, then using manufacturers' representatives becomes untenable. In the same vein, if intermediaries provide a host of functions that the manufacturer does not require, then the manufacturer may be paying needlessly for those functions through margins or commissions. Finally, legal considerations play a major role in distribution. In an effort to control various intermediaries, or to take advantage of the different levels of distributor dependency on the manufacturer, tactics are sometimes employed that raise legal questions.

Exclusive arrangements, for example, are a means of granting a territorial monopoly to the distributor—a situation with which other distributors may have a problem. Alternatively, the distributor with an exclusive sales arrangement in one geographic region may attempt to extend the arrangement by selling the product through branches located in other territories. Manufacturers are apt to respond to this action by dropping the distributor, which will likely prompt a legal suit. Another debated practice is dual distribution, where the manufacturer uses an intermediary in a given territory but also sells direct in that territory. This approach can give manufacturers more leverage when dealing with the intermediary. IBM has used dual distribution arrangements to create competition between its direct sales force and its remarketers.

Price administration is also a questionable tactic because manufacturers try to force distributors—who take title and possession—to charge a particular price or face adverse consequences (e.g., slow delivery). Tying arrangements have been used by industrial firms, but they raise particularly sensitive legal questions. *Tying* occurs when the manufacturer attempts to link his willingness to supply the product, or to charge a particular price, or to meet a particular delivery target to some condition the distributor must fulfill (e.g., providing free warehouse space to the supplier). In another tactic, *full-line forcing,* the manufacturer requires the distributor to carry a complete line of products when the distributor wishes only to carry part of the line. Distributors may feel obligated to carry a full line if the manufacturer has a specific product that they very much want or need.

## Forces Necessitating a Change in Distribution Strategy

Once in place, distribution strategy has to be adapted to changes in the environment, in the market, and in the firm's overall marketing strategy. As the product moves through its life cycle, the market grows and then matures. The number of buyers change, and specialized need segments develop. Existing channels may fail to reach, or to adequately serve, new customer groups and their distinctive requirements.

The purchasing behavior of existing customers is also subject to change as these companies grow, adopt new technologies, and develop new products. They may demand larger quantities, more favorable discounts, and/or more rapid response to their pressing needs. The current set of intermediaries cannot be expected to automatically grow and adapt with the manufacturer's customers. For example, the end-user who decides to adopt a just-in-time inventory system is unlikely to find distributors that have developed the capability to work with such a system, so the manufacturer must be dealt with directly. It will be necessary to modify the distribution strategy and tactics if the manufacturer wants to retain this customer.

As a market grows and matures, another common development is a change in the economics of various distribution alternatives. Thus, a company sales force can become affordable once market penetration reaches a critical level. Conversely, a technically mature product may be more efficiently sold through distributors, freeing up the sales force to concentrate on new or growth-stage products. New channel alternatives also become available over time, perhaps reducing the attractiveness of existing intermediaries. Companies also tend to expand the product line over time, adding alternative versions of an original item, together with product add-ons and complementary products. Proliferation of the product line makes it difficult for the seller to concentrate on any one product without ignoring others. Customers have a more difficult time staying abreast of exactly which products are available. The manufacturer has an increasingly difficult job of motivating intermediaries and, given this situation, will be better off altering the design of the channel.

## Sources of Resistance to Strategy Changes

Manufacturers demonstrate a strong tendency to resist changes in their distribution approach, even while they acknowledge changing conditions in the environment. In most cases, channel arrangements represent a long-term commitment to a partnership. This commitment may be more moral or social, as decision makers are reluctant to simply walk away from an established working relationship. In other cases, they are constrained by a formal legal commitment.

Changes in distribution arrangements take time to significantly affect the market. A time-consuming effort is required to identify intermediaries, evaluate them, establish formal relationships, train the personnel, and work out arrangements for product delivery, service, and returns. Even more time is consumed while intermediaries identify appropriate decision makers in customer firms and establish credibility with them in terms of the manufacturer's product. Because vendors are often preoccupied with today's performance, they may not view distribution changes as a viable strategic option.

Managers also resist change because they fear that an abandoned channel may be picked up by competitors. That is, even when the channel is not economical or does not serve organizational objectives, it is maintained more to hurt the competition than to help the manufacturer. Such behavior is misdirected because the channel will be unattractive to a competitor for the same reasons the manufacturer is considering giving it up. Meanwhile, the manager is ignoring the extent to which current and potential customers are receiving acceptable service.

The decision to modify a distribution strategy can be made, at least in an ideal sense, only when sufficient data exist to justify such a decision. The necessary data are not always available. For example, in switching to a different type of intermediary, or to a direct sales force, not only must costs be estimated for inventory, accounts receivable, training, service, commissions, and transportation, but accurate assumptions also must be made concerning sales volume and revenues under the new arrangement. Loss of both revenue and goodwill during the time period of the transition should also be factored into the calculations.

Resistance to change can also come from middlemen. Intermediaries may refuse to adopt new technologies, such as on-line cataloging and ordering, despite incentives from the manufacturer. New training programs or the use of manufacturer-provided sales aids may be declined. Dropping these unwilling intermediaries may not be possible in the short run, for either legal or practical reasons, especially where the distribution alternatives are few. The industrial marketer may feel that he or she is stuck with the current distribution strategy and will focus more on the other elements of the marketing mix.

A final reason for resistance is that all change creates some amount of disruption. Disruption causes conflict among those who must manage change; a manager's natural tendency is to avoid or minimize conflict. Conservative managers adopt a philosophy of management by exception, where new solutions are not investigated unless the current system goes awry. The result can be missed distribution opportunities and lost profits.

A new strategy may appear only after the "filtering effect" of these forces of resistance has taken place. The result may be either no change or alterations that fall far short of optimal decision making. The industrial marketer who is cognizant of these constraining forces is in a better position to politically address the need for change.

## BUSINESS MARKETING CAPSULE

### *Push Versus Pull Distribution Strategies*

In addition to concerns regarding the types and number of intermediaries to use and the length of the channel, the marketer must determine at what level in the channel to focus the company's efforts. If we assume that the marketer has a limited set of resources at his or her disposal for use in achieving channel objectives, the question is where in the channel these resources should be directed. Should they be focused on the intermediary, on the industrial customer, or even further down, at the consumer level? When the manufacturer employs a middleman who sells to another middleman (e.g., a manufacturer's rep selling to industrial distributors), who should receive the bulk of the manufacturer's attention? The resources here include incentives such as bonuses and prizes, promotional efforts, training programs, and the company's own sales force, among others.

Two possible approaches to this problem are a push strategy and a pull strategy. With a push strategy, the marketer's efforts are concentrated directly on the next, or most immediate, member of the channel. With a pull strategy, the marketer does an end run, circumventing the more direct channel member and concentrating on those further down the channel. The hope is that if demand is stimulated down the channel, it will pull sales through the intervening levels in the channel.

Take the case of Cyro Industries of Woodcliff Lake, New Jersey, a maker of acrylic products. One of these products, Exolite, is used in building greenhouses, among other applications. The company sells Exolite to industrial distributors, who use it to build greenhouses for growers, the end-users.

To stimulate weak sales, Cyro decided to promote the benefits of Exolite directly to greenhouse owners. The strategy was to get growers to specify Exolite to distributors when contracting with them to build greenhouses. The strategy appears to have worked. Sales increased significantly, and distributors who rarely used Exolite began to build as many as 30% of their greenhouses with the product. Cyro successfully used a pull strategy, rather than relying solely on incentives to motivate distributors to push Exolite to customers in need of a greenhouse.

# The Need to Evaluate Middlemen

Once a relationship is established with a given type of middleman, it is good policy to formally evaluate each channel member at periodic intervals. Evaluation provides the marketer with guidance in determining whether or not objectives are being met. In fact, in the absence of clear, measurable objectives, middleman evaluation loses much of its value.

Evaluation provides the manufacturer with a benchmark for identifying which intermediaries are generating favorable results and which are not. In allocating distribution resources, better performers warrant recognition and reinforcement in the form of incentives, promotional support, training, or an extra effort to address their special concerns. With poor performers, management has a dilemma. Will extra incentives serve to motivate them or simply be a waste of resources? Similarly, will punitive measures provide motivation or contribute to a further reduction in their efforts?

Evaluation is also extremely useful in the ongoing process of formulating distribution strategy. Evaluation can, for example, aid in determining whether individual intermediaries should be kept or dropped. In addition, the evaluation process is a source of data for use in analyzing the changing economics of using one type of intermediary versus another type versus a direct sales force. The evaluation process plays an additional role in terms of control. If a middleman is aware that a formal evaluation is being conducted and knows the criteria the marketer is using as the underlying basis of the evaluation, he or she is more likely to strive to perform better on those criteria. This assumes that the intermediary believes the evaluation is reasonably fair and sees a link between performing well on the evaluation and his or her own rewards.

Factors examined in an evaluation of performance can include productivity, profitability, and effectiveness measures. An assessment of productivity seeks to determine the efficiency of middlemen in their use of resources. Examples include sales per employee, asset turnover, or contribution per square foot of warehouse space. Profitability is a measure of financial performance of the intermediary and includes indicators such as return on sales and growth pattern of revenues. Effectiveness is concerned with how well channel members achieve channel objectives and take advantage of channel opportunities. Here, the industrial marketer is concerned with such issues as the number of new accounts versus existing accounts, unmet customer demand, errors in order filling, and number of customer complaints.

There are a variety of ways to evaluate middlemen; this chapter focuses on two. The first is contribution analysis, which represents a more objective technique, and the second is the weighted factor method, which is more subjective in nature.

## Evaluating Middlemen: The Contribution Approach

Contribution analysis was introduced in our earlier discussion of segmentation, product management, and pricing. When applied to channels, it is an approach to evaluating middlemen based on their contribution to indirect (nonassignable) fixed costs and profitability once the direct (assignable) costs have been covered. The question becomes one of determining how much an intermediary contributes to company profitability.

Table 13.6 presents a hypothetical example of a manufacturer that sells all of its output through three industrial distributors. The critical piece of data is the middle-

**TABLE 13.6** Channel Performance Measurement—Contribution Analysis

|  | Middleman A | Middleman B | Middleman C | Total Company |
|---|---|---|---|---|
| Net sales | 12,000 | 10,000 | 18,000 | 40,000 |
| Cost of goods sold (variable manufacturing cost) | 6,000 | 5,000 | 9,000 | 20,000 |
| Manufacturing contribution | 6,000 | 5,000 | 9,000 | 20,000 |
| Marketing and physical distribution costs |  |  |  |  |
| *Variable* |  |  |  |  |
| Sales margins | 600 | 400 | 2,500 | 3,500 |
| Transportation | 300 | 70 | 800 | 1,170 |
| Warehousing (handling in and out) | 12 | 10 | 65 | 87 |
| Order processing | 50 | 10 | 75 | 135 |
| Inventory carrying cost | 38 | 10 | 60 | 108 |
| Annual middleman contribution | 5,000 | 4,500 | 5,500 | 15,000 |
| *Assignable nonvariable (incurred specifically for the middleman during the period)* |  |  |  |  |
| Salaries | 100 | 50 | 900 | 1,500 |
| Middleman-related advertising | 150 | 100 | 500 | 750 |
| Bad debts | 25 | 10 | 10 | 45 |
| Other | 25 | 40 | 90 | 155 |
| **Annual middleman-controllable contribution** | **4,700** | **4,300** | **4,000** | **13,000** |
| Nonassignable costs |  |  |  | 9,000 |
| Net profit |  |  |  | **4,000** |
| Middleman-controllable margin-to-sales ratio | 39.2% | 43.0% | 22.2% | 32.5% |

SOURCE: Adapted from *Sales Force Management*, p. 535, Churchill, Ford, and Walker. © Copyright 2000 by Irwin McGraw-Hill.

NOTE: All figures except percentages are expressed in thousands of dollars.

man-controllable contribution. This figure is obtained by first subtracting the cost of goods sold (of the manufacturer's product line) by each middleman from the sales revenue (i.e., the intermediary's sales of the manufacturer's product line) generated by that middleman. Next, variable marketing and physical distribution costs incurred

458 | Business-to-Business Marketing

by the manufacturer in working with the middleman are subtracted. Then, any fixed costs directly traceable or assignable to the middleman are removed (e.g., special training or promotional materials designed for that middleman). The logic is that a middleman should be held accountable for generating enough revenue to at least cover the cost of producing the goods he or she is selling, plus any other costs directly incurred by the manufacturer as a result of doing business with the distributor.

If the middleman-controllable contribution is divided by the sales generated by that middleman, the result is a profitability index. This index is a good indicator for comparing the performance of various distributors to company objectives. In the example in Table 13.6, middleman C is clearly outperforming the others in sales of the manufacturer's product line; however, after removing the costs incurred by the manufacturer because of middleman C, including production costs, middleman C is contributing less than the others to common nonassignable costs and profitability. In expressing the controllable contribution as a percentage of sales, the picture becomes even clearer. The profitability index of middleman B is almost double that of middleman C. Not only is B a better performer than one might initially conclude, but there also may be inefficiencies in C's operations that are worth investigating.

## Evaluating Middlemen: The Weighted Factor Approach

A second, more subjective, approach to evaluation is the weighted factor method. Where the contribution approach focuses on a single criterion (i.e., profitability), the weighted factor approach lends itself to a large number of different criteria. Implementation of the weighted factor approach consists of five steps. The marketer must first identify the criteria or factors to be used in evaluating the intermediary. In Table 13.7, five criteria have been selected. Other criteria might include new accounts generated, willingness to provide customer feedback, support for new products, and technical services. In addition, an overall category such as sales performance can be broken down further into gross sales, sales growth, sales made versus sales quota, and market share.

With these criteria in hand, the next step is to apply importance weights to each factor. One method is to spread 100 percentage points across the various factors based on their relative importance. This step forces the marketer to prioritize the factors by giving the most points to the more critical performance variables. Thus, in Table 13.7, sales performance is not only the most important factor but is also more than twice as important as any other factor.

The third step is to evaluate each middleman on each factor. In the example, a 10-point scale is used, with 1 representing very poor performance and 10 signifying excellent performance. The analysis can become quite subjective at this point unless the marketer has established clear standards for performance in each category. For example, sales increases in excess of 15% receive a rating of 10 on the sales performance criterion, increases of 13 to 15% receive a rating of 9, increases of 10 to 12% receive an 8, and so on.

**TABLE 13.7** Channel Performance Measurement—Weighted Factor

| Criteria | (A)<br>Importance Weight | (B) Middleman<br>Evaluation | (A    B)<br>Middleman Score |
|---|---|---|---|
| Sales performance | .50 | 7 | 3.50 |
| Inventory maintenance | .20 | 5 | 1.00 |
| Selling capabilities | .15 | 6 | 0.90 |
| Attitudes | .10 | 4 | 0.40 |
| Growth prospects | .05 | 3 | 0.15 |
| Overall performance rating | | | 5.95 |

SOURCE: *Marketing Channels: A Management View* (2nd ed.), p. 353, Rosenbloom. © Copyright 1983 by Holt, Rinehart & Winston Inc.

Step four involves taking the importance weights for each factor and multiplying it by the middleman rating on that factor, then summing these products. The result is a total score representing the middleman's performance.

The final step is to compare these overall performance ratings for each middleman. The marketer cannot assume, however, that low or high relative scores mean poor or good performance. Rather, he or she must develop some standard of performance against which to compare these scores. The intermediary evaluated in Table 13.7 could have a higher score than all other intermediaries but may be short of management's goal that all middlemen receive a score of at least 6.

Also worth noting is the usefulness of the weighted factor approach in selecting a middleman. Trying to determine whether to use a particular type of intermediary, or a specific middleman organization, a marketer would go through the same process of selecting criteria, weighting, and then evaluating the intermediary's potential on each criterion.

# The Role of Logistics in Distribution Strategy

In addition to tackling the problems of design, evaluation, and motivation in distribution channels, the industrial marketer also must monitor the physical movement and storage of goods. Customers are concerned that products are received in the correct quantity, at the required time, using the desired mode of transportation, and in undamaged condition. The managerial decision area that deals with such concerns is physical distribution, or logistics.

Logistics is of strategic importance, regardless of whether the manufacturer uses an intermediary, because it is a key factor considered by customers when selecting vendors. It is not unusual for industrial buyers to rate logistics as the second most important factor, behind product quality, in deciding among alternative sources of supply. Problems in this area can undermine source loyalty with a customer who is basically satisfied with a product. Furthermore, the importance of physical distribution increases with the frequency that a customer organization purchases an item. It should come as no surprise, then, that in industrial markets, customer service is often defined in terms of logistics.

The activities or tasks that fall under the heading of *logistics* are many and varied. They include warehousing, transportation, inventory control, materials handling, receiving, protective packaging, and order processing. Each task has important marketing implications because of the way it affects the value or utility received by a customer. These implications are illustrated in Table 13.8, which presents the tasks of physical distribution as controllable and interrelated marketing variables.

The elements of a company's logistical system interact with one another in a variety of ways. Viewed from the customer's perspective, the system begins with a customer order and ends with the customer accepting delivery of an item. Those responsible for this area must decide how easy to make it for customers to place orders, how long customers must wait to receive an order, the probability that customers will receive incomplete or defective orders, and how customer complaints, inquiries, and special requests will be handled. Underlying these issues are decisions regarding the number and location of distribution points (e.g., warehouses), the mode of transportation to be used, the inventory levels to be maintained at each location, the communication linkages among locations and with customers, and the way in which products are handled and stored. Let us examine each of these five underlying decision areas.

## Warehousing Decisions

Warehouses are used to receive, store, and ship products to customers. They often receive large shipments, such as carload or truckload quantities, and deliver customized orders, and so are responsible for breaking bulk and regrouping products. The principal goal of a warehouse is to move goods, with storage or holding inventory a secondary concern. The more erratic customer demand tends to be, the greater the use of warehouses for storage.

Three types of warehouse arrangements are available to the industrial firm: private, public, and a combination. Private warehouses, or branch houses, are owned or leased by the manufacturer. Although an expensive investment, these facilities can prove to be quite economical when used at or near capacity. They offer greater control over logistical operations and thus improved customer service. A variation of the private warehouse is the company distribution center, whose purpose is constant and efficient movement of goods, not their storage. Alternatively, public warehouses are independent, privately owned businesses that store, receive, and sometimes ship the goods of any number of manufacturers for a rental fee. Some of these, such as com-

**TABLE 13.8** Controllable Elements in a Logistics System

| Elements | Key Aspects |
|---|---|
| Transportation | Represents the single most important activity in the creation of place values and time values; the means of moving goods from the end of the production line to customers in the marketplace |
| Warehousing | Creates place values and time values by making goods available in the marketplace when needed |
| Inventory management | Ensures that the right mix of products is available at the right place and at the right time, in sufficient quantity to meet demands; balances the risks of stockouts and lost sales against the risks of overstocks and obsolescence; and facilitates production planning |
| Protective packaging | Ensures good condition of products when they arrive in the marketplace and maximizes use of warehouse space and transport equipment cube |
| Materials handling | Maximizes speed and minimizes cost of order-picking, moving to and from storage, loading of transportation equipment, and unloading at destination; relates to product protection |
| Order processing | Assists in creation of place and time values by communicating requirements to appropriate locations; relates to inventory management by reflecting demands on current stock and changes in inventory position |
| Production planning | Ensures realization of place and time values by making goods available for inventory; permits planning of warehouse facility utilization and transportation requirements |
| Customer service | Relates place and time values as seen by the company to place and time values as seen by the customers; establishes levels of customer service consistent with marketing objectives as well as with cost limitations |
| Plant location: Warehouse location, facilities planning | Maximizes place and time values by relating plant and warehouse location to transportation services and costs in terms of markets to be served; facilities planning ensures that capacity, configuration, and throughput of warehouse and shipping facilities are compatible with product flow |

SOURCE: *Marketing Channels: A Relationship Management Approach*, Pelton, Strutton, and Lumpkin. © Copyright 1997 by Richard D. Irwin.

modity warehouses, specialize in particular categories of products. Public warehouses are especially attractive when demand for the manufacturer's goods varies considerably. They are much more flexible than private facilities because they can be used on an as-needed basis. Combination arrangements can also be used, such as where a private warehouse is utilized for day-to-day requirements, while public warehouses are employed to meet peak or seasonal requirements.

Deciding on the number and location of warehouses is a function of the geographic dispersion of customers and their purchase patterns. More important than either of these considerations is the level of customer service the firm wishes to provide to customers, as well as what it can afford. Higher customer service usually means more warehouses located closer to customers, but the equation is more complicated than this, as we shall see.

## Transportation Decisions

To move goods between production facilities, warehouses, and customer locations, industrial firms must decide on a mode of transportation and then select particular carriers. There are five basic transportation modes: air, rail, truck, water, and pipeline. These alternatives differ in terms of their relative speed, availability, dependability, flexibility, frequency, and cost. For instance, air freight tends to be the fastest but most expensive, whereas trucking is distinguished by its availability, dependability, flexibility, and frequency. In fact, in many countries, the tremendous growth in shipments by truck during the past 25 years is due to the relative high ratings this mode of transport receives across all the performance criteria.

There has also been considerable growth in the use of freight forwarders to handle transportation decisions. Forwarders take a number of smaller shipments headed to a particular destination and combine them into larger shipments to get better rates. They evaluate all the available modes of transportation and consider any available carrier. Some forwarders also have preferential relationships with particular carriers.

## Inventory Decisions

Inventories serve to balance supply availability and demand conditions while also addressing the uncertainty regarding future sales. This uncertainty leads to the maintenance of safety stocks, which provide the manufacturer with a buffer when forecasts are inaccurate or problems arise with other elements in the logistical system. At the same time, inventory represents a major investment for the manufacturer, and firms have a strong incentive to maintain the lowest possible number of items in inventory consistent with customer service goals. The costs related to inventory include ordering costs and carrying costs (i.e., storage, record keeping, handling, insurance, obsolescence), and these must be offset against the risk of stockouts.

It is not unusual for firms to employ selective inventory strategies, where inventory levels differ based on how fast an item tends to move. The 80/20 principle in inventory management suggests that 80% of sales come from 20% of a company's product line. Hence, it becomes logical to categorize items into fast-, medium-, and slow-moving categories, then maintain higher inventories on the fast movers. These policies must be balanced against the nature of the product in question and how critical the product is to customers' operations.

## Communication Network Decisions

Although fast and accurate communications significantly improves the performance of the entire logistical system, it is a frequently overlooked area. Communication is a two-way function in the logistical system. Information must move from the customer and the distribution points to the manufacturer, and from manufacturer back to both, as well as between distribution points.

Effective logistics requires information that is both accurate and timely. The two most critical sources of inaccuracy are those related to demand projections and to individual customer requirements. Where demand is poorly estimated, the results can be excess or insufficient inventory, premium freight charges, and unsatisfied customers, among other costs. When orders are filled improperly, the manufacturer bears not only all the costs of logistics without a complete sale but also the costs of returned merchandise and again, a dissatisfied customer.

The speed of information flow is also critical. Advances in telecommunications and computer technology, and especially the capabilities provided through electronic data interchange systems and the Internet, have dramatically enhanced the timeliness of logistical communication. These technologies can also result in lower costs. A prime example of this is the Wal-Mart[2] system. The retail conglomerate allows vendors to electronically monitor the sales and inventory levels of their products at all Wal-Mart locations. It then becomes the vendors' responsibility to ensure that their products arrive at the right place and time.

## Handling and Storage Decisions

The final logistical area of consideration, handling and storage, is concerned with movement, packaging, and containerization. This area is less structured than other logistical areas, in part because it is so intimately intertwined with each of them. Handling is typically the greater expense. In general, the fewer number of times a product has to be handled as it moves from the manufacturer to the end-user, the greater the potential efficiencies. This is one of the great benefits of containerization in long distance shipping. The key is for industrial companies to effectively integrate handling and storage decisions into the warehousing, transportation, inventory, and communication systems so as to enhance the speed and ease of movement of products through the logistical system. The end result is a continued shortening of order cycle times and the advent of "real-time marketing."

## Managing the Total Logistics System

The relationships among the elements of a company's logistical system can be quite complex. On the surface, there is an apparent trade-off between distribution costs and the quality of customer service. At a more operational level, numerous trade-offs are involved among all the tasks of physical distribution. To properly manage these complexities, it is essential to consider the total distribution cost concept.

Rather than dealing with each element of physical distribution and individual costs, the total distribution cost concept encourages management to consider all cost elements simultaneously when attempting to achieve desired customer service standards. Reducing any single cost component (e.g., a less expensive but slower form of transportation) to the lowest possible level is likely to drive up other costs (e.g., the need to maintain larger inventories or establish more warehouse locations). Also, reductions in certain distribution costs are made possible by increasing spending elsewhere. An improved order-processing system enables the vendor to lower transportation costs because of a reduction in rush orders and fewer partial truckload shipments.

The marketer must carefully analyze such trade-offs and make compromise decisions with the end-user's requirements in mind. When an intermediary is involved, the marketer has to look beyond the logistical relationship with that channel member and evaluate the entire value chain. Also, in balancing costs, one must not overlook so-called hidden costs. These include lost sales and profits resulting from late shipments, back orders, and customers who switch to alternative suppliers.

Failure to properly coordinate the physical distribution mix results in inefficiencies that distort the relationship between cost and customer service levels. Companies end up not receiving full value—in terms of customer service—for their dollars spent on distribution. Four signs indicate problems: relatively slow-turning inventories, low levels of customer service relative to the company's inventory investment, a high number of shipments among warehouse locations, and frequent payment of premium freight charges. This situation is an invitation to competitors selling identical products in the same market to achieve cost and price advantages.

What is an effective logistics system? A number of different combinations of physical distribution variables are possible, but many may be inconsistent with the level of service that management seeks to provide. Determining the appropriate service level, and then coordinating distribution variables efficiently to achieve that level, is the most fundamental issue in logistics management. Unfortunately, customer service means different things to different customers. Some define customer service in terms of a specific order cycle time—the elapsed time between the initial effort to place an order and the customer's receipt of the order in acceptable condition. Other customers focus on percentage fill rate—the proportion of orders filled at the time of place-

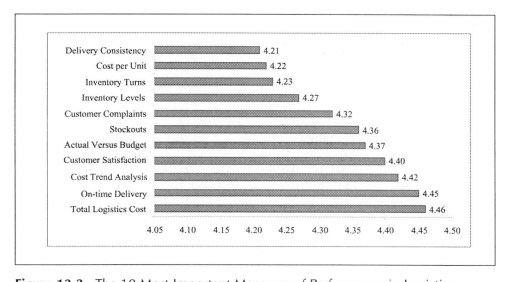

**Figure 13.3.** The 10 Most Important Measures of Performance in Logistics

SOURCE: "Logistics Performance Measurement and Customer Success," *Industrial Marketing Management*, 27 (July, 1998), p. 351, Fawcett and Cooper. © Copyright 1998 by *Industrial Marketing Management*.

ment. Still others are concerned with a combination of factors—ease of ordering, billing accuracy, and percentage of stockouts.

In addition, producers and customers may view service from quite different perspectives. One study of 100 global companies with reputations for outstanding logistical systems reported that cost, on-time delivery, cost trend analysis, and customer satisfaction are the four measures of logistical service most relied upon (see Figure 13.3). Buyer surveys, however often show that customers define service differently from manufacturers and can actually prefer a lower but more reliable service level than that being provided. Customers define poor service in terms of the gap between what they received and what they expected, and it is not unusual for marketers to misunderstand what those expectations were in the first place. As a result, it is frequently possible for manufacturers to improve customer-defined service while cutting total costs.

One reason for "misdefining" customer service is the tendency for producers to place responsibility for logistics in the manufacturing or operations areas, rather than in marketing. Physical distribution is a frequent source of conflict in industrial organizations, often between marketing and manufacturing. Manufacturing is attempting to be cost-effective and manage distribution in a manner that serves production goals; marketing is more concerned with satisfying the customer. An optimum distribution program must balance both cost and service demands. Regardless of where responsibility is placed, marketers must work with manufacturing personnel to achieve distribution objectives. This cooperation requires an ability to reconcile the company's scheduling, capacity, and inventory constraints with the service level needs of cus-

**TABLE 13.9** Advantages and Disadvantages of Each Type of Logistics-Based Strategic Alliance

|  | Advantages | Disadvantages |
|---|---|---|
| Integrated | Maximum reduction of joint costs<br>Highest service level<br>Maximum differentiation from competitors | Investment in dedicated assets<br>Interdependence<br>High investment<br>Slow implementation<br>Difficult to change partners |
| Focused | Ability to keep selected functions out of alliance<br>Easier to implement than integrated alliance | Suboptimal joint cost reduction<br>Limited to competitive advantage |
| Extensive | Short implementation time<br>Easier to switch partners<br>Low interdependence<br>Lower investment than integrated or focused alliances | Low level of customization<br>Suboptimal joint cost reduction |
| Limited | Ease of implementation<br>Low investment<br>Opportunity to evaluate different formats and partners | Limited service<br>Suboptimal joint cost reduction<br>Low commitment |

SOURCE: "Scope and Intensity of Logistics-Based Strategic Alliances: A Conceptual Classification and Managerial Implications," *Industrial Marketing Management*, 26 (March, 1997), p. 145, Zinn and Parasuraman. © Copyright 1997 by *Industrial Marketing Management*.

tomers. Physical distribution is a valuable tool for use by the industrial marketer who can manage it successfully.

## Recent Developments in Supply Chain Management

Recently, interfirm relationships in the supply chain have been the focus of considerable attention. Three topical areas of special note include alliances, single sourcing, and the importance of small suppliers.

A number of industrial firms have begun forming alliances with their customers. Alliances allow a manufacturer to consolidate its market position and become more cost-efficient. By entering into alliances, each party can come to understand the other party's operations, and the total interface can be modified to reduce costs and improve service for both firms. There are a number of different types of alliances. *Integrated* alliances have systems for ensuring prespecified delivery speed and consistency, computer links for information exchange and order status, and joint-inventory programs. *Focused* alliances include relationships where there is a strong commitment of resources to implement a small number of services. *Extensive* alliances incorporate a broad range of services but lack the intensity of integrated alliances. Finally, *limited* alliances revolve around one type of service, like on-time delivery (Zinn & Parasuraman, 1997). Table 13.9 summarizes the advantages and disadvantages of all four alliances.

Buyers traditionally have utilized competitive bidding to minimize price and maintain power, but today's industrial supply chain is too important to rely on divisive negotiations and arm's-length relationships. In a move to lower costs and better coordinate sales and service levels, a number of companies have adopted "single sourcing." One study found that single sourcing resulted in higher-quality products and lower costs (Larson & Kulchitsky, 1998). Some have gone so far as to recommend a certification process for single sources, such as under ISO 9000 standards, to increase the likelihood of success. Although certification is a buyer issue, it is important that both parties work together so that both companies' goals are reached.

Differences also exist between small and large suppliers in terms of their views toward relationships and how much they are willing to invest in them. Smaller firms tend to have a stronger relationship orientation (Kasouf & Celuch, 1997). When dealing with smaller supplier firms, larger manufacturers may find it necessary to provide financial assistance and other forms of help to ensure that the small supplier focuses on core competencies and works to solve problems satisfactorily for the manufacturer. The result will be a stronger and more effective supply chain.

# Summary

Distribution and the value chain, while possibly the least flexible of the elements within the marketing mix, are extremely important strategic variables that must be managed well, continually reappraised, and modified to provide outstanding customer satisfaction at the lowest possible costs. This chapter has examined the nature and scope of value chain strategy from an industrial perspective.

The theme of this chapter has been the role of supply chains in creating value. Intermediaries within the chain add value to the product offerings of manufacturers by providing time, place, form, and possession utilities. This is accomplished through such functions as transportation, storage, credit, customer service, and marketing research. A central tenet in value chain management is that industrial marketers can sometimes eliminate members of the channel, but not their functions. Value chains are utilized by many industrial companies as a form of competitive advantage.

Industrial channels have a number of features that distinguish them from consumer channels. Industrial channels generally are shorter, place higher sales and service expectations on the middleman, and involve different types of intermediaries. The two most prevalent types of intermediaries are manufacturers' representatives and industrial distributors. Characteristics of each were examined within the chapter.

Value chain strategy is concerned with the determination of channel objectives, channel length, channel members, market coverage, and resource allocation within the chain. A number of tactical questions also are pertinent, such as the appropriateness of exclusive arrangements, the design of incentive systems, and the establishment of returns policies. The chapter presented a continuous process model for use in managing distribution strategy. This model consisted of the factors that affect initial distribution strategy, factors that necessitate change in strategy, and sources of resistance to change.

Channels exist in increasingly dynamic environments, and the internal capabilities and requirements of the industrial firm are continually changing. To meet these challenges, all channel members must be continually evaluated. Two approaches to intermediary evaluation were presented—the contribution approach and the weighted factor approach.

Finally, the other side of channel management, logistics or physical distribution, was shown to be a vital part of industrial marketing strategy. Organizational buyers are especially attuned to the logistical capabilities and performance of their vendors. At the same time, supplier firms often place responsibility for physical distribution with production or operations departments. This tendency poses difficulties for the marketer, who must bridge the gap between the firm's manufacturing constraints and the customer's logistical demands.

## Notes

1. www.hyundai.com
2. www.wal-mart.com/

## Questions

1. How is an industrial distributor a "source of value" within the distribution channel?

2. You've done extensive analysis on your distribution channels, which currently include a number of industrial distributors throughout the country. It appears that you could save money by eliminating the distributors and selling directly to your end-users. In spite of this incentive, why might you argue to retain the distributors?

3.  Discuss the pros and cons of using manufacturers' representatives versus industrial distributors if you sold

    ◆ Conveyors and conveyor belts

    ◆ Janitorial supplies

    ◆ Computer terminals

    ◆ Lathes

4.  Why might manufacturers' representatives be considered the elite among industrial salespersons? What are some limitations in using manufacturers' representatives?

5.  What does it mean to "manage" your intermediaries, especially if they are independent companies? What are some tools for managing these intermediaries?

6.  What are some likely sources of conflict between a company that manufacturers standard medical equipment (stethoscopes, thermometers, medicine carts, examining tables, X-ray machines, etc.) and its industrial distributors? Discuss methods for dealing with such conflict.

7.  Discuss the factors that might necessitate a change in the distribution channel strategy once it is in place. Pick a specific industrial product.

8.  Evaluate the pros and cons of the weighted factor approach to evaluating distributors. Why might you use different factors and importance weights for two different distributors?

9.  How might you define and measure customer service levels if you were a manufacturer of gasoline pumps sold to oil companies and convenience store chains?

10. You are a manufacturer of foam core for use in shipping electronics equipment. What are some of the trade-offs you must make in determining inventory levels, the number and locations of warehouses, transportation methods, and customer service levels?

# CHAPTER 14

# The Need for Accountability
## Control and the Industrial Marketer

*Many centralized companies with highly sophisticated
control systems are, in fact, out of control.*
—Gifford Pinchot III

## Key Concepts

| | |
|---|---|
| Annual plan control | Performance monitoring |
| Consumer attitude tracking | Profit center |
| Control benchmarks | Profitability control |
| Control process | Profitability index |
| Control tracking system | Ratio analysis |
| Database management system | Scenario analysis |
| Direct cost | Sensitivity analysis |
| Efficiency control | Spreadsheet |
| Ethical performance | Strategic control |
| Expense-to-sales analysis | Strategic environmental monitoring |
| Full costing | Strategic intelligence system (SIS) |
| Indirect cost | Strategic profit model |
| Marketing audit | Variable cost |
| Performance diagnosis | Variance analysis |

## Learning Objectives

1.  Grasp the concept of marketing control and how control plays an integral part in industrial strategy formulation.

2.  Appreciate practical problems in establishing a control system in industrial firms.

3.  Understand the major categories of marketing control and some of the key concepts, tools, and approaches in each category.

4.  Be able to describe a number of inputs that aid the process of control.

5.  Recognize the need to monitor the ethical aspects of marketing performance, and outline major problems in managing company ethics.

## Accountability and the Marketer

Marketers must be accountable. They must be able to demonstrate that the marketing efforts of the firm are producing tangible results. This is often easier said than done, as the outcomes of successful marketing are not always readily apparent, can be difficult to quantify, and may take considerable time to manifest themselves. Furthermore, performance measures such as sales, new accounts generated, and profits usually are not a function of any one marketing action but instead are influenced by a number of variables. As a result, when trying to assess performance, there is no business function top executives worry more about than marketing.

The management activity through which marketers are made accountable is called "tracking and control" and is the focus of this final chapter. *Tracking* can be defined as observing, recording, or plotting the moving path of some key marketing performance variable. An example would be the pattern in the cost of a sales call from month to month or quarter to quarter. *Control* refers to the prevention or correction of deviations from planned or expected performance levels. A tracking and control system is a combination of measures, tools, and information that act together to maintain actual performance close to desired performance.

A logical question in a chapter on control is "control over what?" In the marketing area, concern is generally with revenues and costs, with more specific interest in key decision variables such as product profitability, sales force expenses, distributor performance, advertising effectiveness, and price variances. The real concern of control, however, is ensuring that the strategies and tactics developed in the marketing plan are achieving management's objectives.

Control, then, must be an integral part of the strategic management process. The detailed measures used in conducting product and market analysis during the strategy formulation process should be consistent with the measures used after the fact to measure performance. Furthermore, the outputs of the control system become inputs into the next planning period. Marketing programs evolve and must be continually adjusted, updated, revised, and improved. A good tracking and control system provides a steady stream of inputs that allow the marketer to make smart adjustments as things unfold over time. Unfortunately, however, many companies approach control as a completely independent activity.

Control systems are a means to an end. A company develops specific measures (e.g., sales per employee, territory contribution margin) that are meant to be indicators of progress toward overall marketing objectives. The danger is in letting the control measure become the goal. A salesperson who knows he or she is being evaluated based on calls made per day (a control measure) will become preoccupied with making as many calls as possible, and not with achieving the company's sales goals. Thus, once employees learn the "rules of the game" as defined by the control system, they can be expected to alter their behavior so as to "look good" according to the "scorecard" that is kept on them. Similarly, then, if advertising efforts are evaluated by top management based on inquiries generated, the marketing manager may spend more money in the trade journals that generate the most leads. The real company concern, however, is in generating names of prospects who are also likely buyers.

Control, or performance monitoring, represents a measurement process. That is, the manager is attempting to measure results at key stopping points (e.g., quarterly) and compare them to some benchmark. Measures are rarely perfect, though, so the ability to ensure that the company has measured what it actually intended to measure must always be questioned. For example, salesperson performance has many dimensions. Finding one or two control measures that comprehensively convey the effectiveness of current selling efforts is difficult. Control measures are indicators; they rarely provide the complete performance picture. This limitation is further complicated by the tendencies on the part of companies both to rely on control measures that are easily quantified and to heavily emphasize sales levels over other control measures.

The need to distinguish between efficiency and effectiveness in marketing activity is a key issue in designing a control system. *Efficiency* is a concern with minimizing the amount of expenditures or resources needed to accomplish a task. *Effectiveness* is a concern with ensuring that the correct tasks are being accomplished. Having one does not guarantee the other; a company could have a very efficient distribution system (e.g., in terms of costs) that is reaching the wrong target market. Control systems tend to place a heavy emphasis on efficiency. The marketing manager must be able to establish a clear, logical relationship, however, between an efficient performance indicator and specific marketing objectives.

Another danger in designing control systems is their ability to stifle the creative energies of marketing and sales personnel. Control systems that attempt to influence the way in which resources are being used (e.g., a salesperson's time, advertising dollars), in addition to monitoring how effectively they are being used, can sometimes undermine motivation and creativity. Control measures provide structure to a marketing task, in the sense that they represent the criteria on which task performance will be evaluated. This structure is a major attribute of control; however, the more structure provided, the less freedom an individual has to approach the task in novel or creative ways. Control systems can become bureaucratic, stifling the employee and encouraging almost mechanical performance to ensure that one looks good in terms of the control measures.

Despite potential problems of overcontrol, an ongoing tracking system tailored to current strategies and tactics is invaluable. In the absence of an effective means of control, the marketing program can stray far off course. This diversion may become apparent only much later, after customers have moved to other suppliers, profits have taken a nosedive, or major opportunities have been missed. By the time corrective action is taken, even more damage is done.

## The Process of Control

There are three elements in the control function:

◈ Establishing standards of marketing and sales performance

◈ Measuring actual performance and comparing it against these standards

◈ Taking corrective action in those areas where performance does not meet standards

Note, then, that control activity is more than developing and using performance measures. There is a formal process involved that also includes goal setting, diagnosing reasons for performance discrepancies, and developing corrective solutions. This process is illustrated in Figure 14.1.

Clearly, if the marketing manager does not have an exact idea of what he or she expects in the way of performance from products, territories, customers, distributors, advertising dollars, or other marketing resources, then control becomes a completely arbitrary activity. He or she has no way to accurately determine how well things are going. Measurable goals need to be established in each of the decision areas within which the manager wishes to monitor performance. A common problem in control is the tendency to establish goals at too general a level, such as for overall sales or market share, rather than for sales by customer type or market share by territory.

Goals must be expressed in terms of *benchmarks* on key control measures. If the control measure is the contribution margin per distributor, then the benchmark might be some specific dollar amount to be achieved at the end of each quarter. The benchmarks are based on the level of contribution the marketer sees as necessary to achieve more general profit goals. Benchmarks must also reflect reasonable, achievable performance levels based on historical trends, current opportunities, and available resources.

A good tracking system requires a strong database so that historical trends in key variables can be plotted and current performance compared against past patterns. An

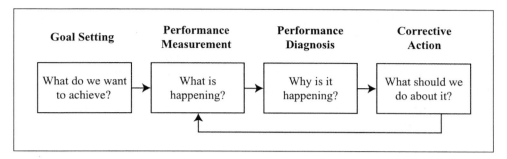

| Goal Setting | Performance Measurement | Performance Diagnosis | Corrective Action |
|---|---|---|---|
| What do we want to achieve? | What is happening? | Why is it happening? | What should we do about it? |

**Figure 14.1.** The Control Process

SOURCE: *Marketing Management: Analysis, Planning, Implementation, and Control* (7th ed.), p. 745, Kotler.
© Copyright 1991 by Prentice-Hall, Inc. Reprinted with permission.

information base must be managed to ensure that raw data are properly categorized (e.g., as a variable or fixed cost, as a direct or indirect expense, as revenue attributable to a certain type of customer or intermediary). Furthermore, the figures must be expressed in the correct unit of analysis (e.g., monthly versus quarterly, net versus gross) and must be constantly updated.

Beyond performance monitoring, the control process is concerned with diagnosing reasons for discrepancies between planned and actual performance. This diagnosis further points to the need for good data. If sales were below expectations, can the problem be traced to some aspect of internal operations, to some unanticipated external development, or to both? Were prices too high, and if so, was this because costs were higher than projected? Or, instead, is the poor sales performance a result of the sales force pushing the wrong products or emphasizing the wrong customers? Perhaps the real problem lies in the sales force's compensation system. In terms of external developments, the problem actually may be related to changes in competitors' prices or promotional expenditures. Alternatively, weak sales may be related to the current economic environment. Information must be collected routinely on internal as well as external factors for the marketer to perform this analysis successfully and pinpoint the real causal factor(s).

The final step in marketing control efforts involves selecting the appropriate corrective action to deal with performance discrepancies. This action can range from doing nothing to a complete change in strategy. Between these two extremes lie several alternatives, such as a modification of marketing or sales tactics, a change in operating procedures, or an alteration of the performance benchmarks. The marketer should not be too quick to modify goals or benchmarks, because this type of inconsistency undermines the credibility of the entire control process. If performance standards were realistic, the logic of control is to find the root of the problem and make corrections. When performance discrepancies arise, the marketer may want to periodically reevaluate the underlying assumptions on which goals for the current period were based.

# Categories of Marketing Control

To organize the marketing control process systematically, the marketer should consider four overall areas in which control is critical. These include the overall strategic direction of the firm, the annual marketing plan, the firm's profitability, and the efficiency of marketing expenditures (Kotler, 2000). Each area requires a different level of analysis.

## Strategic Control

Managers can find themselves so caught up in achieving this year's goals and solving today's problems that they fail to step back occasionally from their ongoing responsibilities long enough to see if the company is missing opportunities. They should ask the question, "Are we taking complete advantage of the markets, products, and channels available to us?" This assessment represents *strategic control.*

The turbulent and dynamic nature of the competitive, technological, regulatory, economic, and supplier environments suggests a need to continually assess the fit between company strengths and/or weaknesses and environmental opportunities and/ or threats. Even with a strong fit, the industrial marketer should look for product areas, services, technologies, customer segments, distribution channels, or delivery systems that the company has not developed, but that could be synergistic with current operations and capabilities.

A tool that is helpful in strategic control is the *industrial marketing audit,* which is a systematic and thorough self-examination of a company's market position. Table 14.1 outlines the areas covered in a typical industrial marketing audit. After conducting such a detailed self-appraisal, management is in a better position to see the total picture of their firm as a marketing entity. With this perspective, it is easier to identify holes or gaps in marketing efforts and determine which resources are being underused or misused.

## Annual Plan Control

*Annual plan control,* the second area of control, represents an attempt to ascertain whether the objectives established in the company's annual marketing plan are actually being achieved. Some of the tools available for this type of control include variance analysis, marketing expense-to-sales ratios, the strategic profit model, and customer attitude tracking.

*Variance analysis* is a method for measuring the relative contribution of different factors to a gap between actual performance and marketing goals. Figure 14.2 provides a graphical illustration, and Table 14.2 presents a numerical example.

**TABLE 14.1**   Checklist of Areas Examined in an Industrial Marketing Audit

I.   The industry
    A. Characteristics
        1. Size (in units produced, dollar sales)
        2. Number of firms
        3. Nature/intensity of competition
        4. Geographical concentration
        5. Interaction with other industries
        6. Product life cycle
        7. Barriers to entry
        8. Regulatory constraints
    B. Trends
        1. Technology and innovation
        2. Prices and costs
        3. Promotional approaches
        4. Other
    C. Firm's position
        1. Size relative to industry leaders
        2. Market strength
        3. Leader or follower
II.  The firm
    A. History
        1. Mission
        2. Growth and expansion
        3. Financial history and position
    B. Goals and objectives
    C. Current strengths and weaknesses
        1. Market
        2. Managerial
        3. Financial
        4. Technical
        5. Market information mechanisms
III. The market
    A. General structure
        1. Number of customers
        2. Geographical spread and/or grouping
        3. Breadth of product use
        4. Switching costs

*continued*

**TABLE 14.1** Continued

     5. Characteristics of current customers

     6. Typical buying process

     7. Nature of buying center

  B. Firm's approach to market segmentation

     1. Degree to which firm has segmented the market

     2. Degree of specification of target markets

     3. Bases of segmentation used: macro vs. micro, other segmentation approaches

  C. Has the firm considered factors that affect the market?

     1. Income effects

     2. Price and quality elasticity

     3. Responsiveness to marketing variables

     4. Seasonality

IV. The product/service mix

  A. List the company's products and services

     1. Depth and breadth

     2. Distinctive features

     3. Economic value to the customer

     4. Limitations of product/service mix

     5. Contribution analysis

     6. Stage of life cycle

  B. Competitive position

V. Promotion

  A. Goals of promotional activities

     1. Personal selling

     2. Sales promotion

     3. Advertising

     4. Publicity

  B. Promotion blend

  C. Personal selling

     1. Organization of sales force

     2. Sales force management

     3. Evaluation of sales force performance

  D. Advertising

     1. Budget in dollars and percentage of sales

     2. Tasks assigned to advertising

     3. Evaluation procedures

*continued*

**TABLE 14.1** Continued

    E. Sales promotion

        1. Budget

        2. Tasks and activities

        3. Evaluation

    F. Publicity

        1. Frequency and Content

VI. Pricing

    A. Goals and role of pricing in the marketing mix

    B. Approach used to set prices

        1. Basis on which prices are set

        2. Flow of pricing decisions within the firm

    C. Prices compared with competitors'

    D. Trade discount and allowances

    E. Financing and credit arrangements

VII. Channels and logistics

    A. Channels

        1. Distribution objectives

        2. Extent and depth of market coverage

        3. Channel design

        4. Channel management

        5. Channel performance

    B. Logistics

        1. Physical distribution organization within firm

        2. Customer service level policy

        3. Inventory and storage

            a. Number of locations of stock

            b. Type of warehouse (i.e., public versus private)

            c. Planned and actual inventory levels

        4. Transportation

            a. Product shipment terms

            b. Mode of transportation used

            c. Type of carrier: common, contract, private

If it is assumed, for the purpose of example, that the marketing plan includes a profit objective expressed in terms of total contribution margin, the first step in the analysis is to identify the variance between actual and planned contribution (Step 1, Figure 14.2). Actual quantity sold is taken times actual contribution per unit. From this total, the product of planned units sold times planned unit contribution is sub-

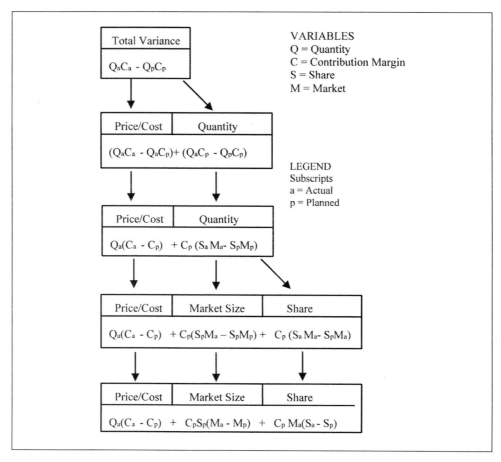

**Figure 14.2.** Variance Decomposition: Comparison With Plan

SOURCE: "A Strategic Framework for Marketing Control," *Journal of Marketing*, 41 (April, 1977), p. 17, Hulbert and Toy. © Copyright 1977 by the American Marketing Association. Reprinted with permission.

tracted. Steps 2 and 3 demonstrate how this variance can be further broken down into a price/cost variance and a volume variance. This approach enables the manager to determine if the overall contribution variance was due to (a) prices or costs that were higher or lower than expected or (b) the number of units actually sold being greater than or less than expected. Steps 4 and 5 attempt to further explain the volume variance. Was the variance due to a difference between the expected market share and what was actually achieved? Alternatively, was the size of the total market larger or smaller than anticipated? The price/cost variance could, similarly, be broken down into its subcomponents to determine if the price charged was less than expected, or if production was more efficient than assumed in the plan.

Variances can be positive or negative. The marketer is concerned with whether performance is above, below, or on target. The performance can be visually plotted

**TABLE 14.2** Analysis of Actual Versus Planned Performance for a Hypothetical Product

| Item | Planned | Actual | Variance |
|---|---|---|---|
| REVENUES | | | |
| Sales (lbs.) | 20,000,000 | 22,000,000 | 2,000,000 |
| Price per lb. ($) | 0.50 | 0.4773 | (0.0227) |
| Revenues ($) | 10,000,000 | 10,500,000 | 500,000 |
| Total market (lbs.) | 40,000,000 | 50,000,000 | 10,000,000 |
| Share of market | 50% | 44% | (6%) |
| COSTS | | | |
| Variable cost per lb. ($) | 0.30 | 0.30 | 0 |
| Contribution per lb. ($) | 0.20 | 0.1773 | (0.0227) |
| TOTAL ($) | 4,000,000 | 3,900,000 | (100,000) |

and monitored using a product (or service) evaluation matrix (see Figure 14.3 for an illustration). Assume the annual marketing plan sets out specific goals for sales, profitability, market share, and industry sales for two products, A and B. The marketer uses the product evaluation matrix to track performance for each product on each of these goals over a number of periods (e.g., quarters, years).

In Figure 14.3, the performances of products A and B have been plotted over three time periods, represented by the subscripts 1, 2, and 3. In Period 1, sales for product A increased at an accelerating rate, classifying it in the growth area. Similarly, industry sales were in a growth stage. Profits were below target, although market share achieved the target goal. In Periods 2 and 3, profitability had been brought into the target range, and the same levels of performance on the other criteria were maintained. For product B, industry and company sales are initially stable, with market share and profitability below target. Market share improved in the second period, but profits remained a problem. By the third period, profits were also on target.

The *strategic profit model* is a second tool for annual plan control. This model enables the marketer to examine how the marketing programs contained within the plan have affected key financial ratios, and ultimately how they have affected returns on investment (ROI). Its use is demonstrated in Figure 14.4.

Bottom line profit, or return on net worth, is pictured as the product of financial leverage times return on assets. Return on assets is divided into net profit margin and asset turnover components, which are, in turn, further broken down. The right-hand column of Figure 14.4 presents examples of marketing actions that might be contained within a marketing plan and shows which financial ratios these efforts would most directly affect. The model shows that the effect of an increase in any marketing

| Company Sales | | Decline | | | Stable | | | Growth | | |
|---|---|---|---|---|---|---|---|---|---|---|
| Industry Sales | Profitability / Market Share | Below Target | Target | Above Target | Below Target | Target | Above Target | Below Target | Target | Above Target |
| Growth | Above Target | | | | | | | | | |
| Growth | Target | | | | | | | A1—►A2.3 | | |
| Growth | Below Target | | | | | | | | | |
| Stable | Above Target | | | | | | | | | |
| Stable | Target | | | | B2 —► B3 | | | | | |
| Stable | Below Target | | | | B1 ↑ | | | | | |
| Decline | Above Target | | | | | | | | | |
| Decline | Target | | | | | | | | | |
| Decline | Below Target | | | | | | | | | |

**Figure 14.3.** Tracking Performance With the Product Evaluation Matrix

SOURCE: "Planning Product Line Strategy: A Matrix Approach," *Journal of Marketing*, 40 (January, 1976), p. 5, Wind and Claycamp. © Copyright 1976 by the American Marketing Association. Reprinted with permission.

expense can be traced to see how profitability ultimately will be affected. Note that an action (such as a reduction in customer order cycle time) by the marketer could affect more than one financial account. Also, revenue and expense items could be both positively and negatively affected. For example, elimination of certain accounts or territories might lessen sales but may reduce expenses even more. Similarly, aggressive sales efforts might raise fixed and variable sales-related costs but may produce enough volume for the firm to reduce manufacturing costs by taking advantage of economies of scale and the experience curve.

Constructing and tracking key *marketing expense-to-sales ratios* is still another approach to annual plan control. Here, major categories of marketing expenditures, such as trade journal advertising, trade shows, sales expense accounts, sales commissions, and marketing research, are each divided by sales and then individually tracked. Benchmarks based on marketing objectives should be set, reflecting the desired level for the ratio. The ratios will fluctuate as expenditures and sales vary over the course of the year. An acceptable range, consisting of an upper and lower threshold, should be determined. Data for the ratio are then tracked periodically (e.g., monthly, quarterly) to ensure that performance is within the threshold levels. This tracking is demonstrated in Figure 14.5.

If any of the ratios deviate from the acceptable range or demonstrate consistent patterns over a series of periods, the control process requires that the marketer attempt to ascertain the cause. Although sales are not directly controllable, they can be influenced. The real danger is in losing control over the amount spent on marketing resources and the manner in which monies are spent.

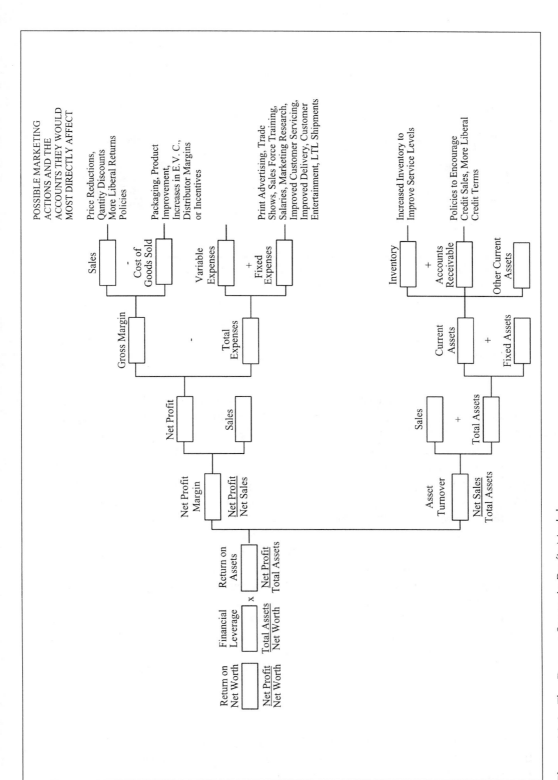

**Figure 14.4.** The Dupont Strategic Profit Model

483

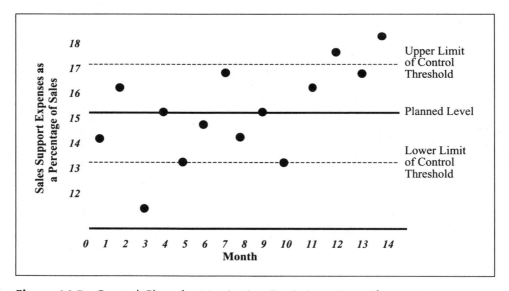

**Figure 14.5.** Control Chart for Monitoring Deviations From Plans

SOURCE: Adapted from *Marketing Management* (4th ed.), p. 839, D. Dalrymple and L. J. Parsons. © Copyright 1996 by John Wiley & Sons. Reprinted with permission.

A fifth method of annual plan control involves *customer attitude tracking* through marketing research. Customers are surveyed to determine the impact of the company marketing programs. This research is especially relevant for tracking performance on communication objectives. A survey might be conducted to see if sufficient numbers of those in the target audience are being made aware of a product through either advertising or a sales call. Similarly, the marketer may wish to learn whether the marketing efforts have had any significant impact on customer attitudes or perceptions.

Effective tracking of customers often requires that the marketer perform longitudinal (over time) studies. Conducting surveys before and after a particular sales or promotional campaign will better enable the marketer to isolate whether changes in key performance variables were due to the campaign itself or to some other factor. When developing survey instruments, it is often desirable to design questions in a way that the study can be replicated periodically. With an ongoing survey program, management can develop a database that assesses trends over time and that provides more opportunity to isolate the underlying causes of these trends, as well as the reasons for temporary fluctuations in the data.

## Profitability Control

Senior management is responsible for achieving overall company profit objectives, but the marketer is, by definition, concerned with the profitability of specific products, territories, segments, customers, channels, distributors, and order sizes.

Quite possibly, for example, a particular customer group, intermediary, or product could be eliminated, causing sales to be lower but improving profitability.

Given the obvious importance of knowing where profits (or losses) are coming from, it is surprising how few managers are aware of the precise net returns the firm actually is realizing on a particular service or market segment in the current operating period. This lack of insight is especially prevalent when a variety of products is being sold in a number of markets.

The ability to examine products, customers, territories, and channels as profit centers is implicit in attempts to perform profitability analysis. The marketer therefore must be able to assign revenues and costs to each of these areas. Of special concern is the need to assign (and hence control) marketing resources.

Perhaps the most valuable tool for use in profitability control is termed the *contribution-margin income statement*. It is based on contribution analysis and contribution thinking, which addresses the question "Is a given product (or segment, territory, or middleman) covering its own direct costs and making a contribution to overhead and profit?" Individual income statements can be derived for products, customers, segments, territories, or channels, which means that each can be a unit of analysis. If the unit of analysis is products, the modularized contribution-margin income statement might resemble that demonstrated in Table 14.3, part A. A territory analysis is provided in part B of the same table.

In Table 14.3, the marketer is responsible for two products sold in two different territories. Revenues, variable costs, and direct fixed costs are attributed to products as well as to territories. Variable costs vary directly with the number of units produced or sold. Direct fixed costs are those that exist only because the product or territory exists; thus, it can be argued that eliminating the product or territory would eliminate the expense. When the unit of analysis is products, direct fixed costs could include expenditures for promotion of individual products as well as individual marketing research expenditures. For territories, the costs of a territorial manager and office space rental represent direct expenses.

Fixed expenses that cannot be traced to the unit of analysis are termed indirect costs. They are treated as common costs, to be subtracted only from the total column. Note that a cost directly traceable to products would be indirect when analyzing territories. The example includes $10,000 in fixed costs that are not traceable to either products or territories; the indirect fixed costs when analyzing products would be this $10,000 plus the $75,400 in rent and salaries that are directly traceable to territories but not products.

Table 14.3 also includes a profitability index for each product and territory. These indexes are calculated by dividing the total contribution of each product or territory by the sales for that product or territory. The result is a performance measure, useful for control purposes. Again, the marketer may want to develop benchmarks for the profitability indexes, against which the current performance of each unit of analysis will be assessed.

One can take this index a step further and include the total investments tied up in a particular product, customer group, or territory. The result would be a rate-of-re-

**TABLE 14.3**   Profitability Analysis of Products and Territories

| Part A: Products | Product A | Product B | Total |
|---|---|---|---|
| Net sales | $400,000 | $420,000 | $820,000 |
| Variable costs | | | |
|     Manufacturing | 200,000 | 189,000 | 389,000 |
|     Selling | 20,000 | 31,500 | 51,500 |
|     Distribution | 40,000 | 10,500 | 50,500 |
| Variable contribution | 140,000 | 189,000 | 329,000 |
| Direct fixed costs | | | |
|     Promotion | 2,000 | 1,500 | 3,500 |
|     Marketing research | 500 | 500 | 1,000 |
| Total product contribution | 137,500 | 187,000 | 324,500 |
| Indirect fixed costs | | 85,400 | |
| Profit | | 239,100 | |

Profitability index: Product A: 34.4%
Profitability index: Product B: 44.5%

| Part B: Territories | Territory A | Territory B | Total |
|---|---|---|---|
| Net sales | 480,000 | 340,000 | 820,000 |
| Variable costs | | | |
|     Manufacturing | 230,000 | 159,000 | 389,000 |
|     Selling | 20,000 | 31,500 | 51,500 |
|     Distribution | 40,000 | 10,500 | 50,500 |
| Variable contribution | 140,000 | 189,000 | 329,000 |
| Direct fixed costs | | | |
|     Rent, territory office | 5,000 | 5,400 | 10,400 |
|     Salary, territory manager | 30,000 | 35,000 | 65,000 |
| Total territory contribution | 153,000 | 100,600 | 253,600 |
| Indirect fixed costs | | | 14,500 |
| Profit | | | 239,100 |

Profitability index: Territory A: 1.8%
Profitability index: Territory B: 29.6%%

SOURCE: Adapted from *Pricing: Making Profitable Decisions* (2nd ed.), p. 117, Monroe. © Copyright 1990 by McGraw-Hill Book Co. Reprinted with permission.

turn index. These investments take the form of assets such as the average inventory level or average amount of accounts receivable. A rate-of-return index for a particular territory can be determined by calculating the ratio of territory net income to territory sales, then multiplying this result by the ratio of territory sales to territory assets managed.

The logic of contribution analysis is that a unit of analysis should generate enough revenue to cover its own expenses—including controllable sales and marketing expenses. This analysis is appropriate for control purposes in the short run, such as the current operating period. Over the longer haul, the marketer may want to use a full-costing or net profit approach, where indirect fixed costs are allocated to individual products, customers, territories, or channels. Allocation of these costs might be made as a percentage of sales or a percentage of direct costs, or (among other possibilities) based on the use of some critical resource. Although allocation methods are, by definition, arbitrary, expenses should be assigned based on some logical and relevant criterion; otherwise, a profitable product or segment can be made to look only marginally profitable by holding it responsible for a disproportionate amount of overhead.

## Efficiency Control

Earlier, a distinction was made between efficiency and effectiveness as concerns in marketing control. In other words, there is a difference between doing things right and doing the right things. The final, and most fundamental, level of control involves the issue of efficiency, which relates to whether the marketer is getting sufficient productivity from the company's marketing resources. More precisely, where profitability control examined the profit contribution of products, markets, and channels, efficiency control focuses on the productivity of specific marketing resources, such as the sales force, trade shows, trade journal advertising, price discounts, and logistics expenditures. The obvious intent is to achieve a given level of performance with these resources, at the lowest possible cost.

The key to this form of control is the derivation of efficiency measures, many of which take the form of singe ratios or indexes. Some examples include the following:

- Cost per sales call
- Sales revenue per sales call
- Advertising cost per inquiry generated
- Advertising cost per thousand buyers reached
- Sales per order size
- Transportation cost per customer
- Sales per inquiry per trade show

◈ Sales per advertising dollar

◈ Repurchase rate

◈ Number of customers lost per period

◈ Average number of stockouts per period

◈ Percentage of customers taking advantage of cash, quantity, and trade discounts

◈ Average monthly number of customer complaints

◈ Average order cycle time per customer

◈ Cannibalization rate

◈ Distributor margins as a percentage of distributor sales

◈ Product returns per distributor

◈ New accounts as a percentage of total accounts

Using these types of measures, the marketer can adjust or adapt the way in which resources are being applied. Efficiency measures might help determine whether sales call frequency should be increased, or whether fewer salespeople could produce the same results. Similarly, these same measures might indicate which trade journals should be dropped from the company's list of advertising outlets, or whether a particular type of appeal is working. The company's service level, which can be a common source of customer dissatisfaction and switching behavior, is also a major source of expense to the industrial marketer. Service levels are subject to considerable fluctuations and should be monitored closely. Efficiency measures can be used to determine how costs and revenues fluctuate with minor increases or decreases in service levels.

Table 14.4 summarizes a study of the control measures actually used by industrial companies. The measures listed were cited most frequently in a large survey of companies. The control efforts of many industrial marketing managers are neither developed all that well nor very sophisticated at present—as witnessed by the heavy reliance on very general sales and control measures. This state of affairs is changing as the emphasis and corresponding expectations placed on the marketing function increase.

# Selected Inputs to the Control Process

## The Budget

The programs and plans of the marketer are usually translated into a budget. The decision to pursue an aggressive penetration strategy with increased selling and advertising efforts involves allocating specific dollar amounts for trade journal advertis-

**TABLE 14.4**  Most Frequently Used Control Measures

1. Products
    a. Sales volume by product
    b. Total contribution margin for each product
    c. Sales volume as a percentage of quota or goal
    d. Market share by product
    e. Net profit for each product
2. Customers
    a. Sales volume by customer
    b. Sales volume as a percentage of quota or goal
    c. Total contribution margin for each customer
3. Geographic area
    a. Sales volume by area
    b. Sales volume as a percentage of quota or goal
    c. Expenses incurred by area
4. Sales force
    a. Sales volume by salesperson
    b. Sales volume as a percentage of quota
    c. Sales expense per sale
    d. Contribution margin per salesperson
5. Order size
    a. Sales volume by order size
    b. Total contribution margin of each order size
    c. Expenses per size of order
    d. Net profit of each order size

SOURCE: "Measures Used to Evaluate Industrial Marketing Activities," *Industrial Marketing Management*, 11 (1982), p. 271, Jackson, Ostrom, and Evans. © Copyright 1982 by *Industrial Marketing Management*.

ing, sales personnel, sales administration, trade show exhibits, and so forth. Furthermore, because the budget is a constrained resource, this decision may mean allocating less to other areas such as distribution or marketing research. For some companies, there is no formal marketing plan and the budget, in effect, serves as the plan.

Budgeting serves the control function in two ways. The first has to do with the usefulness of budgets in identifying problem areas in terms of projected revenues and expenditure levels. The second involves the use of these projected levels to evaluate actual performance. Because the budget contains planned or expected levels of financial performance, the marketer is forced to ensure that budgeted expenditures are sufficient to achieve forecast objectives. If an examination of the budget suggests that profit or sales goals will not be achieved at current prices or spending levels, or

**TABLE 14.5**  Unit Sales Forecast and Total Budgeted Sales

| Month | Unit Sales Forecast[a] Existing Accounts | + New Accounts | × Unit Selling Price ($) | = Budgeted Sales Level ($) |
|---|---|---|---|---|
| January | 2,625 | 875 | 30.00 | 105,000 |
| February | 3,000 | 1,000 | 30.00 | 120,000 |
| March | 5,025 | 1,675 | 30.00 | 201,000 |
| April | 6,425 | 2,475 | 30.00 | 297,000 |
| May | 8,625 | 2,875 | 30.00 | 345,000 |
| June | 7,575 | 2,525 | 30.00 | 303,000 |
| July | 7,200 | 2,400 | 30.00 | 288,000 |
| August | 6,300 | 2,100 | 30.00 | 252,000 |
| September | 5,044 | 1,681 | 30.00 | 201,750 |
| October | 3,900 | 1,300 | 30.00 | 156,000 |
| November | 3,500 | 1,167 | 30.00 | 140,010 |
| December | 2,775 | 925 | 30.00 | 111,000 |
| | | | | 2,519,760 |

a. Based on a goal of 25% of sales from new accounts.

that required expenditures exceed available resources, action can be taken to reallocate funds. Because the budget contains projected revenue and expenditure figures, often broken down by marketing activity, the marketer is provided with a yardstick against which actual performance can be evaluated. Positive or negative performance deviations from budgeted levels help identify company strengths and weaknesses.

Consider the budgets presented in Tables 14.5 and 14.6. The company illustrated is assumed to sell only one product, at an average price of $30 per unit. A monthly unit sales forecast, based on past sales patterns and sales force projections, is provided in Table 14.5. The marketing plan includes a goal of 25% of unit sales to new customers. Unit sales might be further broken down by type of business or territory, which would further enhance the control function provided by the budget. The unit sales are multiplied by the price to produce total forecast sales expressed in dollars.

Expenses to achieve these sales have been budgeted in Table 14.6. They also have been broken out by month and divided into major controllable marketing expense categories. These estimates reflect managerial judgments of what it will take to achieve the sales goals incorporated in Table 14.5. As can be seen, then, the two tables are highly interrelated components of the overall budget. The sales increase in March is reflective, in part, of the participation in a trade show that month and of the expectation that some orders will be taken at the show. Similarly, the marketer has

**TABLE 14.6** Sample Sales and Marketing Expense Budget

| Month | Trade Journal Advertising | Other Advertising | Trade Shows | Sales Commissions[a] | Travel Expense | Customer Servicing | Special Delivery Costs | Marketing Research | Supervision and Other Salaries | Total |
|---|---|---|---|---|---|---|---|---|---|---|
| January | 2,000 | 300 | 0 | 10,500 | 6,000 | 10,000 | 200 | 1,000 | 12,000 | 42,000 |
| February | 2,000 | 300 | 0 | 12,000 | 6,500 | 10,000 | 200 | 1,000 | 12,000 | 44,000 |
| March | 2,000 | 300 | 13,000 | 10,100 | 6,500 | 10,000 | 200 | 1,000 | 12,000 | 65,100 |
| April | 8,000 | 600 | 0 | 29,700 | 12,000 | 10,000 | 200 | 0 | 12,000 | 72,500 |
| May | 8,000 | 600 | 0 | 34,500 | 12,500 | 10,000 | 200 | 0 | 12,000 | 77,800 |
| June | 8,000 | 600 | 0 | 30,300 | 12,500 | 10,000 | 200 | 0 | 12,000 | 73,600 |
| July | 6,000 | 600 | 0 | 29,800 | 10,000 | 10,000 | 200 | 0 | 12,000 | 67,600 |
| August | 6,000 | 600 | 0 | 25,200 | 10,000 | 10,000 | 200 | 0 | 12,000 | 64,000 |
| September | 6,000 | 300 | 0 | 20,175 | 10,500 | 10,000 | 200 | 0 | 12,000 | 59,175 |
| October | 4,000 | 300 | 0 | 15,600 | 6,500 | 10,000 | 200 | 0 | 12,000 | 50,600 |
| November | 4,000 | 300 | 13,000 | 14,001 | 6,500 | 10,000 | 200 | 0 | 12,000 | 62,001 |
| December | 4,000 | 300 | 0 | 11,100 | 6,000 | 10,000 | 200 | 0 | 12,000 | 43,600 |
| Total | 60,000 | 5,100 | 26,000 | 251,976 | 105,000 | 120,000 | 2,400 | 7,000 | 144,000 | 721,976 |
| % of sales | 2.38 | 0.20 | 1.03 | 10.00 | 4.19 | 4.76 | 0.10 | 0.28 | 5.71 | 28.65 |

a. Sales commissions are calculated as 10% of monthly dollar sales.

budgeted added expenditures for advertising and travel expenses to take advantage of the peak sales months of April through August.

The budget aids the control function by forcing the marketer to evaluate whether these expenditure levels are sufficient to accomplish the projected sales levels, and whether these levels are consistent with the resources available. Once the budget is in place, the marketer can use it to determine whether actual unit sales, prices charged, dollar sales, and expenditure levels are consistent with the budget—and identify any major variances. Expenditure levels as a percentage of sales can be monitored and compared to industry standards. By evaluating the productivity of these expenditures this year, the marketer is in a better position to establish the expense-to-sales ratios in future periods and to modify these percentages as the environment changes.

## Data Requirements

The ability to implement the four types of control discussed earlier is built on a strong database. Lack of good and timely data is a major constraint on the control efforts of many industrial firms. Either they do not have the necessary data or the data are not in a form that the marketer can use.

Consider the case of the marketer at an international chemical company who wishes to track something as seemingly basic as average order size, in units per customer, in each of five territories, on a quarterly basis. Where does such information originate? Possibly data on order sizes and customer names can be gotten through copies of invoices available from accounting or shipping, or the sales manager may have field salespeople submit reports including such information. The point is that the marketing manager typically must go to other functional areas in the firm to get much of the internal data required. The information needs and uses of these other areas are likely to differ significantly from those of the marketer. As a result, the data categories, units of analysis, and timeliness of the data kept by those in other departments probably will differ from those needed by the marketer.

Some companies have a controller on staff, and the office of the controller may be able to provide the data. Controllers, however, tend to focus on financial control and to operate more at a strategic level. Even if the information is available through a central company database, the marketer may need to "massage" the data to put them into a usable form.

Assuming that he or she has information on order size by customer, the marketer must group customers into territories (a unit of analysis that may be of no interest to the accountant or company controller) and then separate territorial orders into quarters of the year. Finally, average order sizes must be calculated for each territory in each quarter. At this point, the marketer may also want to break down territories further into companies of different sizes, or from different SIC codes, to perform a segment analysis.

It becomes necessary for industrial marketing departments to adapt their own database management systems from available information sources within and outside the firm. Such systems take random pieces of information and transform them into organized files. The marketer with database management skills is increasingly replacing one who simply made decisions based on the information and analysis provided by others. A simple example of the type of tabular database the marketer might construct to address the problem above is presented in Table 14.7. The database presented would allow for an assessment of average order size not only by territory but also by salesperson, by customer, by product type, and by country. Natural extensions of this database would include the addition of columns for customer four-digit SIC code and for gross margin on each sale.

Construction of a database can also involve political conflict, especially if the marketer is heavily reliant on inputs from other functional areas or departments. Information is often seen as a source of power and influence in organizations. In addition, those in one department may view providing information as a low-priority task. The result can be incomplete information or untimely delivery of data.

## Scenario Analysis

Not only should the tracking system be built on a sound database, but the marketer must also explicitly state any assumptions being made regarding company operations and environmental developments during the control period. The reason for discrepancies between planned and actual performance may be goals based on assumptions that did not hold true.

In any planning process, management is forced to make numerous assumptions regarding market growth, competitor actions, costs of raw materials and components, distributor support, technological change, price stability, and government actions, among others. No matter how much careful consideration and supporting evidence went into these assumptions, the likelihood is that some of them will be violated.

Assumptions that do not hold true can undermine the company's entire marketing strategy. To deal with such uncertainties, it will be advantageous to engage in scenario planning (also called contingency planning). Here, the marketer pinpoints the key assumptions that are most uncertain, then develops *scenarios* representing a best-case, most probable, and worst-case picture of the future in terms of these assumptions. For example, the best-case, or opportunistic, view might include an expectation that the rate of market penetration will accelerate by 10% over the rate assumed in the most probable, or plan, view. The worst-case, or risk, view could include an estimate that the company will achieve only a 90% experience curve instead of the 80% curve projected in the plan view (i.e., costs per unit will drop to only 90% of their original level with every doubling of accumulated output).

Putting together alternative scenarios, the marketer can develop contingency strategies that will be implemented should assumptions prove to be wrong. The control or tracking system comes into play here in two ways. First, the control system not only must monitor marketing performance but also must provide timely feedback

**TABLE14.7** An Integrated Customer Database for an International Chemical Company

| Product Code | Product Type | Product Name | Customer Code | Customer Name | Zone | Country | Territory | Sales-person | Date Last Order | Quantity Last Order |
|---|---|---|---|---|---|---|---|---|---|---|
| 782 | Basic | Toluene | 4161 | Braun Co. | Eur | Swit | 4 | Carpenter | 10/11/81 | 20.9 |
| | | | 2396 | Dagon | Asia | Thai | 2 | Rich | 03/02/82 | 32.0 |
| | | | 7717 | Jones Ltd. | Eur | UK | 3 | Felix | 12/09/81 | 6.0 |
| | | | 4267 | Pinero Co. | SA | Peru | 5 | Howell | 03/03/82 | 13.0 |
| 944 | Fine | Thiazide | 2279 | Roberts Eng. | Eur | UK | 3 | Felix | 04/02/82 | 1.2 |
| | | | 5152 | Wagner Co. | NA | USA | 1 | Wheeler | 09/12/81 | 0.5 |
| | | | 3139 | Nieuwland | Eur | NL | 4 | Carpenter | 10/11/81 | 1.9 |

SOURCE: Adapted from "Conquering Computer Clutter," *High Technology* (December, 1984), pp. 60-70, Cook. © Copyright 1984 by High Technology Publishing Corporation. Adapted with permission.

494

**TABLE 14.8** Scenario Analysis

*A. Annual Contribution Margin*

| State of the Economy | Territory A | Territory B | Territory C | Probability |
|---|---|---|---|---|
| Recession | 3,500 | 2,000 | (500) | .30 |
| Average growth | 3,800 | 4,000 | 10,000 | .60 |
| Above-average growth | 4,000 | 10,000 | 60,000 | .10 |
| | | | | 1.00 |

*B. Contribution Margin Benchmarks: Territory A*

| State of the Economy | 1st Quarter | 2nd Quarter | 3rd Quarter | 4th Quarter |
|---|---|---|---|---|
| Recession | 300 | 1,000 | 1,500 | 700 |
| Average growth | 326 | 1,085 | 1,629 | 760 |
| Above-average growth | 343 | 1,143 | 1,714 | 800 |

regarding the extent to which the assumptions made regarding the current operating period are not holding true. Second, the marketer may need to modify the benchmarks used to monitor sales and marketing performance as assumptions are violated. Acceptable performance levels on the control measures may need to be raised or lowered.

An example of scenario analysis can be found in Table 14.8. In part A, the projected annual contribution margins are estimated for each of three territories. The company has found that sales of its products tend to be affected by overall developments in the economy, which is often the case for industrial firms. Different contribution margin estimates are developed, depending on the state of the economy: recession, average growth, or above-average growth. Each of these conditions represents a different scenario. As can be seen, the territories differ in their sensitivity to economic developments. Territory A is hardly affected, while the impact on territory C is dramatic. In addition, a subjective estimate is included of the probability of each of these three scenarios occurring. If these probabilities were multiplied by each contribution-margin figure, the result would be expected contribution margins.

In part B of Table 14.8, control benchmarks are established for territory A on a quarter-by-quarter basis under each of the scenarios. Actual performance would be compared to these benchmarks to determine whether sufficient progress is being made toward annual objectives. These benchmarks are based on historical data concerning the seasonal trends in company sales over the course of a year. Note that the benchmarks used for control purposes are modified depending on the economic scenario and that, in this case, the benchmarks add up to the annual projected contribution margin. In reality, management may want to set benchmarks at lower levels to allow for some flexibility in quarterly performance figures. The control measures should call management's attention to significant variations in performance, not to minor fluctuations.

## Productivity Judgments and Sensitivity Analysis

Another technique helpful in generating realistic control benchmarks is termed *productivity judgments*. This analysis involves estimating the impact of various changes in each of the marketing variables under the marketer's control. For instance, if discounts are increased or call frequency is reduced, how will sales be affected? Unless this type of analysis is either formally or informally undertaken, establishing control benchmarks will be difficult, for the marketer has no realistic estimate of what to expect from his or her actions.

Consider the case of a proposed increase in expenditures for advertising space in trade journals. The problem is to estimate a sales-response function, which graphically plots sales against some marketing variable, in this case against advertising efforts. The marketer must first obtain data relating purchases of advertising space to sales. This information might come from historical company records (secondary data), where the sales-response function is estimated by extrapolating the past relationship forward to forecast future trends. Alternatively, some form of market experiment could be run, where different levels of advertising are used in different test markets.

Even with data on advertising expenditures and sales, however, it is difficult to determine the precise nature of the relationship, because sales are also affected by other variables, such as prices, competitor actions, and environmental change. Even in terms of the advertising variable itself, frequency of exposure is as much or more a determinant of sales as is the amount of advertising space paid for. The analyst must either control for these other factors or somehow weight their relative influence on sales. In addition, it is likely that the relationship between expenditures on advertising space and sales is nonlinear. Certain levels of advertising may generate increasing returns in the form of sales, but other levels may produce diminishing returns. Simple extrapolations of past trends will tend to ignore the possibility of nonlinearity.

Once the productivity judgment has been made, the analyst can perform *sensitivity analysis*, a kind of "what if?" analysis. Consider the pricing area. Perhaps the productivity judgment has produced an estimate that demand for the company's product is somewhat elastic (e.g., elasticity coefficient of $-1.5$). Based on this estimate, the marketer has projected the levels of revenues, contribution margins, and profits that will be achieved at a given price. Sensitivity analysis could then be performed to see what would happen if the market proves to be more sensitive to price (e.g., a coefficient of $-1.8$). Revenues, contribution margins, and profit would be recalculated at this greater level of elasticity.

A spreadsheet software program is a popular tool for conducting such sensitivity analysis. Electronic spreadsheets represent a useful method for illustrating numerical relationships, or models, which are valuable in evaluating marketing decision alter-

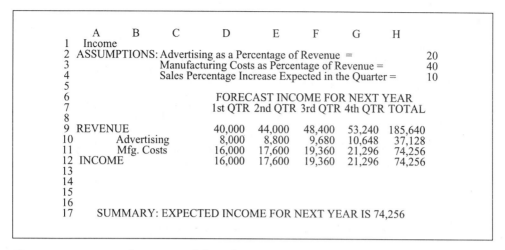

**Figure 14.6.** A Marketing Model With Assumptions

natives. Data are entered in these rows and columns, and can then be manipulated. With a spreadsheet, the marketer can build basic models for use in evaluating each of the elements of the marketing mix. The spreadsheet is built on certain assumptions. Sensitivity analysis can be performed, then, by varying these assumptions.

Figure 14.6 is a simple income-projection spreadsheet with assumptions regarding the percentage of sales represented by advertising and manufacturing costs. It is assumed that advertising is 20% of revenue and manufacturing is 40%. Sales are broken down by quarter and are projected to increase by 10% in each successive quarter. The result is the expected income for the year.

Now, if the marketer wishes to assess the impact of changes in any of these assumptions, he or she enters the change, and the program calculates the results based on the new inputs. Although the original spreadsheet can take considerable time to set up, changes can be made immediately. Figure 14.7 illustrates the results of modifying the assumptions regarding both advertising as a percentage of sales and the quarterly rate of sales increase. This outcome might reflect productivity judgments, such that if advertising is reduced (only 1% of sales instead of 2%), the effect on quarterly sales increases will be only half as much (i.e., sales will increase by 5% rather than 10%). Note that, in this case, although a reduction in advertising is expected to reduce annual revenue, the spreadsheet suggests that profitability will improve.

Spreadsheet analysis greatly enhances the marketer's ability to design a control system that is strategically meaningful. If actual income for the year deviates from that projected in the spreadsheet, this is the beginning point for determining the reasons why. Were the cost-to-sales ratios for advertising or manufacturing greater than expected? If so, were sales lower because the advertising was not as productive as expected? At the lower sales levels, were manufacturing costs higher because of a failure to achieve the anticipated experience curve effect? More complex spreadsheets would enable the marketer to perform detailed analyses regarding some of these questions.

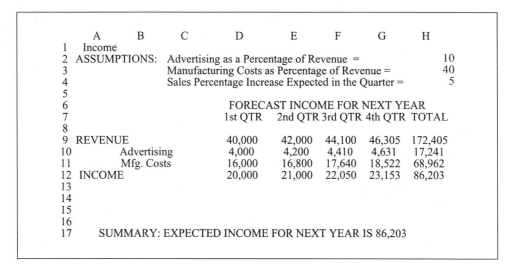

```
        A     B      C        D        E      F      G        H
 1   Income
 2   ASSUMPTIONS:   Advertising as a Percentage of Revenue  =            10
 3                  Manufacturing Costs as Percentage of Revenue =       40
 4                  Sales Percentage Increase Expected in the Quarter =   5
 5
 6                          FORECAST INCOME FOR NEXT YEAR
 7                          1st QTR   2nd QTR 3rd QTR 4th QTR  TOTAL
 8
 9   REVENUE                40,000    42,000  44,100  46,305   172,405
10          Advertising      4,000     4,200   4,410   4,631    17,241
11          Mfg. Costs      16,000    16,800  17,640  18,522    68,962
12   INCOME                 20,000    21,000  22,050  23,153    86,203
13
14
15
16
17       SUMMARY: EXPECTED INCOME FOR NEXT YEAR IS 86,203
```

**Figure 14.7.** A Marketing Model With Altered Assumptions

## External Monitoring Systems

The control process is made much more difficult when the organization experiences change in its external environment. Such change can negate the marketer's assumptions or make control benchmarks unrealistic. Scenario analysis can be useful in anticipating possible changes, but it is rare that scenarios will adequately capture all the changes that take place. It becomes important, then, to stay on top of change.

Data on each component of the environment must be regularly collected, processed, and interpreted. The environment includes everything external to the firm, including the economy, regulation, technology, suppliers, creditors, customers, competitors, the political climate, and nature. Data on these environmental components are evaluated to identify trends. If a clear pattern is recognized, then adjustments may be required—both in marketing strategy and in control benchmarks.

Environmental monitoring should be part of the firm's strategic intelligence system. To aid the control process, environmental monitoring should focus on three types of information gathering: defensive intelligence, passive intelligence, and offensive intelligence (Montgomery & Weinberg, 1979).

*Defensive intelligence* is concerned with helping to ensure that major surprises either are avoided or are recognized and responded to early. Data are collected to determine whether the assumptions on which marketing strategies and tactics were based are actually proving true. For example, current efforts may be predicated on the belief that competitors will maintain current prices, or that energy costs will remain relatively stable. Defensive intelligence serves to send up a red flag if any of the assumptions are being violated. Of course, some assumptions are not explicitly made, but are implicit. As a case in point, a major merger between a competitor and a large conglomerate may not have been expected. Although no explicit assumption was made that a merger would not occur, the assumption was made implicitly because no merger was expected or planned for. Defensive intelligence would serve to pick up signs of a merger possibility.

*Passive intelligence* produces benchmark data against which to compare company policies. If competitors are using a particular sales force compensation program (e.g., 40% commission on sales to new accounts) or spending a sizable percentage of sales (e.g., 20%) on product development, then each of these figures might provide benchmarks against which to evaluate company policies in these areas.

*Offensive intelligence* seeks to uncover areas representing untapped opportunities on which the company can capitalize. Here, the information collection might determine that competitors are overleveraged or are having problems with their distributors. From this information, the marketer might conclude that it will be at least 18 months before the competitor can roll out a particular new product. As a result, heavy investments are made by the company to ensure that the market is well penetrated with its own product before the competitor gets there.

The strategic intelligence system can obtain information from a variety of sources, often at little or no cost. Just a few examples include records on patent filings, annual corporate reports and 10K filings, employment ads, conversations with suppliers, and speeches and public announcements of competitors' officers. It should be readily apparent that, in the so-called information age, a wealth of information is available to the company that takes a systematic approach to identifying and tapping usable sources, and is persistent.

## Analyzing Performance Deviations

This chapter has focused on the tools and techniques of value when monitoring the company's marketing efforts. Just as important is the need to conduct an analysis of the reasons for performance deviations, so that corrective action can be taken where necessary.

Having identified discrepancies between planned and actual performance, it often takes considerable skill and insight to pinpoint the exact causes. The challenge is first to come up with plausible explanations for sales, profits, contribution margins, market share, service levels, customer awareness levels, or expenditure levels being higher or lower than expected. Once these factors are delineated clearly, the marketer must distinguish between *symptoms* and *causes* of performance deviations.

To demonstrate the analytical task confronting the marketer, consider the situation where a meaningful discrepancy between the planned and actual total contribution of a product has been observed. Although unit sales of the product were right on target and the variable costs were as expected, the price charged was actually 10% lower than anticipated. Assume that company salespeople have a range within which they can negotiate prices with customers. The lower average price is not the real cause of the problem, however. The fact that prices were lowered may be reflective of a more fundamental or root development, such as aggressive sales efforts by a competitor. This competitor may have taken away some key accounts, leading company salespeople to go after new accounts by offering lower prices—just to meet sales quotas. The underlying reason for the competitor's successes may be related to a new sales compensation program. Perhaps the real solution, then is a modification of company compensation policies.

For control purposes, a symptom is a condition that indicates existence of a more fundamental problem; a cause is an action that brings about the more fundamental problem. In the hypothetical situation described above, the problem was a loss in competitive position in the marketplace. The cause was the failure to respond effectively to a change in the competitor's sales program. The symptom was the fact that the sales force felt pressured to cut prices in order to meet unit sales goals, thus producing a lower contribution margin.

Analysis of problems, symptoms, and causes should be done in a logical and systematic fashion. Figure 14.8 provides another example, where a decision-tree type of procedure is used. Here, an unfavorable sales deviation has again been observed, and the marketer is anxious to make the necessary adjustments to prevent recurrence of the problem.

The first step is to determine whether sales were below expectations for uncontrollable reasons, such as a change in the environment. If the answer is yes, then objectives and/or marketing programs must be adjusted to reflect the new state of affairs. If the answer is no, then the analyst moves to an assessment of the specific objectives set out in the marketing program. These objectives might include the number of new accounts penetrated, sales by product type, the awareness levels created, or inquiries generated, among others. If the objectives were achieved, then the sales deviation suggests that the marketer has overestimated the productivity of the components of the marketing program. For example, he or she may have expected that 200 inquiries from advertising would translate into 50 purchases, when the actual results suggest that a ratio of 300 inquiries to 50 purchases is a closer estimate of productivity.

If the objectives were not achieved, then the marketer must investigate the design and implementation of the marketing programs. Is the level of program effort (e.g., sales effort, advertising effort, distributor support) equal to the intended level? If the answer is yes, then these levels apparently need to be increased to achieve objectives. This adjustment may necessitate increasing spending in certain areas (modifying the budget) or redesigning the program (e.g., changing the advertising media used or altering the distributor incentives provided). Finally, if the planned level of effort is not being achieved, then the problem lies in execution. The task now becomes identifying the obstacles slowing down program implementation. Possibilities include communication problems, internal opposition to the program, holdups resulting from paperwork requirements, or employees who are poorly trained, unmotivated, or overworked.

The actual problems facing firms may be too complex to lend themselves to a simple solution. The questions in Figure 14.8 may have both yes and no answers. Sales

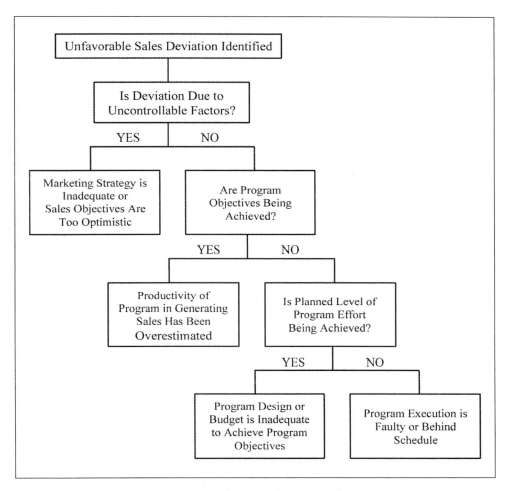

**Figure 14.8.** A Systematic Approach to Analyzing Performance Deviations

SOURCE: *Marketing Management: Strategies and Programs*, p. 398, Guiltinan and Paul. © Copyright 1999 by McGraw-Hill Book Co. Reprinted with permission.

deviations can occur in part as a result of controllable factors but also because of uncontrollable factors. Multiple problems may exist, such as both overly optimistic objectives and behind-schedule program implementation. Problems at one level of Figure 14.8 may contribute to problems at another level. Faulty judgments of program productivity could lead to an improperly designed marketing program.

These complications further emphasize the need for a systematic approach to evaluating why the company performed the way it did. The ultimate value of the control process lies here. Knowing how well goals and objectives are being achieved is vital, but an effective control process should provide inputs regarding future goals as well as direction regarding future strategies and policies.

## Evaluating Ethical Aspects of Marketing Programs

A good control system looks not only at end results but also at how the firm got there. The control system therefore should also monitor the ethical dimensions of the firm's marketing activities. Unethical actions are those that appear to be inconsistent with a sense of what is right. These actions are not necessarily illegal, but they violate generally accepted norms of behavior.

Ethics is frequently a gray area because of differences in people's perceptions of what constitutes an unethical practice. For instance, in a well-known study of attitudes regarding ethical behavior, salespeople and purchasing people differed significantly in their assessment of the ethical quality of every one of 11 business practices (Dubinsky & Gwin, 1981). Examples of marketing-related practices that raise potential ethical dilemmas are shown in Table 14.9.

The ability to monitor ethical performance, as with other areas of control, depends on the establishment of objectives for ethical behavior. Charging fair prices, manufacturing safe products, and using truthful and informative advertising materials are worthy objectives. Firms must balance the need for profit against other motives related to good corporate citizenship. In fact, the blind pursuit of profit objectives typically leads to unethical behavior. For an organization to function efficiently over time, it must adhere to norms defined by more than its minimum required rate of return. This statement is especially true in the industrial market, where exchanges can be for considerable sums of money over long periods of time, and where relationships are predicated on trust as well as a contractual link. Ethical behavior nevertheless sometimes comes at the expense of profits.

The real difficulty in the ethics area has to do with evaluation. How do mangers measure whether their company's marketing and sales activities are ethical? Ethical goals are difficult to quantify, and performance evaluation is subjective at best. Management can develop a set of rules of conduct for issues such as those raised in Table 14.9. Rules are subject to individual interpretation, however, and will not apply to every circumstance that arises. Such rules may be incorporated into a corporate ethics handbook. Buying organizations will sometimes also prepare ethics handbooks and distribute them to vendors.

Underlying the need for ethical control is the fact that corporations are legal entities with unlimited life and limited liability. As a result, there is a tendency to view the actions of a corporation as separate from those of its members. Employees may find themselves doing things in the name of the corporation that they would not do in their own personal lives. In addition, society seems to expect less rigorous standards from organizations than from individuals.

Even so, ethics is a company-wide responsibility and must be managed as such. Marketing managers are often caught in the middle, as they must appease senior managers who pay lip service to responsible behavior but reward short-term financial performance. Marketers are also pressured by competitors who successfully use tactics that clearly conflict with their own company's standards of conduct. Unless

---

**TABLE 14.9**  Some Marketing-Related Practices That Involve Ethical Questions

---

- Having less competitive prices for smaller buyers and for sole source buyers
- Using the firm's economic power to obtain price or other concessions
- Exaggerating vendor problems (e.g., in production, distribution, inventory, or financing) to customer
- Giving preferential treatment to buyers whom top management prefers
- Giving preferential treatment to good customers
- Allowing personalities to affect the terms of sale
- Providing free trips, luncheons, or gifts
- Seeking information on competitors' quotes or other competitive information from customers
- Promising delivery times, knowing they cannot be met
- Exaggerating claims regarding product quality, reliability, or service life
- Understating product safety risks
- Criticizing competitors to get a customer's business
- Announcing new products prior to their development
- Selling a customer a more expensive version of a product, withholding a cheaper version that would suffice
- Making excuses to customers about products that are not yet in stock or sold out
- Ignoring a current customer for a prospect you believe will be better
- Refusing to accept returns of products that are clearly defective
- Replacing components in a currently available product with lower-quality components without informing customers

---

senior management explicitly includes ethical performance in the formal reward and measurement system, it is probably unrealistic to expect those in marketing and sales to exhibit ethical standards beyond those that are pragmatic—defined in this context as behavior that is not somehow penalized in the marketplace.

# Summary

This concluding chapter has explored the concept of marketing control. The control system represents a means to an end; control measures are merely indicators of whether or not things are on track. If the organization has many dimensions of performance on which measurements are taken and feedback is given, it is more difficult for managers to find ways of arbitrarily looking good while long-term company goals suffer. Furthermore, control measures are rarely perfect, making it critical that the marketer continuously evaluate the extent to which he or she is measuring the right things.

As a process, control incorporates four sequential activities: goal setting, performance measurement, performance diagnosis, and corrective action. *Goal setting* produces achievable and measurable standards of performance. *Performance measurement* is the comparison of actual performance to control benchmarks that reflect goals. If performance is outside an acceptable range around the benchmark, *performance diagnosis* attempts to ascertain the reasons why. Once the underlying causes of any deviations have been pinpointed, *corrective action* can be taken to adjust or change goals, benchmarks, strategies, action programs, budgets, or personnel.

In addition to the stages of the control process, there are four levels or categories of control. These include strategic control, annual plan control, profitability control, and efficiency control. These four levels are highly interdependent. A number of tools and analytical approaches for assessing performance at each level were presented. These tools included the marketing audit, variance analysis, the strategic profit model, the product evaluation matrix, marketing expense-to-sales analysis, attitude tracking, contribution analysis, and various efficiency indexes.

Effectiveness of the organization's control efforts can be enhanced by the quality of the inputs into the control system. Inputs can include the budget, an internal marketing database, scenario analysis, productivity judgments, sensitivity analysis, and environmental monitoring systems. Computer spreadsheets were also presented as a helpful resource, especially in conducting scenario and sensitivity analyses.

The complexities involved in explaining performance deviations were discussed. Considerable skill and insight are required to pinpoint the real reason that a given performance indicator is not on target. The manager must be expected to explain and draw inferences from any and all deviations in sales performance, marketing program performance, and marketing cost performance. The key to success in this area is the ability to distinguish among problems, symptoms of those problems, and the actual causes of those problems. Furthermore, problems often exist at a number of levels and interact with one another.

Finally, it is vital to recognize the extent to which a control system emphasizes efficiency versus effectiveness. Both qualities are important, but efficient operations are meaningless if those operations are not effective in achieving overall objectives. In this vein, Pinchot and Pellman (2000) argue that the years to come will increasingly bring control systems that are based primarily on selecting and empowering the right people to manage resources, and not on building elaborate controls to make sure inadequate people do what they are supposed to do.

# Questions

1. Discuss the differences between efficiency and effectiveness in a control system. How could the control system encourage efficiency while at the same time be ineffective?

2.  Performance tracking and control affects each of the elements of the industrial marketing mix. Assume you are the marketing manager at Metcoil Systems, Inc., a manufacturer of pneumatic cranes sold to companies involved in loading and unloading heavy equipment and materials. Identify examples of control measures that could be used to track performance in the product, price, promotion, and distribution areas.

3.  "The marketer must be wary of both undercontrol and overcontrol." Explain this statement and provide examples of the potential problems in either case.

4.  How can annual plan control be used if the company has not prepared an annual marketing plan?

5.  "When using variance analysis, if *positive* variances are found for sales, prices, or profits, the marketer should basically do nothing." Do you agree or disagree? Why?

6.  What might be some of the pitfalls in relying on marketing expense-to-sales ratios in annual plan control?

7.  Contribution analysis has been stressed throughout this book. Explain how contribution analysis can be a useful control tool in managing market segments, products, prices, advertising, and distributors.

8.  What information would you need to use the following efficiency measures?

    ❖ Cost per sales call

    ❖ Advertising cost per inquiry generated

    ❖ Average order cycle time per customer

    How would you obtain such information?

9.  Discuss some of the problems in performing productivity analysis on the likely effect on profits of adding a salesperson to the sales force. What is meant by *scenario analysis*, and how might this approach be useful in evaluating the effect of adding to the sales force?

10. Viceroy Valve finds that sales of its triple-flow valve used in heating and ventilating systems are 20% below target. Outline a systematic process for analyzing this performance deviation.

11. As a sales manager, you have a customer who critically needs one of your main products and can find no other immediate source of supply. Would you find it unethical to charge this customer a higher price than you would charge other customers receiving the same product and delivery arrangements? Why or why not?

# References

Abratt, R. (1986). "Industrial Buying in High Tech Markets." *Industrial Marketing Management* 15 (November): 293-298.

Aijo, Toio S. (1996). "The Theoretical and Philosophical Underpinnings of Relationship Marketing." *European Journal of Marketing* 30 (February): 2.

Ames, B. Charles, and James D. Hlavacek. (1984). *Managerial Marketing for Industrial Firms*. New York: Random House.

Anderson, J. C., and J. A. Narus. (1998). "Business Marketing: Understand What Customers Value." *Harvard Business Review* 76 (November-December): 53-61.

Anderson, P. F., W. Chu, and B. Weitz. (1987). "Industrial Purchasing: An Empirical Exploration of the Buyclass Framework." *Journal of Marketing* 42 (July): 71-86.

Ansari, A., and B. Modarress. (1986). "Just-in-Time Purchasing Problems and Solutions." *Journal of Purchasing and Materials Management* 22 (Summer): 11A-15A.

Avlonitis, G. J. (1984). "Industrial Product Elimination: Major Factors to Consider." *Industrial Marketing Management* 13, 2 (May): 77-85.

Babakus, E., and G. Boller. (1992). "An Empirical Assessment of the SERVQUAL Scale." *Journal of Business Research* 24, 3 (May): 253-268.

Bakos, J. Y. (1997). "Reducing Buyer Search Costs: Implications for Electronic Marketplaces." *Management Science* 43, 12 (December): 1676-1692.

Barry, Kevin. (1990). "Small Firm's Niche Strategy Topples Planogram Biggies." *Marketing News* (January 8): 40-41.

Bellizzi, J. A., and R. E. Hite. (1986). "Improving Industrial Advertising Copy." *Industrial Marketing Management* 15, no. 2 (May): 117-122.

Bennett, R. C., R. J. Calantone, and M. Morris. (1985). "The Implications of Structure for New Product Success." *Proceedings*, Annual Meetings of the Southern Management Association (pp. 235-239). Atlanta, GA: Southern Management Association.

Berkowitz, Eric N., R. A. Kerin, S. W. Hartley, and W. Rudelius. (1997). *Marketing* (5th ed.). Boston: Irwin/McGraw-Hill.

Berthon, Pierre R., James M. Hulbert, and Leyland F. Pitt. (1996). "Structuring Companies for Markets." *Financial Times* (Mastering Management Series), August 16, p. 8.

Berthon, Pierre R., James M. Hulbert, and Leyland F. Pitt. (1999). "To Serve or Create? Strategic Orientation Towards Technology and Customers." *California Management Review* 42, 1 (Fall): 37-58.

Berthon, P., L. Pitt, C. Katsikeas, and J. P. Berthon (1997). "Executive insights: Virtual Services Go International: International Services in the Marketplace." *Journal of International Marketing* 7, 3: 84-105.

Blattberg, Robert C., and John Deighton. (1996). "Manage Marketing by the Customer Equity Test." *Harvard Business Review* 74, 4 (July-August): 136-144.

Bogaty, H. (1974). "Development of New Consumer Products—Ways to Improve Your Chances of Success." *Research Management* 17 (July): 26-30.

Bonoma, T. V. (1982). "Major Sales: Who Really Does the Buying?" *Harvard Business Review* 60 (May-June): 111-119.

Bonoma, T. V. (1986). "Marketing Subversives." *Harvard Business Review* 64 (November-December): 113-118.

Bonoma, V. (1990). "A Marketer's Job Is to Self-Destruct." *Marketing News* 24 (June 25): 10-11.

Bonoma, T. V., R. P. Bagozzi, and G. Zaltman. (1978). "The Dyadic Paradigm With Specific Applications Toward Industrial Marketing," in T. V. Bonoma and G. Zaltman, eds., *Organizational Buying Behavior*. Chicago: American Marketing Association, 49-66.

Bonoma, T. V., and Benson P. Shapiro. (1983). *Segmenting the Industrial Market*. Lexington, MA: Lexington Books/D. C. Heath.

Bonoma, T. V., and B. P. Shapiro (1984). "How to Segment Industrial Markets." *Harvard Business Review* 62 (May-June): 104-110.

Booz Allen & Hamilton. (1968). *Management of New Products*. Chicago: Author.

Booz Allen & Hamilton. (1998). "Six Enduring Principles for Integrating the Supply Web." *Purchasing* 12, 5 (October 8): 26-31.

Calantone, R. J., and R. G. Cooper. (1977). "A Typology of Industrial New Product Failures." *Proceedings*, Southern Educators' Conference (pp. 492-497). Chicago: American Marketing Association.

Campbell, T. (1998). "Saving a Relationship." *Sales and Marketing Management* (February): 57.

Canadian Professional Sales Association. (1998). *1997/98 Sales Compensation Report*. Toronto: Author.

Cannon, Joseph P., and William D. Perreault. (1994). *Buyer-Seller Relationships in Business Markets*. Working paper CRM-WP-94-104, Center for Relationship Marketing, Goizueta Business School, Emory University, Atlanta, GA.

Cardozo, R., and S. Shipp. (1987). "New Selling Methods Are Changing Industrial Sales Management." *Business Horizons* 30 (September-October): 23-33.

Carroll, J. (1997). *Eliminating Barriers to Service Excellence*. Boston: The Forum Corporation.

Case, John. (1990). "Factory of the Future," *Inc.* 12 (August): 72.

Cavusgil, S. Tamer. (1990). "The Importance of Distributor Training at Caterpillar." *Industrial Marketing Management* 19, 1: 1-9.

Churchill, G., Neil M. Ford, and Orville C. Walker, Jr. (2000). *Sales Force Management*. Boston: Irwin/McGraw-Hill.

"Cisco Systems: The Dogfood Danger." (2000). *The Economist* 355, 8165 (April 8): 64-66.

Clark, Irvine, III, and Earl D. Honeycutt, Jr. (2000). "Color Usage in International Business-to-Business Print Advertising." *Industrial Marketing Management* 29, 3: 255-261.

Coase, R. (1937). "The Nature of the Firm." *Economica* 4, 3: 386-405.

Cohen, A. (2000). "When Channel Conflict Is Good." *Sales and Marketing Management* (April): 13.

Cook, R. (1984). "Conquering Computer Clutter." *High Technology* (December): 61-71.

Cooper, R. G. (1979). "The Dimensions of Industrial New Product Success and Failure." *Journal of Marketing* 43 (Summer): 93-103.

Cooper, R. G. (1988). "Predevelopment Activities Determine New Product Success." *Industrial Marketing Management* 17 (August): 249-262.

Cooper, R. G. (1993). *Winning at New Products* (2nd ed.). New York: Perseus.

Cooper, R. G. (1995). "Developing New Products on Time, in Time." *Research Technology Management* 38, 5 (September/October): 49-57.

Cooper, R. G. (1996). "Overhauling the New Product Process." *Industrial Marketing Management* 25, 6 (November): 465-482.

"The Copy Chasers Rules: What Makes Good Business/Industrial Advertising." (1982). *Industrial Marketing* (December): 51-52.

Corey, E. R. (1991). *Industrial Marketing: Cases and Concepts*. Englewood Cliffs, NJ: Prentice Hall.

"The Cost of Doing Business." (1999). *Sales and Marketing Management* (September): 57.

Cox, J. (1985). "Trade Shows Provide Easiest Media Evaluation." *Marketing News* 19 (May 10): 13.

Crawford, C. M., and A. di Benedetto. (1999). *New Products Management*. Boston: Irwin/McGraw-Hill.

Cutler, B. D., and R. Javalgi. (1994). "Comparison of Business-to-Business Advertising." *Industrial Marketing Management* 23, 2 (April): 117-124.

Dalrymple, D. J., and W. Cron. (1998). *Sales Management*. New York: John Wiley & Sons.

Dalrymple, D. J., and L. J. Parsons. (1996). *Marketing Management* (4th ed.). New York: John Wiley & Sons.

Dartnell Corporation. (1997). *Dartnell's 29th Sales Force Compensation Survey*. Palm Beach Gardens, FL: Author.

Day, G. S., and A. B. Ryans. (1988). "Using Price Discounts for a Competitive Advantage." *Industrial Marketing Management* 17 (February): 1-14.

Day, G. S. (1984). *Strategic Market Planning: The Pursuit of Competitive Advantage*. St. Paul, MN: West.

Day, G. S. (1999a) *The Market Driven Organization: Understanding, Attracting, and Keeping Valuable Customers*. New York: Free Press.

Day, G. S. (1999b). *Market Driven Strategy: Processes for Creating Value*. New York: Free Press.

Desiraju, R., and S. Shugan. (1999). "Strategic Service Pricing and Yield Management." *Journal of Marketing* 63, 1 (January): 44-56.

Dichter, E. R. (1973). "Psychology in Industrial Marketing." *Industrial Marketing* 58 (February): 40-43.

Dobler, D. W., L. Lee, Jr., and D. N. Burt. (1989). *Purchasing and Materials Management* (5th ed.). New York: McGraw-Hill.

Dobler, D. W., L. Lee, Jr., and D. N. Burt. (1995). *Purchasing and Materials Management* (6th ed.). New York: McGraw-Hill.

Donath, B. (1982). "Q: What Makes the Perfect Ad? A: It Depends." *Industrial Marketing* (August): 89-92.

Downes, Larry, and Chunka Mui. (1998). *Unleashing the Killer App*. Boston: Harvard Business School Press.

Drucker, Peter. (1954). *The Practice of Management*. New York: Harper and Row.

Dubinsky, A. M., and J. M. Gwin. (1981). "Business Ethics: Buyers and Sellers." *Journal of Purchasing and Materials Management* (Winter): 9-15.

Eisenhart, T. (1989). "Advanced Research Finds a New Market." *Business Marketing* 743 (March): 50-61.

Erb, Martin S., Chair (1980). *Basic Steps in Value Analysis* (pamphlet prepared by the Value-Analysis-Standardization Committee, Reading Association, National Association of Purchasing Management). New York: National Association of Purchasing Management.

Fawcett, S. E., and M. B. Cooper. (1998). "Logistics Performance Measurement and Customer Success." *Industrial Marketing Management* 27 (July): 345-354.

Fisher, R., and W. Ury. (1981). *Getting to Yes: Negotiating Agreement Without Giving In.* Boston: Houghton-Mifflin.

Ford, D., and C. Ryan. (1981). "Taking Technology to Market." *Harvard Business Review* 59 (March-April): 117-126.

Ford, N. M., G. A. Churchill, and O. C. Walker. (1985). "Differences in the Attractiveness of Alternative Rewards Among Industrial Salespeople: Additional Evidence." *Journal of Business Research* 13, 2 (April): 123-138.

Forrester Research. (1998). *On-line Purchasing Futures.* Retrieved from the World Wide Web: www.forrester.com/ER/Research/Report/0,1338,146,FF.html

Foster, Richard N. (1982). "A Call for Vision in Managing Technology." *Business Week* 2740 (May 24): 24-28, 33.

Fournier, S., S. Dobscha, and D. Glen. (1998). "Preventing the Premature Death of Relationship Marketing." *Harvard Business Review* 76, 1 (January-February): 42-51.

Fram, D. (1974). *Value Analysis: A Way to Better Products and Profits.* New York: AMACOM.

French, J.R.P., and B. Ravens. (1959). "The Bases of Social Power," in D. Cartwright, ed., *Studies in Social Power.* Ann Arbor: University of Michigan Press, 150-167.

Gale, B. T. (1985). *Quality as a Strategic Weapon.* Cambridge, MA: The Strategic Planning Institute.

Gartner Group. (2000). *Procurement More Than Just Purchasing.* Retrieved from the World Wide Web: https://gartner4.gartnerweb.com

"Getting to Eureka." (1997). *Business Week,* October 30, 72-75.

Giunipero, L. C. (1984). "Purchasing's Role in Computer Buying: A Comparative Study." *Industrial Marketing Management* 13 (November): 241-248.

Glover, D., S. Hartley, and C. Patti. (1989). "How Advertising Strategies Are Set." *Industrial Marketing Management* 18, 1: 19-26.

Glueck, W. F. (1980). *Business Policy and Strategic Management.* New York: McGraw-Hill.

Gopalakrishna, S., G. L. Lilien, J. D. Williams, and I. K. Sequeira. (1995). "Do Trade Shows Pay Off?" *Journal of Marketing* 59 (July): 75-83.

Gronroos, C. (1983). *Strategic Management and Marketing in the Service Sector.* Cambridge, MA: Marketing Science Institute.

Groocock, J. M. (1986). *The Chain of Quality.* New York: John Wiley & Sons.

Guiltinan, J. P., and G. Paul. (1991). *Marketing Management: Strategies and Programs.* New York: McGraw-Hill.

Guiltinan, J. P., and G. Paul. (1999). *Marketing Management: Strategies and Programs* (7th ed.). New York: McGraw-Hill.

Gupta, A. K., S. P. Raj, and D. L. Wilemon. (1985). "R&D and Marketing Dialogue in High-Tech Firms," *Industrial Marketing Management* 14: 289-300.

Haas, Robert W. (1976). *Industrial Marketing Management.* New York: Van Nostrand Reinhold.

Haas, Robert W. (1982). *Industrial Marketing Management.* Boston: Kent.

Hamel, G., and C. K. Prahalad. (1993). "Strategy as Stretch and Leverage." *Harvard Business Review* 71, 2 (March-April): 75-84.

Hanssens, Dominique, and Barton A. Weitz. (1980). "The Effectiveness of Industrial Print Advertisements Across Product Categories." *Journal of Marketing Research* 17: 294-306.

Hedley, B. (1977). "Strategy and the Business Portfolio." *Long Range Planning* 10, 1 (February): 9-15.

Herbig, Paul, Brad O'Hara, and Fred Palumbo. (1994). "Measuring Trade Show Effectiveness: An Effective Exercise?" *Industrial Marketing Management* 23, 2: 165-170.

Hochwald, L. (2000). "Tuning in to the Right Channel." *Sales and Marketing Management* 152, 3 (March): 66-74.

Honeycutt, Earl D., Jr., Ashraff M. Attia, and Angela R. D'Auria. (1996). "Sales Force Certification." *Journal of Personal Selling and Sales Management* 16, 3 (Summer): 59-65.

Honeycutt, Earl D., Jr., Theresa B. Flaherty, and Ken Benassi. (1998). "Marketing Industrial Products on the Internet." *Industrial Marketing Management* 27, 1 (January): 63-72.

Honeycutt, Earl D., Jr., and John B. Ford. (1995). "A Guideline for Managing an International Sales Force." *Industrial Marketing Management* 24, 2 (March): 135-144.

Honeycutt, Earl D., Jr., John B. Ford, Robert Lupton, and Theresa B. Flaherty. (1999). "Selecting and Training the International Sales Force." *Industrial Marketing Management* 28, 6 (November): 627-635.

Honeycutt, Earl D., Jr., Vince Howe, and Thomas Ingram. (1993). "Shortcomings of Sales Training Programs." *Industrial Marketing Management* 22, 2 (May): 117-123.

Huang, Jen-Huang. (1993). "Color in U.S. and Taiwanese Industrial Advertising." *Industrial Marketing Management* 22 (3): 195-198.

Hulbert, J. M., and N. E. Toy. (1977). "A Strategic Framework for Marketing Control." *Journal of Marketing* 41 (April): 12-21.

International Data Corporation. (2000). *Putting Markets Into Place: An eMarketplace Definition and Forecast* (Bulletin 22501, June). Framingham, MA: Author.

Jackson, D. W., L. L. Ostrom, and K. R. Evans. (1982). "Measures Used to Evaluate Industrial Marketing Activities." *Industrial Marketing Management* 11: 269-274.

Johnston, W. J., and T. V. Bonoma. (1981). "The Buying Center: Structure and Interaction Patterns." *Journal of Marketing* 45 (Summer): 143-156.

Juran, J. M. (1993). "Made in U.S.A.: A Renaissance in Quality." *Harvard Business Review* 71 (July-August): 42-50.

Kajewski, Valerie, Eunsang Yoon, and Gary Young. (1993). "How Exhibitors Select Trade Shows." *Industrial Marketing Management* 22, 4: 287-298.

Kalafatis, S. P., and V. Cheston. (1997). "Normative Models and Practical Applications of Segementation in Business Markets." *Industrial Marketing Management* 26, 6 (November): 519-531.

Kasouf, Chickery J., and Kevin G. Celuch. (1997). "Interfirm Relationships in the Supply Chain: The Small Supplier's View." *Industrial Marketing Management* 26, 6: 475-486.

Keiser, Thomas C. (1988). "Negotiating With a Customer You Can't Afford to Lose." *Harvard Business Review* 6 (November-December): 30-34.

Kelly, Kevin. (1998). *New Rules for the New Economy: 10 Ways the Network Economy Is Changing Everything*. London: Fourth Estate.

Knights, D., and G. Morgan. (1991). "Corporate Strategy, Organizations, and Subjectivity: A Critique." *Organization Studies* 12 (2): 251-273.

Kohli, A. K., and B. J. Jaworski. (1990). "Market Orientation: The Construct, Research Propositions, and Managerial Implications." *Journal of Marketing* 54 (April): 1-18.

Kohli, A. K., B. J. Jaworski, and A. Kumar. (1993). "MARKOR: A Measure of Market Orientation." *Journal of Market Research* 30 (November): 467-477.

Kohli, A. K., and G. Zaltman. (1988). "Measuring Multiple Buying Influences." *Industrial Marketing Management* 17 (August): 197-204.

Kotler, P. (1991). *Marketing Management: Analysis, Planning, Implementation, and Control* (7th ed.). Englewood Cliffs, NJ: Prentice Hall.

Kotler, P. (1997). *Marketing Management*. Englewood Cliffs, NJ: Prentice Hall.

Kotler, P. (2000). *Marketing Management: Millennium Edition*. Englewood Cliffs, NJ: Prentice Hall.

Laczniak, G. (1979). "An Empirical Study of Hospital Buying." *Industrial Marketing Management* 8, 1: 57-62.

Larson, Paul D., and Jack D. Kulchitsky. (1998). "Single Sourcing and Supplier Certification." *Industrial Marketing Management* 27, 1: 73-81.

Levitt, T. (1960). "Marketing Myopia." *Harvard Business Review* 38 (July-August): 45-56.

Levitt, T. (1980). "Marketing Success Through Differentiation—Of Anything." *Harvard Business Review* 58 (January-February): 83-91.

Levitt, T. (1991). *Levitt on Marketing*. Boston: Harvard Business Review.

Lilien, G. L., and J.D.C. Little. (1976). "The ADVISOR Project: A Study of Industrial Marketing Budgets." *Sloan Management Review* 17, 3 (Spring): 17-31.

Little, J.D.C. (1979). "Decision Support Systems for Marketing Managers." *Journal of Marketing* 43 (Summer): 9-27.

Lohtia, Ritu, Wesley J. Johnston, and Linda Aab. (1995). "Business-to-Business Advertising: What Are the Dimensions of an Effective Print Ad?" *Industrial Marketing Management* 24, 5: 369-378.

Lovelock, C. H. (1996). *Services Marketing* (3rd ed.). Englewood Cliffs, NJ: Prentice Hall.

Lynn, S. A. (1987). "Identifying Buying Influences for a Professional Service: Implications for Marketing Efforts." *Industrial Marketing Management* 16 (May): 119-130.

Magretta, Joan. (1998). "The Power of Virtual Integration: An Interview With Dell Computer's Michael Dell." *Harvard Business Review* 76 (March-April): 73-84.

Marsteller, W. A. (1984). "The Changing Environment in Business Marketing." *Marketing Media Decisions* 19, 5 (April): 5-10.

McCarthy, Robert F. (1989). "Hewlett-Packard Misfires Its Marketing Weapon." *Business Marketing* 74 (January): 56-58.

McKenna, R. (1991). "Marketing is Everything." *Harvard Business Review* 69, 1 (January-February): 65-79.

McKenna, R. (1995). *Relationship Marketing*. Reading, MA: Addison-Wesley.

McKim, Robert A. (1999). "Statistical Bidding Models." *Cost Engineering* (December): 40-44.

McQuarrie, E. F. (1991). "The Customer Visit: Qualitative Research for Business-to-Business Marketers." *Marketing Research* (March): 15-28.

Miaoulis, G., and P. J. LaPlaca. (1982). "A Systems Approach for Developing High Technology Products." *Industrial Marketing Management* (November): 253-262.

Minahan, T. (1998). "OEM Buying Survey—Part 2: Buyers Get New Roles but Keep Old Tasks." *Purchasing* 12 (July 16): 208-209.

Mintzberg, H. (1994). "The Fall and Rise of Strategic Planning." *Harvard Business Review* 72, 1 (January-February): 107-114.

Mintzberg, H., and A. McHugh. (1985). "Strategy Formation in an Adhocracy." *Administrative Science Quarterly* 30, 2 (June): 160-197.

Monroe, K. B. (1990). *Pricing: Making Profitable Decisions* (2nd ed.). New York: McGraw-Hill.

Montgomery, D., and C. Weinberg. (1979). "Toward Strategic Intelligence Systems." *Journal of Marketing* 43 (Fall): 41-52.

Morgan, Robert M., and Shelby D. Hunt. (1994). "The Commitment-Trust Theory of Relationship Marketing." *Journal of Marketing* 58: 20-38.

Moriarty, R. T., and D. J. Reibstein. (1982). *Benefit Segmentation: An Industrial Application* (Report No. 82-110). Cambridge, MA: Marketing Science Institute.

Moriarty, R. T., Jr., and R. E. Spekman. (1984). "An Empirical Investigation of the Information Sources Used During the Industrial Buying Process." *Journal of Marketing Research* 21: 137-147.

Morris, M. (1987). "Separate Prices as a Marketing Tool." *Industrial Marketing Management* 16, 2 (May): 79-86.

Morris, M. (1998). *Entrepreneurial Intensity*. Westport, CT: Quorum Books.

Morris, Michael, J. Brunyee, and M. Page. (1998). "Relationship Marketing in Practice." *Industrial Marketing Management* 27, 4 (July): 359-371.

Morris, M. H., and M. Schindehutte. (1999). *Assessing the U.S. Market for Low-Dose, Full-Body X-ray Scanning Equipment* (Research Report 16). Orlando, FL: PenteVisionUSA Consulting.

Morris, M., M. Schindehutte, and S. Zahra. (in press). "Triggering Events and Corporate Entrepreneurship." In G. Libecap (Ed.), *Advances in Entrepreneurship*. Westport, CT: JAI.

Morse, W. J. (1975). "Probabilistic Bidding Models: A Synthesis." *Business Horizons* 18 (April): 67-74.

Nierenberg, A. (2000a). *The Keys to Unlocking a Sales Staff's Greatest Potential*. New York: Nierenberg Group.

Nierenberg, A. (2000b). *New Clients Through Networking*. New York: Nierenberg Group.

"1990 Survey of Selling Costs." (1990). *Sales and Marketing Management*, February 26, pp. 6-106.

Noble, P. M., and T. S. Gruca. (1999). "Industrial Pricing: Theory and Managerial Practice." *Marketing Science* 34, 11 (December): 435-454.

Olsen, R., and L. Ellram. (1997). "A Portfolio Approach to Supplier Relationships." *Industrial Marketing Management* 26 (March): 101-113.

Parasuraman, Z., V. A. Zeithaml, and L. L. Berry. (1988). "SERVQUAL: A Multiple-Item Scale for Measuring Consumer Perceptions of Service Quality." *Journal of Retailing* 64, 1 (Spring): 12-40.

Patchen, M. (1974). "The Locus and Basis of Influence in Organizational Decisions." *Organizational Behavior and Human Performance* 11 (April): 195-221.

Pelton, L. E., D. Strutton, and J. R. Lumpkin. (1997). *Marketing Channels: A Relationship Management Approach*. Chicago: Irwin.

Perdue, B. C., R. L. Day, and R. E. Michaels. (1986). "Negotiation Styles of Industrial Buyers." *Industrial Marketing Management* 15, 3 (August): 171-176.

Peter, J. P., and J. H. Donnelly, Jr. (1995). *Marketing Management: Knowledge and Skills* (4th ed.). Chicago: Irwin.

Peter, J. P., and M. J. Ryan. (1976). "Investigation of Perceived Risk at the Brand Level." *Journal of Marketing Research* 13 (May): 184-188.

Pinchot, Gifford, III, and R. Pellman. (2000). *Intrapreneuring in Action: A Handbook for Business Innovation*. San Francisco: Berrett-Koehler.

Pine, B., and J. Gilmore. (1998). "Welcome to the Experience Economy." *Harvard Business Review* 76, 4 (July-August): 97-105.

Pine, B., D. Peppers, and M. Rogers. (1995). "Do You Want to Keep Your Customers Forever?" *Harvard Business Review* 73, 4 (March-April): 103-108.

Pitt, L., M. Morris, and P. Oosthuizen. (1996). "Expectations of Service Quality as an Industrial Market Segmentation Variable." *The Service Industries Journal* 16, 1 (January): 1-9.

Porter, L. W., and E. E. Lawler III. (1968). *Managerial Attitudes and Performance*. Homewood, IL: Irwin-Dorsey.

Porter, M. E. (1980). *Competitive Strategy: Techniques for Analyzing Industries and Competitors*. New York: Free Press.

Rabino, S., and T. E. Moore. (1989). "Managing New Product Announcements in the Computer Industry." *Industrial Marketing Management* 18 (February): 35-43.

Rasmusson, E. (1998). "The Channels to Watch." *Sales and Marketing Management* 150, 3 (March): 54-56.

Reese, Nancy A., Thomas W. Whipple, and Alice E. Courtney. (1987). "Is Industrial Advertising Still Sexist?" *Industrial Marketing Management* 16, 4 (November): 231-240.

Reuter, Vincent G. (1996). "What Good Are Value Analysis Programs?" *Business Horizons* 29 (March-April): 73-79.

Robertson, T. (1967). "The Process of Innovation and the Diffusion of Innovation." *Journal of Marketing* 31 (January): 14-19.

Robinson, Patrick J., Charles W. Faris, and Yoram Wind. (1967). *Industrial Buying and Creative Marketing*. Boston: Allyn & Bacon.

Rosenbloom, B. (1983). *Marketing Channels: A Management View* (2nd ed.). Hinsdale, IL: Dryden.

Rothwell, R. (1980). "Policies in Industry." In D. Pavitt (Ed.), *Technical Innovation and British Economic Performance* (pp. 291-307). London: Macmillan.

Sager, I. (1998). "A New Cyber Order." *Business Week*, December 7, p. 26.

"Salespeople and Sales Managers Disagree on How to Boost Sales." (1990). *Marketing Times* (July/August): 3.

Schmenner, R. W. (1994). "Service Firm Location Decisions: Some Midwestern Evidence." *International Journal of Service Industry Management* 5, 3: 35-56.

Schonfeld and Associates, Inc. (1998). *Advertising Ratios and Budgets*. Lincolnshire, IL: Author.

Serwer, Andy. (1998). "Michael Dell Rocks." *Fortune*, May 11, 27-34.

Shanklin, W. L., and J. K. Ryans, Jr. (1987). *Essentials of Marketing High Technology*. Lexington, MA: D. C. Heath.

Sharland, Alex, and Peter Balogh. (1996). "The Value of Nonselling Activities at International Trade Shows." *Industrial Marketing Management* 25, 1 (January): 59-66.

Shetty, Y. K. (1993). "Product Quality and Competitive Strategy." *Business Horizons* 30 (May-June): 59-60.

Shuster, C. P., and C. D. Bodkin. (1987). "Market Segmentation Practices of Exporting Companies." *Industrial Marketing Management* 16, 2 (March): 95-102.

Siguaw, Judy A., and Earl D. Honeycutt, Jr. (1995). "An Examination of Gender Differences in Selling Behaviors and Job Attitudes." *Industrial Marketing Management* 24, 1 (February): 45-52.

Sinclair, S. A., and E. C. Stalling. (1990). "How to Identify Differences Between Market Segments and Attribute Analysis." *Industrial Marketing Management* 19 (February): 31-40.

"Special Report: Quality." (1992). *Business Week*, November 23, pp. 66-75.

Spekman, R. E., and L. W. Stern. (1979). "Environmental Uncertainty and Buying Group Structure: An Empirical Investigation." *Journal of Marketing* 43 (Spring): 54-64.

Stedman, C. (2000). "Value-Based Pricing." *Computerworld* 34 (March 13): 11, 58-63.

Stevenson, H., M. Roberts, H. I. Grousbeck, and A. Bhide. (1999). *New Business Ventures and the Entrepreneur* (5th ed.). New York: Irwin/McGraw Hill.

Strauss, G. (1962). "Tactics of Lateral Relationships: The Purchasing Agent." *Administrative Science Quarterly* 7 (September): 161-186.

Trunick, P. A. (1999). "ERP: Promise or Pipe Dream?" *Transportation & Distribution* 40, 1 (January): 23-26.

Tucker, W. T. (1974). "Future Directions in Marketing Theory." *Journal of Marketing* 38 (April): 30-35.

Vroom, Victor. (1964). *Work and Motivation*. New York: John Wiley & Sons.

Waterman, R. H. (1987). *The Renewal Factor*. New York: Bantam Books.

Watson, R., G. Zinkhan, and L. Pitt. (2000). "Integrated Internet Marketing." *Association for Computing Machinery: Communications of the ACM* 43, 6 (June): 97-102.

Webster, Cynthia. (1990). "Industrial Buyers' Level of Involvement With Services." *Marketing Theory and Applications* (proceedings of the 1990 American Marketing Association Winter Educator's Conference) (pp. 69-74).

Webster, F. E., Jr. (1984). *Industrial Marketing Strategy* (2nd ed.). New York: John Wiley & Sons.

Webster, F. E., Jr. (1992). "The Changing Role of Marketing in the Corporation." *Journal of Marketing* 56, 4 (October): 1-17.

Webster, F. E., Jr. (1994). *Market-Driven Management: Using the New Marketing Concept to Create a Customer-Oriented Company*. New York: John Wiley & Sons.

Webster, F., and Y. Wind. (1967). *Industrial Buying and Creative Marketing*. Boston: Allyn & Bacon.

Weigand, R. E. (1966). "Identifying Industrial Buying Responsibility." *Journal of Marketing Research* 3 (February): 81-84.

Weitz, Barton A., Stephen B. Castleberry, and John F. Tanner, Jr. (1998). *Selling: Building Partnerships* (3rd ed.). Boston: Irwin/McGraw-Hill.

"What a Sales Call Costs." (1998). *Sales and Marketing Management* 150, no. 13 (December): 42-43.

White, G. R., and M.B.W. Graham. (1978). "How to Spot a Technological Winner." *Harvard Business Review* 56 (March-April): 146-152.

White, Lynn, Jr. (1962). *Medieval Technology and Social Change*. London: Oxford University Press.

Wilson, David T. (1996). "An Integrated Model of Buyer-Seller Relationships." *Journal of the Academy of Marketing Science* 23: 335-345.

Wind, Y. (1970). "Industrial Source Loyalty." *Journal of Marketing Research* 7 (November): 450-457.

Wind, Y., and H. J. Claycamp. (1976). "Planning Product Line Strategy: A Matrix Approach." *Journal of Marketing* 40 (January): 2-9.

Wirthlin Worldwide. (1999). *Americans on the Job: Part II, The Wirthlin Report—Current Trends in Public Opinion* 9, 1 (January): 1-4.

Wolter, J. F., F. R. Bacon, D. F. Duhan, and R. D. Wilson. (1989). "How Designers and Buyers Evaluate Products." *Industrial Marketing Management* 18 (May): 81-89.

Woolley, Scott. (1998). "Industrial Buyers Are Getting More Mileage Out of On-Line Comparison Shopping Than Individuals Are. Why? E-muscle." *Forbes*, March 9, p. 204.

Zinkhan, G. M., and L. A. Vachris. (1984). "The Impact of Selling Aids on New Prospects." *Industrial Marketing Management* 13, 3: 187-193.

Zinn, Walter, and A. Parasuraman. (1997). "Scope and Intensity of Logistics-Based Strategic Alliances." *Industrial Marketing Management* 26, 2: 137-147.

# Index

# About the Authors

**Michael Morris**, Ph.D., holds the Cintas Endowed Chair in Entrepreneurship at Miami University and is the Director of the Thomas C. Page Center for Entrepreneurship. He also serves on the faculty at the Graduate School of Business, University of Cape Town. In addition, he is the Managing Director of PenteVision, an executive education and consulting firm. He received his Ph.D. in marketing from Virginia Tech in 1983. His dissertation, on organizational buying behavior, won top honors that year from the Academy of Marketing Science. He also holds an M.B.A. as well as M.S. and B.A. degrees in economics. A prolific researcher, he has published three books: *Industrial and Organizational Marketing* (1992), *Market-Oriented Pricing* (1991), and *Entrepreneurial Intensity* (1998). He has also authored or coauthored more than 100 articles in such academic publications as the *Journal of Business Research*, the *Journal of Management, Entrepreneurship Theory and Practice, Industrial Marketing Management, Long Range Planning*, the *Journal of the Academy of Marketing Science*, the *Journal of International Business Studies*, the *European Journal of Marketing*, the *Journal of Business Ethics*, and the *Journal of Business Venturing*. He is also a former Fulbright Scholar (South Africa, 1993). He was twice honored by Pi Sigma Epsilon as its national Faculty Advisor of the Year.

**Earl D. Honeycutt, Jr.**, is Professor of Marketing at Old Dominion University in Norfolk, Virginia, where he teaches classes in sales management, marketing management, and global marketing. He has also served as Chairman of the Department of Business Administration and Director of the Ph.D. Program in Business Administration. Prior to entering academe, he worked in industrial sales and marketing for a division of TRW, Inc. He received his Ph.D. in business administration from the University of Georgia and formerly taught at the University of North Carolina–Wilmington, where he was designated a Cameron Fellow. He has published more than 100 articles in such outlets as the *Journal of Advertising, Journal of Personal Selling & Sales Management, Industrial Marketing Management, Business Horizons, International Marketing Review, Journal of Business Ethics*, and *Strategic Marketing Journal*. He travels extensively to Asia, where he leads Study Abroad trips to the Philippines, and has also taught during the summer at Kitakysushu University in Japan. He was instrumental in forming the Filipino American Student Cultural Center (FASCC) at Old Dominion and currently serves on its board of directors. His family includes his wife, Laura; their one son, Travis, his wife, Angela, and their son, Cole.

**Leyland Pitt** holds joint positions as Professor of Marketing in the School of Marketing, Curtin University of Technology, and as Fellow in Marketing and Strategy in the Cardiff Business School, University of Cardiff in the United Kingdom. He has also taught marketing and electronic commerce in M.B.A. and executive programs at schools such as Warwick Business School, London Business School, Ècole Nationale Ponts et Chaussees in Paris, the Graduate School of Business at Columbia University, and the Graham School of Continuing Studies at the University of Chicago. His particular areas of interest in research and teaching involve marketing and the new electronic media, the staging of consumer experiences, and marketing strategy. He is the author of many papers in scholarly journals, and his work has appeared in publications such as *California Management Review*, *Sloan Management Review*, the *Journal of the Academy of Marketing Science*, the *Journal of Business Research*, the *Journal of Advertising Research*, *Communications of the ACM*, and *MIS Quarterly*. He has been recognized numerous times for teaching excellence, including being named the M.B.A. teacher of the year at Henley and M.B.A. teacher of the year at Copenhagen Business School.